HMS Conway
1859 – 1974

Alfie Windsor
Conway Cadet 1964 – 68

Front Cover: Conway crest courtesy of the Conway Club.
Back Cover: Main Picture, Conway's figurehead today at HMS Nelson, Portsmouth, UK. Image courtesy of Ric Smith MA DMS, digital imagery by Jon Redford.

Extracts from the works of John Masefield used by kind permission of The Society of Authors as the Literary Representative of The Estate of John Masefield.

Photos in Chapter 23 of the Ship under tow and taken from the Suspension Bridge are courtesy of Mr Norman Murcott.

Annotated chart on page 199 courtesy of the Hydrographic Office and Mr R Jones.

Ariel photograph of the Swellies on page 199 courtesy of the Beaumaris lifeboat.

Conway MN Trust Crest in Chapter 42 courtesy of that Trust.

Appendix I-3 courtesy of the Royal Welsh Yacht Club.

First published 2008

ISBN 978 1 905331 31 4

Printed & bound in Great Britain by Bell & Bain Ltd. Glasgow

Published in 2008 by
Witherby Seamanship International
4 Dunlop Square
Deans Estate
Livingston EH54 8SB
United Kingdom
Tel No: +44(0)1506 463 227
Fax No: +44(0)1506 468 999
Email: info@emailws.com
www.witherbyseamanship.com

[58971]

Anyone with maritime connections knows about the training ship *HMS Conway*. Established 150 years ago in response to the demand for better trained officers for the Merchant Navy, and also for a pool of reserve officers for the Royal Navy, she more than met the expectations of her founders.

It is difficult to appreciate that when she started her life as a training ship, there were more ships registered under the British flag than under the combined flags of the rest of the world. This book does not attempt to explain the subsequent decline, but it does show that, given the proper training, the young men ofthis country have a special aptitude for seafaring. The important words are 'proper training', and this is precisely what 'Conway' provided.

I believe that this book is much to be welcomed as a record of a real success story in the long and distinguished history ofthe British Merchant Navy.

CONTENTS

Appendices

PREFACE

I hope you enjoy this book. My name is on the cover but I must thank the hundreds of Old *Conways,* their families and friends, members of staff and other individuals whose experiences and knowledge are shared herein. Without them, this history would have been short and dull. Verbatim contributions are in parentheses. I have followed the convention used by John Masefield (1891-1894) in his earlier history of the Ship, and generally not mentioned the names of individual contributors. Where numbers appear in parentheses after a person's name they indicate their *Conway* years.

I have reviewed thousands of documents and photographs, including every page of nearly a hundred years of Cadet magazines. I could never have competed much of this research without the years of tireless dedication by David Fletcher Rogers (1943-45) and John Southwood (1955-57), who had already saved, copied and scanned endless numbers of documents and images. Once again, I have followed John Masefield and not included cross references to all this source material. Chapters 23 and 24 are exceptions, since they deal with the loss of the Ship. I wanted those chapters to be as full and as authoritative as possible, so they include extensive cross-references to source material. Captain David G Williams (1949-51) deserves special credit for his professional and detailed assessment of the conditions contributing to the loss of the Ship.

I have included many photographs but, as some are fifty or even a hundred years old, they do not all reproduce well. I thought it better to include poor quality images than no images at all.

In a book with naval content, it is very easy to get carried away with the use of initial capital letters and three letter acronyms. I have avoided this as much as possible. However, when referring specifically to one of the three vessels that were *Conway,* I have followed custom and referred to them as the Ship. Similarly I refer to the House, the Camp and New Block. In later years, when *Conway* was ashore but still referred to as a ship, I have reverted to the ship. When naming Royal Navy vessels I have followed convention and omitted prefixes like 'HMS' and 'the.' I have not followed the convention of writing their names in upper case. Therefore I have written *Conway* not *CONWAY,* or the *CONWAY.* Inevitably, I've used a lot of general naval terminology and *Conway* nicknames and slang so there is a Glossary in *Appendix A.* I trust mariners will accept my lapses into lubbers' terminology where it seemed useful.

My eternal thanks to Kat Heathcote at Witherby's for her dedicated editing of my draft, for coping with the vagaries of my punctuation and for enduring my constant enthusiasm for making changes. She has given a beautiful polish to my very rough stone.

Finally I crave the understanding of Old *Conways* everywhere. The most recent *Conway* events described are already thirty-four years old so verifying material has not been easy. I have always attempted to obtain independent corroboration but I received many detailed and fascinating recollections of the same events that totally contradicted each other. Black was white, night was day! I have generally adopted the consensus view, and omitted some recollections irreconcilable with others.

Alfie Windsor (1964-68)
May 2008

CHAPTER 1

INTRODUCTION

There was a time, not too long ago, when the British merchant fleet was larger than the rest of the world's merchant fleets combined. This was perhaps the pinnacle of hundreds of years of British maritime tradition, when Britain ruled the seas and as much as twenty percent of the world's landmass.

This domination created a huge and constant need for young men trained for the challenges of a rigorous life at sea, a life that was hard and required the highest standards of training, performance, resolution and leadership. The training school ship HMS *Conway* existed to answer that demand and became a special part of Britain's maritime tradition. For over a hundred years after 1859, a series of three Royal Navy wooden walls: HMS *Conway*, HMS *Winchester* and finally HMS *Nile*, a hutted camp and then a stone frigate were home to over 11,000 young men training for a life of service as officers in the British Merchant Navy, the Royal Navy and navies and other maritime organisations around the world. *Appendix H* is far from complete but it lists 631 shipping companies and navies, 80 maritime training establishments and 159 uniformed services in which Old *Conways* have served.

Conway cadets arrived as boys and left, about two years later, as men, true to the Ship's motto: 'Quit ye like men, be strong.' Different times called for different methods, so training was constantly changing. It was always physically and mentally taxing, but the end result was invariably the same. Seventeen year old men ready to go to sea and do their duty, a special breed of men, tough, independent, adaptable, reliable and trustworthy. To this day Old *Conways* have a significant influence in all walks of life around the world. Achievements include 26 Admirals, 14 Commodores, 3 Generals, 4 Air Marshals, 4 Victoria Crosses, 3 George Crosses, a George Medal, a Poet Laureate and a staggering array of accomplishments at sea and ashore. A few are listed in *Appendix H*, but whatever Old *Conways* turned their hand to, they succeeded and rose to the top of their professions.

Times change, empires fade, priorities alter, and so our merchant fleet, officers and crew became the first British industry to be outsourced and off-shored. Our reliance on the sea remains unaltered, but without the political will to sustain an independent British fleet, demand for men faded, the ship sadly closed her doors and paid off in 1974. The majority of *Conway* cadets spent a lifetime at sea. While most have retired to safe berths ashore around the world, for those who go down to the sea in ships there is still a good chance that

"you'll find on the bridge a Conway boy."

This is their story.

CHAPTER 2

1857–59 THE FOUNDING

The British Empire was built on the back of international trade, but its foundation was laid by force, a unique, ruthless blend of sea power and military might. At its peak, the Empire straddled over a fifth of the world's landmass and included a quarter of the world's population. The Royal Navy dominated the world's sea-lanes, keeping them open and safe for British shipping, strengthened by control of strategic choke points like Gibraltar, the Falkland Islands, Singapore, Aden, Hong Kong and Simonstown. Merchant shipping was the Empire's glue. Raw materials flowed into the UK from all over the world and British industry exported them again as manufactured goods to captive markets in colonies and protectorates all over the globe. The small harbours around Britain's coast grew into the world's busiest ports – London, Southampton, Bristol, Liverpool, Glasgow and Cardiff each had their specialist international markets. Turnpikes, canals and railways linked these ports to their thriving hinterlands. Such was the scale of the opportunity that Manchester, an inland city, constructed a massive 36 mile long ship canal providing direct access for ocean going vessels.

The British merchant service carried everything and grew exponentially. In the process, some fleets created huge wealth for their owners. Family names like Bibby, Brocklebank, Harrison, Holt and Jardine became household names around the world. By the late nineteenth century, the British merchant fleet accounted for a staggering 63% of the world's total tonnage of shipping material. The demand for vessels and sailors was insatiable, so competition for these scarce resources was fierce. Trade was driven by profit and inevitably some shipowners cut corners to reduce costs; others simply hired the cheapest men available. There was no national training program for officers, many shortcomings in the industry and, for many, safety standards were abysmal, which led to too many accidents and losses. The Government eventually commissioned an enquiry, led by Mr. James Murray, to fire a warning shot across the industry's bows. In 1848, after five years of deliberation, he reported that the merchant service

"was at all times imperilled by the incompetence of British shipmasters."

Many shipowners disputed this one sided view, but in response, the Board of Trade drafted a Bill

"for improving the condition of masters, mates, and seamen, and maintaining discipline in the merchant service."

It became 'The Mercantile Marine Act of 1850,' establishing marine boards in all major ports so that, for the first time, men seeking to be masters or mates in blue water ships would be strictly examined to determine their qualifications and suitability. The boards were also empowered to enquire into marine mishaps. Another even more comprehensive act followed in 1854. From then on, British deep sea vessels had to be commanded and officered by experienced, certificated individuals who had been trained, educated and examined in academic, as well as nautical, subjects.

The Acts carried a clear warning for shipowners: improve the industry yourselves or the Government will do it for you. Annoyed by this meddling, and fearing further legislation, shipowners took the initiative. In 1857, in Liverpool, Mr. Ralph Brocklebank, owner of the well known family shipping line, and Captain Judkins of the American Royal Mail Line (later renamed the Cunard Line) arranged a public meeting to consider

"the arbitrary and oppressive powers vested by the Merchant Shipping Acts in the Board of Trade in cases of casualties in merchant ships, and the manner in which such investigations were conducted."

Similar meetings were arranged in Southampton and London. The Liverpool meeting was attended by local shipping magnates, sea captains, port owners and others in the shipping business. They resolved that

"an association be formed, to be called the 'Mercantile Marine Service Association of Liverpool and the Western Ports,' and to work in close union with similar organisations in Southampton and London."

A committee was formed with James Beazley as the first chairman. Members included Captain John Clint, Ralph Brocklebank, S Graves, Robert Rankin and Samuel Rathbone. The Liverpool MMSA immediately began to consider improvements resolving to

"take every legitimate step to elevate to their proper position the Officers of the Mercantile Marine, and to promote the interests of the service generally."

Significantly they decided,

"to establish schools, afloat and onshore, for the training and education of boys and men for the service."

On 19th April 1858 a committee was formed to consider

"what steps should be taken."

Parallel to these developments in the merchant service, important changes were afoot in the Royal Navy. There had always been a forced flow of seamen press-ganged from the merchant service to the Royal Navy, but the ever growing and conflicting demands of trade and warfare were straining both services to the breaking point. The outbreak of the Crimean War in 1854 demonstrated that the Royal Navy could not operate effectively without a proper reserve of trained officers and men available from the merchant service. The Royal Naval Reserve was formed with 'district ships' stationed in major ports to help recruitment and develop better relations between the two services. The Mersey's ship was HMS *Hastings*, an old, two-deck, sixty gun ship commanded by Captain William Robert Mends RN. He was to play a pivotal role in the founding of *Conway*.

On 12th June 1858, the MMSA committee decided to approach the Government for provision of a ship or vessel to be stationed in the Mersey as a training ship. They met Captain Mends to seek his help and discovered an ardent supporter of a better trained merchant service able to provide a professional Royal Naval Reserve. Captain Mends and the *Hastings's* officers were co-opted onto the MMSA committee. Captain Mends took the project under his wing and developed a detailed plan for the school and an approach to the Admiralty. The goal was simple,

"to train boys to become officers in the merchant service."

They would request from the Admiralty

"a small vessel, fitted up as a training school and placed in the Mersey."

He submitted the application and, on 1ˢᵗ July, Dr. Lyon Playfair attended an MMSA meeting on behalf of the First Lord of the Admiralty to learn more of their plans. He was favourably impressed, promised full Admiralty support and agreed to petition the First Lord, Sir John Pakington, directly for provision of a suitable vessel. Pakington was also supportive as undoubtedly the Royal Navy saw the benefit of better qualified merchant service officers. The investment proved a valuable one. Throughout her life, cadets leaving *Conway* became members of the Royal Naval Reserve, serving with distinction in virtually every major campaign the Royal Navy embarked upon. Many cadets joined the Royal Navy and at least 40 achieved flag rank.

On 16ᵗʰ July 1858, the Admiralty offered to loan HMS *Vestal*, a roomy, 26 gun frigate then lying at Chatham. The committee were not initially convinced. They wanted a vessel

"which could be handled by the boys with little help and could go to sea during the summer months."

However, on 19ᵗʰ July, they agreed to accept *Vestal*. A deputation led by Captain Paton visited the Admiralty formally to accept the offer and discuss arrangements for fitting her out. A gun brig of approximately 250 tons was promised for summer voyages, but this never materialised. The school would be called 'The School Frigate Vessel of the Mercantile Marine Association of Liverpool,' a snappy title that was soon superseded by 'The Mercantile Marine School Ship,' or MMSS for short. It soon became apparent that the cost of fitting out *Vestal* was too great, so the committee asked for a smaller vessel. Old *Conways* might reflect on how close they came to being Old *Vestals*, and New Chums, *Vestal* Virgins! The Admiralty offered instead a smaller frigate, HMS *Conway*, a coastguard ship at Devonport. She was a sixth rate man of war of 652 tons and 26 guns, nicknamed

The First HMS Conway

a Jackass or Donkey frigate. This was a derogatory term because the difference between a Jackass or Donkey frigate and a real frigate was considered similar to the difference between a donkey and a race-horse. She was a 3 masted ship with one covered main gun deck. Her history is summarised in *Appendix B*. On 9th December, the Admiralty formally confirmed the loan.

Captain John Clint, a Liverpool shipowner, went to Devonport to oversee her fitting out. Everything proceeded well and, on 6th January 1859, *Conway* was ready for her transit to the Mersey. The committee advertised for a temporary master, mate and 5 seamen to take charge of *Conway* until her master was appointed. On 2nd February 1859, a committee was appointed to manage the school and its funds. It was decided that she would be moored in the Sloyne, off Rock Ferry slip at the foot of the Bedford Road on the southern, Birkenhead side of the river.

Everything was ready for the Ship's arrival and the school's inauguration. On Saturday 5th February 1859, with a Mr. Paul from the dockyard in charge, *Conway* left Devonport towed by the *Virago,* a 6 gun paddle sloop. She arrived in the Mersey on the evening of the 9th to a welcoming party from the committee and was moored off Birkenhead dock wall. By Monday 14th February she was at her mooring in the Sloyne.

The committee decided to equip her for 120 boys and raised £1,200 in donations and subscriptions from shipowners, shipbuilders, sailors and other interested parties. The Ship was thoroughly cleaned, painted and lime-washed. The main and fore hatches in the upper deck were replaced by double companionways to facilitate access to the main deck. The upper deck between the hatches was removed and covered with a large skylight. A grating was added in the main deck below to admit light to the lower deck. The main deck was originally one large open space, but the fore-part was divided slightly to provide a lavatory on one side and a meat store and scullery on the opposite side. A large simple stove provided the galley and the only heat in winter. The main deck was the original

Rock Ferry Pier (Indefatigable In Background)

gun deck, but the guns had been removed and the ports enlarged to admit more light. It was intended to provide 6 guns for gun drills, but these never materialised so gun drills took place on the *Hastings* and her replacements. The Captain's spacious cabin was fitted out aft on the main deck. The lower deck was modified to provide a small sick bay forward, whilst aft there were staff cabins, a library and a small staff wardroom. The masts were all fully rigged and used by cadets, so small safety nets were provided below each mast. It took several months to complete all these changes, during which time members of staff were recruited and vacancies for cadets were advertised. The Ship was regularly open to visitors and received extensive glowing coverage in the local press. By July 1859, *Conway* was ready.

CHAPTER 3

1859–61 CAPTAIN C POWELL

The First Captain Superintendent and His Staff

The advertisement for a Captain Superintendent to run *Conway* generated 55 applications. The committee selected Captain Charles Powell, Master of the *Anglo-Saxon,* a West Indian mail steamer. He was responsible for:

- the smooth and orderly running of the Ship
- all training, especially with seamanship, boat work and the use of instruments
- cadets' records including details of discipline, training, tuition and examination results
- contracts for the supply of materiel, victuals and clothing.

He was obliged to make a full report to the committee at least once a month on the state of the Ship and cadets.

There were 15 members of staff. The Chief Officer, Mr. Littler, and 4 seamen teachers provided practical seamanship training and oversaw the Ship's daily routine. The Headmaster, master and two assistant masters looked after academic education. The first Headmaster was Mr. Dodson MA, who joined from Greenwich High School to teach navigation, mathematics and the use of nautical instruments. The master, Mr. Hudson, from Chester Training College, taught English and general science. The carpenter taught ship construction and, with 2 stewards and 2 cooks, saw to everything else. An honorary surgeon was appointed, Mr. T Hamilton of Rock Ferry, who also taught emergency first aid.

By early 1859, applications for positions in *Conway* were being received. The Cadet magazine in November 1912 reported that (Captain) W P Lapage

> *"had the distinction of being … the first arrival on the first joining day viz., August 1ˢᵗ 1859."*

All cadets were allocated a serial number and his was 25. He had a successful career at sea, retiring in 1892. John Masefield, in his earlier history of the Ship, claimed the first cadet was (Captain) Howard Campbell. He rose to command in the Canadian Beaver Line and died at sea. He was cadet number 8, but actually arrived onboard before cadet number 1, (Captain) Berkeley Collins. However, as Captain Lapage was subsequently feted by the Conway Club, for this it must be assumed that he was the first cadet.

Captain C. Powell

It was decided to limit numbers to 50 for the first 6 months but there were just 17 cadets on opening day. Average numbers soon grew to around a 100 and from February to July 1860 the average was 101. Cadets wore a uniform of blue cloth with fine gilt buttons embossed with an anchor; jackets had upright collars and gold braid in front of the neck. Caps bore the badge of the MMSA.

Opening Ceremony

The official inauguration was on Monday 1st August 1859. It was covered extensively in the local press. The Liverpool Mercury expended copious column inches, glowingly extolling the virtues of every aspect of the Ship, cadets, staff and routine. The cadets paraded on deck with the Captain Superintendent and the staff as hosts. The committee, their wives and numerous visitors toured the Ship, remarking on the cleanliness, lighting and ventilation. The band of HMS *Nile*, in port on a recruiting drive, played on the upper deck. Naturally there were several speeches. Captain Mends RN considered *Conway*

> "an institution which it was impossible to rate too highly."

The new committee chairman, Captain Sproule, a senior Brocklebank master, was confident that in two years *Conway* would

> "produce a set of boys who would not disgrace any ship in the Kingdom."

To loud cheers, Mr. Brocklebank announced a £5 prize for the cadet making the most commendable progress. After three cheers for Captain Mends and three more for the shipowners who were supporting *Conway* so nobly, Captain Powell took the stage. He confirmed they were all determined to do their best to give a good account at the end of the first half year.

For the first year or so, many cadets served for only a couple of terms, just to get the feel of naval life, but the plan was to accept boys at the age of 13 for a two year course, after which they would go to sea as apprentices. Each year had 2 terms so cadets in their last term were christened Quarter Boys, QBs for short. Apprenticeships at sea started around the age of 15 and lasted 4 years, but the shipping company of Jones, Palmer and Co announced that they would treat 2 years in *Conway* as the equivalent of 1 year's apprenticeship at sea. A boy leaving *Conway* successfully would have completed one quarter of his apprenticeship and so gain a considerable advancement over his contemporaries at sea the title QB adapted to this meaning and, in later years, its meaning evolved again to describe any cadet in his last term. The concession made Jones, Palmer and Co a natural first choice for the best cadets and other companies quickly followed suit! The term QB remained thereafter even though by the 1960s and 70s some cadets were spending 4 years, 12 terms in *Conway*.

Life at sea, then and now, was not for the faint hearted. It was tough, difficult and very demanding. It required men with a steady heart, a firm nerve and a ready hand. As stated in his articles, a ship's Captain truly was 'Master under God' with absolute authority and complete responsibility for the conduct and safety of his crew, vessel, cargo and passengers. A few Old *Conways'* reminiscences illustrate the life a cadet could expect at sea:

Indira ran aground in the South Pacific and the 7 officers (one an Old *Conway*) and 32 crew set off in 2 small boats towards an island,

> *"where natives could be seen gathering. They being hostile no landing could be effected."*

A dhow was sighted and came alongside to offer assistance until the boats realised the dhow intended to take them captive for ransom. After a 'slight scrape' they escaped from the dhow before being captured by another group. They eventually made it to safety.

One Old *Conway* tried to explain daily routine in the clipper ship *Evesham Abbey*.

> *"To give you an impression, just turn out of your comfortable room on some wet night, with the thermometer a little above freezing point. Put on some wet clothes then go out and roll yourself in the nearest pool of water. Add to that the imagination of being knocked down and rolled about the deck, besides the danger at any moment of being washed overboard, there to form a meal for some hungry shark. That will be an approximation of the state of affairs onboard a ship at sea in a gale."*

> *"A very frequent occurrence on long voyages is for the seamen to growl at the Master and owners. But sometimes this discontent goes further and there are disturbances. Let there be no hesitation about which side to take – stand by your Captain."*

> *"One of my men made use of some foul language. I called out to him to stop as I would not allow it. He gave me some impudence. He had a knife in his hand and threw it back as though he intended to give me the length of it...."*

How would you have reacted? There were no police to call, your life appears in danger... The Old *Conway* in question reacted immediately, overpowered the individual and survived by force of will alone.

After being wrecked in *Garston* off Starbuck Island, a cadet straight from *Conway* found himself in the middle of the empty Pacific in charge of a 20 foot lifeboat and 8 hard sailors, all years his senior.

> *"We rigged an oar for a mast and a quilt for a sail."*

One tin of meat and some damp mouldy biscuits were all the food they had and after several days this was almost all gone. The crew literally began to eye up the weaker survivors as a potential meal. He persevered; 23 days and 1600 miles later they all landed safely on Wallis Island and rescue.

> *"One day a drunken Spaniard tried to stab me, but fortunately he missed his aim. I didn't, as I shot him in the arm, breaking his elbow."*

In a 20 year period, 34 old *Conway*s lost their lives at sea washed overboard, falling into the hold or from masts, or from sickness. Not everyone could survive as an officer at sea, so *Conway* tested and prepared boys for these challenges. *Conway* taught cadets how to cope with adversity, take decisions, inspire confidence and lead.

Daily Routine

The Ship's boats were be used to transfer cadets, members of staff and supplies between the Rock Ferry slip and the Ship. *Conway* was therefore always associated more with the Birkenhead side of the Mersey than the Liverpool side. In 1899, Rock Ferry pier was built alongside the slip as one of several Mersey ferry crossing points. The open, deep water mooring was approximately a quarter mile ESE of the river end of the original pier. In 1859, it was a quiet, rural and scenic spot with just

---

And You'll Find on the Bridge a Conway Boy
Captain Matthew 'Chummy' Webb (1860–62)

Matthew Webb joined the Ship at the age of 12 on 20th June 1860. He was popular and quickly earned the nickname Chummy. "We thought very little of him as a swimmer but admired his staying power. He could swim about for an hour without putting a foot on the floor, although in a race he was nowhere."

He left Conway on 1st April 1862 and joined Rathbone Brothers. Returning from the USA in the passenger steamer 'Russia', he saw a member of the crew fall into sea as the ship was making 14 knots in a high sea. The waves were described as "houses high" and "such as no one had ever before encountered."

Webb dived in to rescue him and although he grabbed his cap, the man sank quickly and was drowned. Webb was alone in the water in the middle of the Atlantic for 35 minutes. 'Russia' returned and found him. In a huge understatement accounts record that "he was picked up with difficulty."

In England, he was awarded the first Stanhope Gold Medal, the Silver Medal of the Royal Humane Society and the Medal of the Liverpool Humane Society.

In 1875, he left the sea determined to become the first person to swim the English Channel. As preparation he swam from Blackwall to Gravesend on the Thames, about 19 miles, in 4 hours and 45 minutes. Next, he swam from Dover to Ramsgate, about 17 miles in 8 hours and 45 minutes. At 12.56 pm on Tuesday 24th August 1875, Webb, dressed in his red Conway bathing shorts, dived off Dover Pier to the cheers of a large crowd. He swam strongly, but was swept off course by the tide. At 11.50 pm he was swimming strongly, using the breast stroke at a steady twenty a minute. By 3 am, he showed signs of weakening, his face was covered in salt and blotches but he struggled on. At 10.41 am, he finally stood up in a few feet of water and struggled ashore on Calais beach. It had taken him 21 hours 45 minutes, without touching any boat or physical support. He ate nothing, but drank cod liver oil, coffee, brandy, ale and beef tea. The pilots accompanying him estimated he swam at least 50 miles allowing for the tides. On the 16th September 1875, he visited the Ship and was presented with a pair of inscribed binoculars by the cadets. In 1878, he took up competitive long distance races and extreme endurance events. They took a terrible toll on his body and spirit, so in 1883 he decided on one last big event. He would swim the dangerous rapids at Niagara Falls. Local opinion strongly advised him against it, convinced it was madness. But Webb was sure he could prevail. On 24th July 1883, wearing his red Conway swimming shorts, he entered the water and swam off confidently. As he entered the fast flowing, turbulent waters things quickly changed. He was swept into the whirlpool and did not surface. His body was found a few days later, miles downstream.

The Ship learned of his death with great sadness. In time the Captain Webb Shield was donated as a swimming prize and competed for by the cadets. It is now held by the National Maritime Museum.

a few large houses dotting the shoreline. Cadets would arrive by train at the local station and walk the few hundred yards down Bedford Road, carrying their kit to the slip where they would be taken out to the Ship. The scene today is totally transformed. Rock Ferry is completely developed with housing and large unattractive industrial buildings, and cut off from the Bedford Road by the A41 Rock Ferry Bypass. A long spur has been added to the pier along the line of the old moorings and is now a rather derelict oil jetty.

Conway's organisation and routine were deliberately arranged to closely match that at sea. Cadets were organised into Port and Starboard Watches. In the morning, one watch attended practical seamanship classes on deck, aloft and in the Ship's small boats. There were 4 small boats initially and a large lifeboat was soon added, a donation by a Captain Henderson of London. The other watch attended academic lessons below on the main deck, which could be sub-divided by canvas screens. In the afternoons roles were reversed.

Considerable emphasis was placed on organisation, trust and strict discipline. This was not done in any conscious or overt way. Cadets learned to respond promptly to orders, to accept responsibility for themselves and others, take the initiative, make decisions and generally conduct themselves in a sensible, trustworthy and reliable manner. Perhaps mirroring this, the Ship's motto was taken from the King James Bible, 1 Corinthians, Chapter 16, verse 13:

"Quit Ye Like Men Be Strong."

Modern bibles translate it somewhat differently:

"Be men of courage; be strong."

Rock Ferry from Ship 1936

Mooring from Rock Ferry 1936

Cadets slept in hammocks on the lower deck. They rose at 6 am, washed, exercised, cleaned the Ship and breakfasted at 8 am. The ensign,

"a central white anchor on a blue ground, and in white upon a red ground in each of the 4 corners the letters MMSS" (Mercantile Marine School Ship)

was raised each morning at reveille and lowered in the evening at sunset. Prayers on the main deck followed breakfast and then classes until lunch at twelve. They then had 30 minutes for play followed by an afternoon of lessons. The evening meal was followed by a short break and then a homework period prior to turning in.

Every cadet was personally responsible for the cleanliness of a designated part of the Ship, and the Captain and Chief Officer inspected everything every evening.

The lower deck also served as the mess deck for all meals. Food was simple and monotonous. Each week, a cadet would receive 7 pints of milk, 7 pounds of bread, 14 ounces of sugar, 4 ounces of butter or cheese, 1½ pounds of flour, 1 pound of rice, 1 pound of oatmeal, 5 pounds of fresh boneless meat, 1 pound of boneless salt meat, ½ pint of peas, ¼ of a pound of suet, ¼ pound of raisins and 3½ pounds of potatoes and vegetables. Tea and c-offee were supplied as required. The cadets soon developed nicknames for regular dishes; tea was 'skilly,' cheese and potatoes were 'cheese crap' and bread was

Daily Exercise Late 1860s

'soduk.' An extensive list, including the evocative 'toe nail pie' and 'shit on a raft,' is in *Appendix A*, along with a wealth of other slang terms and staff nicknames used over the years.

As the cadets and staff settled into their evolving routine, all was not well with Captain Powell. He had suffered a number of desperately sad losses in the year since taking command. First his wife, then his child, sister and a much loved aunt died over a period of a few months. He felt the losses deeply and decided he could not cope with *Conway's* growing demands. He resigned his command and in April 1860, he returned to sea. The committee set about finding a replacement at very short notice.

CHAPTER 4

1860–62 CAPTAIN A ROYER RN

Very little is known of *Conway's* second Captain Superintendent, other than his name Captain Alfred Royer RN. The name is very unusual and appears to be of Huguenot origin. He entered the RN prior to 1834 and was a lieutenant and single in 1843. Only one other tantalising clue to his life exists. He published a book of his experiences during the Crimean War, "The English Prisoners in Russia: A personal narrative of the First Lieutenant of HMS *Tiger*, together with an account of his journey in Russia." It was published by Chapman and Halland and must have been reasonably popular, for a second edition was published in 1854. It was also translated into German and published in Leipzig. It is out of print and no copy has yet come to light. His brother, Charles, was also in the RN and rose to the rank of Commander. We do not know Alfred Royer's movements from 1854 to 1860, or how he came to be *Conway's* second Captain Superintendent.

The first Chief Officer, Mr. Littler, also left at some point and Captain Richard Mowll RN replaced him.

Growing Success

The committee and staff had expressed their determination to make *Conway* a success and that seemed to be happening. *Conway* cadets were soon joining shipping companies and demonstrating the quality of their training. She was the first pre-sea training ship established to train merchant service officer cadets and was clearly moving on the right track. Independent confirmation of the Ship's achievements came in 1861, when the Board of Trade officially confirmed that all UK shipping companies would accept 2 years at *Conway* as the equivalent of 1 year at sea. This then made *Conway* extremely attractive to any boy planning a career at sea and was a major contributor to *Conway's* success for over a 100 years. This concession also ended the practice of boys attending *Conway* for just a few terms. From this point on, every cadet would have to undergo a full 2 years of training culminating in passing out examinations. To confirm they had successfully completed a full course, cadets would receive a *Conway* 'Passing Out Certificate of Exemption' when they left.

Perhaps spurred by Liverpool's success, the London MMSA founded a training ship in 1862 and were loaned HMS *Worcester*. Friendly rivalry between the 2 ships was to grow and thrive for the rest of their lives. Imitation is the sincerest form of flattery and the *Conway* model spread until there were over 80 such establishments in the UK and abroad. TS *Mercury* on the Hamble was opened in 1888 and privately financed by Charles Hoare, a wealthy banker. TS *Pangbourne*, another lifelong rival, was founded on the Thames in 1917, South Africa's *General Botha* in 1922 and India's *Dufferin* in 1927 all grew out of *Conway's* ongoing success. These were all officer cadet ships but the benefits of pre-sea training soon spread to seamen as well. In 1863, Captain John Clint, so influential in *Conway's* formation, as well as the Bibby shipping company in Liverpool, decided to set up a training ship for boy seamen. In 1864 they opened TS *Indefatigable*. She was moored close to *Conway* off Rock Ferry. As we shall see, the 2 ships' fates were always to be intertwined. Similar vessels sprang up all around Britain's coast.

A New Ship

As early as the end of June 1860, there were many more applications for cadetships than could be accommodated. It was quickly realised that the Ship was

> *"much too small to afford proper accommodation for the staff and pupils, and to carry out efficiently the training and education of boys."*

There must have been some embarrassment at this admission, as the larger *Vestal* had been turned down in 1858 because conversion costs were too great. Now more money would have to be spent refitting another vessel. The committee petitioned the Admiralty for a larger vessel. The Secretary of the Admiralty, Admiral Lord Clarence Paget, son of the 1st Marquis of Anglesey, inspected *Conway* personally and agreed,

> *"Conway is somewhat confined."*

The local Royal Navy drill ship *Hastings* and Captain Mends RN had been replaced by *Majestic* and Captain Inglefield RN. The Admiralty sought his opinion of *Conway* training and her cadets. He had first hand experience of both, since he regularly taught cadets gun drill and was an enthusiastic supporter. With the support of Lord Paget and Captain Inglefield, the Admiralty agreed to provide a replacement. They offered HMS *Winchester*, a 60 gun Java class frigate launched in 1822.

The Second Conway ex Winchester

Winchester was described as a very comfortable and roomy ship, and *Conway*'s committee quickly accepted her. A brief summary of her career is in *Appendix C*. She was moved from harbour duty in Chatham to Liverpool and, in late summer and early autumn 1861, she was fitted out for school service at a cost of £1,400. The Admiralty agreed that the name *Conway* should be retained for the school ship, so in November 1861 the two vessels exchanged names. The original *Conway* became *Winchester* and was towed away to Aberdeen, where she served as an RNR drill ship. No other record has been found of her, even in the local Aberdeen newspaper; but by 1876, she had been replaced. It is assumed that at some point she was scrapped.

Conway, ex *Winchester*, moved onto the Sloyne moorings just off Rock Ferry pier in the very heart of the busy Mersey shipping scene. Cadets quickly adapted to their new wooden mother. Although she provided more spacious accommodation, there seemed little change in the standard of facilities. After reveille, 102 cadets

> *"had to rush to the wash place with our basins (there were no fitted wash basins) and wait for the basins to fill from four slow-running taps. Cold work in winter for the last few boys, the wash place being in the bows and the hawse pipes admitting air freely."*

Twice a week the cadets combined exercise with cleanliness and bathed at the Cornwallis Street swimming baths. The ferry pier was very busy, so cadets used the slip alongside before marching up Bedford Road to the baths. Rock Ferry was a rural, residential district on the Birkenhead side of the river.

> *"In those days a few minutes walk would take us right into the country."*

En-route to the pier they could see Brunel's *Great Eastern*, which was moored nearby for some time. Her captain visited *Conway* and regaled the cadets with stories of haunting by the ghosts of 2 unfortunate riveters allegedly sealed by mistake in her double hull! She was eventually beached for repair between Rock Ferry and New Ferry, and then broken up. One of her galleys was bought and installed in *Conway*. Cadets frequently explored the beached ship, scrambling in through the narrow screw hole, carefully avoiding the patrolling bailiffs.

Ferries constantly criss-crossed the river between Birkenhead and the great port of Liverpool sprawled along the opposite, Northern riverbank. On a promontory overlooking the Sloyne the ruined buildings and steeple of Birkenhead Priory dominated the scene. Part of the Priory now houses the *Conway* memorial chapel. The huge, world-famous Cammell Laird shipyard was a short distance downstream from the Ship. Busy docks, warehouses and factories lined the rest of the banks opposite as far as the eye could see. Chimneys sprouted everywhere, belching smoke and dirt into the air. For generations this quietly drifted back down onto every surface, so that the whole scene had drained into shades of grime. But in the midst of this industrial landscape, the sky could be a restless wave of blue with the river running from brown to green, and a fresh breeze promising swift passage to the whole world just downstream. Vessels were constantly arriving and departing, muscled hither and thither by busy tugs, many mooring nearby. Many ships passed by on their way to the Manchester ship canal a few miles upstream. Cunard's buoy was very close so cadets could see the splendid new wooden side-wheel Cunarders like *Scotia* and *Persia* and dream of their own future in such vessels. Also moored close by the Ship were two armoured rams built by Cammell Laird

And You'll Find on The Bridge a Conway Boy
Lt. Warrington Baden-Powell RNR
KC Admiralty Court (1861-64)

Warrington joined the Ship in 1861 and went on to become a Master Mariner and the founder of the Sea Scouts. He was undoubtedly a major influence on his younger brother Robert who said of him: "It was under his guidance that I, when a youngster, began my scouting as a Sea Scout. He was himself both a sailor and a boy at heart and so his teaching told. I have never forgotten those breezy times and the things that I learned under him have had their life-long value for me. To the end he remained as he had lived, a sailor and a boy. It was largely thanks to his interest in boys and in seamanship that Sea Scouting became popular in the early days of our movement, so that when the Great War came suddenly upon the nation the Sea Scouts proved able at once to take over the duties of the Coastguards when these were called away to man the fleet. The Scouts watched our Coasts from John O'Groats to the Land's End during the whole period of the War. Also they provided a considerable contingent of signallers, cooks and bridge boys to man the auxiliary fleet. They so acquitted themselves that at the end of the war they received the public thanks of the Admiralty and of His Majesty the King himself." The Sea Scouts were officially incorporated into the movement in 1910 and Warrington wrote the first official Sea Scout manual, Sea Scouting and Seamanship for Boys.

Warrington was also a great exponent of the sailing canoe or canoe yawl. In 1871, at the age of 24, he paddled and sailed a canoe on a cruise around the Baltic Sea that included stops in Germany, Denmark and Sweden as described in his book, Canoe Travelling, published in 1871. In 1876 he became a barrister and was admitted to the Admiralty Bar becoming a King's Counsel.

for the US Confederate forces. They had been impounded by the British Government, uncertain which side to support in the American Civil War. With so much river traffic, other ships often fouled *Conway*'s anchors.

"One afternoon shortly after school the Ship gave an unusual movement and we were adrift."

It was slack water and a ferry helped *Conway* to a position where she could drop her single remaining anchor. When the mooring was lifted for repair, 15 anchors, large and small, came up with it in a compact mass! Increasingly, all these vessels carried Old *Conways* who would return to the Ship and excite the air with stories of the sea, seamen and exotic places. Within weeks of leaving the Ship, cadets might find themselves anywhere in the world. A random selection of their voyages includes Mauritius to Newcastle, Callao (Peru) to the UK, Java to New York, Liverpool to Calcutta, Philadelphia to Hiogo (Japan), Valparaiso to Iquique, and whaling around the Galapagos. One cadet reported a three week voyage that called at Granada, Trinidad, San Domingo, Jamaica, Cartegena, Savanilla, Colon, Limon and San Juan del Norte. Another wrote to his family,

"There are days at sea when I could have wept for very homesickness, and again there were days when the freshness and majesty of the sea seemed to throw a golden glamour over all the surroundings, and I felt that to be a sailor was a glorious privilege."

And You'll Find on The Bridge a Conway Boy
Captain Edward William Freeman

The year of Captain's Freeman's departure from Conway is not known, but it was most likely in the early 1860s. He was to be present at one of the most cataclysmic natural events of the 20th century. He was Master of the steamship Roddam, moored in the harbour at St Pierre, Martinique, when Mount Pele erupted on the 8th May 1902, killing 30,000 people in minutes and completely destroying the town. The damage was caused by a massive superheated mudflow surrounded by scorching fumes and ash travelling at over a 100 km per hour. "Nothing could compare with the immensity of that eruption. The opening of the earth, the pouring forth of lava, the clouds of smoke and steam, the darkening of atmosphere, the rumbling as of thunder. The experience of the Roddam enveloped in burning ashes, was a scene of horror which could hardly be conceived."

Captain Freeman was on deck talking to the local agent at about 7.45 am when they were startled by a tremendous outburst from the mountain. "Scarcely two minutes had elapsed before the whole city, port and shipping were enveloped in a fiery pall of death."

Instantly, Captain Freeman ordered his engine room staff to their posts below and those on deck to slip the cables. The Chief Engineer was scorched to death before he could gain shelter and the same tragic fate befell all the deck officers and most of the sailors, thereby preventing them from slipping the cables.

The ship was lying head-on to the shore, so he ran to the bridge and rang for full speed astern in order to back away from certain destruction and to break the anchor chain so they could escape. Fiercely burning sand was now falling all over the ship. A 3 metre high tsunami hit the ship. The cable parted but the ship was on fire in a dozen places. The bulk of the crew on deck were either killed outright or driven mad with pain from their burns. Fifteen of them jumped overboard to drown or be eaten by the sharks now swimming alongside the ship, almost as if they knew what was coming. The rudder was jammed to one side and he had huge difficulty manoeuvring out of harm's way. Captain Freeman and a few sailors, only one uninjured, struggled for two hours to get the ship out to sea. By now it was pitch dark in the fallout and new fires broke out as quickly as old ones were extinguished. The deadly, fiery shower was falling without intermission, actually setting his clothes on fire and burning the shoes off his feet, but Freeman stuck to his post and ultimately succeeded in bringing his flaming ship and the remnant of her brave crew to safety. The intensity of the falling matter was such that when they arrived in St Lucia the next day, 120 tons of ash had to be removed from the decks. The British Government presented Captain Freeman was with an inscribed cup "…in acknowledgement of his gallantry and devotion to duty on the occasion of the destruction of the town of St Pierre, Martinique, by a volcanic eruption on 8th May 1902."

The Mersey was proving an excellent place to expose boys to ships and shipping, but was not so favourable for her Captain Superintendent. In June 1862, amidst unspecified rumours of 'disturbance' onboard, Captain Royer left and was immediately replaced by the Chief Officer, Captain Richard Mowll RN.

CHAPTER 5

1862–71 CAPTAIN R MOWLL RN

The Third Captain Superintendent

Captain Richard Mowll RN came from a family with a formidable naval tradition in the UK, Australia and the USA. The first known Mowll seafarer became a Cinque Ports' pilot in 1710 and the family have an unbroken link with the sea right up to the present day, with one Mowll a retired Captain RN. Richard was a popular Christian name for the Mowlls, but the Captain Superintendent was nicknamed 'Old Mobby.' The Mowll family history records,

Capt. R Mowll RN

> *"Training ships had a tradition of harsh discipline which hardly fits with the character, so hopefully he was an exception to the rule."*

One cadet observed,

> *"He was strict but kind,"*

so the family traits seems to have run true. He came to *Conway* from the Royal Navy, where he had had a distinguished career. He was Chief Officer before being promoted to Captain Superintendent. He remained in the post for 9 years and brought important stability to the Ship after her formative years. Punishments in his time were simple and effective, mostly consisting of having leave stopped or pocket money cut. He also had more severe forms of punishment. Talking after lights out meant lashing up your hammock and marching up and down carrying it for 2 hours. Another involved standing on deck holding up one end of a bench for long periods. He seemed to have propensity for something called 'black draught',

> *"If we had a dislike for him it was because he gave us too much black draught."*

He frequently prescribed it as a punishment for anyone discovered at morning Divisions with dirty fingernails!

Recollections

> *"I hated scrubbing the upper-deck on winter mornings in bare feet. We had no sea boots. It was cold work, but doubtless was good as a hardening."*

> *"Wednesday afternoon was a half holiday. Those with the wherewithal spent the afternoon in the tuck shop (now The Admiral pub) at the head of the slip."*

> *"I never knew an officer or a master to take the slightest interest in the boys out of school hours."*

> *"There was a good deal of bullying and licking with rope teasers by senior cadets. Another problem at this time was the inadequacy of food but this was finally solved and matters then improved."*

By the end of 1864, there were 4 wooden walls moored in the Sloyne, *Conway*, *Akbar*, *Indefatigable* and *Clarence*. All but *Indefatigable* were two deckers. We know of the first two already. *Akbar* was a tough Protestant reform ship where boys could expect

"hard labour, hard tack and a hard bed."

They would learn there was

"a God, a heaven and a hell."

Clarence was a Catholic reformatory ship that trained boys as seamen for the merchant service. They were not too fond of their alma mater. In 1880, a boy set fire to her but the fire was quickly extinguished. In 1884, 6 boys set a more robust fire and she was burnt to the waterline. The boys went to jail for 5 years and the Admiralty loaned another vessel. In 1886, 10 boys rioted, seriously injuring one master and attempting to kill the Captain. The ringleader went to jail for 5 years, the rest received 12 months hard labour. In 1899, the ship was again burnt to the water. *Clarence* abandoned ship and went ashore permanently to, suitably, the old county prison building renamed as St Davids College in Mold.

The year was divided into 2 terms, one starting in February and the other in August. There was about 2 months holiday a year.

And You'll Find on the Bridge a Conway Boy
Captain John T Walbran (1862-64)

John Walbran joined Conway as a cadet at the same time Captain Mowll was appointed. He was in the first group of cadets to complete their course fully under Mowll's command. He disappeared from the scene for 28 years, so little is known of the man except a brief reminiscence by one of his officers. "There was nothing pompous about the captain; he was a man of warmth and charm who was welcomed wherever he went." In 1892, after a lifetime at sea, he assumed command of the Canadian government steamship 'Quadra' and wrote himself into Canadian history.

For the next 12 years, he patrolled the British Columbia coastline, making maps, servicing lighthouses, searching for missing ships and erecting beacons. He quickly became fascinated with local history, especially the origins of local place names. In 1896, he began writing a book on the subject 'British Columbia Place Names (Their Origin And History).' He researched existing print and manuscript material, but above all he tracked down knowledgeable locals and used his charm to coax anecdotal stories from them and collect vital oral history before it was lost. His book was a seminal work and made a distinctive contribution to the story of West Canada.

For a man so committed to place names and dedicated to British Columbia, it is fitting that Walbran Park, Walbran Valley and Walbran Creek were all named in his honour.

Instigation of the Queen's Gold Medal

Conway's reputation continued to improve. She was now an established success with growing importance in the training of a new breed of professional merchant service officers. An annual report acknowledged,

> *"Many of the leading shipowners of Liverpool will give a preference to the cadets of the Institution."*

On 4th February 1864, HM Queen Victoria acknowledged *Conway's* achievements and announced her intention to grant £50 annually, to be distributed in prizes to *Conway* boys, and to present annually a gold medal.

> *"Her Majesty's wish in the establishment of this prize is to encourage the boys to acquire and maintain the qualities which will make the finest sailor. They consist of cheerful submission to superiors, self-respect and independence of character, kindness and protection to the weak, readiness to forgive offence, desire to conciliate the differences of others, and above all, fearless devotion to duty, and unflinching truthfulness."*

These were high ideals, but they encapsulate what *Conway* strove to encourage in her cadets. They didn't just make fine sailors, they developed into exemplary men who succeeded in every walk of life for precisely those reasons.

The royal announcement continued.

> *"The medal will be open to boys who have been one year onboard the ship, and have received not less than half the total number of marks at the previous quarterly examinations. The commander, after conferring with the head masters, shall select not less than 3, nor more than 5 of the boys whom he considers to possess the qualities for which the prize is given. He shall then submit these names to the boys who have been assembled for the purpose in the school, and each boy who has been onboard 6 months previously to the time of distribution shall then and there vote for one of the boys so selected. The boy who receives the highest number of votes shall receive the medal. These regulations shall be placed upon a board on the main deck, to be called the Queen's Prize List, and the name of each boy who receives the medal shall be recorded upon such list."*

The board, a large framed black board, is now in the Conway Chapel at Birkenhead Priory and it faithfully records the names of all the winners in gold lettering. The first recipient was cadet Oswald Hillkirk. The complete list of winners is in *Appendix E*. Queen Victoria's award helped shape the lives of thousands and, through them, to influence the lives of countless others, which was probably her intent.

The Queen also awarded a prize to the boys competing for cadetships in the Royal Navy.

> *"The prize will consist of a binocular glass, with a suitable inscription, together with £35 towards the expense of the outfit of the boy."*

The then First Lord of the Admiralty gave a naval cadetship, to be awarded by the management committee each year. In June 1866, HRH The Duke of Edinburgh attended prize day and presented the prizes. Nearly 1000 visitors packed the Ship.

And You'll Find on the Bridge a Conway Boy
Kyrle Bellew, Actor (1865-67)

He left Conway in 1867 after a two year course and eventually became a well-known actor. He had an eventful career at sea. During one voyage to the Far East he was swept overboard and picked up for dead in the Bay of Bengal, but survived. Some years later, he washed overboard in the English Channel, picked for dead, but again survived. He spent a short while ashore before the sea called him back. This time his ship was burned and he spent 3 weeks in an open boat. He then spent some time in the Austrian Army, presumably some distance from the sea.

He emigrated to Australia where he had a short career as a public speaker. He was swept up in the New South Wales gold rush but left stranded. Described as having, "a fine appearance and a singularly beautiful voice," he found a troupe of actors and worked his way back to Melbourne. Then, at the grand age of 19, he decided to become a full time actor. One of his old sea captains allowed him to work his passage home - the ship was nearly lost rounding Cape Horn during exceptionally icy conditions. 10 days after arriving back in London he was on the stage. He became a member of Henry Irving's troupe based at the Lyceum.

In 1884, he teamed up with another Old Conway, Frederick John Fagus, who was a celebrated novelist and playwright under the pen name Hugh Conway. His novel 'Called Back' was "one of the most remarkable successes of the last 100 years."

It proved so popular he turned it into a stage play and it ran at the Prince of Wales Theatre from 20th May 1884 for the rest of the year. Kyrle Bellew played the lead. Hugh Conway died in Monte Carlo in 1885 and is buried in Nice. There is a literary scholarship in his name at Bristol University and a stained glass window in his memory at St Stephens Church, Bristol, where he grew up. Bellew meantime formed his own successful repertory and toured the world for 10 years before returning to Australia where he became involved in some successful mining ventures. He died in 1911 in Salt Lake City, USA. Conway training certainly developed adaptability.

"The pupils were all dressed in their neat sailor-like uniform of blue jacket and waistcoat with white trousers."

In 1866, after 7 years of costs, including fitting out 2 ships in succession, the committee was able to announce that all debts were cleared and that they held £500 in their reserves. *Conway* had been fitted out for 125 boys but the record of cadet numbers in *Appendix F* shows a gradual decline in numbers through the first years of Mowll's command. There were 102 cadets in 1862, which increased to 126 cadets in 1864, but then fell back to 117 in 1865, 108 in 1866 and just 94 in June 1867. Later in 1867, it dropped again to just 89, but by June 1868 numbers were back up to 123. The rebound was perhaps influenced by the royal patronage.

1867 Extracts From The 8th Annual Report

This report was more a prospectus than an annual report. It contains no balance sheet but says the balance in favour of the funds was about £700, a significant improvement from the £500 held only one year earlier. It records that £80 had to be spent in changing the Ship's moorings, but there is no information about annual running costs. It is, however, *"somewhat profuse in verbatim reports of speeches and letters that might be well curtailed by abridgment and by omitting repetitions."*

It does tell us something of the aims and daily routine.

"It is designed mainly to train and complete the education of boys intended for officers in the merchant navy. Boys intended for the Royal Navy are also admitted, and receive special training for that service."

"The ship is under the direction of the Mercantile Marine Service Association, which comprises about 900 captains sailing from the port of Liverpool. There is a complete and efficient Nautical and Educational Staff maintained, by whom the boys are carefully and regularly Instructed, and exercised in all the duties of a first-class ship, and receive a general education. No boys are received under the age of 12, or who have passed their 16th birthday. Boys cannot remain longer than 3 years. The boys are taught to sling and lash up their own hammocks; and in summer have to scrub their hammocks and bags. Each in his turn serves as messman for one day to his mess, under the inspection and guidance of the captain of the mess. In turn the boys keep an anchor watch, 2 at a time, for 2 hours. On 2 afternoons in each week the boys are landed for recreation. The captains of subdivisions are boys who, for exemplary conduct, have been selected for these positions of trust and authority. They are exempt from the manual labour of washing decks or being mess men, and there are other privileges attached to the office that make it an object of emulation to the

And You'll Find on the Bridge a Conway Boy
Admiral Sir Sackville Hamilton Carden KCMG RN (1868-70)

Sackville Carden joined the Royal Navy direct from Conway in 1870 and was the first Conway cadet to achieve flag rank.

Prior to the First World War, he saw active service in the Egyptian and Sudan campaigns of 1882-84 and the Benin expedition of 1897. He was promoted Captain in 1899 and Rear-Admiral in 1908. His first command was Nile's sister ship London.

At the outbreak of war he was moved from his position as superintendent of the Malta dockyard to command the Mediterranean fleet. Winston Churchill, the First Lord of the Admiralty, asked him to produce a strategy for the Dardanelles campaign. He proposed a three-stage operation: the bombardment of the Turkish forts protecting the Dardanelles, the clearing of the minefields and then the invasion fleet travelling up the Straits, through the Sea of Marmara to Constantinople. Carden argued that to be successful the operation would need twelve battleships, three battle-cruisers, three light cruisers, sixteen destroyers, six submarines, four sea-planes and twelve minesweepers. Lord Kitchener and Churchill liked the plan and on their advice Prime Minister Asquith approved the operation. Carden commanded the naval forces and launched the first attack on 19th February 1915. The attack was successful but Carden fell ill on 18th March and had to be replaced. His plan was amended to include major troop landings much further south, resulting in the disaster now known as Gallipoli.

Resigning from the British Navy two years later with the rank of full Admiral, he lived in retirement until his death in 1930.

well-disposed. Divine Service is performed on Sundays, and Prayers are read twice each day. Corporal punishment is only administered to boys whose names have been struck off the Good Conduct List, or for first offences of a very serious kind."

In 1871, Lord Dufferin the Chancellor, gave away the prizes and a new annual prize, the Dufferin Prize, was founded for practical seamanship. Captain Mowll had done well. It was acknowledged that the difficulties of managing *Conway* when he took command

"were very great indeed."

Now *Conway* was consistently turning out fine cadets valued by the shipping companies and the Royal Navy.

"Here is the difference between a Conway boy and a 'green' hand. To the 'green' one the officer on deck has to tell him everything minutely: what block, sheave, etc., to put a rope through. To a Conway boy he simply says 'Here, so and so, reeve this' and he expects that it will be done properly. Many a time has our Captain given me the latitude and longitude, and asked me to work a problem that he is working so as to check him if wrong."

Royal patronage had underlined her status and achievements. Numbers had recovered to desired levels. *Conway* was debt free; indeed, it had good reserves. On 9th August, 'Old Mobby' gave notice he wished to retire. He had earned his rest. *Conway* was now an institution, not a novelty. After years of Mowll's inspirational leadership she needed a steady hand to guide her forward.

CHAPTER 6

1871–81 CAPTAIN E FRANKLIN RN

Conway's third Captain Superintendent was another ex-Royal Navy man, Captain Edward Bond Franklin RN. He entered the navy in 1844 and rose steadily though the ranks. In January 1854, he was a Lieutenant; on 20 July 1860, he was Lieutenant Commander on *Banterer* in the East Indies and China. He participated in the capture of the Peiko Forts in 1858 and was Flag Lieutenant to Sir J Hope at the capture of Keh Ding in October 1862. By 1863, he was a Commander and in 1870 he was Captain. He became Captain Superintendent of *Conway* in 1871. He seems to have inspired mixed emotions. One cadet recalled,

Capt Franklin and Staff

"He was a perfect gentleman of the old Navy type, always ready to show kindness, and plainly pained when he found it his duty to award punishment."

Whereas another felt,

"He was sometimes unjust and small-minded."

He remained in post for 10 years, during which time *Conway* was to undergo many changes, not the least of which was a third change of ship. His wife was,

"One of the dearest and best of women with a heart of gold."

Her presence,

"made the Ship more homelike."

1874 May

Scarlet fever broke out onboard, so speech day was cancelled. After at least 2 boys died of the fever, the cadets were all sent home early. The disease highlighted the Ship's shortcoming, the lower deck was poorly ventilated, the sick bay could not cope with the isolation needs of a serious disease, washing and toilet facilities were completely inadequate and there simply was not enough space for the number of cadets. *Conway*, (ex *Winchester*), with one main gun deck, 173 feet long, 45 broad, weighing 487 tons and designed for a crew of 450, was simply too small. The Admiralty were asked if they could replace her with something larger and they came up trumps, offering HMS *Nile*. *Nile* was huge. Two main gun decks, 240 feet long, 53 feet broad, displacing 2,622 tons and designed for a crew of 850. Details of her history are in *Appendix D*.

And You'll Find on the Bridge a Conway Boy
Major Sir Hamilton Gould Adams
KCMG CMGH CB (1871-73)

This cadet went on to prove that Old Conways could be successful soldiers and diplomats. After his period in the Ship he went to sea in the clipper 'Knight of Snowdon'. In 1878, after 5 years at sea, he came ashore and joined the army as a Lieutenant in the Royal Scots Regiment.

His life became a mirror of empire. In 1884, he was in the Border Police in Bechuanaland and later commanded the British garrison there. In 1893 he was caught up in the conflict with the Matabele and commanded the British forces advance from Bulawayo. He fought and beat the Matabele army at the battle of Sengazi. Joining forces with two other columns, the Matabele were finally defeated and he became Resident Commissioner in Bechuanaland. During the Boer War he commanded the Town Guard in Mafeking throughout the siege. He was nearly killed twice by shelling and, on one occasion, he was buried in the rubble of his office when a shell burst overhead. After the war, he became Governor of the Orange River Colony. He was a great race horse enthusiast, and was responsible for the establishment of the Bloemfontein Turf Club. In 1911, he was made High Commissioner for Cyprus and in 1914, Governor of Queensland, where he opened Wondai Hospital in 1915. He laid the foundation stone for Brisbane Town Hall in 1917.

His service was rewarded with the KCMG, CMG and CB. He was returning to the UK from Queensland when he died of pneumonia in Capetown on April 12th 1920.

1875 July 24th

Captain Franklin was despatched to examine *Nile* in Devonport. He found her eminently suitable. She had been built as a sailing ship but converted to steam so she had an engine, a boiler and large coal storage spaces. Franklin proposed a number of changes and improvements. She had to be re-caulked, repainted and generally overhauled. Her engine and boiler had to be removed, the resulting space left open and 220 tons of copper dross and 175 tons of iron added as ballast. The Admiralty provided the mainmast of *Satellite* as a foremast, and the main, mizzen and bowsprit of *Jason* for the other masts and spars to supplement those from *Conway* that could be retained. The work did not start until March 1875, so it took almost a year to complete. The Admiralty agreed that *Nile* and *Conway* would exchange names so that the name *Conway* could be retained on the Mersey.

1876 June 20th

Nile left Devonport towed by *Valorous* a paddle frigate, arriving in the Mersey on 23rd June. *Nile* was berthed alongside the Great (or West) Float and *Conway* was brought from her moorings and secured alongside her. The cadets began stripping *Conway* and moving everything, guns, masts, yards and stores into the new vessel by hand or using hand powered equipment.

"It was fairly heavy work for boys but of course we enjoyed it thoroughly and thought ourselves real sailors."

Nile, When First Converted as Conway

Once everything had been transferred the cadets went home for the holidays and *Nile* was moved to the Rock Ferry mooring. The work had cost in excess of £6,000. *Conway* 2 (ex *Winchester*) was towed away to Devonport early in July. The officers and 163 returning cadets relocated to *Nile*. Permission was eventually granted for the exchange of names on 24th July 1876; so for around three weeks in July, the cadets were actually training in HMS *Nile*. The Old *Conway* (ex *Winchester*) was renamed again as the *Mount Edgcumbe* and loaned as the Cornwall Industrial Training Ship for Homeless and Destitute Boys, more of which is in *Appendix D*.

The first Conway Song was adopted. The words invoke strong principles of comradeship, loyalty, responsibility and service:

> Mine is the Conway, dear old Con-way;
> Sons on every sea.
> I to the dear old ship belong and she belongs to me.
>
> (Chorus) Sons of the Conway, dear Old Conway,
> Sons on every sea.
> I to the dear old ship belong and she belongs to me.
>
> Mine are the Comrades, dear old Comrades,
> Found on every sea,
> Mine are the ships of war, of trade, mine is the ocean free,
> Sons etc.
>
> Mine is the King, as mine the Country,
> Mine is the Lady Queen,
> Mine is the pride, the toil, the peril, mine is the peace serene,
> Sons etc.

Mine are the men who guard the nation,
Watching by day and night,
Mine are the men who serve in silence, strong as the men of might,
Sons etc.

Marching together, sons and fathers,
Listening to the Call,
These to the "Conway" all belong, these are the best of all,
Sons etc.

1876 September

The Royal Navy Guardship *Achilles* broke adrift and crashed down *Conway's* starboard side, smashing ports, boats and the stairway at the entry port. The non-too-observant sentry on *Achilles* reported,

"The Conway adrift and coming alongside!"

1877

Cadets manned the yards when the Shah of Persia sailed up the Mersey to visit Liverpool.

1880

Cadet Möller lost his footing and fell approximately 140 feet from the main topsail, fortunately into the safety nets rigged for the purpose. He survived without injury,

"till then I had thought the nets of little use!"

A strange piece of *Conway* slang came into use. The word 'spare' generally used, eg

"your pretty spare grub,"

meant hand over what you don't want. It was also used in a derisory way to mock or dispute another person's comments. For example one cadet might observe: *"Harrison line is the best shipping line."* To which another would retort, *"Your spare best shipping line."* This strange expression continued well into the late 1950s. The origins and logic of this use are lost but, along with a wealth of other slang decoded in *Appendix A*, it demonstrates that a mangled and impenetrable vocabulary is not the preserve of modern youth.

Attempts were made to stamp out an end of term tradition whereby every cadet hurled their crockery mugs from the main deck to smash in the lower hold; a glorious noise but expensive pastime as the broken crockery had to be replaced. The cadets ignored these interventions and the custom continued for many more years. As a further mark of their independence, other strict rules like 'Smoking not allowed and tattooing forbidden' were also ignored.

"I learned to smoke in less than a week, and had indelible designs done on my arm in Indian ink and vermillion."

1881 September 8th

Cadets provided a guard of honour for HRH the Prince of Wales, his wife, Princess Alexandra, and their children during their visit to Liverpool to open the new Alexandra Dock.

1881

Captain Franklin had now been in command for 10 years. He had organised the smart transition to the third ship and kept training on a smooth and steady course. He retired on 30th September 1881. He was promoted to Rear Admiral on the retired list in January 1900.

CHAPTER 7

A TOUR OF THE SHIP

Doubtless one of the new Captain Superintendent's first acts would have been to familiarise himself with every nook and cranny of the Ship. Let's accompany him on that tour of inspection. I'm sure he will forgive us if we use some un-seamanlike terminology to help us make sense of it all or if our description blurs structural modifications, customs and practices introduced later. Although this is an environment that very few can now experience, the surroundings we shall explore would be very similar to those experienced by the men of the Royal Navy for a couple of hundred years. Many Old *Conways* who have visited *Victory* at Portsmouth have remarked on the similarity between the two ships.

Conway was like a floating multi-storey building with a main entrance, a number of floors and a series of stairs connecting one floor to another. She had a penthouse suite with a private balcony and superb sea views. The cellar, like most cellars, was not often visited, and was dark and dank. On the roof were several masts. Climbing to the very top of these provided wonderful views, even if it was a little blustery. Inside, residents had their own bit of space, but the neighbours could be noisy and it was often difficult to find peace and privacy. But we are touring a ship not a building so walls are called bulkheads, ceilings are deckheads and floors are decks.

Conway Starboard Side

Each deck had a meaningful name:

- The upper deck, originally the spar deck in Nile, was the very top level and completely open to the weather. The most forward section (slightly raised in the photo above) was called the forecastle (pronounced folk-sul, written hereafter as 'Focsle'), while the raised section at the back, ie the stern or aft, was called the poop. The upper deck was just over 200 feet long and about 53 feet wide, but somewhat encumbered by buildings added for *Conway's* purpose.

- The main deck, marked by the upper white band, was where cadets ate and where school lessons were held. It was originally the upper gun deck, but the gun ports had been replaced by windows, and the 34 guns that had engaged the enemy in the Crimean War were long gone, except from one forlorn barrel in the darkest recesses of the cellar where few knew it even existed. The lower deck, originally the main gun deck in Nile, the lower white band, was another original gun deck. This was now accommodation space, the location of the main ablutions and sick-bay. One area on the starboard side was called the quarterdeck, the Ship's 'front door' where visitors boarded.

- The orlop deck, the black area of hull immediately below the lower deck, was where most cadets slept. When fully laden with guns, shot, stores and victuals the Ship would have sat much lower in the water. As a training ship she would never carry such heavy loads so small ports had been cut in the hull to provide some light to this otherwise lightless deck. One of them is visible in the photo, just above the waterline.

The Starboard Gangway and Entry Port

- The hold, which are the bowels of the ship and is below the waterline. Mainly used for recreational purposes.
- The bilge (your cellar) was a final very low space below the hold where the Ship's ballast lay against the hull. Where the other decks were in constant use, the bilge was rarely visited, apart for the cadet responsible for its notional upkeep, and by illicit smokers on their way to their hidden den.

The Ship could only be accessed by boat, manned and operated by the cadets themselves. If the sea was too rough or the wind too strong, no one could get on or off, sometimes for days. This was a mixed blessing. It could prevent teachers coming aboard for lessons (good!), but also stop deliveries of food and water (bad, although judging by the quality of food, many cadets might have said good!). Boats docked alongside at a small platform fixed to the Ship's side. This was connected by the starboard gangway (a short flight of steps) up to the Ship's 'front door,' actually a pair of doors, called the entry port on the lower deck. There was a smaller entry port on the port side used for loading stores.

The Lower Deck

In her fighting days, as a gun deck, it would have been open almost from stem to stern but for *Conway's* purposes large areas had been enclosed to form cabins and other spaces. These divided the lower deck roughly into 3 separate areas midships, bows and stern.

The midships area remained largely open deck.

> *"What immediately strikes one is the seemingly endless length of the deck, which is enhanced by the comparatively low headroom."*

The entry area, called the quarterdeck, was the where the duty officer, cadet captain, messenger and bugler stood their watches - lurking to vet visitors - the nautical equivalent of reception.

> *"The thump of cadets arriving aboard at the lower deck from the gangway and facing aft to salute the quarterdeck was a very distinctive sound."*

Another confirms that the sound he most remembered was

> *"the double rap of shoe soles hitting the duckboard at the head of the gangway as cadets came onboard and saluted the quarterdeck."*

Just abaft (behind) the gangway was a secluded corner where display boards recorded the achievements of notable Old *Conways*.

> *"I particularly remember the one concerning Matthew Webb, the first man to swim the English Channel!"*

In the centre of the deck a small partitioned area housed the gunroom, inner sanctum of senior cadet captains. Originally this was the forward magazine where powder for the guns was stored. The danger of sparks was so great that those working in the magazine wore felt slippers and light was provided from outside the magazine though small glass ports. A painted panel depicting a sailor and ships from her old warship days survives and is in the Maritime Museum at Caernarfon, North Wales. A central table built around the four feet girth of the mainmast occupied most of the gunroom, with bench seats ranged against the bulkheads.

> *"There was a bookcase along the forward bulkhead and a shelf with a row of teasers pickling in salt water to give them the consistency of a steel bar."*

There was a bank of lockers for personal kit and books.

> *"The rest of the Ship's company had only their sea chests to call their own so access to the gun room was a privilege indeed! It was full to bursting if all those entitled were in at the same time. A sliding door completed the feeling of privacy and woe betides any junior who had the temerity to enter without knocking!"*

Outside

> *"was a small two-pound mountain field gun. How it was acquired I do not know. I do know that it took a lot of constant cleaning with emery paper, to keep the bright steel fittings from rusting over!"*

Details of its capture during the Opium Wars had been engraved on the barrel, but years of polishing had removed the engraving! It is now in the Conway Chapel at Birkenhead Priory where, 125 years later, Conways are still proudly polishing it to oblivion. While on the subject of cleaning, a series of steel stanchions about 3 inches in diameter had been installed at some time to help support the main and upper decks.

> *"One of our clean ship duties was to keep these stanchions gleaming brightly with the use of 'elbow grease' and emery paper! I should imagine that in time they were considerably reduced in girth after the constant attention given by generations of Conway boys!"*

Forward of the gun room, a triple set of ladders 8-10 wide and facing aft, led straight up to the main deck, with a second flight continuing up to the upper deck. This was no doubt the main access in the days at sea when hands were called out to tend the sails. A huge capstan dominated the foot of the ladder. Beyond the capstan, across the open deck, on the port side was the port gangway leading outside but with no stair down to the water. The Ship's back door, this was the working end of the operation, used mainly by the water boat that berthed alongside at this point to discharge its daily cargo. Other boats only used the port gangway if wind and tide made the starboard gangway unsafe.

Lower Deck - Triple Ladders and View Forrad

The forward third of the Ship was accommodation and ablutions space, but it was dominated by a huge railed opening originally cut through the decks to install the steam engine. The engines long gone, it now gave light from the upper deck right down to the hold. Cadets recall a constant background noise from all over the Ship.

"Various cries could be heard, rather like street cries of Old London. One was 'Sodduck for spread,' meaning 'I have some bread and I'll swap a piece for a spread of jam.' To overcome this constant noise, so orders and announcements could be heard, a 'still' would be sounded on the bugle."

This required everyone to stop, keep quiet and pay attention.

"There were always a lot of bugle calls mustering: divisions, slack party, working party, duty cutter, number one, juice barge, heavy duty cutters crew, sickbay, cooks to the galley, cookhouse, boathands, boat-hoisting, disperse, hands to wash and so on."

These were often accompanied by incomprehensible announcements rather like announcements on a railway station.

"The cadet making the announcement, shouting so that all onboard could hear, would often ham it up: 'All those taking extra milk FROM SISTER, (heavy emphasis) muster at Sickbay NOW !!'. This referred to cadets whose parents paid for their offspring to receive a glass of milk, issued at Sickbay at 19.30 each day."

Cadets looking for each other also shouted messages up and down this space.

"The call would go something like this, 'Wayyyyy, Smith?' He would reply, from the depths of the Ship, 'Way oh!' Back would come the question, 'Where away?' To which 'Smith' would announce his location, 'Way, orlop deck!' It's surprising how sound could travel. Yet one grew oblivious of the general mayhem going on around, rather, I guess, as people living near a railway or motorway cease to hear them after a time!"

It was also

"where the bugler used to stand to sound 'Lights Out' and, what seemed to be a few minutes later, Reveille"

All routine calls, boats, mealtimes, etcetera, had their own distinctive *Conway* tune - some, like the 'still', copied from the military.

"Blowing a bugle is not as easy as it sounds and the notes range from the near excruciatingly unintelligible, to the pure clear notes of the true 'pro.' These are a joy to the ear and hang like dust motes in the air. Such a sound is unforgettable, and much later I was to hear bugling from Royal Marine bandsmen which nearly moved me to tears. Sadly, the Conway efforts were nearer the former than the latter! The quality of the rendering for Reveille on a cold, wet winter's morning, can make all the difference to one's day!"

On the forward side of this space, two single ladders (actually called hatches in Conway), one going up from starboard, the other going up from port, led to the decks above and below. On the starboard side of the opening was the seamanship classroom fitted with 5 long desks and benches. Opposite *"were 2 small cabins, one for the Headmaster who was the only teacher living onboard, and the other, an officer's cabin, occupied by Mr. Crockett during my time."*

Immediately forward were the night heads, only to be used after lights out; a small space with four urinals and one lavatory for the 200 or so cadets. During the day these heads were reserved for members of staff. The first row of hammocks a little further aft beyond the Headmaster's cabin was reserved for cadets who suffered from wetting their hammocks.

"They were required to sling together, sometimes as many as 4 or 5 unfortunates, and were referred to as the 'piss-quicks' or "water lilies'. The term 'piss-quicks' apparently derived from the 2 flag signal PQ in the International Code signifying: 'I have sprung a leak'.' What the experience did for their self esteem one can only wonder. The night watchman would wake them at two or three hourly intervals to enable them to use said night heads. When cadets kept night watches it was not unknown for them to forget to wake the 'piss-quicks' with inevitable results and punishment to follow."

At the very front of the Ship the bulkheads curved in towards the 'eyes' of the Ship – the hawse pipes in the bows. This was always a very 'draughty' part of the Ship, especially in a gale, as the wind whistled in through the two hawse pipes from each of which a large chain cable led up from the moorings, via the massive swivel. The idea of the swivel, of course, was to ensure that the two cables did not become inexorably twisted each time the tide turned! The inner end of the cable was then secured by turns around the 'bitts,' huge horizontal baulks of timber, supported some 2 feet above the deck by equally massive timber posts. About once a year, under the eagle eye of the Chief Officer, all hands would man a huge four-block tackle laid out along the lower deck and shackled to each mooring cable. At the order 'Heave!' we would slowly drag the mooring swivel clear of the water to enable the bosun to check it was 'free' (to rotate), to repack it with grease, before lowering it down again. This cable area between the hand basins and baths was the 'manger,' so-called because this was where any live meat would have be penned prior to a long voyage!

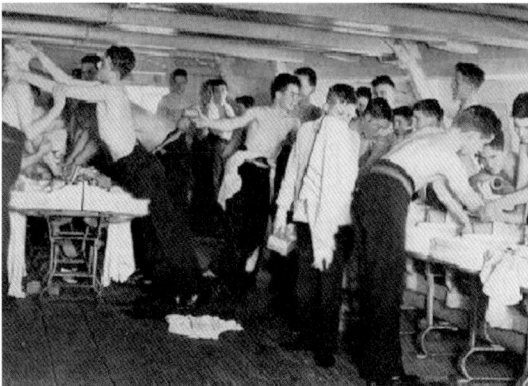

Lower Deck - Washrooms

Lower Deck - Stern Capstan and Hatch

Here on the starboard side were five rows of washbasins, 65 in total for everyone's daily ablutions.

"There was a near normal ritual of having to 'suck' the water from the taps before a miserable flow might give you a basinful!"

On the port side was the communal bathroom, with 14 baths arranged side by side like 2 neat rows of coffins apart from one right up in the bows inexplicably almost at right angle to the rest. These were used by tops in strict routine and then in strict order of seniority.

"I remember the unique smell of hot sea water that characterised bath night when all the tubs were in operation."

Each boy could have a bath twice a week, but water had to be shared. Those under punishment in the coaling party were the second, even third, users of the same bath water, by then usually tepid, so it was said that the most junior cadets often came out dirtier than they went in. New chums had the unenviable task of cleaning the grime from the baths.

"Many is the time someone would have to go up to the boiler house on the upper deck and plead with the donkey man in charge for more steam to heat the water!"

There was a minute cabin with a bath and head for members of staff. The system for disposing of effluent and water was simple. It drained out into a large square pipe on the outside of the Ship and straight into the water, to be dispersed by the tidal stream!

The final third of the lower deck was the area at the stern, where another huge capstan dominated the centre of the deck. Immediately forward of the capstan, in the centre of the deck, a teak railed open hatchway about 8 feet by 4 feet, gave light to the orlop deck below. A similar hatchway was let into the main deck above.

"It is interesting to note that the heavy timber combings (skirting boards) along the midships section still bore indentations made to stop the 'ready use' cannon balls rolling to and fro in their stowage"

Aft of the capstan 2 single staircases (called ladders) led from the after end of the quarterdeck; one down to the orlop deck and the other up to the main deck. Both were reserved for the use of officers and cadet captains only. Around this open space were a series of enclosed spaces.

"The after end is partitioned off as the Ship's sickbay, presided over by resident Sister Parry of daunting presence! This is where daily ailments are attended, and there are a few (actually 7) beds for the occasional casualty."

Immediately forward of the sickbay, against the port and starboard bulkheads were tiny cabins for the Chief and Second officers, the Padre, and a larger classroom used over time as the geography room and the RN Class room.

"As for smells: certainly tar and rope. Also sick bay smells of disinfectant and various medicines; the smell of the canvas from which the hammocks were made,

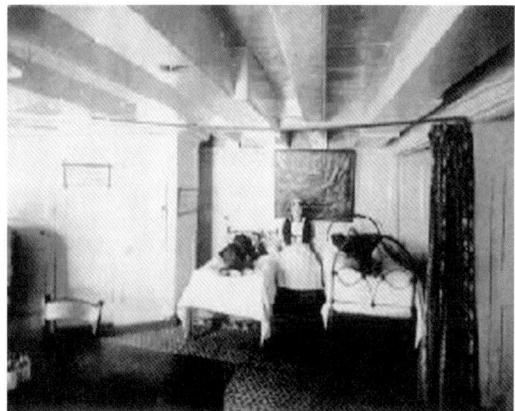

Lower Deck - Sick Bay

the salt air on the upper deck, and brasso polish. The exceptionally strong urine smell emanating from the steel urinal on the on the port side of the lower deck. Sounds? The crying of gulls; the squeak of ropes running through blocks when hoisting boats, and the sound of running feet on the deck as cadets moved forrad along the lower deck to haul on these ropes; the continuous sound of the generator in the boiler house topside; stills; the 'Last Post' at night, and 'Reveille' in the morning."

The Orlop Deck

Taking the stern ladder and avoiding any cadet captains who would immediately award us a punishment for illegal use of the ladder and we would go below to the orlop deck. This was the cadets' main sleeping area and so where they slung their hammocks at night. Apart from 3 small cabins for the Warrant Officers right aft, plus a linen storage area, the orlop was essentially open from stem to stern. The cabins were actually installed in 1938, prior to that the orlop was completely open. To provide daylight, square ports had been cut in the Ship's side, each provided with a wooden 'deadlight.' A line was secured to the inboard centre of this wooden 'plug' and ran inboard. To close the port, the 'deadlight' was pushed outboard, then by means of the line hauled back to take up against the rebated outboard edges of the port, and the line belayed. A series of seven inch diameter pipe-like scuttles were just under the deckhead. They pierced the side to provide faint light and ventilation to the orlop deck. But unlike the orlop deck ports, they were original features. They had an outer, round metal cap, permanently fixed at the end of a threaded rod, which ran inboard with a handle allowing it to be turned, thus tightly closing the outboard end of the scuttle. Under sail, it would have been normal practice to keep them closed.

Orlop Deck Port Side Looking Forward

"The orlop deck was where we boys lived. Completely open either side, virtually from bow to stern, one is confronted by long neat rows of black painted sea chests, ranged against the Ship's side and along the centre line. Each chest had a boy's name stencilled in large white letters. This item was on loan from the Liverpool Sailors' Home, and was returned for another future owner, when the present tenant left the Ship some 2 years later. On opening the lid (secured by a padlock, though one seldom locked anything away as stealing was considered the most heinous of crimes aboard ship in those days), there was a shallow removable wooden tray for one's little bits and pieces, while below, the main part of the chest was used for the stowage of clothing. This was the only privacy a boy could have, and one would use the lid of the chest shut as a private seat, or open as a reclining chair, where you could invite your chum to share, knowing that nobody else, however senior would dream of usurping this right."

"I recall the smell as I sat on my sea chest in starboard Focsle in April 1940; tar, rope, canvas and ... something else. Only in later years did I realise it was BILGES. I walked onboard the Warrior in Portsmouth for the first time and the same combination of smells was clearly evident."

"There were 8 distinct 'areas,' unmarked, but the tribal preserve of the topmen occupying them. The only men allowed to pass unhindered along this deck, were the most senior term, the starboard maintopmen. Anybody else wishing to progress along, or gain access to any part of the orlop deck belonging to a term senior to themselves was obliged to halt at an invisible barrier (where that term's row of sea chests started), and shout out to any member of that term who might happen to be lounging around their sea chests, 'Top, please!' Permission would then be granted, or not. This unwritten code of practice, was scrupulously observed. Even the focslemen, who were responsible for cleaning of the whole of the orlop deck, had to ask this permission before proceeding to sweep that area!"

Starting aft by the cabins

"the central part of the orlop deck was taken up, at the after end, by a long table with benches either side for writing letters, playing games, modelling or some such pastimes."

This was the preserve of the new chums and so called the Nursery. Moving forward was the ladder to the lower deck and hold, then 2 large clothes rack used for hanging reefer uniforms, raincoats and oilskins. Forward again were a storeroom and then 3 more clothes hanging racks.

"The coat racks were good hiding places when dodging the wrath of a CC or when on a knackering expedition or 'borrowing' other tops' cleaning gear. A desperate fugitive would often reach up for the racks and haul himself up so that any pursuers would not see his legs below the bottom level of the coats."

"Then came a large railed opening giving down to the hold, and up to the lower deck. A gangway, giving access to either side of the Ship lay between the racks and this opening and was known as 'the bridge.' It was from here that, as cinema operator later on, I installed the projector. By tilting it, the picture could be directed on to a crude sheet screen in the hold below, where the boys would sit to enjoy this weekly interlude. With no TV, and personal radio sets being things of the future, the showing of these well worn 16mm films on a Saturday night was the highlight of the week! At the beginning of the winter terms (no cinema in the summer), we would pour over the film catalogues to hire what we thought would be popular – Will Hay's 'Destrey Rides Again' and 'Victory at Sea,' are titles which come to mind! During the frequent breakdowns of the antediluvian equipment, and the reel changes, the Ship's company below would break out into ribald song – some of it extremely crude! Strangely enough authority never reprimanded us, though the sounds of our singing

Orlop Deck - Sweeps and Yack Tub

would reverberate around the Ship. Perhaps they believed that we would have to listen to far worse language when we got to sea, so we had better start learning now! Enlightened thinking?!"

"Forward again from this opening, single ladders led up and down to the adjacent decks. Then, to the bows, a large hatch cover, leading down to a provisions stowage, known as the Captain's jam locker. There was certainly jam down there as a member of our term had a key to the hatch cover padlock. It was from here that once a month we would all queue, each boy to be issued with ONE pot of jam! This we would keep in our sea chest to take up to the mess deck at teatime! Many of us of course were supplemented by 'tuck' from home, which we also kept in our chests, hidden from the predatory eyes of our shipmates – no one would ever steal, but if they thought there were rich pickings, they would Cadge! 'Your spare --------?' would be the call! Next to this store was the large, manually operated freshwater pump, with its 2 handles attached to large cast iron wheels. 2 boys at a time would man each handle, so that it took 4 boys to pump water from the freshwater tanks in the hold (which were filled daily from the water boat), up to the various gravity tanks around the Ship. Each top, except for the focslemen and mizzentopmen, were allocated this daily duty on a rotation basis, usually in the evening; each pair of boys doing 5 minute spells. The whole operation lasted about an hour. Meanwhile, the focslemen and mizzentopmen would be required to pump the Ship's bilges, from a vertically handled pump situated at the after end of the orlop deck!"

"Scattered around the Ship at strategic intervals were large wooden tubs (similar to half a large beer barrel), with rope handles, known as 'yak tubs.' These were for litter; and being responsible for the cleanliness of the Ship, the boys were very conscious of nuisance caused by litter throwing. I never remember seeing rubbish anywhere but in these tubs, which in those 'enlightened' days was disposed of by ditching over the side, as was the waste from the galley!"

"I remember the strong smell of Lysol when mopping down, and the smell of the soft soap in the yak tubs on Saturdays, and the dank smell of the Mersey particularly, in the hold."

At night, hammocks were slung the whole length of the Ship, the head lashed to a cranked iron bracket lowered from its stowed position against the deckhead; the metal ring at the foot of the hammock was dropped over a large hook let into the Ship's side. Each hammock, when slung, lay about two and a half feet above the deck and about two feet separated each one from its neighbour.

"Listening to Last Post whilst one was snug in one's hammock and the lights were out (leaving only emergency battery lighting throughout the Ship) could be a poignant experience, whilst Reveille was far less welcome, requiring one to turn out and face another hectic day."

After pipe down, the Ship became strangely quiet

"apart from the occasional cough and one could hear the lapping of the water. I think we probably became accustomed to body odours (given the inadequate washing facilities)"

During the day, hammocks were stored in 2 large bins that occupied a number of different positions over the years. Not all the Ship's company slept on the orlop deck. The lower and main decks were also sleeping spaces at night, as well as the enclosed classrooms, which gave a degree of privacy for the privileged few senior hands and cadet captains who did not have top responsibilities.

"Apart from your sea chest, your hammock was the only thing you could call your own, and to which you could, at night, retreat from the cheek by jowl existence of life onboard. Though not conscious of the fact, social skills soon had to be developed to a high degree if life onboard was to be at all tolerable. This was no place for the outcast or misfit."

The Hold

The hold was a substantial open space left when the engine was removed. The deckhead space was considerably higher than on any of the other decks, probably in the order of 10-12 feet. Being largely below the waterline, there were no

The Hold

openings in the hull so the only natural light flooded down through the large hatch up to the upper deck. The sides of the hold were lined with large freshwater tanks, 5 each side. A small steam operated pump bolted to the forrad bulkhead pumped water from the water boat alongside the port gangway, down into these tanks. The forrad port corner was the carpenter's shop but most of the space was left open for use as a make shift gymnasium where, after working hours the Headmaster would take boys for various gymnastic exercises.

"It was here too that the annual boxing competition was held. These were elimination matches whereby every boy, whether he liked to or not had to take part; each boy being set against other youngsters of similar size, all carefully supervised by the officers. Only once did I box, and being so small, I wasn't in the least bit hurt but, by golly, I was exhausted! I am ambivalent about the teaching of boxing in schools, but it certainly helps to develop self-confidence, and if properly supervised can do no great harm."

Hold - Recreation or Reading Room

It was in this space that cadets lounged on the deck, facing a large cloth screen to watch the weekly cinema projected from the flying bridge across the orlop deck (just visible in the photo). Forward, behind the bulkhead was the main coal-bunker.

At the after end of the hold were 2 main rooms. On the starboard side was what was euphemistically called the games room.

"This consisted, as far as I remember, of one billiard table and that was all."

Squeezed between the games room and the water tanks was a small, enclosed library. On the port side was the cadets' recreation or reading room; the only organised space where cadets could meet and sit comfortably. It had banquette seating on 2 of the bulkheads, and 2 large and 4 smaller free-standing tables and seats for 15!

A narrow fore and aft passage called the tunnel separated the 2 rooms. This was where the propeller shaft had originally run. The bulkhead to the reading room was full height but that to the games room was only half height. The tunnel led aft to another ladder leading up to the after end of the orlop deck. Beneath this ladder, a small hatch, unnoticed by most, led into the stygian gloom of the bilges. We shall hear tales of this place later. Right aft were a cloakroom and fuel bunker. In later years the tunnel was sealed off.

A small group of cadets, the Hold Party slept in the hold – a heterogeneous mixture of young men of varying seniority who also kept their sea chests down there. They had the unpleasant task of keeping the bilges clean and of scrubbing the external waterline

"so that the whole of the Ship is covered weekly."

The Main Deck

Let's promote ourselves to cadet captains so we can legally ascend by the stern ladder from the quarterdeck. Only staff and senior cadet captains were allowed to use the stern ladder as it gave access to part of the Captain Superintendent's private quarters, offices, staff cabins and the officers' wardroom. We emerge onto the Ship's original upper gun deck towards the stern. Once again, this huge deck can be divided roughly into 3 parts, the stern area, midships and the bows. The stern was separated from the rest of the deck by a bulkhead with 2 access doors. There were 3 rows of cabins running fore and aft. Across the stern was the officers' wardroom with large dining table seating 11, a settee and an easy chair. 2 large ports overlooked the water. On the port side were offices for the typists, Captain Superintendent, Chief Engineer and Chief Steward. On the starboard side, from right aft tucked into the curving stern, were a very small cook's bedroom,

Main Deck - Trophies

Main Deck - 'Holy Ground'

a bathroom, the Captain Superintendent's galley, a staff sitting room and a maid's cabin. All these spaces had old gun ports giving changing views of the outside world as the Ship swung to her moorings. Down the centre of the Ship were 2 pantries, a staff bathroom and a separate ladder up to the Captain Superintendent's inner sanctum.

Exiting from this private domain we enter the open main deck space and are faced immediately by another large capstan. Behind us, against the bulkhead, are glass-fronted cupboards holding the silver trophies awarded for activities like pulling, sailing, cross country and rugby. It's light here as there is a large skylight overhead through which the sky and the main mast may be seen. Ranged down either side are 7 gun ports;

> "the square gun ports on the lower and main decks had been fitted with glass casement windows, but the heavy iron rings for manoeuvring the cannon could still be seen embedded in the Ship's side."

The massive trunk of the main mast thrusting down through the deckhead dominates the centre of the deck and here is mounted the large brass Ship's bell. Here too was the 'holy ground,' consecrated by the Bishop, where the padre stood to conduct Sunday services. Cadets holystoned it for hours each Saturday until it was smooth and shining. Forward of the mast double ladders led to the upper and lower decks. Abaft the mast was a large hatchway opening covered by a heavy teak grating.

The main deck served 2 purposes, it was the mess deck where cadets took all their meals, and the classroom area.

> "At mealtimes, the open spaces on the port and starboard sides of the deck were taken up by long metal bound folding tables set at right angles to the Ship's side, with benches down either side. The Cadet Captain in charge of each mess sat at the head of the table, on a stool."

Each mess had 3 'cooks' who, as in RN messes did not cook. The Mugman collected the mugs and skilly, the Messman collected cutlery and butter, the third collected the food.

> "Lost cutlery was rarely replaced, and many is the time one had to eat one's main course with a spoon, or pudding with only a knife and fork! The Chief Steward was responsible for the issue of 'soduk' (bread), 'grease' (butter), and sugar rations for each mess. A staple diet for growing boys, the tiny slab of butter for each mess was meticulously divided into 12 minute portions, one for each member, by the mess's cadet captain. The bread would be brought onboard daily in large wicker baskets, collected from the pier where the local bakery deposited them. It was brought aboard by one of the Ship's boats routinely plying between Ship and shore during the day. These baskets were padlocked in an effort to prevent knackering by permanently hungry boys! But it was possible, occasionally, to prize open a corner and break off a handful of beautifully warm, crusty loaf! Tea, the drinkable stuff, not the meal, was called 'skilly.' It came, ready mixed with milk in large, chipped, brown enamelled teapots, from the galley hatch, where the messes' portions of food were served to the mess cooks at mealtime. The cadet captain of each mess took his food first and then it passed down the mess, those at the bottom watching with eagle eyes to ensure no one exceeded their fair share and so deprived them of their meal."

A small ready use freshwater tank provided water from which the cadets would draw their jugs at mealtimes.

Main Deck - A Mess

Main Deck - Classroom

"The mess tables were swung up and secured by hooks to the deckhead when the meal was over, but lowered again to transform the deck into a series of closed classrooms! This seemingly magic trick was performed by lowering hinged wooden screens, complete with integrated doors from the deckhead, dividing the whole area into 4 self-contained teaching units, complete with blackboard and easel. No doubt today's educationists would throw up their hands in horror at the Spartan facilities, but they were adequate for preparing boys for their future apprenticeship at sea. When school was over, the whole was dismantled very quickly and the deck returned to an eating area or place of recreation. At night hammock bars were lowered into position, and it became a dormitory! Conway taught us to be nothing if not versatile, a habit which has never left me!"

Finally on the main deck, the bows were given over to the galley and cooks' accommodation, arranged around the large hatchway down to the lower deck and hold. On the port side was the galley with one large coal burning range.

"I cannot say that the food was badly cooked, or that there was not enough of it; but boys are always hungry whatever the fare. I think the galley staff did their best!"

Cooks were seconded from the Blue Funnel line.

"And a savoury lot they were too! Perhaps just as well it was a domain not entered into by the boys."

The 16 galley staff, including many Chinese, were accommodated in a miniscule space crammed around the starboard side and the bows.

"Next to the galley, and against the port side was a small room for the exclusive use of the seamen. These were a heterogeneous collection of old salts, gleaned from I know not where, who, under the Bosun were responsible for Ship's general maintenance and rigging, such as painting and renewing of unsound cordage. We boys had little to do with them. A strong smell of shag tobacco permanently surrounded this private den of theirs! Smoking was of course strictly forbidden for the boys not, I'm sure, on health hazard grounds but for a more pragmatic reason, fire!"

This room was converted later into a school master's cabin.

The Upper Deck

Finally, we can take the main ladder up onto the upper deck and fresh air! Immediately in front of us the mighty girth of the mainmast, which seems to climb endlessly into the sky, stayed by a mass of rigging angling here and there in a complex web. Cadets were allowed to climb the main mast.

"You first had to step through the high bulwark surrounding and protecting the upper deck, into the chains, and then by ratlines (rope rungs) between the shrouds, climb hand over hand up the rigging."

The surrounding view must have been a wonderful sight, as there were 5 old wooden-walls anchored close together. The Royal Navy guard ship, *Conway, Akbar, Indefatigable,* and *Clarence.* The timbers of the deck were no longer visible as they had been covered by black asphalt, no doubt for waterproofing purposes. Once again, the deck is in three parts, aft is the poop deck, forward the Focsle, both raised six feet or so above the central upper deck.

Right aft was the poop deck, with the mizzen mast at its centre. It was from the mizzen gaff that the *Conway* ensign (the blue ensign with a castle motif in yellow at its fly) was, with bugler in attendance, hoisted at 'colours' in the morning, and hauled down at sunset each evening. The break of the poop was panelled off, with a glass-fronted door giving access to the quarters behind.

"Amidships, and immediately in front of this door, stood the mighty Ship's double wheel, some 6 feet in diameter; and it was not difficult for imaginative boys to visualise 2 seamen struggling to control the ship under sail in an Atlantic gale!"

Main Deck - Captain's Cabin

Captain's Sternwalk

Upper Deck and Chart Room

Inside The Chart Room

The wheel now has a safe berth in the Royal Navy Museum at Portsmouth, along with the Ship's bell. The cadet captain on upper deck watch was the only cadet allowed upon this hallowed ground, for the Captain's quarters lay immediately below!

The Captain Superintendent's quarters were palatial compared to the two feet of hammock space per cadet! The most impressive feature was the sitting room across the stern. Lit from above by a skylight and set in the massive timber deck beams of the poop, it had two large ports and central double doors leading out onto the stern walk suspended over the water. Only 2 of the large ports were real, the rest were dummies painted onto the hull. This was undoubtedly the most unique penthouse suite in the country! On the starboard side were 2 bedrooms and on the port a morning room and large dining room.

In the centre of the Ship, the upper deck was originally completely open, but it gradually accumulated temporary buildings, particularly during the major refits of 1938. Immediately outside the poop deck was the charthouse,

"a low glass panelled timber structure in which was housed the Ship's chronometer, an Admiralty receiving set (a B.40 if I remember rightly), an HF/DF set for instruction purposes, sextants and charts for the teaching of practical navigation. As would be expected, navigation was taught to a very high standard. There were, of course, no satellite navigational aids whereby even landlubbers can pinpoint themselves on a chart today! Then, it was all sextant angles, heavenly bodies, Admiralty Almanacs and Norries Nautical Tables (Inmans in

Focsle, Foremast and View Aft

Focsle View Over Bows and Figurehead

the Royal Navy). The theory and practise of spherical trigonometry was taught and understood. We were taught the 'Marc St Hilair method of navigation.' Two years or so after I had joined Conway, I was made junior cadet captain of the charthouse and lab; one of my daily duties was to wind, check and log the error of the chronometer against the radio pips which came over on the B40."

Later the chartroom was to be upgraded with more modern equipment.

Immediately forward of the charthouse lay a balustraded and glass covered hatchway, giving light to the main deck. Forward again, and just abaft the main hatchway stood the 'bitts' - short, heavy oaken 'crucifixes' round which the various cordage controlling the movement of the mainsail would be secured. A low timber and glass structure containing the school laboratory took up the central part of the upper deck from the main hatch to the break of the Focsle. Here, the Headmaster taught elementary physics and chemistry.

Forward of this was the Focsle, under which were housed large diesel generators and a 'Scotch' boiler providing steam for various purposes – galley, bathrooms, coal hoist and water pumps. At night, after lights out, the generators would be run down, creating a great hush throughout the Ship. I always used to get a sinking feeling, awakened on an early winter morning by the sound of the diesels being started up again, usually about a half an hour before Reveille! There was a workshop attached to the boiler house, where minor repairs were carried out. Running around the starboard side was a narrow covered walkway to more Ship's heads. This cold and very draughty place consisted of a few urinals and half-door cubicles. Not a place to linger – unless you were an inveterate smoker! The deck over the Focsle was reached by a short ladder on the starboard side, and could be used by any boy. It was a favourite place to lounge and, for the ubiquitous smokers, to lurk behind the large freshwater gravity tank! Here was the foremast and angled up from the deck the bowsprit reached over the bows and the figurehead. Until the refit of the late 30s, a tall, narrow, black and greasy funnel vented smoke and smells from the galley 2 decks below.

"I remember we used to gaze down through a skylight into the galley and see the huge vat of porridge 'brewing' on the stove. Boys have sworn that rats had been seen swimming in this goo! Rats in the Ship there certainly were, the bilges being an ideal breeding ground."

Our tour of the Ship is complete. She would undergo a few modifications over the years but her layout would remain familiar to cadets for the next 70 years.

CHAPTER 8

1881–1903 LT A T MILLAR RN FRGS FRAS

1881 October 1st

Many cadets had hoped that the Ship's First Officer, Mr. 'Strike' Hargreaves would be appointed Captain Superintendent. He was ex-Cunard and very well respected, but he had heart problems, and it was rumoured this this rendered him unsuitable. Instead, *Conway's* fourth Captain Superintendent was Lieutenant Archibald T Millar RN. He had served in small warships, but nothing the size of *Conway*. Little is known of his naval career. In 1862, he was an Acting Second Master. From 1862 to 1866, he served in *Slaney*, a small three gun boat on the East Indies and China station. He became a Master and Navigating Lieutenant in 1867. He retired from the Royal Navy in 1870, joining Messrs Lamport and Holt where he rose to command. From there he applied for the post on *Conway* and was accepted for the position on 4th June 1881. His nickname was 'Lippy' because of a prominent lower lip that thrust out even more when he was annoyed. He was well regarded if not always popular, as various cadets observed:

Lt AT Millar RN

"I would not say he was popular with us, but he certainly was respected."

"I cannot say that we liked him, but he had one great merit, he commanded."

He was an imposing figure,

"the finest looking sailor I have ever seen … with his blue eyes, fresh complexion, white hair with a sheen on it and good teeth."

"He was certainly a noble-looking man."

The cadets quickly nicknamed him 'Lippy,' for his rather heavy lips. Discipline had become a little lax towards the end of Captain Franklin's reign, Millar tightened things up.

"He was a somewhat stricter disciplinarian …. He had found the Ship in a very lax state and pulled her together into working order."

He insisted that all uniforms be purchased from the Liverpool Sailors' Home in Canning Place, standardising the uniform that previously could be bought from any source, using written specifications. The uniform consisted of a blue 'Crimea' flannel shirt.

"There was no doubt about the blue, it came off on everything, neck, hands, underclothes etc., until the shirt had been washed several times."

The cap was a 'Glengarry' style in dark blue with white mottling at the edge. It had a dark blue pompom on the top and long black silk ribbons. Older hands quickly ripped these off as part of the initiation of new chums to *Conway*.

"Methods of annoying the newcomer were legion."

The caps were only worn in the Ship, never in boats or ashore. All kit was provided in a large black sea chest with the cadet's name and number stencilled in white on the side. These battered chests were returned to the Sailors' Home when a cadet left the Ship, then repainted and reissued to another new chum.

As with all servicemen and women, every cadet found they had been allocated a number to be marked on all their personal possessions. This number, once known, was never forgotten, and it had to be marked on all clothing and belongings. In the mid 1960s it was even marked in small brass nails under the sole of shoes. The numbers came from the Ship's registers. The registers were very large tomes (about 4 inches thick) used to record details about every cadet as they joined. Each cadet has 2 facing pages, both having the same number. The left hand page was the cadet's finance ledger showing all fees paid (or not in some cases), less any scholarship monies. The right-hand page recorded school reports, academic results and sports achievements. As each term started cadet's names were entered mainly, but not absolutely, in alphabetical order. For instance, volume 13/36 shows - Webber pages 225, Woodger pages 226, Bissell pages 227, Hayter pages 228 and then Allen pages 229. This volume goes up to page 300, and the next volume 13/37 goes from 301 to 599. The page number for a cadet's entry became his number. It took many years to fill a complete register so there was no chance of 2 cadets having the same number. With 3 intakes a year and courses lasting from 2-4 years, it was quicker to find entries by number than name. The registers are now held by the Merseyside Maritime Museum and copies of individual cadet's entries can be obtained on request.

Starboard Gangway - Prize Day 1883

Captain Millar made a number of improvements to the Ship, including decking the hold and making a lecture hall and gymnasium where once had been a wasteland of ironstone ballast. He introduced a 30 foot model mast to teach rigging, he installed electric lights, pumps and hydrants. He started boxing, fencing and dancing classes, and improved the library. In short he made his mark. He was also an inspirational speaker;

> *"an admirable speaker …. He preached some of the best sermons we ever heard."*

A visitor to the Ship recorded,

> *"The Commander, every inch a gentleman and sailor, conducts the business of the Ship with enthusiasm. His post can be no sinecure, involving as it does the care by day and night of some 170 spirited lads; but his efforts, heartily seconded by an excellent staff of teachers and officers, seemed decidedly successful. The discipline is strict, but that is no fault and is enforced and accepted with good will."*

1884

Captain Millar decided to improve the standing of prefects to encourage boys to excel and seek promotion. The titles 'senior cadet captain' and 'junior cadet captain' were introduced to replace the previous 1st and 2nd class petty officers, or PO. They were also called rates. The term PO continued to be used and, for some time, was interchangeable with senior cadet captain. That use eventually died out but the chief cadet captain and his deputy were also called the CPO and DCPO. They wore gold lace sleeve stripes, broad for a junior and narrow for a senior. More importantly they were allowed to stay up late and to attend a special rates supper, usually of cold beef and ham with beer. Millar was also determined to improve the standard of teaching and adult supervision by replacing a number of instructors. Once a week there were evening concerts or lectures. Captain Millar's wife was always ready with a recitation or to lead the singing of popular songs. She also introduced the practice of donating a bible to each cadet leaving the Ship. He had allowed discipline to slip, but from 1884, much more taut discipline was instituted and the slackness of years stamped out.

> *"We had to leap to the order and be smart at divisions."*

A 'model' mast approximately 10 feet tall was set up in the hold and was very useful for the teaching the elements of rigging and sparring.

1885 February 1st

The 2000th cadet joined the Ship.

1886

160 cadets formed a guard of honour for the visit of Queen Victoria to the Liverpool Exhibition.

1887

The whole Ship's company went to Llandudno by tug for Queen Victoria's golden jubilee, where they feasted on vast quantities of buns and lemonade. The first of November that year saw a very violent gale on the Mersey. Many ships parted their cables, ran aground or were seriously damaged. *Akbar*, a similar size to *Conway*, dragged her mooring and was soon very close along side *Conway*. A powder flat also broke from its moorings and drifted towards the narrow gap between the two vessels.

There was a real danger it might be ground between them with extremely explosive results. Fortunately a ferry managed to get a line aboard the flat and manoeuvred it aground.

1889 May 16th

The first edition of The Cadet magazine was produced. It remained in regular publication until 1974. Initially, it was issued only to serving cadets, but later it was posted to old

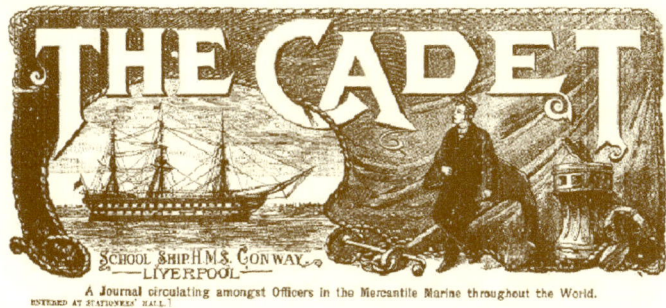

Cover Of The First Cadet Magazine

boys around the world. The first edition described the newly formed Debating Society. Mention was made of the donation of the four-inch breech-loading gun and a quantity of rifles, bayonets and cutlasses for musketry and cutlass drill, then part of the syllabus.

1890

British shipping reached its peak with 63% of the world's steam equivalent tonnage British registered. It had risen from 54% in 1870. Our merchant fleet was larger than the rest of the world's combined. British carrying capacity was four times that of the USA, five times that of France and six times that of each of Germany and Italy. Britain's maritime supremacy was complete and it would remain the principal maritime power until after the Second World War. The population of the UK doubled in the first half of the 19th century and almost doubled again in the second half, triggering a huge demand for imports and creating massive export capacity. From 1865 to 1890, almost 119,000 people a year emigrated from the UK to the USA. The Empire more than doubled in size from 4.5 million square miles and 160 people to 11.5 million square miles and 420 million people. All this trade required ships, British ships, with British officers, fuelling demand for pre-sea training and cadets from *Conway* and her sisters.

Worcester won the first *Conway - Worcester* gig race on the Thames in 1890 by 2 lengths. The race originated after the secretary of *Worcester* a Mr. Bullivent visited *Conway* in 1887. 2 senior cadet captains, Craven and Chase, suggested to him that an annual pulling race be instigated between *Conway* and *Worcester*. After *Worcester* initially declined the idea, Captain Millar eventually instigated an annual gig race for a which a large cup was awarded. There were races every year until 1906. *Conway* won nine times, *Worcester* seven, and there was one dead heat. The races were held again between 1929 and 1939, but *Worcester* won them all. No more races were held afterward, although both ships continued to row gigs and cutters. An annual rugby match was held from 1936 until Worcester closed (the war years excepted).

1891

New cadets were always called new chums; the term is rumoured to have been introduced to the Ship by an officer who had served for many years in Australia where it was in common use to describe novice mineral prospectors. John Masefield's book 'New Chum' described his first days as a *Conway* cadet. It was an experience repeated by every cadet who ever joined the Ship.

"The first day - the noise and strange surroundings, especially the dimly lit orlop deck; the enormous men, especially those veritable gods with gold devices on their arms (cadet captains); the struggle with the hammock, but how comfortable it was as soon as one got the hang of it. The mature appearance of the cadets as compared to the boys of the same age I had left behind at school, some of them looked like hard bitten salts already. Then the confusion of bugle calls, everyone rushing about, lash up and stow, divisions, working sections, rigging and unrigging school and the accompanying language which, I am sure, would have shocked our parents to the core."

New chums were granted 2 weeks grace to learn the ropes, a whole new *Conway* vocabulary and the complex written and unwritten rules. After that, they were expected to know where to go, what to do and when. Failure resulted in swift punishment. In no time at all most new chums assimilated and became indistinguishable from the other hard bitten salts.

"After my first term I felt a lot happier, had made many friends and really began to love the Ship."

"The whole 2 years are a sort of pattern of happiness. A very hard life but a clean one."

On joining, cadets were allocated to a top, rather like modern boarding school houses. The top system evolved over the life of the Ship, adapting to meet changing circumstances. This causes some confusion when cadets from one period read about arrangements in other years. *Appendix G* describes the arrangements for tops and terms over time, and, where possible, the reasons for their adoption. One thing remained constant, during their first term, new chums were always grouped separately from the rest of cadets.

1891 April 26th

A cadet was lost overboard and drowned, the first one ever. He had been skylarking in the chains on the upper deck (a banned pastime precisely because it was so dangerous) and, as the other hands responded smartly to the pipe for tea, he apparently slipped and fell unnoticed into the strong ebb tide. His body was not found until many weeks later.

1892 September 18th

Conway's second Headmaster, Mr. Charles 'Bummy' Barton, died and was buried in Anfield cemetery. He had retired on 31st August, only a few weeks before, after 29 years as Headmaster. He was

"a kind master, a good friend, a cordial messmate."

The early 1890s were another bad period for ill discipline. The Captain Superintendent had formed 'The League' a group of cadets dedicated to avoiding

"all drinking, smoking, swearing and impurity."

It was

"the most hated institution,"

but as it was his pet project. Most cadets joined for fear of making a bad impression. It was believed that those strong enough to ignore the pressure to join were penalised for their temerity. In time, a small band of malcontents, mainly cadet captains, formed the 'Good Cause League,' dedicated to the destruction of Ship's property and causing mayhem. They were very successful in their goals and remained undetected until discovered by accident. The leaders were dis-rated, stripped of badges and buttons and expelled. A number remained and two eventually got very drunk while ashore for their confirmation service. It was decided that they would be flogged rather than expelled. There was mutinous talk of putting the Captain in the coal hole to prevent the flogging, but when all hands mustered to witness the punishment, the Ship's officers and masters were all ranged in front of the Captain.

"It was seen that to get at Lippy we should have to fight men whom we loved. We hissed the Captain's speeches but we did not put him in the coal hole."

The mutiny never happened and the punishment was delivered. The next day one of those punished provoked a serious fight and he was immediately expelled. With the ring leader gone the

"Ship changed for the better."

1895 February 28th

The Mersey was frozen from shore to shore after several days of extreme cold weather – as much as twenty degrees of frost. There was ice constantly in the river, which had already stove in the side and sunk *Conway's* steam launch. The ice rubbed against the Ship damaging her copper lining. Serious leaks began and cadets often spent hours at the large hand pumps emptying the bilges. Temporary repairs fixed the worst of the leaks but it was decided she needed a proper overhaul.

1895 December 15th

The Ship was dry-docked in Bilston Graving Dock for an overhaul. Her hull was scraped; 10-15 tons of mussels and sea-grass were removed, recaulked using 3,500 weight of oakum and pitch, and re-felted with 4,000 sheets of felt secured with 2,300 weight of nails. She was fully re-coppered with 10 tons of copper and repainted. Hundreds of shipwrights worked on the overhaul. On 28th January 1896, 3 tugs returned her to the Rock Ferry moorings to the sound of *Akbar's* band.

1896 April

The Ship was in her 38 year when the 3,000th cadet joined. It had taken slightly less than 14 years to achieve the 1,000th cadet, the next 12 years to hit the 2000th and 11 years to achieve 3,000. *Appendix F* lists the numbers of cadets by year. In the first 10 years the average was 95. In the 10 years up to 1896, the average was closer to 180. Things were obviously going well.

One of the cadets had an uncanny ability to go aloft without disturbing the rigging. He tried many times to catch a sleeping seagull on the yards but without success. Once, watched by a crowd of 50 or so cadets, he managed to touch a gull. His antics were stopped as there was then, and always remained, a quaint but attractive belief that seagulls were the returning souls of Old Conways that should be left undisturbed. This tradition is immortalised in one of the splendid stained glass windows in the Conway Chapel at Birkenhead Priory.

1897

During the summer term, the Captain's daughter Gracie married from the Ship to the brother of a cadet. His second daughter Chrissie

"was sighed for by many senior cadets but, beyond dancing with her, their hopes were not realised."

The photo shows 2 cadets in their Conway uniforms.

And You'll Find on the Bridge, a Conway Boy
John Masefield OM D Litt LL.D Litt D (1891-94)

John was born in Ledbury, Herefordshire, where the family solicitor's business continues to this day. He was orphaned young and brought up by an aunt. It was aboard Conway that Masefield's love for storytelling grew. While in the Ship, he listened to the stories told about sea lore. He continued to read, and felt that he was to become a writer and storyteller himself. After Conway he went to sea but soon realised it was not for him. He deserted ship in New York to become a writer. His poem 'Roadways' explains his calling for the sea.

After many years in New York he returned to the UK. He served as a medical orderly in the Great War even though old enough to be exempt from military service. He became Poet Laureate in May 1930 and was judged to be "everyone's poet and a poet's poet."

He wrote many poems about the sea and a considerable number of verses especially for Conway, including 'The Gulls,' verses for the masting of the new figurehead in 1938 and to commemorate the centenary in 1959. The latter words were inscribed on the lintel of the main entrance to the New Block. He wrote of his Conway years in his book 'New Chum' and was her official historian producing 2 editions of his book 'The Conway' in 1933 and 1953. He is interred in Poets' Corner in Westminster Abbey. A prolific novelist and poet, one of his best known poems is Sea Fever:

I must down to the seas again, to the lonely sea and the sky,
And all I ask is a tall ship and a star to steer her by,
And the wheel's kick and the wind's song and the white sail's shaking,
And a gray mist on the sea's face, and a gray dawn breaking.

I must down to the seas again, for the call of the running tide
Is a wild call and a clear call that may not be denied;
And all I ask is a windy day with the white clouds flying,
And the flung spray and the blown spume, and the sea-gulls crying.

I must down to the seas again, to the vagrant gypsy life,
To the gull's way and the whale's way, where the wind's like a whetted knife;
And all I ask is a merry yarn from a laughing fellow-rover,
And quiet sleep and a sweet dream when the long trick's over.

1899 July 19th.

The Duke Of York, later King George V, visited the Ship and presented the King's Gold medal to Cadet Jackson. This was later presented to, and displayed in, Sydney Cathedral, Australia but was stolen in 2000. The King, drawing on his own long naval career, encouraged the cadets to

"truthfulness, obedience and zeal."

1900

When the *Clarence* boys again burned her to the waterline, a fire extinguisher was installed in *Conway*. A large black water tank was installed

Gracie Millar's Wedding

on the upper deck and connected to the other decks by pipes. Also in 1900, at a cost of £1,000, an electrical lighting system was installed throughout the Ship to replace the oil lamp.

1901-02

Mr. H B Steel, Lancashire County Cricket player, began to coach the cricket team.

1903 May 7th

Captain Millar, who had been ill for some months, died in his cabin of diabetes. Unexpectedly, a new Captain Superintendent was needed.

CHAPTER 9

1903–27 CAPTAIN H BROADBENT RNR

1903 June

Captain Harvey W Broadbent RNR had been *Conway's* Chief Officer since September 1898, so the Ship and cadets had been under his direct day-to-day control for over 4 years. He was obviously very familiar with the Ship's routine, customs and practices, so he knew how things worked. He was selected as the next Captain Superintendent and a Mr. Dibb appointed Chief Officer in his place. Significantly, he was also an Old *Conway,* joining the Ship as a cadet in February 1880, under Captain Franklin, and leaving at the end of 1881, after Captain Millar's first term in command. He was the first old boy to return as Captain Superintendent, establishing a pattern repeated by all his successors.

> *"Captain Broadbent at first sight was a terrifying man whose look froze you to the deck. When inspecting divisions with his tongue pressing out his cheek his set glare made one shudder, but one got to accept his little mannerisms and although held in great respect he endeared himself to all."*

The cadets called him 'Lobster Chops.' He served with Messrs Galbraith, Pembroke and Co, Bibby Line and the Cunard Steamship Company. In 1897, in RMS *Etruria*, in violent weather off Fastnet, he came upon a sinking steamer, the *Millfield* of Whitby. He twice took a ship's boat across dangerous seas and rescued twenty-three men. The rescue took thirteen hours and was described as

> *"a brilliant piece of work."*

He was awarded several medals in recognition of his bravery. On the same trip he met and subsequently married a Miss Wilson of Preston. She was much loved and known onboard as 'Mah Bee' from the Chinese for 'Protective Mother'. He was to serve for 24 years, beating Captain Millar's record tenure of 22 years. To this day, he remains the longest serving Captain Superintendent. He and Mah Bee transformed *Conway*. His first act in 1903 was to change from Association to Rugby Football, a very popular move at the time. Captain Broadbent was also very keen on boxing. During one lightweight final Mah Bee remarked that

> *"his eye is all closed up."*

Captain Broadbent replied

> *"Well, what about it? He can see out of the other one."*

Before the year's end, a fruit store selling oranges was opened in the hold. It was a success and quickly developed into a canteen selling a range of sweets and fruits. This institution survived through to the end of the Ship.

Capt. H Broadbent RNR

1904 July 19th

141 cadets formed a guard of honour at Liverpool Town Hall for the visit of King Edward VII to lay the foundation stone for Liverpool Cathedral. The King presented the King's Gold Medal to cadet W A Galbraith in person.

1904-5

By the dawn of the 20th Century and Captain Broadbent's appointment, Britain's pre-eminent position in world shipping was beginning to slip. Britain now operated 46% of the world's steam equivalent foreign trade shipping, down from the high of 63% in 1890. That fell to 37%, if US domestic shipping, including lake and river traffic, was included. Despite this fall, British shipping accounted for 92% of the British Empire's trade, 63% of trade between the Empire and other countries, and 30% of world trade between none Empire countries. There was still a burgeoning market for *Conway* cadets in the home shipping companies and those in Empire countries, eg the Royal Indian Navy was a major recruiter of *Conway* cadets, as was the Bengal Pilot Service. Fired with enthusiasm Captain Broadbent launched a flood of initiatives.

The galley was remodelled and new ranges installed to replace those obtained from the Great Eastern many years previously. The shore sanatorium was improved. A course of medical lectures, including first aid instruction, was implemented. The original game field opposite the church on St Peter's Road was replaced by 6 acres of newly purchased land in the space now bounded by Knowlsey Road, New Chester Road, Woodward Road and the railway. A tennis court and pavilion were added. Hockey was introduced.

> *"The ground has been made use of in a way never before recorded in the annals of Conway. All hands took to games with zest: minor offences and the black list dwindled away to nothing."*

1905 June 3rd

3 cadets saved a man from attempted suicide in the River Mersey.

1905

After a long and hard life at the hands of *Conway* cadets the Ship's 2 black and white, 10 oared cutters were found to be beyond repair and were cremated in the furnace. Some 4,000 boys had learned to row in them and it was estimated they must have covered over 100,000 miles. They were replaced by 2 twelve-oared cutters made of teak in Bombay Dockyard. They were a matched pair, 38 long by 8 feet wide, 4 inch beams, stepping 2 masts with a dipping lug forward and a standing lug aft. The *Conway – Worcester* gig race that year was a memorable one. We can let John Masefield OM, latterly Poet Laureate and so *Conway*'s most famous son, describe events.

> *"The race was rowed from the powder flat at Eastham to the Ship. For the first 3 minutes the boats were level, both crews pulling with short quick strokes; then the Worcester boat drew a little ahead, and gradually increased the lead to a length. Near the New Ferry Iron Works, one of the Conway midship oars, Number Four, a giant of a man, the oldest man in the race, and the strongest oar in the boat, strained himself, and was hardly more than a passenger for the next 2-300 yards. As a result of this strain, the Worcester boat increased her lead to 2½, and led by this distance at the New Ferry pier. To most people, the race seemed over. As the boats drew near Indefatigable, the Conway's midship oar began to row again, and the cox called on all hands for an*

The Dead Heat

effort. It was blowing somewhat freshly, though with no sea. The Worcester cox took his boat too close in to the ships in the mooring line; this gave the Conway crew a bare chance. At the Indefatigable, the Worcester boat was still leading by two and a half lengths. The Conway crew spurted from this point to the finish. They were on their own water, in the presence of all their friends, who now had the excitement of seeing the boat lift and begin to lessen Worcester's lead. At the Akbar, as at the Indefatigable, the Worcester cox brought his boat too close in to the swinging ship, and lost some of his lead in keeping clear. As they drew away from Akbar, the two boats made the finest finish ever seen in the race. Both crews had lost all nervousness and the short quick arm stokes with which they had begun; they were pulling magnificently with a grand swing that got every ounce on to the stretcher. All present were convinced that the Worcester could not help keeping her lead to the finish. But the Conway rallied and went on from strength to strength. In a moment of intense excitement they drew up to the Worcester boat and made a challenge. Nothing like had ever been seen in Conway rowing, but it still seemed impossible that the Worcester could lose. In the last few desperate strokes the Conway boat crept up, past thwart after thwart, and just carried the red flag up to a dead heat as the gun was fired."

It was the only dead heat in the race's history,

And You'll Find on the Bridge a Conway Boy
Sir Arthur Henry Rostron KBE RD RNR (1885-6)

Arthur Rostron was born in Astley Bridge, Bolton, England, to James and Nancy Rostron. Educated at the Bolton School from 1882 to 1883 and the Astley Bridge High School. Rostron joined Conway at the age of 13. After two years of training, he was apprenticed to the Waverley Line of Messrs. Williamson and Milligan. He joined Cunard in 1895. He is best known as the Master of Carpathia and rescuer of nearly 700 Titanic survivors on the morning of April 15th 1912.

As a result of his efforts to reach the Titanic before she sank, and his preparations for and conduct of the rescue of the survivors, Captain Rostron was lionised as a hero. He testified about the events the night Titanic sank at both the US Senate's and the British Board of Trade's inquiries. Titanic survivors, including American Margaret Brown, presented Rostron with a silver cup and gold medal for his efforts that night.

He went on to become master of Mauritania and holder of the Blue Riband for the west-east Atlantic crossing. He became Commodore of the Cunard fleet before retiring in 1931.

And You'll Find on the Bridge a Conway Boy
James Moody (1904-06)

14th April 1912 was 'The Night to Remember'. The unsinkable Titanic struck an iceberg and sank with huge loss of life. The 6th Officer of the Titanic was James Moody, 6 years out of Conway. Doubtless he would have been amazed at his good fortune to gain a berth in this, the most prestigious liner in a most prestigious shipping company. He was on watch on the bridge at the time of the sinking. He received the fateful message from the lookouts that there was an iceberg ahead. He had earlier told them to be on special lookout for them and initiated the first avoiding action. When it became clear that Titanic would founder he was despatched with the other officers to organise the lifeboats. 5th officer Harold Godfrey Lowe had an encounter with Moody while they filled boats 14 and 16. Lowe remarked that he had seen 5 boats lowered, and one of the next 2 ought to have an officer. He suggested Moody, as the junior officer should go but Moody answered, "You go. I will get in another boat" Lowe survived, Moody did not.

Moody's final actions were recalled by Geoffrey Marcus in The Maiden Voyage. "Chief Officer Wilde's efforts to avert panic, maintain order and discipline, and get the last of the boats loaded and lowered to the water were valiantly supported by the youngest of the officers, James Moody. Long before this, the latter should by rights have gone away in one of the boats along with the other junior officers. But the seamen left onboard were all too few as it was for the work that had to be done. Moody therefore stayed with the ship to the end and was the means of saving many a life that would otherwise have been lost." After overseeing the safe loading of a number of lifeboats, he was last seen alone on deck.

There is a special Titanic exhibition in the Merseyside Maritime Museum, including the Conway Moody Cup. There is a rose marble memorial plaque bearing James's name in the Church of St. Martin on the Hill, Scarborough, and an altar set at St. Augustine's Church in Grimsby in his memory.

There is another monument to Moody in Woodland cemetery, Scarborough, the existence of which was known only to a few members of the Moody family. The headstone refers to his role in the Titanic disaster, and commemorates his sacrifice with the words "Greater love hath no man than this, that a man lay down his life for his friends."

His family donated the Moody Cup, a sailing cup to be competed for annually by Conway cadets. It is on display in the Merseyside Maritime Museum at Liverpool. Old Conways keep his memory alive as once a year it is loaned to the Conway Club Sailing Association, where it is awarded for the best sailing log of the year.

1906

The *Conway - Worcester* boat race was discontinued.

1907 January 19th

SS *Arbutus* dragged her moorings and collided with the Ship, breaking the upper gangway and destroying a cutter.

1907 March

A cadet left after serving 5 years, the longest stay on record!

1908

6 extra acres of land were purchased extending the playing fields down to Hassal/Woodward Road, and bringing the whole area up to 11.5 acres. This left the wooden pavilion in entirely the wrong place but there weren't the funds to move it.

1909 January

The band was formed when the piping of orders was replaced by more audible bugle calls.

1910 July

The Captain Superintendent formed an Old Boys' Association. It was named the Conway Club on December 13th. It thrives to this day, with branches across the UK and around the world. The first president was Major Sir Hamilton J Gould Adams KCMG CMG CB, a soldier diplomat who was something of an absentee landlord, serving abroad for most of his 10 year tenure!

The Sports Pavilion

1912

The curriculum was completely revised. Seamanship afternoons ceased and short periods of seamanship instruction were interspersed into the daily routine. Preparation was introduced 2 evenings a week, with cadet captains taking charge.

1913 July 11th

100 cadets formed a guard of honour onboard the liner *Mauritania* during a visit by HM the King. King George presented the Gold Medal to cadet Raymond Reffell in person.

Of the 26 cadets leaving in July 1913, 21 joined the Royal Navy and 5 the merchant service. There had always been a steady stream of cadets joining the senior service but this was a complete reversal of the norm. In December 1913, the change became a pattern; 21 cadets joined the Royal Navy, 4 more left Conway to take entrance examinations for Dartmouth and just 1 joined the merchant service. In April 1914, 20 of 21 leavers joined the Royal Navy. Even though the war was still some way off, the Royal Navy was clearly preparing for a significant increase in demand.

King's Gold Medal Presentation

1914

When war was declared many officers and crew were called up and the Ship entered a difficult period, without enough staff to train the cadets. Temporary staff came and went very quickly, also called up for war service. However, those who remained managed to pass 100 cadets into the Royal Navy every year during the war. Those seeking Royal Navy entry were educated separately in the 'Osborne Class,' first formed in 1905.

Conway House was opened in February, as a sick bay. It had been purpose built on the eastern end of the playing fields, alongside the Knowsley Road boundary wall. It was a two-story building containing wards, isolation rooms, and a nurse's flat. Captain Broadbent also changed the design of the windows fitted in the old gun ports. The horizontally opening ports with 2 panes in each sash were replaced by 2 vertically opening ports each with a single pane. This gave much more light below decks.

And You'll Find on the Bridge a Conway Boy
Lieutenant Colonel Philip Eric Bent VC DSO (1910-12)

Born in Halifax, Nova Scotia, on 3ʳᵈ January 1891, Phillip Bent left Conway in 1912. He went to sea and had gained his 2ⁿᵈ Mate's ticket when the First World War broke out. He and a friend decided to volunteer. If the authorities had known he was a merchant service officer with a 2ⁿᵈ Mates ticket they would have put him in the Royal Navy. Instead he joined the army as a private soldier in 1914. He was posted to the 9ᵗʰ Battalion, Leicestershire Regiment who were promptly shipped to the killing fields of the Western Front.

Losses were so great that 3 years later, at the age of 23, he was a Lieutenant Colonel commanding his regiment! He was awarded the DSO for bravery. On 1ˢᵗ October 1917, the battalion was ordered to attack Polygon Wood, Zonnebeke, Belgium. The attack was not successful and the Germans responded with a heavy attack and intense artillery fire. The situation became critical and the Allies position was in danger of being over-run. Lieutenant Colonel Bent collected a platoon that was in reserve and, together with men from other companies and various regimental details, organised and led them forward in a counter-attack. Charging forward in front of his men, he inspired them by shouting, "Come on the Tigers!" His actions won the day and secured the position, but during the charge he was cut down by enemy fire. "The coolness and magnificent example of the Colonel resulted in the securing of a portion of the line essential to a subsequent operation, but he was killed whilst leading a charge." His VC is displayed in the regimental museum in Leicester.

1915

New cadets had the same experiences as their predecessors:

"To me the first week was a nightmare. It seemed the whole Ship's company had the perfect right to ask inane questions and many of us went to the bosun to get the 'key for the starboard watch.' The struggle to get one's hammock slung, and when it was slung, and you were asleep some clever dog would land you on the deck and

the trouble began again. It seemed one had barely fallen asleep when a small wiry man with a voice out of all proportion to his size brought us to reality with his call to 'rouse and shine: the sun's burning your eyes out.' After that first week I began to take to the life, it was hard, it was tough, the food was plain but wholesome and of course never enough but at that age what boy had ever enough to eat?"

1916, 1866, 1966, the story was much the same…

1915 August

An Old *Conway* serving in the artillery on the Western Front wrote to his parents:

"In England the people cannot understand this war; until you have seen it, it is impossible to realise – I don't mean the noise of shell fire, that's all part of the game – but the villages, they are terrible – no sound, no people, all shot-shattered houses, broken trees – I cannot describe the terrible sense of calamity. We shall not be beaten. The French will not, the Belgians will not, but everything must be given over to the job."

One of *Conway's* contributions was to obtain new Remington rifles for shooting practice in the rifle range. The growing carnage on the Western Front meant promotion could be rapid, Cadet Eardly Robinson joined the Coldstream Guards as a corporal and after being mentioned in despatches he soon found himself commissioned as 2nd Lt. in the South Staffordshire Regiment.

1916

The Ship was docked for minor repairs twice in the year. First in April, returning to her mooring on 13th, and again in October, after the *Needwood,* a heavy collier, collided with her.

1917 January/February

The Mersey was almost completely frozen over. The cadets could get out of the pinnace in the middle of the river and walk about. An instructor fell overboard and died.

1917 August

The casualty lists published each term in the Cadet magazine were increasing, and Old *Conways* were serving in every theatre of war from Archangel to East Africa, the Western Front to the Pacific Ocean. Two anecdotes serve to illustrate the experience of many:

"Mr. P Barker acting Chief Officer of a merchant steamer was severely wounded in an action with a German submarine, which lasted two hours and unfortunately ended in the loss of the steamer. Mr. Barker was eleven hours in a boat before landing, and then had three hours in a springless cart over rough road before reaching hospital. When last heard from he was making a good recovery. This is the second time he has been submarined."

"T Douglas (1907-11), a corporal RNVR in the Benbow Battalion of the Royal Navy Division, was sent home in October from the Dardanelles paralysed from shock to the nerves. He was perfectly well after six months fighting in the peninsula, when he suddenly dropped. He was several months in hospital and is now at home gradually recovering."

And You'll Find on the Bridge a Conway Boy
Lt. Charles George "Gus" Bonner VC DSC RNR (1899-1901)

Charles George Bonner was born on 29th December 1884 at Shuttington, Warwickshire. Despite living far inland, he knew from a very young age he wanted to go to sea.

At the outbreak of the first world war he volunteered for the Royal Naval Division and was commissioned into the RNR in December 1914. He was awarded the Distinguished Service Cross on the 7th June, 1917, when his ship, Pargust, sank an enemy submarine, he was in charge of two guns which he worked most efficiently.

He was appointed as First Lieutenant of HMS Dunraven, a Q or mystery ship; an armed vessel disguised as a harmless merchantman. On 8th August 1917 in the Bay of Biscay, an enemy submarine UC 71 shelled Dunraven. Dunraven was hit, her depth charges detonated and the stern caught fire. Crew members, including Lt. Bonner and PO Pitcher, stayed hidden as the fire raged waiting for the submarine to close so they could engage her. Lieutenant Bonner, having been blown out of his control station by the first explosion of a depth charge due to shell fire, crawled back into the four inch gun hatch with the gun crew, well aware that it was only a matter of time before the magazine and depth charges below them would explode, and they remained there until it happened.

The gun was shifted bodily, and the gun's crew were blown up in the air revealing Dunraven's identity. UC-71 dove for cover. Dunraven was next hit by a torpedo leaving only two guns manned. UC-71 came back up, shelled Dunraven and again submerged. "The lieutenant was in the thick of the fighting and throughout a whole of the action his pluck and determination had a considerable influence on the crew."

Dunraven eventually sank off Ushant. Lt. Bonner was awarded the Victoria Cross along with PO Ernest Herbert Pitcher. Her Captain, Gordon Campbell, had previously been awarded the VC for his actions in another Q ship. "Their Lordships' appreciation expressed of the magnificent discipline and gallantry displayed by him on the 8th August, 1917, in an action with an enemy submarine. HM the King has been pleased to state that 'greater bravery than was shown by all officers and men on this occasion can hardly be conceived.'" He was invited to spend the weekend with the King and Queen at Sandringham and received his VC in the King's study at York Cottage. He went on to captain his own Q-ship, Eilian.

After the war, he worked for the Leith Salvage and Towage Company from August 1919 until August 1940. He was a very well respected salvage expert. During the Second World War, he worked for the government in charge of salvage in the Forth. After that war, he was flown to Norway to advise on salvage options for the Tirpitz. He died on 7th February 1951 at Edinburgh.

The Admiralty, seeking to increase the pool of cadets available to the Royal Navy, announced that cadets in *Conway*, *Worcester* and the newly opened shore establishment at Pangbourne were henceforth to be enrolled as 'Cadets RNR,' and thus entitled to wear the regulation uniform previously worn by midshipmen RNR. Many old *Conways* regretted the passing of the Ship's distinctive uniform and cap badge, but it was generally acknowledged to be an important recognition of the status of the three establishments, and the quality of their cadets.

And You'll Find on the Bridge a Conway Boy
Captain Edward Unwin VC CB CMG (1878-80)

When he left Conway in 1880, he joined Donald Currie's sailing ships, then P&O and finally the Egyptian Navy, before joining the Royal Navy in 1895. During the war, he was placed in command of the SS River Clyde, an old collier, which had been adapted to land 2,000 troops straight onto 'V' Beach at Gallipoli. Eight ports were fitted in the ship's side level with the interior decks through which sloping gangways could be run out to facilitate speedy landing. Barges were made fast to her port side, which could be used to form a floating bridge if she grounded too far out. When the ship grounded, a hopper on the starboard side would manoeuvre to bridge the gap between ship and shore. 25 small boats were secured alongside, packed with soldiers who were to land first and cover the main disembarkation. V Beach was a natural amphitheatre with perpendicular cliffs on one side and the castle and village of Seddul-Bahr on the other. The beach was steep and covered with barbed wire entanglements to below low watermark. Large numbers of Turkish troops were well dug in around the beach. It was expected to be a very difficult and costly undertaking, probably the most dangerous of all the planned landing beaches.

Captain Unwin beached the River Clyde as planned but the hopper became stuck. He quickly realised that it could not be positioned in time to be of use so he went down into the lighters which had shot ahead as the ship lurched to a halt. He took a line from one of them and swam ashore where he hauled the lighters towards him, assisted by Seaman Williams who had followed him. Standing up to their shoulders in water, they were fully exposed to exceptionally heavy rifle and machine-gun fire from the Turks and became obvious targets. It is reported that for some time 10,000 shots a minute fell in, or close to, the River Clyde. Against the odds they managed to establish a connection with the shore. The army brigade diary records: "Thanks to the extraordinary gallantry displayed by the naval party, the barges were got into some sort of position" As Unwin and Williams held the line taut, the soldiers swarmed forward but under unrelenting, withering fire few got ashore. The sea was soon crimson and awash with bodies.

After about forty minutes, Williams was shot and collapsed into Unwin's arms. Holding him up so he did not drown, Unwin relinquished the rope to other sailors finally coming to their assistance. Unwin was 51, exhausted and frozen from the strain of holding the heavy barges while all but submerged in the sea, surrounded by death and destruction, but he got Williams to safety. Unwin returned to the ship himself needing urgent medical treatment for a heart complaint. For an hour, doctors tried to get his heart to work normally but against doctors' orders he decided to go down into the hopper to try and improve the connection with the shore. Unwin was wounded by bullet splinters in the face and was forced to return to the ship for further treatment. He then took to a ship's lifeboat and still under heavy fire began rescuing wounded men lying in the shallows. He continued until he collapsed through physical exhaustion. He was awarded the Victoria Cross, along with four other men from the River Clyde.

The Captain Superintendent observed,

"… it will make practically no difference as the majority of cadets leaving since … 1913 have gone to … the fleet."

1918 June 4th

Collisions with the Ship were a perennial problem in the Sloyne. Some were vessels attempting to manoeuvre in the fast flowing, narrow channel, but most were vessels dragging their moorings. Almost every year one or two vessels would crash into the jib-boom or drag along the Ship's side destroying boats, railings and rigging. In June, it was the SS *Bhamo's* turn. She collided with the Ship carrying away the jib-boom and the figurehead, a bust of Lord Horatio Nelson. A shortened jib-boom was installed but the figurehead was not replaced for another twenty years! Four weeks later the SS *Elvreda*

"got cross our port bow, fouled our stern and did considerable damage."

It has not been possible to determine the amount spent on these repairs but it must have considerable and ongoing.

1918 November 11th.

"At 11.10 am came the news that the Armistice was signed. Immediately we started cheering. We gave three hearty cheers and sang 'God save the King' and then cheered more. Meanwhile, every ship in the river let off her siren and made a most unearthly row. From Liverpool and Birkenhead docks came a tremendous growl and roar as all the sirens blended their sounds into one. The First Lieutenant came up and said we were to have a half day and work was to stop immediately. There were more cheers and we stowed desks, banging them about a good deal and making lots of noise. Then, we went on to the upper deck. All the ships had tons of flags flying and were hooting away on their sirens, ringing their fog bells and they all put blanks in their guns and let them off with a bang and rockets were going up from the shore and church bells rang. All we could do was ring our little fog bell. However, we hastened to dress ship. We got plenty of rope and tied all sorts of flags and all colours and then stood to attention as they were hoisted while the band played the general salute. There was a stars and stripes at the fore truck, our own ensign at the main and a French flag at the mizzen. At the mizzen gaff we hoisted a huge great Conway ensign. On the bowsprit a Union Jack and tons of burgess, flags and pennants of all colours. … At dinner we made a tremendous row with our knives on the plates and mugs."

One hundred and seventy Old *Conways* gave their lives in the First World War. At least 1,450 served in the three armed forces, including the fledgling submarine service, and countless numbers served in the merchant service. Approximately 220 Old *Conways* were awarded honours and bravery awards, including 3 VCs, 42 DSOs, 48 DSCs, 21 MCs, 2 AFCs and 4 DFCs.

The war had a terrible impact on British shipping. 9,000,000 tons had been lost, nearly half the nation's total capacity. In 1922, in recognition of its wartime service, the merchant service was official renamed the Merchant Navy, and the Prince of Wales was appointed 'Master of the Merchant Navy.' At the end of the war there was a huge shortage of shipping and a surge in pent up world-wide demand. The Government lent 2,000,000 tons of British shipping to the French at very low, pre war 'Blue Book' rates, similarly 400,000 tons to the Italians and retained significant numbers of vessels under requisitioning itself. As a result, British companies suffered commercially while other countries, filling the vacuum, saw commercial rates and profitability soar. The Japanese picked up Pacific Ocean and Asiatic trade forcibly abandoned through requisitioning. The USA also benefited enormously. This subtly altered trading patterns and British ports began to be sidelined. After the war, when other countries could afford to quickly make good their losses, Britain could not. Many British owners, seeing the writing in the wall, sold out while the going was good. In 1919, 7 million tons of shipping were launched worldwide, just 1.6 million tons was British. Britain's share of world tonnage declined to 34.2%. It was the beginning of an inexorable decline, by 1939 it had dropped to 26.1%.

1919 April

At the end of the first complete term after the armistice, 24 cadets left *Conway* and went to sea. Not one joined the Royal Navy.

1920

Conway was created to help build a new breed of better educated mariners for the second half of the 19th Century and that had been achieved. The *Conway* model had been copied across the UK and was still spreading around the world. But a new century had dawned and the British merchant service was evolving again, spurred on by the advances and changes wrought by the war years. Wooden sailing ships had seen their day. In 1860, 70% of British registered tonnage was sail and 30% steam. In 1900 the trend was clear, 94.7% of British registered tonnage was steam and just 5.3% sail. The future lay in iron and steam, engines and technology. Navigation and seamanship skills, largely unchanged for hundred's of years, were adapting. The Editor of The Cadet magazine observed in 1897:

> *"'Ere long the whole trend of sea training will doubtless follow."*

The committee debated whether *Conway* could train young men for this bright new world while ensconced in a relic of the past. The Ship personified their challenge. *Indefatigable* had exchanged their wooden wall for a more modern steam ship, HMS *Phaeton* in 1914. She was moored close by in the Sloyne and must have been a constant reminder that the world was moving on. The committee discussed the possibility of exchanging *Conway* for a modern battleship or cruiser. Captain Broadbent would have none of it. The plans were shelved.

1924 July

HM the King presented the King's Gold Medal to cadet J H Houghton at the Town Hall.

1925

The 1905 'Bombay' cutters were replaced by a pair of matched fifteen hundredweight, twenty-seven feet ten oared cutters specially built for the Ship.

1925 May 15th

Two Americans, Miss K Mayo and Miss M Moyca Newell visited the Ship as guests of Captain and Mrs Broadbent. They were the founders of the New York Apprentices Club, opened as a haven for the cadets and apprentices of the British Merchant Service visiting New York. Young

And You'll Find on the Bridge a Conway Boy
Captain W H 'Tich' Coombs CBE RNR (Hon) (07-09)

Captain Coombs was a quite extraordinary man; physically very short, he was a first class businessman, barrister and public speaker who devoted most of his time to the welfare of others. After the First World War, many shipowners thought little of their officers' welfare, officers could be sacked for frivolous reasons by autocratic owners and many involved in incidents overseas were given little or no support by their employers. As a result, Merchant Navy officers felt undervalued, underpaid and underrepresented. They formed their first union, the British Merchant Service League in 1919; but this failed in 1921. Captain Coombs left the sea in 1921 determined to improve their status and circumstances. He succeeded almost by force of "amiable persuasion" alone. He formed the Navigators and General Insurance Company to enable officers to insure themselves against the loss of their professional certificates following an official enquiry into the loss of a ship, a collision or other accident. They also introduced Emergency Travel Indemnity Insurance to cover costs of emergency travel for husbands, wives and children. It was advertised in the Cadet and heartily endorsed.

In 1925, he wrote and paid for the publication of a book, 'The Nation's Keymen' in which he argued the case for the professional status and role of the Merchant Navy officer.

His work inspired others, and in 1928 he was influential in the formation of the Officers' (MN) Federation through which many British and Commonwealth officers' associations worked together on key issues. In 1932, he formed The Watch Ashore to represent officers' wives. Determined to make the Government improve the lot of officers, he organised a 23,000 signature petition that resulted in the creation of the Merchant Navy Officers' Pension Fund and the Central Board for the Training of Officers for the Merchant Navy. In 1935 he formed the Navigators and Engineers Officers Union.

In 1952, he was appointed Captain RNR, a rare accolade.

men going ashore faced many perils, not least were the 'land sharks' who would entice them into bars and boarding house where they would be plied with drink and encouraged to desert on the promise of greatly increased pay. They could be mugged, robbed or both. Several apprentices were murdered. The Apprentices Club was a safe haven in a dangerous city. They launched this venture in recognition of the kindness shown to American boys in the UK during the war. It was located in the Chelsea Hotel at 222 West 23rd Street, where they rented several rooms on the third floor where the cadets could relax in a home-like environment on their own or participate in various activities. The Club was hugely popular and over 12,000 British cadets visited prior to its closure in 1961. The club went from strength to strength and, in 1947, in recognition of their achievements, Miss Mayo had died but the British Consul invested Miss Newell as an Honorary CBE.

Cadet OD Wilkes left *Conway* and joined the Royal Indian Navy (RIN). Since 1867, a steady stream of cadets had entered the RIN, some 96 in total, but Wilkes appears to have been the last. There were already 64 Old *Conways* serving in the RIN when he joined. One Old *Conway* rose to command the service. Similarly, between the years 1874 and 1917, around 56 Old *Conways* joined the Bengal Pilot Service. In 1927, India opened their own training ship, the *Dufferin,* and this reduced the demand for Conway cadets in Indian marine services.

1926

A new power boat arrived to replace a boat smashed in another collision. The new boat weighed four tons, was thirty feet long and eight feet three inches in the beam. She could average eight knots and carry up to sixty cadets. She was promptly christened the Big Stink. She survived until 1974, but her eventual fate is not known.

1927 March 23rd

Captain Broadbent retired after 29 years service onboard. He and his wife had transformed the Ship with better facilities, extensive sport grounds and a completely revamped syllabus and daily routine.

CHAPTER 10

1927–34 COMMANDER F RICHARDSON DSC RN

The new Captain Superintendent was another Old *Conway* who had been in the Ship between 1900 and 1902 at the same time that Captain Broadbent was Chief Officer. As a cadet, he showed great promise by becoming chiefcadet captain and was chosen by the cadets as the Queen's Gold Medal winner in 1902. At sea, he served first in sail with Potters Brothers, but rose to Chief Officer in the Asiatic Steam Navigation Company. By 1910, he had transferred to the Royal Navy, achieving his first command on HMS *Osprey*. When the war broke out, he volunteered for the naval special forces and served in Q ships. Richardson was awarded the DSC and twice mentioned in despatches. After the war, he remained in command in the Royal Navy until February 1927.

His first act as was to bring training more up-to-date by installing wireless direction finding equipment and to start training cadets in its use. This was followed in 1930 by a gyro-compass, presented by the Canadian Pacific Steamship Company.

> *"Captain Richardson as a captain was always very much above the ordinary. He had a kind heart and knew a fair amount about us boys. I remember him for the thoroughness with which he made rounds on Sunday morning. His white gloves were into every nook and cranny and woe betide the captain of any top if they came away dirty."*

The Captain Superintendent's wife was always an important influence in the Ship and Richardson's wife was no exception. She was described as

> *"ever kind and thoughtful to little boys and sick boys."*

She gave

> *"endless time and trouble"*

Cdr F Richardson DSC RN

to the Ship's festivals, the QBs' suppers and dances and dance suppers.

1927 July 19th

100 cadets were inspected by HM the King at Liverpool Town Hall. The King presented the King's Gold Medal in person.

1928 September 25th

The City of Liverpool acknowledged its inextricable links with the sea and seafarers in a formal ceremony wedding the city to the sea. *Conway* cadets participated in a parade to the pier head and two cadets bore the copper-gilt wedding ring weighing nine pounds, which was symbolically cast into the Mersey.

And You'll Find on the Bridge a Conway Boy
Douglas V. Duff (1914-15)

Douglas was a prolific novelist and writer of boys' adventure stories and could have been a character from one of his own books. He was born in Rosario de Santa Fe, in Argentina, in 1901, and joined Conway in 1914. At the age of fifteen, he joined the Merchant Navy as a cadet in Thracia trading between Liverpool and the Mediterranean. On March 27th, 1917, Thracia was torpedoed in the Bay of Biscay. He was one of two survivors. After being rescued he observed "I lived because of what Conway had taught me." He was quickly back at sea and in "an encounter with German U boats," his leg was broken. He returned to sea again in June 1918 and at the grand old age of seventeen was torpedoed again. Surviving again he was sent to the Black Sea and was involved in the rescue of many Bolshevik fugitives. He never talked about this time except to say it was "indescribable."

After the war, he joined a teaching order of monks in Lincolnshire but discovered he had no vocation. Seeking new adventures he joined the Royal Irish Constabulary. As a keen young constable, he tried to arrest Michael Collins in the main thoroughfare in Dublin. Collins told him not to be so stupid because he was surrounded by bodyguards who would kill Duff before he'd taken a step! In 1922, he joined to the Palestine Police rising to command the force in Jerusalem. The photo shows him in his Palestinian Police uniform.

Leaving Palestine just as Captain Richardson was taking command of the Ship, Douglas took up writing and journalism - at one time interviewing Haile Selassie, the Emperor of Ethiopia.

During the Second World War his escapades continued. He served in the Dover Patrol, set submarine nets in the Suez Canal and broke the German's blockade of Tobruk in a schooner he nicknamed Eskimo Nell.

He wrote about a hundred books in his lifetime, as well as two autobiographies 'May the Winds Blow' and 'Bailing with a Teaspoon.' He also wrote a fictionalised account of his time as a Conway cadet called 'The Sea Whelps.'. He continued writing, broadcasting and television work until his death in 1978.

1929

The Committee considered a suggestion that the Ship be exchanged for a more modern vessel, an old steel battleship or a cruiser. The suggestion was firmly rejected again.

Ever ingenious, two cadets were seen on the upper deck bent over the open galley sky-light. They were armed with two improvised spears made from forks lashed to broom handles and were attempting to harpoon roast potatoes cooking in a pan immediately below them.

"A large crowd of juniors stood spell bound near them watching every thrust."

1930 February

The Lord Mayor of Liverpool (Lawrence Holt) organised a three day Festival of The Sea. A party of cadets formed a guard of honour in the chancel of the cathedral for the main celebratory service. The next day, he entertained the whole Ship's company to lunch at the Town Hall. The Holt family owned the Blue Funnel shipping company, one of Liverpool's most successful fleets. They were already involved in *Conway's* management, and Lawrence D Holt was elected Chairman on 15th July 1934. As we shall see in later chapters, he and the Holt family became inextricably linked with the Ship and over time senior members of Holt's management and other family members including Sir John Nicholson and Mr. Dickie (both partners) plus Julian Holt and Brian Heathcote became influential chairmen or members of Conway's managing committee. Blue Funnel realised significant benefits from this association, achieving a steady supply of well trained apprentices over many years, but the relationship was far deeper than a purely pragmatic one. Lawrence Holt spent a great deal of his own, and his company's money securing *Conway's* future. He paid personally for many repairs and effectively subsidised the Ship for many years. The extent of this munificence is not clear but Holts certainly paid for one major refit and in later years contributed generously to the establishment of the shore base and the docking to which the Ship was proceeding when she was lost. Some years later the laboratories were a gift from Julian Holt and his mother. Many trace *Conway's* eventual closure to the severing of the paternalistic link between the Holts and the Ship.

Cheering The Prince of Wales Ashore

1931 November 4th

The Price of Wales (later King Edward VIII) visited the Ship and personally presented the King's Gold Medal to cadet G W R Graves. The cadets manned the Ship's side to give the Prince a rousing send off. They also formed a Guard of Honour on the pier when the Prince re-embarked for Liverpool.

1932

For two years the cadets, under the guidance of the Ship's carpenter Mr. John Bullis Williams, had been making a model of the Ship to present to The King. It was to a scale of one-eight of an inch to the foot. The hull was cut from a section of African oak from a lower deck fairlead. It was a huge undertaking containing 156 deadeyes and 91 blocks made from old school rulers, metal parts were all from the Ship's copper. There were 120 yards of rigging, 622 bolts (domestic pins) and 1,798

The King's Model

hitches in the rigging (each taking 10-30 seconds to pass). The hull was finished with 16 coats of paint and enamel. It was presented to the King at the palace on 22nd July 1932. It is now on display in the Science Museum in London (and in need of a little care and attention). This venture generated considerable interest in model building and a ship model society was formed. In 1933, they submitted several models to the next ship model exhibition in Liverpool. Instructor Powers's elaborate model of *Conway* received particular praise.

The Ship now owned 12 acres of playing fields maintained by 2 groundsmen. The main sports were rugby in winter and cricket in the summer, as well as tennis.

> *"All boys box; but every boy must know how to sail, swim and row before he may play cricket or tennis."*

> *"I think what gave me the greatest pleasure was watching the many ships coming and going on the Mersey. It taught us all the greatness and romance of the sea and those who serve it; we know those ships and their reputations."*

> *"What impressed me most was the amount of responsibility given to cadet captains, both in the running of their tops and in the management of boats, often under difficult weather conditions; the sound knowledge gained about all forms of boat-work; the fullness of each day with having to run a ship and do a full schooling concurrently. The fact that if one gave one's Conway honour one never broke it."*

1933

The Poet Laureate, John Masefield OM (1891-94) also acted as *Conway's* Poet Laureate, composing many lines for notable occasions. In 1933, he wrote 'The *Conway* Gulls' which commemorated the tradition that seagulls around the Ship were the returning souls of old boys who had crossed the bar and so should not be disturbed, despite the deleterious effects of their calling cards on the Ship's wood and bright work!

They died in the gales' roaring, in the smash
Of some green billow whence they never rose;
Some diced with Death with many lucky throws
Till the last throw, that nulled them into ash.

Some were for all adventure, being rash;
And others died, in thirst and fever-throes,

On frontiers at the furthest that man goes,
Or on the foreman's muzzles, in the flash.

And being gone, they wander home again
Here, to the Ship, and settle on her spars,
Mewing and going gleaning in the sea.

They are our brothers, so let them be,
Old Conways, fellow-sharers of the stars,
Advanced another link upon the chain.

CHAPTER 11

1934 COMMANDER M G DOUGLAS RD RNR

When Captain Richardson left the Ship on 14th June 1934, before the end of term Commander M G 'Monty' Douglas RNR, the Ship's First Lieutenant, was the favourite to take his place. The committee decided not to offer him the post but to recruit a replacement. However, with Captain Richardson already gone, the committee invited Monty to hold the fort, he agreed and was appointed acting Captain Superintendent on 15th June.

He was well respected and regarded with great affection by all who knew him.

> *"No officer has ever had a more winning way with the Ship's company."*

An Old *Conway*, he had been in the Ship as a cadet between 1893 and 1895. He served at sea with a number of shipping companies before becoming a marine surveyor in South Africa. From there he did eighteen months service as an RNR officer before joining *Conway* in 1907 as Second Officer at a relatively young age. At the outbreak of war, along with several other members of staff, he was mobilised. He served in *Charybdis* and then Canadian patrol vessels. He rejoined the Ship in September 1917, just as the title Chief Officer was temporarily dropped in favour of First Lieutenant. In earlier years the term First Officer had also been used.

> *"He always got things done. He would roundly strafe an errant cadet or top and always end his harangue with 'That's all about it' and it generally was.'"*

1934 July 18th

King George V visited Liverpool to open the new road tunnel. He presented the King's Gold Medal to Cadet H Kirby and spoke for some time to Commander Douglas. The King and Queen then went on to open Birkenhead Library where the majority of the cadets paraded. Finally, they left from Rock Ferry Station where a guard of thirty cadets was posted. Providing guards of honour was a recurrent event for Conway cadets, only three days before they had paraded at Liverpool Cathedral for the Hallowing of the Festival of The Seven Lamps. Their presence at festivals, events and commemorations was to increase dramatically during the coming world war when parades were almost a weekly event, sometimes at more than one venue in a single day.

Although a range of sports was available there was no obligation to participate. Some used the opportunity for illicit trips to the cinema in Liverpool.

> *"The procedure was to wear (civilian) grey flannels under one's white (uniform) regulation flannels."*

The enterprising cadets removed their outer layer in the lavatories on Rock Ferry pier and left them with the in the care of the ferry stage attendants. They caught the underground into the city, watched a film and then returned to the pier where they donned their uniforms and returned to the Ship. Unfortunately, as they wandering down the pier in 'mufti' they were in full view of the duty officer on the Ship and his large telescope. Indeed Monty was probably well aware of the practice as he has been a cadet himself not long before. Eventually, one group returned to find the Ship's officers had collected their uniforms. They returned to the Ship where they were put on a charge. The warning was enough and the practice died out or, more likely, the cadets invented a new way to get ashore.

Monty served for just a few months until September 1934 when his replacement took up post. He retired from the Ship but was re-employed again in 1939 as Chief Officer, serving until 1942 when he retired permanently because of ill health.

CHAPTER 12

1934 CAPTAIN T GODDARD RD RNR

1934 September

Captain T M Goddard RD RNR joined the Ship as her new Captain Superintendent with impeccable credentials. He was an Old *Conway* of 1905-07 vintage and winner of the Queen's Gold Medal in 1907. He served at sea for several years, but as an RNR officer he was called up during the First World War. He served in the armed cruiser *Oceanic* before being posted to the Grand Fleet in *Donegal*. After the war, he returned to sea before accepting command of the South African training ship *General Botha* in 1921. He subsequently joined the South African Navy and spent several years surveying the coasts around South Africa. In 1934 he was selected to replace Captain Richardson.

Goddard arrived to a crisis.

Capt. and Mrs T Goddard RD RNR

"When I was appointed in command of Conway in September 1934, Britain was beginning to recover from the world wide trade depression. For the previous few years shipping lines had been badly hit, and the directors were unable to offer good prospects to boys wishing to take up the sea as a career, with the result that there were few applications. Conway was simultaneously hit and the number of cadets onboard during the Summer Term 1934 had fallen to 106."

Numbers had more than halved since the wartime peak, and 1933 saw the smallest intake ever, just 7 new chums. This was doubtless influenced by the continued decline in the British merchant fleet. In 1870, Britain had 63% of world tonnage, by 1914 it was 39% and by 1934 it was just 27%! Foreign shipping companies looked to their own nationals for officers, so *Conway, Worcester* and all the UK pre-sea training ships were suffering. At the same time, there was a significant glut of shipping worldwide; so 1.6 million tons of British capacity was laid up; 40,000 British seafarers were unemployed and officers' pay had been cut. The sea must have seemed a less and less attractive career for boys. Although there were about 300 British shipping companies, the big five, Cunard, Ellerman Line, Furness Withy, Ocean Steamship and P&O controlled over one third of UK registered shipping. If he and the committee could not increase numbers, the Ship might not be sustainable.

Falling numbers weren't Captain Goddard's only challenge. He also found the fabric and facilities in the Ship in serious decline. He was determined to bring the Ship into the 20th century.

"During the twenty-seven years since I had left Conway as a cadet, there had been few additional facilities for training and I found that the Ship's structure had deteriorated badly. I immediately submitted plans for the

renewal of classroom furniture, main deck class rooms to be properly partitioned to make them sound-proof and new seamanship and Royal Navy Class rooms to be made with a laboratory to be built on the upper deck."

His improvement plans stopped the slide in facilities but it was the Second World War that really resolved the deadlier threat of dwindling numbers.

Mr TEW Browne BSc

While we have traced the history of the Ship around the succession of Captain Superintendents there was another body of men also influencing performance and achievements; the Headmasters. Captain Goddard was to be ably supported by the new Headmaster Mr. TEW Browne BSc. He was appointed to replace Thomas Marchant BA who had been Headmaster for the pervious twenty years. His recruitment had been swift. He had applied on 11th July, was interviewed with several others on the 23rd and chosen the same day. He joined on 4th September from Oakham School, but strangely the previous Headmaster remained as a master and did not leave until 25th October 1937! His mission from the management committee was to raise academic standards. This was not to prove easy. Many cadets considering *Conway* naval training thought 'school' was behind them and so had little inclination to academic studies. He immediately established a small science lab on the upper deck, a library, a gym in the hold, re-arranged the timetable and introduced prep twice a week. His diary summarises the state of education he found.

"Junior class age range 12 to 18 – 'How does one teach?' Younger cadets more restless but not in fear of authority. Detention started but no-one used it. Periods go with tremendous verve but more entertaining than educating. Boys too passively enjoying mathematical histrionics. I doubt the value of English teaching. Didn't like the library organisation."

He was equally pointed about his cabin in the Ship,

"small, bare and ill furnished."

Another master was leaving after 28 years service. TEWB, as he was immediately nicknamed, started a new science class in conjunction with Liverpool Technical College, soon broached the idea of an entrance exam to raise standards and set about recruiting a Deputy Headmaster to help he achieve change. It led to the recruitment of a Mr. Carter, called Bogbrush because of his mass of unruly hair. He and TEWB were to become *Conway* institutions. TEWB quickly found that teachers and academic education were second class citizens in the naval hierarchy.

"Commander (Goddard) more distant than I thought. Le Mesurier (the Chief Officer) 'sirs' him but not me."

He realised his lack of nautical knowledge would be a hurdle, so he promptly set about educating himself. His diary records,

"Scudding sail and how to send down yards. Learning navigation – mid latitude and traverse, international code, decided to go for yacht master ..."

TEWB had a penetrating, analytical mind and started delving into technical matters,

> *"… impressed by signals efficiency …"*

but this did not go down well with the uniformed staff. He felt *Conway* put too much emphasis on boat work

> *"… amount of time when at sea handling boats insufficient to justify the time spent."*

He recommended a reduction in the number of seamanship lessons and believed there should be an

> *"educational representative on Shipping Federation Committee" rather than "only case hardened mariners."*

He noted after a few months:

> *"Cadets very anti reduction of seamanship periods and generally against changes."*

He was not deterred. He had a vision for the future, saw a need to improve technical and academic classes and would take every opportunity to further his views. He would fight his corner for the next thirty years and we shall see he was a tireless innovator who made an immeasurable impact. With 'Wah' at the helm and TEWB his right hand man things immediately began to look up.

Another Conway icon, Bossie Phelps, joined in the mid 30s, primarily to coach the gig's crew against Worcester. He proved to be a first class Warrant Officer and remained on the staff throughout the war, eventually leaving to join the staff of Winchester College.

Despite the fall in numbers cadets seemed to relish the *Conway* life:

> *"The only things I can recall are pleasant. The summer evenings spent away up off Ellesmere Port and Port Sunlight in the sailing dinghies with a good stiff breeze to put your gunwales under. The nice clean smell of the Ship on Saturdays after the forenoon 'heave round.' Canteen time when you had some money to spend. The enjoyable afternoons up at the sports field or at the New Ferry open air baths in the summer and reading on the upper deck on a sunny afternoon. It was good to turn into your hammocks at night too."*

> *"I think that the thing that delighted me most was the fact that we were a ship, by which I mean the spirit of comradeship and unity which pervaded the Ship and even to this day those things make me proud I am a Conway."*

> *"Whilst I was onboard I think I learned more about human beings, and how to live with them, work with them and avoid them if necessary than I learned before or since."*

1935 April

One way to attract more boys was to broaden the scope of training; so air training was introduced, the theory of flight and airmanship taught onboard, supplemented by fifteen hours flying from Hooton Aerodrome. This was enough for cadets to obtain their 'A' private pilot's licence and by the end of the summer term several had achieved this Despite its popularity for some, the adoption of air training was not generally like by cadets. Browne was very enthusiastic and started working with the Air Ministry and Imperial Airways to develop an air cadet branch to prepare cadets for RAF Cranwell in the same way the RN class prepared boys for Dartmouth. Air Commodores Tedder and Page visited the Ship on 21st February 1935 to discuss his plans. Air Ministry officials followed a few days later. An Old *Conway* of 1905-07 vintage, Air Commodore Richard Pierse, was Deputy Chief of the Air Staff and he was supportive. However, despite this initial momentum, plans never came to fruition; the Air Ministry decided that supporting *Conway* might prejudice interest from other schools, and perhaps the Committee and Ship's officers were more inclined to remain a naval training ship.

Around this time the Mustard Club came into being; a group of cadets who gathered in the heads for an illicit smoke. Anyone could join so long as they paid the membership fee, two cigarettes for each existing member. Another popular and free smoking haunt was the 'Cockpit.' The hold, site of the old engine and propeller shaft, was the lowest part of the Ship used officially by the cadets. Below it were the Ship's bilges, a low, unlit, dingy and smelly nether world, piled high with ballast and even an old gun barrel. Smokers entered these bilges illicitly through a small hatch under the aft ladder. This dropped them into the old propeller shaft through which they scrambled to an overhead opening which led up into a large but completely enclosed space with good headroom, the 'cockpit.' It was full of abandoned gear including gun carriages, iron ballast and links of anchor chain. It was said that anyone carving his name in the cockpit would die shortly after leaving the Ship. It is rumoured that there were initials carved on every free surface but this is a myth

> *"When I went into the cockpit in 1949 there were very few names carved ... It is of interest that the one member of my term who did carve his name died from injuries sustained onboard his ship, within six years of leaving"*

1935

A Central Board for the Training of Officers for the Merchant Navy was established to promote a uniform national training scheme for deck apprentices. The British India Steam Navigation Company, the New Zealand Shipping Company and Brocklebank were using their own dedicated cargo liners as school ships for their cadets. *Conway* had to adapt her ways. The Captain Superintendent and Headmaster started to discuss the need for a shore establishment. Later that month, they began to share their thoughts with committee members. Early in 1936, Browne extended this forward thinking by sending the Committee and Captain Superintendent proposals for a *Conway* preparatory school, "independent and profitable, 30-40 boys." By February, the local tennis club (Browne played tennis) offered land for a shore establishment.

1936

It was made compulsory for prospective cadets to pass an entrance examination. This was much to the liking of the new Board of Education, which was becoming more and more interested in the Ship. Goddard's and Browne's efforts were bearing fruit and the complement of cadets was steadily increasing and the general standard of education much improved. There was a special RN Class for those seeking entry to the Royal Navy. The system for entry to the RN was diverse and complicated but in the 'olden days' there was a traditional route into the Royal Navy, specifically for *Conways* and *Worcesters* going back to the days of the RNC Osborne. If a boy failed to get a place to the RNC at the age of thirteen and a half, he could have a second shot if he went to a training ship and sat a special exam a few years later.

> *"I went into the RN Class and soldiered on towards what was then known as the Direct Entry Exam for Conway, Worcester and Pangbourne cadets at 17 plus."*

The idea was to fill vacancies caused by drop-outs from Dartmouth and quite a few Old Conways entered this way, including Vice Admiral Sir Archibald Day RN KBE, CB, DSO (1913-14) who was Hydrographer of the Navy between 1950 and 55.

1937

The Honourable Company of Fishmongers awarded a scholarship. Presumably they had a vested interest in well qualified seamen. In February, the Committee and Captain Superintendent discussed the possibility that Rock Ferry pier might be closed and that the Ship would have to be relocated to new moorings. He examined two local alternatives, the Dingle opposite Rock Ferry and Bromborough, a short distance up river. Further afield, he considered Conway on the North Wales coast and Bangor on the Menai Strait. In the event the ferry and pier remained open until 1939, but his investigations were to be revisited within a few years.

Conway recorded a loss of £2,000 in 1936, so Holt decided to delay long overdue pay increases by several months. Although Goddard and Browne were achieving significant improvements, neither man thought their positions secure or sufficiently influential with Lawrence Holt, the forceful chairman of the committee. They felt he interfered too much in their day-to-day work. Most members of staff also felt insecure. But with numbers down, standards poor and finances critical, pressure was inevitable. Holt was a shipping magnate, a businessman used to making tough decisions, not what Goddard or Browne were used to at all. Browne had been half-heartedly applying for better paid jobs at other schools. But by June 1937, he noted in his diary:

> *"Difficulties in school – resolved to leave."*

Goddard was more of an optimist but rumours abounded that he would not last another year. He confided to the Headmaster that he

> *"would resign if he were a young man and could afford it."*

They were both to weather the storm.

1937 July 29th to September 13th

Captain Goddard was concerned that the fabric of the Ship was being neglected. Her last overhaul had been in approximately 1904 and she was beginning to show her age. Goddard arranged a full inspection and this showed the need for a thorough overhaul. The committee agreed and she was moved to Vittoria Dock for the first phase of repairs. The work included repairing damage to the main deck beams and the deck sheathing caused by heat from the cooking range, improving the galley and the heating system, and replacing aged planking between the waterline and the gun ports. 550 square feet of planking was replaced using English oak and extensive re-caulking was completed. The main timbers exposed were found to be in excellent condition.

1938 May-July

Kurt Hahn, a well-known German educationalist with radical ideas, had started Gordonstoun School at Elgin in Scotland. Lawrence Holt who knew him well felt there were synergies between the two establishments. Hahn had introduced a Moray Badge for proficiency and physical fitness after training and Holt wanted *Conway* to do likewise. Hahn and Goddard were keen to collaborate and an 80 foot schooner, the *Maisie Graham* was proposed for joint use, based in Scarborough. The four-masted barque *Lawhill* based in Conway was also considered. *Conway* cadets would henceforth spend considerable time training at sea. Members of staff and the committee visited Elgin and a report was produced. The equivalent of the Moray Badge, the Conway Badge, was adopted but *Conway's* committee eventually decided against the proposals for training at sea on practical considerations of cost and the difficulty of organising regular academic classes under sea conditions, especially the impact of watch-keeping. The committee resurrected the idea of a sailing vessel in 1939 and Captain Goddard visited Gordonstoun for three days. Uffa Fox was consulted about the practicalities, but again they decided against proceeding. When Hahn and Holt created Outward Bound together during the war, these ideas were dusted off and a successful partnership emerged.

1938 July 20th to September 10th

The Ship was moved back to Vittoria Dock for the second phase of renovations. Goddard now wanted to fix the planking from the gun ports upwards, the upper deck, masts, yards and rigging. Some 3,500 square feet of planks were replaced. The decks were all re-caulked with

Carter Preston (left) and The Figurehead

"a hundred men boring bolts out of the planking with oxy-acetylene."

All yards and spars came down; all rigging was stripped, tested and made good. New davits, deadeyes and three new topgallant masts were fitted. The superstructure on the Focsle was removed including the tall, narrow galley chimney so prominent in old photos. All remarked on the fine lines exposed, but these were promptly covered again by a completely new, all-enveloping Focsle structure with new heads, a new boiler and a new water tank. 37 coats of paint were found on the foremast! On 21st September, the committee noted that £17,000 had been spent on refits.

1938 Sunday September 11th

Over a year earlier, at Captain Goddard's prompting, the committee had agreed that the Ship should have a new figurehead to replace the original (a bust of Lord Horatio Nelson), which had been carried away on 4th June 1918 by the SS *Bhamo*. The Conway Club paid it for. Mr. Carter Preston undertook the design and construction. It is a full figure of Lord Horatio Nelson wearing his admiral's uniform, the Royal Navy medal and the jewel of the Bath. His left hand holds a telescope under which is carved the crown of the Merchant Navy. The Trafalgar signal is reproduced on the scrollwork. Preston took great pains to ensure authenticity. To obtain a true likeness he studied various portraits of Nelson and was given unique access to his death mask and his Trafalgar uniform to match colours. The figurehead was constructed from teak, since this was considered a longer lasting wood than the yellow pine normally used for ships' figureheads. A sound decision as the figurehead still survives although now at HMS *Nelson* in Portsmouth (the Royal Navy's Courts Martial Centre). It was not possible to obtain a single block of wood large enough so 3 inch planks were used. It weighs 3.5 tons and stands 13.5 feet high. For the masting (fitting to the Ship), dedication and unveiling ceremony the Ship was brought alongside Liverpool Landing Stage, the only occasion of a wooden wall being secured alongside the stage. Dr. John Masefield OM led the ceremony. At 10.30 am the figurehead was unveiled and Masefield read a poem, 'The New Figurehead,' he had written specially for the occasion.

Ninety nine years ago, the long-dead hands
Fitted your figurehead to lean and yearn
Vant-courier to you as you thrust your way,
Your herald in your going and return,
Seeming to search the seas for foreign lands
Seeming to brood above the burst of spray.

Long perished are those builders, and that form.
We, who are linked to you by subtle ties,
To-day re-dower you, again complete
The Life you had (for us) with head and eyes
To front the running water and the storm
And bear alike, unblinking, sun and sleet.

We give you this as dower, with our thanks,
Old Ship who cradled us and gave us friends
And sealed us to the service of the Sea.
All honour to you till that service ends,
New fo'c's'lemen to fill the dwindling ranks,
And Conway boys wherever ships may be.

Newly Masted Figurehead

This was followed by a service in the Cathedral attended by all cadets.

"If my memory serves me correctly it was a typical dank Liverpool day with Divisions and speeches ad nauseam about both naval and Merchant Navy traditions. I don't remember what I had done on this occasion to deserve it, but I was doggie (messenger) to Lt. Cdr. Couch who was in one of his moods and running around like a chicken with its head cut off. It was not a memorable day for me."

For everyone else it was a splendid day with the Ship finally complete again, well restored and recovering well, from her doldrums days.

And You'll Find on the Bridge a Conway Boy
Captain J C K Kelly-Rogers (1919-21)

In April 1939 April, an Old Conway, Captain Kelly-Rogers, a pilot with Imperial Airways landed his flying boat Connemara on the Mersey and moored next to the Ship. He had reported a "slight engine default" off Holyhead and diverted to the safety of Liverpool where he was able to effect running repairs; a pint of oil from Conway.

This remarkable coincidence allowed a number of cadets to render assistance and be a given a conducted tour before he was able to safely continue his journey to Southampton. He had visited the Ship once before in 1932 in a Southampton flying boat. He was a pioneering flying boat pilot. In 1937, he flew the first Empire flying boat service down the River Nile to Kisumu on Lake Victoria. He then made the first night flight from Kisumu to Durban, South Africa.

His most daring exploit was the rescue of the flying boat Corsair which had made a forced landing on the narrow River Dangu in the North East corner of the Belgian Congo. Corsair had been damaged in the landing and there was not enough clear water for a safe take off. Many attempts were abandoned but it was Kelly-Rogers who eventually got her airborne in 1940 and safely back to Juba.

After the visit to the Ship in April 1939, he piloted the first transatlantic flight by an Empire flying boat, the Capella. Then on 5th August 1939, he piloted the first ever transatlantic air mail flight. He piloted Winston Churchill across the Atlantic many times during the war. He finished his career in charge of Aer Lingus.

1938 December

Perhaps as a result of inspections whilst in Vittoria Dock, and because of a letter from the Admiral Commanding Reserves criticising the condition of the Ship, it was decided to dry-dock her for a major overhaul. She was moved from her mooring on 12th December and dry-docked on 15th. Captain Goddard records:

> *"To decide whether the Ship, which was then a hundred years old, was strong enough, caused a lot of anxiety and thought."*

It was thought many of her oak stanchions might split; so all the decks were shored up with 12inch square baulks of timber. She had a hog of 2ft 6inch, which had to be considered when she took the blocks, and, in addition, the hog was a design feature of all wooden walls; the keel being laid slightly convex from stem to stern to allow for the extreme weight of cannon, shot, stores and victuals mainly stored amidships. Whilst these wooden walls were phenomenally strong sided to withstand enemy broadsides, they relied on the support of the water for much of their lateral strength. They had to be well supported in dry dock if they were not to suffer unbearable strains and simply break in two – or 'break their backs' as it is colloquially known. In other words, there was very real concern that the old Ship might collapse in dry dock. Captain Goddard continues:

"When the Ship was safely in dock and secured, I landed to watch the dock being pumped out. As she was taking the blocks a foreman called out from the lower deck gangway that the Ship was creaking badly and he feared she would break in two. Mr. Dickie, who was standing next to me, quickly replied 'Good, it is the Ship that does not creak that I am afraid for.' Creaking shows that there is plenty of life left in the timbers. Suffice to say that she 'spelled' on the blocks safely and with the hog taken out of her the original lines returned, showing her to be a thing of beauty."

Her last dry docking had been in 1896 and in the 42 years since the underwater portion of the hull had

"deteriorated but slightly."

The copper sheathing had perished and was completely replaced, some 10 tons in total. Incredibly, only one 28 × 12 × 12 oak strake had to be replaced on the port side just below the waterline and a small piece near the stern port. The galley was converted to coke fired. The total cost was £20,000 with £5,000 paid by Alfred Holt and Co.

1939 January 18th

She was returned to her mooring. Captain Goddard had other improvements in mind, including a new central heating system, but he was forced to put them on hold.

"We were fortunate to get as much work done during these three refits for it was intended to effect further repairs and additions at Birkenhead in 1939 but the war intervened and little did we think that the Conway's long years at the Rock Ferry anchorage would soon be ended and she would have to seek pastures new to continue her valuable work. By this time, 1939, we had 180 cadets under training which was then considered to be the full complement, but this was shortly to be increased."

1939

The centenary of *Nile's* launch was celebrated by a special dinner at Liverpool Town Hall, on 2nd May, hosted by the Lord Mayor. On 28th June, the actual day of her launch, the Ship was open to visitors for tea and to observe the moment of her launch. Flowers were arranged on the main deck, a brass band came aboard and played, all hands paraded for a brief speech by the Captain Superintendent for the poop. The Ship's buglers sounded the salute and the band played the National Anthem.

"When I joined Conway, I discovered a remarkably wide mix of young men from a variety of social and educational backgrounds. At one end of the scale we had at least three 'aristos' including a Russian Prince and a Count, and at the other a young chum from a Dorset village school whose widowed mother had brought him up in extreme impoverished circumstances (his father had died in service in the Merchant Navy and the necessary fees were funded by a shipping company's bursary). In between were the well endowed scions of northern industrial families (we called them the 'blanket barons'), sons of expatriate parents who had either been in boarding school since the age of six, with personalities tempered accordingly, or reared by strict non conformist maiden aunts and used to a harsh discipline, and a small number for whom Conway was a last resort in dealing with a difficult boy. But the majority, I suppose, came from seafaring or farming families, or leafy middle class suburban professional or business backgrounds who could afford the fees. Regional accents were very noticeable, as, in some cases were some rather prissy-voweled 'posh' ones. Within a very few days, we new chums had formed sub-sets of mates and were merged into an homogeneous term, controlled by (a) the fact that most of us were where we wanted to be, (b) a desire to avoid the ubiquitous threatened teaser or slack-party, and (c) the rule of privileges - hard to win and easy to lose. We were learning to take orders before being taught how to give them."

New Chums Receive Their Medicine

"The Ship soon became our home. After the refit of 1938 she was well equipped and I personally found she was warm and all enfolding - but far from comfortable - apart from the hammocks, which I took to. The only place to sit on something soft was in one's sea-chest (lid open and tray to one side) or at the mess tables on the main deck on benches (where one sat to study). The recreation room in the hold was devoid of anything sensible to do or even seating, but contained a copy of the Daily Express and Daily Herald (the RN Class had The Times); the library contained an extraordinary assortment of books most of which published no later than 1910. But we made our own life; we did not hate our circumstances; we developed a great esprit de corps; we learned to do what we were told and move at the double; and we became expert at avoiding trouble. And so it went on: we wanted the advantage of the Conway Certificate and entree into a good company - and were prepared to work towards both. The war, of course, provided an impetus to 'do our bit.' Throughout my time I cannot recall any overt bullying; some customary rather idiotic traditional irritations and the natural lording over inferiors by members of the term ahead of you - but bullying, no. Running Conway under the present health and safety regime would have been impossible. Yes, we lost one cadet in a really stupid accident, and I have a mangled big toe due to my own foolishness - but we were learning to take care of ourselves and others."

And You'll Find on the Bridge a Conway Boy
Rear Admiral Douglas Everett CB CBE MBE DSO RN (1911-13)

Many Old Conways went directly into the Royal Navy and the navies of Australia, Canada, Ceylon, Egypt, India, New Zealand and South Africa. At least 40 achieved flag rank. Rear Admiral Douglas Henry Everett RN was one such.

Leaving Conway in 1911, he went directly to the Royal Navy. In the First World War, he served on Zealandia and Resolution. He was Fleet Signal Officer Nelson, 2 Battle Squadron, Home Fleet 1932-1933, and attended the Royal Navy Staff College, Greenwich in 1934. He was Staff Officer (Operations) to Commander-in-Chief, China Station, HMS Kent from 1935 to 1937; and then Executive Officer Ajax from 1937. At the outbreak of the Second World War, he was still in Ajax and fought the Graf Spee in the battle of the River Plate.

As Chief Staff Officer to Force V, he planned the invasion of Sicily of 1942-1943. He commanded the aircraft carrier Arbiter in the Far East from 1944 to1945. After the war he was Commander-in-Chief, Hong Kong 1945-1947; commanded Duke Of York 1947 -1949, and was appointed Flag Officer, Ground Training 1949 -1951. He rounded off his long career as President of the Admiralty Interview Board from 1951 to1952 when he retired.

"The end of the new chums' two weeks grace and the somewhat unofficial punishments given by senior cadets for not asking for 'top.' On one occasion I was on my way to slack party, I had to ask for top a couple of times and was kept waiting a considerable time. When I reported to the slack party cadet captain to do my hour's punishment work (we call it community service today) I received a further half hour for being late."

"One of the new chums was being visited by his parents and sister. They came down to the orlop deck and, as they reached the foot of the ladder, one boy raced past wearing only a vest yelling, 'Help! Rape! Murder!' He was being chased by another cadet with a deck scrubber!"

"One of the pleasantest memories is of cinema nights. They were on Wednesdays when we had just received our clean laundry back. We trooped down into the hold and made ourselves comfortable with our laundry bags as pillows and thoroughly enjoyed the film. And then how good it was to turn in one's hammock at night. There can be few more comfortable places to sleep and we were usually ready for sleep at the end of a strenuous day."

Whilst the cadets went about their unchanging routine Europe was moving closer to conflict once again.

1939 September 9th

At the outbreak of war the Headmaster, Chief and Second Officer were called up and several masters immediately volunteered. More were to follow. Captain Goddard recalled that having so many staff called up

"made us shorthanded but all pulled their weight and the curriculum was fully carried out: I had to assist in the teaching of nautical subjects but as time went on, we were able to complete the staff."

Conway's comfortable existence on the Mersey was about to change forever.

CHAPTER 13

1939–41 THE MERSEYSIDE BLITZ

1939 September

Now the country was at war, it was decided that the Ship needed protection against anticipated bombing raids on Liverpool and Birkenhead docks. Indefatigable cadets came aboard during the summer holidays. So that reflections couldn't help enemy planes find the Mersey, they painted out the Ship's white gun strakes, the upper deck battleship gray, covering it with sand bags, and they fitted black out screens to all 130 ports. They also fitted concrete blast protectors to all hatches and skylights to protect against incendiary bombs. *Conway* was truly ready for war!

By this time there was a marked improvement in the standard of education onboard; and from 1941 until Goddard's retirement in 1949, a *Conway* cadet was placed first in all the annual Royal Navy Direct Entry examinations.

Prepared for War

> *"To extend our service to the country the complement of cadets was increased to 250 and arrangements were made for Gordonstoun School, then at Caersws, Merionethshire, to take cadets for one year of training in our curriculum."*

1940 August 17th

The first air raids on Merseyside began with bombs dropped on docks just opposite *Conway*. They become a nightly occurrence. Between 17th August and 12th November, there were 66 air raids lasting 160 hours. 2 or 3 raids a night were commonplace. They caused great damage and many fires, all plainly visible from the Ship. The strain on staff and cadets was constant. Cadets mounted round the clock fire watches of a cadet captain and 4 cadets.

> *"Taffy Walters, in Conway uniform, and his wife, in spotlessly crisp white hospital uniform, presided over the sanatorium, Conway House, in Rock Ferry where we were incarcerated when stricken with prevalent 'nasties' like pink-eye, etc. They terrified me at first (aged thirteen) but I worked around the playing fields and pumped out the air raid shelter (which was prone to flooding) quite happily under Taffy's eagle eye. But later, after we moved to the strait, and they ran Bryn Mel, the temporary sanatorium, I got to know them, grew quite fond of them, and admired the job they did so scrupulously."*

1940 November 12th

There was a severe air raid and it was blowing a full gale with a strong ebb tide. Captain Goddard recorded that

"the whale factory ship Hektoria, 13,000 tons and with a full cargo of whale oil, dragged her anchors and drifted out to our port side, smashing the out head, lower boom decks and many boats. For some time, she could not free herself and together we dragged Conway's mooring towards the Rock Ferry beach."

All hands were turned out and hastily prepared to let go both anchors. Once out of danger and when it was clear there was no serious damage, they turned in again.

"Eventually, she got clear and left me in a precarious position, demanding a tug to tow our stern to the eastward at the time of the tide to prevent us from grounding on the Rock Ferry side of the river. The collision occurred at midnight and by the following afternoon arrangements had been made for us to be towed to the Vittoria Dock, Birkenhead, to repair the (minor) damage."

They spent the rest of the term and half the Easter term in dock waiting for the moorings to be relaid.

"Facilities for exercising the cadets were difficult and we had to make use of the local park for football and the docks for boat work. However, the air raids and fire watching kept everyone alert until we left on 9th March 1941. During the five months we were in Vittoria Docks, we were fortunate to escape damage from bombing but the day after we left, the street adjoining the dock was badly damaged and the cargo shed alongside where we had been was damaged. We were glad to return to our moorings for we imagined that only direct hits would sink us, but when the enemy commenced to drop magnetic mines into the Mersey our anxiety increased for one lost accurate positions of them due to the strong tides rolling them along the bottom, and one under ours, in spite of our strong hull would, if it exploded, quickly bring to an end our usefulness to the country, for Conway has no watertight bulkheads."

"Conway, with her immensely strong timbers, could stand quick near misses from bombs which exploded on contact with the water. She shuddered and quickly settled down again when a stick of three bombs fell close to the starboard side and another occasion, one on the port side. The explosives were quite near enough to have started rivets in a steel ship."

At this time there were two white Russian cadets, Prince Serge Oblensky and Count Michael Tolstoy. The later was

"born in Germany in 1922 to Russian refugee parents - his father had been an officer in the Imperial Russian Guard. He was educated at the Lycee Empereur Nicolas II in Versailles before joining Conway in January 1939."

He became junior cadet captain over the Chartroom and then senior cadet captain over the Laboratory. He left the Ship in April 1941 and joined the Fleet Air Arm and was lost at sea.

And You'll Find on the Bridge a Conway Boy
The Peirse Family: Admiral and Air Chief Marshall

Admiral Sir Richard Peirse KCB KBE (1873-1875) came from a family of seafarers including two admirals. It is said that his father, a Colonel in the army, to discourage his desire to go to sea sent him to Conway! He excelled and gained entry The Royal Naval College, Dartmouth, where he graduated top of his term. His naval career glittered, he was acknowledged as one of the leading gunnery experts of the day. He fought in the Egyptian War, the Boer War and the First World War as C-in-C East Indies. He was the first naval officer to be made a KBE and was awarded many foreign orders including the French Legion of Honour. "He was one of those brilliant, whole hearted, zealous farseeing sailors devoted to the task of reforming our navy and fitting it for war. He and his kind gave us the navy that pulled us through the First War. The Conway has had few finer sons."

His son, Air Chief Marshal Sir Richard Edmund Charles Peirse KCB DSO AFC, also attended Conway from 1905 to 06. He was Deputy Director of Operations and Intelligence during the Great War. From 1930 to 1933 he was AOC British Forces in Palestine and Transjordan. He was AOC Bomber Command, 1940-1942; AOC-in-C India, 1942-1943 and Allied Air C-in-C, S.E. Asia Command, 1943-1944.

When Conways excelled they did so with elan.

1940 November to 1941 March

The daily routine was adapted to life in dock. Boat work was not very practical and all hands missed the playing fields. Football was played in Birkenhead Park and there were many 'cross country runs' around the docks and streets of Birkenhead. Often cadets would slip off to the cinema when they should have been on a run.

"We also had great fun playing in lorries, tractors, tanks etc., which were in the warehouses awaiting shipment abroad."

There were 250 cadets plus members of staff living aboard.

Arrangements for disposal of *Conway's* sewage and wastewater were primitive by today's standards. Everything drained down a square tube mounted externally on the bows straight into the water. To discharge sewage into a fast tidal river was one thing but to discharge the effluent from 250 + people into a dock for 5 months with no tidal flow was another.

Vittoria Dock - Stern Just Visible

"Disadvantages were the smells emanating from nearby ships and their cargoes, and dirt falling as an almost constant rain of smuts from a ubiquitous pall of coal smoke. Another lasting memory is damp ground-nuts in bulk and their unique stink quite unrelated to the appetising aroma arising from a newly opened packet of salted pea-nuts; the nuts seemed to be a popular wartime cargo and Vittoria dock its principle destination on arrival in England, probably heading towards Port Sunlight and the margarine industry."

The Ship was berthed near a soap factory. The combined smell was described as "awful" which is probably a very great understatement. Cadets were sent home early!

"It has been said that there was no heating in the Ship but there was a primitive form of piped hot water central heating. Indeed, such was my executive promise that in my sixth term I became the working hand in charge of the boiler; a position of great power with possibilities for profit. Apart from stoking the thing I could toast (bake, actually) slices of bread by resting them on the inside of the fire door, closing it for a moment, and then opening again - to reveal a golden brown piece of toast (usually smudged with coal dust, but no matter) I charged one old penny per slice! It says much for the system that I progressed quite rapidly to the higher echelons after that term!"

The bombing intensified. The entrance to Vittoria Dock was very distinctive from the air, even at night, so it was a main bomb aiming target for German bombers. Small incendiary devices landed on the Ship most nights. The cadets scooped them up with shovels and tossed them into the river! During the period in dock there were 15 air raids lasting a total of 69 hours.

"Some lasted from six in the evening to six in the morning"

Many bombs fell on the adjacent sheds and ships. Although one of these raids was recorded as "the worst yet," more intense raids were yet to come. On one night, fires raged along 10 miles of riverbank around the Ship. An Old *Conway* docked downstream in his ship remembers watching the fires and hoping that *Conway* had escaped unscathed.

1941 March 9th

Her repairs completed, mainly recaulking on the port side, a new port anchor stock and running repairs to various boats, ladders and booms, the Ship left Vittoria Dock and returned to her mooring in the Sloyne by 9.45 am. That night there were further air raids.

"One night I was awakened by the crash of bombs dropping near. Our hammocks shook and the nettles vibrated with every explosion."

1941 March 13th

The Captain Superintendent's secretary noted,

"the biggest raid yet. Not a single window left in any house or shop in Rock Ferry."

Five days after returning to her moorings, two magnetic mines, parachuted by a plane flying over Rock Ferry towards South Liverpool, fell into the Mersey. One dropped ahead of the *Tacoma City* (not the *City of Tacoma* as some claim) which was anchored abreast of *Conway*, and the other floating down slowly, its progress retarded by the parachute, just missed the truck of *Conway's* mainmast and fell into the water about twelve yards abreast of the starboard gangway. It was just after midnight and as there was a strong flood tide running Captain Goddard hoped that the parachute would keep the mine from striking the bottom and exploding until it was well clear of the Ship's stern. However it was an ebb tide, so there was a danger that on the turn the Ship might connect with it. He decided the cadets and staff should be got ashore as soon as possible;

"I realised that if the mine exploded where it had dropped or anywhere from there to the stern, the Ship would sink in a very few minutes. I therefore gave the order to Abandon Ship."

One of the Instructors roused all hands, calling:

"Heave O, Heave O, Heave O, a mine is under the Ship and will explode in 10 minutes, Heave O, Heave O, Heave O."

"The cadets were excellent, and for once were really quiet. They dressed quickly and went to their stations."

In two trips the motorboats and the twelve oared cutter ferried everyone quickly to Rock Ferry pontoon. The cutter, also called the heavy weather cutter was normally used when the Mersey was too rough for the motorboats. She was manned by maintopmen, traditionally always the biggest and strongest cadets.

"I remember the excitement of the cutter trips … an impressive stick of bombs falling off Cammell Laird's."

The bowman of the motorboat remembers

"all the river glowing from fires on the Liverpool side."

"We were landed at 2.30 am in the bitter cold and quite dark" Captain Goddard continued, *"Within 20 minutes from the time of calling, just over 200 cadets and staff including my wife's Siamese cat, which made more noise than anyone or everyone, were on the Rock Ferry Pontoon."*

From the pontoon they made their way to Conway House (sick bay), Royal Rock Hotel and the Royal Mersey Yacht Club House where they were kindly entertained and housed.

"We had no gear and slept in our clothes in chairs and the floor."

The only people left onboard the Ship were Captain Goddard, Lt. John Brooke Smith, No 1 motorboat's crew and a steward.

"At about 1:30 pm, the Tacoma City was changing over her dynamos, little realising that the mine which fell ahead of her had drifted down with the tide and had grounded under her bottom. Unfortunately, she stopped a dynamo before starting up another and so for a moment the degaussing current ceased, but sufficiently long enough for the magnetic mine to explode."

"Suddenly there was a tremendous explosion. Looking out of the port we saw the ship next to us break in half, the stern sink and bows swing around the anchor cable. Steam was escaping and men running up to the forecastle, and those on the stern throwing themselves into the water. We didn't waste a second, the boat was manned and we were the first on the scene."

And You'll Find on the Bridge a Conway Boy
Captain Jim Thompson MNI (1939-41)

Jim was the bowman in the boat that helped rescue survivors from the Tacoma City and earlier to ferry the cadets safely to shore as they abandoned ship. He was Junior Cadet Captain of Port Fore top and obtained the Conway Extra Certificate. He was also a keen sportsman who enjoyed boxing, rugger and swimming.

In 1941, after Conway, he joined the Blue Star Line and was appointed to Tacoma Star but was re-assigned at the last moment to Empire Glade. Another Conway cadet, J. Benbow took his place. Tacoma Star sailed and was lost with all hands and Jim had his first lucky escape. Jim's first voyage lasted nearly a year and took him round the world.

His second ship was the Dunedin Star carrying munitions, cargo and passengers to the Middle East via Durban. In diverting to avoid reported U Boat activity, she was holed in mysterious circumstances and, to avoid sinking in deep water, her Master ran her aground on the treacherous Skeleton Coast of SW Africa on 29th November 1942. Her grounding became famous because of the perilous conditions facing the 63 survivors, including Jim, after the ship's lifeboat landed them on the desolate Namibian shore. The coastline is very hot and dry during the day and extremely cold at night. Completely deserted and inhospitable, it is guarded on one side by the fierce surf and on the other by the almost completely barren Namib Desert that runs the entire length of the coast and from 50–160km inland. The crew managed to transmit a distress call and HMSAS Nerine, the Danish Temeraire and the British Manchester Division arrived to render assistance. Despite atrocious conditions they rescued the Master, Chief Engineer and Chief Radio Officer who had remained on the ship along with 42 others. However, Jim and the others onshore could not be rescued. The rescue ships departed knowing that further help was on the way. A large harbour tug, the Sir Charles Elliott, arrived from Walvis Bay but before anyone could be picked up from the shore, she ran low on coal and had to leave. On her passage south, she ran onto rocks and two of her crew lost their lives while trying to swim ashore. Next a South African Air Force plane was sent to drop supplies and water. They had no parachutes so the water was dropped in tyre inner tubes which all burst on contact with the ground. Realising the survivors were short of water, and despite orders to the contrary, the pilot decided to land and pick up as many as he could. He landed safely but got stuck in the sand and was unable to take off again. Other planes dropped daily supplies and water, this time safely by parachute. Nerine returned and floated supplies ashore on rafts. Jim and the other survivors were now reasonably well supplied but as days turned into weeks they wondered if they were ever actually going to be rescued. An army rescue party set off overland and eventually picked up the survivors and took them to Rocky Point where an emergency landing strip had been set up to fly out the women and those needing hospital treatment. The remainder continued overland to Windhoek arriving on Christmas Eve, 26 days after landing.

Jim remained with Blue Star for the rest of the war but fortunately did not have to endure any more excitement – other than being at sea under constant threat of enemy U Boats, mines, aircraft, etc., and a short spell off the Normandy beaches just after D-Day.

After the war, he stayed with Blue Star until the late 1950s when he became a cargo superintendent with BP Trading Ltd, the oil company's stores division. He progressed to senior cargo superintendent and oversaw the loading and transportation of stores and equipment worldwide. In 1958 he became a member of the Honourable Company of Master Mariners and a Freeman of the City of London. In 1974 he was made redundant but undaunted he started his own business L.J. Thompson Marine Services Ltd. - marine cargo surveyors and shipbrokers. It was successful with the majority of its clients large engineering companies overseas. He was President of the Conway Club from 1986 to 1990 and from 1992 until 1996. He was also Chairman of the HMS Conway Trust from 1988 to 2005.

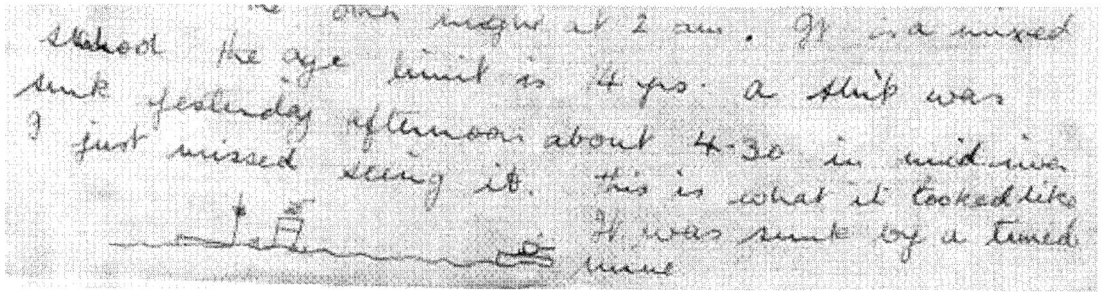

Tacoma City Shown in a Letter Home

Other, larger boats were rushing to the scene from downriver in Liverpool but for a while *Conway's* No 1 motorboat was the only hope for the men in the water. They immediately began rescuing survivors, picking more and more men from the water until, somehow or other, they had crammed most of the crew, 30-40 men, into the small boat.

> *"I wonder how we coped with all those men in No 1 but in an emergency like that it's amazing what can be done."*

Fortunately larger boats then appeared on the scene and the rescued men were safely transferred to them. Their prompt rescue action a success the motorboat crew returned to the Ship. The other mine had dropped by the Conway's starboard gangway, drifted and grounded about fifty feet under the stern and slightly to port.

> *"At daybreak, I had reported the position of the two mines to the Officer Commanding minesweeping flotilla, Liverpool, and was told that a minesweeper would be sent later in the day."*

Manning The Yards

The cadets returned onboard for breakfast.

"Then we landed again in the afternoon and walked about."

"At about 3 pm, my wife, against my order, had managed to get a passage off to the Ship, and before sending her ashore I was giving her tea in the aft cabin when suddenly through the port after gun port, I saw a minesweeper lowering its wire sweep pass close by our stern from ahead. It was too late to get out of the quarters and so I told her that if she wished to see a mine explode she could see one now. At that moment it did and water from the explosion thoroughly washed down the stern walk. The old Ship rose to the explosion and then settled down again with no damage done. I then recalled the cadets onboard."

The padre had been tasked to find immediate alternative accommodation for the cadets until the end of term and succeeded within a few hours! The Headmaster of Mostyn House School, Parkgate, a few miles away across the Wirral, agreed to provide a temporary home.

"We had no dinner and went back to the Ship and told to pack what we could in our hammocks, clothing gear etc. ... We carried them up to Rock Ferry station ... the Ship has been evacuated and we are now at a place called ... Mostyn House School."

With Commander Douglas in charge they worked and slept in makeshift arrangements in the gym and air raid shelters. A plaque at the school commemorates *Conway's* appreciation for this hospitality.

Despite all these vicissitudes, the cadets generally took it all in their stride.

"A few tried to run away by lowering a boat and rowing off at night but they always came back. They were a poor lot but no one thought so at the time."

One popular diversion was sea boot fights, usually on the orlop deck between supper and evening prayers. The gauntlet was thrown down in the form of a sea boot lobbed into the Foretop by one of the other tops. Foretop was home to the largest and strongest cadets including many Canadians. A challenge was never refused and the air would soon be full of heavy flying sea boots. One cadet recalls with notable understatement that

"to step in the path of a flying sea boot was not healthy."

The call to evening muster quickly restored order and cadets turned from trying to knock each other out, to the sober ritual of evening parade and prayers, followed by a mad scramble to retrieve their own sea boots before lights out.

Captain Goddard remained in his Ship through it all, sleeping in a camp bed on deck whenever raids were expected and later proudly reported to the committee:

"Not a day's education had been lost"

during the whole period. He carried a huge burden at this time and his success warrants the strongest of praise. He was in command of a wooden ship strung with miles of rope rigging, soaked in a hundred years' of pitch and tar, and housing 250 young boys and a crew. Incendiaries were falling on the Ship nightly.

"I was surprised at the way an incendiary bomb could penetrate the inch boarding over the chartroom on the upper deck."

He guided the Ship calmly through these difficult times; but his health suffered and his hair turned grey very quickly. He and his wife were well respected by everyone.

"I never heard a disparaging word about him."

With air-raids continuing and intensifying, there were over 200 in 1940, the Captain Superintendent and the management committee realised it was too dangerous to remain in the Mersey. A safer berth would have to be found.

CHAPTER 14

1941 FROM MERSEY TO MENAI

1941 March - April

During the holidays, Captain Goddard urgently sought alternative moorings and facilities. They had to be within reasonable distance of the Mersey so the Ship could easily be relocated, provide an adequate sheltered mooring for a vessel of *Conway's* size, be safer from air raids than the Mersey, and provide adequate shore facilities to replace *Conway's* sick bay and playing fields. The search quickly spread out north and south from the Mersey. Choices were limited. North lay Fleetwood and Barrow in Furness, both targets for air raids and the otherwise open Lancashire coast. Southwest was the Dee Estuary, probably too close for comfort, Conway harbour and then the Menai Strait. Further south Cardigan Bay was very exposed, with no suitable harbours or estuaries. Captain Goddard had already investigated Bangor and Conway as potential alternative moorings in 1937 and it was quickly agreed that the Ship should be moved to a new mooring in the Menai Strait off Glyn Garth, Llandegfan, Anglesey opposite Bangor pier. The mooring was clearly suitable, having been used from 1877 to 1920 by another training ship, the *Clio*. She was one of thirteen industrial training ships around the UK, which trained boys as seamen for the Royal and Merchant Navies. She had closed and been broken up alongside the pier in 1920 but her remains could still be seen at low tide.

1941 May

On 1st May, Hitler ordered a seven day Blitzkrieg on Liverpool and Birkenhead. Bombs, land mines and fire bombs rained down day and night. A group of 681 enemy aircraft dropped 870 tonnes of high explosive and 112,000 incendiaries. May 7th saw a raid that was

"the hardest we had ever experienced."

One Luftwaffe pilot observed:

Bomb Damaged Docks

"It's burning over a wide area down there. The town itself must have suffered immense hits."

Around 65% of houses in Bootle were destroyed and 1,750 people were killed. As many again were injured. The entrance to Gladstone Dock, close to the Ship, was a significant feature used by German bomb aimers. The docks were devastated but the Ship was spared any significant damage. This series of raids confirmed the apparent desperate need to move the Ship and cadets to safety but Captain Goddard and the committee were not to know that the Liverpool blitz effectively ended with this attack. There was one heavier raid in early June, one in November 1941 and a final raid in January 1942. After that the Mersey fell quiet. With hindsight, the Ship need not have been moved at all.

The Committee arranged for Captain Alkins of Blue Funnel to survey the proposed Bangor mooring and he arranged for two anchors to be laid out, NE and SW, with ninety fathoms of cable on each stretched to a mooring swivel. These would be connected to the Ship by fifteen fathom bridles. Given wartime priorities it took until May for the moorings to be laid by the Trinity House vessel *Beacon* and for tugs to become available.

> *"We had been waiting day after day, thinking that the next would bring us word of when we would leave the Mersey for the Menai Strait. Many were the times we were told that we would be moving in a day or two's time, only to find, when the time came, that yet another delay put the time of moving still further ahead."*

> *Whilst at home I received a recall to the Ship. On rejoining I found I was one of only four cadets recalled – myself (James H. Stewart), R.J. Symon, J.S. Fairweather and one whose name I cannot recollect. We were informed by Lt. J. Brooke Smith that the Ship was to be moved to the Menai Strait."*

All four cadets lived locally and so were available at short notice.

> *"The water boat moorings had been taken up and brought onboard. Unfortunately it was found impossible to take the sailing dinghies around with us, though they were brought by lorry later on. Everything in the Ship was made secure. In case we had bad weather, the orlop decks were fitted with deadlights and caulked up."*

All the gun ports were strengthened with baulks of timber.

Eventually a moving date was set. *Conway* would leave her home at Rock Ferry on the Mersey on 21st May 1941. With her departure the Sloyne moorings would be empty for the first time since 1859. The line of four wooden walls ships; *Akbar, Clarence, Conway* and *Indefatigable* would be just a memory. *Conway* was 102 years old and it would be her first sea passage for 65 years.

1941 May 21st – 22nd

> *"The day which we had been waiting for arrived, a crew of seamen came off early. They did the heavier work, the things that could only be done by experienced hands, such as making the towing hawsers fast, slipping our moorings and a hundred and one other jobs that required some experience. The vessel that was to buoy our moorings was standing by in the morning."*

Conway had no motive power and would have to be towed to the strait by two Rea tugs. An Old Conway in his ship on the Mersey was stung to see a Notice to Mariners 'Hulk in tow, Mersey to Bangor'

> *"The tugs came along later, first one then the other, the same tugs that had seen us safely into dock on the last occasion, the Langarth and Dongarth."*

There was also an escort vessel. The Ship's company comprised, in addition to the regular officers, two pilots, two officers, the seamen already mentioned, four *Conway* cadets and two Blue Funnel apprentices, one in each tug. Cadet Stewart was on the forward tug, Symon on the stern tug and Fairweather and the other cadet in the *Conway*.

> *"At 1400 (hours) it began to rain, and everything looked very dismal, but nothing could dampen our spirits, for we knew we would soon be underway. At about 1500 we let go our port bridle. It had been arranged by the*

pilot aboard that we would slip our other bridle at slack water that evening. One tug was already fast forward, and the other tug was soon fast on our stern. At 1821 hours we slipped our moorings and started on a voyage such as she had not made for 65 years. The bell on the (Rock Ferry) pontoon was rung as a parting farewell and the ensign dipped in acknowledgement. The tide was slack so our course took us close inshore in order to avoid a number of merchantmen, which were lying across the river. How the officers and men of those ships must have wondered at seeing one of the wooden walls threading its way down stream, on and past into the distance. Many of them dipped their ensigns in respect to such a venerable vessel. The weather was clearing a breeze setting up from the west, conditions were looking very favourable."

"It was about 1700 when the down river tow started."

"On the way out the Ship was hailed by the Royal Navy Examination Vessel enquiring 'What ship is that?' – it must have been a strange sight to see a wooden walled ship of the line emerging from the gloom!"

"The water boat had been towing alongside the port gangway, but when we got into the channel it was found to be too rough to keep it there any longer. First, one of the tugs was slipped and detailed to take the water boat in tow when we set it adrift. The tug picked it up after some trouble, but was unable to keep up with us. As the water boat was shipping a good deal of water it was decided to leave it with one of the balloon barrage ships anchored along the channel. It sank later that night. We were making fairly steady progress, hardly ever rolling or pitching, which said a great deal for the workmanship of a bygone century. Later that night, the tug which had dropped behind after signalling us for our course, caught us up but it was not thought necessary to make it fast again as we were nearing our destination, easing our speed in order to gain full advantage of the rising tide."

Captain Goddard recalls:

"Entering Crosby Channel (and clear of the more congested areas of the river) the stern tug was let go and made fast forward so the 2 tugs towed the Ship at 3-4 knots. The tow to the Bar Light Vessel, 17 miles from the Sloyne, took 9 hours, nearly 7 of which were against the flood tide, so that we could better keep her under control. A fresh to strong north wind was blowing with a moderate beam sea. Unlike the escort vessel and tugs movements, the Conway was perfectly steady and I doubt whether a pencil would have rolled off a table during the whole of the passage. On previous occasions, when in tow, I had noticed the Conway's grip on the water and realised how important this was when she was under sail. This is entirely due to her deep bar keel. We averaged 7 knots over the ground from the Bar Light Vessel to Puffin Island (off Anglesey) when we stopped."

The escort vessel signalled a farewell message.

"So long and good luck, safe moorings. May you train many more hefty limbed young whelps."

"We arrived off Puffin Island at approximately 6 am the next day and had to wait 2 hours for the tide. One of the tugs, the one standing off, was made fast to our stern once again, for it was going to require some careful piloting to get us to our moorings."

They waited until nearly high water before negotiating the final channel into the strait. They entered the strait at approximately 9 am.

"This was uneventful but the South bend in it between No 1 Buoy and Beaumaris required quick alterations in course with only two feet of water under our bottom. Under these conditions the best method of towing

Conway is to shorten in the two ropes as much as possible when she will answer immediately to any alteration in course. We proceeded slowly up the strait and passing Bangor pier the ensign was dipped to acknowledge the pilot boat's salute."

On sighting *Conway* as she rounded Gallows Point, Captain Goddard's daughter Rosemary, who was acting as his secretary, sent telegrams to all cadets to rejoin the Ship.

"Coming up the strait we were greeted by the sight of the sun breaking through the long rolls of strato-cumulus, tipping their edges with a golden light, it was a suitable setting after such a good voyage, for the arrival of such a great Ship."

Approaching Bangor Pier

Conway's arrival was also generating interest ashore.

"A bird watching historian friend of my father's happened to spot the Conway arriving through his telescope from the roof of his student digs at Plas Menai in upper Bangor. What a surreal moment that must have been. Remember it was wartime so there had been no announcement in the papers or on the radio!"

The Trinity House vessel *Beacon* was waiting to pass the new moorings to the Ship.

"The tugs turned us to face the tide and pushed us alongside Beacon. It took two to three hours to transfer the moorings to us."

"By 8 pm on 22nd May, just over 24 hours after leaving the Sloyne, Conway was riding to her new moorings in the lovely setting of the Menai Strait just off Bangor pier."

All cadet captains rejoined immediately to clean ship and remove the timber from the gun ports. A full 220 cadets boarded her a week later. Gone was the busy, grimy Mersey crammed with ships, the foul smoky air, the hustle and bustle of a major seaport at war and the constant air-raids. In their place were the broad, quiet but challenging waters of the strait, clear air, green fields, open skies and the peaceful city of Bangor. The Snowdonia mountain range and the wooded slopes of the Anglesey shore ringed the horizon. A whole new chapter was about to open.

CHAPTER 15

1941 BANGOR – A NEW BEGINNING

Cadets returning to the Ship were used to the busy Mersey with miles of docks lining both sides of the river, the constant bustling activity of ships entering and leaving port, transiting from berth to berth, bullish tugs thrusting around the river, and ferries constantly dashing back and forth from the Birkenhead piers. Cunard liners moored close by the Ship. A short distance downstream the huge Cammell Laird's shipyard was noisy and busy at all hours of the day and night. The strait was the very antithesis of the Mersey. Bangor and the strait were rural and sedate. On one side was mainland Gwynedd (then called Caernarvonshire), with most of the horizon dominated by the mountains of Snowdonia, which ran down into the sea in the distance. The other bank was the island of Anglesey (now Ynys Mon). At high water, the strait is 1000 yards wide at *Conway's* mooring but, with Bangor pier reaching out 500 yards from the mainland, it left only a very narrow passage at low water exactly where the Ship was moored.

Newly Arrived off Bangor Pier

> *"The shallows extended out from the Bangor shore to within a cable or so of the Conway and at Low Water Springs there was little clearance when she swung to the flood."*

A few houses could be seen clustered by the pier as the city of Bangor was all but hidden by the steep, green wooded banks, which lined both sides of the strait as far as the eye could see.

On one side of the Ship the strait was like a funnel opening out to Conway Bay and the Irish Sea, exposing her to the weather and tides in ways rarely experienced in the Mersey.

> *"The anchorage was exposed to heavy squalls, gales and seas, especially at high water, and on several occasions we dragged our anchors."*

> *"Sometimes we might be cut off from the shore for days."*

On many occasions the 'Z' flag was hoisted, meaning 'Masters cannot be brought off.' At low water the sea retreated exposing the huge expanse of the Lagan Sands. On the other side of the mooring the strait narrowed dramatically to the twisting and dangerous Swellies, and then wound its way several miles to Caernarfon and the open sea again. Ocean going vessels, indeed most vessels, avoided the strait. Nearby Port Penhryn, once busy exporting slate was now only a quiet harbour for small coastal vessels. It dried out at low water. The occasional small passenger trip boat called at Bangor pier. Dickies, the local boatyard, was building motor torpedo boats. Other than that, the waters were fairly empty creating a very quiet mooring. The place could hardly be called a port at all, but that was why it had been chosen. The Luftwaffe was not expected to start bombing Welsh fields.

Naturally, cadets and Old *Conways* had mixed feelings about the move.

> *"Where once we were in the interesting hustle and bustle of our future profession, we seemed suddenly in a backwater and something seemed to leave the old Ship and never returned."*

> *"Many who had sampled both … preferred Birkenhead on the grounds that the Ship was more in touch with marine affairs there and closer to the realities of the mercantile marine."*

To overcome the loss frequent expeditions began to Messers Cammell Laird and to ships of the Liverpool shipping lines.

> *"These trips were undertaken seriously and every cadet had to write an essay on the visit which required his alertness and much observation on his part."*

The visits became a permanent part of the curriculum, enjoyed by cadets, as much because it set them free for a while in the bright lights of Liverpool or Birkenhead. Studious essays describing visits to this or that ship were printed regularly in the Cadet magazine. For Old *Conways*, a visit to the Ship in the Mersey whilst in dock was easily arranged but the number of these visitors dwindled very quickly at Bangor.

The consensus about the move though seems to be expressed by one cadet's views

> *"Having known the Ship in both places, I say nothing finer ever happened to her. She shook off that drab, dirty shore-line, grubby water and foul, smoky air and exchanged it for sunlight on the Welsh mountains, blue water and green grass. Admittedly she lost touch with the bustle of shipping – but first develop the boy and then train the cadet. He will see enough of shipping later –now let's climb Snowden or swim ashore to Anglesey."*

Captain Goddard had no doubts.

> *"What a marvellous training ground we were in. Excellent boat sailing, swimming from the Ship, and an entirely new recreation for us, mountaineering. In the Mersey, every Easter term we had an influenza epidemic onboard, with as many as 10 cadets down at a time. At Bangor during the eight years we were there we did not have one."*

The cadets soon reported back onboard for the new term and recall a myriad of new images.

"There was a certain comfort in returning to our old wooden mother - there she lay, a big black hulk with towering buff masts. The slate grey waters of the strait swung her around on each new tide so the views changed with the every ebb and flow."

The Anglesey shore presented a steep, wooded vista set with a few substantial mansions including the castellated residence of the Bishop of Bangor. On the Bangor side, the view at low tide was of mud flats and the forlorn sternpost of the reform ship *Clio*. The buildings of Bangor University perched up on the mainland hills, and to seaward, the Victorian Bangor pier stood out into the strait. In the distance, across the bay, Snowdonia provided an everchanging scene, mountains white with snow, grey with rain or hazy shades of tan and green.

"Catalina flying boats landed and took off alongside the Ship and the sound of their Pratt and Whitney engines at full power would bring the class in a rush to the ports, ostensibly to view the exciting scene but at heart, to disrupt the lesson."

Bangor - Idyll or Backwater?

The *Clio* had previously occupied the mooring. Locals incorrectly thought she was a reformatory ship, calling her

"the naughty children's ship."

Seeing another warship and uniformed cadets, the locals assumed *Conway* was also a reformatory so cadets did not have too good a welcome at first.

"We had gone in to Bangor pier for provisions and while waiting on the pier one pair of old ladies asked me what I was 'in' for. Puzzled I asked what she meant; she asked what offence I had committed."

The loss of the water boat during the transit from the Mersey created an immediate problem at Bangor. All water for washing, drinking, cooking, flushing the heads, etc., had to be brought from shore and stored in holding tanks. With 220 cadets plus members of staff, a considerable amount of fresh water was needed every day.

"We grew ever more aromatic what with no baths."

Cleanliness problems were quickly resolved. Cadets rowed themselves the three miles to Menai Bridge in the cutter to take baths there.

"By the time we arrived back in the Ship, often after a hard pull against the stream, we were just as sweaty as when we set off!"

At first, water supplies for the Ship were towed out in an old lifeboat. The water was taken from a pipe at the end of Bangor pier. It was bailed out of the lifeboat in buckets, passed through the bathroom ports in the bows and poured into the tanks. A number of milk cans were also filled whenever a boat went to the pier.

> *"We spent the first summer term in the Strait practically without water developing huge muscles lugging milk churns full of fresh water for drinking purposes."*

They were carried to the galley, two cadets per churn, or emptied down a series of pipes rigged to the tanks in the hold by the Ship's Third Officer Mr. Lawrence. This could not be a long term solution so a search began for a suitable new water boat. After a few weeks, searching *Conway* acquired *Indefatigable's* redundant thirty foot powered water boat. As *Indefatigable* cadets had moved ashore permanently due to the air-raids, they were disposing of their Ship, boats and equipment. The boat was named the *Arthur Bibby* (the Bibby Line family were major sponsors of *Indefatigable*, as Blue Funnel's Holt family were for *Conway*) but cadets generally called her the 'juice barge.' She came from the Mersey under her own power. She was fitted with large water tanks capable of holding 1,800 gallons of fresh water, had a very low freeboard and was not particularly manoeuvrable due to her weight and low power. There was no cover at all on deck; the cox'n stood right aft with a wheel driving chains to the rudder.

> *"When we got the boat, it was greatly admired and appreciated by all! It actually had a telegraph to signal the 'engine room,' which gave the cox'n a fine sense of being in command of something worthwhile."*

The engine room was usually full of tobacco smoke!

> *"The engine was an absolute sod to start using a starting handle which required a particular swing to make it kick in, and could break your wrist if it backfired."*

Replenishing the Ship's freshwater tanks was more or less a continuous task.

> *"It was considered a shaggy (easy) number as the regular crew spent most of their time sitting off the pier loading water through a portable pipe, or moored to the port boom discharging water into the Ship."*

As was customary, practical class crews manned the boat during school hours, at weekends or Wednesday half day.

> *"By the next term we had acquired Indefat's water boat and all was back to normal – baths once a week and after coal-hole."*

In 1941, Mr. Lawrence Holt, chairman of the management committee, presented the Ship with *Joan*, a Liverpool fishing-boat called a nobby. *Joan* was a six ton, twenty-five foot, strong, beamy sailing cutter with an 18 hp engine. She was very popular addition but seems to have disappeared from the Ship by 1946.

Cadets were completely responsible for maintaining and operating all the boats, including the water boat for loading and discharging water, for their safety and that of others during trips back and forth between the pier and the Ship no matter what the time of day, weather or sea conditions. All this without any direct adult supervision. This level of responsibility and trust given to cadets, who were still only young men of 13-17 years of age, was typical of *Conway's* approach to developing character and leadership. Officers, school-masters and crew members provided the structure within which the Ship operated. They naturally provided careful oversight but this was at arm's length. The cadets, led by their petty officers (prefects), effectively ran the Ship. They were responsible for the daily routine and good order. They stood watches around the clock, manned boats, organised duties, cleaned the Ship and maintained discipline.

> *"For a lad of 13, life aboard the Ship was an extraordinary experience, both a shock and a delight. Youngsters of 14 and 15 had extraordinary responsibility thrust on them. I recall coxing a motorboat which towed two cutters, one on each quarter, each boat being full of cadets returning from Beaumaris to the Ship, with not an officer nor a lifejacket in sight. A heavily laden motorboat, towing two heavily laden cutters, made slow progress against an ebb tide, until I thumbed a tow from a passing motor trawler. No doubt amused at our plight, she generously passed us a line and towed all three boats back to the Ship."*

Young boys arriving in *Conway* quickly and routinely found themselves placed in similar authority over each other for various tasks, required to take charge and make decisions. No fuss was made about this. Getting used to command, leading men and prompt decision-making was the natural order of things for a naval officer and so to for naval cadets.

With a complex and changeable pattern of tides, cadets had much to learn after the relatively straightforward waters of the Mersey.

> *"The tides and banks were puzzlers at first."*

When *Conway* was moored in the Mersey boats were always able to use the pockets at Rock Ferry pontoon whatever the state of the tide. However, shallow water was something boats, crews had quickly to get used to at Bangor. Invariably cadets landed ashore over Bangor pier - at the slip if water allowed, and if not then by means of the vertical steel ladder at the far outward end of the pier. It was not unknown for cox'ns who were unaware of the shallow depth of the water to end up grounded alongside the slip.

> *"It was quite a long time before we got used to our new surroundings, as the varying directions of the tide puzzled us, until we became accustomed to the intricacies of the various landing places."*

As the cadets acquainted themselves with their new surroundings Captain Goddard and his staff had much to organise. The first pragmatic step was to extend the Summer Term well into August to make up for the lost time. Then there was the difficulty task of securing suitable grounds to replace the Merseyside playing fields. Use of Bangor City Football Club's ground was eventually agreed. Cross county runs were begun along the Anglesey shore and sometimes over the Menai Suspension Bridge and right back around to the pier. With war-time rationing and petrol in short supply, rowing became the preferred mode of transport. Sailing and boat work were possible at all times. Cadets developed practical skills by surveying the strait around the Ship. With miles of quiet, open countryside cycling was encouraged.

> *"We could cycle to chosen haunts ... there we would sit smoking and drinking and feeling very brave. Then we would cycle like mad and catch up with the remainder, our excuse being, if questioned, that old so-an-so's pedal had come off."*

The mountains of Snowdonia dominated the Southern horizon.

"We begged the captain to allow us to walk in the hills at weekends."

The idea was regarded with suspicion at first but then Captain Goddard agreed.

"The first tramp in the hills was quite memorable… we were determined to repeat it."

On July 11th and 12th, 1941 two cadets climbed to the summit of Snowdon. By 1942, cadets had formed the Conway Mountain Climbing Club. Soon, parties of six or eight cadets made regular weekend expeditions into the mountains staying at the youth hostel at Idwal Cottage.

"These expeditions were excellent… and left one greatly refreshed."

The routine would be followed by generations of cadets for the next 33 years. Opportunities for an open-air life were going to be exploited to the maximum.

As the number of cadets was increasing due to the demands of the war the Ship was reaching capacity, additional dormitory space was needed and the small sick bay onboard could not cope with the demands now placed on it. Miss L Johnson of the Johnson Warren Line (later Furness Withy) owned a large summer holiday residence called Bryn Mel above the nearby Gazelle slip on the Anglesey side. She kindly loaned one floor as a sanatorium and agreed that part of the house could be used as a dormitory. Mr. and Mrs Walters, who had run the Conway House sanatorium in Birkenhead, took up residence to manage the place. The 'Bryn Mel Party' quickly became an institution. Every evening a group of twelve, then fifteen and eventually twenty-six cadets went ashore on the last boat accompanied by a cadet petty officer and slept in Bryn Mel.

"The dormitory was a very long room with windows all along the walls – one side looking on to the strait."

They returned to the Ship for breakfast; but in later years they ate at Bryn Mel where the food was always better.

"Your chest etc., was of course in the Ship, I think you did it for about either a week or a month, in I think your third term. Your fourth term was the Outward Bound Sea School at Aberdovey."

In 1941, Lawrence Holt and Kurt Hahn (who also founded Gordonstoun School in Scotland and Atlantic College in Wales) opened the Outward Bound Sea School at Aberdovey. Their aim was to provide a tough survival course for young men whose ships were likely to be torpedoed and who might find themselves in lifeboats. It was decided, doubtless under Holt's influence, that *Conway* cadets should attend a four week course at Aberdovey in their fourth term. Despite its intended vigour and great emphases on physical fitness, *Conways* generally liked the (compared to *Conway*) relaxed routine, for example, getting up at 7.00 am instead of 6.30 am, enjoyed the vastly better food, but hated the morning run followed by a compulsory cold shower; in *Conway* they enjoyed a hot bath once a week whether they needed it or not.

"At this time we were sent to Aberdovey for half a term, which was a wonderful holiday from school, even in February."

One highlight of the Aberdovey course was sailing in their ketch *Garibaldi*.

Garibaldi at Aberdovey Pier

During the war years there was a greatly increased demand for naval officers and *Conway* soon had more applicants than vacancies for its two year course. A special scheme was therefore inaugurated whereby some boys attended Gordonstoun School (which had been evacuated to Broneirion, Plas Dinam, between Llanidloes and Newtown) for a year (three terms) and then joined *Conway* as first term cadets. In their second term they joined the senior hands (*Conway* fourth termers) and left in their 'sixth' term after completing four terms.

It was arranged for a party of Chinese cooks to be provided from the Liverpool seamen's pool. They lived onboard in very cramped cabins on the port side of the main deck, cooked themselves strange looking meals and dressed in odd colours when they went ashore. They were reported to have terrible tempers, no doubt often provoked by experimenting cadets like the Bread Knackers Union who overcame insufficient and poor food by intercepting food deliveries to the Ship, causing discrepancies between amounts purchased and stored.

With the initial excitement of their new surroundings behind them, secure arrangements for watering and coaling, sports facilities in place, adequate accommodation and a new sanatorium, the Ship's company settled into a comfortable routine to wait out the war.

CHAPTER 16

1941–49 BANGOR – DAILY ROUTINE

The daily routine, from 1941 at Bangor, continued as it had for generations of Mersey cadets.

"Conway was run more as a warship than as a merchant ship, with a band and due ceremony at daily divisions. Lots of bugle calls, marching about and saluting. We even mustered an armed guard for ceremonial occasions. I later discovered that when I left in July 1949, in many ways I was better prepared for service in the Royal Navy than in the Merchant Navy. That was the nature of the training, which was far more disciplined than was to be found aboard a merchant ship of the time. Most of us were obviously destined for the Merchant Service and were well, if not specifically, prepared for it."

A certain number of cadets, however, set their sights on the Royal Navy, so a special class was insitituted for those seeking special entry. A great number of *Conways* served in the Royal Navy, the Royal Navies of other Empire countries, even the national navies of foreign countries, including the Egyptian Navy.

Reveille

"Each morning we were woken at 6:30 by a bugler sounding reveille, followed immediately by PT on the upper deck. This was routine in summer and winter, no matter what the weather, and hardened us to the elements."

"When a strong breeze blew in a direction opposite to the tide she would sometimes lie athwart both. At such time the wind would blow though the various openings and make life quite tedious."

PT was followed by a mad scramble to wash and dress, ready for breakfast.

Messdeck

At 7:20, a bugler sounded 'Messmen to the Main Deck' to prepare for breakfast; collapsible tables for each mess were brought down from the deck-head where they were stowed, cutlery and mugs were placed on them. Breakfast was at 7:30. Food was served to nominated cadets from each table who queued at a hatch at the galleys. There was much shoving and pushing, with seniors pulling rank to get ahead. Sometimes there were 'seconds,' and the messmen would rush back to their tables with a dish of potatoes, tip them smartly onto the bare table and hurtle back into the queue, hoping for more.

'The food was poor and sparse; we were given eggs in season - they were strong and fishy. A liquid called 'skilly' was served - it seemed a cross between tea and weak coffee. On Sunday mornings we were given a piece of bacon at breakfast time - the piece was about three inches long. This, with a piece of bread following porridge, formed breakfast for ravenous mouths - we were permanently hungry. Discipline at table was maintained by a particularly painful punishment for misdemeanours, namely 'knuckles.' This involved a miscreant presenting his clenched fist, fingers downward, to the cadet captain who would smartly whack the knuckles with a serving spoon.'

Orders

Bugle calls were used extensively throughout the day to direct the Ship's routine. The 'still' was a special call ordering everyone immediately to stand still and listen to what followed. Distinctive calls (tunes) were then used to summon selected cadets, at a run, to various parts where they were needed. One or more G notes tacked on to the end of these calls indicated which cadets or crews were summoned. Thus the call for a motorboat's crew was followed by one G for No 1 motorboat, two Gs for No 2, three Gs for the water boat and four Gs for the pinnace. The call for a cutter's crew followed by one G summoned the duty cutter crew, two Gs the heavy weather cutter crew. A G was also used to warn of five minutes to Divisions and to start boat races from the starboard gangway. Three Gs might also be used to recall a boat, assuming that its attention could be attracted.

When there was no specific call the duty cadet captain or an officer would bawl out an order into the open space in the centre of the Ship - for example a 'still' could be followed by a cry of 'All hands to the upper deck.' These orders were followed by a two-note, rising 'Carry-on' call when everyone resumed their duties. There was always something to be done so cadets had relatively little free time.

"Everyone was trying to do as little as possible. When people couldn't get out of doing a job then they usually did it well – but they would try hard to do nothing."

Lash Up and Stow Hammocks

"This order prompted a headlong helter-skelter down the hatch ladders, in a race to reach your hammock into which you hastily stowed your bedding and lashed it up with (as I recall) seven equally spaced half-hitches which you laid back on with all your weight before rushing off to fall in line with the rest of your top to present your handiwork for inspection. The last one in the line immediately got three over the backside from the teaser (somebody had to be last!). The inspecting cadet captain then bent your hammock double to loosen the lashings, and then vigorously tugged at the canvas in the

Lash Up and Stow Hammocks

six spaces between the lashings to see if he could expose any bedding. You got one over the 'butt' for each space where bedding could be exposed, and it follows that if bedding could be exposed in one space the canvas could be pulled through to expose it in the other five! And that was just the start of yet another day! Happy Days!"

Rig School

"After breakfast (at 8 am) on weekdays we would descend and, guided by bugle calls, lash and stow our hammocks. This was followed by deckwork ie cleaning Ship during which the band practiced in the Hold, another reason to join the band, to miss deckwork! A further bugle call instructed us to 'Rig School.' This entailed re-arranging the main deck, where we had just eaten, into six classrooms by means of a system of wooden panel partitions."

Wooden beams about eight feet long were placed on the deck in a fore and aft direction. These had pins on their underside, which dropped into holes in the deck. The upper edge of these beams had a groove into which panels were fitted, their upper edges were held in place by large turn-buttons on the deck head. Athwart the Ship there were panels, which were hinged to the deck head, and when not in use lay flat against the deckhead secured by hooks. To rig school the hooks were released and the panels dropped down to hang vertically. Tower bolts into the deck then secured them, keeping them from swinging. A door was built into some athwartship panels to allow access from one classroom to another. The panels next to the Ship's side were unique because they had a device to enable them to clear the heavy frames of the old Ship and the 'knees,' which joined them to the deck beams. This consisted of a small hinged panel incorporated in the main panel. When lifting the panel to the deckhead this small panel was hinged right back so that the main panel would not foul the 'knee' as it was lifted and hooked up out of the way.

Divisions

After the classrooms were rigged there would be a morning parade called Divisions, when all the cadets would wear their uniforms with their brass buttons. To bugle calls they fell in on the lower deck in their respective tops.

Morning Divisions – Monty Douglas Reports to Captain Goddard

"The Captain Superintendent, accompanied by the officer of the day and a senior cadet captain stood on the Holy Ground on the Quarterdeck, situated at the after end of the lower deck. They would be called to attention and the officers and Headmaster would assemble towards the after end, with the cadets lined up on either side of the deck. Captain Goddard would be advised that all were fallen-in and he would appear, acknowledge the salute of the officer of the day and instruct him to "Cawwy – on."

He had difficulty in pronouncing his 'R's. The temporary wartime Headmaster, Mr. Carter, who was fondly referred to as 'Bog' or 'Bogbrush', presumably because of his shock of crinkly hair, would emerge from his office to attend this morning service. A mortarboard perched precariously on his head, he wore a faded gown, his trousers at half-mast, and he usually wore purple socks.

"He was a lovely man and a great maths teacher. He wore a hearing aid which was rumoured to produce 'atmospheric' noises in his ears, so his appearance anywhere brought about a low background hiss from between the teeth of a hundred cadets. Attempts had been made to stamp out this odd habit but it was unsuccessful. On one occasion Admiral Sir Percy Noble, C-in-C, Western Approaches, visited the Ship and made a tour of the classrooms and the hissing was continuous though muted."

At Divisions the Captain Superintendent often read prayers. One became familiar to all:

We commend to Thy care all who go down to the sea in ships
and occupy their business in great waters.
Help them in whatever lies before them.
May they do their duty with cheerful willingness and face danger with courage,
knowing that Thy hand is in all things and that all things are in Thy hand.

Occasionally the Padre led the prayers, but if Captain Goddard felt that the time allocated for praying was being exceeded he would chime in with a *"that'll do Padre, thank you,"* and order the cadet captain to *"carry on."* The brief service over the assembled cadets were brought to attention, the band would strike up and the cadets would march smartly around the deck, the taller boys skilfully avoiding the many protuberances under the low deckhead.

Sunday Services and the Choir

Every Sunday, instead of morning Divisions and school, a religious service was held. Mr. Roberts played the harmonium and he decided that the singing was disjointed and of doubtful quality. This was due partly to the poor acoustics on main deck but mainly because half the assembled congregation was on one side of the Ship and half on the other, with companionways and various other obstructions separating the two sides. His solution was to form a 60 strong choir of cadets with the loudest voices. Quality of voice was quite unimportant. The incentive for joining the choir was a periodic cream tea at his nearby café. Membership of the choir was therefore much sought after.

"Mr. Roberts attended one evening to choose the choir, helped by two burly cadet captains. The selection process was speeded up like this. A small timid cadet would be told 'Paton – sing this! Look sharp now' and the hymn book would be thrust in his hand. With sweet falsetto and perfect tune Paton would start 'He who would true val……..' only to be interrupted by 'That's enough – get out!' and he would be roughly pushed aside. The next cadet might sing atrociously out of tune but in a voice that would not be out of place on a parade ground. 'Right – you're in – stand over there!' The chosen choir was then licked into some semblance of order and with considerable decibel capability, dominate the singing on both port and starboard sides."

School and Masters

On weekdays, after divisions, cadets fell out for school. The school side of the training was in the hands of teachers who came daily to the Ship and they had little sanction against the mischievous cadets, many of whom considered school to be entirely recreational.

"The quality of teaching was questionable as many of the peacetime teachers were away serving in the forces."

Seamanship was taught by a much loved and respected master Mr. C E Lee, affectionately known as 'Hoppy' because he had a false leg from an accident with a snapped wire hawser.

"He taught the intricacies of knots – bowlines and sheepshanks, timber hitches, garrick bends and so forth. He taught us how to rig a jury rudder, how to lay a kedge anchor and how to stow rice and grain and railway

iron. We learnt that the stowage factor of coal was so many cubic feet to the ton, that grain and rice had to be ventilated properly and that mooring ropes had to be adjusted when working cargo. He taught us about handy-billies, single Spanish Burtons, and the mathematics of mechanical advantage and the parallelogram of forces. It was passed down to our class that we should ask Hoppy the stowage factor of rhubarb and indeed one cadet was bold enough to put up his hand one day during a lesson on cargo stowage and asked 'What is the stowage factor of rhubarb, Sir?.' Sure enough, Hoppy went berserk and lashed out with his textbook at the unfortunate cadet who lifted his crooked arm to ward off the blows and was hounded out of the classroom. We never discovered why this question touched off such a reaction."

"Navigation was taught by 'Spud' Murphy, a small laconic man and he was known for his remark 'Reach for your Norries'; this referred to the navigator's bible, Norries Nautical Tables, which provided everything required from log tables to tables of meridional parts, traverse tables, dip of the sea horizon, spherical trigonometric tables and a host of others."

"A harassed young man taught English and he was given a hard time because the subject was considered boring and his classes a time for fun. He would use a padded wooden duster to wipe the blackboard and place it on the front bench. As soon as he commenced to write on the board the duster was passed to the rear bench where it was dropped on the deck. When next he needed the duster he would look at the spot where it had been and say 'Come on now - who's got the duster?' Complete silence and he would walk up the side of the benches, head down, looking for the item. He shouted 'There it is, Hall - it's by your foot.' Hall would promptly kick it forward saying, 'No it isn't, Sir!' This would have the teacher crouching down and when he spotted it again he would shout 'There it is - under you Noble! - give it to me.' And so this farce would continue until the cadets would consent to giving up the duster."

On another occasion, when this master was busily writing on the blackboard, the loose flap on the partition behind it was pushed up, a hand appeared and grabbed the easel and shook it vigorously before withdrawing. The teacher quickly looked behind the easel and seeing nothing continued to write; the hand appeared again and shook the easel. This continued until the teacher went next door and found the culprit who sat at the rear of the next classroom.

"On one occasion, and by a pre-arranged scenario, a cadet asked the English master if he could go to the heads, the master promptly refused permission. A few minutes later the cadet asked again and was refused. After a third refusal the cadet watched his chance and when the master was occupied at the blackboard, silently crept out of the port and clambered up the outside of the Ship onto the upper deck. With the tumble-home (curved side) of the old Ship and the various chains, which supported the rigging, this was an easy task for an agile lad. Later he clattered back into the classroom, disturbing everyone while he noisily regained his seat. The master was flabbergasted and remonstrated with the lad saying 'I told you, you couldn't leave the classroom.' This brought a pantomime type of response from the class 'O - no you didn't, Sir - you said he could go!' The resulting fiasco, I am sure, made the master wonder if he were getting forgetful."

"The teachers had little control over the exuberant spirits who regarded school as a break from the discipline of shipboard routine. Every known device was employed by the cadets to frustrate the attempts of these teachers to teach and it was reluctantly accepted by most that the educational achievements of the Conway were minimal and the true value of the training lay in the producing of young men of spirit and initiative who would become the backbone of Britain's maritime industry."

Such was the indiscipline, a scheme was devised, which the teachers hoped would make the cadets behave during lessons. They awarded merits for good work and de-merits for any indiscipline or bad work. Towards the end of each term each pupil's merits and de-merits would be counted and if he had more merits than de-merits he would have a half-day's break ashore whilst those with more de-merits than merits would have lessons as usual. The cadets soon decided that one measly half day was insufficient incentive to behave for a whole term and the scheme became unworkable.

"On one occasion a cadet whose name I forget had misbehaved and the master said 'Right – take a de-merit.' The cadet promptly said 'Sir, can I have two please, West has got more than me and I want to catch up with him.'"

"Serious misbehaviour in school would result in the cadet being sent to the Headmaster for caning. Mr. Carter was a very mild man and on presenting himself for punishment the cadets would feign fear and he would say 'I don't like doing this but you have been very bad and I have to cane you. It will hurt me more than it will hurt you, I assure you.' He would then reach for his cane, lift it high up and bring it down quickly until an inch or two from the cadet's rear then hold back and land a very weak swipe. The drill then was for the cadet to scream loudly 'Ouch Sir, that hurt.' The disconcerted Mr. Carter would perhaps apply one more similar swipes and dismiss the cadet saying 'There now – let that be a lesson to you. Don't let me see you here again.' The cadet, rubbing his posterior vigorously would depart to continue his behaviour as before. His swipes were as nothing compared to the swipes of the ropes-ends applied by the cadet captains."

Ship's Officers

Naval staff and maritime training were an entirely different affair. Lt. (later Lt. Cdr.) 'Laurie' Lawrence was a genial rotund product of the Royal Navy's lower deck who had made it to the higher ranks. He was the target of a song, sung to the tune of 'If You Ever Cross the Sea to Ireland':

If you ever go across the straits to Conway
Where she's moored five hundred yards from Bangor Pier
You will see old Lawrie dancing on the gangway
Yelling "Get that bloody cutter out of here".

Lieutenant John 'Spooky' Brooke Smith was a tall, bespectacled, and well liked officer who, although a strict disciplinarian, was respected for his impartial running of the daily routine. Under him were the single-stripers or Warrant Officers. At the outbreak of war there were two – 'Bossy' Phelps, a cockney whose family were Thames watermen for generations past and who had won Doggetts Coat and Badge, and 'Ag' Collins, formerly a Royal Navy physical training instructor and boxer. Collins was soon called back up to the Royal Navy. Some time after 1941,. 'Tooley' Lee who was also well liked replaced him. He was an army Warrant Officer, seconded to the *Conway* to teach the

Spooky and Compass Lesson

new-fangled unarmed combat. These stalwarts organised the Ship with smooth efficiency and applied a no-nonsense demand for strict and instant obedience to rules. Under their inspiring leadership the cadets launched themselves enthusiastically, if not always successfully, into all things nautical.

Ship's Boats and Sailing

Looking at the Ship from the land, one could liken her to a duck with her small brood fussing around her. The *Conway*'s brood were a collection of boats - two twelve-oared and two ten-oared naval cutters, the six oared Captain's gig, several sailing boats, the water boat, or 'juice barge,' a sturdy motorboat (No 1) and a smaller motorboat (No 2). In 1946, these were supplemented by the pinnace motor launch (of which more later). The other boats, when in use, lay to a boom which protruded from the Ship's starboard side forward of the gangway. When needed they were allowed to fall astern to the gangway by slackening their lines. This arrangement, common to anchored ships, kept the boats from being bumped against the Ship's side.

> *"John Brooke Smith kept a wall chart with each cadet's name on it and a record of how often they went sailing (which was voluntary in one's spare time - summer evenings and Sundays). The keen types became boathands in their fourth term. We seldom sailed eastward of the pier, usually sailed westwards towards Menai Bridge."*

The cutters could be rigged for sailing with the 'de Horsey' rig. This has short spars and snug sail and mast-plan all inside the boat, a mainsail with perpendicular leech that is boomless for quick handling, and a jib. They were heavy boats but went well in a strong breeze.

> *"Groups of cadets would sail Joan into Beaumaris Bay in the summer months, sometimes entering the River Conway and mooring near the castle. I recall an occasion when she grounded on a falling tide whilst making for Conway and, being deep-keeled, she ended up high and dry on her side on the sandbank. There was nothing for it but to wait patiently for the tide to turn and float her off."*

There were also a Lightning, a fourteen foot Firefly and three clinker built Admiralty class sailing dinghies, which were moored a short distance off, close to the Anglesey shore.

> *"Lumbering through the water, all rope, canvas and heavy fittings they were about as safe as you could get."*

When Admiral Sir Percy Noble visited the Ship, he was rowed ashore in the Captain's gig and the sailing dinghies were manned and instructed to sail professionally near the gig as it made its way to the pier.

> *"The dinghy in which I was among the crew made a close pass in the fresh breeze and when going about the main sheet fouled the cleat and, instead of paying off on the opposite tack, the dinghy promptly capsized giving the Admiral a perfect example of how not to go-about!"*

Cutter's Crew

A cutter's crew consisted of thirteen cadets,

> *"twelve oarsmen and the cox'n, which might have been seen as an unlucky number although we never thought about it."*

Cutters Crew (actually in 1961)

The cox'n was in complete command and gave orders, which, in theory, the rest of the crew obeyed implicitly. He stood or sat in the stern and used a large wooden tiller to steer. In front of him there were six rows of thwarts, each with two oars, one for each side. A cadet manned each oar so there were two oarsmen per thwart, their feet on wooden stretchers to give purchase when rowing. Oars were held with both hands, inboard hand on the loom, outboard hand on the oar shaft. Oars were named, reading from aft, port and starboard, stroke, second stroke, bertha, second bertha, second bows and bows.

"The cutter would lie alongside the starboard gangway, moored fore and aft, port side to, stemming the tide."

The routine was unchanging. Having loaded the boat and shipped the tiller the cox'n barked a series of orders:

"Out poppets."

Poppets were small squares of wood in the gunwale, which were removed leaving rowlocks ready toreceive oars. One bow oarsman would stand by the stern rope, the other the bow line.

"Toss oars."

Five sets of oars were raised smartly to the vertical, blades aligned fore and aft, from their storage placelying along the thwarts (blades forward, handles aft).

-*"Down oars, starboard."*

The starboard side oarsmen (the side away from the Ship) lowered their oars together into their rowlocks and held them horizontally, blades parallel with the water.

"Let go forward, hold on aft."

The bowman let go his line and, pivoting on stern rope, the bows would gradually swing into the stream.

"Let go aft, down oars port when clear," where both bowman would return to their thwart, and toss their oars. Once clear of the Ship port side oars were lowered; it was time for work.

"Standby, give way, together."

The whole crew would commence rowing, taking their timing, or stroke, from the the starboard stroke oar. The lengths of the oars were graded from aft to accommodate the curve of the hull. Stroke was a short oar, second stroke was longer, bertha was the longest, second bertha and second bows were the same length as for second stroke, bow oars were the same length as stroke oars. Blades were thus in a perfectly straight line in the water. The cox'n would steer away from Ship towards shore often with the crew singing in time to the stroke; one popular song had a verse than ran "Heave away! Heave away! From *Conway* to Bangor's a helluva way."

"Feather oars"

was ordered when rowing into the wind or large waves. This meant that as oars were lifted out of the water, the crew turned the blades parallel with the surface to present the narrowest edge to the wind and waves.

"Feathering was not popular as the action strained the wrists."

Pulling was a demanding affair as the cutters were very heavy clinker built boats, weighed down by thirteen cadets and often passengers as well. Each stroke required a long reach forward before dropping the oar into the water, and then pulling it back though the water to the end of the stroke. The end of the stroke meant leaning backwards some way so the oar could easily be taken out of the water, ready for the swing forward to the next stroke. This exercised every muscle in the body.

"The oars were heavy beasts about twelve feet long and solid wood. After a few hours and days pulling we developed calluses on our hands and strong backs!"

Once the cutter got underway it lifted out of the water slightly and the pulling got a little easier, but the boat was also pushing through the waves. Many a new chum didn't grip his oar tightly enough and had it knocked out of his hands by a passing wave and crashed painfully into his chest. Pulling called for absolute co-ordination and perfect timing from all twelve crew-members, team work was everything.

"There were times of course when we wanted to prolong time away from the Ship. We soon leant the art of apparently exerting maximum effort whilst actually doing the minimum of work."

The next series of orders were for coming alongside.

"Bows," warned the crew they were approaching land, moorings or another boat. Both bows oars were 'tossed' or brought smartly out of the water into a vertical position blades fore and aft. The blade ends were briefly brought together or 'kissed' before being lowered and boated on thwarts, blades forward. The two bowmen then took up the bow and stern lines.

"Oars" directed the rest of the crew to stop rowing and hold their oars parallel with the water. The cox'n would then be lining the boat up to come smoothly and slowly alongside without bumping the shore.

"Toss oars" was the signal for the rest of the crew to bring their oars into the upright position with blades fore and aft. As the boat came alongside the slipway the bowman would jump onto the slip,

catch a turn on the slipway chain with the bow rope, let her run until alongside and then check the cutter. Meanwhile the stern man jumped onto the slip and hauled the stern in with the stern rope.

"Make fast" was ordered once in position alongside.

"Boat your oars" was the key for all oars to be lowered into the boat and stowed on the thwarts with blades forward.

It was always smarter to bring the cutter alongside with oars tossed but on occasion more control of the cutter was necessary. This was obtained by keeping the oars on the offshore side, down in the water. They could then be used to slow the boat by ordering *"Backwater,"* ie row astern, or *"Hold water,"* to place oars in the water quickly to take the way off her.

"I can't remember using fenders on the cutters, but perhaps we did. When the boat was carrying cadets as passengers, they would board in strict seniority, the stern seats being most popular, otherwise cramming in anywhere they could, sitting with the oarsman and, if necessary, assisting to pull an oar. It has been said that seamen taught us, but in fact I think we were mostly taught by the more senior cadets, apart from occasional first term seamanship lessons with a warrant officer. What is certain is that we did it over and over again, in darkness and light, in all sorts of weather and conditions, including fog, practically every day for two years. And I don't ever recall wearing a lifejacket or seeing any buoyancy aids or distress flares or any other gear at all, apart from an anchor and line, and a lantern or torch in the dark. Today's Health and Safety industry was a distant prospect; the Ship's routine had its roots in the days of wooden ships and iron men. It did us no harm - no cadet was ever lost despite rowing in winter storms and ripping tides."

Captain's Gig

The Captain's gig crew was made up of senior cadet captains coxed by the chief cadet captain. There were three eighteen foot oars each side and they called for considerable strength because of their length and the narrowness of the gig. The oarsmen sat one behind the other. Steering was by yoke and lines and took some little time to master.

"When I was senior cadet captain in charge of the new chums in Port Focsle we were summoned one day to take Lawrence Holt ashore. He was the owner of Blue Funnel Line and Chairman of Conway's Board of Governors. As it was soon after the beginning of the autumn term we had little experience of the gig. However, we set off smartly from the Ship and, the tide being high, the cox decided to go under the pier and make for the stone slip at the shoreward end alongside the pier. This would save this important personage having to walk the length of the long pier. However, owing to a combination of a strong tide, the cox's inexperience and the small clearance, we managed to enter the gap between two of the pier supports quite off-centre. I can hear the snap – snap – snap as the three oars on the port side broke and deposited the gig on the lee side with an asymmetric problem which was solved by using the remaining oars to punt the gig alongside the slip. Lawrence Holt disembarked without a word."

Weekend Activities

Saturday mornings were for all hands to 'Heave Round,' ie to wash and clean ship including scrubbing and holystoning the decks. In the afternoons, most cadets would be playing rugby at Bangor, later on the green at Beaumaris and at Baron Hill, Beaumaris, cross-country running, sailing or rowing the cutters.

"Cross-country running was part of our routine and sometimes at weekends parties of cadets would be landed on the Bangor shore and made to run along the road, across Telford's magnificent suspension bridge and back on the Anglesey shore to the Gazelle slip. Unscrupulous cadets had been known to hitch lifts in the few passing vehicles which would drop them off a little way from the Gazelle, where they would appear feigning breathlessness and fatigue."

Those not gainfully employed or on duty might be taken for a route march around the lanes just to occupy them for two or three hours on a Saturday afternoon while a few remained on duty aboard.

Cadets occasionally were invited to the Land Army Hostel in Menai Bridge for Sunday tea. It was the home to sixty young ladies doing war work on local farms. One of their number recalls:

"Our hostel became a happy local centre of servicemen. We also entertained young sailors from Conway. Teas usually consisted of kippers on bread but the very young, homesick cadets enjoyed our hospitality."

Smith's Café

"No Bangor cadet will ever forget visiting Smith's café after activities afternoons."

Mr. and Mrs Smith served scrumptious shilling teas; a pot of tea, two thick slices of bread and jam and a piece of cake. For another sixpence you could have beans on toast as well. Many cadets, after a cross-country race, would immediately change and run two miles back along the road to grab a table at Smith's café. Mr. Smith, always wearing a spotless wing collar, was very tolerant and always sympathetic to the cadets. Mrs Smith in her crisp apron, always smiling and kind, baked excellent cakes.

Smith's Cafe

"She worked like a Trojan in her small kitchen spreading butter, cutting cake, spooning jam and filling pots of teas. If ever two people get to heaven those two will, and they will have 'shilling teas' emblazoned upon their haloes."

This brief respite over, cadets would wander back to Glyn Garth slip where a waiting boat carried them back to the Ship for the end of day routine.

"Boarding by the fixed starboard gangway, we would enter onto the lower deck, salute smartly and descend the steep double companionway to the orlop deck and our particular corner where our wooden chest lay against the Ship's side. The wooden chests were provided by the Liverpool Sailors' Home and contained all our gear. Our names were painted in white letters on the front. Most were old and battered having been used and reused by many cadets over the years. A short distance away was the wooden rack where our hammocks were stowed during the day."

Cadets had no privacy and no private space apart from their chest. In accordance with normal naval practice these were never locked, as one's shipmates were trusted implicitly.

Uniform

During the winter term, cadets wore navy blue single breasted jackets similar to battle dress tops called 'SBs,' long dark blue trousers with no pockets, blue collarless shirts with white soft collars, black tie and white lanyard. The senior cadets wore their top buttons undone as sign of their superiority. In summer, the dress was navy blue shorts, blue knee length socks and blue shirts without ties. Sleeves were rolled up very neatly and precisely. At morning divisions, on Sundays, holidays ands other special occasions 'reefers' (best uniforms) were worn – smart double breasted jackets with eight gold buttons and a two inch blue braid stripes on each lapel and a white lanyard. Reefers were hung in the midships coat-racks. Cricket teams wore double breasted jackets or blazers, with white trousers

> "As Cadets RNR we wore a Royal Navy cap badge, albeit one supplied by the Sailors' Home at Liverpool, which was smaller and less expensive than the Royal Navy version. Some cadets acquired a full Royal Navy badge but this was not encouraged."

Following Royal Navy practice during the war years, caps were all black, but after the war white cloth cap covers were once more adopted. White covers were worn from 1st April to 30th September.

> "The change to wearing white cloth cap covers throughout the year came in the early 1950s. White plastic caps followed, which I never much cared for as they had a tendency to go yellow."

> "It was also fashionable in my time to purchase uniform caps from sources other than the Sailors' Home, if one could afford it. 'Jockey peak' versions were considered to be cool (although we didn't use that expression). The warrant officers, 'Taffy' Oliver, Len Flanagan and Ernie Moore wore Conway cap badges, with a Conway Castle as the crown above the anchor and laurel leaves. The officers on secondment (Digby Jones for example) wore Merchant Navy cap badges, or Royal Navy cap badges if they possessed an RNR rank."

New caps were perfectly round and flat like plates. It was customary to remove the cane grommet inside, which kept it in shape, soak the grommet and bend it into a more seamanlike shape and return it to the cap, which naturally assumed what was called a 'shag' and named after the curvaceous cormorant. Officers noticing too great a shag might instruct it to be removed but cadets persevered.

Going Aloft

A popular free-time activity was climbing the main mast (the fore and mizzen masts being out of bounds as unsafe).

The main mast was in three sections mounted one above the other. Where the two lower sections overlapped was a large wooden platform; the old fighting top where marines once stood and fired down on opposing crews. It was from a French marine on one such top that Nelson received his mortal wound at Trafalgar.

"A stout rope net was strung under the main mast to catch anyone who might fall, but no one fell in my time."

The initial climb via the ratlines tied to the rigging (rather like rope ladders) at first seemed easy because they sloped inwards so the body was leaning against them, but it was an awkward climb in that the rope foot-holds were particularly pliable, and it was difficult to achieve a firm foothold with each step. About fifty five feet up, where the first two sections of the mast joined, was the Maintop. It was necessary to climb upwards and outwards around the overhanging 'futtocks' to gain the safety of the top. It was frightening at first because you had to lean out and back to scramble around the overhang.

"I must confess that on the only occasion I went aloft I was white with terror by the time I reached the edge of the Maintop, and I was particularly grateful when another cadet, safely on the platform, recognised my distress, and heaved me up to comparative safety."

Some who could not face this challenging part of the climb could attain the top though a small opening (called the lubber's hole) left in the platform where the Maintop shrouds met the mast. From there a further forty foot

The Mainmast

and much steeper climb led to cross-trees, where a further overhang had to be negotiated roughly at the height of a 10 story building. From there it was a 'simple' climb right to the top of the mast and the truck, the wooden disc approximately 10 inches in diameter topping the mast. Intrepid cadets had been known to sit on the truck some 195 feet in the air.

Cadets were obliged to go aloft only during physical training activities. However, as most cadets and apprentices at sea would have been required to climb various masts for various reasons, acquiring a head for heights was a useful thing.

"I can remember, as a cadet aboard the Drakensberg Castle, being sent up a crappy old 268 type radar mast, above the monkey island, at night, in a gale, to disentangle a halyard that had wrapped around the revolving scanner. Piece of cake after Conway's futtock shrouds!"

"One could also go aloft as a recreational activity with the permission of the cadet captain of the upper deck watch, who stood on the poop deck looking bored. One climbed from the bulwark on the well of the upper deck onto the rigging that led aloft to the Maintop. Climbing as far as the Maintop futtock shrouds was no great problem with lots to hold onto and the ability to rest on the shrouds and admire the view. The first problem arose at the Maintop; to climb on to it one could squeeze up through the lubber's hole. This was frowned upon. The required approach was via the futtock shrouds that led from the edge of the Maintop down to the mast. Unfortunately this meant climbing upside down, as it were, with nothing behind one but space and then, worst of

St Trillo Passes The Ship

all, climbing over the edge of the Maintop, again with nothing behind one but air, to the topmast shrouds when one again had something one could lean forward against, stepping around the edge onto the Maintop and comparative safety. I have seen a cadet freeze whilst climbing the futtock shrouds. A senior cadet climbed over him, putting his body between the cadet and space and giving him confidence to climb back down to the main shrouds. We used to show off to passing pleasure boats, (the St Trillo, the St Tudno and the St Seiriol) which passed through the Strait quite close in summer to and from Menai Bridge, by hanging by our arms from the futtock shrouds, or climbing out on the main yard, or generally putting it about as if we were real hairy sailormen. The passengers loved it and so did we."

"From the Maintop the topmast shrouds lead up to a point about eight feet below the masthead, where one would transfer to the other side and climb down again. It was quite a sight to see the rigging full of cadets climbing up the starboard side and down the port side. It was considered quite good form to have touched the truck. This involved pulling oneself up the mast the eight or so feet between the top of the topmast shrouds and the truck. Quite simple at deck level, but a rather different prospect nearly two hundred feet above the water. I checked it out several times, but felt that I was too young and that life was too sweet to chance it."

Coaling Ship

Another major task early in each term was coaling ship. Coal was needed to provide fuel for the paltry central heating system, the boiler, which provided steam to drive the electrical generator, fuel for the galleys, and steam for the winch, which hoisted the coal from the bunkers down in the bowels of the

The Dirtiest Job Ever Conceived

Ship. This had to be brought from shore and it was a job for all cadets. Tons of coal were dumped onto the dockside at Port Penrhyn, a mile away from the Ship. Each top took it in turn to shovel the coal into large sacks and load them onto the waterboat for towing out to the Ship. Several trips were required. Once alongside, the sacks were winched onboard, carried by hand on trolleys across the upper deck and lowered into the coal bunkers where cadets emptied them. It was hard, tiring and extremely dirty work. After a few hours cadets looked more like 'chimneysweeps.' There was always a competition to see which top could unload a barge in the shortest time. As a reward the fastest top went ashore for a cream tea at Robert's café in Upper Bangor or Smith's café on the road to Menai Bridge.

"This was a masterly carrot for ravenous youngsters and the competition was furious."

The task could take all morning but as soon as the last lump fell down into the coal hole the cadets immediately fell to cleaning the dockside, water boat, barge and the Ship. In no time everything was spick and span as if nothing had happened.

Coal Hole

The various items of coal-fired machinery required a steady supply of coal from the bunkers. A winch would haul sacks of coal from the bunkers to the deck where it was needed, but the sacks had first to be filled and lifted onto the winch; a task for a party of cadets. Another cadet operated the winch from the boiler house, seated on an up-turned yak tub and keeping tally on a chalk board.

"This was probably the dirtiest job ever conceived onboard. It was therefore awarded as punishment for misbehaviour. 'Right – Coal Hole for you!' was dreaded by all because the work was hard and filthy but at one time or another most cadets experienced it."

Boat Hoisting

Following naval practice it was customary at night for the cadet captain of the lower deck watch to hail boats returning to the Ship to see who was approaching. If an Officer was being conveyed the cox'n would respond *"Aye Aye!."* If the Captain was being conveyed the response was *"Conway!"*

Every evening, before slinging hammocks and turning in, various boats were hoisted out of the water. Boats were hoisted on the stout square boat davits which stuck out from the ship's side at an angle of about forty degrees, with falls much as a ship's lifeboats. The rope falls led inboard to two more sets of threefold purchases and finally via snatch blocks to two long hauling parts laid along the lower deck. The hoisting was accomplished entirely manually using cadet-power, a procedure which called for skill and discipline of a high order. The cadets designated to lay out the falls for the boat would be called away first. They would lay out the forrard fall and the after fall in parallel lines and stand-by in the boat under the davits to hook on and pass the wracking lines when hoisted. Stoppers were passed on the cutters and gigs. For the heaviest boat, No 1 motorboat, rackings were passed by two cadets chosen for their height and dexterity. They would call *"Forward (or aft) racking on, Sir"* when they were done. The duty bugler would sound 'Lower-deck' and all hands would assemble on the falls. The cadets would space themselves along the falls, half to the forrard fall and half to the after

"Heave Away Smartly"

fall. The boat would be positioned under the davits and the pulley blocks would be lowered to them and hooked on by the boat's crew, who then held on to lifelines leading from the davit head as the boats were hoisted.

The officer of the day would lean out of a port so he could see the boat to be raised and would shout orders to the cadets:

"Hands to the falls!" – the whole Ship's company would take up their fall and get ready to start heaving.

"Take up the slack forrard" – the cadets would immediately pull stoutly until there was no slack on the forward fall. This would be repeated on the after fall. The boat was now ready to be hoisted.

"Heave away smartly" came next and two crocodiles of cadets would heave on the falls and start pulling aft, a slow tramping with the heavier boats but literally running with the lighter ones.

"Urged on by cadet captains we would go running aft until we ran out of deck at which point a couple of cadets would flake down the rope fall. As soon as you reached that spot you would let go the rope and hare back to the starting point and take hold again. This three inch manila rope was a real joy as it was never exposed to the weather and with constant use and our sweaty little paws it had become as supple as silk."

If the boat were not being hoisted levelly, the order would be given to *"Avast Heaving,"* and then, *"Heave away forrard (or aft)"* would be ordered until the boat was level, when the order would be given to *"Heave away together."* When the boat was in the required position beneath the davits the order to "Avast Heaving" was given. It didn't take long for new chums to learn to heed this order. If not they would run slap into the back of the cadet ahead of them and end up with a clip on the ear.

For lighter boats the order, *"Marry the falls! — Heave away,"* meant bringing the forrad and after falls together so that they could be hoisted simultaneously. With these boats, cadets could literally run away with the falls.

"Avast Heaving. On stoppers" was ordered so cadet captains would pass a rope stopper on each fall; a rope designed to stop the fall running back, so that the inboard end could be secured to a wooden cleat. Taller cadets would leave their place on the falls and seize the parts of the three fold purchases, which were right up at the deckhead, holding the parts together until the stoppers had been passed. The two cadets in the boat would pass the life lines from each end of the boat from the lifting hook and over the davit above to further secure the boat.

"Ease to the stoppers" meant walking back slowly until the stoppers took the weight of the boat and held.

"Light to" (this always sounded like "lie to" to me) meant throwing the rope fall back along the deck so that the slack would allow each fall to be secured to a wooden cleat at the deck head, thus completing the hoisting process. New chums might be advised by their unkind seniors to hold on tight when the order was given; they didn't make that mistake twice. The boat hands secured the boat while other cadets stowed the falls and blocks".

The same routine was repeated until all the boats were hoisted. Every day there would be at least the twelve-oared heavy duty cutter to hoist, and the two motorboats, but a full complement of boats hoisted could include three gigs, two ten oared cutters, a twelve oared heavy duty cutter and No 1 and No 2 motorboats. The Bugler then sounded 'Disperse,' usually followed by the call 'Hands to Wash.' The water boat, the pinnace, the sailing cutter and the sailing dinghies remained on their nearby moorings.

"I heard tell that an inspection of the Ship by HM School Inspectors in the early fifties advised that too much of a cadet's time was taken each day in boat-hoisting, but I don't know what then transpired. Personally, I think that it was time well spent if only because in rough weather this operation taught quick reaction and the faultless response to orders."

There was also a strict injunction against talking on the falls. New chums were sometimes prone to do this during their first weeks of grace but immediately learned the error of their ways. If orders were not promptly obeyed catastrophe could follow as some of the boats weighed several tons. Accidents did happen, but not often.

"This was really tough work and, of course we were all dead tired but as it was the last thing we did before getting into our hammocks there was something sort of comforting about the operation."

Skiving off boat hoisting was not unknown.

"The usual suspects did so on principle, there were plenty of places to hide - behind the tanks in the hold, or on the upper deck."

Turning In

"Dusk would find a lone bugler sounding 'Colours' as the large blue ensign was slowly lowered. Forty years later whilst staying at the monstrous block of flats on the site of the old Bishop's Palace and on a balmy summer evening I could still hear the clean bugle sound of 'Colours' and see in my mind's eye the old Ship lying there, a piece of history and a nursery of hope and adventure."

In the evening every cadet would retrieve their hammock from storage and sling it to one of the iron hooks on the Ship's side and one of the iron brackets, which hinged down from the low deckhead.

"Each of us had about 30 inches of space in which to bed down; the hammocks were cosy and comfortable and sleep came easily to tired youngsters."

Before turning in it was traditional that cadets would tour the Ship and amicably settle any differences they might have had during the day. Hands would be shaken and disputes closed ready for a clean start the next day.

Sunset

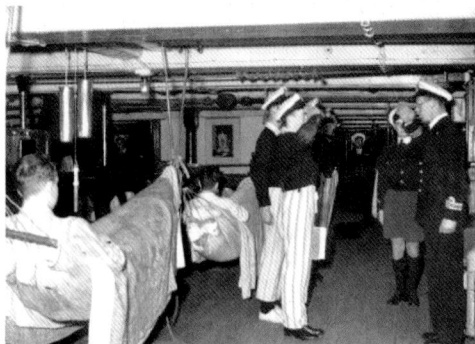

Cadet Captains' Report

"Fifty years later during a Conway Club committee meeting I unfortunately had a particularly belligerent exchange with an Old Conway of 40s vintage. I was surprised when immediately after the meeting he came straight over to me to shake hands and settle our differences before we left or 'turned in.' The idea had died out by my time in the Ship but it struck me as a particularly sensible for men who would have to rub along for long periods at sea."

"At nine thirty the generator on the upper deck would be wound down and a dark silence would fall on the Ship."

Before long the steady sound of footsteps would be heard as the officer of the watch and the chief cadet captain, preceded by a watchman bearing a hurricane lamp, made their way to the centre of the orlop deck. Cadet captains from the various tops would then line up in front of them and, in turn, would step smartly in front of the officer of the watch, salute and report that, for instance, *"Starboard Focsle all correct, Sir. Scuttles shut and bilges pumped, all present!"*

The Watch List would be read out allocating duties for the next day to individuals, boats' crews and those under punishment in the slack party. It was at this hour that official punishment was meted out.

Punishment

"Punishments were awarded for such serious misdemeanours as being caught smoking or insubordination. The punishment party would approach the culprit's hammock, shadows from the glimmering lamp dancing on the deckhead. He would be taken up one deck and in deathly silence, beneath the Ship's bell, he would receive his punishment; usually three or six strokes of the teaser with 12 being given for really serious matters. The swish of the rope's end could be heard all over the Ship, followed usually by a gasp from the recipient. He would then be returned to his hammock to whispered sympathies and to nurse a sore and sometimes bleeding behind. Fortunately, this evening punishment was a fairly rare occurrence as immediate and salutary single stokes with a teaser by the cadet captains kept us in check. The rope's end was administered in this way quite freely and was accepted without malice. The last cadet to lash up his hammock and line up with the rest of his top was often given a whack for being last. Then the hammocks were bent double and straightened; if any bedding showed through then a whack was administered. These arrangements made for speed and competence in hammock lashing."

Daily life was set round by rules and regulations infringement of which, if discovered, usually led to punishment. Discipline was maintained mainly by the cadet petty officers (later called cadet captains), indeed more than one officer has observed that the staff really had little to do with the day-to-day running of affairs, which was down to the cadets. Cadet captains could award punishments for misdemeanours great and small. Some punishments were immediate, one or more strokes across the backside from the teaser wielded by a cadet captain.

> *"There was no particular place for administering the teaser, anywhere where the necessity occurred. Teasers, in my experience, were never used to encourage people to do things, as haul on a rope, etc. That would not have been acceptable"*

Cadet captains breaking rules received upper deck watches or lower deck watches. Buglers typically were awarded extra bugle watches. Cadets could suffer a range of punishments: messenger watches (ie acting as messenger for the duty cadet captain and officer of the watch), coal holes, bunker party and early heave outs. Slack party was another common punishment, which essentially entailed doing whatever extra tasks were deemed necessary.

> *"There were a number of regulars who seemed to spend most of their time on Slack Party."*

Cadets who appeared too often under punishment might occasionally be investigated by an executive officer. The Captain Superintendent reviewed the punishment book every week.

> *"When I was a QB in Conway the Rough Punishment Book was kept in the Gun Room in the charge of the chief cadet captain's (CPO's) valet, customarily a sixth term shag (a QB who didn't get a rate). He used the Gun Room as of right and made up the Watch Lists. At the end of the Easter Term 1949. I found the book lurking in the Gun Room and took it home with me. It is at hand as I write and browsing through it is a delight! Entries were in columns occupying two pages, Name being followed by Offence, Punishment, Meter (that is person awarding the punishment) and Number (being the number of accumulated offences, which disappeared later in the book as the CPO's valet couldn't be bothered to tot them up)."*

Offences and punishments included:

Ringing 11 bells at 8 bells.	1 day's slack
Evading boat hoisting.	1 bugle watch
Insolence.	1 coal hole
Avoiding school.	2 coal holes
Walking in front of Focslemen whilst they were being drilled, and arguing.	1 bugle watch
After continual warning, wearing no lanyard.	1 day's slack
For chipping oak on the main deck with a chipping hammer.	1 day's slack
Insubordination.	1 boiler house coaling
Throwing hammock into hold.	1 coal hole
Continued fooling at band practice.	1 days slack and 1 coal hole
Not turning up for slack party.	1 official stroke.
Breaking rules and refusing to take punishment.	Staff Captain's Reports.

Removing gear from No 7 Mess tin.	1 day's slack
Neglecting his sweep after being warned.	1 messenger watch
Not answering a pipe.	2 days slack party
Bathing on wrong bath night.	1 day's slack

End of Term

"Day followed day in the old Ship and the routine became familiar and enjoyable with the cadets eagerly becoming experienced in the ways of the sea. The anchorage was in an ideal spot with the scenery changing with the seasons and with the wind and sun bringing the cadets a rosy weather-beaten complexion. The crowded conditions and lack of a decent diet did not unduly affect us; nearly all had some sort of 'goodies' sent from home. Peanut butter, biscuits, and cakes were the usual items and some had homemade jam sent by anxious mothers."

Time soon passed and the end of term would suddenly beckon. The tradition was for the cadet captain on watch at reveille to bawl out immediately after the bugle call *"Three cheers for going home three weeks today!"* Of course, there followed loud cheering. A week later, it was repeated and then seven days before the end of term there would be a shout of *"Three cheers for going home seven days today"* and then, six, five, four, three, two and then on the actual end of term day reveille would be played by several buglers with drum accompaniment followed by loud cheers.

The end-of term service, always on the last Sunday of term, was quite moving, even for youngsters of fifteen and sixteen. The service always finished with hymn 577 *'Lord dismiss us with Thy blessing'* – the end of term hymn with the first and last verses sung with great feeling, especially as the Quarter Boys were leaving for good and going to sea.

When a cadet left during term time on appointment to his first ship, he would have toured the mess deck just after breakfast shaking hands and saying goodbye to each cadet.

"The Ship's company would be summoned to the upper deck to man the starboard side. The departing cadet would board a cutter manned by his own term, sometimes a motorboat, which would then leave the Ship and lay off the gangway. The chief cadet captain would call out 'HMS Conway, three cheers for -----!' The cheers would be followed by a Hullabaloo and then the boat would leave for the shore, the departing cadet often lighting up a cigarette in his new role as Old Conway. Hence the unofficial verse to the Conway song:

> *"When I left her at last and I went to sea, a lump was in my throat,*
> *I watched her fade all mistily, through clouds of tobacco smoke"*

On the last evening of term a watch bill was posted for the following term, which showed all the appointments, chief cadet captain, senior and junior cadet captains, boathands, etc. In this low-key fashion individuals learned if they had been appointed, promoted, rewarded or passed over. That evening the whole band would play the last post. On the final day of term the whole band played 'Reveille.'

"At the end of term it was then the practice to send our baggage ashore to Bangor station the night before, where it was held in a convenient store. We kept overnight gear in our white cotton laundry bags, the small

kit-bag. Band members were permitted to take bugles home with them to practice during the leave period, which I did. In my excitement at going home after my first term, I leapt onto the train quite forgetting my luggage and departed Bangor blowing my bugle through the carriage window, only to realise seconds later that I had no luggage. It eventually arrived three weeks later sans a camera and other small articles of value."

During the war, the end of term traditional whereby cadets hurled their mugs into the hold to be shattered with all the others was discontinued.

"The end of term was eagerly anticipated and on the day all the lads were landed (at Bangor pier) to trudge light-heartedly the mile or so to Bangor station carrying an assortment of kitbags."

The fast steam train from Holyhead to Euston, with reserved coaches for the cadets, was boarded at Bangor station. It dropped cadets off at Chester, Crewe, Rugby and London from where they would disperse to their scattered homes. Cadets living in Eire during the war had to remove their uniforms before travelling, if they had landed in Eire in RNR uniform they could have been interned for the duration!

CHAPTER 17

1941–49 THE BANGOR YEARS

1941

At the request of several cadets including, Cadet Bill Nash, Captain Goddard agreed to form an Air Class for those who intended to take up flying as a career. This was not an entirely new venture as there had been an air class in 1935.

"A number of us asked Goddard if we could have an Air Class because we wanted to fly. To his credit he agreed and we started classes in air navigation, meteorology, aircraft recognition, theory of flight, etc."

They visited RAF Mona and RAF Llandwrog and flew in Ansons and Oxfords.

Cadets continued to sleep in hammocks.

"The general opinion was that they were comfortable to sleep in, but I slept in one for two and a half years and I disagree. I adjusted the nettles, and even brought a small pillow from home and smuggled it onboard, but I could never get as comfortable as a half decent bed. Furthermore some miscreant could let you down in the night just for fun."

The majority seemed to enjoy hammocks.

"I still think that sleeping in a hammock is the most comfortable way to sleep."

QBs were allowed to use hammock stretchers which apparently made them much more comfortable.

"Then there was the awful moment in the summer when you had to put the whole kit and caboodle on your shoulders and carry it ashore for scrubbing. At 13 years of age, carrying about 130lbs of wringing wet hammock and contents up and down steep ladders, into a cutter jammed full of cadets and then up the pier to the scrubbing area, was not a happy time. If memory serves, the half hitches were actually supposed to be marline hitches, in that to make the hitch the rope went over the standing part not under. The punishment for such infractions was to take your hammock ashore and double around the parade ground with it. Some of the tough kids would keep going for several hours but eventually collapse face down in the dirt, not moving. The Duty Officer, would just stand there in the rain, staring into the middle distance."

1941 Summer

"I remember a real experience of the sea in the nobby Joan. A lovely summer's afternoon, just a gentle breeze. A crew of about six with an officer in charge, we gaily set sail, clad in short-sleeved summer shirt, shorts and canvas shoes. We had a marvellous day just mucking about in boats. Returning to Bangor the heavens opened, rough seas, high winds and torrential rain. We had no extra clothes whatsoever. I have never been so cold in my life. That certainly taught us a lesson!"

1942

There were 242 cadets. One new chum remembers his first day.

"My first sight of her was from the stone slip at Bangor on a dismal wet day. No 1 motorboat came alongside. The cadet captain in charge was dressed in heavy oilskins with a battered cap on his head, the badge green with salt. He yelled at us 'All aboard my sons and take your last look at freedom for three months.' An awe-inspiring beginning that has remained fresh in my memory to this day."

Approaching The Ship From Bangor Pier

Later that term the whole Ship's company had been landed at Bangor pier for a church service. In the afternoon a severe storm blew up.

"The cadet captain in charge of No 1 took us all back from Bangor pier to the Ship. The waves were very high and the wind strong but in a few hours he accomplished this magnificent feat of seamanship without any aid from officer or instructor."

The BBC had been evacuated from London to North Wales because of the bombing, and broadcasts were made from studios in Bangor and Llandudno. Popular programmes like 'ITMA' (It's That man Again) and Saturday Night Music Hall were made locally and the stars and staff lived in the vicinity. One of the characters in ITMA was Mrs Mop, a charlady whose stock line was *"Can I do you now – Sir?"* Captain Goddard had a look-alike charwoman who came from Bangor several days a week to 'do' for him and Mrs Goddard.

"The Goddards had a coal fire in their accommodation. On one occasion I was bowman in No1 motorboat and had been summoned alongside the gangway to take the Commander ashore. He appeared at the top of the gangway resplendent in his immaculate uniform and lightly skipped down onto the bottom platform. The cox saluted smartly anticipating his boarding when, from above, a bucketful of cold ashes descended in a dense cloud and transformed his uniform into a light grey colour. He probably realised that Mrs Mop had excelled herself and he just shook himself, turned about and re-boarded without a word. The cox just exchanged glances with us – his eyes said it all."

"Robert Robert's café was a landmark in Upper Bangor and was frequented by university students and Conway cadets on the rare occasions when they were ashore. Wartime rationing restricted their cakes and buns but once a week they provided Captain Goddard with an iced sponge cake, which they delivered to the pier with other goodies. The cutter crews which collected these soon became aware of the juicy nature of their cargo and the icing on the sponge cake was picked at by one hand and then another until it was almost bare sponge. As one can imagine this was unacceptable to the Captain who issued dire threats against any of the icing robbers, but the problem persisted. In the end a small wooded chest was made with a hasp and staple and a padlock with two keys, one for the bakery and one for Captain Goddard. The cake was delivered in its chest, to the little kiosk at the head of the pier and a flag was hoisted on the flagpole to advise the Ship that the cake was there. A cutter was then despatched post-haste to collect it. Problem solved!"

And You'll Find on the Bridge a Conway Boy
Captain Edward Robert McKinstry CBE RD RNR (1876-78)

Captain McKinstry died in April 1943. He had been in Conway under Captain Franklin, joining the first term on Nile. "During my two years I was off the good conduct list for six months. No shore leave, had to man all liberty boats, pump water into and out of the bilges, and pump fresh water into the tanks."

As a senior cadet he was promoted cadet captain but still fell foul of the system "I was often Captain of the Slack Party and that was the hardest job of the lot, rounding the others up and clapping them on the pumps but the greatest difficulty was keeping them there." Although the boy fell foul of Conway rules throughout his course, Conway developed the man.

Leaving Conway in July 1878, he was appointed midshipman RNR and joined the British Shipowners Company. His first passage was in 'British Peer', a full rigged sailing ship. Later he transferred to British Merchant commanded by another Old Conway, Captain Moloney.

In June 1885, he passed his Extra Master's exam at the very young age of twenty-four, the first man to do so under new national rules, which allowed the certificate without two years experience in command. He moved to the Pacific Steam Navigation Company and then White Star Line as fourth officer of Adriatic, a crack Atlantic liner. White Star took only the best. He rose fast and by 1889 was first officer in 'Teutonic', a ship that could be quickly converted to a twelve gun light cruiser. Half the crew had to be Royal Navy reservists so his RNR appointment from Conway was a great help. Participating in naval manoeuvres at Spithead he jumped overboard and rescued a man who had fallen, the fourth time he had rescued someone from the sea.

In 1892, he was in command of 'Teutonic' at the age of 31. He also commanded White Star's famous 'Britannic' and 'Germanic'.

It was rumoured in Conway that whilst ashore he had met a young lady and told her he would soon be a Captain, and that when he was, he would return and marry her. True to his word when he was Captain he returned and married her. They set up home near the mouth of the Mersey. Whenever his ship arrived home he blew certain blasts on his siren to announce his return!

"One might say of this active splendid man that he had every fine quality that fits a sailor."

The motor torpedo boats (MTBs) being built at Bangor were tested in Beaumaris Bay and then handed over to naval crews who sailed away to secret destinations.

"One such MTB was anchored just to seaward of Bangor pier when we were sailing the dinghies one autumn afternoon. We were tacking across from the mainland shore in a fresh breeze and when it became apparent that we were bearing down on the anchored vessel it was decided to 'go about' onto the other tack. Shouting 'lee-o,' the cox put his helm down but the dinghy failed to come round onto the other tack continuing on the same tack as before. We gathered speed and despite the cox attempting to steer the dinghy past the stern of the MTB, the stout wooden bowsprit buried itself into the hull of the MTB just a foot from its stern. The officer on the MTB was jumping up and down metaphorically but one of the sailors told us under his breath that we had performed a wonderful service in making it impossible to sail until repairs were made. They were about to sail for the Middle East apparently. The hulls of the MTBs were merely laminated plywood. Two aircraft-type engines powered them; they made a wonderfully loud roar when under full throttle."

Cadets were sometimes allowed out with them on trials.

The 1st XV mainly played against men's teams from the armed forces, but found that what cadets lacked in physical size, they made up for on fitness.

"After running backwards and forwards for an hour or so we began to wear them down. Never more so than in the RAF Pwllheli seven a side tournament 1942-43, which we won against RAF and RN sides. I still have my tankard to prove it."

And You'll Find on the Bridge a Conway Boy
Captain George Hunt DSO, DSC, RN (1930-32

George was born in Scotland in 1916, and at the age of 14 he started his course in Conway. He joined Blue Funnel Line as a junior officer and also spent time in Royal Navy (RN) vessels as a member of the Royal Naval Reserve. As part of the preparation for war in 1938 he was selected along with 100 others to serve full time with the RN. In 1940 he was a survivor from the submarine Unity when she was rammed and sunk in the North Sea. Leter in 1940 he was appointed second in command of HM Submarine Proteus. During the period 1940/41 Proteus sank 12 ships and eventually the submarine 'retired hurt' after a collision with an Italian destroyer the Sattario.

In 1942 he took command of HMS Ultor until the end of 1944. George was the top scoring submarine captain in the second phase of the war in the Mediterranean. He sank 28 ships, totalling 43,000 tons, including one large tanker that was protected by nine surface escorts and five aircraft. He had an unrivalled reputation for accuracy, achieving 32 hits for 68 torpedoes fired. He was awarded 2 DSOs, 2 DSCs and was Mentioned in Despatches twice.

After the war George became a very respected RN teacher – training and examining prospective submarine captains. Other appointments included "In Command" of a Destroyer and the 7th Frigate Squadron an appointment in the NATO Area, Chief of Staff to Flag Officer Submarines and finally Senior Naval Officer West Indies as a Commodore (One star). As flag rank beckoned he decided to retire to Australia. In 1960 he joined the Royal Australian Navy Emergency List as a Captain.

Since moving to Queensland he served with the Company of Master Mariners, has been President of the United Services Institute and was elected Patron of the Submarine Association of Queensland in 1990.

1943

There was a tragedy when a cadet, Joe Paine, attempted to climb down the mainstay and fell onto the physics laboratory on the upper deck and was killed. It was said a broken wire strand pierced his hand and he lost his hold.

"He had just returned to the Ship after an appendectomy. After the usual Saturday 'heave-round' he followed a handful of glory boys who liked to show off by sliding (illegally) down the mainstay. Wearing sea-boots, moving hand-over-hand, he appeared to be progressing well, when suddenly he stopped and gasped out 'I don't

think I can make it.' Weakened by his recent illness he let go his grasp, hung for a split second by his feet, before dropping head first onto anti-fire bomb concrete blocks which covered the lab and main hatch in war time. As you can imagine, it was an awful moment, and affected all who saw it happen in a sort of slow motion, during which we were powerless to help. Joe was unconscious but still alive when we helped get him down to the sick bay, but died not long after."

"I don't recall anyone being blamed at the inquest, but it was a lesson to all concerned as to just how easy it is for a bit of unthinking adventure to have tragic circumstances. Joe's parents donated some chapel furniture in his memory."

The cadet captains set up a scheme to encourage greater sporting competition. Every cadet was allocated to one of six sporting divisions or 'ships' named after notable ships from the war. Cossack's crew wore black favours, Howe's wore grey, Nestor's blue, Ohio's yellow, Rawlpindi's red and Sea Lion's green. Each crew elected their own captain and lieutenant, who then arranged the term's rugby, tennis, cross-country, marching, boxing, rowing and athletics competitions. A Mr. Pledger donated a challenge cup awarded to the most successful crew each term.

"The introduction of the Pledger Cup has proved a great incentive to keenness and rivalry in games and athletics."

The cadets worked out a fair system for scoring the competitions.

1944

"Early in the Spring term the Chief Officer, Digby Jones, mustered senior cadets in the senior classroom in great secrecy to brief us that we were short listed for boat crew duties in the assembly areas prior to D-Day. We anxiously awaited further orders but we were never called."

The war effort involved periodic weeks when funds and morale were raised through 'Wings for Victory' or 'War Weapons Week' and such like. Parades of the services and ancillary organisations like the Red Cross and WVS and Home Guard were held all over Britain. *Conway* provided their band and sixty to a hundred cadets for parades across North Wales. Being the senior service, they led each parade; the bugle and drum band were deafening and the marchers were especially chosen for their smart appearance and perfect drill.

"The drum major, a lantern-jawed lad called Bates, wielded his baton impeccably, hurling it skyward whilst looking straight ahead and unerringly catching it as it spun earthwards."

During one Saturday afternoon practice, a new cadet captain refused to stop for the usual break at Smith's café. As the contingent was negotiating a slight right hand bend the cadet captain unnecessarily ordered *"Right wheel!"* which actually meant a ninety-degree turn.

"We were all pretty fed up, having been marching for an hour and a half. The lads wanted a bit of fun and complied accurately, the first row turned smartly right, climbed a small bank and clambered over a low wire sheep fence and, followed by the other 19 ranks of three cadets, marched across the newly ploughed field until met by a high hedge at the opposite end of the field. The shambles eventually ended by the cadets returning to the lane and protesting that they only obeyed clear orders."

Bored cadets had also conjured up another not-by-the-book response to the 'About Turn' order.

"Instead of smartly turning 180 degrees in four steps with knees well raised, and then marching away in the opposite direction the squad would make eight 'on-the-spot' steps turning through 360 degrees and continue marching in the same direction. This incongruous manoeuvre, performed immaculately was usually done when there were passers-by, whose expressions were quite funny to see."

And You'll Find on the Bridge a Conway Boy
Lt. Cdr. Ian Fraser VC DSC RD RNR (1936-38)

Lt. Cdr. Fraser was awarded the Victoria Cross for 'Special and hazardous duties' in midget submarines whilst attacking the Japanese heavy cruiser Takao in the Johore strait, Singapore on 31st July, 1945.

Ian Edward Fraser joined Conway in 1936. He played rugby for the 1st and 2nd XVs and excelled at boxing, his bouts being noted for their tenacity and commitment. In 1937 he was cox of the Conway gig's crew against Worcester. He left Conway in 1938 and joined Blue Star line. He was appointed Probationary Midshipman RNR in 1938 and in June 1939 was called up to join Royal Oak. He volunteered for submarine duty and was awarded the DSC whilst serving in Sahib in the 19th Flotilla in the Mediterranean. Injury prevented him sailing in Sahib's last cruise when she was lost and all but one of her crew became PoWs. After a short period in command of H44 out of Londonderry, a rather uneventful command, he volunteered for X-craft in March 1944.

His citation reads: "During the long approach up the Singapore Straits, he deliberately left the believed safe channel and entered mined waters to avoid suspected hydrophone posts. The target was aground, or nearly aground both for and aft, and only under the midship portion was there sufficient water for XE-3 to place herself under the cruiser. For 40 minutes XE-3 pushed her way along the seabed until finally Lt. Cdr. Fraser managed to force her right under the centre of the cruiser. Here he placed the limpets and dropped his main side charge. Great difficulty was experienced in extricating the craft after the attack had been completed but finally XE-3 was clear and commenced her long return to the sea. The courage and determination of Lt. Cdr. Fraser are beyond all praise. Any man not possessed of his relentless determination to achieve his objective in full, regardless of all consequences, would have dropped his side charge alongside the target instead of persisting until he had forced his submarine right under the cruiser. The approach and withdrawal entailed a passage of 80 miles through the water which had been mined by both the enemy and ourselves, past hydrophone positions, over loops and controlled minefields and through an anti-submarine boom."

He was also awarded the Legion of Merit of the United States of America.

After the war, he formed Universal Divers Ltd with ex frogmen and colleagues, pioneering the application of wartime underwater skills to the commercial field.

There were often two official parades per day and the cadets could become quite mischievous.

"I recall one instance where the Parade Marshall, a retired cavalry officer, was on horseback. Imperiously he addressed the squad outside the Waterloo Hotel in Bettws y Coed. 'Look here - you chaps. Let's have no

nonsense - heads up - shoulders back, and no slouching.' Such talk from a rank outsider (and a soldier to boot) was quite unacceptable and we soon had a plan to make his afternoon miserable. The Parade Marshall ordered us away. As the senior service, Conway's band and marchers were at the head, followed by the infantry from Trawsfynydd, a contingent from RAF Valley and various scouts, guides, firemen etc,. With a mighty 'thump-thump-thump' from the Conway bass drum, our contingent stepped smartly away marching quickly and with long strides, which soon took us a hundred yards ahead of the rest of the parade. The Parade Marshall galloped up shouting 'slow down - slow down!' Our band master reduced the tempo and the lads took very short steps, reducing progress to a crawl. Soon the rest of the parade bunched up until they were almost marking time. The Parade Marshall, seeing the situation, again rushed up to us shouting 'speed up - you're holding things up.' Promptly, the Conway contingent increased tempo and stride and again were soon many yards ahead. And so it went on the Parade Marshall quite unable to maintain an even speed in the parade because we decided he was to have a difficult time."

Refreshments were provided after each parade, a boon for the starving cadets.

"Volunteer ladies in some chapel schoolroom or village hall provided refreshments and I recall the cadets rushing into one schoolroom and grabbing several plates of sandwiches and elbowing others aside. Being a Welsh speaker I heard one lady remark to another in Welsh — 'Dewcs - mae nhw fel anifeiliaid' - 'Blimey - they're like animals.' We were in fact always ravenously hungry because the food on the old Ship was poor and very scarce. The Crossville Motor Bus Company would then take us to another town, Llandudno or Colwyn Bay, where we would again march and then we would be taken back to the pier at Bangor where the motorboats would come and take us back to the Ship."

The 'heavy weather' cutter's crew remained in use during bad weather when the motorboats had been hoisted for safety.

"There was one occasion when disaster nearly struck one dirty Saturday evening in September. The Padre who had been ashore and was seen on the end of Bangor pier and the order 'Heavy weather cutter away' was given. We donned our oilskins - heavy black tarred garments unlike today's light materials and leapt in turn into the bouncing cutter which had been lying to the boom and which was now alongside the gangway. The cadet captain in charge called 'Let go forrard, Let go aft' and the cutter corkscrewed away from the Ship's side. 'Oars-down, Give Way Together.' The Ship was pointing into the strong wind and tide and Bangor pier was a quarter of a mile astern of the Ship. The wind and tide sped us on and in no time we were rounding to come alongside the head of the pier. The tide was shortly past being full and the ebb was gaining strength so it would entail a hard pull back to the Ship. The cutter was swept past the pier but strong strokes brought us slowly to the floating pontoon where the Padre stood lashed by wind and rain - there was no shelter here. He leapt smartly into the stern sheets and was helped by the cox'n to sit, as it was impossible to stand in the heaving boat. Soon we were away from the pier and leaning to our oars but we made no headway at all. It soon became apparent that we could not defeat the wind and tide and it was decided to make for the Anglesey side where the tide would not be as strong and where there might be some shelter. In the middle of the strait there were four-foot white horses with their tops whipped into sheet spray. We rowers had our backs to this freezing horizontal onslaught but the coxswain faced it as he steered the cutter over to the opposite shore yet keeping the boat from broaching-to and possibly being thrown over. Eventually we crabbed across and headed for the relative safety of the Gazelle slipway. At the head of the slip lay the Gazelle pub, now deserted in the gathering gloom. 'Stand by bowman - get ashore as soon as you can and take the bow rope with you and make fast.' The starboard bowman crouched ready to leap as instructed; the cutter was drifting astern quickly. He leapt onto the seaweed-covered slip and lost his footing letting go of the bow rope. Frantically he tried to retrieve it but the cutter drifted away from him

taking the bow rope too. Suggestions were made to run the boat ashore but the water on the shore edge was a boiling cauldron and it was judged to be safer in the main stream. A cable length downstream a coaster was anchored, its cable taught against the fast flowing ebb. The cox shouted – 'Ahoy there - coaster!' All joined in the shout but there was no sign of life. We rowers felt tired and discouraged but we felt that if we could tie up to the coaster we would be safe. As we passed slowly, driven astern despite our rowing desperately, a figure appeared on the coaster and seeing our predicament, disappeared and reappeared with a heaving line, which he hurled towards us. It fell short and our cox shouted to him to make it fast to a lifebuoy and float it down to us. However, by the time he had attempted this we were well past and before long we were opposite Gallows Point near Beaumaris and we could see in the distance a haze of spume and breaking white water. This was the Dutchman's Bank, the sand bank of the Lavan Sands, which extends from the mainland shore out nearly to Puffin Island. As the ebb progressed, more of the sandbank was exposed. We were now feeling quite apprehensive and thoroughly exhausted. Night fell quickly; no lights showed because of the blackout, the land became just a darker shade than the boiling seas.

"Suddenly, there was a shout from one of the stroke oarsmen – 'Look cox - there's something coming towards us!' Sure enough the crashing bow-wave of a vessel grew closer from the direction of the sea and it was apparent that it would pass about a hundred feet from us. 'All together lads - all shout like mad' shouted the cox against the howling wind. This we enthusiastically did and the vessel could be seen altering course towards us. It was a fast patrol vessel of some 50 tons, which was making for its base at Menai Bridge because of the atrocious conditions at sea. Soon, we were alongside and passing our bowline to eager hands and slowly it tautened as the vessel moved forward. Oars had been stowed inboard and we were slowly towed back up the strait towards the Conway with the bow of the cutter rising high and falling into the troughs throwing sheets of stinging water over us.

"Whilst we had been warmed with rowing we were now rapidly becoming very chilled. The now idle rowers relieved the Padre, who had been bailing water from the stern sheets with a small bucket. The big bulk of the Conway appeared out of the gloom and soon we were alongside the gangway where willing hands leapt into the boat to assist in making fast. One by one we watched our opportunity and leapt aboard and gratefully entered the lower deck, our oilskins dripping. We learnt afterwards that Captain Goddard and the officers had been very worried but as there was no means of communication to the outside world they just hoped for the best. Soon we were tucked in our hammocks after hot drinks; in the morning we were summarily dismissed as heavy weather cutter crew and replaced by another lot of cadets. The bow oarsmen who had leapt ashore on the Gazelle slip had sought refuge at the pub; the landlord let him bed down on a settee in the bar."

1945

As the war came to an end the number of cadets rose to 250.

"I was on the main deck when the announcement of victory was made. We let out a cheer that was taken up by others and immediately the whole Ship's company knew of the victory. We were given 48 hours leave and on VE Day were sent ashore."

At least 166 Old *Conways* were killed. Honours awarded during the Second World War included a

Dressed Overall for VJ Day

Victoria Cross, a George Cross, 22 DSOs, 40 OBEs, 99 DSCs, 2 MCs, 4 AFCs and 20 DFCs. 11 million tons, or 60% of British shipping had been lost. Over 25% of the men in the Merchant Navy lost their lives, and proportionally, casualty rates were higher than in any of the armed forces.

With the war over the Ship's white lines could at last be restored. They had been blacked out in 1939 so that reflections couldn't help enemy planes find the Mersey. On 'victory In Japan, VJ Day' the Ship was dressed overall.

1945 July

Mr. Browne returned, invigorated from wartime service in the RAF. He had struggled since first joining the Ship to redress the imbalances between nautical and academic studies. The uniformed officers' primary concern was technical naval training. The academic masters were supposed to be concerned with general education and were given short shrift if they interfered in technical matters. Differences were exacerbated with officers living in the Ship, whilst masters lived ashore and came aboard only for lessons. Tensions were inevitably underscored by the fact that the Captain Superintendent was in overall command and naturally inclined to nautical rather than academic matters. Although these differences were kept from public view, the cadets, probably sensing the priorities, did not accord academic studies or masters the same status as nautical subjects and officers. When the Headmaster re-joined, he was allocated a residential cabin in the Ship and so became a much more influential part of the daily routine. Educational standards had greatly improved but he knew more could be achieved. He promptly picked up where he had left off. He established gym classes, a drama group, music society and Scout Group. Proposals for Deep Sea Scout Group though were rejected by the Captain Superintendent. Within a few months Browne bounced back and formed an orchestra, who held their first rehearsal on 22nd September.

1946

The new pinnace motorboat was delivered to the Ship by sea from Birkenhead, a gift from Alfred Holts. Before the war they had a vessel, the *Glengarry*, being built in Copenhagen. When the Germans invaded they commandeered her and fitted her out as the armed merchant raider *Hansa*. At the end of hostilities, she was reclaimed by Holts. The pinnace was with the ship but superfluous to

Navigation Exercises in The Pinnace

Holt's needs so they donated her to *Conway*. The pinnace was one a class of small launches used by the Kreigsmarine. Capital ships like *Bismarck* and *Graf Spee* carried two or three, even small vessels like minesweepers might carry one.

"There was a plate on the engine room bulkhead, which said, in German, that it had a capacity for 85 persons in fresh water. It was possible to see where lifting points were fitted so she could be lifted on davits."

Timed in both directions over a measured mile between Gallows Point and near the Gazelle, her speed was 11.5 knots. She was to be a very welcome addition to *Conway's* trio of motorboats. The two motorboats were the long suffering workhorses; the water boat had her dedicated and vital role, now the pinnace provided a greater carrying capacity and power. She was fitted with a small binnacle and used for navigation lessons. The pinnace, like all *Conway* boats was to suffer many and varied indignities at the hands of cadets over the next 30 or so years. 'Each motor boat had a bowman and sternman to handle lines, and a coxswain in charge. The 'official' boats crew coxswain was always a cadet captain but during practical classes even the most junior cadet could find themselves taking charge of a boat. A cadet was also assigned as the engineer to nurse the engines, the term engineer being used somewhat advisedly! Crewing these boats was a sought after privilege. It meant you could be away from the Ship and the watchful eyes of cadet captains, officers and staff for long periods. It presented opportunities to get ashore and always for an illicit smoke. The boat's cadet captain as part of the crew, and so the ringleader of all activities, legal and otherwise, did not count as external authority. The crews were fully responsible for their boats and passengers in all weathers and conditions. Cadets quickly learned valuable, lifelong lessons about boat handling, teamwork, responsibility and most importantly, the creative interpretation of rules.

1946 Summer

"One fine summer's morning I was happily coxing the Juice Barge to Bangor for a refill of water. We all had our little ways of coxing but mine was full ahead/stop, followed immediately by full astern (and prayers). On this particular morning we approached Bangor pier at full ahead until I could see the whites of its eyes, and was receiving nervous and reproachful glances from the bowman. With a carefree flourish I ding-a-linged 'Stop' and was about to follow this with a hearty 'full astern' when, with sinking heart, I heard the bloody engine

stop running. No room to turn - either run up the beach or hit the pier. The pier won and we hit one of the vertical supports with a crashing crack I can still hear in bad moments of memory recall. The pier still stood, the barge did not sink, the bowman caught the side as he was being projected overboard and the engineer got burned as he flew over the overheated engine (serve the b.....d right too). So, all was well, and when the crew pulled me off the engineer, we tanked up and blithely returned. Alas Spooky had been watching our shenanigans through the main entrance telescope and I was summarily dis-rated (only temporarily) and left to stand on the quarter deck as a dreadful warning to other coxes with fast and loose ideas of seamanship."

HM The King Inspects Cadets 1946

During 1946, the Board Of Admiralty decided that the Captain Superintendent of *Conway* (along with those of two other training ships, *Arethusa* (now displayed at the South Street Seaport Museum in New York) and *Mercury* (now restored as *Gannet* in Chatham Royal Dockyard) would, from then on, be granted the honorary rank of Captain RNR.

"On cessation of hostilities, we had to give up use of Bangor City Football Club's ground and use our other field on Beaumaris Common instead. This was a two mile walk from the Ship, which, with changing into football kit, meant an hour and a half from the time of leaving the Ship until a game had started. The disused Victorian gaol, complete with treadmill and condemned cell, were our changing rooms. You had to be careful to leave the cell doors open as they had snap locks - you can imagine the rest. In the summer the pinnace would tow us round to Beaumaris Pier in the cutters, which saved a long walk as buses were out of bounds."

Eventually better facilities were found at Baron Hill on the Bulkeley Estate above Beaumaris.

"Memories of my time onboard? The whole Ship's company diving over the side, some from the nettings, in a swimming race to the Anglesey shore. Practising the pipes on the stern walk and being asked to move to the starboard side (away from the captain's office), mountaineering teams setting off for a weekend at a stretch, sailing as a crew in the local yachts (Dragons and Menai Strait class), the excellent Chinese cooks, the Welsh 'Quarters' char (Mrs Mop to all) who rode a bicycle around the lower deck, and many more memories – all pleasant."

1947-48

England was still recovering from the Second World War so many items were still rationed.

"From memory we were allowed one pot of jam per month, eight ounces of butter between six. Some food arrived cold. One night I found a wire scourer in my cabbage and on complaining was told that I needed the iron."

A song popular with the cadets went,

"The Conway's the pride of the Blue Funnel Fleet, Plenty to do and ---- all to eat !"

The food became so bad that it was decided to bring this into the open by organising a strike for better meals.

"When it became time to hoist all boats up to their night positions, which required all the Ship's company, we all pretended to lay on the ropes without pulling, even the cadet captains were in on the plot and continued to shout the usual orders. Finally, when the situation became obvious, we were assembled and kept at attention until the officers were informed of our reasons. It was agreed that the matter would be examined and the food improved on condition that our action was never to be repeated. Sadly, the small improvements made did not last long."

"Another cadet and I decided that we would go for a midnight row in the small skiff, which was hoisted above the gangway each night. We crept onto the gangway and carefully lowered the skiff as quietly as possible. To us it sounded very noisy as the ropes and derrick creaked. Finally in the water we had forgotten the bung so we hastily and loudly stamped the bung in whilst the water flowed in. Casting off we glided with the current until we were about 50 yards astern of the Conway. At this point a ghostly apparition appeared on the gangway and a voice echoed 'Skiff come back immediately.' Unfortunately for us it was Captain Goddard resplendent in dressing gown. We returned quickly and were to report to the Captain's cabin next day where we were quizzed about our joy ride. We were given some punishment but not too severe and survived for other adventures."

1947

"I took part in the cross strait swim. We started in the car park at the root of Bangor pier at high water slack. We ran down the slip and swam alongside the pier with one's supporters cheering you on, to the finish

line at the top of the Gazelle slip. The winner in 1947 was a Bermudan boy called Harry Lancaster. He was a marvellous swimmer and his swallow dives off the poop rail were great to watch. As far as safety was concerned, we were escorted by the cutters and the emergency boat."

1947 Summer

"In my day the Summer Term Prize Giving was the great occasion attended by Parents and the Great and the Good of the Shipping World. The Right Honourable S. Barnes, MP, Minister of Transport presented the prizes."

Prizes included the King's Gold Medal, the Trinity House Prize of a telescope and aneroid, the Mercantile Marine Service Association watches for the greatest proficiency in all branches of training and education, the Derby Prize for the Management of Boats, the Royal Indian Navy Prize for Rule of the Road (an aneroid), the Langton Prize for Practical Navigation and Nautical Astronomy (a telescope), the Hon Company of Master Mariners' Prize for Nautical Astronomy (prismatic binoculars), the McIver Prize for Seamanship (an aneroid), the Dodd Prize for Proficiency in Engineering and Science (a sextant) and The Drew Cup, presented by Mrs Drew in memory of her son, lost in HMS E14. There was also the Moody Cup for Boat Sailing presented by relatives of J.P. Moody, lost in the RMS *Titanic*, the Harley Shield, presented by Mrs Harley in memory of Lieutenant W.R. Harley RN, killed in a flying accident. The Marconi Prize, presented by the Directors of the Marconi International Marine Communication Co Ltd, for Sound Signals in The Morse Code, was a Broadcast Wireless Receiving Set.

The Focslemen's Derby was resurrected for the new chums. In earlier years it had been called The Obstacle Race.

"As a humble new chum I well remember it, my term were the unwilling entrants. The derby was held towards the end of term and received the tacit approval of the duty officers as they must have been well aware of what was going on. Without the option, the new chums were assembled wearing gym gear, one evening at the after end of the orlop deck. The course extended along the port side of the orlop deck, across to the starboard side at the Foretops, back along the starboard side to Starboard Focsle, down the after stairs to the tunnel, along the tunnel and into the hold where the course ended. The jumps consisted of sea-chests at intervals along the deck, arranged so that the runners had no option but to jump over them. The Ship's company lined the route, equipped with teasers and ropes' ends, which they liberally applied to encourage greater speed and participation from the new chums. The piece de resistance was the final jump at the end of the tunnel. A gym mat was held up by two cadets each side, obscuring a yak tub full of water placed such that everyone jumping over the mat would land in the yak tub and receive a soaking. In the narrow tunnel it could not be avoided. It was a mean spirited occasion and, I believe, was the first derby held for a number of terms, there being a certain degree of fallout following previous events. It may have been the last to be held aboard the Conway, certainly no more were held in my time (I left in Summer Term 1949)."

1947 Winter Term

"In my second term, I was bowman on No 2. She had a small diesel engine, which was a devil to start from cold. We had to use heating plugs, small cardboard tubes like a half smoked cigarette. We put a match to these until they were smouldering and then screwed them into plugs in the cylinder head. After a few minutes we swung the starting handle with the compression lever open and when enough speed had built up, we closed

the lever, and hopefully she would fire and run. You had to judge the timing right, too soon and she was too cold, too late and the heating plug had gone out and we had to begin again. This was the winter term, January to Easter, and it may have been better in the summer. I seem to remember trying to smoke one of the starting tubes, but although it looked like a ciggie, it tasted even worse than the Turf and Bar One ciggies, which were all we could afford. But at least we had an excuse for carrying matches! She was steered with a proper wheel, whereas No. 1 had tiller steering and a petrol engine. No 2 was also a lot smaller and much easier to hoist at night. The pinnace was usually moored at the starboard boom at night and the juice barge lay alongside the port midships or, if the weather was bad, out on the port boom."

1948 Spring

Every part of the Ship was the responsibility of one of the tops. They cleaned it, maintained it and effectively 'owned' it. Convention demanded that 'visitors' from other tops had to ask for permission before entering or crossing any space. This meant calling out 'Deck please,' 'Hatch please' etc., as appropriate at every unmarked boundary. Once one of the 'owning' topmen had granted permission, you could proceed, but the owner might first demand some forfeit like a song or recitation. Even a short journey could be a trial, as a typical trip to empty the yak tub *(rubbish bin)* for Port Focsle cadets illustrates. First it had to be dragged up the steep hatchway ladder from the orlop deck to the lower deck, having requested 'Hatch please' of the appropriate cadet. Then 'Deck please' to move from the hatch onto the lower deck, then 'Hatch please' to step onto the main hatch for a double haul up two decks, then 'Deck please' to gain the upper deck. The final request was 'Tunnel please' to get into the tunnel to empty the tub. The whole process was repeated in reverse to return to the safety of port Focsle on the orlop deck. This arcane ritual continued in modified from up to the closure.

Should one wish to dispose of some article such as a magazine, or spare slice of bread, it was the custom to call out *"Quiz"* (Who). The first person to respond *"Ego"* (I) would be awarded whatever was being disposed of.

1948.

"Climbing out along the yard just beneath the Maintop was accomplished by standing in a rope slung beneath the yard, the 'horse' I believe it was called, and holding onto a metal rail secured on the foreside of the yard just below top centre. At the end a stay from the mast above could be usefully held on to. Anyone falling would have probably bounced off the bulwarks overboard, or more fortunately fallen straight into the sea or unluckily into a passing cutter or motorboat. There was a cadet in my term who Captain Hewitt referred to as 'the monkey man.' It was his wont to walk out along the yard and stand at the end, and he habitually wore boots. He was said to have stood on the truck, although I did not witness this. His nickname was 'Boris Trotsky.' Boris had the reputation of being bolshie, he was certainly eccentric but was a very nice fellow. Extremely tough, people did not mess about with him but I never knew him say a bad word about anyone or harm others in any way."

Members of the band wore a badge on the left sleeve of their reefer uniform, a castle enclosed in a laurel wreath.

"As a new chum I lusted after one and dreamed of going home at the end of my first term wearing the super little badge and holding my left arm at a slight angle so that it would be readily visible to be admired.

Accordingly, I enrolled to learn to play the bugle in order to join the Band and gain that badge. Learning to play wasn't too difficult as there were only five notes to blow, but learning all the bugle calls I found to be extremely taxing. By some stroke of misfortune I was appointed as Duty Bugler before I was quite ready for my debut. Shortly after the afternoon watch began, Mr. Crockett, the duty officer, told the cadet captain to call away No 1 motorboat. I knew this call and performed quite adequately. He then ordered 'Boathands' to be called. 'Whistle it please,' I asked the cadet captain. He did so, and I blew the bugle. To my surprise and relief, boathands appeared. Things seemed to be going well. Call 'Working Party' said Mr. Crockett, 'Please whistle it,' I asked the cadet captain, He did so and I repeated it on the bugle. A group of irritated Mizzentopmen appeared. 'Call away Maintopmen,' said Mr. Crockett. 'I'm not bloody whistling it said the cadet captain' who then told Mr. Crockett I didn't know the call. 'Well tell him to call away the Foretopmen,' which the cadet captain announced I didn't know either. 'Well what call does he know?' asked Mr. Crockett looking slightly peeved. 'Slack Party, Sir.' 'Well call away Slack Party.' So I did, eight times that afternoon. No one else got a look in and I had to swear the Messenger to secrecy, otherwise they would have lynched me."

"There was a cadet named Minter, who climbed to the end of the bowsprit (quite a normal activity, in fact we used to climb down and sit on the figurehead on Nelson's head). Sitting at the end of the jib-boom at the end of the bowsprit, Minter offered to jump in and swim to the guest-warp (a rope suspended around the hull just above water level for boats to secure to and for cadets who fell in to hold-on to whilst awaiting rescue), provided that everyone watching gave him half-a-crown. Being sufficiently encouraged he duly jumped, but I don't think he collected many half crowns; five shillings a week pocket money wouldn't allow for such gestures, even for the pleasure of seeing Minter leap off the bowsprit."

1949 Easter Term

There were 275 cadets onboard, the highest complement ever. There was a large intake so the quarterdeck division was formed of surplus new chums. Mike Llewellyn was appointed their senior cadet captain. 'His' new chums won the Hobson Cup for the best maintained part of the Ship. They were responsible for the 'holy ground' on the quarterdeck, situated at the after end of the lower deck. The Quarterdeckmen not only hand-scrubbed this section of the deck, but holystoned it with small hand held holystones. It came up so well the Quarterdeckmen decided to holystone the whole of the adjacent deck, for which they were responsible.

"Quite soon one could see where our responsibility ended and the Mizzentopmen's began. Ironically, Captain Hewitt advised against the practice because he thought it might wear out the teak decking, quite apart from annoying the Mizzentopmen who were not much inclined to holystone anything."

"Each Mess was issued with cutlery, mugs and water tumblers for twelve cadets at the commencement of term. Broken or vanished items were not replaced until the following term. It was not unusual towards the end of term to be reduced to eating a roast dinner with the aid of a spoon. Those unfortunates who had to wait to use someone else's mug might be left with only the dregs from the tea pot. This could be circumvented by drinking tea from either the mess sugar basin or the mess butter dish once their contents had been distributed. The sugar basin was preferable, being deeper and usually containing a residue of sugar. The butter dish was a last choice, being rather shallow, easily spilled and usually somewhat greasy."

Every cadet about to complete his training had to choose the shipping company he wished to join. An 80 page booklet 'What Company Shall I Join?' existed to provide advice on the 37 most popular companies. Each was described in terms of its fleet, types of trade, ports, length of voyages, application process, terms of employment, wages and premiums, accommodation, approach to training and promotion prospects. The Captain Superintendent would also advise cadets, giving them an insight to life in different companies rather than just the basic facts. He could also help match the cadet's temperament and abilities to an appropriate company. Cadets were allowed to apply to only one company at a time, but if the first choice had no vacancies they could opt for a second choice.

"It always seemed to me that Blue Funnel with its midshipmen offered the very best of training to prospective deck officers. A unique shipping company in so many ways, self insured it was said, with the course lines inked in on the charts so that in the event of disaster another Blue Funnel ship would arrive in support within three or four days along the same course, even a hostel for the middies at Liverpool when leaving or joining a ship. I sailed with a number of ex Blue Funnel middies and they were usually a cut above the average. It is reasonable to say that Alfred Holt's was the preferred shipping company at the Conway in 1949. Captain Goddard tried to persuade my mother Blue Funnel was a better choice than the Union-Castle, and I have no doubt that in terms of cadet training he was perfectly correct. However, they didn't trade much to South and East Africa and they didn't possess a fleet of beautiful lavender hulled ships!"

Tom Goddard, in his last few terms, frequently took prayers at evening quarters.

"He possessed a wonderful speaking voice, which resounded around the lower deck. The small speech idiosyncrasy added to, rather than detracted from his delivery. Particularly impressive (especially on a winter's night after a long spell of boat-hoisting, with a force seven blowing, the old Ship quietly creaking, and her movement perceptible in the slight swaying of the ranks of the opposite watch) was his rendering of the doom-laden words of Ecclesiastes chapter 12, verses 1-8. 'Remember now thy Creator in the days of thy youth..........Vanity of vanities, saith the preacher: all is vanity.'"

One cadet could not settle in the Ship and absconded with considerable skill.

"He used the light two-oared skiff, which at night was hoisted on a simple purchase by the gangway. He got up in the night, lowered the skiff, rowed to the pier and legged it into the dark. Eventually, his parents brought him back. After the third repeat escape it was rumoured that Captain Goddard suggested sarcastically to his parents they might like to buy the skiff."

Two other absconders found their way to Ireland, while two more were found camping out on the Wirral.

This was the last term at Bangor but, before we can move forward to the Summer of 1949, we should understand why everything was about to change again.

CHAPTER 18

1945–48 A TIME FOR DIFFICULT DECISIONS

At the end of the war *Conway's* management committee faced three difficult questions:

- Whether to remain in Bangor or return to the Mersey?
- Who would replace Captain Goddard who was due to retire?
- How to adapt courses and the curriculum to meet the shipping industry's changing needs?

Their decisions would shape *Conway's* future for many years

A Long Term Home

By 1945, the cadets who had experienced life on the Mersey had left so all cadets now viewed Bangor as their natural home. However, some members of staff and the committee had an enormous emotional attachment to the Mersey and, with the war over, they assumed the Ship would return to her proper place there. For others, Bangor and the strait had proved to be a better location, despite the more exposed nature of the mooring. Sailing and boating opportunities were improved, the strait was a healthier place than Liverpool and access to the mountains had proved extremely popular. Regular ship visits to the Mersey provided an adequate if not ideal replacement for the busy maritime activity of the Rock Ferry mooring. Along with these emotional ties there were other, more compelling, reasons for making long term decisions about the future.

The demand from shipping companies for cadets was at an all time high and was expected to increase. With 250 cadets the Ship was already at her capacity and 26 cadets had to sleep ashore every night. Teaching space was similarly stretched. The Ship was not big enough and it was feared she would fail an imminent Board of Education inspection because of overcrowding. *Conway's* great rival *Worcester* was experiencing similar challenges. Prior to the war they had been given the *Cutty Sark* as extra accommodation and she had been moored near their ship. During the war, they had relocated to a shore establishment. By 1945, the *Worcester* (ship) was in a very poor condition, had lost most of her masts and only kept afloat by a large salvage pump. She was returned to the Admiralty but sank and broke her back in 1947. To replace her and *Cutty Sark, Worcester* acquired the faux three decked ship *Exmouth*. She looked like a wooden wall sailing ship but was built in 1904 of iron and steel and was 300 feet long. She had been purpose built as a cadet training ship and so had many improvements over the converted hulk previously used. With good headroom, proper classrooms, heating, lighting and staff accommodation she lacked the elegance of her predecessor, but was far more suitable for the purpose. Members of *Conway's* staff visited *Worcester* to compare notes.

Adding further pressure for change, the land based sanatorium and dormitory at Bryn Mel, and Bangor City Football Club's playing field had been loaned only for the war years and now had to be vacated.

The committee had been discussing these issues for some time but pressure was building. On 12th November 1945, the committee's secretary, Mr. Wilson, wrote dramatically to the Headmaster

"We must find another home for Conway."

He did not explain what he had in mind but there were four broad considerations:

- Should the Ship remain in the Menai Strait, or return to the Mersey where they already owned 12 acres of playing fields?
- Whether to replace the Ship with something larger and more modern, or to keep the Ship and supplement her with a second vessel to provide additional space?
- How to provide adequate shore based facilities, such as playing fields with direct access to the Ship, if they remained on the strait?
- The final and radical option was to replace the Ship solely with a shore establishment.

Captain Goddard and Mr. Browne were convinced that the strait was the best long-term home but would not countenance a purely shore based solution. They eventually won the day and Goddard recorded,

"It was agreed that if suitable fields could be found together with a shore establishment, the Ship would remain in the Menai Strait. I was instructed to search for such a place."

The committee did not rule out replacing the Ship and a number of potential replacement vessels were examined, including Scott's *Discovery*. Mr. Browne recorded that *Undine* and *Gamecock* were examined on 19th February 1946 but recent research shows *Undine* was a submarine and *Gamecock* an American clipper declared derelict in 1880! Doubtless there were other, as yet, undiscovered vessels of the same name. These alternative vessels were all judged unsuitable.

A number of potential shore bases were examined. On 21st January 1946 Browne and Goddard visited Treborth Hall, owned by Colonel and Mrs Davies. It was situated on the mainland between the Menai Suspension Bridge and Telford's Britannia Bridge, and had excellent buildings and grounds. Browne felt it

"suitable – good shape, additional out-buildings. Space for 100 boys. Good playing field."

However, it had a major drawback; the only direct water access was to the notoriously dangerous Swellies, which were completely unsuitable as a new mooring for the Ship. The alternatives of leaving the Ship at Bangor or finding a mooring further beyond the Swellies would leave the Ship too isolated from the shore establishment. Despite this, Goddard obviously felt Treborth Hall had potential because the committee meeting on 23rd January formed a Treborth Hall sub-committee including Captain Brown, Mr. Wilson and Mr. Heathcote. Thus emboldened the committee finally resolved to sell the Rock Ferry playing fields. Mr. Browne confided to his diary that this was an *"irrevocable step."* After seeking the requisite approval of the Minister of Education, the playing fields, sports pavilion and sanatorium acquired in 1904 and 1924 were sold on 17th June 1946 for £12,515. The Minister directed that the proceeds must be applied towards the costs of adapting the new premises at Anglesey. The Ship would be kept; there would be no going back to the Mersey.

The Treborth Hall sub-committee first met on 2nd February following which, on 12th February, Captain Goddard produced a *"scheme for bunks/wardrobe in units of two."*

By the 15th, the chairman Lawrence Holt was

"building up objections to Treborth to get the price down."

Later he would sweep aside all objections. On 19th February, Captain Goddard received a letter from Wilson saying Treborth was a complete white elephant although

"no reason given for this complete about face."

The next day Lt. Brooke Smith talked with Mr. Holt and Mr. Heathcote who implied a shore base was years away. Another letter followed on 25th saying the alterations required at Treborth were too expensive. He mooted the possibility of taking over *Indefatigable's* base at Plas Llanfair on Anglesey, adjacent to the Britannia Bridge. This seemed an unlikely option as *Indefatigable* had only rented the premises from the Marquis of Anglesey in 1944. Browne *"thinks chairman is against the general policy"* advocated by the Captain. This letter was clearly a shot across Goddard's bows because at the committee meeting on 28th February, Mr. Wilson said the expenses of Treborth were too great and the plans were abandoned.

Another property considered at the same time was Sir Richard Bulkeley's Baron Hill estate just outside Beaumaris on Anglesey and only a few miles from the Ship. Mr. Browne writes of his visit on 26th January 1946, with Captain and Mrs Goddard:

"Building in the hands of the military. Seven big rooms with panelling and plasterwork. Difficulties – heating, repair and decoration."

Its elevated position boasted breathtaking panoramic views across the strait to Snowdonia and the mainland. It would provide magnificent playing fields and Goddard eventually negotiated temporary use of the fields to overcome the loss of Bangor Football ground. Although close to the Ship, it was still divorced from the Gazelle Slip by the busy main road from Menai Bridge. With Treborth Hall disqualified, Baron Hill was revisited on 24th March. A case for its use was produced but in July it was still found wanting and firmly crossed off the list. A property called Craig-y-Don was considered but the 5th September committee meeting had concerns about

"the cost of levelling the site."

An un-identified property owned by Lord Penrhyn was also considered. Committee visits to both were arranged for 25th September. At the same meeting, the option of another vessel was resurrected because

"the committee realised that Conway would fail a Board of Education inspection due to overcrowding."

The Admiralty was approached and on 13th December 1946 they offered the free loan of the 350 ton schooner *Alk*

"if Conway can bear the cost of the refit - £2,000."

It was decided this was

"no answer to overcrowding"

and not pursued. By 31st October.

"Wilson despairs about the cost of Craig-y-Don, swing back to Penrhyn."

The Board of Education inspection eventually passed without incident on 14th March 1947. Fortunately, they were sympathetic to *Conway's* special circumstances and the attempts to find additional space. As the committee prevaricated, members of staff were becoming increasingly frustrated at the lack of a decision. The Government was approached for assistance with costs and, after initial negotiations, Mr. Browne thought the

"chance of a Government grant is good; possibly have to accept some 'free' boys (Direct Grant) but this we do now."

This hope was also to wither on the vine.

Meanwhile, behind the scenes, Captain Goddard had quietly been hatching a new plan, and on 18th December he broached it with Mr. Browne. They would move the Ship to Plas Newydd, the Marquis of Anglesey's estate further along the strait where they could also obtain extensive shore facilities.

"The idea was entirely his and he made the first contacts with our good friends the Angleseys."

Plans were obviously advanced because he and Browne visited the estate with the estate manager three days later on 21st December. Two thirds of the main house had been occupied by the United States Intelligence Corps during the war but they had now vacated it. Captain Goddard was immediately convinced.

"This part of the house, in wonderful condition, could accommodate 100 cadets and staff and provided excellent dining rooms, kitchens, etc. There were stables, which could be converted into classrooms, laboratories, gymnasium, etc. There was a boat dock, sports pavilion and playing field with ground suitable for more football fields and tennis courts. With Snowdonia only a few miles to the south, I thought the site and prospects ideal."

After further visits in January, Browne noted Goddard's *"extraordinary optimism"* for Plas Newydd. With the Marquis's agreement he took the plans of the house and grounds to *Conway's* management committee on 14th February 1947. The Captain Superintendent reported they were *"pleased."* Browne's diary records otherwise:

"Wilson seems to doubt not only Plas Newydd but the need for a shore base at all,"

considering it

"worse than Rock Ferry."

On 12th April, Browne, Goddard, Holt and Wilson visited Plas Newydd and a further obstacle emerged. The Marquis was concerned for his privacy and did not want to allow use of the dock or the main estate approach road, preferring *Conway* to build their own. Road access was easily resolved by agreeing use of a smaller, side entrance to the estate. By the end of April use of the dock remained unresolved. Browne feared

"Plas Newydd likely to slip away like Treborth. Intention seems to be to get engineers to show we couldn't afford it."

By 22nd May Wilson had reportedly *"gone off the Plas Newydd idea."*

The committee also

"wanted to know whether it was possible to take the Conway through the Swellies and if so, was there an anchorage with sufficient swinging room near the house. The anchorage would have to be near enough for a quick passage to the boat dock by motorboat but far enough to thoroughly exercise the cutter's crew when rowing."

We shall return to Captain Goddard's detailed planning and preparation; but suffice to say he became convinced a safe transit could be made. After 21 months of frustration, the committee met on 21st June 1947 to consider Goddard's proposals.

"I considered this (transit) possible and accordingly informed the Committee of Management and to enable them to come to an agreement over the house etc I also stated that after, a preliminary examination, I was sure of a safe anchorage."

He was amply supported by Mr. Browne who said a shore base was essential if they were to extend courses, and was highly desirable anyway. The committee accepted Goddard's assurances and decided the Ship would move to Plas Newydd but the debate raged for a little longer. As late as November 1947, the secretary to the committee was arguing that the Ship should remain at Bangor. Captain Goddard's son in law, then acting as his aide, recalls:

"He was finally instrumental in steering the committee in the direction of Plas Newydd."

The committee recommended that Plas Newydd be adopted subject to the negotiation of suitable terms. By late June, rent was set at £800 per annum for the use of part of the main house including the library, dedicated use of the stable block, use of various sports fields and the dock. This was an incredible bargain as the committee were spending £300 per annum on crockery – part of which cost was the cadets' end of term tradition of smashing all their mugs by throwing them down into the hold. On 26th November 1947, it was agreed that *Conway* would use

"part of the Plas Newydd mansion, a stable block, a wharf and parts of the grounds."

The die was finally cast. The Ship would be retained and moved to Plas Newydd. A shore establishment would be opened there to supplement Ship based accommodation and provide modern classrooms and playing fields. Despite these general agreements, it would be 12th October 1951 before the detailed lease was finally signed, over two years after Conway moved in!

A New Captain Superintendent

The war had placed considerable strains on Captain Goddard and he was not well. He was also approaching retirement and at the November 1947 committee meeting he confirmed he that he would stay

"I think about two years," enough time to see the Ship safely transferred to Plas Newydd and the shore establishment opened.

Prudently, the Committee had already begun to seek a replacement. Some hint as to the characteristics desired of the new man could be gleaned from previous appointments. The last three Captain Superintendents were Old *Conways* so the new man was likely to be the same, or at least to have experience in one of the other major training ships. for example Captain Goddard was an Old *Conway and* previously had been Captain of South Africa's *General Botha* training ship. The last three Captain Superintendents had been appointed after 27, 25 and 22 years service at sea so the new man would likely have been a cadet in the early 1920s, also ensuring a certain minimum of length of service available to command *Conway*. He would probably be an RNR officer, perhaps even Royal Navy. He might well have served as a *Conway* Officer. Mr. Browne's diary identifies a number of the candidates:

- Lt. Cdr. Horrey of the Royal Indian Navy's training ship *Dufferin*.
- Lt. Cdr. C. I. C. D. Lane, one of *Conway's* officers. Browne thought *"Holt has a fixed conviction that Lane not the right man for Captain"* whereas Browne thought *"he would be better than Goddard."*
- Hoyle, Chief Officer *Pangbourne* who later became Captain of TS *Mercury*.
- Whyatt from TS *Mercury*.
- Captain Eric Hewitt RD RNR (*Conway* 19-21) ex Royal Mail and with distinguished wartime service in the RNR. Captain Hewitt had actually been approached by committee member Sir John Nicholson as early as 1945, when Nicholson had been impressed by Hewitt's work in Singapore. However, Mountbatten asked Hewitt to join him in India which he felt obliged to do. Nicholson kept in touch and approached him again in India where Hewitt agreed to apply for the post.

Perhaps unsurprisingly, Hewitt was chosen and joined the Ship as Staff Captain in March 1948. Despite this title, he actually fulfilled the role of Chief Officer.

"When I joined on a year's trial on both sides, it came as almost as big a shock to me as it had done 30 years previously. To find myself in what had been Monty's cabin when I was a cadet, with somewhat primitive ablutions and oil lamps after 10 pm and grub not dissimilar to what I remembered as a cadet it was a bit of a jolt. I don't think it took me a week to decide what I wanted, and what made me decide was that the same spirit permeated the Ship that I had known as a cadet."

Of the staff he said *"No man could have a better team to work with."*

Curriculum Changes

Three things were forcing change on the shipping industry and so on *Conway*.

First, Britain's pre-eminence at sea continued to fade. In 1939, Britain operated just over 25% of the world merchant fleet tonnage. There were 1,869 vessels over 3,000 gross tons, a total of 12,233,920 gross tons, but this was still less than capacity in 1914. There were 197 shipping companies, down from the 300 or so in the late 1920s. They were organised into large 'shipping conferences,' essentially collaborations, which set freight rates and generally inhibited innovation and expansion. A myriad other pressures were impacting British shipping. As the Empire was granted independence, nations like South Africa, Ghana, Nigeria and India created and favoured their own merchant fleets over Britain's. These new navies naturally competed on other local routes so as British control over the India routes slipped, trade with Burma and China also reduced. In turn, other organisations like the Bengal Pilot service and the Royal Indian Navy, long recruiters from *Conway's* ranks, began to recruit their own nationals. The US Foreign Assistance Act essentially ensured that 60% of US cargoes had to be carried in US flagged

Capt E Hewitt RD RNR

and manned ships. Most of the Americas quickly followed suit to protect their own interests. Bilateral trade agreements restricting shipping arrangements began to proliferate and many foreign governments discriminated in favour of national flags and subsidised national companies. Britain suffered most from these changes. Although tanker trade was booming, burgeoning air travel meant passenger liners were disappearing, by 1948, only 22% of world capacity was British. To continue to attract the best boys, *Conway* had to ensure her cadets found preference for the decreasing number of places available with shipping companies. It was a case of adapt or die.

Secondly, the curriculum also had to keep abreast of technical changes like electric and hydraulic deck cranes replacing steam driven winches and derricks, the introduction of steel hatch covers, and the development of radar which was having a significant impact on navigation practices. The size and speed of ships was increasing, eg the size of the average pre-war tanker was 12,000 deadweight tons, this would leap to 37,000 deadweight tons by 1953.

Finally, and perhaps most importantly, the whole maritime industry was shifting to the view that boys should complete their academic education at normal state schools before starting pre-sea technical training. The School of Navigation at Warsash proved the trend. It opened to provide pre-sea training to boys *after* they had completed their academic education. Other local education authorities started to provide training for cadets and officers. The Merchant Navy Training Board (MNTB), set up in 1937, began to develop plans for future training. These trends threatened *Conway's* whole existence.

In 1939, Browne had attended a meeting in Nottingham to discuss the 'Rigidity of the Navigation Schools.' It convinced him that *Conway* training must change with the industry it served. The war years intervened but in 1945 he found a willing accomplice in Captain Goddard. They planned a two pronged attack. First, to maintain a steady flow of new entrants, and second to adapt training to the industry's evolving needs. Whilst they agreed on strategy, they did not always see eye to eye on tactics. In March 1947, Browne enthusiastically recommended a strengthened collaboration with Outward

Bound at Aberdovey, if only to secure access to their yacht the *Prince Louis*. Captain Goddard refused, he was a very pragmatic man and had little time for Kurt Hahn's 'ideas.' By way of compensation, he agreed a new regime for prep.

To ensure a steady supply of cadets, Browne began talks with several prep schools to see if he could encourage them to recommend boys to a course at *Conway*. By the end of September he noted:

> *"Clear that Conway would find favour with prep schools if it could take boys at 13½ to 14 for a 3 year course, put in Latin as alternative for entrance exam to French and Spanish."*

By the end of 1945, he produced a draught five-year plan for change, which included closer links to a number of feeder prep schools, opening a junior division (effectively *Conway's* own prep school), changing from School Certificate examinations to GCEs (being introduced nationally in 1951) and introduction of a three year course. He consulted the Minister of Education who recommended several changes to the plan and then, after consulting Lord Winster, the Minister of Civil Aviation, the Headmaster included an Air Training Plan.

The proposed changes would come at a price *Conway* could ill afford, so Browne enquired of the Ministry of Education about grant-in-aid conditions. This was followed soon after by an application to the Government for funding to assist a new shore establishment. The winter of 1946 and 1947 was very cold with heavy blizzards. In January, Mr. Browne struggled to a meeting with Mr. Heathcote, a committee member, to discuss the MNTB's plans for the industry only to be advised that they didn't know that themselves! On 22nd May, Mr. Browne had an important meeting with Lawrence Holt and Mr. Wilson.

> *"Wilson gone off the prep school ideas"*

and was even vacillating about Plas Newydd. Instead of the Headmaster's proposed three year course, Holt preferred a concentrated one year course under the auspices of the Ministry of Transport. On 30th May, with suspicious timing, proposals for shortened courses also came from Captain Wakeford of Southampton. Naturally Lawrence Holt was supportive and Browne was not. Wakeford's proposals were to fit into the MNTB scheme *(sic)* in order to obtain the full support of the industry and aid from the Ministry of Education on the technical side. Browne described the ideas as "vaporous" and glumly concluded:

> *"Plas Newydd most unlikely, then, as competition stiffens, lose cadets and sink back to the 1930s."*

The Headmaster stuck to his guns; a three year course was the right solution. In March 1947, it emerged that the percentage of cadets gaining an 'extra' *Conway* Certificate had fallen. This was attributed to a reduction in the standards of entry to meet the demands of the war years, to changes in staff in those same years and also to overcrowding. This substantiated Browne's stance that improvements to entry standards, training and a shore base were necessary, and, no doubt, disposed wavering committee members in his favour.

Lt. Commander Lane, a proud and enthusiastic member of staff, shared their desire for improvement. In 1939, he expressed a trenchant view of *Conway's* training.

"I feel very strongly that more attention should have been paid to explaining to cadets what life at sea was really like, what each grade of officer and each department actually did every day and, more importantly, how and why they did it. I can't remember a single occasion on which a captain or any other officer from a ship in Liverpool was invited to lecture to the cadets. Our own officers helped of course but they had often been away from ships for some years and were not always abreast of current developments. Visits and discussions with serving officers would have been of inestimable value. More visits should also have been arranged to the docks so that we could see things at first hand."

Whilst the introduction of ship visits had inadvertently addressed some of his criticisms, *Conway's* training had remained largely unchanged for a long time. The end of the war acted as a turning point for the industry. Life at sea was changing; the demands on a master mariner were changing; shipping companies and the whole industry were changing.

The newly appointed Captain Hewitt also wanted change. He proposed alterations to the Conway Certificate, recruitment of more boys from abroad and renaming *Conway* an Apprentices College. He was also most concerned that the syllabus remained relevant to shipping companies' needs and so began forging closer links with their Marine Superintendents. Their input was not always welcome.

"Elder Dempster would rather have a cadet after one term at Aberdovey than two at Conway."

Shaw Savill proposed shorter sandwich style courses, further fuelling the one, two or three year course debate.

Options were put privately to individual committee members to gain their support. Views became entrenched and discussions tense. Matters were to come to a head on 21st June 1947, at a committee meeting that was probably one of the most important in the Ship's history. They met to choose between a one or three year course and to make final decisions about the future of the Ship and/or a shore base. Dr. Mountford (Vice Chancellor of Liverpool University) and Mr. Magney (Director of Education for Liverpool) were invited to provide expert advice. Probably to Browne's surprise, they adopted his proposals. The final key decision had now been taken; a three year course would be introduced, not a one year course. However the decision was revisited several times and the three year course did not actually start until 1952. Reflecting the greatly increased capacity the shore establishment would provide, the Headmaster boldly suggested that cadet numbers should increase from 250 to 300.

The final piece of the mould, which would shape *Conway* for the next twenty-one years, was now in place.

CHAPTER 19

1949 THROUGH THE SWELLIES

In January 1948, with final objections overcome, Captain Goddard and Mr. Browne started detailed planning for transferring to Plas Newydd. Organising the new shore base seemed to fall mainly to the Headmaster, while Captain Goddard arranged the new mooring by the house, and the Ship's transit through the Swellies. This was all to be completed so that Plas Newydd could be occupied from September 1948. It actually took until April 1949.

Planning the Transit

It was not possible to take the Ship around Anglesey and to enter the strait from the Caernarfon end because the bar there was at least 4 feet too shallow. The Ship would have to be moved 5.3 miles from her mooring off Bangor pier along the narrow strait to Plas Newydd. Most of the transit was easily navigated; but the section between the two bridges, known locally as the Swellies, was fraught with potential dangers. The channel was extremely narrow, twisting and shallow for a ship of *Conway's* size. The Swellies had extremely unusual tidal conditions with potentially strong streams and unexpected eddies. Steep wooded slopes either side of the bridges meant winds were funnelled unpredictably through the space further complicating matters for a high sided vessel like the *Conway* under tow and with no means of independent propulsion. Admiral Lord Nelson described the Swellies as

> *"one of the most treacherous stretches of sea in the world"*

and no vessel remotely approaching her size had ever been taken through. The complexity of local tides meant that timing would be crucial to ensure enough depth of water for the Ship, so Captain Goddard decided that a survey of the Swellies and the potential mooring was necessary.

Captain Goddard can describe preparations in his own words.

> *"The Admiralty was approached with a view to undertaking the survey but unfortunately no vessel or surveying officer could be spared. Having had experience in hydrographical surveying, I undertook to do the work. I first ascertained that the Menai suspension bridge was 100 feet above high water ordinary springs and the Britannia tubular bridge 101 feet and, by striking my stump topgallant, the height of the masts above the waterline was 96 feet. But, as the Bridge heights were calculated on a Liverpool 29 feet tide and I reckoned on getting through on a 31 feet tide, I estimated 2-3 foot when I passed under the suspension and 3-4 under the tubular."*

The first issue was resolved; the Ship would just fit under the 2 bridges across her route!

He engaged the assistance of one of the masters, Mr. M Woods, Lt. Brooke Smith and several cadets, who *"did all the sounding by Douglas machine, handled the motorboat and did the tide recording. They all gave me valuable help."*

This small group first erected a number of marker beacons and then undertook a very detailed survey of the new mooring so that

"almost every tenth foot had a sounding."

The survey would have been an onerous task only possible around the short periods of high and low water slack. They worked mainly at weekends.

"No 1 motorboat took these officers down to Plas Newydd and embarked on a series of continuous soundings aided by a sounding machine clamped to the gunwale."

He made a chart of the mooring to a scale of 1: 2500. The extent of his survey of the Swellies is not clear; but a full survey would have been an enormous task, requiring far more resources than the small party allocated. There is no record of a wider body of cadets being engaged in this task so it must be assumed that the Swellies' survey was sufficient but far less exhaustive.

The planned transit of the Swellies consisted of a number of apparently simple legs, but each was fraught with difficulty:

- Passing under the Menai suspension bridge, the first leg was a gradual curve to starboard (the right) to pass through the 91 feet gap between Swelly Rock and Price's Point. The Ship's beam was 54 feet.

- A very sharp adjustment to port (the left) around Price's Point was then needed to stay in the very narrow channel. If the Ship swung too wide here she would be swept ashore on Gored Goch island.

- A fairly straight run followed between the mainland shore and the dangerous Cribben (Devil's Teeth) Rocks. This was the narrowest part of the channel, hardly wider than the Ship herself.

- Finally a slight adjustment to starboard would pass the Ship safely under the centre of the tubular bridge and out of the Swellies. Timing was critical to ensure sufficient depth of water over the Cheese Rock that sat right in the middle of the channel approaching the tubular bridge

He gradually evolved his approach.

"From the suspension bridge to Price's Point I anticipated no difficulty but then it was necessary to take a 4 point turn to port as soon as we cleared the Swelly Rock in order to get the tubular bridge transit beacons in line. On this transit I could run down to the narrowest part of the channel at the SW end of the Gored Isle where I would have 4 feet under my bottom and soundings showed there was a width of 84 feet between the 22 feet contours (Conway's draught aft) which, as the ships beam was 54 feet, would give me 15 feet clearance each side. In the Swellies, slack water occurs 1 hour 20 minutes before High Water and the stand of the tide at Extraordinary Spring Tides is 13 minutes, extending to 18 minutes at neap. At these former times streaming 9 knots in the Pinnace, I could not pass Price's Point when trying to make the passage to the South West from Price's Point to the of the end of the Gored Isle, so I consider the tide at half flood to be 10 knots."

Others recall *Conway's* fastest motorboats unable to make headway against these strong tidal streams.

Captain Goddard was well aware of the serious dangers he faced and of the many variables outside his control. But, as his knowledge of the Swellies increased, he became more confident that with a following stream, rising tide and good timing he could pass the narrowest and shallowest sections safely.

> *"To be safely towed through, the Conway would have to be at the Menai suspension bridge 1 hour 20 minutes before high water at the beginning of the stand of the tide and make the passage during the 13 minutes it lasted. I considered this possible and accordingly informed the Committee of Management. I think my experience as a hydrographical surveyor and the desperate need to get her through to open up the Conway Shore Establishment made me decide it was possible."*

Whether this 'desperate need' overshadowed other considerations is not clear. The senior local pilot Mr. Richard John Jones with generations of family experience of the strait behind him agreed.

> *"Given good weather, I am confident we can get the Conway safely to Plas Newydd,"* he said.

According to the daughter of Lt. Col. Davies (he owned Plas Talgarth, which had been seriously considered for the shore base), her father 'masterminded planning' for the transit. Davies owned Gored Goch island where he spent as much time as possible between April and October.

> *"He became an acknowledged expert on the Swellies, and used to give talks about them."*

He too thought the transit feasible. Not everyone was convinced, as Captain Goddard admits:

> *"It created a lot of interest amongst the North Wales seafaring fraternity, who had declared the undertaking to be a foolish one."*

The Cadet magazine records: *"the consensus of local opinion seemed to be on the pessimistic side ... it was decided to risk taking the Ship through the Swellies."*

The transit was a calculated gamble. It may have been possible to get her to Plas Newydd but no thought appears to have been given to the infinitely more complex task getting her back out again for her long overdue refit in Birkenhead.

Preparing the New Mooring.

Captain Goddard wanted the Ship to be moored off Plas Newydd so that in future, ship and shore based activities could be integrated seamlessly. A mooring had to be created as none existed. After a preliminary examination of the strait around Plas Newydd, he found a potentially safe anchorage in the stretch of water running north and south between the house and the small defunct slate port of Port Dinorwic. The Ship would have 44 feet under her keel at low water ordinary springs and a swinging radius of 396 feet.

"It afforded the facilities and distances we required and the heavily wooded bank on the Anglesey side gave excellent protection from westerly prevailing winds. This anchorage had one drawback but it had to be overcome. The nature of the bottom was rock and stones, bad anchoring and holding ground under normal conditions and methods."

He could not rely on anchors in this seabed so would bury four large Admiralty Pattern anchors in the shore instead. Two of these were the spare *Conway* anchors from the Ship, four tons each with huge wooden stocks. The other two were brought to Port Penrhyn from *Conway's* old mooring in the Mersey, along with the huge old mooring swivel. They were five ton Admiralty anchors, seventeen feet long with iron stocks. They had had their upper flukes and stock bent over so they did not protrude above sea level on the old Mersey mooring.

The mooring was planned in the form of a giant X. At the centre a series of three large mooring rings would connect via a two and a half inch sixty-three foot cable to a swivel. Two bridles connected the Ship to the swivel, which rotated allowing the Ship to swing with the tide without twisting the cables. From the centre, four arms of two and a half inch mooring chain cable stretched diagonally under water to the banks on either side of the strait. The shortest arm was 658 feet in length, the longest 1037 feet. At the end of each arm, an anchor would be buried midway between the high and low water marks. Each anchor would be backed up by an eight ton, five foot concrete cube buried inshore from it. The Ship's old anchor cables would be wrapped around the flukes to connect the anchors to the concrete blocks. The old Mersey anchors were placed in the mainland shore where they remain to this day. The anchors from the Ship were on the Anglesey side and were left with their flukes and stocks projecting six feet or so out of the ground. Local workmen prepared the concrete blocks but cadets dug the graves for the anchors by hand. They had to work quickly in the short period either side of low water.

"The cadets worked like navvies, often covered head to foot with mud until dark."

With ground prepared, the huge anchors could be transported individually from Bangor to the new mooring. This dangerous and difficult task was undertaken by the cadets using the Ship's boats, under the watchful supervision of Lt. Brooke Smith. Each Ship's anchor was suspended between two of the cutters in line astern, the anchor fluke was connected to the leading cutter, the anchor ring to the following cutter using four inch rope. Both boats were towed by the pinnace in line ahead. Counterweights were put in the opposite end of each boat to trim them. Smooth calm water was necessary when the anchors were being transported for the cutters had only about four inches freeboard and towing had to be steady. A cadet was stationed in each cutter, armed with a sharp axe ready to cut the anchors free if the cutters swamped. The weather was kind, but as the first anchor was taken through the Swellies the second cutter sheered around in a very worrying fashion.

"Fortunately, all other boats stopped when they saw us as their wash might have swamped the boats."

Once over the prepared grave, the axes swung in unison and the anchors dropped smoothly alongside their new homes. Released from the deadweight both cutters jerked upwards almost throwing their crews overboard! On the next day, the second Ship's anchor was moved but the counterweights were adjusted and the forward cutter very nearly swamped. Only furious rebalancing of the counterweights prevented a disaster. Then a coaster steamed past and

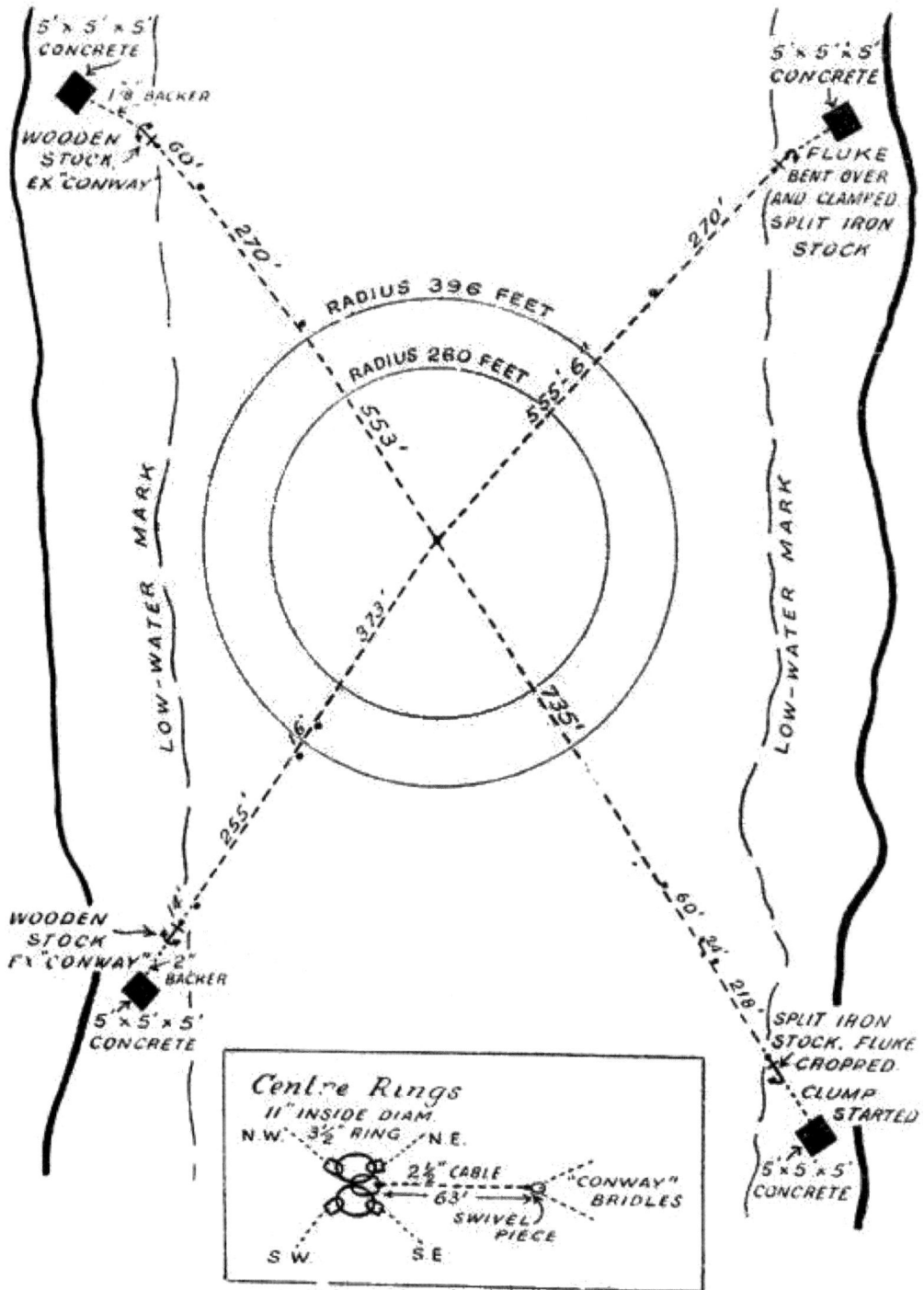

Plan of The Plas Newydd Mooring

Transferring The Mooring Cables

"there was some violent signalling until she slowed down."

Over the next two days the old Mersey anchors were brought safely through and positioned by their graves. These were transported on a platform constructed across two cutters lashed side by side as the 'in-line' method was proving too dangerous! With the aid of hydraulic jacks, the cadets manhandled the anchors into their graves. This careful treatment meant they could be recovered, one in 1968 by Lt. Brooke Smith and cadets using the same basic technique to lift it as he employed to plant it. It is now displayed proudly outside the Merseyside Maritime Museum in Liverpool. The second was recovered in 1987 by a team from the Seiont II Maritime Trust, led by an Old *Conway*, and now sits outside the Caernarfon Maritime Museum.

"It now remained to transport the cable and this was done by building a platform between the two cutters and flaking down on it two shackles each trip. On arrival these were dropped and shackled to the anchors and stretched along the banks between the high and low water contours to await the Liverpool and Glasgow Salvage Association's ship Ranger to connect it to more cable that she was bring from Liverpool."

The cable was also transported by the cadets. At the same time, to lighten the Ship to reduce her draught for the passage, a considerable amount of equipment was transferred by the cutters to Plas Newydd.

"I thought the world of Captain Goddard. The whole of my first term seemed given over to trans-shipping the mass of equipment necessary. These were our games periods during this term. Everything had to negotiate the Swellies, using a catamaran built from two 36 foot cutters, and this is not the easiest of tows. It did mean there was much less rowing in cutters until we were settled at Plas Newydd and the catamaran was turned back into two cutters! Filling the heavy platform with several shackles of chain makes it a very heavy displacement and ill-behaved tow."

Between the 4th-11th April 1949, the *Ranger,* under the charge of an Old *Conway*, Commander Smith RNR, completed laying the complex mooring. Goddard was well pleased with the outcome.

"When finished, with the four legs hauled taut, the centre mooring ring was only 30 feet north of the position I had anticipated it would be. All this work, with the exception of the Ranger's part, was done by the cadets under my guidance and indeed it was valuable experience to sling anchors between cutters, transport them to positions 6 miles away and through difficult water and such that in all probability, they will never do again in their sea careers."

The *Ranger* secured to the new moorings and stood by to transfer them to the Ship when she arrived.

The Transit.

"I decided to make the passage on April 12th 1949, when there was a 31 feet Liverpool tide."

At 8 am, two Menai Strait pilots, Mr. Richard John Jones and his son Mr. John Richard Jones, boarded the Ship. Two Liverpool tugs, the *Minegarth* and the *Dongarth* from the Rea Towing Co Ltd of Liverpool were in attendance to move the Ship. At 8.30 am pilot Richard John Jones moved to the forward tug *Dongarth*, which was under the command of Capt D Duff. The second pilot boarded the *Minegarth* astern. *"A gale was blowing and it was raining heavily despite which thousands of sightseers crowded vantage points on both sides of the Strait."* They were to be disappointed.

"Unfortunately, a strong south west wind was blowing that day and after several fruitless attempts by the tugs to get heaving lines aboard, I decided it was too risky to make the passage."

There were 3 more days during which the tides were right for the transit.

Captain Goddard recalled:

"April 13th was a 30 feet, 6 inch tide and a boisterous fresh wind blowing from the south west, but I decided to go."

Approaching The Suspension Bridge

It wasn't raining but he acknowledged:

"The conditions were far from ideal."

The tugs were secured to the Ship by 9 am *Dongarth* again forward and *Minegarth* stern to stern so she could steer the Ship. After a final discussion between Captain Goddard and the pilots in the *Conway* they returned to the tugs and the Ship let go her mooring. One of the cadets recalls the moment.

"A very clear memory is letting go the mooring off Bangor. Several tackles were used, the hauling part of the smallest heaved the next one an inch at a time so the next one came in a fraction of an inch at a time, and so on! It took an age and the biggest was a steel wire rope that was stoppered off with three chain stoppers, in the usual way. The mooring bitts were about six feet diameter and vertical so a loop of wire was being delicately laid around this when all three stoppers slipped, with a crack like a gun shot! I was perfectly placed to witness this! How many people were near at hand, I've no idea, but there were a great many but all so well placed it resulted in not one single bruise! It did make us far more careful with stoppers, and such like, because it seemed to take an age to pull the slack back in the several tackles for a fresh purchase!"

They got underway at 9:32 am, followed by a small flotilla of private boats and watched by thousands from the banks.

"The watching crowds cheered the vessel's progress through the strait."

Onboard the *Conway* were Captain Goddard and his wife, Captain Hewitt, officers and members of the crew and a BBC recording unit. That week's Radio Times carried a feature on the transit and one cadet described the event for the popular 'Children's Hour'. 14 cadets had remained onboard at the end of the Spring Term to help with final preparations, but as the Ship got underway one had gone ashore. Mrs Goddard realising there were now 13 cadets aboard insisted to her husband that one should take passage in a motorboat leaving a more auspicious 12 cadets aboard. Captain Goddard ordered several cadets off and into a boat. They must have departed looking crestfallen because they were allowed to return before the Ship reached Menai Bridge.

Above: Passing Under Scylla's Eyrie
Centre: Abreast The Platters
Below: Arriving off Plas Newydd

"We started off in the Pinnace and I'd felt so sick and so mad about this. I was on cloud nine, as soon as we climbed onboard I viewed everything through rose coloured spectacles."

Another cadet recalls:

"We boarded in time to see the impossible sight of Conway's masts squeezing under the bridge."

"I got under way two minutes late and this gave me twenty eight to get to the bridge. I had previously instructed the pilot on the tug to do this part of the journey in half an hour."

There was a strong head wind so the tug took forty minutes.

"By the time I was under the bridge, the ebb tide had commenced to flow. I think Odysseus had much the same feelings as I when he passed under Scylla's eyrie and with Charybdis waiting to do weird things with the tides. However, the bridge did not obstruct my main trunk, there being about three feet clearance, and I was soon abreast the Platters where we altered to close under the Gwynedd Bank before hauling out again to pass between Price's Point and the Swelly Rock.

"These two negotiated safely, there was a four point turn to port to get her on to the tubular bridge beacon's transit. Unfortunately, a squall on the port bow slowed the turn and the ebb tide took the Ship towards the Gored Island I signalled the tug to head over to port but for five minutes we were towed alongside the island, within five feet. However, we gradually got clear and at the beacon before the tubular bridge we had got over the transit line."

There is an element of dramatisation here as "five feet" from Gored Island would have taken the Ship straight onto Cribben Rocks! This slight diversion meant they also passed the Cribben Rocks with only 10 feet clearance to starboard. The final obstacle was the Cheese Rock, which they expected to pass with only four feet under the keel. Captain Goddard was not concerned,

"if she did ground … she would free herself on the flood … We alerted course for the centre of the south arch, passed under it with a good clearance and then into deeper water".

"Conway was the deepest draught-vessel, 22 feet aft, and the largest ever to have passed through the Swellies and I was glad when it was accomplished."

The Ship was safely through but it had been much more of a roller-coaster ride then expected. One of the cadets was

"very impressed by the behaviour of the tugs, one towed, and the other steered. I knew all about the perils of the Swellies, I'd heard all the frightening stories but again, due to lack of experience, did not appreciate the finer points of travelling through the narrower parts. However, squeezing such a large ship though such a narrow place was hugely impressive!"

Captain Goddard paid high tribute to the pilots and they were later presented with an engraved bowl as a token of *Conway's* esteem.

Long blasts from the two tugs heralded her leaving the danger area. As they passed the front of Plas Newydd the Marquis's standard dipped in salute.

"The remainder of the passage was uneventful and we were soon alongside the Ranger to take over the moorings. The time taken to pass through the Swellies was 18 minutes."

The whole voyage took one and a half hours.

Preparing Plas Newydd.

This was

"managed and supervised by Mr. A Wilson, the indefatigable Honorary Secretary who made a great success of it."

However, he was based in Liverpool, so much of the day-to-day work devolved locally. While Captain Goddard remained closely in touch with progress much of the local responsiblity for preparing Plas Newydd and organising shore based routine seems to have fallen on the Headmaster. A range of buildings and facilities had to be prepared.

Part of the main house (Plas Newydd) was to be converted into small dormitories for a hundred cadets, with two tier wood panelled bunks and personal lockers, ablutions, a sick bay, staff cabins, a galley and a large mess deck. The Marquis agreed that *Conway* could use his library. A tannoy system would be fitted throughout and a telephone exchange was to be installed. The nearby stable-garage block was to be given over entirely to *Conway* as a gym, labs, classrooms and staff accommodation. Initially it was agreed the two buildings would be named Cook and Ruthven, but these were subsequently changed. *Conway*'s portion of Plas Newydd would be the Nelson Block (colloquially called The House) and the stables the Kelvin Block. The Liverpool architectural practice of Gornall, Kelly and Partners was chosen to produce detailed plans with Kelly directly involved. Initial dormitory design could accommodate only eighty-eight cadets, so a committee member suggested

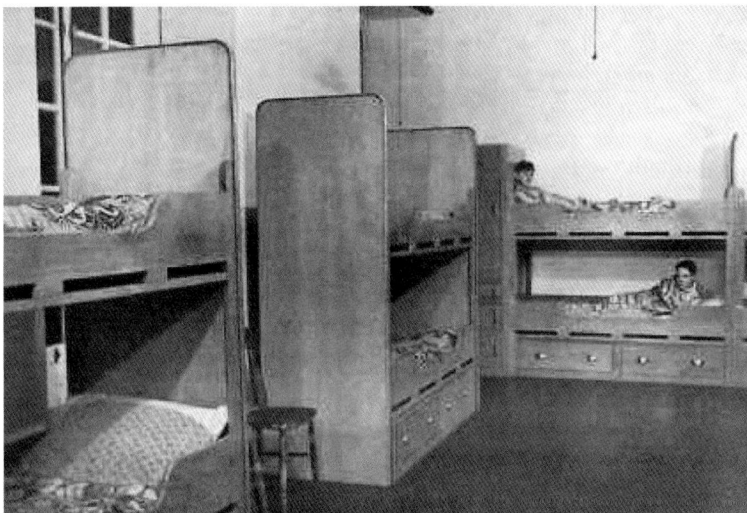

Bunks at The House

The Dock

"throwing out bathrooms and using the gym as sleeping place."

Even the Chairman Mr. Holt joined into the fray with specific ideas about how the shore establishment should operate.

"Chairman wants simplicity with spirit of hospitality."

Browne demurred,

"when he goes to the length of having buckets instead of showers."

The shore establishment would not be allowed to become too comfortable compared to the Ship!

The Marquis's private tidal dock and slip was to be organised for use by the cadets along with use of a large room for seamanship, a bosun's locker and loft. A number of davits were to be installed, and a binnacle. The sea water swimming pool was to be renovated and the small changing rooms turned into a navigation room. With the help of the cadets, Captain Goddard made plans for the necessary alterations.

"These were effected and the dock is indeed a valuable addition to the many amenities provided by the estate."

For sports, a large field at Maes Y Fan was to be laid out with rugby pitches, the three tennis courts tidied up and the sports pavilion renovated. A large flat grassy area behind the house was to become the cricket pitch and athletics track; few cadets realised that underneath it was large water storage tank!

Another stone building behind the pavilion was allocated for the cadets' 'tuck shop cum café.' The cadets would soon adapt their own routine and the woods behind the tuck shop became a popular meeting place for illicit smokers. Mr. and Mrs Walters moved from Bryn Mel, he ran the tuck shop and is remembered by generations of cadets for his loud proclamations of

"beans on toast and a cup of Cawfeeeee!."

She was the Nelson Block Nursing Sister.

Mr. Wilson was masterminding the financing of the move and improvements. By September 1948, these had reached £40,000 with only £20,000 promised by 4 shipowners. He had worked tirelessly behind the scenes for years and had built up *Conway* and MMSA reserves from £400,000 to £1.5 million. He was suffering from overwork and felt his efforts were not valued. However, Captain Hewitt fully appreciated his work.

"Terms of contract (for Plas Newydd) show … how astute he is."

At some point, Lawrence Holt had confided to him that he intended to retire from the *Conway* committee and as Blue Funnel's chairman in 1953, and that he would recommend Sir John Nicholson to replace him as Blue Funnel's chairman. Wilson decided that he would resign at the same time.

Mr. Browne threw himself energetically into planning while also working on the organisation of the shore establishment and arrangements for the new three year course. The Captain Superintendent would retain overall command, but Mr. Browne clearly expected to have control over the shore establishment. A power struggle developed between Captain Goddard, as incumbent Captain Superintendent, and Captain Hewitt as Captain Superintendent designate and the Headmaster. This came to a head in May 1948. Captain Hewitt expressed concerns that Browne's ideas

"gives Browne control over the Executive Staff ashore."

Browne noted,

"EH fears he could not maintain full control"

and countered that, with the Captain Superintendent living aboard, and the Headmaster living in the shore base, only the Headmaster could be in charge there. Captain Hewitt was not happy with these arrangements and by the end of the month he was

"in doubt whether to stay."

Mr. Browne's empire building evidently also upset Mr. Wilson, culminating in a letter from him to Captain Goddard saying,

"Plas Newydd was none of Browne's business and to keep his nose out."

Mr. Browne wrote back saying he could not operate under such conditions. The disagreements dragged into 1949, but were eventually resolved in Captain Hewitt's favour. In January 1949, Captain Hewitt made it very clear that Mr. Browne would not obtain greater responsibility than he already had as academic Headmaster. One of *Conway's* officers would be Chief Officer of the shore establishment reporting to the Captain Superintendent. Browne's proposal for academic house masters and uniformed divisional officers was over-ruled. There would just be uniformed divisional officers. Their relationship continued to be very mixed. At one point Browne noted admiringly,

"Hewitt has great thoughts – adopted his ideas with little hesitation;"

but later ruefully recording that he was

"Mr. Browne, not 'Tom' anymore."

However, neither man allowed these personal differences to leak into public view. They were to work closely together and achieve enormous improvements for next fourteen years.

CHAPTER 20

1949 A TOUR OF THE SHORE BASE

Plas Newydd From The Strait

Plas Newydd was a few hundred yards along the shore from the Ship's new mooring, set in a break in the miles of dark trees that lined the Anglesey shore. It was set back about a hundred feet from the water behind a wide expanse of well tended grass sloping down to a solid crenulated seawall with a small integral boathouse. The dock was to the left but the house dominated the strait. Built by the architect James Wyatt, it was a grand 18th century 'stately home.' Three stories tall, the ivy clad ashlar stone building mixed gothic and classical styles. The front of the house included three large bays and the roof line was punctuated by several small domed turrets. It was aligned almost north south alongside the strait with acres of beautiful grounds and mesmerising views to Snowdonia. One old boy, returning in 2006 for the first time in fifty years noted:

"The sheer beauty of the surrounds that we so casually took for granted, oh what callow youth!"

The Dock

Like many cannily positioned Welsh buildings, the house was set back into a small fold of ground, which sheltered it like an upturned collar. From many angles the house was almost hidden from view as out of the weather.

Leaving the Ship by boat, a few minutes motoring or pulling arrived at the Marquis's private dock, which had been handed over to *Conway*. It was a small, sturdy, professional looking affair, perhaps reflecting the influence of Admiral Lord Clarence Paget, son of the first Marquis and CinC of the Mediterranean fleet in Nelson's day. On the left a solid stone built sea wall projected at an acute angle, thirty feet or so out into the strait with a narrow walkway along the top. Depending on the state of the tide the walkway stood six to twenty feet above the water. Goddard added a small platform to the end of the walkway, projecting over the strait, from which cadets could practice heaving the lead. On the inside of the seawall a wide slip angled down from the dockside into the water, providing boat access at all states of the tide. It was fitted with rails and a capstan so boats could be hauled out of the water for storage, inspection and repair. The dockside, tucked under the wooden slope, curved around to a long low stone building built into the hillside. Part was the bosun's locker smelling darkly of tar and hemp, the rest the seamanship classroom where cadets learned their trade. It was wood lined with benches along two sides. It had two large splendid models of cargo vessels in glass cases and the walls, ceilings and deck were covered with ropes, pulleys, lights, chains, anchors and many strange nautical devices that new chums would soon come to master. Outside on the dockside there was a ship's binnacle next to a small 'radar room' full of other mysterious equipment. The dockside was always full with boats stored or being repaired, fuel tanks, boat davits with which the cadets practiced lifeboat drill and boat hoisting. Depending on the time of day there might be groups of cadets preparing to go sailing, busy in and out of the seamanship room, receiving sextant instruction from the Captain Superintendent or splashing noisily in the large sea water pool, which formed the opposite side of the dock to the slip. Sloping up next to the seamanship room a tarmac track wound it way up into the trees providing a fleeting glimpse of the seawall promenade and the house.

The northern half of the house, now called the Nelson Block, was allocated to *Conway*. The unprepossessing entrance was at the back, tucked right under a high walled slope. Access was via a small semi-enclosed yard. Inside the ceilings all seemed un-naturally high to small new chums used to normal domestic buildings. Immediately opposite the entry was a small cubby used by the officer of the day and duty cadet captain. It contained a tannoy system for broadcasting messages and instructions. To the left were the galley, a large mess deck and a hobbies room. The hobbies room gave access to an outside area where a hut would be erected to house a full sized snooker table. A short dark corridor ran to the right. To the right of the entrance door, opposite the cubby, a few steps lead to a small room, which would house the telephone exchange and act as an office. On the other side of the corridor were the cadet captains' gun room *(private study)* and a flight of narrow stone steps to the two upper floors. A door, strictly out of bounds to cadets, led out to the Marquis's lawns leading down to the strait. The two upper floors were for dormitories but on the first floor was a large library with over 3,000 volumes.

On both dormitory floors a long central corridor ran left and right from the stairs. To the left were entrances to a number of small dormitories, some with adjacent washrooms. At the far end the corridor was blocked by a fire escape door into the Marquis's private, and strictly out-of-bounds, quarters. Each dormitory was fitted with sets of wooden bunks and accommodated eight to twenty cadets. Mauritania was the largest and as a sop to superstition there was no bunk 13, just a 12a. Upper bunks had odd numbers and were occupied by the starboard watch. Lower bunks were even numbers and were occupied by the port watch. Each cadet had a wooden cupboard and drawers for his uniform and other personal items. These were all subject to random inspection by cadet captains, with immediate punishment for untidiness. Some dormitories had splendid views along the strait to the Britannia Bridge or to the Ship in the distance. Across the strait Snowdonia dominated the skyline. Those on the back of the building looked out onto the blank wall at the back of the House! Dorms all had large vertically opening windows but Mr. Drake would berate cadets who left windows open when the central heating was switched on.

The Seamanship Room

> *"In his tired, patient voice he would announce: Close that window; you may want to turn Anglesey into a tropical island but the heating's not up to it!"*

To the right were the main heads and showers. A dog-leg in the corridor led to a number of other small rooms. On one floor these were fitted out as staff cabins, on the other as a small

The House Library

Dormitory Overlooking The Strait

sick bay and ward. On the top, second, floor, inside a window overlooking the courtyard, a patent life saving harness was installed. In the event of a fire cadets could strap on the harness and sort of abseil themselves down the outside of the building. It was a moot point how many would be saved in this way and how many burnt to a frazzle as they queued patiently for their turn. Presumably those on the first floor were expected to jump. The floors were covered in highly polished brown or red lino. Every inch very shortly became 'sweeps' cleaned to gleaming perfection twice a day by cadets.

In an interesting comparison with modern times, one group of old boys touring the dorms in 2004 found the bunks and cupboards replaced by single beds and the windows adapted so they could open only partially. The place was then a young people's outdoor centre and the tourists were assured the changes were all due to health and safety risk assessments. There was a danger that children might fall out of a top bunk and sue, or not realise they might fall out of an open second floor window. The same mentality seemed to hold sway at the dock. Where generations of *Conway* cadets took full control of motor, sailing and rowing boats in all conditions without any adult supervision and quickly learned valuable lessons in team work, leadership and responsibility; modern youth is obliged to sit through laborious safety briefings encumbered by foul weather gear and life savers. *Conway* instructors threw cadets in at the deep end; we picked up the challenge, survived and thrived. Pity the modern instructor and children so constrained by legislation and hidebound by fears of litigation. How can young people excel if not challenged or trusted?

Outside, the courtyard was accessed by a narrow sloping road that led up to the Kelvin Block. This contained a gym, classrooms, laboratory and staff accommodation. From here roads led off to the sports fields and dock and continued up to *Conway's* main entrance off the lane from Brynsiencyn

Laboratory

Kelvin Block and Cromlech

to Llanfair PG. On the grass across from the Kelvin Block was a large stone prehistoric megalithic structure called the Cromlech (crom means 'bent' and llech means 'flagstone.' It was more correctly a dolmen, the remains of a prehistoric stone chamber tomb. Although many supplies would be brought daily by boat from Port Dinorwic, three miles along the strait, the Ship's postal address was now the village with the longest name in Wales, Llanfairpwllgwyngyllgogerychwyrndrobwllllantysiliogogogoch

(Welsh for Saint Mary's Church in the hollow of the white hazel near a rapid whirlpool and the Church of St. Tysilio of the red cave.). Fortunately the name was always abbreviated to Llanfair PG.

With the Ship conveniently moored nearby, the splendid shore base with its excellent educational and sporting facilities and the nearby mountains for adventurous training, *Conway* launched into what might be judged as the peak period of her existence. Some consider that, at this point, she changed from being purely a training ship to become a sea school.

Ship, Dock and Plas Newydd

CHAPTER 21

1949–50 OPENING THE SHORE BASE AND A CHANGE OF COMMAND

A Change In Command

Captain Goddard was determined the Ship's move to Plas Newydd and the opening of the shore base would be his swansong, after which he would retire and Captain Hewitt would assume command. Several years later he reflected on his period in command.

> *"During the fifteen years of my command of Conway, the Ship had received many alterations and had been moved about a lot. The number of cadets and their standard of education had improved and so I am satisfied in thinking that definite progress has been made to keep Conway abreast of the times. The Summer Term 1949 was my last. Our project was accomplished and Conway was given a new lease of life."*

His son-in-law, Commander Bruce 'Fancy Pants' Andrews DSC RN (34-36), added, particularly of the move of the Ship,

> *"Not a bad crowning achievement and one that took a considerable nerve."*

On 26th July, at the end of the summer term, Captain Goddard formally handed over command to Captain Hewitt.

> *"Divisions were piped on the lower deck and, after a short speech from both Captain Hewitt and Captain Goddard, we all shook hands with Captain Goddard, after which a presentation was made and we were dismissed."*

With her husband's retirement Mrs Goddard also left. She was very well liked.

> *"Mrs Goddard did more than anybody to improve the tone of the Ship by setting a splendid example on the social side and not sparing herself in the effort."*

Capt Eric Hewitt RD RNR

She was elected a life member of the *Conway* Club. The Goddard's finally left the Ship on the 28th after all hands manned the sides and gave three rousing cheers to send them off. Captain Goddard's early years had been traumatic with huge obstacles to overcome. Although popular with the cadets, he had not always received the full support or trust of the chairman, committee, his executive team, Headmaster or masters. Indeed, many doubted his ability or that he would survive. The war years transformed everything. He became an inspirational figure guiding everyone safely through the hazards of war, the transition from the Mersey to the Menai Strait and the opening of the shore establishment at Plas Newydd. His successor was to face even greater challenges and to overcome them with equal verve.

The New Shore Base

1949 Summer Term

For the first term off Plas Newydd arrangements remained the same as at Bangor and all the cadets lived in the Ship. The new location proved popular.

The Marquis Inspects The Guard of Honour

"The Plas Newydd moorings cannot be compared to those at Bangor – they are far superior in every way. It is more peaceful and colourful for a start. The new playing fields are much better."

1949 October 21st

On Trafalgar Day, the shore base was officially opened. The official programme explained it was

"made necessary by the continued excess of applications over vacancies onboard the Ship … The developments are designed to allow for a greater number of cadets and to give wider scope and opportunity to the system of training."

The shore base was described as the Shore School, which

"gives HMS Conway roots ashore so that in the years to come Conway training may endure undeterred by the passage of time."

The ceremony was held in the yard of the Kelvin Block. At 2 pm the buglers sounded a 'Still' and the Marquis inspected an armed Guard of Honour. The Marquis, Chairman of the Management Committee and Captain Hewitt all said a few words with the Marquis formally declaring the 'Shore School' open. The cadets marched past and were dismissed. The buildings and Ship were open for inspection by parents and visitors. Tea was served on the Nelson Block mess deck. The log records,

"Dressed ship overall. All boats wore ensigns. Ship open to visitors."

The shore establishment was finally occupied and once more cadets found themselves comparing the old and the new.

"I think the general feeling among the older hands was that ashore one 'played' at sailors' whereas in the Ship we were sailors."

"Instead of bugles or a boatswain's call there were announcements over the tannoy."

"The discipline in little things was a great deal stricter than onboard."

The start of the new regime did not all go well. *Conway* lost the annual rugby match against their arch rivals from *Worcester*.

Ship, Dock and Plas Newydd

For the first time ever, new chums spent their first term ashore, but they could see the Ship from Plas Newydd.

Ship From Focsle's Nestor Dorm

"On our first day in that stately home we were able to look out from our dormitory window, across the narrow straits, at the anchored Ship, listening to the rhythmic echo of her diesel engine in the boiler house on her upper deck, and watching her swing slowly with the changing tide. Our thoughts were chiefly concerned with wondering what life onboard would be like. If we were excited, which we certainly were, we were probably also a little afraid for a new and utterly different life awaited us. Even ashore, we needed to undergo a speedy transition. We soon learned that floors were decks, ceilings were deckheads, and walls were bulkheads. Going to the town of Bangor still entailed 'going ashore,' corridors were alleyways, lavatories were the heads and the main entrance to the house was the gangway. Those of us who were detailed to lay the tables for meals were summoned over a loudspeaker system by a bosun's pipe, followed by the order, Cooks to the galley."

"We were given an early introduction to the ship herself, as shore-based cadets went aboard on Sundays for divisions and divine service. And there was the institution of the Captain's welcoming tea party. This entailed sitting at a large circular table in the captain's comparatively luxurious quarters at the stern of the Ship, next to spacious windows on the inside of a balcony known as the stern-walk. The teapot was passed anticlockwise, irrespective of rank, and in a somewhat tense atmosphere, we were asked to say a little about ourselves over tea and cake."

"I was in the first term to occupy Plas Newydd shore establishment where we stayed for one term before joining the hammock brigade onboard. The cadets who preceded us thought we were being given soft treatment but I well remember ALL the ship's company making good use of the new fangled showers ashore as there were only a few baths aboard and one had to sign the bath book each time it was your top's turn to use them. As I remember both taps initially were so hot that even water from the cold tap had to have cold water added from a churn, can't remember where that came from though. As you would imagine, after half the top had bathed both taps were bloody cold! The trick was to try and get the happy medium in the pecking order. Baths were only allowed one per week, as also was a change of underclothes. As we were charged for laundry some types economised and I remember one friend wearing his blue working shirt all term and being proud of the fact that the red stitching, which was part of the makeup of the shirt, was almost invisible at term end. I expect he would be horrified now if one of his kids tried that trick!"

The new showers at the House did not work very well and required constant maintenance by Jock Marshall, the handyman. They were randomly either scalding hot or freezing cold; and warning signs had to be hung by the shower room hand 'hot only' or 'cold only.'

"My term was the first to spend a first term in the house, and we went round the Marquis's part several times. The part I loved was the library where we were allowed to read, but not take away the old books, some printed back in the seventeenth century. I was privileged to be able to read the first chapter of a first edition of Gulliver's travels while one of the Marquis's footmen stood close watch over us to make sure we treated them with the respect they deserved. Whenever I smell the odour of a really old book nowadays, it takes me back to that library."

"I served one term at the house before braving the (imaginary) hardships onboard the Ship. It is funny that I can hardly remember anything about life in the house, apart from spending one or two evenings in the Marquis' library, yet I still have vivid impressions of life aboard. Also I can hardly think how we got all our belongings into those tiny sea chests, which had to be kept tidy for rounds."

Parties were put to work to clear out the open-air sea-water pool alongside the dock.

"This was a dirty and sometimes wretched task as the sludge and filth lay feet thick and this was increased every high water as the pool filled from the strait."

1950 January

A new prospectus was issued. The Ship aimed

"to give a sound general and technical education to boys desiring to entering the Merchant Navy and Royal Navy."

The Chief Officer was Mr. Geoff Drake Master Mariner. The Executive Officer Ashore Lt. John Brooke Smith RNR Master Mariner. The Second Officer was Mr. L LeBesque Extra Master Mariner. There were 12 technical, i.e. uniformed, staff including the Captain Superintendent and 11 academic staff, including the Headmaster. The prospectus concluded with fine words:

"No finer environment could be obtained for instilling into youth the finest qualities of our Royal and Merchant Navies. Add to the advantage of such surroundings the experience of many years of training, sound British games, good food, oceans of fresh air and the unequalled Spirit of the Conway and your picture of a perfect environment is as complete as it is unequalled anywhere in the world today."

More mundanely the committee wrote to Captain Hewitt and Mr. Browne reminding them of the need for economies as the fitting out of Plas Newydd and shifting the Ship had severely depleted *Conway's* reserves.

Daily Routine.

Cadets in the shore base quickly settled into a new daily routine.

"We were roused at 6.30 am by a voice over the loudspeaker exhorting us to 'Rise and Shine.'"

Donning sports rig everyone went for a quick sprint out of the grounds.

> *"How can one forget those early morning runs at 0600 down to the Brynsiencyn cross roads and back, still dark, bright moonlight and sometimes a heavy frost."*

On very wet days the gym and mess deck were used for PT.

> *"These savage amusements were not very popular, but they certainly woke one up!"*

At 6.45 am cadets washed, dressed for the day and made their bunks. Normal winter working rig was a variation of battle-dress, a blue serge lumber jacket and trousers, a blue shirt with detachable white collars and black tie. All was rounded of with a naval cap. In summer battle dress was replaced with blue shorts, blue shirts and regulation length blue stockings. Best uniforms or 'reefers' with their gold buttons, white lapel stripes and neck lanyards were worn for Sunday divisions, church and other special occasions.

Starboard Hold Dormitory

Breakfast consisted of porridge, followed by a kipper or a piece of bacon, or an egg, or beans on toast (these came in daily rotation). Three slices of bread, and butter (enough for two slices if spread very thin) washed down with a cup of skilly (tea).

> *"After breakfast all hands turned too and cleaned ship until 8.30 am All hands except those on duty then fell in for divisions (parade), in the courtyard if it was fine, in the gym if not. After being inspected the cadets marched past the senior officer who took the salute."*

School lessons followed, four in the morning and three in the afternoon. These were for a mix of academic and nautical subjects. Two evenings a week there was preparation, the other evenings being free for clubs and societies or simply for the canteen. The officers and masters worked tirelessly to encourage and support a wide range of clubs. One such endeavour was the *Conway* Ornithological Society, which started around September 1949. Two cadets found they shared an interest in birds; they were soon joined by a third and by the end of the next term they had a well organised society with its own library, cupboard, records, organisation, weekly meetings, rules and fees! They organised weekly field trips and even managed one weekend trip. Within a year it was a fully fledged operation with fifteen members, accepted as an alternative to sports. The Snowden Scouting Group went from strength to strength. The shooting club was also popular and a .22 range was set up in the tunnel in the hold.

The promised *"oceans of fresh air"* were guaranteed on Wednesdays and Saturdays as they were sports afternoons. Rugby or hockey in the winter, cricket in the summer. Sailing, rowing, cross-country running, athletics and boxing figured large all year round. The Haig Trophy continued to engage parties of cadets in long, competitive mountain treks interspersed with practical problem solving exercises such as trying to splice a rope underwater.

Saturday mornings ashore were dedicated to very thorough cleaning, known as 'Heave Round', in preparation for Captain's Rounds at 11. Captain's Rounds in the Ship were on Sunday. Woe betide any cadet and his cadet captain if Captain Hewitt found a speck of dust or lack of polish anywhere. Every week, each officer assessed the tops' performance giving marks out of ten for each of 'Top spirit, zest and enthusiasm,' 'Conduct and discpline,' 'Deck work, cleanliness and neatness,' 'Appearance of cadets, dress and cleanliness,' 'Cutter,' 'Drill and PT,' 'State of division's boat,' 'Evolutions, working section, reeving falls etc,' 'Tidiness of orlop deck near chests' and 'Any other points.'

The Senior Executive Officer also assessed each top but gave up to 20 marks each for 'Deck work' and 'Discipline.' The Captain Superintendent marked each top out 30 for 'Deck work' only but could allocate up to 10 marks for other categories if he saw fit. The top with the most points at the end of term won the Hobson Cup. Competition was fierce as the winner chose which of the motorboats it wanted to run the following term.

"The water boat was most popular as her run was to Port Dinorwic for water, and at Port Dinorwic were cafés, girls and the chance to smoke in peace!"

The cutters were considered the booby prize inevitably going to the division with the least points.

After dinner, evening divisions were held on the mess deck and 'pipe-down' was at 9.45 pm.

The existing top and watch system was adapted to accommodate the shore establishment. Initial plans were that the top system would continue afloat and the system of 'ships' introduced at Bangor in 1943 would be adopted ashore. In fact tops, watches and 'ships' were integrated into a completely new approach. There were now five tops or divisions, Focsle who wore yellow edging on their sports vests, Foretop red, Maintop blue, Mizzentop green and told (who seemed not to have had colour). Each top was divided into port and starboard watches. On joining, new chums were allocated to a top and watch irrespective of term, age or size. Generally, they would remain in that top until they left the Ship. Each top therefore had a fairly even mix of cadets from the youngest to the most senior, so the previous groupings into 'ships' for fairer sports competitions became superfluous. This retained the even distribution of ages and sizes for inter-top Pledger Cup sports competitions achieved by the 'ships' arrangements. In the Ship, Maintop worked the main deck, Foretop the upper deck, Mizzentop the lower deck, Focsle the orlop deck and Hold the hold and bosun's stores. In the Nelson Block, the new dormitories were all named after prominent merchant ships. Several of the names previously used were retained as names for dormitories. The Royal Navy ships' names were not retained. Focsle berthed in Andes and Nestor dormitories, Foretop in Ohio and Rangitiki, Maintop in Rawlpindi, Mizzentop in Jervis Bay and Orontes, and hold in Mauritania. Each top (or strictly speaking division) onboard would have one senior cadet captain and two junior cadet captains. Ashore there would be a senior cadet captain (the deputy chief cadet captain) in overall charge and five junior cadet captains, one for each division.

CHAPTER 22

1949–53 SHIP AND SHORE

Coal and Water

Even at this seeming idyll, a perennial problem remained; supplying the Ship with coal and water. Disposing of waste was not a concern; it all went direct into the Strait to be flushed away by the tides.

In the first few years at Plas Newydd, coal for the Ship was delivered in ninety large sacks at Port Dinorwic and then transported by the boats to the Ship. By 1952, coal was dumped onto the dock at Plas Newydd in large heapstogether with sacks. The whole Ship and shore base were involved, organised into parties for various activities. All motorboats, cutters but not gigs were towed ashore. Sacks were filled by one party, conveyed to the slip by another, loaded into the boats by another. The boats were towed to the port gangway;

Above: Water Boat (Probably Aground) at Port Dinorwic
Below: Water Boat Discharging Alongside 1951

> *"We would sometimes try to make the juice barge roll, in a high-spirited attempt to alarm Brooke Smith into thinking that the cargo would be tipped into the Menai Strait!"*

Sacks were hoisted to the main deck by one group, dragged to the main deck bunker entrance hatch by another party and emptied by another. The empty sacks were returned to the boats that then left for another load. The rig of the day was 'jockstraps and sea boots' so all hands were decked out in what ever they wanted - rugger shirts, shorts, boiler suits, bandanas, head coverings, anything in fact. By noon the operation was complete and the Ship and the dock were returned to their normal pristine condition. Meanwhile, the showers in the school block were overloaded with filthy bodies. At other times, bags of potatoes were transported by a special two wheeled trolley from the house to the dock and then out to the Ship.

Water had to brought by boat to the Ship twice a day, sometimes more. The water boat's crew now had to collect water from Port Dinorwic, or PD as it was known, one and a quarter miles away. Their daily routine began at 6 am They would take the water boat to PD, run hoses from a hydrant and commence filling the water boat. Once full they returned to the Ship and pumped the water out. At 8.30, wherever they were, they were relieved by a 'practical class' crew. After a day's school the water boat crew returned to their boat at 4.30 pm and continued loading and pumping often until 9 pm at night. The slip at Port Dinorwic dried at low water so constant re-positioning was required.

> *"During bad weather it was often difficult to get alongside the slip but the officers never interfered with the coxswain's decision."*

They were actually several miles away anyway!

> *"I learned more about initiative and responsibility in that capacity than I have ever done before or since."*

> *"We accidentally grounded the Juice Barge on a Thursday morning practical at Port Dinorwic slip. Strangely… just a few yards from the café! Two unusually unpleasant petty officers, and the rather unhappy boat's crew, re-floated the vessel at something like 11 pm the same evening at the top of high tide."*

> *"I was also present on another occasion when the same imposing vessel had to be hauled over some yards of shingle with the aid of balks of timber, white lead, tallow and about fifty cadets. The water boat had grounded broadside on, above the shingle bank near the Port Dinorwic slipway at the top of a spring tide. Captain Hewitt was heard to be remarkably forthright with the boat's crew that he judged had done their best to deprive the Ship of water for a month."*

As it was suspected that grounding was a convenient way to spend a few extra hours ashore, and not a sign of poor seamanship on the part of boats' crews, a system of 'practical demerits' was introduced for those putting boats ashore. The water boat remained afloat thereafter.

1949

> *"The Seamanship Officer was the ex-Royal Navy heavyweight boxing champ. He was so formidable that on the dreaded occasion that I had to heave the lead for examination purposes from a platform over the reeds, I knew I couldn't get it over the top and, sure enough, I felt the line go slack when it was vertically over my head. With the class watching, and him glowering below, my only thought was not to damage his 14 pound lump of lead. I looked up and the missile was descending, I caught it like a cricket ball and it drove me right across and into the chains. The lead was clutched to my chest and I dared not move until ordered to do so. After a while I stood up festooned with rope, and a subdued titter of laughter ran through the class. Another five minutes passed and we were all frozen in time, until the oracle spoke, 'Well at least he tried, get down off there you bloody fool' and gratefully I descended the ladder, which shook with my trembling. I was very relieved when I went to sea to find they had electronic depth sounders and my erstwhile skill of heaving the lead was obsolete."*

The Padre formed the Conway Snowdon Scout Group with the Rector of Llanberis, and cadets spent odd weekends staying in the Rectory. A group of about 8 cadets would go to Port Dinorwic on Friday evening and catch a bus to Llanberis.

"I think there were about 6 groups all told. We would stay in the vicarage Friday and Saturday nights. During the day we would climb a mountain in the area if the weather permitted, if not we would go on a low altitude hike. Any spare time we had we would work on the standard scout activities. The rector of Llanberis would act as scoutmaster. Mountain first aid seemed to be the thing we concentrated on most. Although we did not wear scout uniform we did work for the scout badges. We found it a nice way to get away for the weekend with very little discipline. It seemed to be very popular with the smokers."

The groups would return to the Ship on Sunday evening. Each year Patrols competed for the Haig Trophy. This required a variety of hikes and following of clues, solving of puzzles and completing of challenges. The sort of thing that outdoor team building organisations still do today.

"One winter, with a group of cadets, we climbed up the side of the Devils Chimney in the mountains and got lost in a snowstorm and came down on the wrong side of the mountain and had to walk 14 miles back to Capel Curig."

Sometimes they would climb on Conway Crag, part of Clogwyn Mawr in the Llanberis Pass. The crag had been named by the Climbing Club of Great Britain after cadets first climbed it on 23rd March 1946.

"I remember the Padre because one day, when committing the ashes of an Old Conway to the deep from one of the two 'pulpits' on the quarterdeck, he forgot, or had not noticed, that during the service the Ship had swung on her moorings and the wind was blowing in such a way that the ashes, when spooned over the side descended down and through the porthole of the cabin underneath, which just happened to be his. As we were going down the hatch after being fallen out from the parade we were treated to the sight of the Padre sweeping up ash from the floor of his cabin saying 'Dear oh dear oh dear' The second committal was via the dustpan and brush!"

1949 June 20th

Air Chief Marshall Sir Richard EC Pierse KCB, DSO, AFC, RAF (1905-07) attended a special memorial service and unveiled the new roll of honour and honours boards. The aft part of the lower deck had been altered to take the boards of the 1914-1919 and 1939-1945 wars, with a painting of Nelson between them. Framed citations for *Conway's* four VCs and GC and the ace submarine officer Commander GC Hunt DSO and bar, DSC and two bars (1920-22), hung nearby, adding to the atmosphere. The memorial service was conducted by the Bishop of Bangor.

"The Roll of Honour was fitted to the athwartship bulkhead of the cabin just above the starboard gangway. With lights in the deck head shining on these boards the scene during the silent hours appealed to me as something to be most solemn, and I am sure that these emblems of gallantry and

Nash's Fly Past

sacrifice will impress upon the generations of cadets under training that the creating of the Conway tradition demanded, most fully the price of admiralty and the necessity and duty to live up to the Ship's motto 'Quit Ye Like Men, Be Strong'."

The honours boards are now safely preserved in the *Conway* Chapel at Birkenhead.

1949 August

Cadet Basil Nash left the Ship in 1943, having been an instigator of the Air Class in 1941. He joined the RAF and eventually qualified as an pilot, flying maintenance tests flights from RNAS Stretton near Warrington. In August 1949, he qualified as a Mosquito pilot and flew a Mosquito over the Ship. His Observer took a photo, reproduced here, as he flew past. Basil was obvious a very confident pilot given his height above the water, proximity to the Ship and the steep wooden bank just out of shot to the left!

1950 March 18th

Cadet JH Ivor Lowe fell from the Captain's stern-walk and was drowned.

> *"One of our tasks onboard was to clean this area. This involved casting a bucket, on the edge of a long rope, into the Strait to fill it with water. Lowe leaned over the edge of the stern-walk rail to haul up his bucket in such a way that he was directly over the pail. While changing hands in the heaving process, and leaning yet further outwards to grip the rope as far down as possible, the weight of the water in the bucket pulled him over the edge of the stern-walk rail and he fell into strait."*

It happened in foul weather and it is thought he hit his head and was stunned.

> *"No 1 motorboat went to his rescue and Ferris Morton (49-50), who was a strong swimmer, dived in to attempt to save him, unfortunately to no avail as poor Ivor, wearing oilskins and sea boots, was a deadweight and Ferris couldn't hold him. Sadly he sank and was lost. Ferris was awarded a Royal Humane Society Certificate for his gallant attempt."*

> *"According to the tale related onboard, he was drowned, in part because his sea boots filled with water, dragging him down. From that time onwards, we were never allowed outboard, at the chains, for example, without wearing sea boots at least one size larger than normally required, so that, in theory, the boots might be kicked off if we fell overboard."*

> *"Everyone onboard was deeply touched. I realized that in Conway we had joined a fellowship. I was very much impressed and very proud."*

His body was found on 2nd May on the shore about two miles from the Ship. Lt. John Brooke Smith formally identified the body. The inquest at Plas Newydd on 3rd May recorded a verdict of accidental death. The Cadet magazine recorded that

> *"He was buried on 5th May at Rhyl, 56 cadets attended his funeral, their slow marching through Rhyl at the head of the funeral cortege being a very sincere tribute to their late shipmate."*

The Headmaster recorded that he had

"never been more moved."

1950-52

"There were three memorable warrant officers aboard the Ship. Ernie Moore, Jackie 'Gunner' Mayne and John 'Taffy' Oliver. All three had a very big hand in teaching the basic skills of seamanship as well as being very instrumental in maintaining shipboard, and shore-based discipline. They taught us how to march, salute in the proper naval way, stand at attention 'with the thumbs in line with the seams of the trousers,' tie knots and hitches, splice rope and wire, sew canvas, send and read morse and semaphore, and a multitude of other skills and disciplines, which certainly stood me well in later life."

Ernie Moore was perhaps the most colourful, certainly in his use of language.

"My first memory of Ernie was when he told us that we were not allowed to have sheath knives with points on. It was apparently against the Ship's regulations. This was immediately followed by a warning that, if any of us were so unsailor-like as to spoil one of a sailor's most important tools by breaking the tip off a knife, we would have him to answer to."

One day, as the pinnace was coming alongside the gangway in fairly heavy weather, the bow man was having a great deal of trouble in picking up the mooring wire with the boathook. Ernie, leaned over the top of the gangway and in his nice London accent said,

"Come on my son, your mother might have waited nine bleeding months for you but I'm not going to."

To many cadets though, Ernie and his wife were father and mother figures.

Gunner Mayne was probably the most energetic of them all.

"From him we learned that Whale Island was the axle on which the British Royal Navy revolved. Without it, the Royal Navy would probably have foundered long before. Everything he did was 'on the double.' Consequently he expected that everything we did should also be 'on the double' As our drill master he taught us not only to march, salute, stand correctly, but also to have pride in our accomplishments. I think many of us learned from him that, although tasks might sometimes be difficult, they are never impossible."

John Oliver was the quietest of the three.

"His lilting Welsh accent was always controlled and he never seemed to have to raise his voice much at all. For a couple of terms he was my divisional officer and I found him to be very considerate and thoughtful. The other thing I remember about him was that his initials, JO and the way he wrote them, were extremely easy to forge. This was a great benefit when one needed a note or a textbook label initialled by your divisional officer. Something I took advantage of on a couple of occasions."

"Three great men. It's more than fifty years now, but I still remember them and am indebted to them for all the things they taught me."

1950 Summer

The first cross strait swim from Vaynol dock to Plas Newydd dock was held and the newly presented Vaynol Cup was won by cadet David Nutman. The following year, it was won by Bill Sylvester. He was a new chum so everyone was surprised at his achievement especially when he then went on to win the 600 yard down strait swim for the Drew Cup. The cross strait race was an annual feature for the next 24 years but, no one ever came close to Bill's wining time of 7 minutes 13 seconds.

And You'll Find on the Bridge a Conway Boy
Captain David Nutman FNI (1950 -51)

Conway brought out the sportsman in David. As well wining the Vaynol Swimming Cup he was a member of the Caernarfonshire schools relay team at the AAA Championships in Cardiff, June 1951 where he first met his future wife, through an Old Conway. He was also a strong member of the 1st XV rugby team, which beat Worcester in the Autumn of 1951.

David's sea-going career reflected a life that is impossible for seamen today. It started with Bibby Line in the Leicestershire on charter to British India Line running between London and East Africa. Subsequently he served on passenger liners between Liverpool and Rangoon, and then in troopships between Liverpool/ Southampton and Hong Kong/Korea/Japan (Kure). He obtained his 2nd Mates Certificate in 1955 and Mates in 1957. Moving on to Elders and Fyffes in 1959 he served on 'Banana Boats' running to West Africa (Tiko and Fernando Poo) from Garston, Liverpool. Later he moved to the Avonmouth - Jamaica service (Kingston, Bevans Wharf, Oracabessa, Port Antonio and Montego Bay).

In 1960, he came ashore and worked in the financial sector until 1978 when the sea finally called him back. He joined Canadian Pacific Ships, as Extra Second Officer on a very large crude carrier. He obtained his Masters Ticket in 1980 while serving as Second Mate and Mate on containerships on the North Atlantic service. After more time in bulk carriers, he was promoted Master in 1986 and at long last achieved the coveted title of 'Captain.' He continued to serve as Master on bulkers, container ships and specialised Ro-Ro ships till 1990.

Then, forty years after leaving Conway, he finally came ashore settling, like so many Old Conway, close to the sea on the Wirral. For the next five years he was a Nautical Surveyor with the Department of Transport, carrying out random inspections of passenger pleasure craft in North West England, Wales, from Barmouth to Silloth (Coastal), the Lake District and even the canals from Skipton to Birmingham. "The Lake District had a very good 'bush telegraph.' I could be sure that within 30 minutes of my arrival at the first lake, be it Windermere, Ullswater, Coniston or Derwentwater, all the operators in the district would know that the Department Inspector was around."

He remembers "a life of fun and sorrow, the peculiar and the absurd, but especially the brotherhood of those who went to sea."

Fittingly it started and ended with Conway, he was President of the Conway Club from 2003 to 2005 and is currently Chairman of the Friends of HMS Conway.

1950 July 19th

HMCS *Crescenti* under command of Lt. Cdr. 'Skinny' Hayes DSC RCN and an Old *Conway* entered the strait to visit the Ship. She was on a training cruise and carried 70 Canadian navy cadets. *Crescent* entered the strait at Caernarfon only just managing to clear the bar at high water. She moored off Port Dinorwic and a series of exchange visits and sporting fixtures were held. The Canadians narrowly won the gig race even though they were 4 years older than the *Conway* cadets. On leaving, *Crescent* steamed up the strait past *Conway* before turning and steaming past her again

HMCS Crescent Passes The Ship

and back out to sea. At 375 feet she remains the longest vessel to have visited the strait. There was so little room to spare that when she turned her Focsle party were able to reach out and pull branches off the trees on the shore, which they presented to Lt. Cdr. Hayes.

1950 November.

"I was on the 100th Course at Aberdovey. Those course members who came from industry, hated it and thought the food and conditions appalling. We Conways thought we were in paradise! The morning shower water was fed direct from a mountain stream, which cascaded down a rock face behind the shower area. Invigorating to say the least. We resided in six huts, each named after a first world war naval hero. I was in Jellicoe and others included Fisher and Sturdee. During the course we all in turn went for a cruise on one of their two ketches, Warspite and Garibaldi. Each cruise was for six days and was captained by Alan Villiers of Mayflower and BBC fame."

1951 January

Lawrence Holt presented the bell of the *Nestor* for the Nelson Block. It was hung in a frame outside the gangway entrance hall and used by watch keepers to sound the time. It is now in the *Conway* Chapel at Birkenhead.

1951 June 19th

Food was described as *"horrendous"* and *"pretty gruesome."*

Junior cadets at the foot of the mess had always had short rations but the situation now seemed much worse.

"I can remember the senior cadets eating the lion's share of any meal and the junior cadets at the bottom of the table getting very little."

Upper Deck Sweep 1951

War time rationing was still in effect; so there were small portions anyway.

"In order to survive we relied on parcels from home and snacks in the canteen after games. We were only allowed one parcel a month from home so the usual practice was for four cadets to get together and arrange with their respective parents to send the parcels at weekly intervals so that the group shared one parcel each week. The contents were, by request, very basic. Not gourmet, but solid enough to stave off the hunger pains of young, active, growing teenagers."

The quality of the food, or lack of, eventually led to a food strike on 19th June 1951. How the whole shipboard complement of cadets learned about it without it coming to the attention of the administration is a mystery,

"especially as we prepared for it for a couple of days ahead."

The Headmaster thought that many of the masters secretly supported the cadets.

"On the appointed day, everyone onboard stashed quantities of sodduck and grease and other types of cooking foodstuffs in their chests. When the day arrived we went to the mess deck and when the breakfast food arrived at the messes, we poured all the condiments we could find into it and returned it uneaten, and spoiled, to the galley. Lunch and supper were treated the same way. We heard that the administration was furious, and the story was that Captain Hewitt accused all hands of attempting mutiny."

He threatened to withdraw his letters recommending QBs to shipping lines, a step that would have had serious consequences for their careers. In fact, Captain Hewitt thought the strike was originated, not by the QBs but by the term below, but he knew that pressure on the QBs would be most effective way to avoid any recurrence. When they left the Ship in December 1951, Captain Hewitt refused to shake their hands. He told the chief cadet captain he would consider the complaint if it was properly submitted. It then transpired that complaints had been made before but never got past the Chief Officer, Mr. Drake. He was summoned to a meeting with the Captain Superintendent after which he appeared 'a crumpled man.' Two senior committee members talked of

"an unpleasant air of fear of the Captain Superintendent onboard."

The cadets gave Captain Hewitt a new nickname, 'von Hewitt', although this did not last long. For a few weeks after the strike there was a distinct improvement in the quality of the food.

"It didn't last though."

1951

"Aft of the Nursery on the orlop deck was the hatchway to the hold, leading down from aft to forward into the tunnel (the old shaft tunnel), along which new chums had to run the gauntlet of older hands as they staggered with their hammocks into or out of the hold. On cinema nights the front row of the stalls was composed of a pile of hammocks, on which senior hands sprawled to look up at the screen at the forward end of the hold."

Under the hanging coats between the foretops on the orlop deck was a large hatch cover, leading down to the provisions stowage, known as the Captain's jam locker.

"Occasionally, about half an hour after lights out, a shadowy figure would arrive and disappear in among the coats. The creaking of the hatch would be heard once, then a second time and two or three of the marauder's grateful pals would each feel the weight of a two pound tin of jam drop into their hammock (could be painful, but worth it). I admit to being the receiver of stolen goods, along with other hungry Foretopmen who benefited next morning. His nickname was Jammy."

"Another memory was of the snooker table down in the starboard hold. On a windy night the old Ship would roll slowly and that played havoc with my game. Opposite the snooker table was the library, a lovely quiet room panelled in dark wood and with comfortable banquettes where one could curl up with a good book."

"The healthy fresh air, which swept along the orlop deck where we spent a large part of our time, came through holes that had been cut in the hull, apparently to provide more ventilation."

The openings did have wooden plugs but they tended to blow out on the colder windier days of winter.

"I recall a tale told of a visit by the Worcester rugby team who complained of the lack of fresh air in the tween decks. Plugs were removed from the ships side and the winter winds did blow! Almost immediately there was a request to replace the plugs! This did nothing to enhance their reputation."

"We did lead a Spartan life in those days. But despite all that, I still think that my days onboard were the happiest and most carefree of my life (until I retired, that is)."

1951 July

Sister Parry SRN retired after 20 years onboard. She was

"a good-humoured and gentle lady who made being sick a pleasure. I never knew her get ruffled, though she had plenty to try her patience."

1951 November 10th

For cadets who lived onboard their sea-chest was extremely important. The large black chests were provided from the outfitters in The Sailor's Home, Liverpool.

"It was your home from home, it stored all your possessions and it was the only area of the Ship where you were afforded privacy. If you wanted a quiet read, or a few minutes for private thoughts, you sat on your chest and all the other cadets understood that you wanted to be alone and respected that right."

"You never owned your chest but, when it was time for you to go onboard, at that time for most cadets in their third term, it had mysteriously appeared on the orlop deck. Some old name had been scraped off and in its place your name had been painted in large white block letters. Incidentally, the paint could be scraped off easily and many an Old Conway received a nickname through having his name altered by his shipmates. When you opened the lid there were 3 shallow trays, about 2 to 3 inches deep, 2 small and 1 large. Underneath was the main part of the chest. This is where you stored nearly all of your clothes, shoes and even books. The top trays were used for smaller items and often had mouldy sodduck and other festering items of food. I recently visited the Conway Chapel in Birkenhead and was amazed to see how small the chest actually was. I think they must have shrunk over the past 50 years." (They had actually been cut down for use in the New Block)

"Chests were usually unlocked. Occasionally, you might find that someone had 'borrowed' one of your text-books, but theft was extremely rare. You learned very quickly that you do not steal from shipmates."

However, on 10th December a theft was reported. This led to the chest search.

"At the end of lunch one day we were told that we would all remain at our messes on the main deck. No explanation was given and we had no idea why. What happened next was an exercise in masterly organisation. Using every staff member available, every chest onboard was searched. In small groups we were escorted to our own individual chests and each one was searched by a staff member as its owner watched. The missing object, which initiated the search was never found. I don't know how much contraband was unearthed that day but I can guess there were more than the few laboratory rubber-bungs found in my chest. (Used for plugging the bath plughole on Foretop bath night). A few strokes from the teaser and all was forgotten. Three cadets, however, were suspended because the contraband they had were packets of contraceptives. Fortunately the Board of Governors, led by Mr. Holt, reinstated them."

1952

"Communication from Ship to shore was by semaphore signalling between the poop and the dock."

"No one onboard had a radio. News was gleaned through copies of The Times, in the reading room. The Ship's newspaper, started by Mr. Kingsford, was displayed in a slanting glass-covered desk on the lower deck, and occasionally illustrated in my time by second officer GAB King, from Shell Tankers, who produced water-colours of life onboard. The Liverpool Echo was also displayed in this case."

The new Padre, the Reverend Turner, joined from TS *Mercury*. He was small and wiry, an Olympic long distance runner who had represented Great Britain in the Marathon at the 1936 Olympics in Berlin.

View From Ship to Shore

Hammock

"He was an exponent of the Finnish Style of running, which meant keeping your heel down and literally sloping over the ground to save energy. To make it more effective you had to lean forward slightly at a specific angle to provide the necessary thrust to maximise forward motion. In his day he could cover the ground at truly remarkable speed and was the very devil to keep up with."

As Padre, he was allotted the task of holding and distributing pocket money to cadets.

"We received five shillings a week in pocket money, hence the phrase "Yes, yes, here's your five shillings."

It was paid in the form of a book of chits, which could be exchanged for lights meals, sweets and chocolates in the shore canteen. Change was given in cash.

"We were always hungry! Sweets and chocolates were still rationed in 1953, as Britain continued to feel the effects of the war."

I think the Menai Strait One Design dinghies came in 1952."

The dinghies were specially designed for the strait waters in the early 1930s by Mr. W.H. Rowland of Deganwy, for the builders Morris and Leavett of Gallows Point, Beaumaris. They were a 20 foot sloop with a lifting centre plate that could be sailed at any state of the tide. There were 17 in the class, of which *Conway* had 6; GP 8233 *Taeping*, GP 8234 *Ariel*, GP 8235 *Lightning*, GP 8431 *Flying Cloud*, GP 8342 *Simba* and GP 9433 *Sobroan*. All but one are still in the strait, most moored at Beaumaris.

In the Ship cadets continued to sleep in hammocks.

"Once hammocks were safely slung, and we were comfortably settled for the night, a bugler would sound the Last Post. If this was expertly played, it could be a very moving moment. Sleep, like death, should ideally

involve a trusting surrender, and there was something strangely humbling and comforting in this knowledge, underlined as it was by the evocative notes of bugler. In sharp contrast, reveille was often something of an unpleasant jar! Reveille was sometimes played by a tall and likeable cadet. He used to help out in the boiler-house, and wished to go to sea as an engineer, but he was a terrible bugler! I remember how, one morning, a cadet, who slung his hammock near mine, said that he would refuse to turn out, on the credible grounds that the marvellously inexpert notes from his bugle could not possibly be recognised as reveille!"

For daily use, coal had to be transferred from the coal hole to the ready use bunkers in the boilerhouse on the upper deck. Coal bags were filled by a party of cadets and winched up a relatively narrow shaft by a steam dolly winch.

"It was while engaged in this one day that a dramatic accident happened. A cadet was lifting the handles of a heavy coal bag onto the metal hook on the end of the winching cable, when his hand became caught fast between the handles and the hook. Panicked shouting by his shipmates was mistaken by the winch operator, topside, for 'Heave away!,' which he promptly did, and the unfortunate cadet rose from our midst and swiftly disappeared into the shaft. Matters were made worse when shouts of 'Vast heaving!' were heeded, and the cadet became suspended, motionless half-way up the shaft. The winch operator peered down to see what was awry, and once he realised what had happened, he evidently decided that it was better to continue winching his human cargo upwards, rather than lowering the cadet back into the coal hole. Finally topside, and released, the victim was quite understandably in a state of shock but not, as far as I remember, seriously injured."

"There was a time when Catholics were not eligible to be Conway cadets, and even when Catholics were eventually welcomed into the shipboard family, they were not entitled to be cadet captains, until this ban too fell away. There was, however, a Catholic tradition, which had long been observed in the Ship, and in all ships of the Royal Navy. For immediately on coming aboard, cadets knew that they had to face aft, and salute. How many knew what, exactly, was being saluted? When all England was Catholic there was a crucifix, or a statue of the Virgin and Child on the quarterdeck, and it was these Christian symbols that were being honoured. I would love to have sung the Conway song with my shipmates, but was never able to do so because it was only sung at divine service, which Catholics did not attend."

They were taken instead by boat to Port Dinorwic and then by bus to Caernarfon where they attended the local Catholic Church.

"While waiting on the upper deck for the boat, which would take us Catholics to Port Dinorwic, the strains of that lovely hymn, Eternal Father, Strong to Save would waft up from below, and I wished that I too were below in fraternal solidarity, and joining in."

1952 February 6th

"In my first term in the House, before going out to the Ship, I was among a group of cadets attending a mathematics class in the Nelson Block when the history master, Mr. Kingsford entered and spoke quietly to the mathematics master, Mr. Miller, who was facing the blackboard. Mr. Kingsford left, but Mr. Miller did not turn to face us until at least a minute had passed, and we were keenly aware that something dramatic had happened. What could it have been? Eventually Mr. Miller turned to say 'I am sorry to have to tell you that His Majesty the King has died.' We could not believe it. Why? Almost certainly because the King had been such a quietly inspiring and affectionate presence throughout the war, when we had been children.

An awareness of His Majesty was somehow inseparable from any thoughts of the national pride, which so frequently needed expression in that war. For this reason he seemed to be an essential and permanent presence, much as our parents were an essential and apparently permanent presence."

"I was in Signals class with Jackie Oliver. One of our party asked to go to the heads. While there he was tuned into the BBC on his crystal set and heard the news and mournful music. He rushed back to class and told Oliver who asked him how he knew. He then delivered a bollocking for listening to a radio in the bog and not concentrating on bodily functions. At the end of the class, Oliver dragged the poor guy to see Brookie who delivered another bollocking for listening to the radio. Brookie then dragged the poor guy to see Hewitt who gave him a third bollocking. Hewitt told Brookie to get the upper deck watch to signal to the dock watch to phone the house and tell the duty telephone operator to phone the BBC in Bangor to confirm the news. 'Yes, true' said the BBC. Frantic semaphore conveyed the news from the dock to the upper deck watch who, after many repeats, passed it to Brookie. All hands were mustered on the upper deck for general salute and the ensign was lowered to half mast."

That morning, an hour or two before we heard the shattering news, a cadet had accidentally hoisted the *Conway* ensign, on the flagstaff ashore, upside down, and he was later tortured by the belief that this very public and acutely embarrassing mistake had somehow caused the death of the King!

"It was soon announced that, as Cadets in the Royal Naval Reserve, we would be required to wear black armbands for a period of mourning. I think it true to say that we were aware of being part of a solemn and prolonged historic occasion."

1952 May

The Padre decided they needed a mast at Llanberis rectory for scouting ceremonies, so one was prepared in the Ship and towed to Port Dinorwic by one of the motorboats. The Conway Scout Group then walked the 12 miles from Port Dinorwic to Llanberis carrying the flagpole on their shoulders.

Throughout the period 1950 to 1953, the Headmaster and Captain Hewitt continued debating the curriculum and organisation of *Conway* internally, with the committee and with others. These were perhaps driven by an apparent slippage in educational standards. There were disagreements in committee over technical training for junior cadets after Blue Funnel's representative said they had

Carrying The Mast to Llanberis

"reached the limit of taking Conway's lame ducks; it was giving Conway a bad reputation in the company and with the Board of Trade."

There had been difficulties in placing some cadets because of their low mathematics marks. Ideas came and went. A favourite seemed to be a purely academic two year course at Plas Newydd followed by two or three terms in the Ship dedicated to practical nautical training. Under pressure from Captain Hewitt, attendance at the Aberdovey Outward Bound courses was stopped and consideration given to collaboration with Eskdale Mountain School instead. There were even meetings to discuss greater collaboration between *Conway* and *Worcester*, including combined exams and passing out certificates, perhaps presaging a combined establishment. Discussions were held with Pangbourne about introducing a GCE A level course. While the debate ebbed and flowed, the three year course, approved in 1947, finally started in 1952. *Conway* training now provided two options:

- The new 3 year course accepted boys between the ages of 13 years and 6 months and 14 years and 9 months. The first year would not count towards sea time seniority. There would be one intake a year in January, with a maximum of 125 cadets.

- The established 2 year course accepted boys between the ages of 14 years 9 months and 16 years 6 months. There were 2 intakes a year in May and September, each of up to 50 cadets.

Despite all the heartache over the introduction of the 3 year course, the editorial of the Cadet magazine in January 1953 reported on the first year of the new course

"… the experiment has been a great success and its popularity is growing … there were far more applicants for the second course coming in the New Year than we can possible accept."

The *Conway* Certificate was revised to align with the new General Certificate of Education. The front remained the same but the back now listed the passing out exam results for each subject. To be awarded an Ordinary Certificate a cadet must have reached at least the Fifth Class, have been at least six terms in the Ship, be at least 16 years of age and have achieved a 50% mark. For an Extra Certificate the cadet also had to have reached

"65% of the aggregate of twice his term percentage plus thrice his examination percentage plus his executive percentage, and have obtained a pass standard in Maths, Navigation, English and Spanish or History/ Geography."

1952 June 14th

Mr. Drake and four cadets travelled to Birkenhead to collect the pinnace, after some repairs, and bring her back to the Ship. They broke down three times en route and eventually were left drifting for over eight hours in very rough conditions out into the Mersey estuary almost to the bar lightship. Rockets and smoke signals eventually attracted the attention of the Royal Iris ferry, which arranged for the New Brighton lifeboat to tow them safely back into dock.

1952 November

The exhaust pipe on the juice barge broke and all four of the crew suffered extreme CO_2 poisoning. The medical officer Dr. Reid feared they would die but fortunately they all recovered.

1952 December

Two cadets ran away from the Ship, one was persuaded to return but the other did not.

During the holidays prospective cadets would attend for interview and to sit the entrance exams.

"In December 1952, at just 14 years of age, my father put me on a train to Bangor in North Wales. For a boy unused to travelling anywhere that could not be reached on his bicycle, this was a journey of some magnitude and, as it turned out, it was a journey that was to set the course of my life in so many ways. The purpose of this journey was to attend a written examination and interview for a place at Conway. It must have been the beginning of the Christmas holiday, as there were few serving cadets in evidence, only those who had stayed behind to 'look after' the fifty or so young applicants. Holiday or not, from the moment of my arrival at the House, I was conscious of an atmosphere of organisation. My arrival was noted against a typed list and I was allocated to a dormitory. Then a meal was served on the mess deck followed by a conducted tour of the House. All these events were controlled to a timetable; orders were broadcast by a cadet with a bosun's pipe over the tannoy, with a somewhat rotund Lt. Cdr. Lawrence standing in the stairwell demanding that we all 'keep to starboard' as we hurried from place to place; impressive stuff for a boy from the fells above Bassenthwaite Lake! Not much sleep that night, but in the morning, early, there was just enough light to make out through the elegant dormitory windows, the famous wooden ship "Conway" lying to her mooring in the tide and in silhouette against the Snowdon range. Everything was still and quiet but then, 'Wakie, Wakie, Rise and Shine!,' suddenly shattered the peace. This was no invitation to the guest applicants to make their way to breakfast; it was an order to be obeyed at once! Bathroom, get dressed, make bunk, muster on the mess deck along with various other instructions, all executed with the urgency expected by the duty cadets. After breakfast, the mess deck was cleared away and it became the examination room, mathematics in the forenoon, English in the afternoon. Then, after tea, interviews got under way and, when my turn came, I found myself facing an officer and a teacher who turned out to be friendly enough! The following day, after breakfast, those applicants facing very long return journeys were free to depart while the rest of us were ferried in motor boats, again crewed entirely by cadets, (not a member of staff in sight), out to the huge black and white Ship. Although shown around various parts of the vessel, we applicants had no experience of ships upon which to draw and found it difficult to take everything in apart from the massiveness of her structure and fittings. In the short time available to us however, I do remember that we were invited to climb the mainmast shroud; but just a few steps up the ratlins and our initial enthusiasm was quickly replaced by our instinct for self-preservation! Our visit to the Ship probably lasted no more than half an hour and soon we all returned home to await our results. After what seemed like an eternity, the postman brought the news that I had been accepted to join Conway for a two-year course commencing after the Easter holiday in 1953."

1953

The chart room, or chart house, on the upper deck was in regular use.

"From very early in our first term we had instruction in the use of sextants with Captain Hewitt and we were checked off on his personal list as having been up, out and over the main mast - we had several sessions with

him. Apart from the sextants - I suppose that was why it was locked (but so was the spud locker) - there were some charts, of course, Decca, a Kelvin Hughes sounder, Brown's gyro, a deviascope - barograph, not Loran, D/F and a telegraph."

Forward of the mainmast was the so-called science room, no longer used for science as this endeavour had been transferred to the shore base. It was where 'Spud' Murphy now imparted the art of navigation.

Sextant Class With Capt Hewitt 1952

"I remember an incident in the old science room. The instructor, while sitting at the teacher's desk, swung his legs and knocked over a large chemical foam fire extinguisher. Anxious as always to help, the cadets all rallied round and were eventually successful in getting the extinguisher through the door onto the upper deck. Not however, before almost all the foam was discharged. The classroom, the instructor and most of the cadets looked like something from Scott of the Antarctic."

"During our first term we were taken onboard the Ship and introduced to the idea of going aloft. Most of us, I believe, were a little apprehensive. The safety-net under the main mast rigging did not look too secure and did not really help in quelling any nervousness. However, as time went on I enjoyed going aloft. In the summer term when the weather was warm and sunny the main top was an ideal place to lie and soak up the rays. It was also an ideal place for the smokers as, when they were lying flat on the top, they were invisible from the Ship. There was also no chance of any authority figure coming upon you without warning."

Morning Divisions

The occasional cadet performed feats that can only be described as hair-raising.

> *"One cadet during my time would go out to the end of the yard on the footropes, climb on top of the yard and then saunter nonchalantly back to the rigging along the yard. It was rumoured that he could stand on the main truck but I never actually saw that feat performed."*

In 1952, the BBC was making a TV show about North Wales and included in it were a few shots of the *Conway*.

> *"In order to impress the viewers with our daring and skills the main mast was dressed with cadets. A number of us ran up the rigging and then spread out on the crosstrees and the yards, using the footropes. I'm sure it looked very impressive to the viewers but the thing which impressed most of us was the BBC cameraman, whom nobody saw, running up and down the rigging while carrying and using a large TV camera."*

> *"Conditions in the Ship were tough but there was an air of homeliness that is hard to describe. When one got back late after a day of boat duty, or even slack party, perhaps cold and soaked to the skin, you could hang your wet togs up in the drying room, luxuriating in the heat from the steam pipes and then go down to the orlop deck to your sea chest and relax with a book and maybe some tuck you had hidden away for such an occasion as this. My memories of my chest (port side of the orlop deck overlooking the hold) are always warm and cosy - unless some stupid bugger had left a scuttle open and the wind was getting in! If you wanted to be really quiet you could go down to the reading room at the after end of the hold, having requested Top of course, and curl up in a corner of one of the settees there with your latest letters or a book."*

Friday night was always fish and chips night.

"I remember as a new chum, in my position at the bottom of the mess, all that was left by the time it reached my place, were two chips. I got up left the table with my plate and approached the officer of the day, Ernie Moore, with my complaint, must admit I felt like Oliver Twist."

Ernie listened to the complaint, looked at the plate with the two chips and said

"Well lad you had better go back to your mess and eat them before they get cold."

"Every once in a while we would be faced with the dreaded operation of hoisting the swivel. The four enormous anchors which held our old wooden mother captive in the middle of the strait were all connected by huge chain anchor cables to a giant swivel more or less under the forefoot of the Ship. From there two more cables led up to the hawse pipes. Now, in a perfect world this would allow the old lady to swing lazily to and fro with every change of the tide. First with her head towards Menai Bridge then towards Port Dinorwic; but every once in a while she would get her knickers in a twist. At the next slack water, every cadet would man all the boats with the hope of hauling the Ship's stern round and getting the twist out of the anchor cable. Some hope, so Operation Swivel would be put into gear. Lifting tackles would be laid out, double Spanish burtons, triple Spanish burtons - anything to get a better mechanical advantage, which would help us lift the equivalent of a Cromwell Tank off the bottom of the strait. Finally, when all was set up, Brookie, his circular glasses glinting with concentration, would calculate the exact moment when the curtain should go up. Hoisting boats was nothing like this. Little by little the filthy black monster would appear above the surface until the order; 'Vast heaving!' would allow us to catch our breath. Then stages would be rigged and the Slack Party would be sent down to chip off all the barnacles and grunge and pump fish oil into the bearing. Iron pipes to act as tommy bars would then be stuck in to the upper and lower halves and the stronger cadets would sweatily heave back and forth till all was loosened up. After that, Eric, the rest of the officers and probably a surveyor from Liverpool would climb into the pinnace for the 'great inspection.' There was more gold braid down there than you could shake a stick at! The heads under the Focsle were out of bounds for the day. You can imagine if some chump pulled the chain at the wrong moment! When the OK was given, the whole operation would go into reverse and the monster would slide back into his lair for another year or two"

Inspecting the swivel was not the only maintenance required. *Conway* was a wooden ship, and by 1953 she was 114 years old. Her sisters were all long since scrapped and there were very few similar vessels surviving She had last been dry docked in 1938 and a long overdue overhaul had been further delayed by the war. In the post war years all energies were focused on establishing the shore base and achieving a smooth change of command from Captain Goddard to Captain Hewitt. By 1953, the ship was badly in need of a refit. A comprehensive survey identified the extent of the work. It was to include a proper central-heating system, to replace all coal fired equipment with electric power (an underwater Ship to shore power cable was considered), a 'dramatic' redesign of the Ship's internal layout and accommodation and a new copper bottom! The work would be organised by the same Mr. Dickie who had completed the 1938 refit, and was planned to last just four weeks. She would have to be dry-docked, and that meant a move back to Birkenhead.

CHAPTER 23

1953 THE LOSS OF THE SHIP

At 8.15 am on Wed 14th April 1953, *Conway* slipped her mooring off Plas Newydd and was taken under tow for the first stage of her return to Birkenhead for a refit. This was intended to prepare her for at least another twenty years service. As she moved away down the strait on that bright fresh morning, no one knew that within a few hours, under the fearful gaze of the thousands who waited to cheer her under the Menai suspension bridge she would run aground and break her back. Britain's last commissioned, floating wooden walled ship of the line would be a sad wreck. This chapter deals with the story of that day; but the simple chronology presented needs to be understood in the context of the weather, tides and other physical conditions that make the strait such a difficult stretch of water. That is covered in Chapter 24, Two Bridges Too Far, a definitive study of the very unusual physical conditions, unique to the Menai Strait, which contributed to the loss of the Ship.

The Plan

The Menai Strait is a 19 mile narrow and twisting stretch of water between the island of Anglesey and the Gwynedd coast of North Wales. The nearest entrance to the strait, at Caernarfon, was too shallow for the Ship, so to get to Birkenhead she would have to leave by the Penmon entrance. That meant a return through the Swellies, one of the most dangerous water channels in Britain. The Swellies are bounded at one end by the Britannia bridge, also commonly referred to until the fire in 1970 as the tubular bridge, and at the other end by the Menai suspension bridge. The tide enters the strait first from the south-western end at Caernarfon, and somewhat later (having passed around the island) a stronger flow of tide enters from the north-eastern end at Penmon. The two tidal streams are said always to meet between the Menai suspension bridge and Penmon. While the southwestern entrance acts more like a normal estuary, the presence of these two dissimilar tides in the same waterway results in very unusual tidal conditions throughout the rest of the strait. In particular, the northeast-going flood stream in the Swellies reverses its direction while the tide is still on the rise, thus the tide continues to rise after the direction of the stream has reversed. Exactly when this occurs is heavily dependent on atmospheric conditions. While the southwest flowing stream is nearly always stronger than the northeast flowing stream six hours later, there are times during strong southerly winds out at sea when over several consecutive tides there isn't any south-westward flow in the strait at all. Conversely, strong northerlies at sea can occasionally result in a southwest-going stream of awesome strength. Moreover, both northerlies and southerlies will vary both the duration of slack water in the Swellies and the time it occurs. Quite clearly this is not at all the sort of place where you can expect to move a ship simply by following a timetable, as was eventually attempted.

Planning the transit of the Swellies was almost impossibly constrained by two quite contradictory considerations:

- Cheese Rock sits underwater directly in the middle of the narrow channel exactly where Conway would enter the Swellies. At 22 feet draught *Conway* needed at least 24 feet of water over the rock to pass safely. This depth was possible only on the very few highest tides in the year. Her entry to the Swellies had to be delayed until there was this sufficient depth of water.

- On the other hand, *"It was vitally important for the Ship to be out of the Swellies before the tide turned against her"*[4] since, once the southwest-going stream sets in on a big tide it gathers momentum with remarkable rapidity and could quickly overpower the tugs, this encouraged the earliest possible entry into the Swellies.

So, owing to the deep draught of the Ship, the choice lay between either waiting for positive clearance over Cheese Rock in the hope that the tugs would prevail against the rapidly accelerating contrary stream, or making an earlier transit in order to avoid that contrary stream but with the risk that she might find the bottom on Cheese Rock. But even if she had found the bottom no real harm would have been done since it was a rising tide. Captain Hewitt's calculations were therefore based on the highest tide of the year, and were determined so that he could pass safely over Cheese Rock. But, unknown to him, and quite understandably, his calculations appear to have been based on false parameters.[6] It thus seems that because of this,

"exact timings were eventually fixed and stress was laid on the critical point of the timetable, which was to pass under Britannia Bridge at 9.20 am"[7]

As we shall see, everything was to hinge around his rigid adherence to that specific time.

This dependence on the highest tide of the year did not fit well with the need to minimise the effect on training. It was decided to shift her first from Plas Newydd back to her old mooring off Bangor pier. She would spend the summer term there[8] and all the cadets would move with her, the accommodation at Plas Newydd being temporarily vacated.[8] At the end of the summer term she would be towed to the West Float dry-dock at Birkenhead for refit during the long summer holidays.[9] To further minimise disruption, the Easter holiday would be reduced to

"no more than a token ... but to give a week's additional summer leave instead. At the same time this will give the ship repairers an extra week."[8]

Similar arrangements would apply in reverse for her return in September of that year.[8]

Preparation

For Captain Hewitt, this was to be one of the most important tasks of his period in command. Although discussions about a refit had had started by February 1952,[3] it was April 1952 before there was sufficient agreement[1] for him to begin planning the passage. The Plas Newydd mooring lay within the jurisdiction of the Caernarfon Harbour Trust, which extended from seaward of the Bar in the west, to Britannia Bridge in the east. Thus in 1952, the Harbour Trust was advised of *Conway's* intended move to Bangor the following April. Some reassurances must have been sought for one of the earliest letters in the Trust's *Conway* file is a reply dated November 1952, in which Capt Hewitt, on behalf of Committee, confirms that the matter was raised at a recent meeting and that the MMSA accepted full responsibility for the movement of the Ship.[40] He also began gathering navigational and tidal data from the Harbour Master at Caernarfon and tidal data from Bidston Observatory on the Wirral.[7] The most obvious source of vastly superior information was the local pilots whose family had been piloting vessels through the strait for several generations, but for whatever reason they were never really consulted. Captain Hewitt seemed to have arrived at some early conclusions as the Headmaster recorded in his diary that

> *"No problem for small boats at HW slack (2 hrs before Liverpool). Avoid going through with the first of the east going (flood) stream for fear of Price's Point or Swellies Rock."*[10]

Captain GAB 'Gabby' King (*Conway's* Second Officer) recorded at the time that *"serious preparations"* only began early in 1953 but that planning rapidly began to

> *"dominate the lives of all of those of us onboard."*[9]

He also records that in the Spring Term of 1953

> *"taking soundings and current rates became part of the curriculum."*[11]

Why this was necessary is not clear since this had already been done in 1949 by Captain Goddard. Captain Hewitt was already on the staff then and had remained in the Ship for the transit from Bangor in 1949 so he was familiar with the extent of Goddard's survey work but perhaps was not satisfied with it. Interestingly, at the time of writing, no records have been found of *any* contact between Captains Hewitt and Goddard in 1952 or 1953. Captain McManus, in his more recent assessment states that Captain Hewitt made several passages through the Swellies in the Ship's No. 1 motorboat at high, low and slack waters and also observed the tides from the shore.[12] However my review of the Ship's log book for the period April 52 to April 53 identified only the following specific activities.[13] All are within a few weeks of the shift:

16th March 1953	Captain Hewitt and Captain Miller to Swellies at slack water am/pm.
25th March 1953	Laid marker buoy off Glyn Garth for Ship's mooring.
27th March 1953	Captain through Swellies to Bangor.
28th March 1953	Captain with pinnace to Bangor.
29th March 1953	Captain to Bangor in No 1.
30th March 1953	Captain, Captain Miller and tug masters through Swellies in No. 1.
10th April 1953	Captain through Swellies with Caernarfon Harbour Master to buoy channel. Three extra buoys were laid as an aid to the transit of Cribben Gutter.
11th April 1953	Transfer marks on Church Island adjusted.
12th April 1953	Captain through Swellies in pinnace.

This number of trips seems somewhat at odds with claims of extensive and early surveys. It is possible that other journeys were made but not recorded, however the log books were normally scrupulous in recording movements of *Conway's* small boats, especially through the Swellies or when Ship's officers were present. Although useful in familiarising Captain Hewitt with the topographical features of the passage, these trips, in a small boat drawing only inches of water, would have been of little value in assessing the reaction of a deep ship to any undertow effects of the tide in the Swellies's narrow channels. Inexplicably, the Menai pilots, with unrivalled knowledge of the strait, were not consulted at this stage. However, another Old *Conway*, Captain James Miller (*Conway* 1925-27), who was a Liverpool pilot and so not familiar with the Swellies, did accompany Captain Hewitt on a couple of these exploratory visits.

On 7th July 1952 the Ship's log book records

> *"Draughtsmen from A Holt and Co measuring up the Ship for plans."*[13]

Copies of their very detailed plans are online at www.hmsconway.org.

Captain Hewitt's control over planning seems to have been limited to local arrangements at Plas Newydd. When it came to questions of tugs, personnel, and responsibilities WH Dickie (no connection with the Dickies of Beaumaris), the *Conway* committee's Honorary Superintendent Shipwright in Liverpool appeared to be in charge. Strangely, apart from *Conway* management committee meetings on 28th January and 25th March 1953,[13] records of only one meeting between Mr. Dickie and Captain Hewitt have been found; the Ship's log book recording Mr. Dickie visiting on 11th February 1953

> *"in connection with the refit."*[13]

Dickie arranged the tugs, recruited the Liverpool pilot, James Miller allocated him the liaison role between

> *"Conway, Menai Pilots, tugs etc"*

Miller was Blue Funnel's preferred Liverpool pilot and would pilot the Ship up the Mersey on the final leg of her subsequent transit from Bangor to Birkenhead. Dickie also called a key planning meeting in Liverpool on 24th March to which Captain Hewitt was not even invited.[14] Captain Durant of Rea Towing, in his report to the Inquiry, confirms Dickie's lead role,

> *"We were first advised by letter from Messrs. Alfred. Holt and Co., dated 13th February 1953 signed by Mr. Dickie, of the projected movement, in two stages, of HMS Conway from Menai Strait to Birkenhead... we were requested to have two tugs available for the various moves......."*[14]

When it came to a critical decision about the number of tugs to be employed, Captain Hewitt and Pilot Jones requested three but were over-ruled by Conway's management committee.[7,12] Captain Hewitt clearly had little influence over most planning.

Conway had been shifted many times on the Mersey by the Rea Towing Company's tugs as Captain Durrant, Rea's Marine Manager, confirmed, most recently using the same two tugs and their tug masters.[14] Two tugs had used on the passage from Liverpool to Bangor during the war. Similarly, only two were used for the transit from Bangor, through the Swellies, to Plas Newydd in 1949. That transit though had been with a following stream and so was much easier. Against the tide, the return would be a far more challenging affair. *Conway* had no engines and so was incapable of independent manoeuvre in the twisting channel, and her anchors formed part of her permanent mooring so she had no means of anchoring in case of emergency. According to Captain Hewitt's son, Michael, both Hewitt and the Senior Menai Strait Pilot Richard Jones considered that three tugs were needed.[12, 15] The Inquiry confirms that Pilot Richard Jones had *"asked for three tugs but it was assured that two were ample for the job."[7]*

However, when challenged, he admitted that

"his experience of towed ships was negligible."[7]

Michael Hewitt says he understood from his father that, in rejecting the request for three tugs, Dickie argued that he arranged hundreds of tows a year and, when Captain Hewitt supported Jones's views, bluntly enquired how many tows Hewitt had organised?[15] Dickie thought two sufficient. The Inquiry also noted that

"It was not feasible to have one ahead tug on each bow and one astern, owing to the narrowness of the channel."[7]

Captain Durrant told the Inquiry that he was requested

"to have two tugs available... also one of the Tug masters who was present when Conway had made her previous move."[14]

In so doing Captain Durrant carefully reminded the Inquiry he had more than complied with the request; providing the same two tugs that had brought *Conway* through the Swellies to Plas Newydd in 1949 and both tug masters from that transit.

On 19th March 1953, the Captain visited the Admiralty, who owned the Ship, but the reason is not recorded.[13]

"On 24th March 1953, Mr. Dickie held a meeting at Birkenhead to discuss the operation with Captain Durrant, Captain Duff (Rea's Supervisory Tug-Master) and Liverpool Pilot Captain Miller. Captain Hewitt and the Menai pilots were not invited to the meeting.[12, 14, 16] Captain Durrant noted that "It was then arranged that the above named - except Mr. Dickie - would proceed to Menai on March 30th to complete arrangements, on the spot, with Captain Hewitt, HMS Conway, the Caernarfon Harbour Master and Menai Pilots."[14]

One can but speculate if there was something lacking in the relationship between Mr. Dickie and Captain Hewitt.

On 30th March 1953, as agreed, Captains Duff, Durrant and Miller went to the strait for their first formal discussions with Captain Hewitt, Captain Rees Thomas, the Caernarfon Harbour Master and the strait pilots. This was the first time the latter had been involved or even consulted.[16] The date for the transit was fixed for Tuesday 14th April 1953, depending of course on suitable weather.[12] This would be the second of three successive days of spring tides. On page 184 of his autobiography, Captain King claims that the shift was planned for the 13th but delayed for twenty-four hours at the last minute because of deteriorating weather.[11] This is not recorded in the Ship's log book (King was duty officer on both days) nor can I find any other corroboration for this earlier date. However the Ship's log book does confirm the deteriorating weather with a falling barometer, increasing winds, and ships' boats dragging their moorings.[13]

The meeting then moved on to consider timings. Captain Thomas recommended passing under Britannia Bridge at 9.25 am, using timings based on Caernarfon Bar. He estimated that there would then be 10-15 minutes slack water. Captain Hewitt's observations at Britannia Bridge indicated that Slack Water started 10 minutes before Captain Thomas's timings. He therefore intended to arrive at Britannia Bridge at 9.20 am, so as to have 5 minutes in hand.[12] While passing under the bridge even before the time recommended by the Harbourmaster lent a retrospective air of respectability to the operation in the light of what eventually happened, this does seem slender reason for fixing the vitally important time when the Ship would pass under the bridge upon which the success of the whole operation depended. It was more likely that 9.20 am was (erroneously) seen as the earliest time when a vessel of 22 feet draught could pass over Cheese Rock, but which would have focused unwelcome attention on the questionable presence of such a ship at Plas Newydd.

A final briefing meeting, to include the tug masters, was arranged onboard *Conway* for Monday April 13th, the day prior to the move.

Durrant[14] and McManus[12] confirm that all aspects of the operation were discussed and agreed at the 30th March meeting. Afterwards Captains Hewitt, Durrant, Duff and Miller, with the two strait pilots, went down to the water's edge by Britannia Bridge and watched the tide turn.[14, 16] The Ship's log book records that they later went through the Swellies in No 1 motorboat.[13]

Early on Monday 13th April, the tugs arrived from Liverpool and made their way past the Ship to Port Dinorwic.[13]

In the afternoon, Captain Hewitt took the tug masters FA Brown (*Dongarth*) and F. Cooper (*Minegarth*) through the Swellies in *Conway's* motorboat about one hour before low water.[7] This would have shown them very clearly the restrictions and obstacles to navigation they faced. On their return from this inspection, the boat picked up Messrs. Duff, Miller, Pope (Marconi Representative) and Durrant from the Plas Newydd dock[13] and all proceeded onboard *Conway* for the final planning meeting before the shift the next day. The meeting involved Captain Hewitt, Captains Brown, Cooper, Miller, Duff and Durrant.[12, 14] The Inquiry did not record that Mr. Pope was present although he clearly came onboard with the rest of the party.[7] The Swellies trip and the visit of all these individuals is not recorded in the Ship's log book. The strait pilots were excluded from this meeting,[16] even though this was the meeting to fix the final timetable and arrangements, details that Captain Hewitt would refuse to deviate from on the day. Indeed the Inquiry acknowledged that the only time the local pilots were consulted was on 30th March, observing that on no occasion did a meeting take place involving all concerned.[7]

"The exact timing of each point of the move was finally fixed and agreed upon,"

as were other arrangements and dispositions.[7] These can be summarised as:

- *Dongarth* would secure forward under command of F A Brown accompanied by the junior Pilot John Richard Jones. They would be in direct radio contact with Captain Miller (responsible for all communications) in the Ship. The Rea Towing Company representatives confirmed *Dongarth* alone had sufficient power to tow *Conway* against the tidal stream expected and to counter the effects of the stern tug.[14] They knew their tugs and had towed *Conway* many times before.

- *Minegarth* would make fast with her stern to *Conway's* stern. She would be under the command of F Cooper. *Conway* was a 'dead' ship with no motive power or steering of her own. The question of *Minegarth* needing to slip her towing spring and assist *Dongarth* forward after clearing the Swellies was discussed which, while an acknowledgement of the stronger tide expected on the other side of the bridge, was thought unlikely to be necessary. It was deemed essential to keep *Minegarth* astern in the Swellies for effective control of the Ship in the narrow channels.[7] Provision was therefore only made for one tug forward. This decision was to have fatal consequences. *Conway's* Second Officer, 'Gabby' King was to be in charge of the stern party and communications with *Minegarth*.

- Captain Hewitt's proposed times for passing each point were reviewed. 9.20 am was confirmed as the starting time when the Ship would pass under Britannia Bridge. It was stressed that this was the critical point of the timetable. It was only forty-five minutes before predicted local high water (Liverpool minus 2.00), which was dangerously late on the tide for a ship that had taken 18 minutes to complete the inbound transit with the stream flooding behind her.[17] But being a rising tide the Ship was restricted by her excessive draught until she had clearance over Cheese Rock, and it would have been easy for Captain Hewitt to misinterpret the ambiguous title on Captain Goddard's chart and arrive at the false conclusion that he wouldn't have the Ship's draught over the rock before 9.20 am, which would seem to explain that being fixed as 'the critical time,' although in reality the Ship could have passed over the rock with the last of the tide behind her up to 40 minutes before then.[5] The 9 cables passage through the Swellies from Britannia Bridge to the suspension bridge was estimated to take about 15 minutes. This assumed there would be a 10 minute period of slack water starting at 9.20 am.[5] This was based on Captain Hewitt's observations on smaller tides, which failed to recognise that the duration of slack water in the Swellies varies inversely with the height of the tide, and which duration and the time it occurs are both further conditioned by atmospheric pressure and the strength and direction of the wind.[18] Based on this over optimistic premis it was estimated that the tow should pass under the suspension bridge and so leave the Swellies between 9.35 am and 9.40 am. By the time the tow arrived at the suspension bridge it was agreed that the West going stream would have started and would already have attained a rate of 4 knots. This rate (only 5 minutes after the stream was estimated to start) was based on Captain Hewitt's and Captain Miller's observations (on smaller tides), and, according to Captain Durrant it was confirmed by both strait pilots.[14] But it must be very doubtful that all should have been so positive about such high precision performance by a tide that is known to be heavily influenced by the weather, and within minutes of its start, when the actual time that tide would turn was itself a very mobile response to a number of little understood variables.[18] Shortly after the 1949 transit Captain Goddard said

  "A knowledge of the tides is of primary importance though for during high spring tides 'a maximum rate of 10 knots is usual', which considerably limits the safety periods."[41]

- But, the Ship was now inextricably committed to passing under Britannia Bridge at precisely 9.20 am the following morning.

- Mr. Pope, the Marconi representative, confirmed that the walkie-talkie radios (brought down with the tugs) for communication between the Ship and the tugs had been tested with the tugs down channel and found to be satisfactory. They would not prove so reliable in actual use.

- The Liverpool pilot Captain Miller would be in charge of communications with both tugs.[14] Tugs were to acknowledge or reply to orders by agreed blasts on the whistle if they could not respond over the radio. In case of complete radio failure semaphore would be used. Cadet Ian Grindrod would be the signalman on the foredeck.[19] Cadet Mike Begley, who would be the stern signaller on the poop under direction of the Second Officer, still has the semaphore flags he used that day.[20]

- Captain Hewitt, on *Conway's* Focsle head would be in command throughout. He would be advised by the senior Menai pilot, Richard John Jones.

- Lt. Cdr. John Brooke Smith, the First Officer, would be on the foredeck acting as liaison with a team of cadets as runners, including Cadet Noel Roberts from Beaumaris, the youngest cadet onboard that day.[21]

- The Second Officer was in charge of the stern party based in sick bay.[11]

- Crew members and the rest of the *Conway* cadets would be allocated around the Ship.

- Catering staff would be in the galley and the Captain's steward, Walter William in his cubby.

- Captain Hewitt's wife, son Michael and daughter and some members of staff would accompany the Ship as passengers.

- Mr. Hampson, the science teacher and a keen amateur photographer, would be onboard to create a full photographic record of the day.

- The gigs were to remain hoisted onboard but the motorboats would follow under their own power, manned by cadets. No 1 motorboat would tow the 3 cutters.

Before following the day's events, let's quickly examine the passage she was about to attempt. I am grateful to Richard Jones, the great-grandson of the Ship's pilot and current Caernarfon Harbour Master for his permission to use his chart of the Swellies that shows *Conway's* planned and actual courses, to the Beaumaris Lifeboat web site for use of their aerial photo of the Swellies and to Norman Murcott of Llangefni for use of many of his excellent photographs taken on from the suspension bridge.

First, the Ship had to be moved from her mooring off Plas Newydd and positioned ready to transit the strait at the appointed time. The passage of the Swellies will be described in a number of legs:

1. They had first to cross from the northern (Anglesey) shore, A on the photo, to the southern (Gwynedd) shore to enter the main channel under the right hand arch of the Britannia Bridge. Point 0c on the chart, B on the photo.

2. They then had to pass safely over the first major hazard, Cheese Rock, midway between points 0c and 1c on the chart.

3. A cable's distance from the bridge to the marker pyramid on the Gwynedd shore they would shape course slightly to port *(the left)*, midway between points 1c and 2c on the chart to line up on the transit markers that defined the safe passage through Cribben Gutter past Cribben Rock. The top of the rock is just breaking the surface to the right of point C on the photo but on the day it would have been completely submerged. The navigation channel is to the right of the rock, close against the wooded Gwynedd shore.

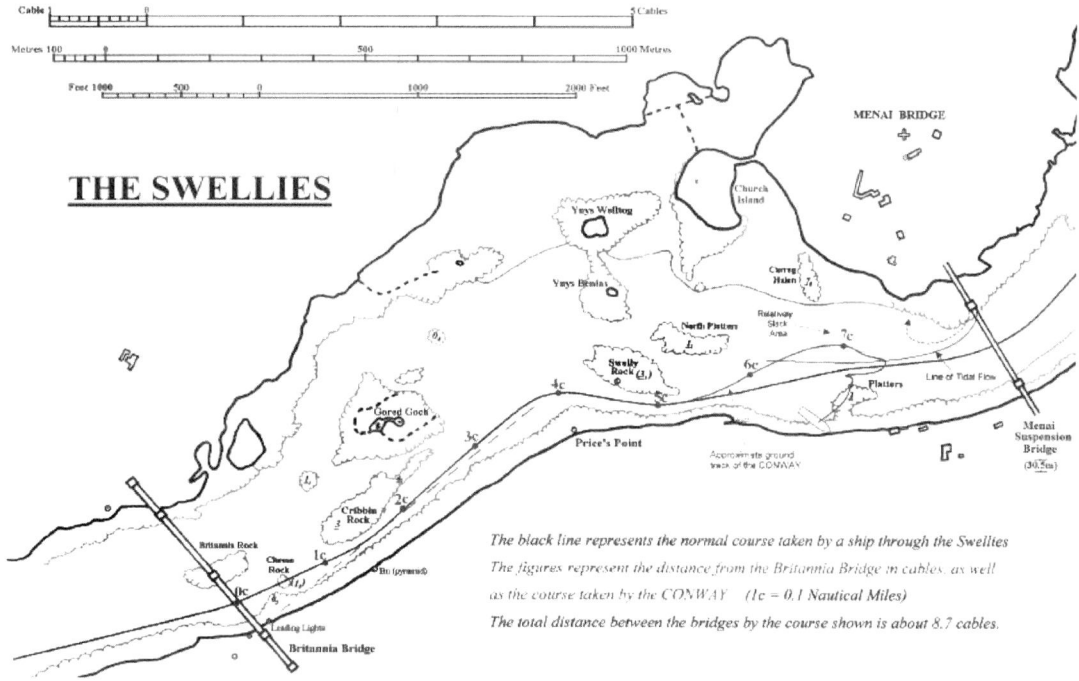

The black line represents the normal course taken by a ship through the Swellies

The figures represent the distance from the Britannia Bridge in cables, as well as the course taken by the CONWAY   (1c = 0.1 Nautical Miles)

The total distance between the bridges by the course shown is about 8.7 cables.

Chart of Actual and Planned Route Through The Swellies

Ariel View of The Swellies

4. At Price's Point (4c on the chart, D on the photo) she had to haul out to clear off lying dangers.

5. A sharp alteration to starboard *(the right)* would enable Swelly Rock to be cleared. The rock is visible to the right of point E on the photo, although on the day this too would have been underwater and so a major hazard to the Ship.

6. With Swelly Rock astern (point 5c on the chart), and when the cross on Llandesillio island was just forward of the beam, they would have to haul out again to make offing past the Platters Rocks until the boathouses on the Gwynedd shore were abeam before steering to pass under the centre of the suspension bridge. The Platters are to the right of point F on the photo.

All these manoeuvres had to be completed within eight ship's lengths which, with the degree of control needed in the narrow channel, presented an obvious challenge for tugs on long scope single hawsers.

The Ship would then pass under the suspension bridge, out of the narrow and twisting Swellies and into the much wider and fairly straight channel to her temporary mooring between Glyn Garth (G on the photo) and Bangor pier, also just visible in the photo as a faint white line out from the Gwynedd shore. However, clearing the Swellies did not mean she was clear of danger. Depending on prevailing conditions, the two tidal streams meet somewhere between the suspension bridge and Penmon at the strait's north-eastern entrance (well beyond point G on the photo). The Ship would probably have to stem a still building stream all the way to her Bangor mooring. The ability of one tug to tow her through this stream would remain critical long after exiting the Swellies if she was to gain her mooring.

The rest of this Chapter describes events as they unfolded, starting the previous evening.

6 pm Monday 13th April

It was early evening when they

> *"hove cables short for test purposes."* [13]

The Ship would have been unusually quiet as the holidays had started and the cadets were all away. Second Officer King, when he completed the log that evening, recorded that that the whole crew were onboard ready to slip and that Captain Miller (Mersey pilot) and 16 cadets were onboard to assist the next day.[13] For one of those 16, Cadet Noel Roberts, it was his first night onboard. He had only recently joined and had spent his time so far in the shore base. He lived at Beaumaris so Lt. Cdr. Brooke Smith invited him to join the party of local cadets who would assist the officers during the transit. He remembers rigging his hammock that evening little knowing it would be the first and last time he would ever sleep in the Ship.[21] The duty officer's first entry in the log the next day said that 17 cadets had been onboard overnight[13] so one more must have crept onboard after 6pm, or he miss-counted the previous evening!

At sunset the watch keeper J H Squires hung out the anchor lights and at midnight he recorded that the barometer was steady at 29' 14" and the wind, calm.[13]

All the planning was over. In just a few hours the transit to Bangor would begin.

Tuesday 14ᵗʰ April - Letting Go

Second Officer King was duty officer that morning and J H Squire was watch keeper.[13] According to King's entry in the Ship's log book, Tuesday 14ᵗʰ April dawned

"cloudless, fine and bright"

with the wind Calm force 0, although by 8 am there was a light north westerly (force 1-2) across the strait, he recorded the draught as: Forward 19 feet 10 inches, Aft 21 feet 10 inches and Mid-ships 20 feet 10 inches.[13]

Captain Hewitt thought it

"seemed a most favourable day for the attempted passage, fine and sunny with little or no wind." [22]

The Inquiry recorded conditions as

"clear and sunny, with a flat calm and light breeze." [7]

Captain Durrant judged the conditions

"almost ideal for the operation." [14]

In his house, 'Ceris', on the Gwynedd shore by the suspension bridge, Lt. Col. Davies recorded a

"fine morning, with just a light breeze from the North, but certainly not enough to worry about." [23]

Lt. Col. Davies was a keen local sailor who knew the waters very well. He was considered an authority on the Swellies and had helped Goddard plan the transit in 1949. He owned Gored Goch island in the middle of the Swellies, living in the house there for many months every summer.[33] It was an encouraging and positive start to the day.

Despite the seeming halcyon conditions in the strait, it was the situation out in the Irish Sea that had greatest effect on the tides,[17] and here the wind was north westerly force 6 increasing 7 with gusts up to force 10.[18] The Liverpool pilot boat's log book also recorded a north west wind force 6, increasing to 7 during the morning.[7] This was very bad news for it would have the effect of adding significantly to the strength of the southwest-going stream.[18] The Inquiry report observes

"It is somewhat surprising to us that the party had no knowledge of the stormy conditions prevailing at sea at the time Conway was to make the passage. Local knowledge may well have been that, under such circumstances, abnormal conditions might be encountered. It seems clear, from the time Conway took to do six cables (9.23 am to 10.10 am), that something very unusual was taking place, possibly a strong undercurrent which is known to occur in the channel." [7]

This is an obvious reference to the Southwest Residual (the SW-going non-tidal current in the strait) that is known to be heavily influenced by winds in the Irish Sea.[17]

5.00 am (approximately)

The tug crews down at Port Dinorwic started their day.[14] With a well planned timetable events onboard *Conway* started to unfold with satisfactory precision and she soon began to bustle with activity.

6.30 am

6.30 am Adjusting The Black Balls

Anchor cables were hove in and the Ship put on slips.[7] Last minute adjustments were made to the two black balls in the starboard mizzen ratlines that warned other vessels that *Conway* was under tow and not under power.[32]

6.50 am

The two tugs left their anchorage and made their way up to the Ship.[14] About the same time the pilot boat was making its way from Caernarfon to the Ship carrying the Joneses, father and son, who were discussing the weather and plans. Jones senior remarked that he would like to enter the Swellies earlier than the time set by Captain Hewitt.[24]

6.55 am

The tugs came alongside a few minutes ahead of schedule.[13]

7.35 am

Dongarth was fast forward and the cadets commenced heaving cables short.[13] *Conway* had no mechanical capstans and it was noted that the leads to the bollards were not particularly clean.[11] *Dongarth*, the forward tug, was secured through *Conway's* starboard hawse pipe using two hawsers, a 4 inch towing wire and a 12 inch towing spring *(large ropes)*.[14]

Minegarth was secure aft. As there were no structural arrangements for securing a towrope astern 'Gabby' King and his small working party of cadets and crew had been obliged to a somewhat Heath-Robinson solution. The 2 stern towing springs came inboard through 2 of the 3 sick bay ports on the lower deck. The ports used were the third and fourth ones on the port side. They opened over the stern of the Ship and had been specially strengthened for the purpose. The large mizzen mast passed down through Sick Bay so King simply turned *(wound)* the springs around the mizzenmast 9 times and then stoppered off *(secured)* further forward.[11] King observed

"This was a solid enough way of making fast but not one which was easily slipped in an emergency."[11] Presumably this was the approach used for earlier tows on the Mersey, from Liverpool in 1941 and from Bangor in 1949.

7.55 am

The two Menai pilots arrived at the Ship,[13] and separated to their respective stations in the Ship and the forward tug. The senior pilot, Richard Jones, who was to remain onboard approached Captain Hewitt and expressed the view that in the light of the conditions he thought the Ship

"a bit late." [16]

Hewitt's response is not known.

Capts Hewitt, Millar and Pilot Jones

Captain Hewitt, Captain Miller and Pilot Jones senior went to their position on the Focsle head. Even though it was a clear day all three wore dark coats over their uniforms with upturned collars and gloves, it was clearly a brisk day.[32]

They were ready to cast off and begin the transit so the forward tug relieved the strain on the Ship's cables, which were to be slipped to marker buoys.

8.05 am

Port and starboard cables were ready for slipping.[13] The Headmaster on the shore took some cine film of the next few minutes before going down to the dock to watch the Ship pass.[25]

8.22 am [13]

With the cables eased, all hands (including the cadets) hauled up the swivel,[26] the anchor cables were slipped to 2 three-inch wire pennants and the pennants themselves buoyed to an attendant boat.[11] Accounts vary but between 8.15 am and 8.22 am *Conway* was free of her mooring and her passage had begun.

From Plas Newydd To Pwllfanogl

The first leg of the transit was very simple, a wide, deep slowly bending channel to the Britannia Bridge.

8.25 am [13]

With the Ship stemming the northeast-going flood stream she was facing Port Dinorwic ie the wrong way. She therefore had to be swung to face in the direction of the Britannia Bridge before proceeding. Cadet John Ellis, having assisted with the heavy work

8.25am Starting to Turn The Ship

of casting off, which required all hands, went below and aft to the starboard gangway where he left the Ship and took charge of No 1 motorboat, which was to follow her to Bangor, towing the three cutters. From this new low vantage point he thought that the wind seemed *"quite strong."*[27]

The Ship was also accompanied by the pinnace and No 2 motorboat, although it has not been possible to ascertain who was onboard them. A number of other small private boats milled about as spectators.

8.31 am [13]

With the turn accomplished and a following tide Conway moved away with little effort from the tugs[7] Captain King remembers the moment vividly,

> *"To those ashore it must have presented a brave spectacle and for those of us onboard it was a moment of excitement and exhilaration."*[1]

On shore, the Headmaster Mr. Browne, with Captain Goddard (who had brought the Ship safely from Bangor to Plas Newydd, albeit by the skin of his teeth), Mr. Alfred Wilson (Hon Secretary of Conway's management committee), Dr. Wilson Read (the Ship's medical officer), Mr. and Mrs Walters and Mrs Drake watched her depart before driving to the banks of the Swellies outside Menai Bridge where they would have a grandstand view of the passage though the Swellies.[28] The Marquis of Anglesey's pennant at Plas Newydd dipped in salute as the Ship passed.[9] Conway's ensign dipped in acknowledgement.

Almost immediately, Captain Miller found difficulties communicating with the stern tug. Conway could transmit messages to *Minegarth* but could not receive them from her, so whistle and simple semaphore signals were adopted as previously agreed.[12]

8.45 am

> *"The passage to the Britannia Bridge was uneventful, the tugs towing easily to arrive at the bridge at the agreed time of 8.45 am"*[7]

This observation was slightly misleading. The actual point of arrival was Pwllfanogl Creek some distance short of the bridge on the Anglesey shore.[22] Captain Durrant followed the Ship to Pwllfanogl in one of *Conway's* motor boats, and watched her pass under the Britannia Bridge before landing (presumably at *Indefatigable*) to go by road to the suspension bridge where he would have a grandstand view as the Ship negotiated the Swellies.[14]

8.50 am [13]

Captain Hewitt ordered the Ship to be stopped and held in position (approximately at the point marked A. on the photo on page 212). Captain Hewitt intended to hold the Ship in this position and then set off so as to pass under the Britannia Bridge at 9.20 am, exactly as planned.

The highly experienced local Pilot Richard Jones, who probably knew the waters better than anyone, was of course looking at the water rather than his watch. The northeast-going stream would have been weaker than usual, suggesting that when the stream reversed direction the contrary stream was likely to be a lot stronger than anticipated by the planning committee. He immediately objected strongly to holding the Ship,

>*"Oh no Captain - we must keep her going"* [16]

The Chief Steward, Lloyd Walter Williams, was delivering mugs of tea to Captain Hewitt and the pilots and overheard this exchange. He confirmed that the pilot said they should go immediately otherwise they would be too late.[29] Captain Hewitt's reply seemed to imply that he was waiting for some important visitors to arrive on the suspension bridge.[29] This rumour of 'VIPs' has had long legs but there has been no other mention of visitors expected on the bridge and of course there was no way Captain Hewitt could possibly know if they had arrived or not. It was possibly a reference to Captain Durrant, from Rea Towing, who had just disembarked to go to the bridge. But Captain Hewitt was not holding the Ship for the convenience of spectators, his overriding concern was the depth of water over Cheese Rock, which his calculations suggested would not equal the draught of the Ship before 9.20 am (apart from any effect of the wind, and unknown to Captain Hewitt, the Ship had better than her own draught over the rock as early as 8.40 that morning[30]). Given the many months of quite unprecedented planning, which reflected the obvious concern about the very feasibility of the outward transit, perhaps the most astonishing fact was that all the planning had been purely theoretical, and no thought had been given to correlating soundings over Cheese Rock with the nearby tide board, which would have eliminated all the guesswork.[31] Instead, on the day, Captain Hewitt adhered rigidly to his committee's timetable and told the pilot:

>*"The Ship goes under the bridge at 9.20 am hours and not one moment before."* [16]

The main opportunity for completing the transit that day had been lost.

9.08 am

Captain Hewitt knew that to pass under the Britannia Bridge at 9.20 am they would need to move off from Pwllfanogl a few minutes earlier in order to work across from the Anglesey shore to the Gwynedd side, and to line up for the very narrow channel under and beyond Britannia Bridge. He gave the fateful order for the forward tug to resume headway. Captain Durrant's report states that the tugs held her off Pwllfanogl from 8.45 am to approximately 9.15 am.[14] The log book records it was from 8.50 am until 9.08 am.[13]

As they passed the buildings of the TS *Indefatigable*, on the Anglesey shore, her colours dipped in salute.[11] It was fitting that *Conway's* last acknowledgement came from *Indefatigable*. The two ships' fates had always been intertwined. They had long been neighbours on the Mersey, and *Indefatigable* had followed *Conway* to the safety of the strait during the war. *Indefatigable* paid off in 1995. The statue of Admiral Lord Nelson on the Anglesey shore looked on as Conway's figurehead of Admiral Lord Nelson, glided by. The tugs manoeuvred the Ship across the strait and aligned her to pass between the centre and right hand towers and into the Swellies at point 0c on the chart, B on the photo.

9.08 am Moving off From Pwllfanogl

9.23 am

Just 3 minutes later than planned, *Conway's* bow passed serenely under the bridge.[13] Captain Hewitt remarked to the pilot that they were 3 minutes late. The pilot answered that they were early rather than late,[7] a strange observation given he had wanted them to proceed much earlier.

Lt. Col. Davies lived in Ceris, the red brick house on the Swellies' Gwynedd bank hard by the suspension bridge.[33] He was in his garden on the banks of the strait

"I heard the tugs whistle as they passed under the Tubes."[23]

He observed that

"the wind was freshening very much, and had gone round to the North East, a bad quarter as it always affects the tides … the wind would increase the rate of flow of the tide. It was obviously going to be a near thing."[23]

Captain Durrant of Rea Towing, now on the suspension bridge, reported that, at 9.40am, the north westerly wind had

"freshened considerably"

and that it was noted

"by a local pilot stationed under the Britannia Bridge"

that the anticipated 10 minute slack water period did not materialise. The south going ebb stream set in immediately at 9.20 am.[14] Instead of 10 minutes of towing through relatively slack water, the stream had set against them before they even started. The identity of this 'local pilot' has never been established. The two Menai pilots were part of the tow and no arrangements had been made to have anyone else under the bridge. Several locals seem to have given themselves the title of 'pilot' and 'Taffy' Oliver, one of the Ship's Warrant Officers, was also credited (quite incorrectly) with being a local pilot so it may have been any of them. None were official Trinity House pilots but the unnamed individual's observations certainly bolstered the party line at the later inquiry.

The Britannia Bridge and Cheese Rock

The Headmaster, Captain Goddard, Mr. Wilson and the rest of his party were by now standing on the main Holyhead-Menai Bridge road waiting for their first sight of the Ship as she cleared Britannia Bridge (there is still a lay-by on the A5 at this vantage point today, although over 50 years of tree growth now limits the view they would have had). The Headmaster's timings are a little out, but his autobiography recalls:

"The old Ship came under the bridge a little ahead of time, like a stately dowager preceded and followed by alert young pages. We stood, filled with a mixture of pride and apprehension."[28]

It is interesting that he, like the pilot, thought them a little early. The

"alert young pages"

were of course the Ship's small boats and cutters. The Headmaster's more contemporaneous diary says,

"walked down and watched her enter the Britannia Bridge at about 09.30."[25]

This conflicts somewhat with his autobiography.

This was anticipated to be a most critical part of the transit because the Ship could ground on Cheese Rock. Timings had all been calculated to provide sufficient depth of water to avoid this. That morning's soundings of the Ship had shown a draught aft of twenty-one feet and 10 inches so they needed at least that depth of water over Cheese Rock, plus a safety margin. As they passed under the Britannia Bridge Cheese Rock lay directly in their path, just 300 yards ahead. No doubt everyone held their breath. However, in just a few minutes Cheese Rock was cleared without incident. It must have seemed to Captain Hewitt as if all their careful planning had been vindicated and that the rest of the transit would be relatively plain sailing. Nothing could have been further from the truth.

As a result of the manoeuvre to cross the strait and enter the Swellies, the forward tug was on the Ship's starboard side. They were now approaching point 1c on the chart, Price's Point was directly ahead so they had to make a slight adjustment to port in order to pass through Cribben Gutter.

Approaching Cribben Gutter - Tug on Starboard Bow

Cheese Rock To Price's Point

They were at point 1c on the chart and now had to transit the extremely narrow channel called Cribben Gutter to point 3c approaching Price's Point. *Conway* almost filled the channel, Captain Goddard, in his planning in 1949, estimated they would have only 15 feet of clearance on each side. The heavily wooded Gwynedd shore was very close on their right, Cribben Rock was equally close on their left and beyond that Gored Goch island. Captain Hewitt had laid three special buoys alongside Cribben Rock to guide the tow through this extremely narrow channel.[13]

Communications with the forward tug were now working smoothly. The forward tug, having completed the slight change of course, was now on the Ship's port (left) bow.[32] *Conway* was aligned on the two diamond navigation marks on Church Island and the distant Anglesey shore. For some reason, Captain Hewitt had actually adjusted the Church Island mark on 11th April.[13]

In Cribben Gutter - Tug on Port Bow

Pilot Jones and Capt Miller

9.26 am

The marker buoy on Cribben Rock was close abeam to port[13] - they were roughly midway between points 1c and 2c on the chart. On their left, Captain Hewitt's extra marker buoys alongside Cribben Rock sat perfectly upright, but almost as soon as they were past spectators on the bank said they began to tilt confirming that the stream had reversed against the Ship.[9] This supports the party line that the tide turned earlier than expected[7] but does not entirely fit with Captain Durrant's assertion that the unidentified local pilot under the Britannia Bridge had noted the tide turning at least 6 minutes earlier at 9.20 am.[14] Lt. Col. Davies from his garden below the suspension bridge observed

"the ebb tide beginning and the wind increasing."[23]

Captain Hewitt and the pilots knew how much their progress now relied on the timing and force of the stream against them. It was already much stronger than expected so they were only making very slow headway and slipping behind schedule.

The Ship, filling up the very narrow channel, was further accelerating the flow of water around her hull. Down in the sick bay Captain King could feel the Ship being buffeted in the turbulence. He watched the stern tug *Minegarth* sheering from side to side trying to hold *Conway* on course.[9] *Dongarth* began to belch black smoke as she laboured forward.[32] Cribben Gutter was eventually cleared without incident. As King peered out of a side port the trees on the shore seemed to be crawling by.[11] The Ship was not making the progress necessary to clear the Swellies before the stream became too strong for any progress to be made. One of Mr. Hampson's photos clearly shows the tension in the faces of Pilot Jones, as he watches the dangerously close Gwynedd shore, and Captain Miller as he relays instructions to the forward tug.[32]

By the time Gored Goch was abeam, Pilot Jones, believing the transit unlikely against the earlier than expected counter stream,[24] advised Captain Hewitt to reverse the role of the tugs and drop *Conway* back below Britannia Bridge to await the next tide. It would have been a relatively straightforward manoeuvre. The rear tug, stern on to the Ship, was facing in the correct direction and it would have been a short, straight dash with the stream. With hindsight, it was the last realistic opportunity to extract the Ship from the danger she faced. Captain Hewitt confirmed to the later Inquiry that he declined Jones's advice.[7] The suspension bridge was tantalisingly close ahead, they were making progress and the *real* danger of Cheese Rock had been cleared.

9.35am The Ship From The Suspension Bridge

9.35 am

Price's Point Beacon (point 4c) was at last abeam to starboard.[7] It had taken 12 minutes to cover a distance of 4 cables from Britannia Bridge. The timetable anticipated that by 9.35 am (9.40 am at the latest) they would have passed out of the Swellies. In reality, they were only half-way through and almost at a standstill against the stream.[14] The suspension bridge was

"black with onlookers"[11]

and the expectant crowds now had their first clear view of the Ship as she emerged from behind Price's Point.

Price's Point and Swelly Rock

Having cleared Price's Point, a sharp alteration to starboard (the right) was required to bring them into the constricted Swelly Passage between Swelly Rock (nowadays marked by a large beacon) and the Gwynedd shore. They would face a short but difficult transit to point 5c on the chart, where they would manoeuvre again to pass under the suspension bridge. The narrow channel from point 4c to 5c funnels and greatly accelerates the speed of the stream. Captain Hewitt told the Inquiry he knew that this

"was where the tide always runs the most strongly."[7]

Turning Around Price's Point

With a vessel the size of *Conway* this would be like threading a needle and called for manoeuvring of the highest order from Pilot Jones, the tug masters, and Captain Hewitt.

The two tugs began to turn the Ship. The stern tug eased *Conway's* stern towards the Anglesey shore. At the same time the forward tug eased her bows around into the narrow channel. The two tugs could not communicate directly or see each other so this would be a tricky manoeuvre. Captain Miller acted as the go between relaying instructions and messages. To the spectators on the suspension bridge it probably all looked easy as the Ship quietly turned in front of them from head-on to side-on.

When Swelly Rock was abeam, the wind strengthened and changed direction. The Ship was coming more into the influence of the wind outside at sea. The Inquiry recorded a range of opinions. Pilot Jones thought it NE force 2-3, most others agreed it was NW.[7] Captain McManus in his later evaluation using cine film shot at the time, estimated the wind to be Northerly force 5.[12] Captain King onboard thought it from the NNW,

"quite blustery and gusty."[11]

But away from the shelter of the strait, the wind at sea was a lot stronger.[18] This was the worst possible wind direction as it was pushing even more water than normal out of the Irish Sea into the north-eastern entrance of the strait, reinforcing the strength of the southwest-going stream into the Swellies and against the Ship.

9.40 am

Captain Durrant, now on the very centre of the suspension bridge, observed the scene:

9.40 am "Virtually stationary"

"at 9.40 am looking from the suspension bridge, the tow was practically stationary, with the forward tug, Dongarth, towing at full speed against the stream but making no progress. In this situation, apart from minor tacks to port or starboard, Conway continued stationary head to tide, but edging gradually towards the Gwynedd side under the pressure of the strong north westerly wind against her port side. Careful observation of the rate of passage of floating kelp borne on the tide, which already appeared to have the character of a race, indicated a rate of at least 8 to 10 knots." [14]

An average of 4 knots had been expected. [11]

Pilot Jones asked for more power from the forward tug and again advised Captain Hewitt to back out of the Swellies as he now believed the transit to be impossible given the force of the stream against them. [24] He said very quietly:

"Captain, we must go back,"

Captain Hewitt replied:

"You don't seem to understand do you? The ship must go on." [16]

At the Inquiry, Captain Durrant, Captain Duff and the two tug-masters all agreed that under the prevailing conditions to go back would have been impossible. [7] Their views were not disputed by the Inquiry although the Ship would not have had to be turned, as both tugs were already stern-on to the Ship exactly as in 1949. It was perfectly feasible, if a little tricky, for the direction of the tow to have been reversed by the tug on the bows dropping off her power so the stern tug could take up the lead. She had been brought through in 1949 in this way, with the same tugs, tug masters and pilots. She would have been stern first, but that would have been of little account to a 'dead' tow.

9.45 am (approx.)

Captain Hewitt observed

"She was not going very fast but appeared to be making headway," [22]

perhaps explaining why he decided for a second time not to heed the pilot's advice to reverse her out. Very slowly, Swelly Rock was cleared.

Approach to The Suspension Bridge

9.45 am

The Ship was now just ahead of chart point 5c and barely making progress against the stream. Captain King observed:

> *"We were caught in the worst part of the channel with nowhere to go."*[11]

Lt. Col. Davies confirms

> *"By the time Conway came in sight by the Platters, she was only just moving and obviously things were tricky."*[23]

From Swelly Rock

> *"the prudent navigation demands that the Ship should haul to the northward in order to get on an offing of the Platters before making for the centre of the suspension bridge,"*[7]

ie, she should follow the route shown by the black line on the chart. However, the recommended course would have kept her in the middle of the strengthening stream. The main line of tidal flow is clearly marked on the chart, the direction being influenced by the shallows around the Anglesey pier of the suspension bridge. This creates an area of water in the Swellies, marked on the chart as Relatively Slack Area, which is not moving with the full force of the stream. Pilot Jones junior, on the forward tug, realised that if they headed off towards the Anglesey shore, through point 6c towards the Relatively Slack Area at 7c, they would avoid the worst of the current and probably be able to make some forward progress. He guided them across into this slower moving water.[24]

9.50 am

Jones's diversion had enabled them to make some forward progress and they were now abreast the Platters in the Relatively Slack Area where the Ship was held for a while. Some sceptics doubt this manoeuvre ever occurred, but the record confirms it did. On the suspension bridge

> *"observers noted what they remarked to be a sheer to port (the Ship's left)."*[7]

The Inquiry thought this was a natural aligning for the suspension bridge, in reality it was Jones junior re-directing the Ship.

From their distant vantage point near the Britannia Bridge, Headmaster Browne and his party watched:

> *"We saw her pass the first of the danger points, the Swelly Rock, and approach the Platters; then I spoke my relief to Watson. ...'.what should we have done if she had grounded?'"*[28]

Later he recalled

In Relatively Slack Water

"Wilson and I conferred that we had been thinking how we would grapple with the problems of her loss and thankful that they would not arise when she seemed to sheer over to the Anglesey shore and then turn again. She then appeared quite stopped and we gasped 'she's touched on the Platters!' For fully 2 minutes she was still." [25]

Because of the acute angle of their viewpoint and their distance from the Ship, they too were misinterpreting Pilot Jones junior's manoeuvre described above. Photos too, clearly show the Ship out of the main stream close to the Anglesey shore. [32]

Capt Hewitt Ponders His Options

Very soon though they would have to pull back out into the main stream to get into the channel to pass under the suspension bridge. Pilot Jones senior doubted they could make any headway once back in the main stream; he apparently had an alternative but risky strategy. Slightly ahead of them near point 7c, between Carreg Halen and the suspension bridge, there is a deep pool with depths ranging from 25-48 feet at low water. The stream eddies around it but the pool is outside the main flow in a slight counter current. Pilot Jones senior wanted to place the Ship into this pool and hold her there for four hours until the strength of the stream had abated. [16, 24] Many dispute that this advice was ever given. It was not mentioned at the Inquiry and no record of it has been found other than from the Jones family. However, independent corroboration has now been discovered. Mr Ball, Bosun's Mate, confirms that this manoeuvre was proposed by the pilot, but rejected by Captain Hewitt. [43] The pilot had already twice advised Captain Hewitt the transit was not possible and offered an alternative to secure the Ship's safety. It seems perfectly reasonable that the pilot would continue his professional responsibility especially with the Ship now in extremis. The deep pool exists and the pilots knew where it was. Pilot Jones's proposal was a brilliantly inspirational emergency manoeuvre, which may well have succeeded.

9.50 am Moving Back Into The Stream

It is a cliché to say that command is a lonely place, but at that moment Captain Hewitt must have known just how lonely it was. He had been in many exceptionally difficult circumstances during the war and always brought his ships to safety. His decisions so far on the day had proved correct. He must have had great confidence in his own judgement. The pilot could advise but not order; only Captain Hewitt could make the final decision. It was in the character of the man that he did not flinch from this. Conditions were deteriorating by the minute. He had to choose between going forward and remaining where they were; in dangerous waters with the possibility of grounding on the falling tide. They had not made the progress they expected but they were still just clawing forward. With the suspension bridge tantalisingly close the safest option seemed to be to press ahead, no matter how slowly. But passing the suspension bridge would have been a false dawn. There was no magic line draw underneath the bridge with dangerous currents on one side and calm safety on other. The stream originated somewhere two miles further along the strait towards Garth Point so it flowed just as strongly on the other side of the bridge. Shortly before 9.50 am Captain Hewitt made up his mind. They must get the Ship out of the Swellies. He ordered the tugs to ease *Conway* back into the main stream. They might yet make it.

Before The Suspension Bridge

Back out in the stream conditions were dramatically different to those expected just a few hours before. Captain Miller told the Inquiry

> *"it was not a true tide, but just a swift moving, confused mass of water."*[7]

From 9.23 am to 10.10 am, *Conway* had only made good 6 cables over the ground, which is barely half a knot.[12] The tugs were clearly fighting a losing battle. They were approximately 350 yards from the suspension bridge[11] but they could make no more headway. The Inquiry confirmed,

> *"Conway was not now moving."*[7]

The forward tug was not powerful enough to take her forward and with the stream surging ever faster and becoming more turbulent it might not be able to hold her either.

9.54 am [13]

With the pilot's concurrence Captain Hewitt ordered the stern tug let go and brought forward to provide extra power.[7] Captain King recalls

10.12 am Minegarth Claws Her Way Forward

"a breathless messenger arrived from the poop deck instructing us to let go."[11]

He and his small working party now had a Herculean task. They were faced with a 12 inch towing spring and a 4 inch towing wire wrapped 9 times around the mizzenmast and

"drawn bar-tight"

by the constant tension from the stern tug.[9] It took

"a prolonged struggle"

just to free 2 turns of the top spring.[9] The confined space of the sick bay, with only 6 feet headroom, was now a very dangerous place.

"It became obvious that the tug would have to slip the wires if we were not to take all day and risk life and limb."[11]

The quickest option was for the tug to cast off from her end, but the stream was so strong that the tug could not come astern sufficiently for her slip hook to be knocked out.[9]

Eventually, in desperation, King ordered most of the working party out of the sick bay and a few of them attacked the wires with axes.

"At last we managed to cast off, the last turns smashing the sick bay to match-wood as they flew clear through the gun port."[11]

but fortunately not injuring any of those present. The Rea Towing Company later submitted a claim for the wires and springs lost including various lengths

"retained on stern mooring deck of Conway when tug slipped."[14]

10.10 am[13]

The stern tug was finally free. The Headmaster and Captain Goddard, still back by the Britannia Bridge, were watching with trepidation

"The stern tug cast off and went round to try and pull her bow over … we got in cars and drove to Colonel Davis's house and went down to the shore."[25]

Captain King believes it took about 20 minutes to slip the tug.[11] After letting-go *Minegarth* had to complete a 180° turn and recover the springs now in the water. She had a top speed of 10 knots but was still swept 400 feet astern of *Conway*. *Minegarth's* Skipper Duff recalled

"She was going every ounce she could go but still going astern."[14]

Minegarth gradually clawed her way past *Conway* to make fast ahead of the Ship. Time was slipping by and the force of water was unrelenting. Skipper Duff said later

"Under the strong tidal conditions prevailing it would have been impossible to place Minegarth under the bluff bow of Conway in a position to pass or receive a towing line directly from the Ship, and likewise impossible for the crew of the Ship, owing to her design, to make a speedy connection through the small hawse holes half way down her bows."[14]

The possible need for a second tug forward had been discussed at the final planning meeting but those present had decided it would not be necessary and so no provision was made.[7]

Captain McManus takes up the story. *Minegarth*

"therefore decided to go ahead of the forward tug and attach a line to her and tow in line ahead of her. Such an unusual procedure is fraught with danger, and was a plainly desperate measure. She passed a 6 inch rope to the Dongarth and the Dongarth passed an 8 inch rope to the Minegarth. With the 2 tugs towing in tandem the Dongarth, with taut lines to the Minegarth ahead of her and an equally taut line to the Conway astern, found her manoeuvrability seriously restricted."[12]

The Inquiry considered

"The manoeuvre was brilliantly executed."[7]

10.20 am

Minegarth took up the strain ahead of *Dongarth* and the combined efforts of the 2 tugs produced a slight but noticeable headway towards the suspension bridge.

"Conway started to move ahead."[23]

Captain King recalls

"There was a hope that both tugs might be able to hold the Ship where she was for 2 hours until the force of the ebb tide eased … but the hope was as slender one."[9]

This seems at odds with reality as the ebb was known to increase to 10 knots, well outside the capabilities of the tugs. Perhaps this was a miss-attributed confirmation of Pilot Jones's proposal around 9.50 am to hold the Ship in the deep pool near Carreg Halen.

According to the Ship's log, at 10.09 am,[13] 'the pilot boat secured herself to port to give extra power'; rather like an ant pushing an elephant. However this time cannot be correct as the pilot boat is clearly not alongside in any of the pertinent photos.[32] The pilot boat must have come alongside shortly after 10.20 am as the photos taken from that time show her in position.

10.20 am Minegarth and Dongarth Take Up The Strain

The Grounding

Their challenge might now seem to be just a question of raw tug pulling power versus the strength of the stream. But if you narrow a channel of flowing water it flows more quickly generating turbulence and eddies. That is why broad, calm rivers suddenly turn into boiling maelstroms where the banks narrow. Dr. Toby Sherwin, Marine Science Labs Menai Bridge explains:

"The generation of eddies in the Swellies is non-linear. It requires only a small increase in the strength of the stream to produce a disproportionately large increase in the size and strength of the many eddies"[34]

Dongarth, Held Head and Stern, Lists Dangerously

The wide area of strait above the suspension bridge was significantly narrowed by the encroaching shoreline and the piers of the suspension bridge, accelerating the flow of water under the suspension bridge. *Conway* and her tugs were compounding the problem, acting like a plug and further narrowing the channel, making the stream flow even faster and more turbulently around the Ship. Without a stern tug to hold her steady the Ship was sheering about wildly.[13] It was for precisely these reasons the planning committee had decided not to provide a second tug forward.[7] The closer the Ship was pulled towards the suspension bridge, the worse things got. The treatment was killing the patient! In barely 10 minutes, it would all be over.

From his vantage point on the shore right opposite the Ship, the Headmaster recorded,

"The two tugs were straining hard to hold her but we could see that the tide had now started to run to the southward and they lost ground."[25]

Captain Durrant, watching from the suspension bridge, was under no illusions about the dangers, not just to *Conway* but to his two tugs and their crews. Indeed the tug crews were now in greater danger than those on the relative safety of the Ship. He reported to the committee that

"Dongarth, held head and stern by tow ropes, was severely hampered in her manoeuvring ability, and at one point was listed to her gunwale in her efforts to hold Conway up to wind and tide."[14]

Captain Durrant recounts the rest of the saga.

"At 10.30 am, without warning, when Conway was abreast of Platters Rocks, and there appeared to be good hope of the tow making the bridge and passing through, she took a violent sheer to starboard, apparently forced by an eddy of overwhelming strength. Her forward end passed over the Platters, the Ships forefoot digging into the bank adjacent to and shoreward of the Rocks. This disastrous sheer occurred, and was concluded, in a matter of seconds."[14]

Unnamed observers ashore spoke of

"something in the nature of a tidal bore as Conway took her final sheer."[11]

Lt. Cdr. John Brooke Smith later wrote to his mother

"the tide suddenly came down like a mill race and the tugs could do nothing"[35]

Lt. Col. Davies, one of the closest observers on shore, confirms

"A big surge of tide came down: it always does come in sudden rushes, especially with the winds in the North East. It struck Conway on her port bow and she started to sheer over to starboard, towards us. Simultaneously, the leading tug's hawser parted and off went Conway on a wild rush across the channel, towing the tugs like a puppy on a string. She came over the Platters (just scraped them I'm told), just missed the boat houses, and took the shore some 50 yards further west. The tide slewed her stern round a bit, and there she stuck."[23]

She was firmly aground in the Davies's front garden.

The Headmaster also recorded the final moments

"For 10 minutes it was give and take and then quite suddenly it happened. She took a sheer towards the Caernarfon shore and the tide and wind together were more than the tugs could hold. They strained, belching black smoke; a hawser parted and we all said 'My God!, she's gone!' and without a shock or sound she brought up gently but firmly on the Caernarfon shore."[25]

His autobiography records events somewhat more lyrically.

"Conway's bluff brows swung over towards the shore ... and carried her irresistibly across the Platters. We saw her masts cant and come upright again as her keel touched and then slipped over the rocks into deeper water, and then her stem touched the shore... the bows of the old Ship kissed the shore so gently that I was convinced no damage could have been done."[28]

Captain Goddard, standing with the Headmaster, knew *Conway* better than anyone. He thought otherwise

"That is the end." he said.[28]

The press, watching from the suspension bridge, suddenly had a much more dramatic story to tell. It would be front page news with dramatic stories and photos in the next morning's national editions. The Daily Mail enterprisingly organised a plane to take an aerial shot showing *Conway's* position and just how close she had come to clearing the Swellies.

10.25am The Moment of Impact

The Ship's log records she grounded at 10.25 am[13] Other reports confirm the gentleness of the impact. Cadet Owen Roberts, freed from his duties in the aft party, had come up on deck and was standing right behind Captain Hewitt.

"As we grounded, Eric swayed forward, I swear he bit right through his cigarette."[26]

While others attended to affairs of state, Roberts, upholding the best traditions of *Conway* cadets, went foraging. The galley was deserted but the range had shifted off its base.

"Behind was the biggest pile of compacted dead cockroaches you could ever imagine."[26]

Enough to put him off his foraging!

Durrant reported to the Inquiry that after she grounded

"the tow lines eased momentarily, the ensuing and suddenly increased strain caused the Minegarth's 6 inch line to part, but her 8 inch line, plus the Dongarth's 2 hawsers connected direct to the Conway, continued to hold."

Durrant's timing, from his eerie on the suspension bridge, conflicts with that of the Headmaster[25] and Lt. Col. Davies[23] who were both on the shore within yards of the Ship. They observed the hawser part when *Conway* was struck by the sudden tidal surge *before* she crossed the Platters. This earlier parting was confirmed by Captain King who also agreed that she touched briefly on the Platters.[9] However, they all agreed, and the Inquiry confirmed, that only one hawser parted so the forward tug remained secured to the second tug and so to the Ship. This is clearly confirmed by the photographic record.[32]

10.40am The Tugs Try to Pull Her off

With the tide already falling there was precious little time for the tugs to get the Ship afloat again before she would literally be left high and dry.

"The tugs were eased over to a position in which the hawsers were leading aft across the Conway's bows, and from where they continued their efforts to haul her stem off the bank. Those efforts were restricted by the necessity, and difficulty, of keeping the tugs head on to the racing tide, plus the very small radius of action available in the rocky channel."[14]

As they began their struggle, the pilot boat cast off and moved away from the Ship.[32] Both tugs continued heaving at maximum capacity for at least another 10 minutes without success. Captain Hewitt realised she was hard ashore, and at 10.45 am he ordered the tugs to let-go.[13] She was 1,100 feet from the suspension bridge on a heading of 118°[14] As the towing hawsers slipped off the Ship all hope of saving *Conway* went with them. The tugs proceeded immediately to Menai Bridge pier to await developments.[14]

Lt. Cdr. Brooke Smith immediately began taking soundings all around the ship[9] as the pilot boat came back alongside.[32] The soundings were not encouraging, two thirds of the hull was safely on the Platters shelf but about 50 feet[9] of her stern was unsupported and would be suspended over 31 feet of water at low water.[14] The tide was falling and only time would tell whether the strength of her construction would be able to support the huge loads, which were already being applied to her wooden frame.

Taking Soundings Around The Ship

Wooden wall fighting ships like *Conway* were massively strong but contained a potentially fatal design flaw. No single tree was long enough for the keel so it had to be constructed from several lengths joined together. These joints were weak points. Sir Robert Seppings, the Ship's designer and constructor, observed in 1814.

"The strength of a ship, let its construction be what it may, can never exceed that of its weakest parts."[44]

Conway was phenomenally strong transversally, with 13 inch square frames spaced only a couple of inches apart and clad inside and out with thirteen inch thick planking, resulting in sides over 3 feet thick of virtually solid oak. It was her armour against enemy cannon shot. This was further braced transversely by rows of deck beams at 7 feet vertical intervals and oversize oak beam knees *(wooden brackets)*, which extended to the deck below. By contrast, the keels of these ships were surprisingly puny. Tapering towards bow and stern and having a maximum section of only 19 inch square amidships, usually of elm, and made of up to 8 lengths each not less than 25 feet long, which were simply laid over each other with scarves *(matching diagonal cuts)* and fastened together with a regulation 8 nails. Because of this the keel contributed nothing at all to longitudinal strength. The support of the water was vital to keeping them secure. These ships are best thought of as a primitive compound girder, relying on the longitudinal planking of their multiple decks supported by a system of stanchions (posts), which together with their hull planking provided their longitudinal rigidity. While all of this was said to be 'bolted' together, these 'bolts' did not have threads and nuts as we now think of bolts. They were no more than nails, albeit typically an inch and a quarter in diameter, which were laboriously hammered into pre-drilled undersize holes. So these ships were notoriously weak longitudinally, and they must have worked abominably in a seaway. Indeed, to quote C. Napean Longridge in his analysis of Nelson's ships,

"All of these ships started to hog (arch their backs) as soon as they took to the water."[36]

Conway was stronger than most due to Seppings's revolutionary system of diagonal bracing, but she still needed the water to support her keel. As the tide fell she was losing that vital support. Cadet Noel Roberts clearly remembers the ominous creaks and groans, which started almost as soon as she grounded.[21]

Aground

The Ship's boats stood off for a while but at 11.10 am[13] they came alongside, Captain Hewitt ordered ashore all those onboard not required and then instructed that the Ship's papers and records to be landed.[9] Within an hour of grounding the local fire brigade had brought pumps onboard to assist the Ship's pumps.[9] An unrelenting effort then ensued:

"Almost immediately all hands – officers, masters, 17 cadets and catering staff began lightening ship to help her lift off at the next high tide and a shuttle service began with No 1 and No 2 motorboats and the pinnace carrying equipment from the Ship to Menai Pier and then by truck to Plas Newydd. We worked like this until late at night when it became apparent that the Ship was hard and fast."[27]

A similar story was told in the September edition of the Cadet magazine.

"As soon as the Ship struck every effort was made to salvage records, memorials and trophies, and our gratitude to those who helped in this work can never be sufficiently expressed. The cadets and staff who had returned to the Ship for the passage worked until they could hardly stand, and valuable assistance was also given by the Commanding Officer and men of the Royal Army Service Corps at Menai Bridge, and by the National Fire Service officers and men of the same township, and it was thanks to their help that so much of the portable equipment of the Ship was saved."[22]

Lightening Ship

As this determined salvage began tentative arrangements were made for an attempt to re-float the Ship on the next high tide at 9.45 pm The tugs waiting at Menai Bridge were ordered to stand by again at 8.30 pm A third tug was ordered from Liverpool to provide additional assistance, but after leaving the Mersey at 2.30 pm the tug (the *Grassgarth*) was forced to return to port owing to bad weather. Arrangements were made to despatch another tug, if possible, from Liverpool at midnight.[14]

A large crowd gathered on the shore and banks of the strait to take photos, look for souvenirs, and view the Ship. They got there by trespassing across Lt. Col. Davies's garden.

"Within minutes spectators from far and wide descended on us in swarms! After a lot of damage and theft the police came to our rescue; everything is shut and bolted."[23]

Captain King recalls that by 11 am, the Ship was beginning to

"creak and groan as the strain came on the inadequately supported after end."[11]

By midday, the sounds were becoming more and more alarming, until early in the afternoon the decks aft began to

Unloading at Menai Pie

"pancake down into each other."[11]

Lt. Col. Davies from the shore

"heard ominous creaks and reports."[23]

Onboard, Lt. Cdr. John Brooke Smith observed,

"At first we thought we might be alright. Then, as the tide fell, great bangs and cracks commenced and beams 4 feet across broke, and stanchions bent like hairpins."[35]

At 2 pm,

"the sounds of tortured wood and metal were becoming more ominous … and became almost continuous."[9]

Then,

"One of the 3 inch steel pillars on the main deck bent perceptibly and sheared with a loud report as the deck head dropped an inch or two."[11]

The decks were curving in a slight gradient towards the stern and some planking was beginning to open. A huge main beam under the beak-head fractured causing a large bump to appear in the deck.[9] The Ship simply could not survive the damage being done.

At low water it was found that *Conway* was ashore for three quarters of her length with almost all her port side alongside the West Platters on a bed of sloping rock and gravel.[9] From outside no sign of the disastrous internal collapse was visible, which explains why initial newspaper reports said the Ship was to be re-floated and repaired. Indeed the press were to continue speculating for some

Aground - Almost Low Water

time about how the Ship was to be rescued and restored. One paper carried a detailed report on how *Conway* was to be repaired and then sent to the USA as a training ship! For those more directly involved the truth was clear.

> *"The Writer earlier in the day had made contact at Menai with Captain Nelson, Nautical Adviser to Mr. Lawrence Holt, and with him boarded the Conway during the afternoon just before Low Water. The outlook then appeared very bad, with the after end of the Ship sagging downwards from the main mast aft and a continuous sound of wracking, twisting and rending timber, and rushing water below. As the tide fell, the forward end of the Ship dried out, but the after end, which was in deep water, fell with the tide and the Ship eventually broke her back. She is now a pitiable sight inboard, and though from the bridge she may still appear something like her old self, inside the picture is vastly different, for the beams and planks are broken, stanchions buckled and twisted, and decks which were once over 6 feet high are now only 4 feet apart."* [14]

This inspection was

> *"just before Low Water"*

and already there was

> *"rushing water below."*

The Ship was mortally wounded within a very short time of grounding despite external appearances.

Cadet Ellis was still busy ferrying papers and gear to Menai Bridge pier.

> *"I recall while manning one of the boats I took out to the Ship Lawrence Holt who visibly had tears in his eyes as we approached the Conway. With him was the Marquis of Anglesey. On coming alongside the Ship the tide was very low so both men in beautiful suits, bowler hats and overcoats had to climb a Jacobs Ladder to reach the bottom of the fixed Ship's gangway. Later in the day I had changed duty and was loading trucks when they came ashore and Lawrence Holt stopped me and asked if I was a Conway boy. I must admit I thought the question a bit odd as I was in uniform, but he was very upset."* [27]

Local quarry men volunteered to help; and a lighter was obtained to increase carrying capacity. [35]

At around 4 pm, Captain Hewitt ordered everyone ashore for safety until the tide began to make again after low water. [9] Once completely high and dry there was a danger the Ship would roll onto her side. Meanwhile Lt. Col. Davies had invited Captain and Mrs Hewitt and their children to spend the night at his house and it became the command centre for recovery work.

> *"Poor chap! ... to lose his Ship and his home all in a moment was grim indeed, and perhaps, if she turned over, all his furniture and belongings as well."* [23]

Later, the Hewitts moved into a house lent by the Marquis, who also provided accommodation at Plas Newydd for 7 other members of staff with cabins in the Ship. [35]

Lawrence Holt with his Nautical Adviser, Captain James Nelson, Alfred Wilson (Secretary to the Committee), Mr. Wilson (Alfred Holt's Construction Department) and Brian Heathcote and arrived at the scene again at 5.30 pm They viewed the Ship from the beach, where her fore part was then high and. dry, and then adjourned, to await further inspection an hour before high water at 8.45 pm[14]

Around 7 pm, 30 or so men and boys returned onboard and began unloading again into half a dozen motorboats, racing against the clock to save as much as possible before high tide.[9] In the early evening Captain King remembers rescuing a large Russell Flint watercolour of the Ship. In his autobiography he wondered what happened to the painting.[11] I can report that it hung in the Stone Frigate until paying off in 1974, when an Old Conway bought it. It hangs safely and proudly in his dining room to this day.

As the tide began to flood (*come in*) again the hope was that she would float sufficiently before the water could flood in through her stern ports. Many years before, in order to increase ventilation, ports had been cut in the orlop deck well below the design level for openings in the hull. They had been perfectly safe while the Ship was afloat and very lightly loaded but would now provide unstoppable ingress for the water if the Ship's natural buoyancy did not lift her in time. The Ship was lying on a sloping bank, her stern still in water and some hull timbers had also opened wide. The Ship failed to lift and soon water flooded through the lowest of the stern ports and then through her after orlop deck ports.[9]

The Ship Fails to Lift

"*Then the tide began to rise and the pumps were useless. It just flowed in through ports and filled up the orlop deck, and after end of the lower deck, wardroom and Captain's office on the main deck.*"[35]

At 9 pm, Captain Hewitt, Lawrence Holt and one other visited the Ship again. They soon realised the Ship could not be saved. The order for a third tug was cancelled. Deteriorating conditions onboard *Conway* made it clear that further attempts to tow her off would be useless.[7]

The salvage teams continued working into the evening but, as darkness fell, they were forced to cease work. At 10 pm[9]

"*We were then ordered back to Plas Newydd for the night. Of course when we got there we were all very hungry and thirsty having had nothing since breakfast at about 6 am. However, nobody had thought of salvaging food from the Ship and all that could be found was some bread, butter and jam but not enough tea, coffee or cocoa to make a full pot, only a small amount of each, so it was all put into the one pot and boiling water poured in. The subsequent brew came out looking something like tomato soup and had a distinctive flavour but we all enjoyed our late night supper.*"[27]

The last few onboard then prepared to leave the Ship. Second Officer Gabby King was the last man to leave her. He recalls

> *"The fuel supply for the generator was set with enough diesel to ensure that the gangway was cleared and we were all in the last boat before it ran out. With the boat punching into the stream, the low hum of the Ship's generator died away as the fuel supply was exhausted, the lights flickered, slowly faded to orange, and then went out abruptly. The Ship had died."* [11]

Constructive Total Loss

At low water, 5.00 am, on the following morning (Wednesday, 15th April), a further inspection of the Ship's interior was made by Lawrence Holt and party, plus representatives of the Liverpool and Glasgow Salvage Association team from the *Ranger* with the Salvage Officer Len LeBesque (an Old *Conway* and former *Conway* Second Officer).[7] They determined that conditions had deteriorated overnight, following which a decision was made to call off, for the present, any further attempts at re-floating.[7, 14] The tugs *Dongarth* and *Minegarth* therefore left Menai Bridge for Liverpool, at 9 am arriving Gladstone Dock at 3.30 pm[14]

Axe Wielding Cadets Take A Break

> *"For two more days we continued salvaging what we could from the Ship. We rotated our tasks from moving things from the Ship to the boats, manning the boats, loading the trucks at Menai Pier and discharging the trucks at Plas Newydd."* [27]

Lt. Cdr. John Brooke Smith masterminded recovery operations

> *"We have worked each day dismantling fittings and saving gear. The mess was indescribable. We break down bulkheads with axes to get things out of cabins, dismantle stoves, climb down into store rooms wading in congealed cornflakes and flour and mud to find broken plates and cutlery. Today we got out of the stores about 200 blankets, counterpanes etc. The Captain being so high up has had everything saved, and I have got all my stuff. I can break any lock now with one blow of an axe!"* [35]

Lt. Col. Davies's house continued as the

> *"unofficial shore base for the Ship"* [37]

Huge effort went into recovering every cadet's sea-chest. The Headmaster recalls,

> *"Set off soon after 8.00 am, went onboard with a couple of men, Seaman Owen and Cadet Noel Roberts. We started salvaging chests, first rigging lifelines to give us a purchase on the slippery sloping deck, then getting a line on each chest in turn and hauling it up hill to the main hatch where was a tackle rigged to heave it up to the lower deck."* [38]

Chests were floating everywhere,

"we lug them out at low tide, you can barely stand up (mud and slime). Sometimes we hoist the chests out of the water with a hook and the handles come off and they fall back. All the books are in them."[35]

Once salvaged, everything in the chests was turned out on the dock and they were hosed down. Skinner earned a new nickname, 'Winkle', from his continual advice

"You've gotta get all them winkles out of the corners."[39]

Salvaging Sea Chests

Cadet Rob Cammack recalls the disorienting effect of working in the Ship as she lay angled into the water

"Although I was not on the Ship at the moment of the disaster I travelled north the following day to help with the salvage of personal effects etc. I have to admit that as we were scrambling about on the orlop deck fishing out sea chests, I just had to sit down on one of them and cry my eyes out. I was not the only one either. A strange thing was that, after being below for some time, coming up on deck one would feel that the whole horizon was tilted over at an angle. It took quite a while for this to wear off."[39]

The Headmaster experienced a similar disorientation

"It was a queer sensation once you got inside the Ship, the slope of the deck without any outside terms of reference gave a queer feeling of nausea almost akin to sea sickness until you were used to it. The two and a half inch solid steel stanchions were bent and twisted, the deck had a great hump amidships and an abrupt change of slope just abaft the mainmast. On the upper deck the deck had lifted and cracked away from the sides and the rigging on the starboard side strained so that the tar was being squeezed out of the lanyards. I went into the geography room and had the sensation that the water surface of the strait, and not the deck, was sloping up towards the suspension bridge. Then I found myself looking through the lower part of the glass of the port – under water as the level rose and the stream gushed through every crack and joint. By this time the level was above that of the coaming around the ladder and a great cascade was pouring down into the Hold."[38]

This all confirmed the Ship was beyond saving.

On Thursday evening, 16th April 1953, Mr. Alfred Wilson issued a press statement on behalf of *Conway's* management committee.[14] HMS *Conway* was a constructive total loss, she was beyond repair or recovery.

Notes

1. Conway Management Committee meeting 29th March 1952.
2. Diaries of TEW Browne, 10th March 1952.
3. Diaries of TEW Browne, 28th February 1952.
4. Correspondence and telephone conversations, Captain Gwyn D Pari-Huws (44-45). Former Caernarfon Harbour Trustee.
5. Appendix Loss Figure 8.
6. Appendix Loss Sections 10,11 and 12.
7. Report of The MMSA Sub-Committee of Inquiry. Privately published.
8. The Cadet Magazine January 1953. Copies held in the Conway Archive in the Merseyside Maritime Museum.
9. Death of a Veteran by Captain G A B King (Conway's second officer and in charge of the aft party). Published in the BP Apprentices' magazine in 1953.
10. Diaries of TEW Browne, 7th March 1952.
11. Autobiography of Captain G A B King (Conway's second officer and in charge of the aft party).
12. The Loss of the Conway by Captain Brian McManus (Conway cadet 42-44). Privately published.
13. HMS Conway Ship's Log Books (1951 to 14th April 1953). Held in the Conway Archive at the Merseyside Maritime Museum.
14. Rea Towing Company Report by Captain Durrant to the MMSA Inquiry dated 16th April 1953. Privately published.
15. Personal recollections of Michael Hewitt, son of Captain Hewitt.
16. Interviews with the Emrys Jones (Caernarfon pilot). Son and grandson of the two Menai Strait pilots with the Ship, by Captain David G Williams.
17. Chapter 24: page 241.
18. Chapter 24: The Wind.
19. Interview with Cadet Ian Grindrod, signalman on the foredeck.
20. Interview with Cadet Mike Begley, signalman on the poop deck at the stern of the Ship.
21. Interview with Cadet Noel Roberts one of Lt. Cdr. Brooke Smith's runners on the Upper Deck.
22. The Cadet Magazine September 1953. Copies held in the Conway Archive at the Merseyside Maritime Museum.
23. "The Sorrowful Saga of the Conway," private papers of Lt. Col. R Davies.
24. The Loss Of The Conway by R J Jones great-grandson of the senior pilot on the day. Privately published.
25. Diaries of TEW Browne, 14th April 1953.
26. Interview with Cadet Owen Roberts part of the stern working party under Captain King.
27. Interview with Cadet John Ellis, one of the 17 cadets onboard at Plas Newydd before casting off, and then coxswain of No 1 motorboat during the transit.
28. The Skyline Is A Promise an autobiography by Wing Commander TEW Browne MA MSc (Headmaster of Conway 1934-64). Published by Rondo 1971 SBN 85619 000 4.
29. Phone interview with the son in law of Walter 'Little Willy' William, Captain Hewitt's chief steward.
30. Appendix Loss, Section 5, Figure 9 and related text.
31. Appendix Loss, Section 5, text referring tide board and note 11.
32. Photo archive of the loss at hmsconway.org
33. Letter and conversations with Mrs P.M. Vivian, daughter of Lt. Col. Davies.
34. Correspondence and telephone conversations in the production of Appendix Loss, between Captain D Williams and Dr.. Toby Sherwin, Director of Estuarial Research, Marine Science Laboratories, Menai Bridge, who was fascinated by the physical aspects of the loss.
35. Letter from Conway's Chief Officer. Lt. Cdr. John Brooke Smith to his mother.
36. The Anatomy of Nelson's Ships. C. Napean Longridge. Nexus Special Interests Ltd.

37. Letter from Lt. Col. Davies to a family friend dated 17th April 1953.
38. Diaries of TEW Browne, 17th April 1953.
39. Email from Cadet Rob Cammack who helped with the unloading the day after the grounding.
40. Letter from Captain Hewitt to the Caernarfon Harbour Trust dated November 1952.
41. Article in Sea Breezes magazine by L G Fay entitled 'Career of the *Conway'* reproduced in the August 1949 Cadet Magazine which quotes Captain Goddard.
42. On a New Principle of Constructing His Majesty's Ships of War a paper by Robert Seppings published in the *Philosophical Transactions of the Royal Society of London*, Vol. 104, 1814 (1814), pp. 285-302.
43. Tape recorded interview with Mr Ball, Bosun's Mate onboard that day.

CHAPTER 24

TWO BRIDGES TOO FAR

Chapter 23, 'The Loss of the Ship', provided a chronology of the events culminating the loss of the Ship. It analysed *what* happened, but did not explain *why* it could happen. I am indebted to Captain David G Williams (49-51), for the following incredibly detailed analysis, which fills that gap. His 21 years as a First Class Pilot (Home and Overseas), licensed for and fully experienced with, all classes of ship up to and including 100,000 tons, gives him a unique insight into the loss. Supported by the investigations of oceanographers and a wealth of scientific, meteriological, tidal and other material, his analysis is a definitive study of the very unusual physical factors, unique to the Menai Strait, which were allowed to contribute to the loss of the Ship.

Menai Strait Tides – Overview

The tide enters the Irish Sea from the north and south of Ireland, and meets and separates in the vicinity of a line between Morecambe Bay and Dundalk, leaving both coastlines south of Dublin and Liverpool firmly in the zone of the tide from the south. High water Liverpool occurs about 6 hours after high water at Cobh and the Lizard, and the tide as it rises enters the Menai Strait from the southwestward. However, the severe physical restrictions of its narrow and shallow southwestern entrance inhibits the full development of the tide in the Strait, so the tide isn't rising in the Strait as fast as it is in the surrounding Irish Sea, and as the bulk of the tide rushes round Anglesey, an hour or two into the new young flood the tide in the northeastern entrance starts to overtake the height of the water back down the Strait. This naturally means that the tide will now want to start to enter from the north; but for a while this is resisted by the inertia of the stream, which the even higher water level outside the southwestern entrance continues to press strongly northeastwards through the length of the Strait. The effect is thought to heap up the water somewhere in the Bangor end of the Strait, and this increasingly precarious heap is pressed ever westwards by the mounting disparity in water levels, and is further destabilised on encountering the highly irregular underwater topography between the two bridges. But at about this time the flood at the southwestern end is beginning to weaken, and no longer able to resist this mounted potential from the north. So while the Strait starts to fill through its south-western entrance, the last hour and a half of the flood comes in from the north, and in between the flood stream running one way and the flood stream running the other is what the Admiralty Pilot describes in atypically venturesome language as:

"A brief period of uneasy uncertainty while the water doesn't know which way to go;"

and it's local practice in the Strait to call this period slack water, or more commonly 'The Slack.'

Note: The term slack water is universally taken to mean that short period either side of High or low water when there's no detectable rise or fall in the tide, and no movement either way in the tidal stream ie it's a short period at the top or bottom of the tidal curve when the totally unstressed water is said to be limp, or slack. But here in the Swellies this so called slack water occurs about an hour and a half before high water, at a time of still vigorous tidal activity, when the highly stressed water is in a state of uneasy equilibrium between two opposing dissimilar streams. When on a big tide it goes 'Slack' in the Swellies the whole surface of the water becomes covered in the strange whirlpool like markings that are unique to this stretch of water, providing very visible evidence that the water is anything but slack, but is in fact in an extreme highly charged state of stress.

When high water does occur, the ebb stream in the Strait will naturally run southwestwards in common with the tidal movement in the rest of the southern portion of the Irish Sea. But for the previous hour and a half, the flood stream in the Strait has been running that way anyway, so there's no clear distinction between the flood and ebb streams. But to add further confusion, in the Strait it's the local practice to call all of the south-west going stream 'The Ebb,' even though the first hour and a half of it is actually the second phase of the flood. This gives rise to the apparently unique phenomena, that unlike, anywhere else in the World, in the Menai Strait not only does the tide rise strongly right throughout the period they call 'The Slack,' but even after the direction of the stream has reversed it goes on rising strongly for the first hour and a half of 'The Ebb.' Captain Goddard (ship's first term at Plas Newydd):

"We were highly amused by the antics of the tide."

Note: To avoid otherwise inevitable confusion, for the rest of this work I will refer to 'The Ebb' and 'The Slack' in parentheses as these terms are used in the Menai Strait, to distinguish them from the commonly understood meaning of ebb and slack in conventional tidal terminology.

North Eastern Entrance to The Menai Strait

Menai Straits Tides In Greater Detail

But the streams in the Menai Strait are not tidal streams, but are instead a response to differences in the water levels, which result from the frictional stress on the tide induced by the physically restrictive environment. Thus, although not tidal streams, the differences in water levels taht promote the flow are themselves the product of the tide, thus drawing the distinction between tidal streams and tide generated streams such as occur in the Menai Strait. The two locations in the Strait with the greatest frictional resistance are its narrow and shallow southwestern entrance at its one end, and the tortuous rock-bound Swellies near its other. These limit the water entering the Strait when the Irish Sea is flooding, leaving the water level lagging behind the sea level in the second half of the flood, and conversely, since water cannot exit the Strait quickly enough to keep pace with the falling tide outside, the water level in the Strait remains above sea level during the latter half of the ebb. Thus, not only are there times during the tidal cycle when the water flows right the way through the Strait one way or the other as one might normally expect, but there are other times when in response to the water level in the Strait being either higher or lower than sea level at its ends the water flows either into the Strait or out of it through both its entrances at once. This effect is best appreciated by studying the excellent page of hourly chartlets published by the Royal Welsh Yacht Club (RWYC) under the title: 'Menai Straits Tides At A Glance [Appendix I-3], which if studied in conjunction with the Marine Science Lab's 'Mean Spring Tidal Conditions in the Menai Strait' will give clear insight into the causes of the varying directions of the stream during a typical semi-diurnal tidal cycle. [Appendix I-4]

Figure 1, which is self-explanatory, not only compares the direction of flow with the differences in water levels, but also shows how these differences vary with the highest, lowest, and average height tides. Clearly, the physical restrictions of the Strait will have greater impact on the greater volume of water trying to get through per unit time on the bigger tides, thus producing the bigger differences in the levels as shown in Figure 24.1. This naturally results in a stronger stream on the bigger tides, not as a direct response to the bigger tide in the usual way, but in response to those bigger differences in water levels.

Dr Toby Sherwin (Marine Science Laboratories, Menai Bridge):

"There are times during neaps when slack water just seems to go on and on, and others at springs when there's hardly any slack water at all."

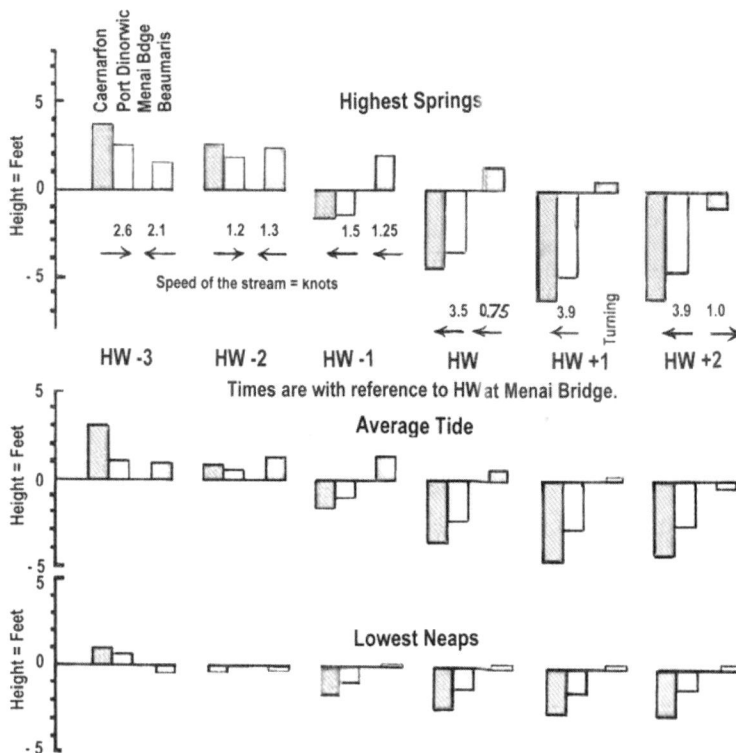

Figure 24.1: Water Levels Along The Strait Above/Below The Level At Menai Bridge

We can see this very clearly in Figure 24.1. The change from positive to negative parity in water levels is very much more clearly defined on the bigger tides than it is at neaps when the change is a feeble and much more gradual process. Notice how much the same change, which takes 4 hours on average tides, takes only half that time at highest springs, while the total change at neaps for the full 5 hours shown is equalled in less than an hour on the bigger tides. This more clearly defined reversal in the relative water levels on the bigger tides translates into a more decisive and immediate reversal in the direction of the stream. So, the first fact of importance here is the higher the tide the earlier 'The Slack' and the shorter its duration.

Figure 24.2 shows the same information but at shorter intervals around the reversal of the stream. Notice the build up of water east of Menai Bridge (Beaumaris) on the bigger tides that isn't present at neaps (the water heap?), and the potential this has for the immediate strength of the subsequent southwest-going stream. Also the marked descent through level parity on the bigger tides of Caernarvon and Port Dinorwic relative to Menai Bridge and Beaumaris, and that within 15 minutes after level parity there is already a 40 inch difference between the levels at Beaumaris and Port Dinorwic on highest springs, compared with a difference of only 6 inches at neaps.

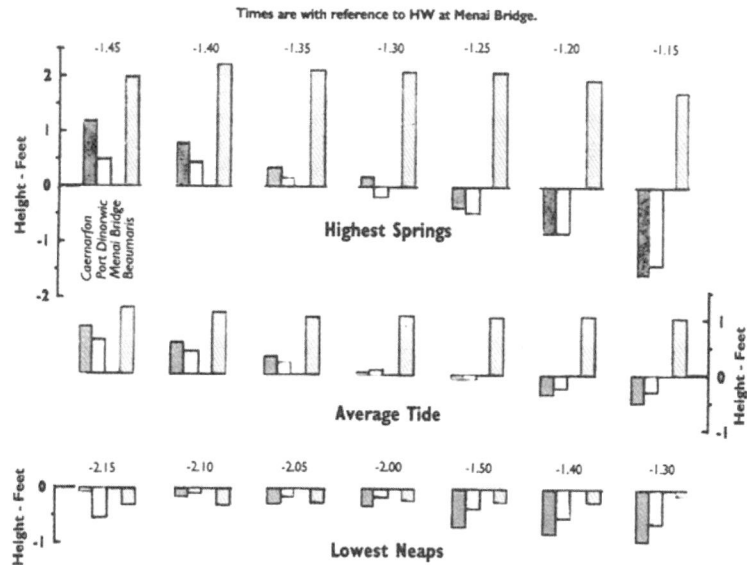

*Figure 24.2: Water Levels Along The Strait Above/Below The Level
At Menai Bridge Around The Reversal of The Flow*

But the reversal of the stream doesn't coincide with level parity. Instead the inertia of the existent stream causes it to continue flowing for a while ('uphill' as it were) until it all comes rushing back again much like sluicing water back and forth by up-ending a bathtub. Thus, unlike conventional tides, where the beginnings of the new stream are barely perceptible and only very gradually become apparent, on a big tide in the Menai Strait the onset of 'The Ebb' is unusually marked, and gathers momentum very rapidly. Not only is the new stream reinforced by the carry-over beyond level parity from the other, but being delayed beyond level parity, by the time 'The Ebb' sets in on a big tide there is already an appreciable difference in water levels. The combined effect can sometimes be quite dramatic. I remember several occasions sitting out on the port chains on summer evenings at the Plas Newydd mooring, when the silence of the evening was suddenly shattered by a single swiftly moving wave traveling against the direction of flow, which went unnoticed in deep water, but which fizzed and cracked sharply as it exploded its energy noisily along the shallows of the Gwynedd shore, leading to much fanciful speculation as to what this sinister, sudden intruder might mean, was it the wash of a ghost ship etc.? Looking back on it a lifetime later, what we had witnessed was of course a tidal bore. A tidal bore is formed when the tide rises at such a rate that it forces the tidal wave front to move at a faster speed than a shallow water wave is able to at that depth of water. This causes a shock wave to be formed, the visible evidence of which is a wall of water backtracking against the direction of flow. Nowhere have I ever seen any reference to a tidal bore in the Menai Strait, but I've no hesitation in stating that there is one because I've seen it myself on several occasions. It's not a very big one, and likely only occurs on the highest tides. By contrast the tidal bore in the Amazon (for example) can attain a height of 17 feet and travel inland for up to 50 miles.

The Swellies - Looking NE Towards Bangor

Looking SW Towards Plas Newydd

The Southwest Residual.

In addition to the tide generated streams in the Menai Strait, there is also a non-tidal current, which is referred to quite simply as the 'Southwest Residual,' and is thought to be a dynamic reaction to the energy expended by the tide upon the restrictive environment of the Strait and the consequent difference in tidal range at its ends.

Although not invariably so, the Residual is dominantly southwestward, and explains why the southwest-going stream is typically stronger than, and lasts for longer than the northeast-going stream 6 hours later. This results in a net westward transport of water through the Strait, which in environmental terms explains why the Strait is a lot cleaner than but for the Residual it otherwise might be.

The Wind

As might be expected, the strength of the Residual varies with tidal range. Variations in wind stress also reflect directly on the SW Residual, with Northwesterly winds augmenting it, while Southwesterly winds reduce it or even turn it towards the NE. This has self-evident and opposite effect upon the strength of both the NE and SW-going streams, both the commencement of 'The Slack' and its duration, and the all important time when 'The Ebb' will begin.

Admiralty Pilot:

> *"The streams in the Swellies, and to a less extent in the Strait northeastward and southwestward of the bridges, are affected by winds outside at sea: winds with a southerly component holding the water up, winds with a northerly component causing the stream to turn to the westward earlier. With strong northerly or northwesterly winds both the rate and duration of the southwest-going stream are increased, and the southwest-going stream may begin about a quarter of an hour earlier. Strong south or southwesterly winds have the opposite effect."*

Dr. Toby Sherwin:

> *"In Simpson et al page 252 there is a formula which reads:*

$$U = -11.2 - 0.057W^2 \cos D - 3.67(R - 3.6) cm\ s^{-1}$$

which expresses the enhancement of the flow due to the Residual at Plas Newydd. If we ignore the effect of direction (the cos D), with a northwesterly wind the Southwest Residual could increase by 0.057 x (wind speed)^2. Thus the effect of the 16 m s^{-1} wind that day would be to add to the immediate strength of the Southwest-going stream as much as an extra 15 cm s^{-1}, or 3 knots at Plas Newydd, and quite obviously by a lot more than this in the narrow sections of the Swellies."

Sub Committee Report:

"It seems clear, from the time Conway took to do 6 cables (9.23 to 10.10), that something very unusual was taking place, possibly a strong undercurrent which is known to occur in the channel,"

From the Investigating Subcommittee report, [Appendix I-1] it's clear that Captain Hewitt was firmly of the view that the tide turned precisely at some predetermined time of the day, and that transiting the Swellies was no more than passing the Ship under the tubular bridge at precisely that time. But according to the RWYC, 'The Slack' in the Swellies can usually be expected any time between Liverpool -2.15 and Liverpool - 1.45, which depends upon a permutation of 4 primary variables, the interval between high water at Menai Bridge and Port Dinorwic, variations in the Liverpool Tidal Constant, Atmospheric Pressure and the height of the tide. The strength and direction of the wind and the consequent extent of Residual activity will further advance or retard the time when the stream will reverse direction. It would therefore be naive in the extreme for us to believe it in any way possible to determine in advance the time when 'The Slack' will begin and end on any given day, yet page 1 of the Subcommittee Report is almost entirely devoted to describing the compilation of a detailed timetable solely to ensure that the Ship entered the Swellies at the precise time of day that evidently it was firmly believed that a 10 minute slack would begin. The report states that Captain Hewitt went to the tubular bridge on several occasions to check for himself the time the water slacked there. The report continues (to a final briefing meeting aboard *Conway,* to which the local pilots were not invited):

"The exact timings were finally fixed and agreed, and stress was laid on the critical point in the timetable, which was the time under the tubular bridge at 9.20 am."

Sadly, Captain Hewitt took no account of the wind. On the fateful morning, the wind in the Strait was a mere Northwesterly 1-2, but outside in the Irish Sea where it really mattered, the Liverpool Pilot Boat's log recorded Northwesterly, 6 increasing 7. It was also a very unstable wind with Bidston Observatory recording gusts up to 49 knots (storm force 10).

Together with the highest tide of the year, these were precisely the conditions which could be expected to result in an unusually strong Southwest Residual, producing an early reversal, brief period of 'Slack,' promptly followed by an unusually strong Southwest-going stream. Conditions for the outward move could hardly have been more unpromising. But in the shelter of the Plas Newydd mooring there was no indication of this. Captain Durrant:

"The early morning weather was fine and bright with a light north-westerly wind blowing across the strait. Conditions appeared ideal for the operation."

But in its report, the Investigating subcommittee was to comment later:

> *"It is somewhat surprising to us that the party had no knowledge of the stormy conditions prevailing at sea at the time 'Conway' was to make the passage. Local knowledge may well have been that, under such circumstances, abnormal conditions might be encountered."*

Barometric Pressure

Of course, anything that alters the water levels relative to each other will alter the time of level parity, and thus also change the time when flow reversal occurs. As early as 1747, Gissler discovered the inverse relationship between sea level and atmospheric pressure (1 cm change in sea level for each 1 mb change in atmospheric pressure). In 1964, Prof J.G. Harvey established that in the Menai Strait atmospheric pressure has a much greater effect on water levels than does the wind, and that:

> *"in the Menai Strait there is a particularly close inverse relationship between water level and barometric pressure 12 hours earlier."*

This might at first be thought to have uniform effect along the Strait, and so not interfere with the normal mechanics of level parity. However, Harvey's paper continues:

> *"A decrease in atmospheric pressure brings about the largest increase in mean water level at Caernarfon and Port Dinorwic (relative to Menai Bridge and Belan). Perhaps surprisingly, as well as having more influence (than the wind) on the overall mean water level, atmospheric pressure also has a greater effect (than the wind) on the differences in water levels between the various positions in the Menai Strait."*

This makes it plain that changes in atmospheric pressure were yet another highly significant factor affecting both the strength of the stream and the time when flow reversal will occur.

Tidal Constants

It's the practice in the Menai Strait to quote the times of the tides there by reference to the time of high water at Liverpool (45 miles away!), which assumes a constant time difference, or Tidal Constant on Liverpool. But to quote Reed's Nautical Almanac:

> *"Tidal Constants are not in fact constant, and may vary quite appreciably with changing astronomical conditions."*

But it isn't only the interval on Liverpool that concerns us. The time interval between high water at Menai Bridge and Port Dinorwic isn't constant, and variations in this interval will also alter the time of level parity and flow reversal. From graphs drawn in association with constructing the bar charts From the Figures it can be shown that a given difference in the duration of that interval alters the time of level parity by about half that difference. It had been my intention to wade through the tide tables to determine to what extent this interval varies, which is no more than to make an academic point. Sufficient to say that in the 25 tides I did examine in making these bar charts, high water at Port Dinorwic varied between Menai Bridge -twenty minutes and Menai Bridge –fifty-two minutes, a difference of over half an hour. This one variable on its own is therefore enough to alter the time when the stream reverses direction by as much as a quarter of an hour.

Barry Youde, himself a former Liverpool pilot and now a marine lawyer, questions the difficult position his godfather, the Liverpool pilot CJ Miller, was placed in as liaison between *Conway* and tugs, and that anything which might be construed as an act of pilotage would automatically place him in breach of Section 30(3) of the 1913 Pilotage Act, which created criminal liability for any pilot who is not licensed for a District who pilots or attempts to pilot a ship after a pilot licensed for the District has offered his services. But I really don't think there was any sinister motive in this. Here we have a ship about to be moved by tugs completely unfamiliar with a unique and impossibly difficult waterway, under the command of a captain, pilot and officers none of whom had any experience whatsoever in handling a ship with tugs. The situation was utterly bizarre. The obvious solution was to place onboard someone like C J Miller who was thoroughly familiar with directing Liverpool tugs, to act as a go-between Command and tugs, and there his responsibility ended. He played no part whatsoever in the decision making process.

Navigation Overview

The Southwestern end of the Swellies at low water was photographed from the tubular bridge on the line of the southern transit markers through Cribbin Gutter (far right). To give scale to the photo, the nearest point of Cribbin Rock (left of the Gutter) is about 700 feet from the camera. The surface width

Southwestern End of The Swellies at Low Water on A 10M Liverpool Tide

between Cribbin Rock and the Gwynedd shore (extreme right) is about 150 feet. The wind locally was southerly force 5, but might have been stronger than this outside at sea, so the water level shown here might be more generous than usual. When *Conway* passed through here outward, at Liverpool - 2.00, there would be about 19 feet more water here, which may be judged against the buildings on Gored Goch.

It was generally assumed that since the Ship had gone through the one way she could equally as well go back the other, but the two transits are completely different. Inbound, if you are caught by the reversal while still in the Swellies (as indeed Captain Goddard was) then at least the tide will be turning with you. So it's perfectly safe to start the inbound transit as soon as the water is seen to be going 'Slack.' But given the rapidity with which the SW-going stream develops on a big tide, through fear of being caught by the reversal this is a luxury, which cannot be afforded when outbound, and it's the local practice to make the outbound transit with the last of the NE-going flood. It must be almost a criminal act that Captain Hewitt actually planned to meet the south-going ebb in the Swellies, which is in complete contradiction to all local advice.

The pilotage of the Menai_Strait has been exclusive to the Jones family for well over 100 years, and the knowledge gained has been passed from father to son over many generations, and yet the Subcommittee Report records

"No occasion was mentioned in which a full conference of all concerned included the local pilots."

Ships are entering and leaving ports all over the World all the time, but nobody expects the captain to have any part in this, that's what the pilot is for. The captain's job is done when he presents his ship at the outer limits of a pilotage district, and doesn't start again until the pilot has taken him back out to sea again. So what on Earth was Captain Hewitt doing fussing about over matters he couldn't be expected to know anything at all about, even to the point where he pro-actively excluded the Trinity House pilots every opportunity he could?

While aboard *Conway*, it was believed the Ship was leaving with plenty of time in hand, the Pilots boarded at 7.55 am and expressed the view they thought the Ship 'a bit late.' Accounts vary, but between 8.15 am and 8.22 am Conway slipped her mooring and was under weigh. The ship had been stemming the NE-going flood, so she had to be swung before proceeding. However it is stated that she was turned easily and proceeded towards the Bridge with a following tide and very little effort by the tugs. At 8.50 am Captain Hewitt had the Ship brought up just short of the bridge.

Pilot Richard Jones immediately objected strongly:

"Oh no Captain - we must keep her going,"

to which Captain Hewitt replied very firmly:

"The ship goes under the Bridge at 9020 hours and not one moment before."
(Verbally - Pilot Emrys Jones)

Dr Toby Sherwin:

"The zone of slack water travels westwards, so when it goes slack at the tubular bridge it has already been slack many precious minutes at the suspension bridge. You really can't afford to wait for the slack at the tubular bridge; you do have to go in with the tide behind you. This also means the slack lasts longer for the inbound vessel which carries the slack with her, than it does for the outbound ship which goes against it."

Notice too that the Royal Welsh Yacht Club advise yachtsmen to aim to be passing Menai Bridge at the commencement of 'The Slack' when inbound and when outbound - Menai Straits Tides at a Glance [Appendix I-3] In other words they advise making all of the outbound transit with a following tide, starting about 20 minutes or so before the anticipated time of 'The Slack.' This is exactly what the pilots wanted to do but Captain Hewitt would not allow it.

It's perhaps not surprising that there are serious variations between the Sub Committee Report and the version of the incident as recalled by the pilots. It's clear that the Sub Committee sets out to show *Conway* and those in charge in the most favorable light, and in its effort to do so is in many instances downright misleading eg

"The pilot checked with Captain Hewitt that the time of arrival at the tubular bridge was 9.20,"

absolutely outrageous; nothing could be further from the truth, by 9.20 am the pilot wanted to be at least at Menai Bridge.

"The passage to the tubular bridge was uneventful, the tugs towing easy to arrive at the tubular bridge at the agreed time, although the pilots agreed no such time. Conway had her bows under the tubular bridge at 9.23 am Pilot Jones agreed that, if anything, Conway was early rather than late."

Gets worse doesn't it? Gives the impression the Ship had an uninterrupted tow, passing under the bridge at 9.23 am. Sorry, but we do have the Ship's log which tells a very different story. From the pilots' perspective, and in line with local advice, by 9.23 am the Ship should have been somewhere between Menai Bridge and Bangor, not just passing under the tubular bridge. By no stretch of the imagination could the Ship be regarded as being 'early.'

We've seen why, in the Menai Strait, the higher the tide the shorter is the period of 'Slack,' and that a wind in the Irish Sea with a northerly component will further curtail its duration, so that on the day in question with the highest tide of the year and a force 6/7 (gusting up to 10) Northwest wind we cannot be at all surprised that Captain Durrant's observed:

"The anticipated 10 minute slack did not materialise. The south going Ebb set in immediately (the flood ended) at 9.20 am" (See Durrant's Report - Appendix I-2)

Note: Captain Durrant was not a local, and not familiar with the oddities of the Menai Strait tides, so we do have to excuse him for believing that slack water was synonymous with high water. This leaves me with having to point out that in attempt to clarify what he says, in this instance only I have paraphrased his statement.

At 9.40 am, after the head tug had struggled for 20 minutes with diminishing speed as 'The Ebb' relentlessly gathered momentum, Capt Durrant describes the Ship as making no further progress when, by carefully timing Kelp weed borne on the tide, he estimated that the tide (which he describes as having the character of a race) had already reached a rate of 8 or 10 knots. Blue Funnel Pilot James Miller described it as:

"not a true tide, but a confused mass of swiftly running water."

The Menai Strait Pilot stated that conditions had become abnormal. 2nd Officer GAB King said the stern tug found it almost impossible to come astern against the tide sufficiently to slack the towing springs so the slip-hook might be knocked out. It took 20 minutes before the tug finally freed herself from the Ship. Lt. Commander Brooke-Smith stated:

"The tide suddenly came down like a mill race."

Stern tug skipper Cooper said that after letting go from Conway's stern, his tug was

"going every ounce she could go (10 knots) but was still going astern. The tide was most severe."

Observers on the shore spoke of:

"something like a Tidal Bore."

All this only 17 minutes after she'd entered the Swellies.

Thanks to Geoffrey Haskins (40-43), himself a former Hydrographic Surveyor, we now know that what was believed to be Goddard's chart is, in fact, one of a set of three being a complete survey of the Menai Strait by Commander James Kerr, and dated 1872. [(Appendix I-6)] Referring to the chart title, the tide at the suspension bridge is unlikely to differ noticeably from the tide at Menai Bridge pier, nor is the tide at the tubular bridge likely to be noticeably different from the tide at Pwllfanogl. But from the chart title we can see that high water at the tubular bridge is a full 51 minutes before high water at the suspension bridge only 18 cables away, and when the tidal range is 22.5 feet at the suspension bridge it is only 19 feet at tubular bridge. This, together with the multiple different Chart Datum in use in the strait, posed an obvious problem for Commander Kerr in reducing soundings on his chart against some common denominator. But despite the big differences in the tides along the Strait, it is perhaps surprising that Mean Tide Level (MTL) is common throughout its length. Here then is a common reference level which can be used anywhere in the Strait. So Kerr's solution was to avoid Chart Datum altogether, and instead he reduced his soundings against a stated rise and fall (thus automatically about MTL). Nor for the purpose would it matter what rise and fall he used. As it happens he chose to use 22.5 feet which is a bit unfortunate, because that is also what the chart title states to be the rise and fall at Menai Bridge, thereby introducing scope for confusion. Since the chart title clearly states that soundings between the bridges are reduced for the same rise and fall as Menai Bridge, it would be all too easy to fall into the trap of adding back to soundings the height of the tide at Menai Bridge at any instant in order to figure the depth at that time at any given point between the bridges. But with a moment's reflection, this cannot possibly be the case. After high water tubular bridge the tide will be falling there while it is still rising at the suspension bridge. Even though the tidal range is less at the tubular bridge, because the tide is so much earlier there, in the hours leading up to high water tubular bridge the water level there will always be higher than at the suspension bridge. But after high water tubular bridge the situation becomes reversed, and in the hours that follow it's the water level at the suspension bridge that will always be the highest. So, it simply isn't possible to have a time/height correction to soundings that is common to all soundings between the bridges.

Instead, using James Kerr's chart to figure the depths, you first have to add to soundings half the stated rise and fall (11.25 feet) to bring soundings to MTL, then add/subtract the actual height of the tide above/below MTL, using the Menai Bridge tide for soundings at the suspension bridge, the Pwllfanogl tide for soundings at Britannia Bridge, and some form of sliding scale to interpret the difference between these two extremes for soundings at any intermediate point in between. This very unusual procedure is certainly not made obvious by the chart title.

The Draught

For a ship which it was said could only make the transit on the highest tide of the year, the draught was of supreme importance, yet we don't really know what that draught actually was. At the Inquiry Pilot Jones stated the draught as 21 feet forward and 21 feet 10 inches aft. Captain Hewitt gave the draught as 19 feet and 6 inches forward and 20 feet aft, a hugely important net difference of 1 foot and 10 inches (which even on a big Spring tide is the equivalent of a 25 minute delay in time) yet this the Committee passed without comment. For the purposes of this work we will use the greater draught, the 21 feet and 10 inches quoted by Pilot Jones, and round it up to 22 feet, bearing in mind that if Captain Hewitt was correct then he would have had 2 feet more clearance, or a 25 minute time advantage over that suggested by this work.

Figure 24.3 shows the error resulting from wrongly computing Cheese Rock depths by reference to the height of the tide at Menai Bridge. The Marine Science Labs at Menai Bridge produce individual Tide Tables for each of the places along the Strait, which include the predicted height of the tide at Menai Bridge at hourly intervals throughout the year. Close examination of these latter show them simply to be the standard semi-diurnal sine curve, which given the effect on the tide of the restrictive environment may not faithfully reflect reality. But in the absence of anything better, Figure 24.3 also uses the sine curve to show the height of the tide above MTL at Menai Bridge, and the consequent (erroneous) depth over the rock which would result from using Menai Bridge to figure the depth. This may be compared with Richard Jones (junior)'s actual measurements taken on 22nd February 2000.

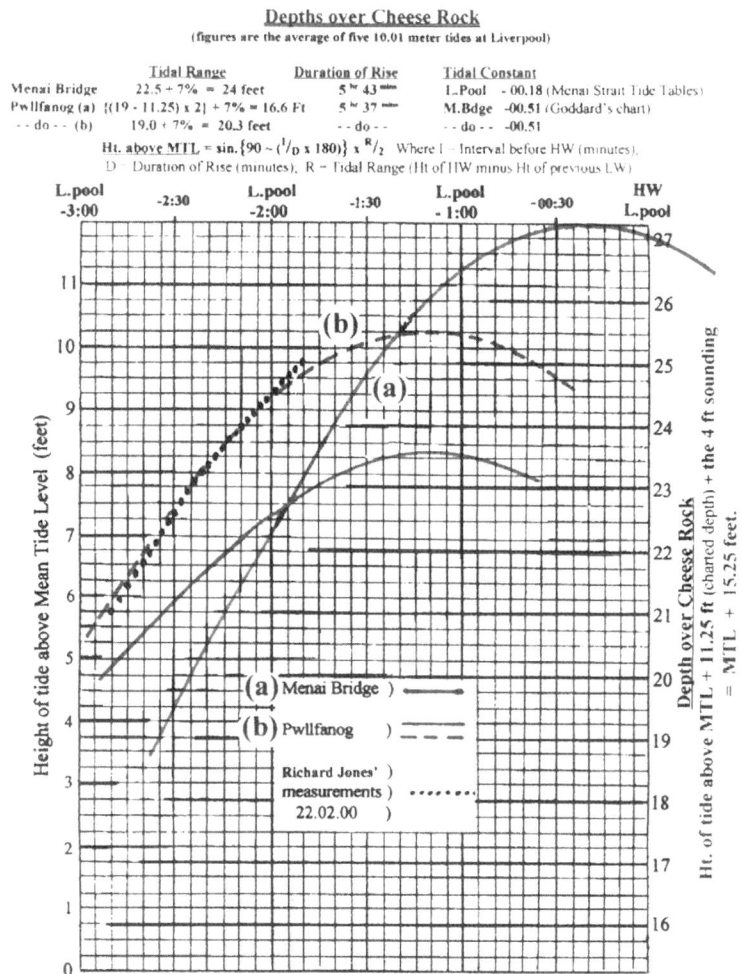

Depths over Cheese Rock
(figures are the average of five 10.01 meter tides at Liverpool)

	Tidal Range	Duration of Rise	Tidal Constant
Menai Bridge	22.5 + 7% = 24 feet	5ʰ 43ᵐⁱⁿ	L.Pool - 00.18 (Menai Strait Tide Tables)
Pwllfanog (a)	{(19 - 11.25) x 2} + 7% = 16.6 Ft	5ʰ 37ᵐⁱⁿ	M.Bdge -00.51 (Goddard's chart)
-- do -- (b)	19.0 + 7% = 20.3 feet	-- do --	-- do -- -00.51

Ht. above MTL = sin.{90 ~ (¹/_D x 180)} x ᴿ/₂ Where I - Interval before HW (minutes),
D - Duration of Rise (minutes), R ~ Tidal Range (Ht of HW minus Ht of previous LW)

Figure 24.3: Depths of Water Over Cheese Rock by Reference to
the Height of the Tide at Menai Bridge

High water Liverpool that 14th April morning was 11.18 am. Now let us suppose that Captain Hewitt was misled by the ambiguous title on the chart, and fell into the trap of wrongly believing that to figure the depth over Cheese Rock he must add the height of the tide at Menai Bridge to the 4 feet sounding. The erroneous result of doing this is the subject of the Menai Bridge graph, which as you see shows 22 feet (*Conway's* draught?) over the rock at Liverpool -2.00, or 9.18 am that morning. This would certainly explain Captain Hewitt's fixation on

"0920 hours and not one moment before."

In his mind, this was the earliest possible time the Ship could pass over the rock, so he would have had no patience with the pilot's insistence that the Ship be put to the rock half an hour sooner.

But before being able to continue, it becomes necessary to explain a couple of our expressions to our non-nautical readers. Please refer to Figure 24.4. What Commander Kerr's chart refers to as 'Rise and Fall' is what today we call the 'Range' of the tide, which is the difference between the height of high water and the previous low water on a rising tide, or the difference between the height of high water and the following low water on a falling tide. The two are seldom the same, but it's the range on the rising tide that is commonly quoted and is the only one that concerns us here. The 'Rise' of the tide is the height of that tide at high water above charted depth. Without going into too much detail, the tides are regarded as oscillating about Mean Tide Level. Thus twice the height above MTL at high water equals the Range of that tide. On a chart such as James Kerr's, where soundings are reduced for a Mean Springs Range of 22.5 feet, from Figure 24.4 you will see why the Rise of that Mean Spring Tide equals its Range.

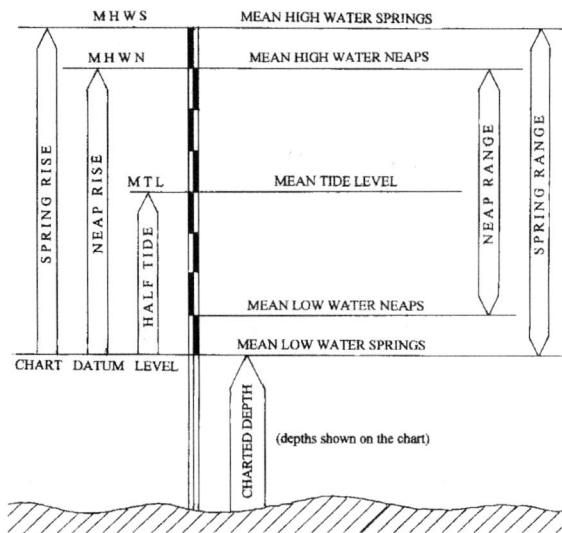

Figure 24.4: Diagrammatic Representation of the Tides

The chart states that at Pwllfanogl the Rise at springs is 19 feet. Therefore, Range = (Rise -11.25) x 2, which gives us the Range at Pwllfanogl as 15.5 feet at Ordinary Springs. Add 7% to this and we get 16.6 feet as the Range on the highest tide of the year. Half this Range (8.3 feet) plus 11.25 feet (MTL) plus the four foot sounding over Cheese Rock gives us the depth over the rock at high water on the highest tide of the year as 23' 6." Working the sine formula on a Tidal Range of 16.6 feet produces the curve (a) in Figure 3, which (just like erroneously working the depth on Menai Bridge) again shows the Ship would have bare clearance over the rock at Liverpool -2.00 (9.18 am), yet again confirming Capt Hewitt's conviction

"0920 hours and not one moment before."

But there is something very wrong here. In Masefield Captain Goddard states:

> *"on this transit I could run down to the narrowest part of the channel at the SW end of the Gored Is where I would have four feet under my bottom,"*

an obvious reference to the least depth, which is Cheese Rock. But according to graph (a) in Figure 24.3 he could not have had more than 18 inches under his keel even on the top of high water. Moreover graph (a) disturbingly bears not the slightest resemblance to Richard Jones (Junior)'s actual physical measurements. So let's look at this chart title a little more closely.

The title states

> *"soundings are reduced to low water springs, NE of Britannia (tubular) Bridge for a rise and fall of 22.5 feet, to the SW for 19 feet."*

So west of the bridge 19 feet is indeed both the Range and the Rise at Pwllfanogl, but east of the bridge it's no longer the Rise, but it still remains the Range. Now that we know that east of the bridge 19 feet is the Range (not the Rise) at Pwllfanogl, this paints a very different picture.

Instead of the 16.6 feet Range we had previously concluded, adding the 7% to the 19 feet Ordinary Springs Range at Pwllfanogl now gives us a Range of 20.3 feet on the highest tide of the year. Reworking the sine formula for this new Range produces the curve (b) in Figure 3, which as you see coincides precisely with Richard Jones' measurements, and it is this that clinches it for us.

Conway was by far the deepest ship ever to have transited the Swellies, at a draught right outside the pilots' experience, so we do have to sympathise with Captain Hewitt's reluctance to accept the pilots' advice regarding the available depth. Indeed Emrys Jones, who dismissed this question as

"*there was plenty of water,*"

told me that in his day he regarded 17 feet and 6 inches through the Swellies as the

"*absolute maximum.*"

However, his need to berth at Caernarvon on the last of the NE-going flood meant he regularly 'powered' these little ships through the Swellies against the flood about an hour before 'The Slack' when there would be a lot less water. But full marks to Richard Jones (junior) for physically measuring the depth over Cheese Rock on 22nd February 2000, although that he saw the need to do so doesn't say too much for his family's prior knowledge of that depth.

From this analysis confirmed by Richard Jones (junior)'s measurements, the reality was the Ship had 22 feet over the rock as early as 8.38 am that morning (Liverpool -2.40) [see Figure 3], and had no reason at all to be brought up at 8.50 am and held to for that fatal 20 minutes at Pwllfanogl. She could have been kept going at 8.50 am as the pilot recommended. Given the 15 minutes the Ship took between Pwllfanogl and the bridge, this would have put him over the rock around 9.05 am (Liverpool -2.13) with (at least) 18 inches (possibly 2 feet more [see 'The Draught' above]) over the rock and the tide behind him. Given Captain Goddard's

"*18 minutes between the bridges*"

in similar tidal circumstances, the Ship would then have been under the suspension bridge around 9.23 am, or about the time the tide turned at the tubular bridge that morning, or shortly after it had turned at the suspension bridge, so even this ("Keep her going") was a bit late on the advice of the RWYC. But sadly Captain Hewitt knew better. But the really astonishing thing is that Captain Hewitt did not see the need to correlate soundings over Cheese Rock with the nearby tide board on the bridge, which would have eliminated all the guesswork, leaving him in harmony with the pilots, and perhaps then he would not have fatally delayed the Ship until 9.20 am. Indeed, while the plan called for the Ship to be through the Swellies in 15 minutes, by 10.10 am, after 47 minutes the Ship had only made good 6 cables and was at a complete standstill with another 3 cables still to go. Clearly by delaying until 9.20 am, the Ship was far too late, the situation absolutely hopeless and the Ship in grave danger. When Pilot Jones said very quietly:

"Captain, we must go back," Captain Hewitt replied:

"You don't seem to understand do you? The ship must go on." (verbally - Pilot Emrys Jones)

Witnesses at the Inquiry agreed that going back would not have been possible. Captain G D Pari-Huws (44-45) counters this convenient assumption

> *"But why ever not? It might have <u>looked</u> a bit kack-handed, but both tugs were stern on to the Ship and the tidal circumstances were exactly the same as they had been in 1949."*

Instead, the decision having been made, with great difficulty the stern tug was finally slipped and sent forward to assist the head tug. But even both tugs towing ahead together made very little, if any, difference. Short of going back, there was nothing more which could be done, and Captain Hewitt had made it plain that going back was not something he was prepared to consider.

So finally the Report states

> *"At some time between 10.20 and 10.30 am (between 57 and 67 minutes after she had entered the Swellies) with both tugs towing ahead but making little impression, when abreast of the Platters Rocks, Conway took a sudden and violent sheer to starboard, took charge, and went ashore over the Platters in a matter of seconds."*

The Ship had grounded half an hour before high water Menai Bridge, less than 6 inches below the top of the highest tide of the year (see Figure 3).

When all attempts to tow her off proved futile it was decided to leave further efforts until high water on the following afternoon's tide, so the tugs left the Ship to await instructions at Menai Bridge Pier. Meanwhile, as the tide ebbed, the stern lost its support while the fore ship was held firmly on the Platters so hogging the Ship appallingly, collapsing her decks and opening up her seams. When the next tide made, the stern failed to lift and water poured into her mercilessly confirming she was mortally wounded. On Thursday evening, April 16th 1953, in a press statement, Mr. Alfred Wilson, Secretary to the *Conway* Committee declared *HMS Conway* a total constructive loss.

The subsequent Investigating Subcommittee Report (see Appendix I-1) has been termed a 'whitewash.' Captain G. D. Pari-Huws:

> *"The ship was gone and could neither be salvaged nor replaced, but there was a lot more to lose than just the Ship. For*

"Mortally Wounded"

an establishment which set out to teach others navigation to lose its own ship in circumstances which seriously questioned the competence of those in charge could not be allowed to happen. There was nothing to be gained but a great deal to be lost by embarking on a head-hunt. The Committee was not a bunch of fools, they knew perfectly well what had happened, but they saw it not in the general interest to reveal it."

I remain firmly of the view that left to their own devices the pilots would have got her through, as they have done for thousands of other ships both before and since. Why *Conway* stood out alone in finding it necessary to interfere with, ignore, countermand and defy the pilots is not at all obvious, but for so doing she did pay the ultimate price.

Captain David G Williams (Rtd First Class Pilot) (49-51)

CHAPTER 25

1953 RECOVERY

It took a while for the news to spread to Old *Conways* around the world, but eventually everyone learned the sad, unbelievable truth. The Ship was gone.

On 23rd April, the management committee met for the first time since the loss. Two questions had to be addressed. Who, if anyone, was responsible for the loss of the Ship, and, if *Conway* was to survive, how to accommodate the cadets when they returned for the summer term?

The Inquiry

The committee quickly came to the most delicate item on the agenda, the loss of the Ship. It was reported that neither the Admiralty, who actually owned the Ship, nor the Ministry of Shipping planned to hold an inquiry. In fact, Captain Hewitt said that when he reported the loss to the Admiralty they more or less replied that as they had nothing to do with her for the last 77 years they were not interested. Lawrence Holt's family had a long, almost paternal relationship with *Conway* and he said his conscience was troubled. He felt there should be an inquiry into the loss. The committee decided they would have to conduct it themselves and set up an investigating sub-committee consisting of:

- Brian Heathcote (Assistant Manager, Alfred Holt and Co.) as Chairman.
- Mr. L. O'Brien Harding (Partner Bibby Line).
- Mr. Alfred Wilson (MMSA General Secretary and secretary to the *Conway* committee).
- Captain G. Ayre (Port of Liverpool Harbour Master).
- Captain A.G. Peterkin OBE (Retired Harrison Line Master and Liverpool Pilotage Committee Nautical Adviser).
- Captain James Nelson, who was present for part of the time.
- Lord Norbury (*Conway* cadet circa 1908-1910) Manager, International Paints Merseyside, however illness prevented his participation.

The sub-committee's work would be a delicate affair. The events had been front-page national news for days. The Merchant Navy's premier officer cadet training ship, with a veteran Captain RNR in command, experienced naval officers and a management committee of the great and the good of Liverpool shipping had just lost their ship in a stretch of water acknowledged to be extremely treacherous. One might even question what such a veteran ship was doing there in the first place? Captain Hewitt had resolved to resign, but members of the committee approached Mrs Hewitt and with her solid support convinced him to remain in post.

The inquiry sub-committee met on 5th May 1953 and heard accounts from:

- Captain Eric Hewitt, Captain Superintendent

- Richard J. Jones, Menai Strait Pilot. Captain Frank Durrant, Marine Manager, Rea Towing Company. F.A. Brown, Tug-Master *Dongarth*.
- F. Cooper, Tug-Master *Minegarth*.
- James Miller, Liverpool Pilot.

None of the *Conway's* officers attended, not even Lt. Cdr. Brooke Smith, who had been in charge of the forward party or Captain King in charge aft. No independent or expert witnesses were called. But to use the word 'witnesses' is probably to misunderstand the nature of this inquiry. Heathcote was about to become chairman of *Conway's* management committee and other committee members had been party to the planning and decision-making. The inquiry was an internal damage limitation exercise.

> *"The ship was gone and could neither be salvaged nor replaced, but there was a lot more to lose than just the Ship. For an establishment that set out to teach others navigation to lose its own ship in circumstances that seriously questioned the competence of those in charge could not be allowed to happen. There was nothing to be gained and a great deal to be lost by embarking on a head-hunt. The Committee was not a bunch of fools, they knew perfectly well what had happened, but they saw it not in the general interest to reveal it."*

They carefully countered all the obvious issues. The channel was too narrow for two tugs forward. There was no reasonable need to have made provision for a second forward tug. The timing of the passage as planned was correct, the tugs were powerful enough for the expected conditions, no tug available could have countered the surge that drove the Ship ashore, an unidentified local pilot conveniently confirmed that the tide turned early (earlier than recorded by any other spectator), communications were effective at all times. Everyone involved had done his utmost. Planning was

> *"correct"*

the tug masters' manoeuvre was

> *"brilliantly executed."*

The sub-committee's unanimous conclusion was that Captain Hewitt and the entire team had acted with

> *"the highest standards of skill and seamanship."*

Participants were obviously singing from the same hymn sheet. The local pilots who struck a few discordant notes were neutralised; their requests for an extra tug were invalid because they didn't understand towing, their repeated advice to turn back was considered impossible by everyone else, the committee even disqualified the pilot's views on wind conditions. The two pilots honoured with a silver cup for their part in the successful 1949 transit were ignored before the transit and neatly sidelined afterwards. Despite all this tidiness, glaring anomalies remained unresolved:

- The need to bring the stern tug forward
- was *"clearly foreseen in the preliminary conference"*

- yet no provision had been made for it.

- Captain Hewitt gave *Conway's* draught as 19 feet and 6 inches forward, 20 feet aft, but the logbook said 19 feet and 10 inches forward, 21 feet and 10 inches aft. Pilot Richard Jones gave the draught as 21 feet forward and 21 feet and 10 inches aft. No one questioned these discrepancies, even though her draught was a critical factor in planning the earliest time for clearance over Cheese Rock.

- An average towing speed of 4 knots was planned, yet when the tow reached the suspension bridge the stream was expected to be running at 4 knots. Clearly, this meant that very little headway would be possible. The tugs' maximum speed *when light* was 10 knots, yet Captain Goddard was on record in the Cadet magazine as saying that the ebb stream could reach speeds of 10 knots, so quite how the tugs were supposed to manage if such a stream were encountered was unclear. How had these assumptions been adopted when Captain Hewitt, the tug masters and local pilots had all participated in the 1949 transit and knew first hand what the conditions could be like? Perhaps we begin to see a reason why the local pilots were so completely excluded from the planning.

- The impossibility of reversing the Ship out of the Swellies was not questioned, even though that was exactly how she had been taken through in 1949 under the same tidal conditions, by the same tug masters and pilots, and with Captain Hewitt onboard.

The Inquiry concluded that the grounding was due to the exceptional condition of a 10 knot stream, when everyone assumed a maximum of only 4 knots. With a mild slap of the wrist for appearances sake,

"It is somewhat surprising to us that the party had no knowledge of the stormy conditions prevailing at sea at the time,"

the inquiry was done. I can do no better than quote Captain Brian McManus in his later analysis,

"by closing the stranding episode quickly the Conway Committee wisely minimised both the personal stress experienced by those directly involved, and also the potential for fruitless recriminations."

A transcript of the Inquiry Report is in Appendix I-1

Close or Continue?

The committee meeting on 23rd April also considered the future. A lot of preparatory work had already been done and any doubts were quickly swept away. They agreed immediately; *Conway* must continue and a replacement vessel should be sought. *Discovery* was suggested. A new nautical college would be built on the shores of the strait at a cost of £200,000, funded by donations from shipping companies. A temporary hutted camp would be built near the canteen to accommodate cadets until the new college was ready. In the September 1953 edition of the Cadet magazine the chairman of the management committee acknowledged,

"one (person) in particular made continuity assured, the Marquis of Anglesey came forward immediately with practical help in our extremis and ensured that we could go on. We shall not forget his kindness for many years to come."

The huts would cost £20,000 to build and a further £20,000 to fit and furnish. The Chairman Lawrence Holt announced that Alfred Holt and Co would pay

"the whole cost of the salvage"

although he already knew that the Ship was not salvageable. Cunard offered to do

"anything to help."

Despite the upbeat nature of these public pronouncements the committee faced huge uncertainties over the coming months. The Marquis had quickly agreed a site for the temporary huts but he and the committee could not agree the best site for the new college. An Admiralty Committee on the general training of naval cadets made proposals for a new state college, mirroring Browne's three year course with entry at 13½ and greater emphasis on general education and preparation for GCE. It seemed *Conway* might have to compete as a private school with high fees against a well-appointed state endowed college. The reputation of Southampton was growing amongst ship-owners at *Conway's* expense. It was feared that, to survive, *Conway* would become the second line for less able boys of better off parents or have to be indirectly subsidized by the education committees. The cost of the new college quickly rose to £250,000 and shipping companies did not flock to contribute. £100,000 was pledged, by Lawrence Holt providing Cunard agreed to match it. The committee meeting on 23rd July recorded,

"we will be lucky to get £100,000 and £250,000 out of the question."

There were doubts whether cadet numbers could be maintained, even talk of reverting to a simple one year course. It seems the committee were thinking the unthinkable; *Conway* might have to close within 3 years. However, this time the tide turned in *Conway's* favour and positive announcements flowed. Sites for the new college and the huts had been agreed with the Marquis; a vessel would be obtained and moored in the strait,

"from which all boat work will be practiced;"

and the chairman further confirmed

"we shall have our own seagoing craft big enough to take a whole term of Conway to sea for a voyage as part of their training."

It would be owned by a shipping company and based in Liverpool. The number of cadets would remain at 250-300 boys. Funding would be found for the new college no matter how long it took. We shall return to the saga of the new college, but it would be 10 years before it opened!

A New Chairman

In June 1953, Lawrence Holt resigned as chairman of Blue Funnel, the family firm and, after 19 years, as chairman of *Conway's* management committee. Despite some rumours, this was unconnected with the loss of the Ship. He had first announced his desire to retire in 1949. He had been prevailed upon to remain but in the middle of 1952, nine months before the loss, the committee finally accepted his resignation and voted on his successor. He was replaced as *Conway's* chairman by Brian Heathcote and in Blue Funnel by Sir John Nicholson, who also joined *Conway's* committee. Captain Hewitt paid strong tribute to Holt at Prize Day in July 1953. He was appointed

> *"when it was essential that new ideals, vision and energy were required, for Conway was then behind the times in the education she provided. Under his guiding hand a new spirit pervaded the Ship, the curriculum was amended, and the Ship received recognition as an efficient secondary school. The vast resources of Mr. Holt's family business were put at the Ship's disposal and all departments gave advice and help so that not only were the educational facilities improved but also the hull and fittings. A large programme of refit was put in hand. His retirement … will be a grievous loss to us, for it has been an inspiration to all onboard to have a chairman whose watchword was always 'Service'."*

Mr. Heathcote was introduced as a man with

> *"like ideals"*

and

> *"there is no man better to see the obstacles overcome and we look forward with confidence to his years in office."*

As part of his first address to cadets, Mr. Heathcote demonstrated a deep understanding of *Conway* with a rallying cry, which resonates to this day.

> *"Tradition doesn't reside in the timbers of an old ship. It doesn't reside in bricks and mortar. Tradition is in us. It is the use we make of the examples of the past, to embellish it, to enhance it, and then to pass it on to the generations yet to come."*

Captain Hewitt felt that one tradition, the singing of the *Conway* Song on Sundays, should end as the words were less appropriate without the Ship. Cadets simply disagreed and so he allowed the singing, no matter how tuneless, to continue. Captain Hewitt wrote to John Masefield asking him to re-write some of the verses to reflect the loss of the Ship. Masefield replied that

> *"though the words may be inappropriate, the tradition was the thing and no change should be made."*

The Captain Superintendent eventually concurred, observing that

> *"although 70 years separated Masefield from the cadets of that day, the strong sense of continuity joined them."*

Conway would survive providing a new home could be readied in time.

CHAPTER 26

1953 UNDER CANVAS

Until the temporary hutted camp was built there remained the immediate challenge of how to accommodate the cadets so that training could continue during the summer term.

Captain Hewitt and Mr. Browne urgently sought alternative accommodation for the 170 or so cadets who would otherwise have returned to the Ship. Within two days of the loss, the Headmaster visited Plas Coch, another large but old and dilapidated house built in 1569, a mile or so along the road from Plas Newydd.

> *"Accommodation for 200 boys using large barn, attic stores. A rabbit warren of long rooms and would be a death trap in event of fire, which with the large amount of old dry wood would be a risk."*

When the water was tested it was found to be unsatisfactory. The accommodation offered by Lord Penrhyn in 1948 was re-examined but also rejected. The Royal Navy suggested that *Conway* shared the Royal Navy College at Dartmouth as it was half empty. Perhaps not co-incidentally, the Times Educational Supplement ran a special feature describing *Conway* as 'The Dartmouth of the Merchant Navy', but it was decided that too much had already been sunk into Plas Newydd. On 19th April 1953 a temporary tented camp was proposed on the Plas Newydd estate. After examining sites on Druid's Field and at the canteen, they agreed on 22nd to use Maes y Fran, the upper rugby field. The committee confirmed that the tented camp was an acceptable solution to immediate accommodation needs, but only for one term.

The Royal Army Service Corps at Menai Bridge were approached and agreed to loan *Conway* 23 large khaki marquees and 2 smaller tents.

> *"They were on loan from the Army and were so dilapidated they must have been hidden since the Crimean War."*

They were about 18 feet wide and perhaps 24 feet long. On 25th April 1953, they were erected on Maes Y Fran in 5 hours. During the holidays cadets received a number of letters advising them about arrangements for the next term. RN Class cadets were instructed to report back on the planned start date of 25th April 1953, all other cadets were separately advised to return on 6th May. When they returned to start the summer term, instead of a wooden wall ship in the strait, they were to live in tents in a windy field, albeit one with spectacular view of Snowdonia and

The Tents on Maes Y Fran

Snowdon. On clear days the Snowdon Mountain trains could be seen puffing smoke on their way to the summit.

Each division was allotted 5 marquees each sleeping 8-10 cadets on iron bedsteads. Each cadet's sea chest was next to his bunk. Additional marquees were provided for duty staff, the chief cadet captain and recreation. The gunroom marquee was larger than the dormitory marquees and in the centre of the camp. Two small bell tents were set up near the camp entrance for the duty cadet captain, messenger and bugler.

"They were bell tents, and I seem to remember that they were hired from the Army. I think that there were about 10 cadets per tent, sleeping. We had to go to the Kelvin block to wash or shower."

Arrangements were superior to the ones onboard as there was an adequate supply of hot water. Additional toilet facilities were rapidly provided, although they were about 400 yards away from the camp.

"They built a sort of brick privy (I wouldn't call it a head) in one corner of the field and getting there on a wet rainy night was a bit of an adventure."

"It was amazing how quickly we got back into a routine not too dissimilar to life onboard."

The previous organisation was maintained as far as possible. 'Lash up and stow' changed to lifting all the side curtains of the tents and hanging out the bedding to dry, it never seemed to stop raining that term.

The early morning scramble in the Ship for exercise on deck was replaced by PT in the centre of the camp where morning divisions were also held. One tradition to die that term was that of calling for three cheers for going home, perhaps caused by the lack of a single spot where an announcement could be heard and responded to by all cadets.

4 new wooden class-rooms, well-lit and heated, were built in the Kelvin Block quadrangle (in 2008 only one remained and that was showing its age). The only really unsatisfactory item was the dining accommodation at the Nelson Block which, having been originally intended to accommodate 100 shore based cadets, now had to accommodate almost three times that number.

"This was overcome by having two sittings for meals and rearranging the school timetable so that time should not be wasted. None of this would have been possible had it not been for the efforts of the galley and pantry staff, who, with surprisingly few complaints, adapted themselves to the changed conditions."

This term was a critical one for *Conway* and her cadets. The Ship had been lost and nothing was certain, cadets were

"in a sort of a daze,"

hardly believing that the Ship had gone.

"When we were in the tents none of us really believed that the old Ship was a total loss. We used to have long discussions as to how to re-float her. We used to go aboard quite a lot to salvage stuff, and even with the water creeping up the after end of the lower deck she still seemed alive and real."

Fortunately, the chief cadet captain that term was Bill Silvester and he made a crucial difference. With his quiet authority and much valued guidance the cadets adapted to their new surroundings and made it through this most difficult term.

"Although the weather was most unkind for the greater part of the term the cadets seemed to thrive under canvas. A full month elapsed before anyone was admitted to sick bay, and he had taken too great an advantage of one of the infrequent appearances of the sun, and suffered accordingly. After his discharge, browner and wiser, sick bay remained comparatively empty apart from a few minor accident cases."

The cadets took to their new surroundings with aplomb.

"After we returned at the beginning of the Summer Term and having spent one night in one of the tents the Captain asked me if I was warm enough with only one blanket as I was from Bermuda and a much warmer climate. I said No! So we had additional blankets issued. It was quite cold in the tents at night and as I recall we were quite comfortable with the extra blanket."

Happy Campers

"We had iron bedsteads with every imaginable invention to keep the rain off and, of course, our sea chests salvaged from the Ship (I still can't bear to say wreck). The tent walls, about four feet high, could be rolled up leaving the whole tent open to the air. Very nice on warm days and also useful after rain to help dry things out."

"It rained like hell all the time and we used to rig up waterproof hangings over our bunks to keep the water off. We also had to fix ourselves some kind of duck boards due to the mud. Every couple of weeks we had to move the whole camp a few yards one way or another to find fresh grass. The places where the tents had been before, clearly marked as muddy ovals."

"We had to put planks under the feet of the camp beds to stop them sinking in the mud overnight and rig a groundsheet over oneself to keep the drips off."

"I had some ex US army camouflaged ponchos cum groundsheets which I strung up over my bunk and a second one made a sort of tablecloth for my chest. They kept the worst of the rain off"

"One of our greatest enemies were the sheep who used to scratch their backs on the tent guy ropes in the middle of the night. Even worse, they could get their heads stuck between the two parts of the guys and someone would have to get out in the rain and free the offending beast. As I was junior cadet captain I could usually pull rank on the wetter nights, but I took my turn when it was drier."

The Kelvin and Nelson Blocks and the dock were about 15 minutes walk away so Bill Silvester asked to be allowed to have a bike sent from home as his feet were acting up after an operation (a lot of his foot bones were held together with wires) and this was granted. Of course this prompted other cadets to apply for bikes giving reasons from flat feet to dandruff. A large number of bikes appeared from somewhere and soon most people had one and were cycling madly everywhere.

"We were allowed to use bicycles to make the trip to the Kelvin Block and back, but it was very muddy at the time, so riding the bikes was far from smooth. There were no roads, only muddy tracks or fields, and these were ordinary road and racing bikes with very narrow tyres."

Many cadets were too far away to get bikes from home and used to cadge lifts from the more fortunate cadets.

"You could often see three or four chaps on one machine wobbling down the lane from the rugger pitches."

Above: Davies and Silvester (seated) and Bike
Below: Cycle Race

"Bill Silvester, the chief cadet captain, was more or less the instigator of the famous bicycle races, run on the dirt-track principle. We hurtled round a small oval track, black mud instead of cinders, and he was often the winner. However, the number of calls in sick bay for sprains etc. and the growing pile of smashed bikes decided him to put an end to the racing. When he said 'Enough' we all stopped. No questions asked. He did things like that by force of character and personality alone."

Another cadet recalls

"The mud was terrific! Members of staff were not too worried about the mounting number of cuts and bruises but went overboard about the destruction of so many bikes. They reckoned they would get it in the neck from the parents. As the number of bikes reduced each bike carried more and more passengers from the camp down to the school block, a lot of them just collapsing on the way so that the path along by the rhododendron plantation started to look like a rather poor junk yard - finally they were all banned. Those that had survived, of course."

That term's New Chums had last seen the Ship during their tour after their entrance exams a few weeks previously.

"I found myself onboard a steam train heading for Bangor, the train was thronged by cadets in uniform; such anticipation. We were loaded into the waiting Crossville buses at Bangor station and then the general hubbub stilled to a respectful murmur as the bus swung onto the suspension bridge. The order "Off Caps" rang out and all eyes turned to look at our Conway, barely a quarter mile distant, partly submerged and hard aground on the Platters Rock; silent thoughts."

This 'off caps' tradition was to continue well into the late 60s. If no caps were worn cadets simply turned to face the wreck site and fell silent for a moment. The New Chums were spared the tents and went straight into the Nelson Block.

"I think it was quite amazing that the Committee and Staff were able to live up to their 'business as usual' promise so well. Obviously there were some problems, not least the improvised catering arrangements, but by and large, Conway training and its naval discipline were maintained to a high standard; a credit to the staff and to the cadets. We New Chums were introduced to seamanship and boat work by rowing the 12-oared cutters and sailing various craft in the strong tidal streams of the Strait, we practiced our bends, hitches and splices, we had timetabled classes in all curriculum subjects and we took part in physical training, athletics and the usual summer sports. Under the direction of our cadet captains, we kept our accommodation at the House spic and span, learned our parade-ground drill, mustered for Divisions, including Captain's inspections, and attended prayers morning and evening as well as church service on Sundays. My parents claimed they hardly recognised their 'grown-up' son upon his return home for summer leave, such was the maturing effect of Conway life and training."

1953 June 15th

Just a few weeks after the start of term, there was the coronation of Her Majesty the Queen, and all hands were given a few days off in which to proceed home for the celebration. Not long after that there were two further events: The Queen's Coronation Fleet Review at Spithead and her tour of the nation.

Cadets were excited to hear that some of them would attend Princess Elizabeth's coronation ceremony at Westminster Abbey, and that 120 cadets would attend the Queen's review of the fleet at Spithead from aboard the cruiser *Dido*.

"… As her engines were in mothballs, she had to suffer the indignity of being towed out to her position in the review lines! As an added introduction to the Royal Navy, cadets were taken in a trip round the Isle of Wight in the destroyer Trafalgar, giving us the opportunity to sense the atmosphere aboard a modern warship. The Royal yacht Britannia, having only recently been laid down, the Queen inspected the fleet from the Admiralty despatch vessel Surprise. A 21-gun salute was fired as the Surprise sailed down the lines of ships, dressed overall, and a picture of cadets lining the deck of the Dido, one of them clearly wincing from a deafening gun report, appeared later in the 'Everybody' magazine. In the afternoon of the review day, we were invited to the quarterdeck of the Dido to drink the health of the new Queen, before being given shore leave in Portsmouth. I wonder whether this overall experience inspired any of the cadets to join the Grey Funnel Line rather than the Merchant Navy. At any rate, it certainly underlined our honorary RNR status."

When it was known that her tour would pass along the North Wales coast from Caernarfon to Bangor, all hands were ferried to Port Dinorwic to line part of the route.

"We cadets were well-drilled in our No.1 uniforms, stood for an age in a straight line along the pavement fronting the sombre grey buildings of the village and then, when the motorcade eventually arrived carrying the Queen and Duke of Edinburgh, it was travelling so quickly that we were convinced they had not even noticed us!"

While cadets made the best of life in their tents, there was considerable activity behind the scenes. By the time they returned for the winter term further magic would have been worked.

CHAPTER 27

1953-6 THE END OF THE SHIP

As soon as it became apparent that the Ship could not be salvaged, a prolonged dispute arose about ownership of and responsibility for the wreck. The legal aspects of maritime jurisdiction, ownership of vessels, liabilities of Royal Navy ships, insurance etc., combined to create a minefield for those involved. The arguments would drag on for over three years.

Abandoned and Forlorn

Following the loss, the MMSA's main concern was the continuation of training, not the future of the Ship. They immediately wrote to the Admiralty, in effect, terminating the loan and 'returning' the Ship! They also wrote to the Caernarfon Harbour Trust advising that the Ship was now a matter for the Admiralty. The Admiralty inspected the Ship on 12th July 1953 and replied that it was unable to accept responsibility for the consequences of the actions of others outside its control. While this absolved them of any obligation to recover or repair the Ship they seemed to accept that the wreck was now theirs. A team of Royal Navy specialists arrived and secured the Ship to the shore with heavy cables to prevent her floating off. They also placed warning lights in the Ship.

Since 1875, the Ship had been insured for £5,000. The insured sum was demanded from the underwriters by the Admiralty within days of the wreck taking place. The underwriters paid up as she had been formally declared a constructive total loss. Late in June, the Headmaster recorded in his diary

"Future of the Ship itself subject of much argument – whether it belonged to the Admiralty or to the underwriters."

The underwriters though would not accept responsibility, paying over the insured sum was the end of their involvement.

The management committee meeting on 21ˢᵗ January 1954 discussed responsibility for the wreck and any damage it might cause. Newspapers reported locals complaining that large baulks of timber and fittings were floating off her and causing a hazard to small boats in the strait. There was increasing concern

"that her inevitable fascination for small boys was luring children into perilous games around and aboard her."

The committee were advised that if an incident occurred and any injured party could prove negligence on *Conway's* part then the MMSA's indemnity insurance would cover the costs but they would become responsible for the wreck. If negligence could not be proved then *Conway* was clear of responsibility. On 6ᵗʰ May 1954, the Admiralty formally accepted the findings of the MMSA inquiry giving credence to the argument that *Conway* was not liable for the wreck.

Meanwhile, the wreck was deteriorating badly. She was still intact and recognisable but was severely twisted, her sides collapsing inwards, her back clearly broken by the tides and the fierce streams and eddies through the Swellies. In plain view to traffic on the suspension bridge she was a sad reminder of that terrible day. Every trip over the bridge must have been torture for Captain Hewitt, and the officers and committee members involved. Although the strait was not a busy waterway, the wreck was close alongside the very narrow channel and so a danger to passing shipping. If she broke up her huge timbers, possibly even large sections of hull, could obstruct the channel or be swept out into the Irish Sea and along the coast, presenting significant dangers to shipping; rather like shipping containers lost overboard today. Perhaps sensing the implications, within a year the Admiralty formally announced that they were abandoning the wreck. One of the many letters in the Admiralty file, dated November 1954, is unambiguous:

"My Lords .... feel they have no legal, or even moral responsibility."

However, they could not just abandon her, they had to abandon her *to* someone, normally the authority having jurisdiction over the coast where grounding occurred.

Unfortunately, no one seemed to have formal jurisdiction over the stretch of water where the Ship lay. The Caernarfon Harbour Trust was responsible for the safety of navigation from seaward of Caernarfon Bar in the west to Britannia Bridge in the east. The (then) Beaumaris Borough Council were responsible for the strait from Puffin Island in the east, to the Suspension Bridge in the west. Neither party was responsible for the Swellies. This might explain why Captain Goddard, in 1949, and Captain Hewitt, in 1953, took it upon themselves to erect additional navigation aids in the Swellies to help their passages. There was no doubt that the wreck lay on the approaches to the Port of Caernarfon, and presented a danger that portions of the wreck might break free and obstruct the fairway, so closing the port, which was still visited regularly by small coastal tankers and other vessels.

Eventually, as the vessel had been formally abandoned, a private individual boarded the wreck and attempted to take possession. To avoid the further complication to which this situation would lead, the Caernarfon Harbour Trust exercised their formal rights over wrecks in the approaches to their port and assumed possession in May 1954. The Harbour Trust appealed to the (then) Ministry of Transport and Civil Aviation who replied that:

> "...the Minister had no funds which could be made available for removal of the wreck."

The Trust sought advice from Trinity House, the (then) Docks and Harbours Association, and of course Legal Counsel. Meetings were held at the Admiralty in London and at Caernarfon with the Secretary to the Admiralty in attendance, but still the matter went unresolved. Officialdom reiterated that responsibility now lay with the Harbour Trust.

The Trust had very few funds to pay for dismantling and removing the wreck but eventually the Admiralty indicated that financial assistance might be forthcoming and that meanwhile the Trust should seek quotes for the work. The work was put out to tender and correspondence between the Admiralty and the Trust discussed the various applicants. The contract was awarded to a Cardiff firm on 30th July 1956, for the sum of £47,200. This sum was to be paid to the contractor for disposing of the remains of the Ship, which contained thousands of tons of potentially useful wood, 220 tons of copper ballast, 175 tons of iron ballast and hundreds of tons of other metals. Her hull's copper sheathing alone consisted of 3,409 sheets of 18 ounce copper, each 4 feet by 1 foot and 2 inches - approximately 10 tons of copper! Today, the contractor would probably have been paying for the privilege of reclaiming these raw materials!

The Headmaster's diary says that by 13th October 1956 the contractors had started dismantling work. They adopted a fairly entrepreneurial approach, selling off useful items to all comers. Lt. Cdr. Brooke Smith purchased sections of the main mast, which were eventually erected at Plas Newydd in 1964. The owners of Thurnham Hall, near Lancaster, bought the ornate doors to the Captain's cabin, where they hang to this day. Colonel Davies who owned land access to the wreck expressed his concerns to a friend in a letter dated 18th April 1953

> "If some breaker strips the hull as she lies, will he do it by water, or from the land?"

With uncanny prescience he speculated,

> "Burn her? Let her lie?"

Fighting The Fire

On the night of Tuesday 30ᵗʰ October 1956, a fire broke out onboard. She was a wooden ship strung with miles of rope rigging, soaked in 117 years' worth of pitch and tar. She burned furiously

"from stem to stern"

for over 18 hours, breaking up significantly in the process. Flames leapt from her ports. Four large explosions occurred when gas bottles exploded, one flying 150 feet though the air onto the shore in a blaze of sparks. The sky was lit up for miles. The local fire brigade were quickly on the scene. After 3 hours struggling on deck, they seemed to be bringing the flames under control when a stiff breeze blew up and ignited a firestorm they could not control. Forced ashore, they were unable to fight the fire effectively and had to wait for low water, by which time it was too late.

By a strange quirk of fate, as the fire raged, a party of cadets was returning from a rugby match on the mainland. Passing over the suspension bridge

"we found the Ship on fire, stopped the coach and the traffic, and gave a Hullabaloo":

> *Hullabaloo! Hullabaloo! Hullabaloo! Ba La!*
> *Conway! Conway!*
> *Rah! Rah! Rah!*
> *Pieces of eight, Pieces of eight,*
> *Pieces of nine and ten,*
> *We'll cut the throats of everyman*
> *And sew them up again.*
> *Dead men tell no tales!*

Eventually the fire burned itself out. All that remained were the stumps of masts and a twisted mass of smouldering timber in odd shapes barely recognisable as sections of hull and deck. One cadet remembers

"the strait was almost impassable for days and weeks after with flotsam."

Newspapers reporters flocked back to the scene and *Conway* was again front page news. The terrible news spread to Old *Conways* around the world. She had gone in a final, fitting blaze of glory. Over the next few days the newspapers widely reported the fire was caused by a

"workman's oxy-acetylene torch."

Rumours abounded but none was ever substantiated. The most popular was that while a welder's torch was being used in the paint locker, a spark fell into a seam where it smouldered unnoticed for several hours before bursting into flames after the wreck had been vacated for the night. The Harbour Trust issued an official statement broadly confirming this, saying she had been

"set alight by a welder's torch."

The contractors objected that this inferred them to be liable by reason of

Smouldering Remains, Focsle Askew

View From The Suspension Bridge

"neglect in their duty of care."

The contractor obviously had good lawyers and the Trust's statement was quickly changed to

"set alight by vandals."

The contractors also had a sharp accountant. Their contract was for the removal of the wreck, which had been substantially achieved, albeit with hardly any effort on their part. They submitted their invoice for the full value of the contract. The Caernarfon Harbour Master was so incensed that the contractor's task had been materially reduced, he attempted to withhold part of the agreed payment. While he doubtless had the moral high ground, the legal view was that the required result had been achieved. Full payment was made. The Harbour Trust was eventually only required to make a token contribution; in the end, the public purse made up the balance.

Today, no trace of the Ship is visible from the suspension bridge. However many large timbers remain on private land on the steep wooded bank by the foreshore. Timber from the lower deck has been tested (by Dublin and Bangor Universities) and identified as African Oak (Oldfieldia Africana, a tall hardwood tree from the wet evergreen forests of West Africa, which actually is not an oak at all). The foreshore is littered with metal debris but this also is not accessible to the general public. Below the water the hull, though much reduced, is still substantially intact along with various items of equipment, including the old donkey winch spotted recently by a diver. Cadets, staff and locals rescued many timbers and items and their whereabouts and use are recorded on www.hmsconway. org. The most unexpected of these is the Bangor diving couple who rescued enough timbers to build a beautiful fitted kitchen!

With the final end of the Ship another chapter in *Conway's* proud history came to a close but the last line of the *Conway* Song gave direction to those remaining: Carry On, Carry On, Carry On.

CHAPTER 28

1953 A TOUR OF THE CAMP

Cadets returning for the winter term found another incredible transformation. The tents were gone and in their place was a substantial camp of 18 wooden huts to accommodate the 200 cadets and staff who previously had lived in the Ship.

"We cadets were amazed to find that an entire hutted encampment had been designed, built and landscaped on land behind the cricket pitch. On brick foundations, the new huts were basically of timber construction, with pitched roofs, insulated and centrally heated. They were light and airy and altogether a pleasing replacement for the emergency bell tents."

Above: The Hutted Camp in 1954
Below: Hold and Mizzentop Huts

The Camp, as it was to be called, had been erected in front of the canteen on a paddock of the estate's Dairy Farm, close to the main road, just inside the estate boundary wall and alongside the driveway. The huts, appropriately painted a shade of battleship grey, were set around a quadrangle with an inner perimeter pathway enclosing a large grassed area divided by four paths A number of large mature trees remained around the site. The ground sloped gently down from the Camp to the athletics track, then to Plas Newydd and finally the strait.

The *Conway* Club had arranged for shipwrights, from Alfred Holt and Co., to undertake the difficult job of removing the figurehead from the wreck and transporting it to Plas Newydd for re-masting at the Camp. At the start of term it was recumbent at the approach to the Camp, but before long it was masted on the roundabout, which formed the entrance to the Camp at one corner of the quadrangle. Behind the figurehead was the quarterdeck hut containing offices. Entered over a wide veranda, it housed (left to right) Captain Hewitt's Office, his Secretary's office, the watchkeeper's office or guardroom and the gun room (cadet captains' common room). The name plate from the stern of the Ship was mounted on the veranda. Following the buildings clockwise, behind the quarterdeck was a long mess deck, assembly and galley hut with a small room at the far end reserved for the Galley Trogs *(kitchen staff)*.

> *"The cooking was still done in the kitchen, down at the House, and the 'hot' food was transported up to the camp."*

Next to this was a gap with a small flag pole and yard arm where the signal of the day was hoisted. This was in a corner of the quadrangle where the path turned and ran in front of a row of 7 huts set at right angles to the path up to the canteen. First was the recreation hut with a small library/ reading room on the left and the games room on the right with a snooker table. It looked out over the cricket pitch/athletics field.

> *"It was quite a warm pleasant place, it had some odd pictures on the wall, which were cartoon illustrations of old nautical sayings like 'Between the devil and the deep blue sea.'"*

It contained a large glass cabinet in which were posted sports fixtures, away match results and reports and items of interest. The next 6 huts were dormitories for port and starboard Focsle, port and starboard Foretop and port and starboard Maintop. The path then turned right onto the next side of the quadrangle. Off to the left was a small boiler room hut then, set back, was the granite dairy building (now the National Trust cafeteria). This contained the canteen, a store room, carpenter's workshop and 2 classrooms.

Around the back was a small hut containing 2 more classrooms. The next hut contained 4 staff cabins, initially home to Messrs Hutchinson, Parry, Kingsford and Fozard. Finally on this side, at right angles to the path, in a small hut was the masters' common room. The path then turned another corner for its last leg back to the figurehead roundabout. There were 5 more huts at right angles to the path. The first 4 were dormitories for starboard and port hold then starboard and port Mizzentop. The last hut, alongside the figurehead, was divided for the Chief Officer 'Brookie' and Padre Turner.

Captain Hewitt had worked another minor miracle in just a few weeks and they were ready for occupation when term began. The next edition of the Cadet described the scene.

> *"They had grown, not like a rash of mushroom buildings, but like a miniature garden city; the fine trees had been left untouched and broad walks intersected pleasant squares of grass, which day by day grew more lawn-like. A miracle had occurred, and everyone recognised it and paid tribute to the architect who had planned it and the contractors who had so speedily followed his directions."*

The article went on to acknowledge the past, but set sights firmly on the future.

> *"The pride taken by cadets in their accommodation is only equalled by the pride they formerly took in their decks and though all without exception would gladly forsake the spaciousness and convenience of life ashore for the cramped inconvenience of the Ship, if she could again be restored, there are many advantages in the present set-up. There is a well-known saying that your last ship is always the best, and this is a truth, which*

all Conways will find if they follow the sea as a career, and while we still have cadets who commenced their training on the old Ship it is not always easy to realise the advantages thrust upon us, but nevertheless, they do exist. The mid-day rush for classes being taught ashore but living onboard has gone, the light in the dormitories far surpasses that onboard with less resultant eye-strain, the long waiting for a boat before and after games is no more, but perhaps the greatest advantage is that the executive officers, instead of running the Ship's routine, now have more time to exercise personal supervision over cadets in their divisions and to teach them the craft of the seas. The change from a ship to a shore base had meant many changes in daily routine, not all of which have been as successful as anticipated, but faults had been rectified as they became apparent. 1954 should see a great step forward."

Some thought the huts were Army surplus, because they looked like military huts but they were new and custom built to similar dimensions as the huts already erected at the Kelvin Block the previous term. The architects, Kelly, Gornall, were already designing the new college building. The huts were

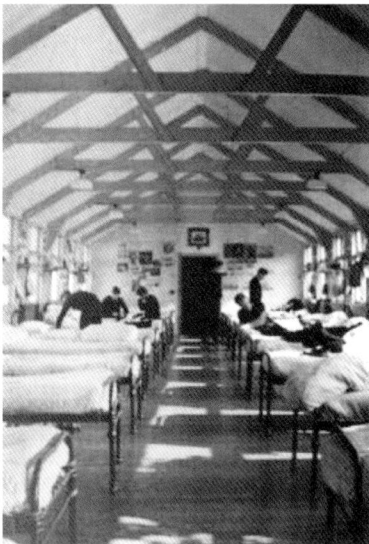

Starboard Fore 1963

very spartan. They had basic central heating but it was not very effective and, as a rule, windows were all left open. Each dormitory housed about 20 cadets. A row of 10 iron bedsteads ran down each side with each cadet's black, wooden sea chest beside the head of his bed. A small shelf was placed above each bed for a display of personal items with a hook below for one's cap. A towel was folded though the foot of the bed. No more sleeping in hammocks, although the hammocks were retained as covers for the bed springs. There were no curtains on the windows, apart from in the senior cadet captain's cabin.

On one side of the main entrance was a tiny, single-berth cabin for the division's senior cadet captain or one of the "unattached" senior cadet captains like the SCC Boats. Opposite the cabin was a single head, a room for hanging reefers and a small oilskin, sea boots/rugby boots room where anything wet or muddy was dumped before putting on foot clouts from the nearby clout can. Competition for the Hobson Cup (the smartest and cleanest top) remained fierce and maintaining the huts' highly polished wooden floors was an important part of this competition. All 4th termers downwards therefore had to put their feet on pieces of cloth called 'clouts' and skate across the floor to improve rather than damage the shine. The senior terms did not use clouts.

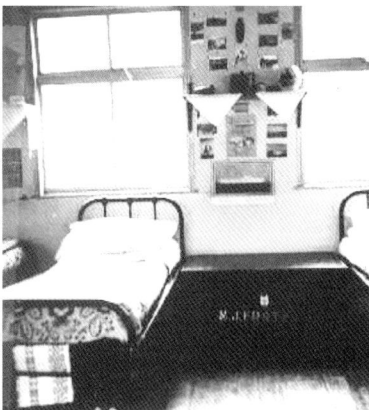

Forster's Bunk

"The worst job was the floor area in the corridor between the front door and the hut entrance, as outdoor shoes were still worn and senior hands plus stroppy QBs would often wear their rugby boots until they got into the oilskin room. Next worst was keeping the windows spotless and crystal clear, the slightest mark could easily be seen from inside either in daylight or at night from the light of the adjoining hut, requiring seemingly endless return visits to the offending window."

The first bunk inside the main sleeping area was for the junior cadet captain. Unlike all the other bunks, his was placed along the bulkhead rather than at right angles to it, providing a little more personal space than other cadets. Opposite was the clout can. He was at the door end to prevent any potential night time departures and was the one who gave permission for visitors to enter. As you gained seniority you moved further down the hut, so QBs and shags were at the far end of the hut where there was a fire door. Sometimes a second junior cadet captain bunked by this door.

> *"In our time lead seals and wires were instituted on the fire door push bars. However, unscrewing the eyelet screw on the doorframe that the wire went through did allow a few nocturnal escapades without the need to break the seal."*

The Captain and his family had moved into an apartment in the Marquis's house. Sick bay, some staff cabins and accommodation for new chums remained in the Nelson Block (along with a billiards room and mess deck for their use. The Headmaster, Mr. Drake and Pug Bayliss had small cabins in the Nelson Block. The Kelvin Block continued as the gym, classrooms and washrooms, with two more classroom huts. The dock continued as the base for all boating and practical activity although it was now out on a limb rather than the central transfer hub between Ship and shore.

> *"Much of the gear previously in the Ship's Chart House was now kept in the Seamanship Room on the dock. There was also some rather antiquated electronic equipment (Loran presumably) that I never saw being used. The Kelvin depth-sounding equipment, with its many fathoms of high grade steel line, was set up on the side of the dock. The binnacle, with its brass cover, was in the seamanship room and there was another less impressive binnacle set up outside to which you could fit an azimuth ring and practice taking bearings. There was also a dry card compass set up diagonally opposite Eric's office in the Camp."*

CHAPTER 29

1953–63 CAMP DAILY ROUTINE

The Camp was formally opened by the Marquis on Trafalgar Day 21st October 1953. Captain Hewitt observed,

> *"we look ahead to the new Conway emerging from the wreck of the old, sloughing off the faults of the old system, but keeping ever bright the glory and strength of our heritage."*

The daily routine continued largely as before, although things like boat hoisting, coaling ship and the coal hole were no more. Few concessions would be made to being ashore rather than in the Ship. *Conway* was referred to as a Ship not a school, so floors were still decks, walls were bulkheads and motorboats continued daily to Port Dinorwic rather than having deliveries by road from the closer Llanfair PG.

> *"Our enforced transition from life afloat to life ashore was complete. Conway was very much alive, back on an even keel and our training moved forward much as it would have done onboard the Ship. Inevitably, our proficiency in boat work and certain other aspects of seamanship suffered through a comparative lack of opportunity and may not have matched the skills of those cadets who served in the Ship. But it is equally possible that our academic abilities benefited from a more regularised school day and better classroom/ laboratory facilities. I found my two-year course in that wonderful environment a most enjoyable experience, it passed by almost too quickly and had it not been for the prospect of joining my first ship, 'to see the world,' I would have been sad to leave. Many times at "Conway," and since, have I been thankful for my parents' foresight and sacrifice in sending me there for what was probably the most defining stage of my life."*

Standing Orders

Captain Hewitt published Standing Orders for the executive duties of the Chief Officer and Divisional Officers at the Camp and the House. There appears to have been no equivalent for the Headmaster or academic Term Masters. He wrote the nine pages of orders neatly into a book without a single alteration or mistake. Lt. Cdr. Brooke Smith was designated Chief Officer Camp and was also Divisional Officer Mizzentop. He was responsible for the

> *"care, maintenance and cleanliness"*

of all the huts, the dock and boats, for the daily Ship's log, the defaulters (punishment) book and for the recruitment and performance of staff like

> *"shipwrights and seamen."*

All Camp Divisional Officers reported to him. Most importantly,

> *"he is responsible for the practical training of cadets and will maintain the Practical Class Book showing duties assigned to each cadet and will endeavour to see that, provided efficiency is not impaired, all cadets have an equal opportunity to take charge of boats during school hours."*

The Second Officer, Mr. Drake, was designated Chief Officer House, responsible for the health, welfare and general performance of the junior cadets.

Reveille

Morning reveille, at 6.30 am, was by bugle call, following which energetic cadet-captains set about rousing any laggardly sleepers.

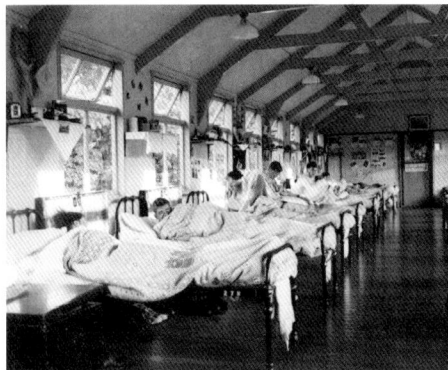

Reveille

> *"I'd never heard anything like it before, and found something thrilling and energising in the clear, plangent notes, which seemed to cut the growth of sleep away like a scythe. Later, of course, I reacted automatically to its summons, hardly registering the bugler's efforts. Cold winter mornings brought cracked notes from frozen lips and amused scorn from the bleary audience."*

Air Bedding and Wash

> *"There were no washing facilities at the Camp, only a lavatory in each divisional hut and a couple of drinking-fountains. The washbasins were a quarter of a mile away in the Kelvin Block, and at reveille you leaped out of bed, feverishly dragged on plimsolls and whatever else you thought appropriate to the weather (or simply retained pyjamas alone), grabbed your previously laid-out towel and washing-kit, and galloped along the tarmac driveway from the Camp quarterdeck to the ablutions among a horde of others in similar disarray. On summer mornings it was exhilarating, with the panorama of Snowdonia set before us as a backdrop to the playing-fields and the pseudo-castle, which was the Kelvin Block; on winter mornings though, the only light came from the old Ship's oil-lanterns set on low pedestals at a few places along the way. In the gloom, and perhaps rain or snow, cadets collided with one another and tripped over one another and the bodies of the already-fallen, and the air was heavy with muffled, profane exclamation. It was a glorious stampede, ending at the washbasins where, regardless of your time of arrival, your turn at the taps depended on your term seniority. New chums accordingly came last, faced with the prospect of punishment on a late return to the hut. QBs reserved (unofficially) a bank of washbasins for their exclusive use, while senior cadet-captains enjoyed the comparative privacy of a smaller wash-room to one side, where preparation for the day ahead was a relatively civilised and consciously leisurely, if not languid, affair. The duty officer would scour the huts to make sure no shirkers were left behind but there were always a few who would escape the net and remain unwashed for that day, and probably several more."*

Meals

3 full meals per day were provided. They were cooked in the galley at the House and brought up to be eaten in the Camp mess deck hut. Breakfast was at 7.00 am.

> *"200 hungry cadets, plus the officers and resident teaching staff, sat at trestle tables. 'Cooks to the galley' was sounded about 5-10 minutes before each meal as a signal for designated cadets to proceed to the mess deck to lay out the tables, collect water, tea, food etc. Seating on each table was strictly in order of seniority. Food was passed down the table from seniors to juniors with the inevitable shortage at the foot of the table."*

Galley staff were employees of Alfred Holt's shipping company and a few locals. Food was mediocre in quality and not very appetising, but every last scrap was eaten. Junior cadets could still be imposed upon by their seniors.

"I was told that one of the QBs was having a lie-in and would take his breakfast in bed. It was set aside for him, but after clear up decks I dropped it in the galley gash-bin and went on with my morning routine. It was interrupted by a message from the QB in question demanding my presence in one of the Foretop huts, where I was arraigned before a kangaroo court and treated to a short painful session of unofficial retribution and warned to keep silent about it, on pain of worse. Of course, everyone including cadet-captains knew about it, but it got no further as far as I know, the officers seemed unaware of it and I said nothing. The outcome though, was that I got slightly more to eat thereafter, and there were no more orders for room service."

Boat Work

After breakfast at 7.30 am, the duty motorboat crew would make for the dock and the daily run to Port Dinorwic between breakfast and school a different crew each day took the pulling gigs and cutters for a run no matter what the weather or water conditions.

Above: Cutters Crew 1959
Below: Gig Race off PD

"First sight of the oars engendered a feeling of faint incredulity, how on earth was such a massive spar to be moved, let alone handled with intent? 'Toss oars' on a cold winter morning meant sitting with the oar raised vertically blade up while icy seawater ran copiously down the loom and over the hands. It also ran up the arms of the green and unwary. The 6-oar gigs were quite different, actually a pleasure to pull and cox, and the inter-divisional gig races were always exciting."

In winter the oars often had first to be released from the ice, which had frozen them to the thwarts. Everyone else cleaned ship under the supervision of the cadet captains. before morning divisions. Anyone feeling unwell, or fancying their chances of bluffing their way out of cleaning or boat work would make for sick parade in the house at 7.45 am

The Dock was the domain of the bosun, 'Bullshit' Owen, and his mate, Ernie Ball, who had a snug room above the bosun's store in the stone building, which also housed the seamanship room.

"Mr. Owen, a small wiry North Walian, regarded us with shrewd circumspection, given to the utterance of homilies on anything from the handling of rope to the hazards of cold stonework: 'You'll get piles sitting on them cold stones, boy. Oh, yes, and then you'll remember me.' Turning to Ernie,

always a pace or two in the offing ' – won't he, Ernie?' But Ernie, stolid West Country, apple-cheeked and slow-spoken, never answered beyond a slow smile and a nod. But he was a kindly man, very patient with a cadet's apparent imbecility, though the patience was leavened with mild sarcasm. 'A splice, is it, boy? Well, you could keep a small parrot in it with room to flap its wings. Give me that spike. Now look….' "

Quarterdeck Duties

The duty cadet captain and duty messenger took their places in the guardroom where the barometer, logbook and leave book were kept. Every cadet captain (except senior cadet captains) and every cadet took their turn in these duties as appropriate to their rank, unless some poor soul with extra watches as punishment took their place. Band members provided the duty bugler. The Ship's bell was hung outside the gun room on a large wooden frame, seemingly made from blackened telegraph poles. The duty messenger rang the time using the Ship's bell.

"At one time there was a system of duty signallers. One stationed at the camp, one near the cromlech and one at the dock. There was also a new-chum signaller on the ramparts of the Marquis's House. In theory it was possible to send a message by semaphore from the camp to the dock via the house or vice-versa, but in practice it was quicker to send the duty messenger."

Above: Quarterdeck 1957
Below: Ship's Bell 1957

Signal of the Day

Everyday a new signal was flown at the Camp mast by the junior cadet captain 'flags and clocks,' using the International Code and requiring knowledge of the sequence of halyards.

"For example, in 1961

- *12th February. DFS NCG TI 1st sub 2nd sub 5: Church service 1115*
- *15th February. LEX P5312 P04 1st sub 6: My position by observation is lat 53° 12'N, lon 4° 06'W*
- *28th March. DNZ FTP: Commencing examinations*
- *5th April. 7 RA 1st sub NIX: Seven-a-side rugby.*

It was, of course, the old 1934 code, which contained the incomprehensible model verb, 'to glean.' I could never work out how it was used, or why it was necessary, and Brookie's somewhat rambling explanations merely shrouded the whole thing in profound mystery. For instance, the signal on 3rd February, 1961 was QJO (Are you gleaning) AFZ (Weigh anchor). My reaction at the time: total incomprehension."

Divisions

On weekdays, morning divisions were held in the central quadrangle at 8.50 am. In the event of really bad weather, the mess deck was used.

"The chief cadet captain would report to Eric who was and was not present; the Padre (Rev.. Turner) would lead the prayers and hymns; each divisional officer would inspect his cadets drawn up in files of three and finally the band would lead a short march-past during which the salute would be taken by Eric or Brookie in front of the guardroom."

When it came to time for prayers, Roman Catholics (RCs) were ordered to fall out and stand in the doorway of one of the huts with the cadets on sick parade. At the end of prayers, RCs fell in again for the march past. There was some consternation at the beginning of one term because two new chums who had just joined were Muslim and they stayed put for prayers as the order did not say

"RCs and Muslims Fall out!"

The situation was soon rectified.

Cleaning Ship and Weekend Rounds

All cleaning, painting, minor gardening, path-sweeping, etc,. in and around the Camp was performed by cadets, plus the usual scrubbing and polishing of decks and cleaning windows etc.

Captain's Rounds 1961

"The Camp mess-deck had scrubbed boards, done by a working-party from the responsible division on Saturday morning, perhaps joined by a group under punishment, the Slack Party. It entailed scrubbing on hands and knees, using hot water with dollops of soft-soap and handfuls of soda crystals thrown down by the cadet captain in charge. It brought the boards up to a pale, sterile rawness and hands to a red-rawness, stinging for hours afterwards, particularly under the nails."

Every Saturday morning, all the boats and the dock area were inspected during Captain's Rounds. Cadets would stand in fear and trembling alongside their area waiting for Eric to run his glove over the surfaces.

"Hold cadets operated an incinerator at the back of the huts nearest the road. This was a big wire cage for burning leaves, garbage, etc,. with a standing area for dustbins. The Menai Bridge Council bin lorry once caught fire after collecting Conway bins from the Camp, causing acute embarrassment to Eric who meted out severe punishments to everyone in sight."

Members of Staff

School

Following divisions, cadets were dismissed to attend school lessons or join other activities. There were 4 lessons before lunch, with a 15 minute 'Stand easy' break mid way, and 3 lessons after lunch. Academic staff wore their gowns and were punctilious in doffing their mortar boards when saluted by passing cadets. The maths master was 'Sprogs' Carter,

"an amazing mathematician who worked out logs mentally, and was totally ambidextrous so he would write the number with one hand and the log with the other simultaneously."

"He had a hearing aid. It gave us amusement to suddenly go dead quiet so he thought it wasn't working and would turn it up full, then we would resume the noise."

Lessons ended at 4.00 pm, with a 15 minute break for milk and cake to fortify cadets for sports.

'Sprogs' Carter 1961

Sports

Sports continued to figure large on Wednesday and Saturday afternoons. In winter, rugby was a religion. The 1ˢᵗ XV, Pug Bayliss's pride and despair, used to get a special breakfast to build them up and had to come back from summer leave a week early to begin training.

"Breakfast was often porridge topped with cornflakes followed by bacon and eggs and deep fried bread, which was as hard as a rock outside but soft inside - and on good days baked beans all well covered in HP, sauce and washed down with skilley (tea). This was after everyone else and we did not discuss the amount of food we consumed in case it caused a problem with the starving great unwashed."

Sailing was always popular and the main alternative to cricket and athletics in the summer term.

Fife Sailing Boat

"The MSODs (Menai Strait One-Design) were super boats, half-decked, carvel-hulled Bermudan sloops, that put up a good performance without threatening to drown their crews, they were all but impossible to capsize. There were 2 sailing-cutters, heavy gaff-rigged wagons with loose-footed mainsails controlled by a sheet running through a murderous block. They had centre-plates on tackles, and were heavily-rigged. The sails were No.2 canvas, which seemed to be woven from steel thread when wet, but they sailed well in a stiff breeze, when it could take 2 cadets to hold the tiller up against the constant tendency to fly up into the wind. They were totally safe, even when driven hard on the wind with the lee gunwale under and green seas pouring in: junior cadets enjoyed the privilege of doing the pumping, often enough driven to superhuman efforts by sheer terror."

A matched pair of Fifes, 'Morwys' and 'Thelma', specially designed for the strait were popular boats. The highlight of the summer term was the Beaumaris Regattas. Boats were towed to the scene through the Swellies, usually by the pinnace. The gathering-place and start line lay off the well-known pub, The Gazelle, where officers and masters accompanying the boats could relax, and where we could sit on the low wall of the foreshore car-park to eat our packed lunches.

"In my first summer (1960) I crewed an Enterprise owned by the senior cadet captain of the Hold. He was a farmer's son, a pleasant man from West Wales, who managed his boat well enough despite a withered left arm, legacy of a shooting accident. He used his teeth to handle the main-sheet, which impressed me no end."

Cricket, athletics and tennis were other popular summer sports. In the winter terms boxing was compulsory.

Cricket 1963

"I discovered to my alarm that you had to box for your division, and the opening fights were pretty bloody affairs (mine among them) with cadets matched by weight alone, which often meant no match at all in ability. As the weaklings and the inept fell out, things got more scientific, and towards the end some pretty work was done; one or two cadets reached schoolboy national standard. There were also fights against Worcester and Pangbourne. A small number of cadets took up judo, but it was viewed as an aberration by most, with something slightly distasteful about it."

Cadets on Crib Goch

Mountaineering weekends continued to be very popular

Canteen

On non-sports days some cadets had hobbies, others participated in one of the organised clubs or spent what little free time they had in the canteen where tea, coffee and snacks were served to the ravenous and generally. Initially it was run by the Mr. and Mrs Walters

"You could get simple cooked meals there, baked beans or poached egg on toast, for example, to be eaten in, which was by far the safest way of spending pocket-money. The alternative, carrying out a handful of Wagon Wheels, crisps, biscuits or whatever, risked confiscation by Maintop QBs acting as models of customs officials at a border crossing."

When they retired it was taken over by the kindly 'Ma' Basham and her husband.

"She was stout, rosy-cheeked and wide awake to cadets' ploys and subterfuges."

She was a surrogate mother figure to generations of cadets. Their daughter's presence behind the counter was guaranteed to boost sales.

Tea and Evening Prep

After tea at 6.30 pm, there was Prep from 7.15 pm to 8.45 pm supervised by cadet captains, during which, on Fridays, the Padre (Rev. Turner) handed out of pocket money.

"He brought round a lot of loose change in a small blue cloth drawstring bag, tightly clutching the pocket money account book under his arm. How precious that shilling (or maybe two for the better off ones) was for the canteen; a slice of buttered toast or two, beans on toast and maybe a Murphy, but that only for a special occasion or to ward off real hunger."

Dancing Classes

These were a voluntary evening activity paid for by a few cadets.

"They had two main advantages. They got you out of prep and you got to meet Girls!"

They were held in the winter terms, perhaps with an eye to a future in passenger liners.

"Friday evenings were spent on the House mess-deck, cleared for the purpose, where a record-player was set up by the large woman who ran the show and her less formidable assistant, about whom we speculated wildly and probably inaccurately. It was a week-about routine; we danced alone or with girls shipped in from a school somewhere safely distant. One or two incipient romances germinated, but on the whole we were a pretty graceless, clumping lot suffering from more or less embarrassment."

Evening

Everyone turned in at 9 pm Immediately before turning in was a time for more cleaning and polishing of 'sweeps.'

"Polishing the deck in the hut was a sort of pagan ritual, worship of the great god 'Ronuk,' performed on hands and knees last thing in the evening before evening rounds. The Ronuk polish was applied, or 'laid,' by wrapping a dollop of it in an absorbent rag (the clout) and working it through the material onto the boards of the deck by main pressure while shoving the polish-sodden bag about in a suitable pattern of movement. Other polishers would follow astern, bringing the waxy coating up to a luminous, improbable lustre, wary of the gigantic splinters, that could spring out of the wood. The boards were raw pine. We'd be in pyjamas, so would get into bed (hastily, as the round's party was seen approaching) still grimy with Ronuk and associated dirt, which would have to be suffered until reveille and the morning wash at the Kelvin Block. On one occasion an over-zealous (or tardy, or panicky) cadet jumped into bed still grasping the oozing Ronuk clout, with predictably messy results."

Once cadets were in bed evening rounds began a final inspection by the duty officer to ensure no one was missing, that fire door seals were intact and that all was spick and span. Cadets lay smartly to attention in bed, eyes to the ceiling with their bedding smartly tucked in and crisply folded.

"We waited for the duty officer to make his way towards the hut for evening rounds. Being in Port Hold you could see him progress up and down Starboard Hold with his small entourage and then there was a last minute scramble into bed to lie to attention, as through the stillness one heard the muffled voices as the cadet captain reported the hut as 'all present and correct' or 'x present, y in sick bay' etc., and a shout from the doorway of 'Rounds.' Then the advancing loud footsteps as the team marched the full length of the hut. I think we all learned to use the full powers of our peripheral vision to try to see who and what was going on, particularly if the footsteps stopped. The moment frozen in case it might be something on your shelf that shouldn't be there. The sigh of relief when it turned out to be someone else who was for the high jump. This was followed by that brief period of relaxation

before the sound of the Last Post drifted across the Camp, and then, precisely on the last note, all the hut lights were switched off (by, I think, the chum in the bed next to the entrance door) in unison. A certain amount of whispering (reading with a torch under the bedclothes - a punishable offence) before the junior cadet captain exerted his authority with a few judicious shouts down the hut and then silence descended and sleep ensued."

It was absolutely forbidden to be out of a hut between lights out and reveille, which naturally motivated many to find ways and means of escaping for a cigarette or for an nocturnal tramp to the nearest pub in Llanfair PG.

The House

New chums in their first year were accommodated at the House, with Geoff Drake in charge.

"His sardonic turn of phrase and dryly trenchant tone of voice was eminently mimicable, and most cadets tried their hand at it, with varying degrees of success."

He was a kind man, but a measured disciplinarian, not open to manipulation by cadets.

"The first time I heard him speak was when he addressed all new chums and three year cadets on the House mess-deck on the first or second day of term. He said 'There's a sea-boot in my office. It's been there since the middle of last term. Is it too much to expect of the cadet concerned that he notice that he's got only one sea-boot, and would he mind collecting the other forthwith?' This was greeted with silent delight by his admirers (most cadets) and exaggerated resignation by the disaffected. He projected a very pronounced personality, rather ascetic, dry, humorous and wise, the wisdom indicated by his goatee and moustache. He was diabetic, and cadets were under instructions to administer the sugar he kept about his person if he ever went into a diabetic fit; I never saw it happen."

New chums were allowed a short period of grace to learn the ropes, a mass of formal and informal rules, arrangements, customs and privileges. During this period they normally escaped punishment for infringements, receiving warnings and explanations instead. They were however fair game for a range of pranks ordering them to

"Go to Sick Bay to be measured for your sabre,"

or

"Go and ask the Duty Officer for red oil for the port lamp,"

and

"See the Chief Officer to get paint for the last post."

All of which spoofs resulted in red faces for the poor new chum and amusement for the officer consulted.

"In the second term we all moved to the Camp. At the Camp there was a strict hierarchy as follows:
- *Second and third termers were 'chums.' Any fifth or sixth termer could call 'chum' at which all second and third termers rushed to the caller, the last to arrive got a job ranging from making coffee or running a message to occasional just plain harassment.*

- *Fourth termers were still junior but did not 'chum.'*
- *Fifth term were seniors - some were junior cadet captains.*
- *Sixth term were QBs - Quarter Boys in their final term before going to sea."*

Junior cadets therefore had three gauntlets to run: overall conduct monitored by officers and staff led by the Captain Superintendent, the official rules enforced by the cadet captains led by the chief cadet captain, and the unofficial privileges enforced by the QBs led by the King Of The Woods. Reconciling the three was never easy. Complying with one often meant falling foul of the others.

> *"I can remember the joy of the power I felt as a new QB of shouting 'Chum' down the length of the hut and the last one to arrive (sliding on clouts of course) ended up with some shoe spit and polishing to be done. QBs didn't clean their own shoes if it could be avoided. Very often it was the same rather slow reacting chum who ended up with most of these tasks. I suppose we all thought, 'Well we had to do it as a chum so they can too.' How good it felt when you were in your second of your terms up at the Camp and the shout of 'Chum' no longer applied to you."*

"Life Was Tougher In the Ship"

Cadets would not be too coddled.

Motor Boat Alongside The Slip 1956

> *"The huts in the Camp were non too warm in the winter. Remember, every other window open and the hot water boiler turned off at 9 pm Just great big bundles of oilskins, duffle coats etc., heaped on top of cadets' beds trying to keep warm for the duration of the night, waiting for reveille and a very swift dash to the Kelvin Block to wash."*

Compared with the tents,

> *"we were definitely spoilt by having a very nice tarmac road leading from the huts to the washrooms. It was also a hell of a lot closer! The central heating in the huts though was something else. We had a three inch circular pipe filled with lukewarm water running around the hut. During the winter months when every other window had to be open, I used to sleep on my stomach with hands wrapped around the pipe. I have never to this day complained about central heating."*

Another cadet fondly recalls how

".... many a day I used to wake up covered with a fine blanket of snow - bliss! Maybe that's why I am not too keen on skiing."

Church

On Sundays, a full reefer-uniform divisions was held followed by a church service in the temporary chapel set up in the gym.

"Padre Turner was regarded with mixed feelings, something of an unknown quantity to be tested with circumspection, half-curiosity, half-boredom. He was cultivated by cadets interested in motor-cars on the off-chance they would get a high-speed run along the A5 in his Jag."

The full ship's complement could not fit inside the gym so every Sunday a different party of cadets would march two miles down the road to Llanedwynn church to join the Marquis of Anglesey in his private chapel near the Moel-y-Don ferry.

"It was quite tiny and I suppose not more than a dozen of the Marquis's family and retainers present. The Welsh lady organist, nick-named Boogie-Woogie Annie, dressed in a long, sheepskin coat and woollen hat (winter and summer) would entreat cadets to sing up by raising her hand palm upwards. Cadets would start to bellow at full volume and she would frantically try to quieten things down again only to be met by whispering voices. One cadet was detailed to hand pump the organ often with drastic consequences - either a force 10 or a flat calm."

RCs continued to travel to Caernarfon.

Slash Creek

A popular Sunday afternoon activity was a visit to Slash Creek, a sandy inlet on the Anglesey side of the strait towards Port Dinorwic. Cadets would row a gig down and ground it in the creek where they were out of site of the House and the mainland.

"We would swim, sit in the sun, chew the fat etc and row back in time for tea. A great afternoon on a hot summer's day."

Shore Leave.

A lucky few might have time to 'go ashore' for a few hours. A bugle call summoned them to the guardroom where they were inspected to ensure they were smart enough before removing their lanyards and 'taking the Liberty Boat ashore', ie walking out of the main gate. Going ashore was another convention that gave no ground to not being in the Ship. If you missed the liberty boat (parade) you obviously could not get ashore!

"You signed out for shore leave with the duty cadet captain and signed back in on your return."

Sometimes returning cadets were expected to turn out their pockets to ensure they were not bringing cigarettes or other contraband.

"There was a rose border at right-angles to the gun room in front of Eric's office and, on one occasion, several of us hurriedly buried our fags and matches in there when we were lined up returning from Sunday leave to have our pockets turned out in the gun room."

Haigh Trophy

For many years this had been a competition between Snowdon Group patrols but, at some point, it changed to an inter-divisional summer term competition. It was a mixture of orienteering and team building. It was a day-long map-reading exercise decoding directional clues and climbing several mountains with a few tests of initiative, 'incidents, thrown in along the way, all against the clock.

Haigh Trophy - Snowdon The Easy Way

"The day would start very, very early. Teams were taken by coach and dropped off at various start points on the circular route in the mountains where they were handed the first clue to set them on their way. It would be well after 7 pm before we got back to Camp."

One year, when the circuit was around Snowdon, two teams were taken to the summit in a special open train.

"One test was to sound the middle a lake using of Kelvin deep-sea sounding apparatus, a glass tube in a metal container attached to the lead. The problem was two-fold: to rig a means of getting the lead out to the middle of the lake, and to get the discolouration of the glass tube necessary to gauge the depth of water against the boxwood scale. The first was done by stretching a line across the lake with a pulley-block made fast to its mid-part carrying the sounding-line, and the second by the simple expedient of arming the open end of the tube with a pinch of salt."

Because this was a salt water device measuring a fresh water lake, success depended on adding the salt, yet no salt was provided. However, on arrival each party was provided with bags of crisps; the old fashioned sort with small bags of salt in them. Many cadets happily sprinkled the salt on their crisps before realising the error of their ways.

Another involved

"diving into ice cold water to place a panel over a hole and then pump out the water. It was supposed to be a submarine that had sunk and the idea was to see if we could work out how to raise the sub. We also had to build a bridge across a small river/stream or build a raft from 45 gal oil drums and float your team across."

At each of the challenges there would be a very cold officer or teacher waiting to make sure all teams played the game, to allocate points and hand out the clue to the next challenge.

"I participated in 1960 for Hold Division. It was a scorching hot day and we had no water with us so the few mountain streams had to suffice for quenching our thirst when we found them and then, luckily, we found a milk bottle, which we took, and filled as opportunity arose along some stages with us. I am sad to say that despite our sterling efforts Hold ended up with the lowest score of 50.6 points. The first task, set by Geoff Drake, was to remove a heavy boulder from the body of 'Charlie' without further damage to

his anatomy. I expect we killed the poor dummy. At another base our attempts were not too impressive; 'Hold arrived but planning beforehand was not a noticeable feature. Turner climbed up one tree quite well but had no clear idea of what he was to do when there.' As Turner and I were used to climbing the tree between Port and Starboard Hold for a smoke, we could have put it to good use that day if no officers had been around!"

"I feel tired out thinking of those mountain days - but great fun even at the time."

Cross Strait Swim

The race happened in the summer term each year. The strait was always freezing cold and fleets of jelly-fish skulked around awaiting the unwary. It started from the dock during low slack water, cadets swam across the strait to the Vaynol side where they went round a moored boat and swam back to the dock. Everyone who was capable was expected to participate, no matter how long it took.

"Each divisional officer had to assess the capability of the cadets to do it and, if in doubt as I was in the first summer, had to do a trial in the pool. There were no consequences for failure in the swim itself as putting in the effort was considered satisfactory."

Those few judged unsuitable, or smart enough to skive off acted as coxes/strokes etc., for the rescue boats, which were manned mainly with junior cadets.

"There were a lot of us in the water at the start, all full of vigour and churning the stuff to white."

The throng quickly became very strung out with swimmers spread right across the strait some already well on their way back while the slowest swimmers were still doggy paddling over the first leg.

"Upon getting out of the water we were all chivvied up to the seamanship room to dry off and change back into uniform."

Everyone then doubled back up the hill to the mess-deck for tea and cakes.

"When you had done it gave a sense of achievement no matter how long it took."

QB and Chum Books

A ritual towards the end of one's time was the compiling of a QB Book.

"In this your term-mates were invited to leave marks of their regard or other sentiment, with complete frankness. In fact the entries, in the form of letters, tended towards the conciliatory and sentimental as the prospect of the final parting took on an aspect of reality, alarming and even dismaying to some, despite the exciting prospect of a first ship. It began to dawn on us that the lachrymose displays of earlier terms of QBs had legitimate grounds. The Conway effect was unique and profound, and the more loudly it was scoffed at the deeper it had penetrated its victim's spirit."

Two such letters are reproduced below, the authors first naming the shipping company they were joining:

Brocklebank

> *Dear -----,*
>
> *I must say that I think QB books an absolute load of crap, but nevertheless I will endeavour to write something which, no matter how inane and stupid it may seem, will bring you some sense of satisfaction (?!) when you read through it in later years.*
>
> *You're only fault this term is that you are taking things too seriously, apart from that you're doing not badly at all as Senior ----. We have had some good laughs together both this term and in preceding ones, for funnily enough we seem to have the same sense of humour. As this term draws to a close I think all us are beginning to realise just how much Conway was a way of life to us and that we will be actually sorry to leave.*
>
> *What more can I say but to wish you all the very best in the future and that I hope I see you again in later years. Remember you are always welcome at my home where you will be given a traditional Scottish welcome, whatever that may be —*
>
> *Good luck,*
>
> *----------*

King of the Woods

Senior cadets would abscond into the surrounding woods at every opportunity for a quick smoke. This was a serious punishable offence if caught by cadet captains or officers. A new tradition quickly started, that of "King of the Woods." This was an unofficial appointment, a QB, usually a tough nut, elected by the rest of his term as their top dog. Often it was the person they thought had most deserved but missed promotion to cadet captain. His word was law in and out of the woods.

QB Oars

An unofficial trophy for leavers was the QB oar, an ash cutter-oar blade to be decorated, then signed by one's term-mates. The problem was to get one's hands on a broken oar, which in the normal way would have been well-nigh impossible. In such cases the obvious recourse was to break one 'accidentally' during pulling practice.

> *"This was done by pulling hard, then suddenly lifting the blade clear of the water and shoving the loom violently forward. It seldom broke the oar, but often sprang it, to be written off by a disgusted (and knowing) Mr. Owen, who then turned a blind eye to its efficient disposal by the vandal concerned."*

Judging from the number of surviving QB Oars, *Conway* must have had to buy new sets of oars every few years.

In later years, the practice of Chum Books evolved and displaced the QB Book. These were often started on joining as new chums and took the form of personal diaries and scrap books of daily life.

P&O

Dear -----,

At last we are leaving this God Forsaken Establishment and we are both away to sea. Although I will be sorry to leave the place on the last Wed I think I will be glad to finish with school days and start earning a little money. I reckon you feel the same way.

I must say we have not always agreed but I think our arguing days are over, at least I hope so. I think on the whole we have been the best of pals and I hope, as you wrote in my QB book, we will manage to keep contact by mail and then someday we may meet in some hot, stinking Malayan Port!

I and ----- will be, I think, the ones who will miss you the most because we have always been together. We even managed to meet each other in the leaves. So don't forget if you get transferred onto the UK run, there is always a spare bed at the address I've given you. If you haven't got that long just pop in and see us – you will be most welcome.

Just for laugh's sake I'll bet you £1 you get married before you are 35 – you can hold me to that, OK?

Well, -----, the best of luck in 'British and Irish' (no offence) and roll on the time when you get command.

All the best.

End of Term

Prize giving, awarding of sports colours and announcement of rates for the following term was done on the mess deck at the Camp on the last night of term. However at the end of the summer term, if the weather was good, it was done on the sports field with a dais rigged for the staff. This was followed by a mad scramble by those promoted, and honoured with a colour, to sew them on and display them accordingly by the time we boarded the buses for Bangor station the next morning.

"I can recall riding a double decker in the pitch dark, with some young band shag hanging off the boarding platform giving Menai Bridge a loud reveille on his bugle as we rattled through to the station."

There was a good deal of sentimentality about at the end of term:

1953 QBs at Bangor Station

"Some QBs, leaving for their first ships or whatever, seemed more or less overcome by maudlin regret, and even remorse where they looked back on a career of mild infamy among the lower orders. At the customary line-up of departing seniors – rated and unrated – to be shaken by the hand by all the rest in solemn procession, I was astonished to see hard men in tears, including my erstwhile persecutor, who astonished me even more by saying he hoped I'd forget the affair in a spirit of forgiveness. Well, as a general rule we harboured no resentment over such things, and it was so in this case, but how does one forget one's time as a Conway cadet? Not possible!"

CHAPTER 30

1954–63 THE CAMP YEARS

1954 Spring

There had been many staff changes.

"G.A.B. King had been replaced as Second Officer. Miller, John Oliver and Bert Mandeville were gone and there was an older PT officer nicknamed Winkle who later died in the gym. The Padre was E.A. Turner. Sanderson and, later on, Fozard taught Spanish, Phillips taught geography and the history master was Paul Kingsford. Ernie Moore, Howard Davies and Hutchison, were there and Preen taught English. There was an officer called 'Arry Parry' a Welsh fellow and an seconded officer whom we called 'Glooppy,' a gangly individual who insisted on bringing his head down to his hand when saluting instead of the reverse procedure. Another Welshman, 'Bongo' Jones, taught mathematics and the Reverend 'Cupid' whose real name I never learned. 'Sprogs' also taught maths and was the Deputy Head Master. If we wanted to side track him from maths, which only the minority could follow, we used to ask him about electronic computers. Even in those days he would happily talk about computers for the entire lesson. We did a fair old number in mental torture on poor old 'Cupid.' Once, as each cadet stood at his desk to get a project marked, they would surreptitiously insert a drawing pin through his gown and into the wooden floor. The end result was spectacular, as 'Cupid' finally arose from his chair he reached the end of his gown tether, and with a resounding ripping noise crashed over the back of his chair. I'm afraid he gave up on attempting to teach us in the end, which is entirely what we deserved."

"Our classroom in the Kelvin Block was adjacent to the gym, and another spontaneous idea between lessons came when an unlucky cadet was demonstrating his prowess on the wall bars. He proudly hung with arms outstretched halfway up the wall, whereupon his wrists were immediately seized and lashed to the bars. All hands then retired to the classroom leaving him in situ. The poor lad lasted to about twenty minutes into the next lesson before his howls of pain had the teacher gasping in disbelief through the windows at his predicament. We were young then... seemed like a good idea at the time."

"Once, when coxing No 1 power boat and coming alongside one of the cutters, the bowman was a tall

Figurehead at The Camp

thin new chum, and the engineer yelled 'Jump - you'll make it in two!' The poor lad jumped but hadn't noticed that the painter was snagged. I shall never forget the look of astonishment on his face as his forward trajectory changed to a vertical descent! The stern man came rushing out of the fore cabin at the splash (and laughter) but didn't remember to take the cigarette out of his mouth until after we had completed the rescue - fortunately no one noticed."

When towing other boats back to their moorings, it was not done to let the other boat pick the buoy before slipping the tow line. One approached the mooring at full power and, depending on tide etc, the line was slipped short of the buoys. There was a lot of hooting and jeering (at the power boat cox'n) if the other boat had to get out oars or be picked up for a second attempt.

In 1954, after the coronation, the Queen made a tour of Wales.

"I was in the crew of the No 2 motorboat that day. The 3 motorboats ferried all the cadets to Port Dinorwic, and they lined both sides of the main street to salute the motorcade. Those of us in the boat crews were wearing our battledress and blue shirts with the soft collars. Naturally we weren't to be associated with the others in their No 1 uniform, so we were at the other end of town, sitting on the wall of the bridge, overlooking the dry dock. As the motorcade approached we all leapt to our feet and saluted. The Duke of Edinburgh was in the car. I saw him burst out laughing as he saw us and he drew us to the Queen's attention, and she turned and laughed too."

Captain Hewitt seemed adept at gaining publicity for *Conway*, an excellent way to attract new boys. In March, the BBC visited and filmed the *Conway* song and a march past and this was broadcast on 13th April. In June there was an article in the Liverpool Post and Pug Bayliss made a speech on the radio. Following the success of their previous visit, the BBC agreed to return for a full 10 days of filming in 1957, providing they could erect 20 large floodlights around the Camp.

1954 August

The Headmaster took the gym team to Sweden for 3 weeks to compete in an international competition.

1954 September

Wg. Cdr. Browne ruefully announced

"GCE results very poor. Trying to cover a four year course in less than two years with sometimes inadequate grounding."

1955 January

The first consideration was given to providing a GCE 'A' level in a new Special Studies course, which would incorporate the special RN Class. The course was launched within the year and the old RN Class, the first started in the Ship, came to an end.

1955 Summer Term

"It was the last but one day of term and Lt. Frankyn (an RNR officer on a year's secondment), found his car wouldn't start - there was a cupful of sugar in his petrol tank. That evening, at divisions, Eric said that if the culprit didn't own up then summer leave would be delayed from 1000 to 1800. Nobody owned up, and nobody split so we were all held back. There must have been a dearth of national news that day and the Daily Express (or perhaps the Liverpool Post) ran the headline 'Silent 200 gated for 8 hours' with lots of pictures and journalese! We all assumed that the culprit was one of my term who had been punished by the officer a couple of days earlier but he denied it even though we kicked his backside!"

"A group of us had been climbing Snowdon for the weekend and, on our return to the Rectory in Llanberis, learned we were snowed in with little prospect of return to Port Dinorwic in time to catch the launch back to the Conway on Sunday evening. We agreed to walk back via Caernarfon and the Menai Bridge, a distance of 21 miles. We set off on Sunday evening and all went well until about 2 am when tiredness and the bitter weather were beginning to tell on some of the group. By this time, faced with the conditions, tiredness and the distance ahead, we decided that a short cut through the tubular railway bridge might ease all these difficulties."

The bridge consisted of 4 large metal rectangular box-section spans, like tunnels suspended on piers. The 2 main spans were each 460 feet long, with 2 shorter spans linking to the shore. They were completely unlit and just wide and tall enough to accommodate trains.

"Having cut across the Vaynol estate to the bridge we split into 3 groups, the lead off group as they approached the halfway point in the tunnel would flash their torches to indicate that all was well. The sight of the torch flashes set off the second group who would follow the same procedure. I was with the third group, who once again set off on seeing the flashes from the second group. For the first few yards, at both ends of the tunnels, the two tunnels inter-connected, thereafter they singled up into their own tubes. It was pitch black inside with no light whatsoever and all there was to guide us through were timber planks running alongside the rail track. It was an eerie and claustrophobic atmosphere, the rhythmic sounds of feet upon timber planks and the sensation of someone in front or behind, as we moved at the double. After what seemed an age there was a sudden change in our rhythm and a pressure on the ears; there was a train in the tunnel behind us! A cold feeling of fear gripped us. I stumbled and fell across the railway track striking my head upon something hard. Momentarily I lost all consciousness and with it all sense of foreboding. In those few seconds I lay there, then I saw this bright light bearing down on me and a loud rumbling sound. I threw myself sideways and lay perfectly still, the wheels of the 3 am Holyhead express, passing within inches of my head. Seconds passed, I raised my head and saw the red lights of the last carriage in the steam and smoke that outlined a silhouette of the tunnel exit within yards of where I lay. I went to raise myself, placing my hand on a warm and moist object. Cadet X had been in front of me and for one horrendous moment I thought it was him without his head! I moved to lift him and found to my relief that it was a kit bag with warm engine oil at the neck of the bag. I remember running from the tunnel and jumping over a wire fence and rolling down the embankment where I rejoined the others. We arrived back at Plas Newydd exhausted just after 4 am on Monday morning."

1955 Winter Term

Rugby matches were played on the 4 rugby pitches at Maes Y Fran, where the tented camp had been in 1953. These were all rather sloping and it was decided the 1st XV needed a better pitch. The Worcester match was relocated to the cricket pitch but then it was agreed that the field in front of what later became the New Block could be used. The chums and others were employed, stone picking until it was completely clear and suitable for the tough men of the 1st XV to throw themselves around on.

1956

The new and very impressive 36 page prospectus issued in 1954 by Captain Hewitt was revised. *Conway's* official title changed from Cadet School Ship HMS *Conway* to The HMS *Conway* Merchant Navy Cadet School. Her role remained unchanged, to produce

"A steady stream of British mariners trained in sea-craft and character to shoulder the responsibility of vigilant watch on the high seas and to give leadership by example in the responsibility of command."

Boys were trained by

"toughening the fibre of body and spirit to meet the challenge of hazard, emergency and duty at sea with courage, strength and resource."

To achieve this Captain Hewitt had 11 technical staff, 12 academic staff, a chaplain, medical officer (Dr. Jack Dubberley) and two nursing sisters (Mrs Walters and Miss Griffiths). All but 8 were resident in the ship. Divisional Officers at the Camp were:

- Mizzentop: Lt. Cdr. J Brooke Smith RNR.
- Foretop: Lt. R.E. Parry RNR.
- Maintop: Lt. Cdr. WA Hutchinson RD RNR.
- Focsle: AC Moore RN.
- Hold: Mr. Howard Davies Master Mariner.

Divisional Officers at the House, also called the Junior Divisions were Mr. G Drake Master Mariner over Mizzentop and Hold, J Oliver RN over Foretop and Maintop, and CE Skinner RN over Focsle. The syllabus in the first 4 terms mainly prepared boys for GCE 'O' level examinations, but nautical subjects were taught from the outset, becoming the main focus once GCEs were completed. A new Seamanship GCE was introduced. A Special Studies class existed for those wishing to take 'A' levels or planning a career in the Royal Navy, the Army or the RAF.

1956 Easter Term

The rugby 1st XV had a very successful season winning 8 out of 11 matches and scoring 146 points. D M Johnston represented Welsh Schoolboys in matches against France and England

1956 June 14th

Captain Hewitt was appointed ADC to the Queen. The committee were delighted at the free publicity this would bring!

Standing : Capt. E. HEWITT, R.D., R.N.R. ; F. G. JONES, A. P. WOODHEAD, E. L. WAUGH, D. F. C. BURDETT
J.A. STEVEN, D. M. M. SHAW, Mr. K. BAYLISS
Seated : M. M. RUSHFORTH, B. WILSON, T.G. DICKINSON (Capt), D. M. JOHNSTON (W.S.S.R.U. Cap.) J.K. ORCHARI
Front Row : G. L. BEATTY, R.P. FROST, F.I. HOPKINSON, B. COOPER
Played 11; Won 8. : Lost 3 : Points for 146 ' Points Against 91.

1956 1ˢᵗ XV Easter

The next day Wg. Cdr. Browne issued an instruction to the lower III that tame jackdaws could not be brought into class.

"MacNamara's is quite astonishing, it will fly the length of the class room to perch on his arm and I'm told that one of the three or four birds came down and perched on the shoulder of one of the parents watching the QGM voting."

These astonishingly tame birds became a regular feature of daily life. On 6ᵗʰ July

"At divisions, 'Jack' the jackdaw searching for treasure in Fozard's trouser turn-up, at the end of prayers flew over to perch on Mr. Skinner's shoulder, greatly to the amusement of the cadets. Tonight as I was writing letters he came into my study and tried to grab the pen as I was writing. He was most interested in the papers and particularly in the desk pen-holder into which he poked his beak several times and then regurgitated a

MacNamara and His Tame Jackdaw

couple of large stones, about ¼ inch in diameter, and a tiny snail. He hopped around and then appeared to settle on my shoulder but he then misbehaved himself on my jacket and I had to put him out."

On the 22nd July,

"as the boys were falling in for church I noticed the jackdaw lined up at the end of the file and taking his dressing. He followed the boys in and we had to take him away before service started."

The bird's antics continued until 8th July 1957, when

"the little jackdaw died last night. He had flown into the galley and mistaken a bowl of fat for water and got into it before anyone could stop it. The chef washed it in warm water but though it perked up a bit yesterday it wouldn't eat anything and this morning Crawley found it dead."

1956 Summer Term

Two new identical gigs were built by Dickies. They were towed in tandem from Bangor to Plas Newydd by the pinnace, with a crew of cadets from Hold Division under the watchful eyes of Mr. Howard Davies. The existing gigs continued for a few more years but were in a very bad state. When *Conway* paid off in 1974, the new gigs were transferred to *Indefatigable*. When *Indefatigable* closed in 1995, the gigs were rescued by The Friends Of The *Conway* but found to be in a terrible condition. They were recovered in the hope that one might be restored from the remains of the rest but they later disappeared from what had been thought to be a secure storage yard.

1957 February

The committee were advised that *Conway* would make a loss of £1,000 by the end of the year, largely due to the cost of books and paper.

1957

Charlie Nicholson was the Chief Engineer and taught ship construction and engineering. He had a slide rule about 3 feet long, which he used to carry on his shoulder like a rifle! A poem appeared in the Cadet magazine entitled '*Conway* through the Alphabet.' The letter C was:

"C is for Charlie with his Massive Slide Rule, Everybody agrees It's the Biggest in School!"

In July Robertson sat on a scythe – 12 stitches.

Influenza hit the ship in September. On 24th, 20 or 30 cadets were ill but by 30th

"Over 100 down with flu."

1957 November 28ᵗʰ.

75 cadets formed a Royal Guard at Llanfair PG station for HRH The Duke of Edinburgh, who detrained there on his way to a visit to Menai Bridge.

1958 February 3ʳᵈ

Sister Parry died. She had ministered to cadets in the Ship, at Bryn Mel and Plas Newydd. A tower of strength and always sympathetic, there was

> "less malingering aboard Conway under Sister's supervision than in the sick bay of a warship."

1958

Starboard Main hut had a valve radio on the bulkhead half way down one side of the hut.

> "This was supposed to be switched off between lights-out and reveille, but officially we were allowed to listen to the Saturday night play so the volume could be increased during its transmission. We all looked forward to the occasion."

A few cadets had their own radios around, which everyone would congregate to listen to the latest tunes. Unfortunately the only decent station was Radio Luxembourg.

> "This was extremely frustrating, as reception was not always good. We fifth termers held a meeting to discuss how we could listen to more music. It was decided to form the IHN (inter hut network), to broadcast our own music."

A radio and record player were set up as the broadcasting centre in starboard mizzen hut. A network of wires was then secretly installed connecting all the huts.

> "These were laid while doing gardening duties, despite some query about our enthusiasm from a couple of the officers."

Any cadet could join IHN by purchasing a set of earphones and making a weekly contribution of sixpence.

> "Each week members voted on their favourites, producing our Top 10 or 20. Funds were handed over to the cook who purchased the latest records from Bangor. Noel Jackson, from Antigua and owner of the radio, was the DJ, and W Anderson, from East Africa, manned the record player suspended under a bunk opposite with two torches for lighting. We broadcast every night until we left Conway in December 58. What happened after that I have never found out."

The whole thing was completely illegal and with wires strung inside all the huts and around the whole Camp it was amazing they were never discovered. Their only close shave came one cold morning when Lt. Cdr. Brooke Smith surprised Jackson and Anderson having a lie in.

> "He queried the number of wires coming in but we managed to talk our way out of that!"

And You'll Find on the Bridge a Conway Boy
Lionel (Ken) 'Buster' Crabb GM OBE RNVR (1922-25)

Lionel Ken Crabb left Conway in August 1925 without having excelled, other than winning the Third Class prize in 1924. "He was a man averse to fitness, a chain smoker, who could only swim 3 lengths of a swimming pool." He joined the Lamport Holt Line. At the outbreak of war he tried to transfer to the Royal Navy but was refused on medical grounds. He instead became a Merchant Seaman Gunner, which enabled him to transfer 'by the back door' to the Royal Naval Patrol Service that used trawlers to clear mines at sea. Naval doctors soon found he had a weak left eye and banned him from further sea service. He volunteered for mine and bomb disposal duties and was posted to Gibraltar in 1942 to make recovered mines and warheads safe. He later became a recovery diver. On the 7th December 1942 the Italians attacked vessels in Gibraltar at night using human torpedoes from the Olterra, an Italian merchant ship docked in Algeciras in neutral Spain. Crabb scouted Gibraltar harbour in the dark not knowing whether a bomb might explode. His work as a diver took steely courage and bravery earning him the George Medal in 1944; the second highest gallantry award a civilian could be awarded. He developed advanced diving techniques, providing the Royal Navy with new ways of defending and attacking ships. He received an OBE in December 1945.

He spent some time searching the bottoms of ships in Haifa in Israel for limpet mines placed there by the Jewish Forces in 1948. He retired but was recalled to active service in 1951 and released again in 1955.

He disappeared in mysterious circumstances on the 19th April 1956, while diving near the USSR warship Ordzhonikidz in Portsmouth harbour. The Soviet leaders, Khrushchev and Bulganin were based in the cruiser for a state visit. Many conspiracy theories surround his disappearance. Officially, the Admiralty declared that Crabb was missing presumed drowned while testing secret underwater apparatus in Stokes Bay, Portsmouth. There were rumours that Crabb was working for MI6 gathering intelligence on the Russian ships, was discovered and killed. Others think he experienced technical problems that led him to drown. One extreme theory is that he was captured and taken to Russia where he became Captain Lev Lvovich Korablov in the Soviet Navy! Eden's government decided it was not in the public interest to disclose details of Commander Crabb's death. A corpse was found in Chichester Harbour, West Sussex on the 9th June that year. It was badly decomposed and without a head or hands. It was hastily identified as Crabb's and buried in Milton Cemetery, Portsmouth.

The IHN was quite professional and later was recorded onto a reel-to-reel tape recorder in one of the classrooms behind the canteen. Discovery was inevitable,

> *"I returned for my QB term to find a staff member ripping up all the wires and that was the end of that."*

Many cadets came from overseas particularly East Africa. From the mid 50s, there were always a number of cadets from Malaysia, apparently under an agreement between the UK and Malay governments for the training of deck officers. They would fly home with BAOC and Captain Hewitt made the bookings for their flights himself. His main contact at their office in Liverpool says that he was very demanding as he cared that BOAC would be doing the right thing by his cadets. She liked dealing with him as he knew what he wanted and she appreciated the effort she made for the Cadets.

> *"During my first term at the House there was a big stink (and quite rightly so) as the bullying by some QBs was really bad. The details escape me, but I think it was a QB hanging by the arms from a beam in one of the huts dropping onto a prone chum's chest, which I believe caused some broken ribs. This was the extreme, but there was some other bullying."*

One cadet attempted to hang himself, after younger cadets bullied him.

> *"He actually hanged himself but was found by 2 boys who pushed a desk under his feet and went for help. Another came in and found he had pushed the desk away and was again hanging."*

He survived. Captain Hewitt read the riot act and lectured the older boys on their responsibilities to the younger ones. One aspect of bullying carried over from the Ship was being put in the Derby.

> *"It was organised by the QBs in the form of a race. Various obstacles were set up on the sports field at Plas Newydd, over and under which you had to crawl while the QBs beat you with sticks or knotted towels, all interspersed with well placed kicks. To get around the course could take some 10 minutes, in the process of which you got mud on your clothes, which was a logistical problem as you had no change of clothes. If you didn't perform well enough in the Derby, or if they were not satisfied, they put you around again, presumably to ensure that you moved at a greater speed."*

This was all accompanied by frenzied blasts on the bugle to encourage the fainted hearted in this very organised affair. To be told that you were in the Derby was sufficient to create the utmost dismay. One of the cadets who endured the Derby in 1958 became deputy chief cadet captain in 1960. He was pleased to report:

> *"in my sixth term there was no bullying per se going on, as I kept a close watch to head such hysterical behaviour off at the pass."*

However, after he left a new chum recalls:

> *"Bullying in 1960 was a part of the culture but, when I joined along with a few others who were largish in size it started to die out. I like to think that, as the 1960 intake grew in seniority, we stamped out most of the bullying."*

Conway would test your metal but only in the very rarest of cases was that inadvertently to breaking point. Another new chum in 1960 has a positive view of the tough and challenging regime

> *"Conway and her sisters weren't there to nurture the runts of the litter: seagoing required personal traits that revolved about self-reliance and self-sufficiency, and the motto, 'Quit ye like men, be strong' wasn't an idle conceit. It had been carefully and deliberately chosen by God-fearing men in something of a God-fearing age, and if some of us scoffed at it, I think most kept it in mind for possible private use in a tight corner later in life."*

One such tight corner faced an Old Conway when his ship was boarded by armed pirates off Chenai, India, in 1997. He calmly secured his ship against the pirates and mustered all hands to repel boarders, which they eventually did. Tough training obviously helps with tough situations.

1958 April

The Staff and Mrs Hewitt 1959

The long running debate about the quality and nature of *Conway* training continued unabated. Three things were always at the heart of the debate; the balance between academic and technical training, the length of courses and the age at which boys should join. Committee members were all deeply involved in shipping and so could judge the value of the *Conway* product first hand. Sir John Nicholson reflected the views of many in a letter to Captain Hewitt, observing that shipping company entrants direct from grammar schools were often of a better calibre than *Conway* boys. He proposed that academic education should be left to ordinary schools and that boys attend *Conway* only after GCE O Level for a purely technical, one year course. Numbers would be almost halved to 150. There was strong opposition from Captain Hewitt and the Headmaster as these ideas had first been discussed in 1947 and kept resurfacing. They doubted *Conway* could attract 50 boys per course or survive on half the income. The Headmaster observed that

> "...a post GCE entry puts Conway in direct competition with 15 other schools offering same course with full remission and no fees."

He returned to his long cherished ideal, a 3 year course with the first 2 purely academic ashore, and the last purely technical in a ship. As Headmaster *he* would run the shore school and the Captain Superintendent the ship. Thus, a bitter disagreement between Hewitt and Browne surfaced once again. At one point in May 1947, Captain Hewitt had threatened not to take up his appointment as Captain Superintendent because of the Headmaster's constant manoeuvring for more control and greater recognition for academic staff. The two men were both strong characters with firmly held views and their personal relationship fluctuated behind the scenes as they clashed constantly over organisation and training. However, they joined forces resolutely against a 1 year course and within the month the proposals were disapproved. However, in a conference with marine superintendents in July, several favoured a 1 year course, re-igniting the debate. The Marine Society decision to award grants only for post GCE course provoked protest from *Conway*, *Worcester* and Pangbourne. Early in 1959 staff attended a conference on sea training and remission organised by the Ministries of Transport and Education for the Heads of Nautical Schools. The need for *Conway* to align training with the shipping companies' needs was never far from anyone's mind.

1958 June

There were Pakistani cadets for several years and on 6th June, one of them named Hasan, won the Queen's Gold Medal.

And You'll Find on the Bridge a Conway Boy
Sir J Busby Hewson (1918-20)

In 1959, Sir J Busby Hewson became the first Old Conway to be appointed a High Court Judge. He showed early promise in Conway, gaining prizes in his first and last terms for English, Mathematics and Navigation. He played for the 1ˢᵗ XV and was Chief Cadet Captain in his last term. He achieved an Extra Conway Certificate and joined the Canadian Pacific Steamship Company and the RNR from Conway.

He eventually gained his Extra Master's certificate and became a Commander RNR, having served in the RN throughout the war. He came ashore in 1933 and was called to the Bar in 1936. He was appointed to the Probate Divorce and Admiralty Division but most of his legal work was associated with maritime matters.

"There was quite a 'constitutional crisis' about this as Captain Hewitt had misgivings about putting Hasan's name forward on account of Pakistan being a republic."

In 1962, an American, Marks, was under consideration and there were similar concerns. Buckingham Palace was consulted and no objections were raised so his name was included in the list, but he did not win.

1958 September

HRH The Queen Mother made a private visit to Plas Newydd. She visited the dock and observed cadets undertaking various activities.

1958 December

The sailing boat *Flame* was purchased for £1,800.

1959

The Queen's Gold Medal was won by Cringle on 19ᵗʰ June. He was obviously very popular choice wining with

"more votes than all the others together."

2 days later *Worcester* beat *Conway* in a gig race by ¼ length. Over 900 spectators attended.

Flame 1959

One of the perks of being in a sports team was that it got you out of the ship for away games. There was pleasure out of all proportion in spending a few hours in a coach driving to venues around North Wales and of food in some other school. Ruthin, Rydal, Colwyn Bay, even near-by Llangefni became greatly anticipated jaunts. For the lucky few in the 1ˢᵗ XV there might even be a trip to our greatest rivals, Pangbourne near Reading and *Worcester* on the Thames

"I couldn't get into a rugby team so gave Mr. Fozard's hockey a try so I could escape Conway for a bit on away match days. Junior Leader's Tonfannau (near Tywyn, later a hostel for Ugandan Asians, now closed and flattened) was a bit tough, Bangor Normal College (Ladies), boy they took no prisoners, and RAF Valley with Vulcan bombers doing touch and go landings alongside the hockey pitch stand out."

The highlight of the Gymnastics team year was an exhibition display at the Llangefni summer show.

"I joined the Snowdon Group as an escape tactic. The Friday evening motorboat to Port Dinorwic and then off by bus to Llanberis youth hostel with our Peak cigarettes was a real joy. I even followed the Beagles (Mrs Hewitt's hobby) once or twice for a chance to get out. Come to think of it, all the books I had read before going to Conway about prisoner of war camps and what the inmates did for escape and evasion tactics stood me in good stead during my couple of years."

Port Fore Hut 1959

The cross-strait swim had a major jelly fish problem in 1959 and several swimmers were badly stung. One from Hold got into so much trouble he was hauled out, brought to shore and rushed to Bangor Hospital. He was in severe shock and could not easily breathe, which was a real concern.

"The swim across the straits and back was okay once you got started. I remember getting back to the slip and finding it difficult to believe how heavy my legs felt when getting out of the water."

"One Saturday afternoon, I was on 1st XV stretcher party at the top rugby pitch and was gripped by considerable abdominal pain. I ended up being carried to the sick bay at the House on the stretcher I was supposed to be helping to man. Medical methods at the sick bay were somewhat limited and Sister gave me laxative tablets (on the assumption, I presume, that any pain in the lower body region was bound to be due to constipation) which exacerbated my condition into peritonitis."

There was a chicken pox and scarlet fever epidemic onboard, which were knocking people down like nine pins.

It was *Conways'* centenary year and the QBs that summer were referred to as the Centenary QBs. A service of commemoration and thanksgiving was held at Bangor cathedral on 28th July, followed by the Centenary Prize Day and parade at Plas Newydd. The guest of honour was Lord Cilcennin (previous First Lord of the Admiralty), and there were over 250 invited guests plus parents and nearly 300 cadets. Decca Radar Ltd presented a radar set to the ship. Lawrence Holt unveiled a plaque dedicated as

"a tribute to her glorious past and as a mark of faith in the future of the school."

John Masefield wrote a special verse for the occasion:

A hundred years ago, when ships were wood
And rigging hemp. This ship of ours began
With hope (mans best begetter of all good)
For England's props, the ship and sailor man.

There in the Sloyne, abreast Rock Ferry pier
This August day began the thing desired
The "Conway" (with her future lying near)
The words of hope were uttered, hearts were fired.

Relic of those old "ships" are with us still
Some of the hope has been achieved, but more
Waits for the living "Conways" to fulfil
In all the seas that ring this planet's shore.

"Up with her 'Conways' all; abandon fears,
Let us do better this next hundred years.

John Masefield.

Cadets attended the Trafalgar Day parade and service in St Paul's, London.

"A Master at Arms from Whale Island Gunnery School appeared some time before and educated us in the art of marching!"

The first night was spent on the P&O passenger ship *Himalaya* in Tilbury. The following day there was a special presentation on stellar navigation at the Planetarium. We lined up with loads of other naval cadets and several bands and marched up to St. Paul's for the service. After that some local cadets went home for the night, accompanied by a fellow cadet.

"My favourite memory of that day was the pride I had in our band, which had been thoroughly well knocked into shape by a couple of Marines and to my delight managed to completely drown out the Worcester band, which marched behind us. Their flutes could not compete!"

Another cadet remembers,

"Fozard conjuring on the return journey – the look on the ticket collector's face was that of a man who was not sure if his eyes were deceiving him."

The *Conway* band and marching cadets were in great demand at this time. Parties of cadets would be sent to Liverpool for the annual Battle of the Atlantic commemoration parade; Lord Mayor's Day in Bangor; investitures at Bangor Cathedral; visits by dignitaries to local towns, such as the Duke of Edinburgh's visit to Holyhead. The band was very smart and professional in spite of its reputation amongst cadets for being full of shags ie untidy, lazy fellows.

"Lt. Cdr. W Hutchison led a trip on the yacht 'Flame' in the summer of 1959, which I was fortunate to be involved in. We joined her in Holy Loch and, after a day of familiarisation on the Clyde, we sailed back to the Menai Strait via Arran, Stranraer, Laxey IOM and Moelfre Bay. We experienced strong winds and

foggy calms, anchoring most evenings until the next day. It was a terrific experience, which I thoroughly enjoyed and wouldn't have missed for the world."

1959 September

2 cadets borrowed Hutch's motorbike, visited Bangor and stole 75 pairs of shoe laces and a window latch. This led to a magistrate's court appearance and subsequent expulsion.

"At the police station xxxxx admitted taking the motor-cycle for a dare. In a statement he said he was a fifth term cadet at HMS Conway and added 'At Conway it is a tradition to do things that have not been done before and I suggested that we should borrow Commander Hutchinson's motor-cycle, but that was meant more as a joke then. At about 11 last night we took the motor-cycle from the cricket pavilion and we pushed it for about 2 miles before starting the engine.' At the back of the High Street they admitted to stealing the shoe laces through an open window and the window latch through a broken window."

The lawyer said on their behalf, in mitigation, that

"they are subject to impersonal discipline and naturally look for an outlet for their vigour and spirit."

Others contented themselves with forays across the fields to the back door of the pub in Llanfair PG after lights out. One had to have a little light relief! It seemed to have been an unfortunate term; 8 other cadets were sent home early and 2 were expelled when it transpired they had been imprisoned in Switzerland during the holidays for stealing watches.

"Jay 'Birdie' Hooper was a Maintopman in my term. He was a talented sailor and a stalwart of the sailing group. He eventually represented Bermuda in the 1968 Mexican Olympics, I can't remember what class he competed in but, considering the number of skilled Bermudan helmsmen, he must have been pretty good."

"I remember when Margaret Hughes was murdered down Beaumaris way. She was sexually assaulted and strangled. Over 2,000 men were fingerprinted and palm printed. From memory they caught a Dutch seaman in Liverpool and he was charged with her murder. All the cadets were fingerprinted, they returned the prints to us after they'd been checked."

"One of the cadets in our term was reputedly a Russian Prince, apparently with high connections He became a bugler - his renditions were atrocious, and it was a bit like 'guess the command' when he was duty bugler. He'd roam the musical scale looking for 'G.' To his credit, he totally ignored all jibes, and stuck with it, until you could eventually at least make a good guess at the calls. One memorable day, when he was the bugler in the morning colour party, someone

Figurehead and Cadets 1959

had stuffed a rag up his bugle. He marched out to the flagstaff, blew furiously into his sabotaged bugle as the ensign was raised, only to have a confused cadet who was hoisting the ensign stop in mid hoist, while he removed the offending rag. His red face was visible even at a distance."

"I was King of the Woods during the summer term of 1960 when I was a leading architect of a fairly magnificent smoking den in the woods. This den was also used on Sundays by a select group of church parade dodgers. Time spent at the den in the summer sunshine provided a short but welcome break from authority, allowing also for the luxury of unhurried smoke and quality time with your mates. The Marquis's gamekeeper eventually stumbled upon our den and Eric announced that, despite its ingenuity, those concerned must demolish it forthwith. He added the caveat that no action would be taken against those who had shown such enterprise provided it was done without delay and for us to note that future visits to the woods thereafter would be punished without hesitation. Subsequently we took to climbing the magnificent sycamore tree between port and starboard hold huts for a clandestine smoke."

"We grew used to being lightly knocked about by cadet-captains with their casual laying-on of teasers, and thought nothing of it; but when it was official things were altogether different, being arraigned before a panel of cadet-captains in the gun-room was a serious business. I was given a taste of it when acting as cook on the mess, hurrying back from the galley hatch with a couple of mess-tins I dropped the potatoes. There were no survivors and the mess went hungry, no question of a replacement supply, every potato was marked in the cash-strapped victualling that prevailed. The result was an appearance before the inquisition, headed in suitably dignified and sombre fashion by the CPO, who asked me a few questions the answers to which seemed to me to be absurdly obvious. Everything was entered in the punishment book, and I got four across the backside with a teaser. It hurt, and the bruises lasted a good 10 days, admired by all. Admiration wasn't sufficient incentive though, and I dropped no more potatoes."

1960

2 cadets were found smoking in one of the Marquis's bedrooms. A maid came in so they crept under the bed to hide, but left their feet sticking out. Swedish gymnastics had completely dominated European school physical education programmes since the 1840s. In 1960, Mr. Roland Palm, a Swedish gymnast, visited to train boys in gym. He was popular but could only remain for one month as there was no staff vacancy for him.

In September cadet C Williams from Barmouth was presented with a Royal Humane Society award for bravely assisting in the rescue of a man and woman stranded on the bar at Barmouth sands in freezing conditions and rough seas.

1960 December 2nd

Ernie Moore RN retired and was presented with a tray made of mahogany from the Ship. He was a Londoner and a very colourful character. Ernie and his wife were father and mother figures for many cadets.

1961

"I remember the culture shock of the first few weeks in the ship. My first dormitory was Nestor. The sea of unknown faces, the confusion of where to be or where to go, the sounds of amplified orders, bugles and whistles.

To me it was quite head spinning and only stabilized by the relative sanity of the classroom, and as some of the unfamiliar faces became people with names. Two were quite memorable characters. One would entertain us after lights out with exotic stories of life in very far away Northern Rhodesia (a little different from my life in Altrincham), another had an amazing repertoire of enjoyable stories ranging from humorous to ghostly. They helped us all to forget our homesickness and relax us into deep sleep."

"I remember spending hours hollowing out a new piece of chalk and filling it with match heads. Cupid managed to set it off when writing with it on the blackboard. His reaction was priceless. A puzzled expression came over his face when confronted with a piece of chalk erupting like a roman candle. Then it dawned on him that he had been had, just as it went out. 'Yes! Very clever,' he said, 'Now can we get back to Pythagoras.' Placing bits of plastic set squares in the heating elements of the class fan heaters used to give off vast amounts of black smoke too. God, he was a good sport."

1961 March

It was agreed that time in the Special Studies (A Level) class would count towards remission time.

1961 November

"As a senior rate in my last term I got an invitation to the St Winifred's School dance. The dancing-party went by coach to be met at the main entrance by a formidable cohort of mistresses who funnelled us through iron-bound double doors, which crashed shut behind us with a groan of dry hinges and grinding of heavy locks not unlike theatrical representations of a medieval jail. At the affirmative answer to a cry from somewhere ahead of us, 'Are all the Conway boys in?', we were hustled along a short passage to emerge in the school assembly hall like early Christians at the Coliseum. The mistresses were seated at the back of the hall in terraced ranks, eagle-eyed and purse-lipped, and we received instructions to choose our partners from the 6th form only, presumably to protect the younger girls from premature corruption. We danced industriously for nearly 3 hours before release for refreshments. The girls knew a way out of the building via a sort of priest's hole, and led us in a well-planned rota of small groups into the open air among the laurels and rhododendrons of the grounds. There was also an accommodating pub nearby, where I downed a guilty Mackeson before returning to the fray with my partner for the evening."

1961 December

Cadet captains were not immune from rule breaking although it was perhaps more important that they did not get caught.

"After rounds I joined most of the senior rates in Port Main's cabin, gathered together with permission from the OOD, tempered with a warning not to misbehave. He couldn't have known about the great cache of hard liquor clandestinely amassed in small lots during the term at away rugby and hockey matches. The party was ostensibly based on the contents of food-parcels sent from home and accompanying soft drinks. We started on the gin, vodka, Dubonnet, scotch and VSOP cautiously enough, diluting it with Guinness and mopping it up with cold roast chicken, cake, cheese, sardines, shortbread, biscuits, crisps, ham and suchlike delicacies, believing ourselves to be all but totally silent. By the time the last dregs had been absorbed however, half the Camp must have been aware of Port Main as the epicentre of a small earth tremor, finally subsiding by around 0230. Next morning I had a splitting hangover. One senior cadet captain was discovered in a comatose state propped against a fire-extinguisher under the big tree in the centre of the Camp and, at divisions, the CPO

and senior CCs were stiffly elaborate in their saluting and other evolutions, pale-faced and tight-lipped. We actually believed no-one knew about the debauch, but of course it was common knowledge by breakfast-time. Drink was, of course, strictly prohibited. If Eric had followed it up, almost the entire corps of senior rates would have been dis-rated, probably with consequent loss of our places with shipping companies. I just count my lucky stars, that's all."

1962

"I was in charge of the dock one day when the phone rang. I picked it up and said, 'Yahaa! Lt. Cdr. Parry here' in excellent imitation of him. The reply came back, 'That's damned funny! Lt. Cdr Parry here, too.' And it was! I put the phone down, and started worrying. By the time I saw him later in the day he just gave me a long hard look. Another good sport!"

"Parry did have a sense of humour alright, I went out the back gate one day and donned my yellow jumper and blue jeans to meet my girl friend. We went into Bangor, collected her dog and went for a walk. Blow me away Parry walked up the main street towards me. He looked me in the eye and he turned away up a lane way very quickly, I went the other way up another street, I thought that's it, I'm a goner! Monday morning in class he bounced in and drew his hankie from his sleeve and asked whether we had all had a good weekend. He said the weather was lovely, ideal for taking one's dog for a walk. He looked at me and that was it. Everyone else thought he was off his trolley."

"We were offered the chance, for a shilling, to view the mural paintings by Rex Whistler in the Marquis's part of the House. I thought I'd better go, although I was not one for art. The mural, of the view over a village looking down on to the harbour has stayed with me since then. The 3D affect of the steps with the cigarette, which had been left smouldering on the step, gave one the impression that it could be picked up and smoked. The Greek columns looked so real that we ran our finger across the columns in an expectation of feeling the sculptured design. It was pointed out to us that if we looked at the sky we would see the impression of a sailing ship that had been painted over by the artist and was to be finished on his return from the war, but sadly he was killed at D Day."

Plas Newydd is now open to the public and the mural is a highlight of the tour but I doubt they will let you run your fingers over it today!

"A bonfire had been built for Guy Fawkes night. The event had been rained off and the following day our class had Geoff Drake. The bonfire was totally waterlogged and Geoff Drake sent two of us down to the dock with instructions to bring back two buckets of TVO each. Once we got back we were allowed to pour two of the buckets of TVO over the bonfire. He lit a newspaper and stuck it in the bonfire, which ofcourse started to burn. Once the fire took hold he told one of us to chuck one of the remaining buckets over the bonfire, which was done immediately. The result was a colossal black mushroom of smoke and flame. Fortunately we were upwind of the fire, but maybe he'd thought of that. The second bucket went on too, but we were already getting blasé about it."

Jellyfish were a problem for the cross strait swim every summer, but 1962 was the year of the Portuguese Men O'War with huge tentacles. Cries of

"Je-ee-e-ll-eeee Fishhhh"

could be heard frequently.

"The boats were out picking up people who either got stung or were just tired out. By the time I got back to the dock thinking I was the last one, the tide had changed. I looked back over the strait and there were groups of cadets still in the water trying to avoid the jellyfish. The disturbance caused by a group seemed to keep them at bay. I didn't enjoy that day one bit."

Lt. Cdr. W. Hutchison committed suicide in his hut near the canteen.

"His cap always looked way to big for him, great guy, but with demons."

He had been on the Artic Convoys to Murmansk. He joined the staff around 1955 and was Maintop divisional officer at the Camp from 1960 to 62. *"Very much respected in my time."*

Lt Cdr Hutchinson 1960

"Held himself very erect and probably used a little alcohol, totally understandable. Have never forgotten him, but he was an enigma."

"He was hugely respected and I do not remember anyone ever saying a bad word about him. I had several long discussions with him in my final term, and although he was sometimes challenged by Johnny Walker, I have nothing but good recollections of his concern and helpfulness."

"He was a totally fair and honest man and personally I respected him hugely. He was someone you could talk to or ask questions of and as far as I was concerned he genuinely tried to help."

"I was Flags and Clocks and to get the signal of the day I was one of the first into Hutch's cabin, every day. However, on this particular morning Fozard and Parry got there before me. I saw what had happened but they shuffled me out telling me to say nothing to anyone."

The police came and everything was dealt with quietly and the day's routine was hardly disturbed.

"It was as if nothing had happened, which I suppose is why so many of my era cannot remember it. For me it was certainly a great shock as I had a great respect and liking for Hutch. Working with him every day we had sort of repartee going."

1962 April Fools Day

At dead of night, 2 cadets were dragging the small wheeled gun from the House up to the Camp. They were going to tie it to the door of the duty officer's cabin so he could not get out on April Fools Day. The duty officer was Alan Ollerton.

"A shadowy figure bent himself onto the ropes and gave us a very welcome hand. We tied it to the door and suddenly realised that the extra hand was non other than Alan himself. He made us do a couple of extra journeys back and forth to the Kelvin Block before finally returning the cannon to its rightful place."

The next morning Brookie's bike had gone missing.

"Unable to find the bike or the culprits, he paraded the whole ship's company around the large tree in the centre of the huts. He walked around and around the tree haranguing all hands about the loss of his bike."

What he did not realise was that his bike was securely tied to the topmost branch of said tree. The cadets could all see it and were trying very hard not to laugh or point it out.

"Needless to say he soon realised where his bike was hiding – I vaguely remember early heave outs for all hands!"

1962 Summer

A cadet took an MSOD out in a full gale in order to prove they could be capsized. The only result was that the mast got snapped clean in 2.

2 gigs were on the outfalls in the dock ready for the next day's divisional rowing final. The division that thought they had drawn the, 'slower' boat crept down to the dock during the night and swapped the colour plaques over. All went well until the boat keepers went onboard the next morning to prepare the boats and quickly noticed that they were not working on their own boats. Punishments followed for the miscreants.

Ernie Ball's Retirement

1962 October

An event of great significance to generations of *Conway* cadets occurred when the Merchant Navy and Airline Officers Association presented *Conway* with a copy of the film 'Fire Down Below.' It was to be watched and re-watched, seemingly without end forever!

The Bosun's Mate, Ernie Ball retired.

1962 November

Wg. Cdr. Browne developed proposals for 2 year pre-sea training course for engineers. This had first been suggested by Captain Hewitt in 1958, who also wanted a course for pursers. It would include mechanical drawing and chemistry, prepare them for entry to technical college and earn 6 months remission. The idea was well received but never got off the ground. However, many cadets left *Conway* and joined shipping companies or the Royal Naval Engineering Service as engineering cadets and pursers, often because their eyesight had fallen below the standard required to be a deck officer during their course.

1963

"I used to rent 2 buses, twice a term, for 2 guineas each and charged one and three pence for each cadet to travel to Bangor. I could cram over 50 cadets on both upper and lower levels, so you can see the return on investment

was considerable. The ship only hired buses to bring us back from Bangor, so to get there was a very long and tedious walk/hitch hike."

This went on for 3 terms until the staff started asking who had actually made the arrangements.

"Eric lambasted me when he found out that I was making a profit out of my fellow cadets and the deal was outlawed!"

Undeterred, another he found another deal that was real money maker.

"We used to get a new suit of best reefer uniforms every year. In your second year, the first year's suit was kept for second best. If you were in a 3 year course you'd get another new suit, which meant you had 3, and didn't need the original issue. Well, I used to go around the chaps who had just received their third set and buy them. I paid as little as 1 shilling - up to two and sixpence. I'd then cut off the buttons and sew on ordinary black, plastic buttons. I then made a deal with Mrs. Basham, she ran the canteen, and sold the 'almost new' Sunday suits to her for 10 shillings. She in turn sold them to the workers on the farm at Plas Newydd, as Sunday best for Chapel. I probably went through 20 - 30 complete suits over a 2 year period. Not a lot, but if you remember, we 'plebs' only got 1 shilling a week for spending money."

This budding entrepreneur now runs a large car dealership in North Carolina so *Conway* obviously helped him find his way in life.

"I was the engineer on No 1 and we had made the usual evening run to PD to take the bosun home. We had 2 stowaway cadets onboard for a fag run. We disembarked the bosun and 2 of us shot up to the café to buy cigarettes. Meanwhile No 1 was doing ever decreasing circles off of the concrete jetty awaiting our return. It was an ebb tide and with a thump they grounded right on the edge of the jetty, ending up bow down and the stern in the air at low tide. Panic stations all round. Another motorboat came down and they were so busy gloating at us they came in too close and beached themselves. More panic! Somehow the story got into the newspapers under the headline 'Red faces for the Navy.' The boats lifted safely off on the tide."

In the very cold winter of 1963 and 1964, there was a very thin layer of ice on the strait.

"One start of an Easter term the weather had been so cold that the away matches were cancelled due to the hard ground, so we all went to climb Snowdon, up the back way and down the railway side. We climbed Snowdon in wellington boots and greatcoats. Brooke Smith and Kingsford said at the summit that if any cadets beat them down they would buy a beer for them. I think 6 or 10 cadets beat them down."

CHAPTER 31

1964 ANOTHER REBIRTH

From Concept to Construction

On 6th May 1964, the Nautical College approved by the committee in 1953 finally opened. It had been a protracted and difficult birth.

The firm of Gornal, Kelly and Partners of Liverpool were employed as architects in 1953, with Mr. Richard Kelly FRIBA, personally leading planning. On 12th November 1953, a survey of the preferred site on the banks of the strait identified a 40 foot drop from the back to the front of the site, but a splendid outlook over the strait if trees were cleared. His original proposal was for a 2 storey building hugging the natural contours of the land and facing the strait. The entrance hall would overlook the strait with offices on one side and administration services on the other. It would have a central assembly hall, with mess deck below and galley on one side, flanked by dormitory wings. When Mr. Kelly delivered these plans in January 1954 the cost was £300,000. In October, a swimming bath was added at a cost of £4,700 but a separate navigation and seamanship block, costing £40,000, was rejected. In January 1955, a model of the new building, now incorporating classroom wings, was presented to the committee for approval. Costs had risen to £400,000, including £10,000 for furniture. Once the site was cleared he thought it would take 2 years to build.

In September 1955, after 17 months of fund raising, only £100,000 had been secured despite initial grand promises from Blue Funnel and Cunard, but that jumped to £200,000 within a month! Despite the slow start, shipping companies clearly came to believe in the concept of a nautical college. By January 1956, pruning of facilities had reduced costs to £360,000 and £260,000 had been promised. In May only £30,000 more was needed. The committee thought that enough funds had been committed to allow work to start and signed a contract for ground clearance to begin in February 1956. The official opesning would be in the ship's centenary year of 1959.

Lack of committed funds meant costs had to be reduced, more people wanted to tinker with the design. Captain Hewitt's ideas for an entrance mezzanine floor were opposed by the architect but eventually agreed. The Marquis naturally had concerns about the siting and impact of this massive building on his land so he wanted to approve the plans before any public announcement was made. The Headmaster wanted more space for science labs, technical staff were not satisfied with arrangements for seamanship and navigation, more married quarters were needed, others wanted a separate staff wardroom. Work did not start as planned, slippage soon ran from months into years and prices started to escalate. The Marquis agreed that one row of huts at the Camp could be retained as classrooms, a much cheaper solution than new bricks and mortar. Even with the classroom wings removed, costs had increased to at least £400,000, mainly driven by the legal construction standards for the dormitory wings. The ground-hugging nature of the planned building was turning out to be a very expensive solution. At the committee meeting in October 1956, as the wreck of the Ship was being broken up, progress stalled completely and a fundamental review of plans and priorities was arranged. Matters got worse in 1957 when a key grant application to the Leverhulm Trust for science laboratories was rejected and the Marquis refused a separate seamanship and navigation building above the dock.

In May 1958, Mr. Kelly returned with a modified plan that was the basis for the eventual building. He proposed a single 'T' shaped building with a 5 storey accommodation block parallel to the strait and a combined mess deck/assembly hall, entrance hall and offices at right angles to it. The building unfortunately turned its back on the strait and plans to clear the shore line were dropped. A house for the Captain Superintendent would adjoin one end of the dormitory block. There were no classrooms but provision was made for these to be added as wings either side of the entrance hall when funds permitted. Until then all teaching would be in huts retained at the Camp. The final price was still expected to be £450,000, of which only £50,000 still had to be found. The committee returned to the idea of a partial replacement for the ship and allocated a budget for a small sailing vessel. The year 1958 dragged into 1959 and at long last Wg. Cdr. Browne got his way over the science labs; they would be added on top of the mess deck. In July the committee approved these plans and started negotiating the lease with the Marquis's agent. A year was required for detailed drawings, quantity surveys and tenders. With 2 years for building, late 1963 was pencilled in as the opening date. Companies were invited to tender for the work and, on 15th October, the Committee awarded the main building contract to Leyland Construction of Preston. Over 26 main sub-contractors were engaged and Leyland's Managing Director took personal control of the whole project. Just as everything seemed to be falling into place the committee dropped a bombshell, they could not agree the terms for the lease with the Marquis. As no compromise could be reached, building work was put on hold on 2nd December 1960. The issues were eventually resolved and work began again in late in 1961. However, according to a legal opinion obtained years later,

"although Heads Of Agreement for a lease were initialled, no lease was actually prepared, let alone executed."

Mrs Hewitt Lays The Foundation Stone

The whole site was put strictly out of bounds to cadets as the builders began clearing the site of trees. Mrs Hewitt laid the foundation stone on 1st August 1961. It was 102 years to the day since the very first cadet, (Captain) Howard Campbell, joined the ship. By reducing costs (the swimming bath and seamanship/navigation block were dropped, and Mrs Lawrence Holt and Julian Holt paid for the science labs themselves), the two classroom blocks (planned for a later Phase 2 extension) were included in the original build for a cost of £66,000. Small flats were included on each floor at the west end of the accommodation block at a cost of £500 each. The main assembly hall and mess deck building was of

Dormitory Wing Under Construction

steel frame construction. The accommodation wing had a reinforced concrete frame. The classroom wings and other smaller building were brick built.

"I was duty motorboat crew and we had to move the contractor's flat top barge around the area while they were constructing the main sewer drain - direct into the strait as they did in those days."

By January 1962, the structural framework was in place, in May the outer walls were taking shape and by September 1962 the outer structure was almost complete. There was a delay of a few weeks because of a strike in 1961, and the severe winters of 1962 and 1963, but building was completed in time for occupation in the Winter term of 1963. Over 300 cadets would pay fees of £261pa each, but in 1964 annual council rates alone would be would be £4,000.

The final costs of the building, furnishings and ancillary costs such as removing the Camp, were expected to exceed £500,000, with most subscribed by shipping companies. The Captain Superintendent acknowledged the key contribution of all Old *Conways*:

"if they had not upheld the traditions we try to teach, the shipowners would not have felt it worth their while to donate half a million pounds to see their like perpetuated."

The New Block was only the start of a grand strategy. Phases 1 and 2 were the accommodation facilities and classrooms of the New Block. Phases 3 to 7 envisaged additional staff houses, a seamanship/navigation block, gym, swimming pool and chapel. At some time in the future an Engineering Block would be built.

What's in a Name?

Initially, the building was going to be called the 'Queens Building' but the name was abandoned when it was realised that the Queen would not be able to perform the opening. Lt. Cdr. Brooke Smith suggested that it be named 'Conway.' This was agreed and formally announced in the May 1964 edition of the Cadet, although it was rarely used in practice. Strangely, a few months later, the official programme for the opening ceremony referred only to 'The New Buildings.' While Watch Bills generally used the term 'College,' the most common name for 11 years was the unlovely 'New Block.' The prospectus for the chapel introduced the name 'New Conway' building. After *Conway's* closure the politically correct but illogical 'Conwy Centre' was used for a while but at long last the name has now settled down as 'The Conway Centre.'

The Conway Cadet School Ltd

Since 1863, Conway had been run by the MMSA as an unincorporated institution, with the MMSA acting as guarantor owning all assets including leases on land and property. By 1963, the MMSA had acquired significant leaseholds at Plas Newydd on *Conway's* behalf and were obtaining even more for the New Block. The MMSA decided it was necessary for this property to be vested in a more formal way and so to transfer ownership to a company limited by guarantee and not having any share capital.

The company was called 'The Conway Cadet School' but this was quite distinct from the ship's formal name of 'The HMS Conway Merchant Navy Cadet School'. The Articles of Association referred to it as a Trust controlled by a governing body of members who all had to be members of the MMSA.

The company's key objects were:

"To acquire and take over the assets of The HMS Conway Merchant Navy Cadet School … and to continue and extend the work of the said School…,"

and

"to provide education and training and religious instruction and services for boys particularly those intending to become officers in the British maritime and air transport services and the armed forces."

A raft of other objects and articles dealt with organisational, procedural, financial and management arrangements. The subscribers (no titles were given) were:

George Ayre, Wallasey, Shipmaster (retired).
Arthur Baptiste, Liverpool, Shipmaster (retired).
Arthur Litherland, St Helens, Shipmaster (retired).
Philip Savery, Colwyn Bay, Shipmaster (retired).
Eric Shaw, Heswall, Shipmaster (retired).
Charles Vaughan, West Kirby, Shipmaster (retired).
Frank Wilkes, Liverpool, Shipmaster (retired).

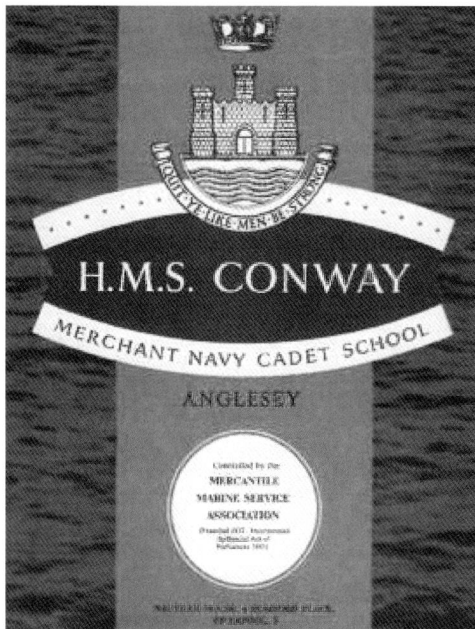

Prospectus Cover

These gentlemen became the first committee members, along with Charles Birchall, William Coombs, Lelsie Harding, Julian Holt, Alwyn Hughes, Harold Magnay, Sir James Mountford and Sir John Nicholson. The latter became the Trust's first Chairman. The Committee was to have no less than 14, and no more than 24 members. Half these were to be elected from the Council of the MMSA, the other half to be co-opted

"shipowners, educationalists and other persons having a bona fide interest in the objects for which the Trust is founded,"

but who did not need to be members of the MMSA. The company was incorporated on 25th April 1963, certificate number 758795. 105 years and 6 days after the MMSA had originally set up a committee to plan Conway they relinquished direct ownership to the new company. While the MMSA retained over-all control, an arm's length arrangement had been introduced. An updated prospectus was issued

Change of Headmaster

Not only was the organisation of *Conway* changing, it was time for the Headmaster Wg. Cdr. Browne to retire but when, in November 1962, Captain Hewitt suggested that Wg. Cdr. Browne stay on until he was 70, Browne was not willing. He wanted a change (not to retire) so they agreed a replacement should be sought. In October 1963, the Headmaster's position was advertised in the Times Educational Supplement. There were 35 applicants and interviews started in January 1964. On 27th February the position was offered to Mr. Basil Lord and he accepted.

29th July 1964 was Wg. Cdr. Browne's last day as Headmaster. In his diary, he wrote a neat play on words:

> *"The end of Tom Browne's Schooldays but the Lord will be with us."*

He had joined the Ship on 19th September 1934 when there were just 4 academic staff, one of whom was part time. Browne noted:

> *"Periods go with tremendous verve but more entertaining than educating … mathematical histrionics … doubt the value of English teaching … didn't like the library organisation … classes bored … trouble with classes, too much talking."*

He obviously felt a lot needed to be done. Within months, he was advertising for a Deputy Headmaster (Mr. Carter joined on 1st March 1935), had started science classes in conjunction with Liverpool Technical College, proposed an entrance exam to improve standards and had introduced flying classes. He bought a physics lab for £45 and a chemistry lab for £110. Very soon, he was discussing *Conway* education with the management committee, Admiralty, Ministry of Education, Ministry of Aviation, Worcester, Dartmouth, the Shipping Federation, even Imperial Airways! He was going to make changes. He dedicated 30 years of his life to *Conway* apart from a short break in the RAF during the Second World War. He never relented in his pursuit of improvements and opportunities for the cadets. He masterminded the development of the new 2 and 3 year courses, the introduction of GCE O levels and then the 'A' level Special Studies class. He encouraged every officer, master and cadet to every sort of out-of-school activity from a Scout Group, to Duke of Edinburgh's Award Scheme, from Ornithology Society to a Debating Group. He planned and organised the annual Haigh Trophy competition. His diaries show he was constantly evaluating standards and seeking ways to improve technical training and academic education. He could be a thorn in the side of the technical staff, who felt he was overstepping his academic responsibilities, and was never happy with the lower status accorded to masters than officers. This led inevitably to clashes with Captain Goddard and later with Captain Hewitt, but both men were as one in their dedication to *Conway*. In his valediction Captain Hewitt said,

> *"He has left his mark on thousands of cadets and will always be remembered with affection … He joined the Ship when she was educationally in the doldrums and is leaving her on the crest of a wave … The list of all he has done is infinite."*

He left a team of 14 highly qualified and motivated academic teaching staff. Ordinary mortals might have retired but not TEWB. He was given a world cruise by Blue Funnel and afterwards became Headmaster of a school in Canada. He published his memoirs in 'The Skyline Is A Promise' in 1971.

The Conway Chapel

While plans were laid for the new college, the old boys under the auspices of the *Conway* Club decided that a Chapel should be built adjacent to the new buildings. Mrs Hewitt promptly raised several thousand pounds through fairs and fetes as the Club launched the Centenary Appeal Fund to pay for it.

Mr. Kelly produced plans in September 1962, described by the Headmaster as a

"small scale Coventry Cathedral to cost £70,000."

These too were scaled back and the Club eventually launched an appeal for £40,000 with a target date for completion of 1971. The Marquis kindly gave the land alongside the new Mess Deck and over the next few years cadets started stone picking to remove every last pebble from the proposed site. It is rumoured that in 1964, cadets under punishment spent months clearing the stones from the left hand side of the space and dumped them on the right. In 1965 they were cleared for the right and dumped on the left and so on ad infinitum until the builders arrived with a JCB and scrapped the site clear in minutes. In the meantime, the old mess deck hut from the Camp was erected for use as a chapel behind the new galley-staff accommodation. It was still in place in 2007 and used as the *Conway* Centre shop.

Moving into the New Block

At the end of the summer term 1963, the building was finally completed and cadets left their huts for the last time and headed home for the holidays. There were no cadets left who remembered Captain Hewitt's magic wand in 1953 creating a tented camp in a matter of days and then the hutted camp in just a few weeks. But he waived it again with spectacular effect.

"The camp came down during the summer holidays, when we came back for the winter term it just wasn't there."

Even the foundations for the huts had gone. It's rumoured the huts were sold and still litter farmyards and fields around Anglesey.

The New Block was first occupied on 18th September 1963. As at the Camp, the port and starboard watches of each top had their own dormitory, now with 26 bunks, and a small cabin for the senior cadet captain. The junior cadet captains continued to occupy the bunks just inside the doors. The bunks had been moved down from the Camp and each cadet still had a bed-head shelf for a personal display. This at least would have felt familiar. One change was not so welcome.

"They took our sea chests during the hols and cut them down to foot lockers. We were very upset when we came back and saw the destruction of these. We had chest of drawers instead."

The comparisons ended there. All the dormitories were now housed in a single, centrally heated, five story block called the 'Cadets Wing.' Focsle were on the top floor with Foretop, Maintop and Mizzentop successively below them. The ground floor contained common rooms and the main sports changing rooms and ablutions. The port dormitories were on the left looking towards the strait, the starboard to the right. The ship was, in theory therefore, facing the strait with the main entrance, always called the quarter deck, appropriately towards the stern. This was a hang-over from the original 1954 plan, which had all the buildings facing the strait.

The north classroom block was occupied at half term and the south in the first term of 1964. There was universal praise for the new classrooms.

> *"Mrs Basham's takings at the canteen plummeted when cadets faced the half mile hike from the New Block rather than the short dash from the huts."*

Despite all the changes of accommodation, the officers, masters and general regime remained pretty constant. The early morning dash in pyjamas from the Camp to the Kelvin Block in all weathers was replaced by an early morning run from the New Block to the site of the old huts in all weathers!

> *"Many cadets at the time of purely huts pedigree thought the New Block was for sissies and too easy. No doubt the last ship based cadets in 1953 thought the same of the cushy life in the huts."*

> *"I suppose the camp was sort of more military when you think of films of people doing National Service, whereas the New Block was more educational establishment."*

> *"No doubt the New Block was a softer touch than the Camp, which I am sure was also the case when the ship was lost and the camp created, but the facilities were so much better and if I remember anything much about that term was how good it was."*

> *"There was definitely a different feel to it, maybe because of the newness of the building as opposed to the Camp, everything was bricks and plaster instead of wooden planks and wooden walls, proper classrooms and science labs etc. The dining hall and the kitchens in the New Block were light years ahead of the old mess deck at the Camp. Food was better I think, but that might have been QB seniority."*

> *"Having spent my QB term in the New Block, the thing I really remember was the vast improvement in facilities, especially the classrooms. The huts in the Kelvin Block and behind the canteen in the Camp were pretty basic and falling apart by the time they came to the end, whereas the New Block seemed to enjoy all the latest in educational thinking and facilities."*

Official Opening

Eventually, it was agreed that Prince Philip, already familiar with *Conway*, would perform the opening ceremony.

> *"Well that was a good excuse for more stone picking. Every bit of grass round the New Block had hundreds of cadets crawling on their hands and knees picking up every stone that was in sight for days on end. We were convinced some sadistical b***d was putting them back down as soon lights out went."*

6th May 1964 was set for the official opening ceremony. It was decided that the Duke would pay a quick visit to Indefatigable to celebrate their centenary en route to *Conway*. It was an overcast day but earlier rain had moved away. The visit was timed to perfection. At 12.00 pm sharp, the cadets fell in by divisions on the parade deck facing the figurehead, the opposite way to normal so they would be facing the Duke as he came along the main drive from *Indefatigable*. He arrived at 12.10 pm, accompanied by the Marquis who was Deputy Lord Lieutenant of Anglesey. The Duke was

"How Long Have You Been a Cadet?"

The Formal Opening Ceremony

introduced to Sir John Nicholson (chairman of the management committee) and then Captain Hewitt. A general salute was ordered and the Royal standard was broken at the truck. He then inspected the parade and stopped at one of the shortest boys to asked how long he'd been a cadet, not realising he was a brand new new chum.

"My eye's jogged from side to side as I counted the hours since I'd joined. Then, while he waited for an answer I asked myself was it four days or three? Did I need to clear my throat? Did I need to add 'Sir' to the end of my answer? I realized that HRH was probably a master of mental telepathy so I'd better get it right. As I prevaricated the smile on Hewitt's face gradually became more tight lipped. I finally decided that it would be OK to say something regardless of the truth: 'Three days.... Sir.' "

HRH moved on to take the salute at a march past as the band thundered away in their best tradition. Lunch was in the Captain's house with the dignitaries and their wives plus the Headmaster, Mrs Holt (widow of Lawrence Holt) and Mr. and Mrs Harding (vice chairman of the committee). After lunch HRH and party met the architect, builder and others associated with the development, inspected the fine model of the Ship installed on the quarterdeck and Gordon Ellis's splendid mural of the Ship. He moved to the platform on the Assembly Hall to declare the New Block open and addressed the assembled cadets and visitors, observing that *Conway* reflected his personal belief that

"Education is not a system for accumulating facts, it must prepare people to meet the responsibilities and challenges of civilised life."

In very good spirits and obviously enjoying his visit he unveiled a commemorative plaque on the quarterdeck and toured the New Block and the dock where cadets were frantically sailing, pulling and motoring every one of the 26 small boats. No-one capsized, collided or ran aground (for a change). Finally, at 3.25 pm, HRH went ashore from the parade deck, cadets giving him a resounding send off. Everything went according to plan, cadets were given an extra day's leave and at last the building was open.

Conway originally opened on 17th August 1859 with just 17 cadets in a small warship on the Mersey, and no grounds. Her founders could never have imagined that 105 years later over 300 cadets would be assembled outside a purpose built modern building on the Menai Strait surrounded by acres of playing fields and with a fleet of small boats. Her cadets had established a world-class reputation; wherever there were ships you would find on the bridge a *Conway* boy. The staff who had lived through the loss of the Ship, the tents and the uncertainties of the previous 10 years could never have foreseen what Captain Hewitt and Wg. Cdr. Browne would achieve. It was more like a miracle than a new beginning. It's difficult to imagine the monumental effort of will it must have taken Captain Hewitt to pick himself up from the loss of the ship, to persevere and arrive at this proud day. It must have seemed the absolute pinnacle of *Conway's* achievements. It probably was, and for now, a seemingly bright and promising future beckoned. Yet another phase of *Conway's* life was beginning.

HRH with Ship's Model

Leaving The Mess Deck

CHAPTER 32

1964 A TOUR OF THE STONE FRIGATE

The New Block was designed to accommodate approximately 230 cadets, but the mess deck and galley had to cater for up to 350, allowing for staff and a 100 or so cadets from the Nelson Block. The access road from the Kelvin Block approached from the south at right angles to the frontage and the building was well screened by woodland, so there was no grand, sweeping view of the buildings. Once onto the parade deck the imposing building emerged although a narrow band of trees hid the strait from view. How much more impressive it would have been if it had faced the strait as originally intended. Anglesey limestone proving too expensive, all exterior walls were rendered in a roughcast finish naturally coloured grey to match local stone as closely as possible.

The New Block and Chapel in 1972 With The Strait Visible Top Right

It was aligned broadly north-south, parallel to the strait and was 'H' shaped. The eastern side (left above) was the two storey entrance hall flanked by single height classroom blocks. The west side (right above) was the five storey accommodation wing. The mess deck/assembly hall and galley, with laboratories above linked the east and west buildings.

The parade deck was used for morning divisions. At the north end, the figurehead had been remasted facing down the deck, under a carefully preserved oak tree. The figurehead is now at HMS Nelson,

Portsmouth. At the south end, the main topmast and topgallant mast, purchased from the Ship's breakers by Brookie, had been stepped together with a yard and gaff. In the photo the yard and gaff have been removed for repair and are lying under the tree bottom right. A safety net allowed cadets to go aloft. To the west of the parade deck was the 1st XV rugby pitch.

The New Block was entered through a columned porch of Portland Stone and three pairs of glass panelled doors over which was inscribed, in capital letters, John Masefield's verses written for the centenary celebrations in 1959.

The Ship's bell was hung outside to the left of the entry porch. Timekeeping bells were rung by the duty cadet.

The doors led to a spacious entrance hall always called the quarterdeck. A splendid large model of the Ship (now in the Royal Navy Museum, Portsmouth), post room and staff room were on the left. The duty cadet captain's and messenger's room and a waiting room were on the right. The log and leave book were kept here. Stairs either side of the entrance led up to the Captain's, Headmaster's and other offices on the first floor. The Ship's wheel was on the top landing, although this too is now displayed at the Royal Navy Museum. Captain Hewitt's insistence on this office mezzanine floor had created a bright three storey space magnificently filled by Gordon Ellis's 16 foot by 10 foot painting of the Ship at Rock Ferry. It remains in place to this day; and every child visiting the *Conway* Centre receives a brief explanation of the painting and *Conway* in general. The painting was the privately commissioned gift of Mr. Leslie Harding (the Vice Chairman of the committee and partner in Bibby Brothers and Co) in 1963, especially for the New Block entrance. He wanted to ensure that, as first hand memories of the Ship passed away, there would be some tangible reminder of *Conway's* origins for future cadets. Mr. Harding chose the highly appropriate words, which hang with the painting, from the 1660 Navigation Act:

The Parade Deck

Top: Main Entrance
Below: Entrance and Painting

New Block Floor Plan

'IT IS UPON SHIPS AND SAILORS UNDER THE GOOD PROVIDENCE OF GOD THAT OUR WEALTH, SAFETY AND STRENGTH CHIEFLY DEPEND."

Words that, which still ring true today but with an import that would soon be ignored by politicians.

Side doors led through inner lobbies (with a small office and staff head) to the north and south classroom wing but cadets were not allowed to use these short cuts. In fact most cadets rarely visited the quarterdeck other than for the end-of-term ritual of team and class photos.

The 2 classroom wings were mirror images of each other. 8 classrooms along a central corridor, 5 facing the parade deck and small heads either side of a central rear access door. They were numbered S1 to 8 and N1 to 8. One south classroom housed an extensive library. In each wing 2 classrooms could be opened into one larger room.

Another set of double doors on the quarterdeck gave access to the double height combined mess deck and assembly hall used for meals, evening divisions, prize days and other such events. It was 90 feet long and 49 feet wide with rows of dark oak tables and benches, neatly laid out but swept smartly aside for evening divisions. At the quarter deck end was a small dais where staff could eat, although they also had a private wardroom to one side. A stage, 45 feet wide and 20 feet deep, fitted with lighting and sound systems occupied the opposite end of the mess deck. There was a large storage area under the stage – soon in use by 'Spider' Webb's rock band for practice sessions. While 'our' mess tables are still used, the benches are now stored under the stage. A risk assessment apparently indicated they represent too great a risk for modern children safely to negotiate, so each child now has a nice safe single seat! Where a *Conway* cadet was trusted implicitly to climb

The Mess Deck

The Laboratories

a 60 foot mast or steer a rowing crew unsupervised through miles of rough seas, modern children cannot be trusted to negotiate a wooden bench unsupervised! Traditional wood panelling was everywhere but the large, circular lighting chandlers had a modern '60s' feel to them. Very large windows at first floor level lined both sides of the mess deck, making it very light and airy. Side doors on the north side gave access to the large modern galley and servery, above which was accommodation for the galley staff. An open corridor on the south side provided access to a paved terrace and grassy area where the chapel would later be built.

Above the mess deck, accessible from the quarterdeck and aft deck, were three fully equipped labs, a lecture theatre with stepped seating, a dark room and work room.

The mess deck's south corridor also led to backstage or the aft deck, a double height open area around the back of the stage with coat racks for wet weather gear and a glass topped display case used for news and items of interest. Stairs led up to the labs above the hall with heads on a small landing. The central heating and hot water boiler room and an electricity sub station were beneath.

The sloping nature of the site required a long, wide triple flight of stairs with short intermediate landings, leading from back stage down to the cadets' accommodation wing. Although parallel to the strait there were, at best, only partial glimpses of water from this wing as the foreshore had not been cleared of trees as originally planned. The stairs led down to the south end of the building. To the right was a 5 storey tower containing a lift, absolutely out of bounds to cadets who were expected to use the stairs, the Chief Officer's cabin and a connection to the Captain Superintendent's house. To the left a very long corridor ran the whole length of the wing to another tower with Matron's cabin and a small first aid room on the ground floor. Along one side of this corridor were in turn, Foretop and Focsle common rooms, the cadet captains' gun room, an ante room, games room, reading room and finally, Maintop and Mizzentop common rooms. Half-way down on the left, in an annex, were large locker/changing rooms, 2 drying rooms, 24 hand wash basins, 20 showers and 12 heads shared by all cadets.

The 4 upper floors were all dormitory floors identical in layout, with 2 dormitories per floor. Each floor was the preserve of a single top and the old tradition of visitors having to request 'top please' before entering was preserved. At the centre of the building, between each pair of dormitories and over the ground floor ablutions, was a washroom and heads and a large trunk store. Mizzentop's trunk room was the chief cadet captain's cabin, provided with the fine wooden dining table. At the south end of each floor was a small self-contained family flat for members of staff. The north end provided 2 bachelor cabins, each with a small sitting room, bed recess and bathroom.

The House remained unaltered but the old washrooms at the Kelvin Block were changed into classrooms; the 2 huts there were renovated as navigation and seamanship rooms. The gym was improved.

Conway was originally housed in a sixth rate frigate, then a fourth rate frigate, finally a second rate ship of the line. Now, she was undeniably a first rate stone frigate. What might be achieved with such glorious facilities?

Accommodation Wing

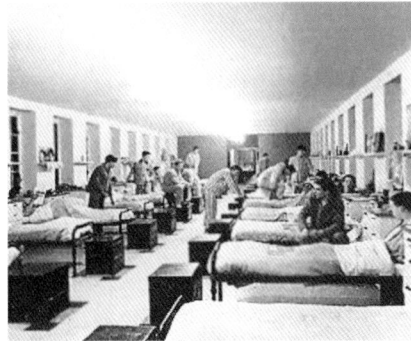

A Typical Dormitory

CHAPTER 33

1964–68 STONE FRIGATE DAILY ROUTINE

Reveille.

The day began at 6.30 am (6.45 am in winter) with reveille played upon the bugle.

> *"The Duty Bugler used to have to get himself up and be on station outside the port changing rooms door in the New Block five minutes before reveille. Bugler's dress was pyjamas with reefer jacket and cap. I would warm the mouthpiece in water beforehand as it was often bitterly cold."*

As reveille sounded, there was a mad dash for the heads as the duty officer (later the duty master) marched through the dorms calling a variation on

> *"Wakey, wakey, rise and shine,"*

or

> *"Show a leg, show a leg, show a leg,"*

or

Front of The New Block 1964

> *"the sun's burning your eyes outside"*

for the benefit of any loafers. Those under punishment of an early heave out were up 30 minutes earlier doing physical exercises as expiation of their sins. A new chum recalls his first morning:

> *"Woken at 6.30 am by a loud bugle rendition of reveille to find an ancient mariner (Mr. Drake, the Foretop divisional officer) in his uniform striding through the dormitory yelling 'Hands Off Cocks, on Socks' followed up by a threat that 'the last man standing will receive an Early Heave Out,' a rude awakening in many ways!"*

Morning Run

All hands then dashed to the lower car park for an en-mass run, often in pitch darkness and freezing winds, up the main drive to the anchor light that hung on a post half way up the drive. If it was *very* bad weather everyone did PT outside their common room on the ground floor corridor.

The duty motorboat crew were excused the run and went straight to breakfast before doubling down to the dock. There they rowed the skiff out to the mooring, no matter what the weather or water conditions, and picked up the motorboat for the morning run to Port Dinorwic to collect the reading room and masters' papers, not to mention the illicit cigarette orders.

Wash and Make Beds

The day started with a fast wash and brush up, beds were made and gear stowed, the dormitory was prepped and cleaned.

Standard Royal Navy uniform was worn at all times. 'No.8s' were the normal daily working rig, blue shirts, a blue 'woolly pulley' and long trousers in the winter, shorts, long socks and shirtsleeves in the summer. Shirtsleeves had to be folded up very neatly and equally, not just rolled in a slapdash way, shorts and long socks had to be of regulation length, hair had to be kept short and, despite being seamen, beards were not allowed, even for those who could manage to grow one! Everyone wore a clasp knife on a lanyard with a single wide blade, a fold out marlin spike, and a black handle with cross hatching to improve the grip when wet.

> *"They were used for rope work in seamanship lessons and boat work, and great for carving one's initials on the Marquis of Anglesey's trees. The fold-out marlin spike came in handy for splicing work, making complex knots like a monkey's fist and undoing shackle pins."*

On Sundays and for going ashore No 1 dress reefers were worn with a spotless white lanyard around the neck under the collar and looped into the top pocket, slack for plebs, and bar tight across the lapels for QBs and rates. White shirts with detachable starched collars were worn so every cadet had an invaluable collection of front and back studs without which the collars could not be fixed to the shirts. We even had the odd wing collar for special occasions. Best shoes were 'spit and polished' by hand, sometimes for hours, until the toe caps were better than mirrors. The greatest crime was to stand on a chum's polished toes.

> *"40 years on, at a reunion, we all looked down to see beautifully polished shoes, a few with exemplary shiny toe-caps. Old habits die hard!"*

Cooks to the Galley

The bugler sounded '1ˢᵗ G', which summoned the duty cooks to the galley.

> *"We all had to take turns doing 'cooks,' laying the mess, fetching the grub from the galley, cleaning up etc. Each mess had a junior cadet captain in charge and our junior cadet captain demanded immaculate manners; we were not allowed to make chip butties, we had to eat jam sandwiches cut into quarters, we couldn't start before he did, and when he finished, so did we. It was like dining with the Queen!"*

Breakfast and Meals

While the cooks were doing their stuff everyone else assembled back stage to wait for the bosun's call, which at 7.00 am would finally summon them to flood in for the meal.

The bosun's bell was sounded by the chief cadet captain so ensure quiet before grace, gabbled through by the duty cadet:

> *"Bless this food O Lord, for the support of our bodies, and grant our souls Thy heavenly grace. No 'Amen,' just the scrape and crash of wooden benches and the clatter of cutlery as the cooks for each mess dashed to the galley to collect the first course from the galley trogs."*

Messes were tables of 8 cadets, usually seated top to bottom in order of seniority, which was the same direction in which the food was passed down once delivered from the galley by the duty cook. A typical breakfast was eggs of some form perhaps with bacon, ham or sausage, a loaf of sodduck (bread) along with 'grease' (butter) and 'spread' (jam). Sugar butties were a favourite. Milk and hot water were provided to make instant coffee or skilly (tea) in giant skilly pots. There never was enough food so you learnt to eat very quickly so your cook could get back to the serving area in case there was any 'spare.' Every meal, finished with another grace.

During breakfast, the post cadet captain would arrive and start laying out the mail on the top tables.

> *"Following grace we sat expectantly while he called out the names of those with letters or, better still, parcels. Parcels normally meant extra food!"*

Others found way to generate their own mail.

> *"For a laugh I wrote to the Chinese Embassy and asked for a copy of Chairman Mao's Little Red Book. They must have thought they'd penetrated the Royal Navy as a large box full arrived soon after. I panicked, expecting to be suspected of subversion."*

Every cadet had a small display space above their bunk where they were expected to create a personal display.

> *"In 1967, someone had the bright idea of writing to airlines and embassies masquerading as the 'HMS Conway Travel Club' and asking for posters. Soon the dorms began to look like travel agent shops, with huge posters everywhere. It all came to a guilty halt when the Irish Embassy sent boxes and boxes of travel literature."*

Clean Ship/Boat Work

After breakfast, time was allocated to 'sweeps.' Every cadet fit for work and not on some other duty cleaned their allotted part of the buildings.

Every day one of the divisions provided the cutter or gig crew for early morning rowing.

> *"A quick double down to the dock was followed by a row along the strait, either towards Indefatigable and the Britannia Bridge, or towards Port Dinorwic where we could gaze up the long garden walk cut by the Marquis through his woods with a stone bench over looking the strait."*

If the sea or weather was very bad the crew emulated the 'heavy duty cutters crew' of old and replaced the duty motorboat crew for the run to Port Dinorwic.

> *"It was a long row to PD, especially against the tide or in winter when your hands froze to the oar shanks and one's buttocks became numb from the cold wooden thwart, your exhaled breath would be thick about the boat as the coxswain upped the stroke against the tide. Battling a large cutter oar at 18-20 strokes per minute single handed was very hard work."*

In finer weather, the crew might steal a few minutes ashore.

"Port Dinorwic was just a few long terraces of granite cottages and the café/shop where we picked up the papers and fags. The dock then was derelict. It was an old slate dock, built out of slate and with slate debris and rusty machinery everywhere, and the tracks of the old narrow gauge railway line, which ran up into the mountains to the Llanberis Dinorwic Quarries, once the largest in the world. One morning we followed the rails past the lock gates and the tidal dock up to the dry dock, which was completely filled by the St Trillo, a trip boat, which still made occasional transits of the strait. The railway line disappeared into a small tunnel under the main road but we didn't have the time to go any further."

Motor Boat Picking Up Boat Crews

"I was coxswain of No 1 during my last term and did the daily paper (and fag) run to PD. We used to have a mug of tea and some toast followed by a fag in the café at PD before heading back. One particular Sunday we spent longer than usual in the café, but not to worry it was a rising tide. After the leisurely break we all sauntered outside to find No.1 high and dry, half on and half off the slip. It was an ebb tide. Coxswain (me) now in major panic mode. What to do? After a few minutes a workboat motored passed, I took command of the situation and flagged him down. Entering into a non-Lloyds Open Form Salvage agreement (packet of fags) he pulled the boat off. Everyone leapt onboard and we started up at full ahead to regain time. Terrible vibration so had to slow down. Turns out the shaft was bent whilst aground. Swore aforesaid crewmembers to silence. I got away with it, although no one could work out why No.1 suffered from vibration all of a sudden. I awaited the dawn knock of the Marine Accident Investigation Branch with trepidation. Is there a statute of limitations on these things?

"My No. 2 boat crew smuggled contraband from Port Dinorwic on a grand scale, in fact I still watch the news to see whether any names I recall are linked to the latest container load of illegals unearthed at Dover!"

"A classic prank was to send some unsuspecting new chum to report to the bosun as 'Skiff's Engineer': poor victim would find himself in charge of a one-man rowboat. (Don't ask me how I know)."

'Flags and Clocks' was another duty.

"I had the job for 2 terms. What a doss it was! I remember having to sit in Dhobi Clarke's cabin, await the 8 o'clock signal on the radio, then note the variation of the chronometer, set my watch, and then check all the clocks in the ship and hoist the signal of the day. If the chronometer was more than about 2 minutes out I used to unscrew the bezel and move the hands to a more accurate setting. Not the best thing to do to a precision instrument."

The flag locker was in the Kelvin Block.

"It was on the right as you went through the archway. It was very handy for ducking out of cross-country runs and I spent most of my time there when I should have been elsewhere. There was a fireplace in the room, so

on Saturday, if the film was no good, a select few would gather up the sodduck and spread after the evening meal, take it down to the flag locker, make a fire and have toast and jam."

The signal of the day was an ongoing convention.

"I made up a few dubious signals, which amazingly where not picked up on. One in particular was 'I have lost my anchor two miles west of Liverpool pier head' This would have placed it somewhere in the middle of Birkenhead! All through my last term I was hoisting similarly inventive signals and no one ever noticed."

Divisions

Morning Divisions

At 8.45 am, another 'G' was sounded prior to Divisions held outside on the parade deck (inside on the mess deck only if it was pouring). Cadets fell in by port and starboard watches facing the mast, Focsle nearest to the figurehead and the band to one side by the mast. Tallest cadets were on the ends of each rank, the smallest in the middle in order to present a graceful curving outline of heads rather a random series of peaks and troughs. Platoon cadet captains would call their platoon to attention and 'dress them off' so they were also neatly spaced. The chief cadet captain was in charge of the parade and issued most orders.

"We would stand to attention for the raising of the Conway ensign to the sound of the bugle. The Colours were raised to the top of the mast, except on sombre occasions such as the death of the former King, the Duke of Windsor."

The Captain Superintendent, accompanied by the duty officer, would take the parade. After 1968 they were replaced by the duty master on weekdays and the Headmaster on Sundays. At one point each platoon cadet captain had to double over to the chief cadet captain and line up to report any absences. They would step forward, salute, make their report, salute again and return to their platoon. Salutes were always the Royal Navy way, 'long way up, short way down,' hand open flat but parallel to the ground and angled so the saluted person could see only the back of the hand and not the palm.

"Dhobi Clark, being an Royal Navy man, was always very smart at this manoeuvre. Some of the Merchant Navy master mariners were a bit more haphazard."

Saluting apparently took its rise historically as a show of empty hands demonstrating that the 'visitor' was not armed. The Navy, being completely trustworthy, did not need to show an empty hand like the other services and so deliberately tilted the palm away from sight. The poor chief cadet captain had instantly to memorise long lists of cadets missing on duty, in boat's crews, sick or not on parade for other reasons. Once all the reports were in the chief cadet captain marched over and reported the whole list to the duty officer who was standing close enough to have overheard the original reports and so was able to validate a full and accurate report. The occasional loud rebuff to the chief cadet captain for a missed name was quietly appreciated by the assembled cadets. The chief cadet captain ordered *"Parade - Off Caps"* which was performed in perfect unison with 300 cadets silent chanting *"up, two, three, down"* to remove their caps. Prayers followed, led by the padre and then *"Parade - On Caps"* to the same furtive chanting. The Captain Superintendent or duty officer might make an announcement then a march past was ordered. The bass drum thumped out the rhythm, the band stepped off with a stirring roll of drums, crash of cymbals and a medley of bugle notes vaguely approximating to the chosen tune, followed smartly by each platoon in turn. The parade marched around the parade deck with *"Eyes Right"* then *"Eyes Front"* ordered as each platoon passed and saluted the Captain Superintendent who returned the salute. Mr. Lord recalls his first Divisions in command. He wore his gown and doffed his mortar board to each salute but decided this was a bit ridiculous and stopped. After Divisions cadets were dismissed to school.

School and Staff

School was from 9.00 am to 4.30 pm, with a morning break at 11.00 am and lunch at mid-day. 'O' level classes included a mix of academic subjects English, Maths, Physics, Geography, Chemistry, History or Spanish. Spanish was the logical foreign language for seamen given its spread across Central and South America and in other pockets around the world. Technical O/OA level subjects included Marine Science, Seamanship and Navigation. 'A' level classes were mainly English, Maths and Physics and completed in one year. It was not unusual for cadets to leave with 10-12 good O levels passes and 2-3 good 'A' level passes.

> *"We had a rum mixture of masters and divisional officers but all were on the whole good fellows once you got to know them."*

The Headmaster was Basil Lord known as 'Basil,' 'Lordy' and 'Foxey' after a TV hand puppet of the time called Basil Brush. Geoff Fozard was a short, plump man with a sleek, black, brylcreamed hairdo and a Latin look, naturally he taught Spanish (later he was also the Focsle divisional master).

> *"He had a parrot in his cabin, a mean spirited bird which would dive bomb you with shit when provoked."*

Mr. 'Dodo' Woolley, had a habit of rubbing his hands as if washing them, while licking his lips and then adjusting his glasses, which were heavy rimmed. He was the studious sort, very intelligent and had various degrees and PhDs; he taught marine science. Maintop divisional master in later years was 'Booooks' Barker, so named because of the way he said

> *"Get your booooks out lads."*

He was a very commanding individual with a heavy Scouse accent. He used to frown on cadets making chip butties or 'chipped potato sandwiches' as he called them. He taught physics. Mr. Paul Kingsford, 'Ning Ning' to some, 'Sping' to others was the ardent coach of the rugby colts who exhorted us to play with

> *"fire in your bellies."*

He taught history by rote with huge lists and anagrams to help us remember them. He was ex-army and had fought at Alamein. He was not a man to be crossed and usually exuded authority as he strode around the school. Others of note were 'Sprogs' Carter – maths teacher, an older Yorkshireman whose lips caused him to spit as he talked and who, without his hearing aid, was deaf as a post.

"Then there was 'Lads' Goodey who looked decidedly Mexican. He taught maths and sport and always, as we thought, bullshitted about his exploits climbing the north face of the Eiger and Everest. That was until we saw a National Geographic TV programme featuring 'Lads' striding ahead of an Eiger expedition with his faithful black labrador dog. It transpired that he and his wife were both well respected climbers."

Then there was 'Dithery Dan' who taught Geography.

"I cannot remember his real name but he was a very skinny man with a terrible shaking affliction as he chain smoked his way through classes, with Players No 6. We liked him as you could sneak a fag in the back of his room unobserved or more likely un-cared about."

After the Reverend Turner left in 1969, the new Padre was the Rev. Alex Harrison. Seconded from the Missions to Seamen, he was a tall man, ex RAF with a gold-toothed smile, slicked hair and oily smile. He coached the bantams rugby team.

Dhobi Clark With Princess Marina Inspecting Cadets at Llandudno

The naval or technical staff wore uniform most of the time. Maintop divisional officer, Lt. Cdr. 'Dhobi' Clarke, was ex Royal East African Navy.

"He spoke with the heaviest naval officers' accent drawing out all the words for expression. He was a very good navigation master."

He took his divisional officer's duties more seriously than most, regularly briefing his cadet captains on their duties and the behaviour he expected of them. It showed, as Maintop were frequently winners or runners up in inter-divisional competitions. 'Boo Boo' Davidson was Focsle divisional officer; short, stocky and quietly spoken, quite unassuming in his manner.

"He was my favourite. He wore second mate's uniform, he had a terrible stutter especially when aroused, when he would say Buh-Buh Buh Bloody Hell boy, hence his nick name. Foretop divisional officer was Geoff Drake, he had the most extraordinary vocabulary and a strange drawling way of talking."

Mizzentop divisional officer was Lt. Commander John Brooke Smith, 'Brookie' the Ship's longest serving officer. He and his family were *Conway* legends, his father was a *Conway*, and so were three of his brothers. He loved the old Ship and *Conway* was his whole life. He wore round glasses and a smile never seemed to be far from his face. He had a nasty a habit of appearing when you least wanted him to, hence his earlier nickname of 'Spookie.' He was slow to rouse, almost gentle most of the time, but very forceful when he found slackness or ill discipline. 'Gonk' Barratt was a bearded, fat squeaky voiced Merchant Navy officer who wore the same blue suit all year without cleaning it and suffered terrible dandruff. He was the inspiration for the 1st XV's team mascot. He had a penchant for teaching self defence by instructing us to carry, at all times, umbrellas and rolled up newspapers to, as he put it,

"Jab-em-in the balls."

Afternoon Tea

Small bottles of milk and cakes were served outside, behind the galley block after lessons.

Sports and Free Time

Pool 1963

The rest of the afternoon was devoted to activities and sports on Wednesdays. Any free time was filled by visits to the canteen, lazing around, hobbies or cleaning your gear. In the summer term the outdoor seawater pool was popular, so long as it hadn't filled up with jellyfish.

"Ordinary cadets weren't allowed radios but the rates had radio and record players and we listened to the music of the time."

In 1970, afternoon classes and sports sessions were reversed so classes ran until dinner.

Dinner

A single 'G' around 6.15 pm called cooks to the galley, followed by the evening meal.

Preparation

After dinner, a 'G' announced prep from 7.00 pm to 9.00 pm Each class retired to their classroom under the supervision of a cadet captain and worked in studied silence. Talking or messing about quickly earned punishments of early heave outs or extra watches.

"Request to go to the heads was normally refused so we all learned to control our bladders."

During late afternoon/evening, 'Sunset' would be sounded by the bugler in time with the duty watch keeper lowering the colour from the mast.

"One chap thought it would be interesting to see how fast I could play Sunset, lowering the colours at rate of knots to my frantic rendition. Needless to say we both got extra watches, which gave us plenty of time to get it correct."

Any cadets in sight of the ensign turned to face the mast, stood to attention and saluted.

Evening Divisions

Another 'G' summoned cadets to the mess deck for a final parade. Evening Divisions assembled in long lines, Focsle at the front then Foretop, Maintop, and Mizzentop. Whereas Focsle were under the constant gaze of the Captain Superintendent and duty officer at the front, Mizzentop could relax somewhat out of sight at the back. Once again absences were reported via the chief cadet captain to the duty officer. The list of duties for the next day were read out from a daily watch bill including the names of the duty officer, duty cadet captain and messenger, duty bugler, duty cutters crew, slack party, early heave outs an so on.

"The Padre would read some meaningful moral story and we were dismissed."

Rounds and Lights Out

After a quick check of sweeps to ensure all was neat and clean, everyone prepared for bed. The routine then was identical to that at the Camp, personal displays were expected to be in smartly laid out, bedding was to be neatly tucked in with just the right amount of sheet showing, cadets lay to attention in bed waiting for the final check of the day. The senior cadet captain waited at the dormitory entrance for the duty officer and chief cadet captain to arrive and, to a call of "Rounds" from the chief cadet captain the three of them would walk smartly through the dorm inspecting everything as they went and making sure every bed was occupied or accounted for.

Finally, the bugler sounded a final 'G' and the 'Last Post' at 10.00 pm to signal 'Lights Out.' No-one was now allowed to talk or get out of bed and the duty officer and chief cadet captain could be expected to prowl the dorms from time to time to ensure everything was in silent order. Some officers were noisy enough to warn of their approach and naturally found blissfully quiet dorms. Others seemed to sneak around on tip toe so that their voices would suddenly call out of the darkness awarding punishments left and right to those out of bed, talking or reading by torchlight under the bedclothes. Many dorm junior cadet captains allowed some quiet chat between neighbours, especially the QBs, but if things got too loud a bellow of 'Pipe Down' immediately delivered silence, or punishment for those who didn't respond quickly enough. The senior cadet captains in their cabins, attended by their valets would make toast and hot drinks, and visit each other to socialise. The chief cadet captain entertained in his cabin between the Mizzentop dorms. His valet usually had to traverse one or more floors to get there, evading the duty officer on the way in order to prepare new watch bills, write up the punishment books, make toast and generally sort out any problems from the day. The officer's knew the chief and senior cadet captains' day did not end with lights out and so seemed to give them and their valets some leeway. Even if caught they were rarely actually punished for being out of bed.

Saturday

Captain's Rounds

Mornings were similar to weekdays except there was more time for cleaning sweeps. After divisions it was Captain's Rounds at the dock, House and Kelvin Block. Captain Hewitt, telescope under arm, prowled every sweep in turn, accompanied by the chief cadet captain and the appropriate junior cadet captain. The cadet(s) responsible for maintaining it stood to attention in hapless anticipation of what he might find. Hours of effort might be nullified by a smear of polish or dusty corner. Every least comment was treated as a plus or minus point towards the inter-divisional Hobson's Cup. Once the shore sweeps had been inspected, the Captain embarked in the Captain's Gig to be rowed by the specially selected Captain's Gig Crew around every one of the 25 or so small boats on their moorings. The chief cadet captain coxed the gig, which had a marvellous brass tiller yoke and was expected to come smoothly alongside every boat, coming to a complete halt right alongside without touching, no matter what the conditions. No one was excused stress on this day! In every boat the crew were waiting to attention for inspection and a casual word could reward or destroy hours of scrubbing and polishing.

"We learned a hard and invaluable lesson. If a job was your responsibility it was 100% your responsibility. If you got it right you got the praise but stumble or fail and there was nowhere to hide."

Sports

Rugby, hockey, and cross country were the main winter sports, with sailing, athletics, cricket and tennis in the summer. Sailing often involved trips through the Swellies to Beaumaris with all the sailing dinghies towed behind a motorboat.

"Memories flood back of trying to right a dingy turned turtle in a huge blow off Beaumaris, and wondering who the hell thought it was a good idea for us to wear those heavy white naval woollen roll necks…at the age of 12, wet, it easily doubled my body weight!"

Boats to Beaumaris

Rugby was organised into teams by age group. The Padre coached the youngest boys who competed to play in the Bantams. Mr. Kingsford developed the next age group in the Colts. Finally Ken Baylis took the senior boys, who competed to play in the first and second XVs. The rugby strip was 10 horizontal bands of red and white but the 1st XV had just 4 broad bands of red and white. Those selected for teams who played well could be awarded colours for the sport at the end of term prize giving ceremony. Colours were a postcard sized white cloth badge with an appropriate crest, which could be sown onto a track suit. Outstanding 1st XV players received a red rugby cap with silver edging and a smart tassel, almost identical to that awarded to Welsh internationals to this day.

Tennis was played on the 3 courts alongside the athletics pitch and was always something of a minority sport. The coach was Mr. Fozard, often supported by Mr. Kingsford.

Athletics and cricket were mainly conducted on the large flat area below the Sports Pavilion, actually the top of the Marquis's private water reservoir. Some of the more dangerous events, like the javelin, were in a corner of the 1st XV rugby pitch.

Conway competed regularly against a number of schools including Langefni, Bangor Grammar, John Brights, Rydal (a private school in Colwyn Bay), Manchester Grammar, Wallasey, Friars, Lindisfarne and Ruthin School. The standard of rugby

was always good and cadets were regularly selected for Caernarfonshire (now Gwynedd) and North Wales school teams. The highlight of selection to any team were the away matches on the island, along the north Wales coast but sometimes as far afield as Liverpool, Manchester and Ruthin. Every winter the 1ˢᵗ XV played Pangbourne and *Worcester*, one at home and one away. This entailed a night away and these matches were always the hardest fought of the season. It was always more difficult playing away to Pangbourne and *Worcester* as *Conway* had no supporters to face down their assembled ship's company.

Evening

Saturday evening was often film-night. Everyone attended except for those under punishment on slack party. The mess deck was rearranged theatre style. The projector was a cranky noisy machine that had seen better days. At the end of each reel there was a quick pause to change reels, sometimes they had not been rewound before being sent and so started upside down. The poor operator had to endure loud jeering as he fumbled to rewind and reload the miscreant film. They were never particularly good films, 'Fire Down Below' was a regular, otherwise it was some grainy black and white Royal Navy training film or a promotional film from a shipping company.

Sunday

Morning

The morning was split between Divisions in No 1 uniform, followed by Captain's Rounds at the New Block. Every nook and cranny was inspected and judged.

Church

> *"I was i/c port classroom heads and spent many a morning, Brasso in hand, polishing the pipes till you could see your face in them. Then on Sunday rounds, standing at attention at the entrance to the heads when Basil poked his head through the door, grunted and said 'carry on,' the mixture of relief he had not found anything to criticize, and the frustration of yet again not having received a compliment that would count towards the Hobson Cup."*

Church followed Divisions in a large wooden hut below the Galley Block. It had been the messdeck hut at the Camp. The altar was set up in the middle and the padre conducted services from there. Captain and Mrs Hewitt sat opposite and the cadets sat in rows either side, facing along to the altar. QBs naturally sat at the back where they could feign indifference to proceedings.

> *"Hewitt had a strange way of kneeling for prayers, never on both knees. He knelt on one knee, rested his elbow on the other and then shielded his forehead with his hand."*

Today, the church hut is the *Conway* Centre's shop. Once the new chapel had been built by the *Conway* Club, services moved to that splendid building. After church was letter writing, prep, then lunch.

Afternoon

There was some official free time, unless you were under punishment. Most used it to 'make do and mend' – carry our repairs to clothing.

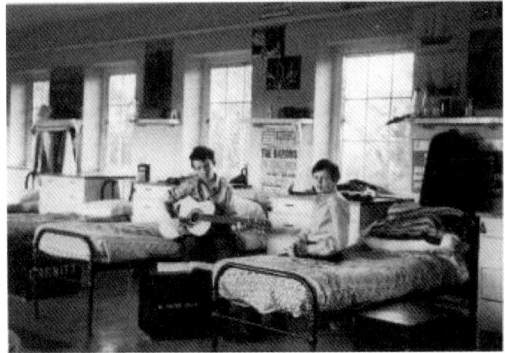

Spare Time in Focsle 1973

> *"We each had a little cloth bag called a 'housewife' but pronounced ' hussif,' full of needles and thread, scissors and other bits and pieces with which we could sew on buttons and make other running repairs to our clothes."*

A few had time to go ashore.

> *"After lunch we would fall in for the liberty boat (always made me laugh that, the liberty boat being the car park by the port dormitories)."*

If cadets passed muster with the duty officer they were given permission to 'go ashore' for a few hours. After 1968, weekends away were allowed twice per term.

> *"We could leave on Friday afternoon after school to stay with relatives and friends but had to be back by lights out on Sunday. Cadets from overseas or with no relatives to visit sometimes accompanied boys who lived nearby, but for those who stayed in school the daily routine was changed somewhat to allow a more relaxed weekend."*

Mountaineering Expeditions

These weekends continued to be very popular. Groups of 6-10 cadets would prepare an itinerary and set off from the ship on Friday afternoon, get themselves to the mountains where they would walk and scramble around their chosen itinerary. They would camp out for 2 nights and return to the ship on Sunday evening. Expeditions were written up and handed over to the Duty Officer for checking and filing. There were a few gash tents but cadets often just took their bed liners as make-shift hammocks, lashed them up in the trees and slept under the stars.

> *"I remember one weekend in 1967, a group of 4 of us camped on the hill way up above the Aber Falls. The slope was so steep our hammocks were at ground level at one end and about 5 feet up in the air at our feet! We were swinging away in our hammocks, yarning away in the silence of the Welsh mountains, fire burning quietly when the local forestry warden appeared demanding to know who we were and what the hell we thought we were doing with a fire on 'his' hillside. He was all set to turf us off but once he realised we were Conway cadets - we were allowed to stay!"*

There was no adult supervision, cadets were completely on their own, yet in almost 20 years no one ever was injured or needed rescuing.

Some cadets evolved the concept beyond that intended.

> *"2 of us more senior cadets used one such trip as a cover for a camping weekend with our dancing class partners in a quiet corner of a public park by the strait in Bangor. The rest of our party (younger cadets chosen with*

great care) were despatched into the mountains as planned. The 2 of us changed out of our mountaineering kit into smart civvies on the way into town. To the surprise of the rest of the group, when we reached Bangor we left them to their trek while we made for the park. We had a relaxing time with our young ladies, lazing in the sun, wandering along the foreshore, gazing across the strait and constructing our walking notes (based on an emotive vision of conditions in the mountains - and quick cross checks with the rest of our bemused group back in the ship on Sunday evening). On Saturday afternoon, knowing no fear, I sauntered into Bangor with my young lady on my arm without a care in the world. Unfortunately Mrs Lord had decided to go shopping that day. Wandering up the High Street we came face to face. I looked at her and nearly died, she looked at me - for a very, very long time (perhaps it was just the bright lobster colour I had turned), then at my partner, then back at me. I thought 'that's it, my promising career as an senior cadet captain is about to crumble....' Obviously being a very busy lady (and perhaps a bit short sighted?) she said nothing and walked on. Like the condemned man I made the best of the rest of the weekend and scuttled back to the ship on Sunday evening expecting the worst. Nothing happened. I awaited the deadly call from Lordy, Eric or Brookie all day on Monday. Nothing happened. After several more days of sweating nothing happened. What a nice lady."

Punishment

Members of staff were always around, but essentially the cadet captains continued to be responsible for running the ship and maintaining order. The cadet captains could award punishments to more junior cadets caught breaking the rules. A senior cadet captain could award greater punishment than a junior cadet captain. Most punishments were one or two 'early heave-outs' – being woken at 6ish to undergo rigorous physical exercise, 'slack parties' which meant undertaking the dirtiest jobs needing to be done, or 'extra watches,' which usually had miscreants on duty when other chaps were at the pictures, relaxing or doing whatever they did on a Saturday evening or Sunday afternoon. All punishments had to be recorded in the punishment book kept by the chief cadet captain's valet. The chief cadet captain monitored entries to ensure no one was being singled out unfairly and that punishments fitted the crimes. Once a week the Captain Superintendent inspected the book. Woe betide the chief cadet captain if Captain Hewitt found any whiff of impropriety.

More serious offences merited attendance at a formal process in the Gun Room. The chief cadet captain adjudicated. The offender was marched in and the alleged offence read out. The awarding cadet captain would explain the reasons for the charge and the offender was invited to offer an explanation. The chief cadet captain might dismiss the charge, issue a warning or award a punishment. The difference with the Gun Room was that punishment could include up to six strokes or 'cuts' with the teaser. In many public schools at the time prefects were allowed to administer corporal punishment to other pupils. It was a dying practice and through the period at the New Block its use fell away until it stopped altogether.

"When I was chief petty officer I preferred not to use the teaser on some hard cases as they hardly considered it a punishment at all as it was too quick and easy. Slack parties and extra watches were much more effective because they took away a person's free time and left them to contemplate the error of their ways."

The teaser was a 2-3 foot length of thin rope, back spliced at one end to make it thicker and then 'whipped' (bound) with fine twine so it was pretty unbending. It was kept in a milk bottle of salt water, which stiffened it even more. The chief cadet captain nominated a senior cadet captain to deliver the cuts and the offender had to bend over in the Gun Room and receive them on the spot. It was pretty painful to receive just one stroke so six was a serious matter. When cuts were awarded one or two was the norm, six very rare. The teaser could bruise, even cut skin through trousers. After receiving the cuts there was the ritual of shaking hands to indicate a punishment fairly given and stoically received.

"On knocking on the gun room door and shouting out 'Gun room please' I entered where the chief cadet captain sat behind a large desk with the teaser in its bottle standing menacingly on it, and the punishment book in front of him. Also present were most if not all the senior cadet captains and the accusing cadet captain. The charge was read out and a response asked for. The punishment as I remember was a choice - 2 cuts or 4 days extra watches as runner during the week ends. I chose the cuts. This was administered by an senior cadet captain not of my division. I was required to bend down with the back of my head up against the wall so I couldn't 'ride' the stroke. The senior cadet captain swung it and hit my backside. He did seem to get some pleasure in being able to get the second one on top of the first, which was quite painful - in my case when I looked there was a welt which had split and was weeping a little."

Some cadets never received a cut, many learned the lesson and rarely reappeared, a few were repeat offenders and seemed not the least concerned.

"The teaser was always painful and sometimes a boy might not take it well. There were often tears in the eyes of recipients so as chief cadet captain I quickly learned to wield this hard justice with great care. Eric was always very thorough in his examination of teaser punishments and would cross examine some of my judgements very firmly."

Anyone promoted to cadet captain who had not received cuts as a punishment had to receive 3 cuts from a brother cadet captain as a warning of the pain he could inflict. Needless to say very few people managed to escape cuts before promotion.

To expect one boy to judge and then physically to beat another might be considered distasteful even barbaric today, but that was once the perfectly acceptable norm in schools across the country. Of all the hundreds of contributors to this book not one has claimed any lasting damage from the teaser.

QBs continued to exploit their positions with chores and impositions on the junior cadets. There was no organised or persistent serious bullying although some QBs might have used a lanyard to encourage a sluggardly cadet and more than one thump was administered for cheeking a senior or to settle a dispute.

QB Bags

As part of the seamanship exam, each cadet sewed himself a QB bag of canvas, yarn and rope. About 18 inches tall and 10 inches in diameter they required competent use of a sailor's palm to stitch the heavy canvas using a number of special stitches. The drawstring rope handle was decorated with a number of different styles of fancy knot work and the whole bag ornamented with inked patterns and pictures. They were useful bags and many wore out through over use before courses were finished.

Extra Certificate 1968

Terminal Course Reports

On completing his course, every cadet received a bound report of each term's progress and achievements in a blue covered Terminal Report and yellow covered Executive Report. Performance in every subject was commented on, and the Captain Superintendent added his own assessments of the term. Physical progress was also recorded with height, weight and chest measurements all carefully recorded. Those that qualified also received their *Conway* Passing Out Certificate.

End of Term

There was a prize-giving assembly on the last night of every term.

> *"After the evening meal the mess deck was cleared of tables and we all sat in long rows facing the stage. Eric would proceed to hand out prizes, sports colours etc., and of course appoint the cadet captains for the following term. (What I wonder is the collective noun for cadet captains? A punishment of cadet captains?). He'd call out the names and their appointments starting with the chief cadet captain. The honoured few would march smartly up to him, collect their badge, piece of cloth or whatever, perhaps receive a few chosen words, salute and march back to their places. These perambulations were all supported by varying degrees of wild cheering and clapping depending on how well the individual was regarded by the rest of the cadets."*

The last morning continued the well-worn ritual of an very early bus ride to Bangor station accompanied by discordant bugle blasts before boarding the reserved coaches in the train. All travel to or from *Conway* had to be in full No 1 reefer uniforms. Uniform and caps were surprisingly useful to smooth the buying of beer and cigarettes in the train's bar. At each stop, Crewe, Rugby, London. more and more cadets detrained and dispersed around the globe.

CHAPTER 34

1964–68 STONE FRIGATE YEARS

1963

The first chief cadet captain in the New Block was Tony Coates.

The old Hold division finally disappeared with the closure of the Camp and was relegated to an overflow dormitory (Mauritania) in the Nelson Block. If there were too many cadets for the divisional dormitories they were allocated to Mauritania instead, either individually or in pairs by cadet numbers.

"I had a Snipe sailboat and capsized in the strait in a real blow with Caldwell and nurse. She had a wooden leg (you could hear her 'clonk' around the halls of the house at night when she was doing her rounds). When we went over, her wooden leg got caught up in the centreboard housing and she almost drowned as the lee side went under water! Bit hair raising for a few minutes."

"I remember the utter confusion I caused as a new chum rowing a cutter for the first time. It was a different world, orders may as well have been in Serbo-Croat. I kept catching crabs, losing time, missing orders, how should I know that I was 'second bertha' and the cox was shouting at me? It got off to a bad start when we got into the boat. It was so cold the oars were frozen to the thwarts. I assumed we would just go back to the warmth of the House but no, we chipped the ice away and pulled up and down the strait in the extreme cold, in a stiff wind and with freezing waves breaking over the bows from time to time. Years later I toughened up and raced in my divisional cutter's crew. What a great start in life!"

Cutter Sailing

1964 Spring

Influenza struck the ship

"with a virulence we have only once before experienced since the war,"

noted the Headmaster. It affected cadets and staff alike. After a very taxing term, but unconnected with the previous term's illness, Sisters Griffiths and Hughes retired after 10 and 2 years service respectively. Both were thanked for their kindly ministrations and wholehearted participation in wider activities. They were replaced by Sister Evans.

The Duke of Edinburgh's Award Scheme was revived, perhaps influenced by HRH's attendance to open the buildings. 9 cadets began preparing for their awards, 3 cadets, Mike Warner, Marks and Mike Dunham, being selected to be one of 6 Englishmen to participate in the 1964 tall ships race in a square-rigger.

"4 of us wound up in Gorch Foch and 2 in Danmark. I had my seventeenth birthday halfway across the Atlantic on a square-rigger and, of course, my first ship to sea was square rigged. It took the holidays and a term so I missed my proper QB term and had to come back after my mob had left. It was a bit difficult after tasting real freedom but I think that I was unofficially cut a fair bit of slack!"

1964 May

There were 298 cadets. A group of 4 cadets spent 14 days aboard the Royal Navy frigates *Nubian* and *Londonderry* for a round trip cruise from Portsmouth to Lisbon. They watched the start of the tall ships race, in which *Conway* cadets were participating.

1964.

"In my first term we were given a couple of weeks grace to learn the ropes. Strange things like you can slouch, walk, march or double up (run) from the House to the edge of the Kelvin Block, you should walk smartly across the front of the Kelvin Block, but you must double from the Kelvin Block to the corner of the New Block and then only ever march ie in-step and with arms swinging smartly on the parade deck. Each of these legs being no more than a few hundred yards. Why?"

After your period of grace, any transgression of rules spotted by of a cadet captain could result in punishment, often cuts from the teaser delivered after a mini court marshal in the gun room.

"I remember getting unofficial cuts on a number of occasions, administered almost exclusively by lanyard - not nearly as bad as official teaser cuts, but sore enough given that invariably I was wearing pyjamas."

'Spud' Murphy retired after nearly 26 years unbroken service teaching navigation and as the editor of the cadet magazine. *Conway* cadets around the world owed their navigating ability to his teaching. He retired to continue his other love, as an alderman of Beaumaris.

Mayor's Parade Bangor 1966

'Greasy' Fozard taught Spanish.

"He swept into our first lesson in his gown and said 'I am going to teach you Spanish. This is the last time I will address you in English. Siéntese."

Bemused at first,

"we very quickly learned the meaning of sit and stand, how to enquire and respond about the weather and how to ask a person's name and tell them your own. That's really all I ever took in."

"The choice in my day was between Spanish and History. I chose History because Mr. Kingsford was guaranteed to get you through 'O' level. Can't help feeling that Spanish would have been more useful for a life at sea though"

Cadet D Jones (61-63) presented a new drum major's mace.

Mr. Basil Lord MA joined as Headmaster and was immediately thrown into the complexities of preparing for the introduction of the new Ordinary National Diploma (OND) in Nautical Studies. Cadets now had a number of ways to qualify for a life at sea:

- Those not expecting to achieve four 'O' level GCE passes could work towards a *Conway* Leaving Certificate (Ordinary, First Class or Extra).

- Those achieving four 'O' levels qualified to spend two or three terms post 'O' levels to work towards Part 1 of the OND and a *Conway* Leaving Certificate.

- To spend an additional 6 terms post 'O' level working towards 'A' levels and a *Conway* Leaving Certificate.

1965

The first OND course in Nautical Studies started as a one term course culminating in an examination for Part 1 of that qualification. It was anticipated that Parts 2 and 3 would be completed post *Conway* and prior to obtaining a second mate's ticket, and that some would progress to the Higher National Diploma, even a BSc in Marine Studies.

Cadet J Blattman won first prize in an essay competition organised by the Seafarer's Association and the College of the Sea.

The Royal Navy offered free flying scholarships during the holidays to *Conway* cadets over 16 years of age and with 3 'O' levels.

New Chums Fall in at The House

One of the year's new chums reflected on his experiences.

"Conway taught us team work, to be competitive, loyal yet adaptable. When I joined the Ship I suddenly found myself part of a number of peer groups and had to balance the seeming irreconcilable loyalties these placed on me. First there were my term-mates, the 30 or so boys who had joined with me and who would remain together for our 2 year course. As new chums it was us against the world, especially during the first few weeks grace when we had to learn the ropes, customs and practices. Each of us was also allocated to one of 4 divisions. Each division thus had cadets ranging from the rawest new chums to the most seasoned QBs, but we shared an absolute loyalty to our top and each other. We shared dormitories, paraded together, were responsible for the maintenance and cleanliness of discrete areas of the ship and we competed in sports against other tops. This top loyalty cut right across the natural bonds with my term-mates. Other peer groups and loyalties coalesced around sports teams, boat crews, hobbies and personal interests. In our final terms some of us became cadet captains, responsible for preserving 'law and order', while the rest remained QBs committed to breaking and circumventing every rule. I learned to accommodate these conflicting demands. Survival obliged me to be flexible and adaptable, to compete fiercely with an individual one moment, say in a rowing race, but defend him equally robustly moments later as a member of my term and then accept that as individuals we might differ greatly in our approach to the rules. I never found it difficult to reconcile these conflicting expectations. It benefited me throughout my life."

And You'll Find on the Bridge a Conway Boy
Robert 'Ian' Jackson (1965-68)

A Typical Day at The Office

Ian left Conway when the British shipping industry was in serious decline and a lifetime at sea was no longer guaranteed. He joined one of the best companies, Cunard Brocklebank, later moving to Kuwait Shipping and then Texaco in London doing demurrage work. In 1976 he came ashore and joined HM Coastguard serving at St Anne's Head in Milford Haven, Oban and Liverpool before moving to Walton on Naze as District Controller of Thames CG in 1989.

After 18 years, he transferred to the Maritime and Coastguard Agency as a Counter Pollution and Salvage Officer in the Eastern Region, covering from Berwick to Portland Bill. His work involves auditing ports for Oil Pollution, Preparedness, Response and Co-operation Convention compliance and assisting authorities with counter pollution planning and exercises. He is part of the UK response team for pollution and salvage incidents within UK area of jurisdiction working with the Secretary of State's Representative for Marine Salvage and Intervention (SOSREP) or the Counter Pollution branch of the MCA. As part of the team Ian acts as the on call officer for the whole of the UK for a week at a time, taking the first call from the Coastguard of any pollution incidents and reports of broken down vessels that may pose a risk to the UK's coast. He then either runs the incident or makes the decision to escalate it to a national response. Oil in the water offshore is the responsibility of the Government and response may involve spraying dispersants from aircraft, booming and/ or oil recovery. He has been involved in many vessel incidduts such as the Manaar Star, LT Cortezia, City of Sunderland and numerous others. And then there was the MSC Napoli!

On the 18th January 2007, when the MSC Napoli became a casualty in the English Channel, Ian responded to support the salvage work and set up the Salvage Control Unit (SCU) at Weymouth coastguard station. His work involves dealing with Ministers, Salvage companies, P and I clubs, lawyers, cargo interests, local authorities, environmentalists and many other organisations. The vessel was taken in tow by French salvage tugs and was towed towards UK waters due to weather conditions making the French coast untenable. The tow took shelter in Weymouth Bay awaiting better weather to round Portland Bill. In the early hours of the 20th January the Salvage Master announced that the vessel was sinking and SOSREP ordered the vessel to be beached in Weymouth Bay as close inshore as possible and in the least sensitive area of what is one of the most highly protected environmental areas in the UK. It was the first time a vessel has been deliberately beached on the UK shore. The vessel was beached 1 mile off Branscombe beach in Dorset. Led by the Dutch firm SMIT, a major salvage operation started. Many containers were washed overboard and onto Branscombe beach and became front page news as hundreds of people descended on the beach to carry off everything they could. Eventually all the containers remaining were removed and the vessel was cut in two by strategic use of explosives and the forward section was taken to Belfast to be recycled. SOSREP and the MCA also had to oversee the huge amount of work undertaken ashore at Portland Port to receive the salvaged containers and to dispose of damaged and unwanted cargo and containers. The removal of the stern section is still underway, a year after the initial grounding, and Ian is still involved.

"We all wore a knife on a lanyard at all times, it had one large blade and a marlin spike."

They were an essential tool not a potential weapon. That is until one junior cadet captain supervising a prep class one evening, probably meaning to scare a transgressor, threw his knife at a younger cadet.

"The vein in the cadet's thigh was pierced and the lad spent a lengthy time in hospital. It was a terrible accident and the cadet captain was disrated. But it was the only incident of its sort I ever heard of."

The mast was stepped at the southern end of the parade deck. Although always referred to as the mizzen mast, it was in fact the main topmast.

Stepping The "Mizzen" Mast

1966

A group of cadets travelled to Gareloch to compete in the 5 day Mudhook Regatta, a schools and universities sailing championship. 57 universities and schools participated and *Conway* came fourth, their captain, Peter Dickie, observing

"we were pleased but not satisfied."

Attendance became an annual event but subsequent performances never matched this first achievement.

A second party of 15 cadets embarked on a short cruise in the *Nevassa,* courtesy of the British India Steam Navigation Company. *Nevassa* was a school ship taking parties of school children on short educational cruises. The cadets boarded at Liverpool and disembarked at Southampton.

In Andes dormitory, a cadet had something stolen from his locker. This was a terrible offence as cadets never locked anything away, always implicitly trusting their fellows. No one owned up to the apparent theft and a deadline was imposed on the grounds that, if no one admitted the offence, everyone in the dorm would be called to the Gun Room and receive three cuts.

"The deadline passed and we duly presented ourselves. Perhaps the busiest Gun Room session in all time?"

"During breaks from classes someone started a new game, I think called 'Buck Buck.' We had teams of 8 or 10. One person as 'captain' would stand with his back to a classroom wall and the rest of his team would pack down against him like a rugby scrum, but in one long line along the tarmac road. One at a time, members of the other team ran at the end of the line, dived onto the back of the long 'scrum.' As he dove forward, the captain started yelling 'buck, buck' at the top of his voice and the bent over cadets started jumping wildly up and down trying to dislodge the opposition who had to hang on for dear life and crawl along the backs of the gyrating scrum."

The aim was to get the whole team on top of the scrum.

"No one ever succeeded but we had fun trying. It was the most bruising experience, especially when you were inevitably bucked off and onto the tarmac road, closely followed by your team mates."

After their 'A' level exams, 7 cadets and Mr. Howard-Davies sailed the MSODs *Ariel, Flying Cloud* and *Lightning* clockwise around Anglesey. They sailed 87 miles and took 4 days.

In 1950, Mr. Kingsford had launched the ever popular The Ship; a weekly broadsheet of prose, poetry, sketches by cadets and staff. It was displayed on the reading board on the Ship's lower deck. Publication had died with the Ship and lack of a suitable home mitigated against its rebirth in the Camp. Suddenly, in 1966, it re-appeared as The Sheet and was displayed in the cabinet back stage. Mr. Drake became editor of the Cadet magazine.

1966 Winter Term

"The country needs men of this calibre"

There were a number of staff changes at the end of the year. 'Pug' Bayliss resigned after 18 years service. He was a well liked master, best know for his fanatical devotion to the 1st XV rugby team but also a great organiser of the main summer athletics competition and the boxing. He suffered from a debilitating hearing defect but ignored doctors' advice to take things easy, Captain Hewitt observed that

"he preferred to wear himself out than rust out."

Unfortunately, he left rather smartly under something of a cloud after inappropriate behaviour towards a junior cadet. A sad end to an otherwise illustrious career. Mr. Williams, the ex-Chief Steward, retired as wages and records officer after 20 years in the Ship. He had served Hewitt and the pilots tea in 1953 as they waited at Pwllfanogl Creek to take the Ship into the Swellies on her last voyage. Sgt J.B. 'Ocka Jock' McLeod RAF, one of the warrant officers and divisional officer for focslemen at the house, died. He had been in the Ship only 3 years and used to regale cadets with his exploits as an engineer in MTBs during the war. He was short, red-headed and sprightly. Mrs Broadbent 'Ma Bee' died. She was the 97 year old wife of a previous Captain Superintendent and had been an extremely popular lady. Finally, at the end of term Mr. Payne the English teacher also departed. These changes seemed to have a marked effect on the term. Captain Hewitt observed in the Cadet, perhaps with the departure of 'Pug' Bayliss uppermost in his mind,

"There are some terms so depressing that the sooner they are forgotten the better."

He went on to heap praise on the senior gun room team mentioning

"the magnificent work put in by the senior cadet captains under the chief cadet captain and deputy chief cadet captain"

and evoking Churchill's words that

"the country needs men of this calibre."

They are pictured (left to right), front row D. Stocks (Focsle), J S Kirk, C. Massie Taylor the chief cadet captain, his deputy Alec McNab (a great sportsman who would practice the hurdles wearing heavy mountain boots). Back row, M. Winn (Foretop), R. 'Tiny' Pace (Maintop) and C. Chubb (Mizzentop).

1967

"I was in the 1st XV that was caught red-handed by 'Ning Ning' in the Caernarfon Arms in Birkenhead after we'd just played Birkenhead Grammar. We were all on Captain's Report on the Monday, where Eric managed to scare us all witless before decreeing that all 1st XV away matches were cancelled for the rest of the season. The drink must have been good for us, we beat Pangbourne the next term."

In one memorable boxing final in the gym, the chief cadet captain (CPO) ended up fighting the king of the woods (KOW).

"It was a much anticipated fight, I think every non-rate on the Ship was rooting for the KOW with just those in officialdom rooting for the CPO. They were both tough men, the CPO probably the bigger of the two but the KOW a tough Scouser. It was an absolute bloodbath with the audience going mad between rounds. It all went quiet when KoW went down and the CPO Massie Taylor won the match."

1967 Summer

The average number of 'O' level passes was 6.7, two more than the national average for grammar schools.

The format of the Haigh Trophy changed in 1967. Originally a mountaineering competition for the Snowdon Scout Group, it had become an inter-divisional competition. To allow more cadets to benefit from its challenging format each division would now enter 2 teams, with the B team following a slightly less physically demanding course. The course that year was typical. Starting at Bont Newydd below Aber Falls it was a semi circular route scaling Llwytmor 2,700 feet, Foel Fras 3,092 feet and Drum 2,592 feet, a steep descent to Hafod y Gwyn (near Roewen), a climb over the Tan y Fan ridge to Cefn Coch stone circle and finally back to Llanfairfechan, approximately 14 miles of mountain walking and a total ascent of 4,240 feet. Directional clues involved things like Spanish translation and mathematical calculations without which the next destination could not be determined. Waypoint tests included 2 mathematics challenges, navigation, science and first aid. Points were awarded for time taken over the route, accuracy of map references, problems solved and expedition logs. Mizzentop won.

1968 Easter

The guest of honour for prize day was Captain WE 'Bil' (spelt that way deliberately) Warwick CBE RD RNR (1926-28), Captain designate of the new Queen Elizabeth 2.

And You'll Find on the Bridge a Conway Boy
The Warwick Family (1926-57!)

The Warwick family are another Conway dynasty, with four family members attending Conway over two generations. Brothers William (26-28) and Norman (48-49), and William's sons Eldon (55-56) and Ron (56-57). They had a unique family connection with Cunard.

Commodore WE 'Bil' Warwick CBE RD RNR (26-28), was junior cadet captain in Conway at Rock Ferry. Close to the end of his course a representative from the Mogul Line visited Conway to recruit apprentices to join a new ship being built in Scotland. Bil applied and was accepted. His Discharge Book shows him as joining the ship on the 25 October 1928 so he may have had to leave Conway a bit earlier than usual. Interestingly, the Discharge Book records him being signed on as a Junior Officer throughout his time as an apprentice. He went to India on the ship and did not return for several years having obtained his 2nd Mate's and First Mate's tickets before doing so. Eventually he returned to the UK and joined Cunard. He became Master of the Queen Elizabeth and the Queen Mary, and was the first Master of the Queen Elizabeth 2 in 1968. He later became the fourth Conway appointed as Commodore of Cunard in 1970 and retired in 1972.

Bil's brother Norman Ralph Warwick (48-49) was in Conway for the final year at Bangor and the first term at Plas Newydd. He eventually went to sea in the Silver Line.

Bil's son Eldon John Warwick (55-56) also attended Conway joining the year after the Camp was opened. He served his time with Brocklebanks and worked for several companies before retiring in 1997 after serving in command for about 20 years.

Bil's younger son Commodore Ronald 'Ron' Warwick OBE RNR LLD FNI (56-57) was also a Conway cadet. He first joined the Port Line and after obtaining his Second Mate's Certificate in 1961, he spent the next several years sailing with various companies to gain experience of different types of ships. In 1967, he became chief officer of a cargo ship and by 1968 he had obtained his Master's ticket. He joined Cunard as a third officer in 1970. For one brief day in 1970 they both served in Queen Elizabeth 2 as she was moved in Southampton harbour. He was Chief Officer when Queen Elizabeth 2 was requisitioned by the government for service in the Falklands campaign and holds the rank of captain in the RNR. Ron first sailed as Captain in 1986 on Cunard Princess, and also sailed in command of the Cunard Countess and Cunard Crown Dynasty before his appointment as Master of Queen Elizabeth 2 in July 1990. He was the first Captain of the new Queen Mary 2 and the fifth Conway Commodore of Cunard from 2003 to 2006 when he retired with 36 years of company service. Ron describes an encounter with a large wave during very bad weather in 1995 en route to New York in Queen Elizabeth 2. "The wind speed was recorded well over 100 knots ... We were hove to and riding out 30-40 foot waves. It was a dark night ... The sea was nearly white with foam and driving spray lashing the ship. The rogue wave was sighted right ahead looming out of the darkness and it looked like we were heading straight for the white cliffs of Dover. The wave seemed to take ages to reach us ... it broke with tremendous force on the bow. An incredible shudder went through the ship followed a few moments later by two smaller shudders. The QEII withstood the wrath of the ocean despite hundreds of tons of water landing on the bow. There was some superficial damage such as bent railings and buckled deck plating. No passengers or crew were injured. It can be quite difficult to gauge wave height but in this case the crest of the wave was more or less level with our line of sight on the bridge ... 95 feet above the sea surface. This was the largest wave that I have ever encountered and I cannot begin to imagine what effect it would have had on a smaller vessel!" Canadian weather buoys nearby confirmed the wave's height as 98 feet.

1968 Spring Term

The 1st XV, learning nothing from their previous escapade, were caught in a pub in Betws-y-Coed on the way back from an away game.

Capt 'Bil' Warwick Inspects Maintop

> *"Mr. Kingsford would always drop us off in the village and very pointedly tell us that he would be in the bar of such and such a hotel 'just in case you need me.' Unfortunately the new master, Mr. Harris, was not aware of the subtleties of this arrangement and wandered into the small bar where we were all packed in smoking and drinking! We were all on Captain's report and Eric roasted me as I was a senior cadet captain and supposed to set an example. I felt very hard done by as I was actually over 18 at the time but he didn't strip me of my rate."*

1968 Summer Term

The Ship's 5 ton anchor embedded in the strait (on the Anglesey side furthest for the dock) was lifted by Lt. Cdr. Brooke Smith, assisted by a group of cadets. Brookie lifted it in the same way he placed it almost 20 years earlier. A cadet recalls the experience.

> *"I was a digger. We had to dig the mud from around the anchor at low water, so it could be broken out. Once it was all clear, at low water, two cutters were lashed to the anchor, one either side of it using cross boards, and when tide flooded the anchor broke free."*

It was in excellent condition although the stock had been removed in 1949. The cutters were towed back to the dock and the anchor lifted with the life boat davits. It was then lashed down on one of the fife trailers and towed up to the New Block adjacent to the mast, where it was left while someone decided what to do with it. It is now on display outside the Merseyside Maritime Museum at Liverpool. The second anchor (the one closest to the dock) was lifted between 8th and 10th September 1987 by a group from the Seiont II Maritime Trust Caernarfon led by an Old Conway and is displayed outside the Caernarfon Maritime Museum.

Cadets Bligh, Petty, Powell, Rogers, Surens and Williams participated in the Welsh Schools National Athletics Championship. The best performance was by Petty who came third in the hop, skip and jump with a personal best of 42 feet 10 inches. John Bligh captained the 1stXV,

> *"he was our gentle giant – much bigger than the rest of us and so great in the line-out."*

He was selected to represent Wales for an Under 19 game against France.

Epidemics of mumps and then German measles played havoc with the term's sporting activities as no-one was allowed out for 6 weeks.

The MSODs were sold and replaced by 3 GP14s, with another 3 to be built by cadets.

The Breeches Buoy competition was won by Foretop, the invigilating coastguard concluding it was an

"almost faultless display"

in a time of 4 minutes and 5 seconds. This competition was always a term highlight with the rockets flying noisily in a cloud of smoke over the dock to be secured by the wreck party on the opposite sea wall. How many *Conway* cadets must have participated in this ritual over the years? How many ever used a breeches buoy thereafter?

Breeches Buoy Competition

CHAPTER 35

1965-69 NEW HANDS ON THE TILLER

Voluntary Aided Status

The average number of cadets in 1964 was an all time high of 307 and the annual fees were £352. Building the New Block had been a long and expensive process so cash reserves were at a very low ebb. Income in 1964 was £110,590, but expenditure was £114,560, creating a deficit of £3,970. The method of calculating fees was simple; anticipated everyday running costs were divided by the number of cadets. Extraordinary expenditure seems largely to have been paid by Blue Funnel (Ocean Fleets) through the good offices of Julian Holt, the Chairman of the Management Committee. Later that year it was calculated that *Conway* needed a minimum of 310 cadets to remain viable but numbers were below that, and dropping. Financially, *Conway* could not survive.

The committee, Captain Superintendent and Headmaster agreed they had to find new ways of supporting *Conway*. For obvious reasons they first approached Liverpool Education Authority who considered the proposal for 6 long months before a party of councillors led by Ethel Wormald visited the ship in 1965. Liverpool eventually decided they could not undertake the task alone and approached 4 or 5 other authorities, essentially those bordering or close to the Mersey, including Cheshire, to see if a consortium might be formed to run *Conway*. Cheshire dropped out but discussions with the others continued until approximately July 1966 before foundering. This was devastating news. The committee decided *Conway* would have to close and to make the announcement at Speech Day, Summer 1966. With just one week to go they received an unexpected call from Cheshire County Council offering to step into the breach and take *Conway* over themselves. This incredible turnaround was engineered by one man at Cheshire, Bertie Dues, who simple decided that *Conway* could not be allowed to close. After much debate internally they agreed to make *Conway* an offer, doubtless seeing the incredible potential of the facilities at Plas Newydd for use as a general outdoor educational centre as well as a specialist naval school. They envisaged a gradual transition to become a sixth form college of the sea. Julian Holt arranged for additional funds from Blue Funnel to tie *Conway* over while this last ditch salvage attempt was attempted. The Ministry of Education became involved and they strongly advised that *Conway* seek Voluntary Aided Status, indicating that the rules could be adapted to accommodate *Conway's* circumstances. By February 1967 it was clear that voluntary aided status might mean the Headmaster taking over from the Captain Superintendent, and possibly the loss of the ensign, the title 'HMS,' for pupils to be called cadets or even to be members of the RNR. These were all unwelcome changes but things were desperate

> *"It is either accept this voluntary aided (status) or shut up shop within a year."*

Cheshire was the only game in town. Or was it? *Conway's* two arch-rivals, *Worcester* and Pangbourne, faced the same challenges but followed different courses.

HMS *Worcester,* on the Thames at Greenhithe was founded in 1862, just 3 years after *Conway*. By 1964, she had fewer cadets than *Conway* but decided to respond by an aggressive move to capture greater 'market share.' In 1968, just when *Conway* was saved by voluntary aided status, *Worcester* merged with the King Edward VII Nautical College to form a new body; the Merchant Navy College at Greenhithe. Later the South London College and the Department of Navigation of Sir John Cass College were integrated as well. The syllabus was extended to include engineering, radio and second Mate and Home Trade Certificate courses. Even this could not generate sufficient income and at some point they too obtained voluntary aided status with the Inner London Education Authority. However, in 1974 when *Conway* was nearing her end, *Worcester's* strategy seemed to be succeeding as a huge complex of new buildings were constructed at Ingress Abbey on the Thames. *Conway* did consider the merger route. Wg. Cdr. Browne's diaries show that as early as January 1959 Sir John Nicholson the chairman of the management committee suggested

> *"Direct grant status, approach to Worcester to align policies."*

However, by April it was concluded that *Worcester's* aims differed from *Conway's* as the former was

> *"obsessed with pushing boys to practical applications, whatever general level of education."*

Although close contact was maintained with *Worcester's* plans, *Conway* decided against merger. Despite the Merchant Navy College's success, funding problems, arising from Mrs Thatcher's abolition of the Inner London Education Authority in 1989, forced the college to close.

Pangbourne Nautical College was founded in 1917 on the banks of the River Thames, near Reading, UK. Although never entitled to be called HMS Pangbourne, cadets were permitted to wear the same Royal Navy uniform as *Conway* cadets and followed a very similar regime, training boys for the sea by developing leadership, self-discipline and service. As late as April 1964, *Conway*, Pangbourne and *Worcester* were discussing the possibilities of a shared syllabus but by July 1964 Pangbourne had selected a dramatically different course. They decided to become a fully-fledged public school. Despite *Conway's* fears about the attendant loss of uniforms, titles and ensigns, Pangbourne was allowed to retain them all. Today, most nautical aspects of training have been shed but Pangbourne survives and is the only school in the world allowed to wear the RNR cadet uniform and the blue ensign. They are co-educational, have 400 pupils who join at age 11 or 13 and over 90% stay on for 'A' levels before going to university. Relatively few now go to sea. TEW Browne spent 30 years trying to build a similar model at *Conway*, Basil Lord who followed him shared similar goals but came on the scene too late to achieve them. *Conway* could have followed this route but chose a different path, one that ultimately proved a dead end.

A number of accommodation alterations and developments were required to achieve the minimum standards set for a voluntary aided school. These included staff bungalows, a new engineering block and improvements to the gym and art room. Cheshire could not fund this capital expenditure as all such funds were provided centrally. The department granted £20,000 toward the costs but this did not cover all of them so some other source of funding had to be found. Voluntary aided status meant that it would no longer be appropriate for the MMSA to manage *Conway* and, at the Ministry's suggestion, it was agreed that the British Shipping Federation(BSF) would replace them, fund the balance and take a controlling interest in *Conway*. By March 1967 they were in detailed negotiations with *Conway*. They allocated approximately £250,000 for the work but as they were also funding developments costing £500,000 for the new National Sea Training School at Gravesend, they were determined to contain *Conway's* development costs wherever possible.

During 1967, negotiations came to a successful conclusion and agreement in principle was reached with Cheshire Education Authority that,

"it should maintain the school"

and with the BSF, that

"it should take over the trust (ie the Conway Cadet School Ltd company) and its finances."

Proposals were submitted to the Department of Education and Science and on 5th February 1968 the department published a Notice of Intent in the press. A last minute hitch almost scuppered all the plans. As part of their inspection of *Conway's* facilities, Cheshire's medical officer ruled that the seawater swimming pool, fed by the waters of the strait,

"could prove a serious public health hazard."

Cheshire announced they would not proceed unless a new covered, heated pool was built with a filtration plant and changing rooms. This would cost £30,000. Cheshire did not have the funds, and neither the department nor the Federation could find any extra funding. To avoid falling at the last hurdle they all agreed to approach the *Conway* Club to see if the £40,000 already donated towards the planned chapel might instead be spent on the pool and some staff bungalows. It is not clear how this problem was resolved but Cheshire obviously received sufficient guarantees about the pool as the money was not diverted from the chapel and a new pool was not built. However, in November 1969, the Federation were still discussing the possibilities of a combined building with a chapel at ground level and a pool in the basement.

Vesting Day was set for 5th April 1968, but was delayed by a cabinet reshuffle when the minister most involved, the Right Honourable Patrick Walker and his key maritime adviser, Dr. Noel Thompson, were moved to another department. On 19th July 1968 the new minister, Alice Bacon, declined to grant voluntary aided status as some last minute objections had been received from other education authorities. They were concerned that Cheshire could maintain artificially high numbers by accepting boys from other areas, obliging other authorities to pay the fees. The other authorities would lose control over their budgets. What parent would not seek a well subsidised high quality boarding school education? Ministry of Education officials had foreseen this possible challenge from other authorities and assured Cheshire and *Conway* that the Ministry would unequivocally support Cheshire, and insist that other authorities had to pay *Conway's* fees if a child chose to attend. The new Minister would not allow those assurances. A high powered delegation from the Federation and Cheshire visited the Minister on 22nd, she refused to allow what had previously been agreed but a compromise was found. She would allow voluntary aided status on condition that Cheshire agreed to consult other authorities before accepting boys from them. This ensured that those other authorities had the final say over whether to commit their funds to education at *Conway*. The seed planted by this decision took 6 years to grow and was the final cause of *Conway's* closure. As an educational charity *Conway* was already under the general jurisdiction of the Department in accordance with the Charities Act 1960. Eventually, on 25th (according to the Federation) or 26th July 1968 (according to the Club's legal opinion) *Conway* became a voluntary aided school by order of the Department under the provisions of section 15(2) of the 1944 Education Act. The department's legal instrument, formally sealed on

28th, was to be reviewed every 3 years. 2 other important conditions were attached; as soon as possible *Conway* should become a sixth form college, and the 13 and 14 year-old intake should be phased out.

Ownership

On 31st December 1967, a transitional committee under Julian Holt assumed practical control of *Conway* until legal formalities had been completed. On 30th May 1968 the MMSA finally relinquished control of the *Conway*. Ownership of the *Conway* Cadet School Ltd, including the New Block and all *Conway's* assets' transferred to the BSF who appointed all the Company's Trustees, all but one directors of the Federation. They in turn appointed the new management committee, 12 were nominated by the Federation, Cheshire were invited to nominate the other 6. Only Julian Holt remained from the old MMSA committee as a Company Trustee and committee member. From that day on, Cheshire were responsible for operating *Conway*, specifically for education, employing all the staff and most maintenance. However the Federation, not Cheshire, had overall control of *Conway*, as they owned the *Conway* Cadet School Ltd. In the words of the legal opinion obtained by the *Conway* Club later,

> *"BSF thus effectively replaced MMSA in the administration of the school."*

Conway's new chairman, Mr. Stanley Grant Fowler MBE, was the Deputy Chairman and Managing Director of the New Zealand Shipping Company and the Federal Steam Navigation Company. He had served in the RNVR, was also a director of the Australind Steamship Company and went on to a senior position in P&O Group. The new management committee comprised the Chairman of the Federation, the General Secretary of the Merchant Navy and Airline Officers' Association and representatives of BP Tankers, Furness Ship Management, Esso Petroleum, Dalgliesh and Co, British and Commonwealth and Ocean Fleets (a grouping of at least 13 companies such as Blue Funnel, Elder Dempster and Glen Line). In no way therefore can it be claimed that when the MMSA relinquished control, *Conway* lost her vital link with the shipping industry. The BSF probably represented a strengthening of that bond.

Cheshire also nominated a powerful group to the committee, including the chairman and deputy chairman of the county council, the chairman of the education committee and the head of the council's finance committee. They brought formidable educational and organisational skills to the table.

For some reason, the Plas Newydd leases owned by the *Conway* Cadet School Ltd were not transferred to the Federation. The legal opinion obtained by the Club in 1973 observed that in 1963 there were formal leases between the MMSA and the Marquis (dating from 1949) for the use of the Nelson Block and Kelvin Block, but that there appeared to be no lease for the area used for the Camp. Finally, while no lease had been formally executed for the land on which the New Block was built, there was a properly initialled Heads of Agreement for it, although this could not be found! Interestingly the lease negotiated in 1968 included allowance for

> *"The use of the Nelson Block only for short residential courses managed by Cheshire or for training cadets for the Merchant Navy."*

The MMSA transferred all its interests in these arrangements to the *Conway* Cadet School Ltd company when that was formed in 1963. It might be expected therefore that when ownership of the company passed to the Federation, so too would the leases, formal and otherwise. This did not happen. The legal opinion continues

> *"What appears to have happened is as follows: MMSA and the company must presumably have surrendered to the Marquis all rights under the existing arrangements. What the MMSA and the Company received in return is not known."*

Cheshire, not the Federation, then negotiated a 999 year 'head lease' direct with the Marquis (backdated from 25th March 1961) for the Nelson Block, Kelvin Block, the land on which the New Block sat, sewage works, playing fields and dock. It was signed on 2nd April 1968. Three days later Cheshire and the Company (read The Federation) signed a Heads of Agreement for a sub lease of the Kelvin Block, New Block land and sewage works, although this sub lease was never executed. The Nelson Block, dock and playing fields were not included. These arrangements were all carefully concluded on the same day but before the Department was due to grant voluntary aided status and take a strict oversight of *Conway*. The Federation owned the New Block buildings but Cheshire owned the main lease for the land on which they stood. This convoluted solution was to work in Cheshire's favour later.

Captain Superintendent To Headmaster

The most significant change flowing from the new arrangements was that after 109 years the post of uniformed Captain Superintendent lapsed, to be replaced by that of academic Headmaster. In February 1967 Captain Hewitt had announced that he planned to retire in 1969. When the Federation and Cheshire took control in July 1968 he hoped that he would be able to serve out his last year but this was not to be. The life saving voluntary aided status soon turned out to be a double edged sword. Schools supported with taxpayers' money had to comply with rules set by the Department of Education and Science. Cheshire had no option, a fully qualified Headmaster had to be in charge; Captain Hewitt would have to go. He was very bitter to be pushed out after having overcome so many adversities to keep *Conway* afloat but he acknowledged

> *"Life is changing. The shipowner wants a different sort of man"*

With typical candour he admitted,

> *"I do not consider I am the right man to stay and deal with it. I am too old fashioned and set in my ways."*

Mr. Basil Lord BA

At the Conway Club dinner in 1968, at the end of his last term, he ruefully observed

> *"I am the only man I know who has lost the same ship twice."*

In August 1968, he began a year's sabbatical leave, retiring formally in August 1969.

Mr. Basil Lord BA, Headmaster since 1964, found himself in complete command of *Conway*. He was educated at St Paul's School, where he was a foundation scholar, and Hertford College, Oxford. His studies were interrupted by war service in the Royal Navy from 1944 to 1947. After achieving his degree in Natural Sciences he became a teacher. For 15 years he taught at Manchester Grammar School, Welbeck College (a specialist military engineering school) and Glasgow Academy. His wife Mai had worked at Southampton University. Captain Hewitt observed

> *"I am handing over to Mr. Lord a very different Conway to the one I inherited, but ... with his younger approach to education and training he is bound to see her go from strength to strength."*

A complete list of Captain Superintendents and Headmasters is in *Appendix J*.

From Ship To School - Everything Changed, Everything Stayed The Same

Mr. Lord was determined that *Conway* would prosper and a new prospectus was issued indicating her future course

> *"Increasing emphasis is being placed on post GCE 'O' level work and it is hoped Conway will develop as a unique sixth form college with a nautical bias."*

Conway's training had always been 'Education for the sea' ie training boys for a career at sea. Mr Lord sought a vital lifesaving change that would broaden the school's appeal by focusing on 'Education through the sea'. Some would still go to sea, but henceforth the school would prepare pupils for a range of nautical careers, including oceanography, marine insurance and shipping company management. Naval traditions would be maintained, pupils would still be cadets, wear RNR uniform and follow a strongly naval routine. Water based activities would remain important but the overarching aim would no longer be to turn out cadet navigating officers. New GCSE and 'A' level subjects such as Marine Science and Marine Biology, could be introduced, but plans to purchase a motor fishing vessel to take cadets to sea for short training cruises foundered when Cheshire refused to foot the bill.

Voluntary aided status was a seismic change because now every aspect of *Conway's* management, organisation, staffing and operation would have to comply with national educational standards and procedures. Cheshire, having assuming responsibility for *Conway's* educational routine, legally had to implement those standards and procedures. The first casualty, as we have seen, was Captain Hewitt. The post of Chief Officer died at the same time, Lt. Cdr. Brooke Smith becoming housemaster of Mizzentop. The Federation had firm views about *Conway's* future as Mr. Lord made very clear when he proposed the toast to 'The Ship' at the 1969 Old *Conways'* dinner.

> *"When I took charge of Conway last year, I was given a directive by the governing body that Conway was to be organised not as a ship but as a school – a school with a strong nautical bias. Thus in responding to the present toast I am in a somewhat difficult position because the ship no longer exists, save in your minds and memories. In one sense this has always been so for the concept of the ship has been something separate and individual to each one of you."*

While the rest of his speech avoided the word 'school,' from then on the Cadet magazine displayed a split personality when it came to terminology. 'School' largely superseded 'ship,' and, for example, 'mess deck' became 'dining hall.' The number of bursary staff increased significantly to come into

And You'll Find on the Bridge a Conway Boy
Captain Eric Hewitt RD RNR (1919-21)

Eric achieved the rare accolade of a Double Extra Conway Passing Out Certificate. Accepted into the RNR he spent 6 months with the fleet before completing his Merchant Navy apprenticeship with Glen Line. He passed his second mate's certificate in June 1924 and moved to Royal Mail Lines. He obtained his first mate's certificate in 1927 just before his 23rd birthday and his Master's in 1930. He was promoted Lt Cdr RNR in 1936.

He was called up to the RNR in 1939. He was appointed take a tramp steamer filled with concrete and dynamite from London to Dover. Under fire from the German guns at Cape Gris Nez, he manoeuvred her into position as a block ship at one of the entrances to Dover harbour. Clearly, the operation's successful outcome pleased their Lordships and he was commended for his skill and determination in surmounting many difficulties and bringing an important and hazardous operation to a successful conclusion.

In November 1941, in command of the Flower Class corvette Aster and the sloop Shoreham, he served in the Indian Ocean, Persian Gulf, Red Sea and Mediterranean. He was promoted to Commander in 1942 and took part in Operation Husky, the invasion of Sicily, in 1943.

On 13th August 1943, he was mentioned in Dispatches after the slow Mediterranean UK convoy MKS 21, with 40 ships he was escorting, was attacked by 47 He 111 H-6 torpedo bombers off Alboran Island. The attack was repulsed and at least 7 aircraft were shot down. Admiral Andrew Cunningham, C-in-C Mediterranean, wrote: "I congratulate you, the escort force and convoy against heavy harassing attack. The enemy got a sore head he is likely to remember." He participated in the Normandy landings. In February 1944 he was attached to Capt Walker's famous Liverpool-based anti-submarine flotilla in command of the Black Swan Class sloop Whimbrel, which became his favourite ship. At the end of the war he went to Bergen to take the surrender of the German U-boats.

In 1945, as the youngest serving Captain in the RNR, he was on Admiral Lord Louis Mountbatten's staff in Singapore controlling the sea transport arrangements of the whole Far East. In May 1947 Mountbatten brought him Delhi to supervise the withdrawal by sea of British forces from India. He was confirmed in the rank of Captain RNR at the early age of 40. He became Conway's Staff Captain in March 1948 and Captain Superintendent in 1949.

He established Conway's new routine on shore and afloat at Plas Newydd, and saw her through the dreadful loss of the Ship in 1953. He masterminded the next term in tents and the creation of the hutted camp. When the New Block finally opened in 1964, after 10 years of struggle, he had achieved a minor miracle. Conway had been rehoused in modern buildings, with extensive laboratory and classroom accommodation and excellent playing fields. He worked tirelessly with the Headmaster and Committee to extend and improve technical and academic training so Conway supported the shipping industry's needs.

He was ADC to HM The Queen in 1956, High Sheriff of Anglesey in 1971, a Younger Brother of Trinity House 1950 to 1995, an auxiliary coastguard and President of the Conway Club 1969-72.

He was ably assisted by his wife 'Fanny,' indeed TEW Browne believed it was her determination and support that motivated him through Conway's most difficult times. He was not always popular with cadets, as his early nickname of 'von Hewitt' demonstrates, but every cadet from 1949 to 1968 will acknowledge his positive influence over their lives. If the Ship was our old wooden mother he was our stern father. The Cadet magazine acknowledged "their steadfast championing of Conway's cause over 20 eventful years and the ever-constant service so freely given to the Ship we all hold we all hold in such affection."

In 1968, they retired to Penmon overlooking the strait. Fanny died in 1984. Eric died on 13th December 1995, aged 91, as a result of inhaling fumes from a fire at his home. Nearly 400 people attended his Memorial Service.

line with staffing levels set in national agreements between county councils and the unions. Divisional officers had to become housemasters, all technical staff (who were at least Master Mariners or senior officers and so hardly unqualified) had to qualify as teachers or leave. Mr. Lord ensured that the few without the right piece of paper were able to study and obtain their teaching certificate. The cover of the revised prospectus in 1970 unfortunately displayed a representation of the Ship that was such a caricature it must have had Old *Conways* turning in their graves.

Mr. Lord instigated a huge improvement programme. Six New Block classrooms were converted into dedicated navigation, seamanship and geography rooms, the gym was re-floored, new staff houses were built, the sailing fleet was modernised and No 1 motorboat received a new engine and face-lift. The syllabus was revised. The library was refurbished and additional books ordered. The wooden classroom huts at the Kelvin Block were refurbished as technical workshops and an art room. A 9 hole golf course was laid out and facilities for archery provided. Plans were produced for an indoor pool, a large engineering block and more staff housing to be built on the area to the north of the New Block. He summed it all up succinctly

> *"We are not stagnant; we are alive; we are developing."*

Chief cadet captain Harboard supported his outlook at the annual *Conway* Club dinner

> *"We have good reason to look back with pride, but we must also look forward with faith that Conway, revived under the new structure, will carry on the training of men competent in many fields."*

Other aspects of the routine were unchanged, ship visits, talks by representatives of shipping companies, the school dance and theatre visits continued. Inter-divisional sports were contested as keenly as ever although badminton replaced boxing. Cadet captains still effectively ran the daily routine themselves with undiminished keenness. At the Old *Conway's* dinner, chief cadet captain Alfie Windsor, the last to serve under Captain Hewitt, expressed the cadets' views:

> *"Some believe Conway was a better ship than she is a building and that in coming ashore we have lost a lot of our former character. I am here to put the record straight. Conway now is as good as she ever was and the cadets in her intend to make sure that, whatever happens, she remains that way."*

Once again staff and cadets adapted to a new future.

1969

> *"I imagine things remained much about the same for the first term or so under Mr. Lord. We certainly still had divisional officers and also house masters. In Mizzentop, the divisional officer was Brookie and house master 'Puff' Harris. I can remember the teaser being used in 1968 but very rarely and I think it became verboten in 1969. Officers were permitted use of the cane; I know that for a fact because I got 6 from Dhobi for smoking."*

Televisions were installed in the common rooms.

> *"The 4 divisional day rooms (on the ground floor) were rarely used but the games room was always in use. The 2 snooker tables were very popular."*

With Cheshire now in charge

"The intake of 1969 naturally contained a very large number of boys from Cheshire."

The editorial in the Cadet magazine noted:

"Conway is adapting with quite remarkable facility to the changes that have come upon her in the last 12 months, for most of them are not radical change. The development of the industry we serve has dictated many of them, and the others are due to our changed circumstances. But there are more and more radical changes too and we must be prepared to accept and adapt to these."

A new subject, Marine Science, was developed by 'Dodo' Woolley involving many wonderful subjects such as meteorology, plankton and whales. It was adopted by the Associated Examining Board as a new GCE 'O' level.

The Rev, Alec Harrison was seconded from the Missions to Seamen and became the resident padre replacing the Rev. Turner.

Cadets were invited to participate in a science fair at Bangor University and demonstrate a piece of scientific equipment interesting to the general public. Under the expert guidance of Mr. Woolley, cadets Christie, Croker, Morgan, Roberts, Sandy and Walker, decided to demonstrate a model-ship testing tank. They duly constructed a 16 feet by 2 feet tank, which held a ton of water. An overhead gantry on rails towed the models so measurements could be taken. Scale models of No. 1 and No. 2 motorboats and a cutter were constructed. A BBC crew visiting the fair invited the team to compete in the BBC's Science Fair series.

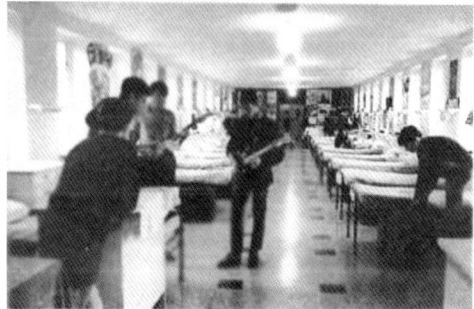

Spider Webb (right) and Ken Huggins

The won their heat in Manchester and appeared in the final in London, coming second by one point. As a result they were invited to compete in the European 'Contest For Young Scientists 1969' at Eindhoven, in the Netherlands. They won a first prize of £1,000

"to support their excellent research work."

Following a tradition started in 1962 by the Scorpians band, Steve 'Spider' Webb formed a rock group with Pete Brown on drums, Bill Philp on rhythm guitar and Ken Huggins on bass.

"Mr. Woolley lent us his excellent valve amplifier and helped us design and build the bass speaker cabinet in the physics lab."

They performed at the ship's dance in the summer of 1968.

"On one occasion, when we played a gig at the Bangor High Girl's school, he came along to keep an eye on his precious amp ... just as well as he was needed to carry out running repairs on it."

A *Conway* institution ended when the Liverpool Sailors Home closed in 1969. Mr. Bird the manager of the outfitting department had measured over 2,000 cadets in his time,

> *"when they joined, when they left, some when they married. I saw them growing out of their uniforms, I saw their collars grow too tight, I saw their shoes wearing out, but they never grew out of their raincoats. I made sure these were supplies that would still fit them when they married. It always made me smile when the new chum, standing there with his cap over his ears and his raincoat down to his ankles, told me that his collar was too tight."*

Monnerys were the new official outfitters. The building was demolished in 1976 but the Liverpool Sailors' Home Trust was set up to support organisations training and assisting seafarers and their families.

1969 October

The Cadet magazine, published every term since around 1890 became an annual publication, Issue 296 in October being the first since September 1968. The practice of including a list of cadets joining the ship and where from was discontinued.

The commanding officer of the RNR training centre in Liverpool arranged for *Mersey* to visit Holyhead for a week so that parties of cadets could spend a day at sea. This proved very popular and another visit was arranged in 1970.

CHAPTER 36

1970–73 THE FINAL YEARS

1970

The Haigh Trophy expedition came to an abrupt end

"when a thick fog descended."

Displaying brilliant initiative, of which all cadets would be proud, the Focsle and Foretop teams made for the safety of lower ground and entered the first building they came to for shelter, a pub, where they spent the rest of the day and part of the evening before catching a bus back to the ship.

There were some changes to accommodation arrangements. The chief and deputy cadet captains moved into the Gun Room on the ground floor and the large trunk rooms between dorms became studies for the upper sixth.

1970 May 23rd

The Britannia Bridge caught fire during the night and burned in a most spectacular fashion. Given its occasional use by cadets as a short cut to the mountains, many Old *Conways* hearing the news must have immediately suspected who might have been responsible, but some local boys owned up to starting the fire accidentally. The tubes of the bridge were lined with wooden sleepers and, over the years, these had become soaked in diesel and oil from passing trains. A few senior cadets crept out in the dark and took the pinnace and other boats down to watch events at close quarters. A BBC camera crew reputedly caught them on film. On another night

"we collected souvenirs in the cutter, this was done in the company of rates and senior cadet captains so, if not officially sanctioned, was definitely less punishable."

The bridge tubes were damaged beyond repair and were replaced by an open deck over a metal arched bridge.

"The arch sections were fabricated in a yard just below Port Dinorwic, and then taken up to the bridge on barges to be hoisted into position. It was quite eerie to be out on the strait early in the morning and have a huge tug and barge combo loom out of the mist and head up towards the bridge."

Later, a road deck was added on top to relieve pressure on the Menai Suspension Bridge.

1970 Summer Term

Because of the dangerous state of the Britannia Bridge, transits to Beaumaris for sailing regattas became impossible. However sailing remained very popular with 82 cadets in the sailing group and a fleet of 2 Fifes, 6 GP14s and 2 Mirror dinghies. By the end of the summer, only 4 cadets had not achieved at least a third class coxswain's certificate. Petty and his crew came second in the national schools regatta.

The pinnace, a stalwart of *Conway's* small boat fleet since 1946, finally reached the end of her life. She had Kitchener Gear so, instead of a gearbox, relied on two curved moveable rudders closing across the rear of the propeller to redirect the thrust to go astern. It jammed increasingly often in the most embarrassing situations. Then, after a hard life, the engine, an old Gardner diesel that operated on the wartime mix of tractor vaporising oil (TVO), finally gave up the ghost. She was brought out of the water onto the slip for inspection

"I lost the top of my little finger to the starboard leg we were attaching. I remember picking it up and putting it back on the end and going off to see Sister Jones and being taken off to Bangor Hospital. It knitted back on but never grew to match the rest of the finger."

The pinnace's corroded iron nails were continually being replaced and under the cadets' gentle ministrations she had been holed, beached and repaired several times. It was decided the pinnace was beyond economical repair and should be scrapped. She was beached in the dock, stripped of fittings and a working party ordered to set fire to her.

"We had great difficulty setting her alight, mind you we were using TVO!!"

1970 June 7th

Mrs Coombs, widow of Captain Coombs, laid the foundation stone for the new chapel. The Bishop of Chester officiated.

Many cadets participated again in the sponsored 18 mile Island Walk in support of UNICEF. The padre noting that

"no one disappeared en-route."

1970 October

There were 19 members of staff, 7 for nautical studies and 12 academics. Mr. Carter the Deputy Head had joined in 1935. Lt. Cdr. Brooke Smith, previously Chief Officer but now housemaster of Mizzentop, had joined in 1940. Seven others had joined between 1949 and 1956, the rest had all been appointed by Mr. Lord. W. Davidson was housemaster, Focsle, and Lt. Cdr. P.J. Clarke RD, RNR was housemaster Maintop. Mr. N.A. Johnson was housemaster, Foretop.

Lt. Cdr. Edwin Parry resigned and returned to sea after toiling unremittingly for 14 years to teach cadets navigation.

"He had the most remarkable way of pronouncing horizon, making it sound more like 'horry zon'."

"We had our bad eggs, a couple of seniors were sent down for bullying."

In a disturbing endnote to the year the Cadet magazine carried an article highlighting

"the discourtesy between cadets themselves, between cadets and staff, and between cadets and visitors so frequently displayed, and the general untidiness, the litter scattering proclivities, which there is little effort to control. The damage wrought to the structure and fittings of the School."

And You'll Find on the Bridge a Conway Boy
Rt. Hon. George Iain Duncan Smith MP (1968-72)

Iain Duncan Smith joined Conway in January 1968 when he was nearly 14. During his sojourn he was a Focsleman and a drummer in the band; usually more a marker of a rebel than a leader. He was a competitive sportsman and was awarded 1st XV colours in the Autumn of 1971, playing as fly-half alongside Clive Woodward at centre. He was captain of the cricket team in 1972 and played for the hockey team. He won the Lawrence Holt prize for History in 1972 and left Conway with 3 'A' levels and 8 'O' levels.

From Conway, he went to Perugia University in Italy, then to Sandhurst after which he joined the Scots Guards, with whom he served from 1975 to 81. He served in Rhodesia at the time of that country's independence and in Canada, Germany and Northern Ireland. Retiring from the Army he was a director of GEC/Marconi from 1981 to 1988, a Director of Bellwinch Plc from 1988 to 1989 and Publishing Director of Jane's Information Group from 1989 to 1992.

Entering politics, he contested Bradford West in the 1987 General Election and was Vice-Chairman of Fulham Conservative Association in 1991. The next year he was elected MP for Chingford. Over time he was a member of the Standards in Public Life (Nolan) Select Committee, the Members' Interests Select Committee, the Administration Select Committee and the Health Select Committee. From 1992 to 97 he was secretary of the Conservative Back Bench Foreign and Commonwealth Affairs Committee and a member of the Conservative Back Bench Defence Committee. Following boundary changes he was elected Member of Parliament for Chingford and Woodford Green in May 1997 with a majority of 5,714 and has held the seat ever since. From June 1997 he was Shadow Secretary of State for Social Security, and in June 1999 he was appointed Shadow Secretary of State for Defence.

Aged 47, he was elected Conservative leader in September 2001, at the time of the 9/11 attacks on America. During his two years as Leader of the Opposition he supported action against Afghanistan and Iraq. He forged close links with senior members of the US administration, relationships that still prosper today. As Conservative leader he led the party towards a greater emphasis on public services. His policies on school choice and NHS reform are still at the heart of today's Conservative agenda.

When he lost the Conservative leadership in October 2003 he established the Centre for Social Justice. He remains a respected and influential MP, Conway's most successful politician. Life is not all politics. In 2003, he published a novel 'The Devil's Tune' and he continues with sport, "I play for the Parliamentary football team and I think I am right in saying we were the last team to play at Wembley before they tore it down."

This was not a new phenomenon, there had been other periods in the past when standards changed and Old *Conways* lamented the good old days.

1970 December

Mr. Lord, determined to have a very strong impact on academic standards, announced impressive 'O' level results. Over 70% achieved a pass in English language, only 2 out of 50 failed English literature, maths had only 1 failure out of 22 candidates and in all other subjects results exceeded the national average. He was steering a successful course, taking *Conway* from sea to land, she might no longer be called the Ship but she certainly was going to be just as good as the School.

1971

> *"When I joined, Conway took boys for a 3 year 'O' level course, and/ or as sixth formers for a 2 year 'A' level course. The nautical bias was there for the 'out of school' activities, and the curriculum included seamanship, navigation, and marine science 'O' levels. The whole ethos and daily pattern of life and work was still firmly Conway and things nautical, but educationally it was a standard boarding school."*

An ONC in Nautical Science was offered (the other pre-sea colleges were offering OND), and Engineering Cadetships led to an OND in Engineering, and a Marine Engineering Technician's Certificate. A busy series of ship visits was undertaken to Ocean Fleets, British and Commonwealth, New Zealand Shipping, Furness, Ellerman, Blue Star and Port Line vessels. Groups of 20 cadets at a time also spent short periods at sea on *Mersey* on her RNR training cruise.

The school changed to one intake a year in September 1971. There were 182 cadets and while this was below the desired optimum, no reduction in entry standards was contemplated. The sixth form was the largest ever at 40, compared to only 6 in 1969. Mr. Lord's desire to establish a sixth form college seemed to be bearing fruit.

> *"I wanted to stay on at Conway for 'A' Levels but there was no course available for 'A' level navigation or astro physics, which were the subjects which I loved best so I left and went to sea. It was a real wrench that last week or so when we knew we were leaving our friends to actually go out into the world. Conway on the whole turned out a well rounded individual well disciplined with social skills, a good education and a strong sense of right and justice, in most cases better than what actually exists in our world."*

Jack Isbester, extra master, was seconded to *Conway* from British and Commonwealth for 12 months as Director of Nautical Studies and Deputy Headmaster.

> *"Whenever he addressed the mess deck his cap was always tilted backward, hands behind back and he rocked on his heels like Dixon of Dock Green."*

Orienteering was quite the rage nationally and Jack was much enthused about it. He would run cross country races with cadets.

'Bog Brush' Carter 1961

Mr. Goodey, who had taught maths since 1966 left to join the Nelson Field Studies centre as a climbing instructor. Mr. Johnson left to join the British Forces Education Service as Head of English in Dortmund. Mr. Bamber left to return to Pakistan, which meant the 1st XV had to coach themselves for one term. The greatest loss was the retirement of 'Bog Brush' Carter after 36 years service. He joined the Ship in 1935 as a maths teacher and Deputy Headmaster. During the war years, when TEW Browne was away on active service, Carter was acting Headmaster. Generations of *Conway* cadets had reason to be thankful to him for giving them a sound grounding in maths that came from patient teaching and an insistence on accuracy. He was invaluable in initiating Mr. Lord into the

> *"mysteries and uniqueness of Conway.,"*

Lt. Cdr. Brooke Smith ruefully observed that he and Mr. Kingsford were now the only true *Conways* left.

2 new staff houses were completed at the north end of the cadets' wing and the Headmaster hoped that 4 more would be built in the near future. The staff flats in the new Block were leased at a rental of £78 pa, which included the provision of heating and water. A separate charge was made for electricity consumed. The flats were unfurnished and fairly small. Any member of staff who rented one of these flats was obliged to act as duty master approximately every fifth day. If he was a house tutor, the £78 was waived. If he was a housemaster, the rental was similarly waived and he received a special payment of £210 pa. Meals were provided in the Ward Room for members of staff when on duty, but full board for the family of the staff member was not provided. The uniformed staff did not receive any uniform allowance.

1971 Summer

The HMS *Conway* Sailing Club was born and accepted by the Royal Yachting Association. In a busy series of regattas they won 7 out of 9, most importantly beating Rydal School to make up for a complete whitewash in the rugby against these arch rivals.

1971 October

The Old *Conways'* non-denominational, memorial chapel was finally completed at a cost of £40,000 and was presented to the school by the *Conway* Club on behalf of Old *Conways* and parents. Lord Anglesey most generously offered to donate the land for the site, providing *Conway* raised the money for the building.

> *"One gets the impression of spaciousness and modern clean lines. I can remember the excitement generated when we watched the steeple being raised on our brand new chapel."*

The cadets also raised some of the money for the chapel including a fund raising sail around Anglesey. The 6 GP 14s (*Taeping, Ariel, Lightning, Flying Cloud, Simba* and *Sobroan*), each crewed by 2 cadets and escorted by 2 safety launches, circumnavigated the island in 3 days.

The Conway Chapel at Plas Newydd

> *"The original idea was to raise money but the major factor involved was the challenge of taking the dinghies around the island."*

It was announced that the Cadet magazine could no longer be produced in its traditional form and that alternative formats were being considered. Cheshire auditors had reviewed its viability and judged it uneconomic, with a circulation of just 500. Mr. Drake resigned as editor, a 'temporary' position he had held since 1965.

On a brighter note, Alderman Patrick Parle 'Spud' Murphy was called to the bar at the age of 71. He led a busy life. He was Mayor of Beaumaris in 1960, chairman of Beaumaris Harbour Committee, a member of the Beaumaris Port Health Authority, an associate of Royal Institute of Naval Architects and a member of the Institute of Navigation. In his spare time since retiring as *Conway's* navigation master he had been studying law. He was a Master Mariner, commanding his first ship before he was 30.

1971 Christmas

Lt. Cdr. John Brooke Smith retired after 31 years service.

And You'll Find on the Bridge a Conway Boy
The Brooke Smith Dynasty (1893-1963)

Brookie Leads a Parade at Bangor

Below: Brookie at The Dock

The Brooke Smith family were Conway legends, with five family members, over three generations, serving as cadets.

Captain Louis Brooke Smith RNR (1893-95) was the patriarch. He sailed in clipper ships with Carmichaels and Stewarts obtaining his extra Master's square rigged certificate in 1903. He served in the Boer War and the first world war. He was marine superintendent of the Meteorological Office for 19 years and organised the system of weather observations by ships at sea and the shipping weather bulletin. He was elected a Younger Brother of Trinity House in 1919. His eldest son John (25-27), fifth son Frances (34-36) and sixth and youngest son Guy (44-46) as well as grandson Bruce (61-63) all followed him to Conway.

John - 'Brookie' was the Ship's longest serving officer, joining in 1940 and retiring in December 1971. He was born on 14th February 1911 at Fretwell in Yorkshire. He left Conway as a senior cadet captain with an extra certificate. He was appointed Midshipman RNR and joined Alfred Holt and Co, later moving on to the New Zealand Shipping Co. By 1939, his eyesight deteriorated to such an extent that his sea-going career was over, however as a Lieutenant RNR he was mobilised during the war and transferred on a short-term loan to the Ship. The loan lasted 31 years.

"As a divisional officer he was superb. Very smart in dress, encouraging, very strict but always fair. His austere countenance hid a great shyness but he gained the greatest of respect." He had an extraordinary knack of appearing at the scene of any crime or misdemeanour when you least wanted him to, hence his earlier nickname of 'Spooky.' He wore round glasses and a smile never seemed to be far from his face. *"He was slow to rouse, almost gentle most of the time, but very forceful when he detected slackness or ill discipline."*

Captain Hewitt promoted him from divisional officer to chief officer and arranged for him to be awarded the honorary rank of Lt. Cdr. RNR. He was in the Ship for her transits from the Mersey to Bangor in 1941, from Bangor to Plas Newydd in 1949 and from Plas Newydd in 1953 when the Ship was lost. He found the loss deeply distressing and he did more than any person to ensure that the very best of Conway traditions continued. He served as chief officer until 1969 when Cheshire abandoned the title and he was obliged to become a housemaster. He served faithfully but was unhappy about the changes and the loss of long held traditions. He loved the old Ship and Conway was his whole life. He retired at the end of 1971 to Brook Cottage in Haskerton. He died on 23rd December 1990 and was buried in the local churchyard

Guy (44-46) was a cadet in the Ship at Bangor at the same time that his elder brother John was an officer. One evening as duty officer John read "The following cadets are on slack party – Adams, Baker, Brooke Smith…" a great cheer went round the Ship. Both brothers took this in good heart. After Conway, Guy went to sea but later joined the British South African Police in Rhodesia before retiring in South Africa.

And You'll Find on the Bridge a Conway Boy
The Brooke Smith Dynasty (1893-1963)

Lt. Cdr. F.H. Brooke Smith GC RD RNR (34-36) was a cadet in the Ship on the Mersey. A Sub-Lieutenant Royal Naval Reserve he was torpedoed in the second world war and then volunteered for mine disposal duties. In December 1940, having previously defused 16 mines, a mine fell on the fire-float Firefly in the Manchester Ship Canal, landing inside the deck locker alongside the engine-room. It failed to explode. When Sub-Lieutenant Brooke Smith arrived to deal with it, he found it was firmly wedged, but by using a rope he was able to pull the mine slightly clear of the engine-room casing and then, lying on the sloping engine casing, head downwards, he managed to place a safety gag in the bomb-fuse. The clock of the fuse then started to tick, but he stayed where he was and finally managed to stop it before the inevitable explosion occurred. He had dealt successfully with many unexploded bombs, but this was the first time that he had used a safety gag on a bomb-fuse and he had to do so in most difficult circumstances as he was compelled to work by touch, without being able to see the bomb fuse at all, and his chances of succeeding and of escaping with his life were regarded as very small. He also dealt with a mine in allotments 50 yards from Short and Masons aircraft factory in Macdonald Rd, London.

Lt.Cdr. F.H. Brooke Smith GC

Later, he helped train divers for Suez Canal clearance. After the war he was a senior officer on passenger lines between New York and Bermuda. He was killed in a road accident near his home in Woodbridge. His medals are on display in the Imperial War Museum in London.

Bruce (61-63) was a cadet in the Camp when uncle John was chief officer, but by now Brookie must have been accomplished at dealing with family members as cadets. Bruce was senior cadet captain Focsle in the summer term of 1963 before going to sea with the Royal Mail Line. He later joined the RAF becoming an instructor teaching pilots to fly.

1972

There were 180 boys in total, still organised in 4 divisions but the traditional port and starboard watches were now called platoons.

"I left in 1972, and for the first time ever less than half of us actually went to sea. However, the Conway experience set us up for life, whatever we were to do. Our year had the notoriety to agitate for change. Why did we have to wear reefers to go on leave? Eventually we were permitted to wear 'civvies' so long as we passed inspection prior to going on leave."

Mr. Lord recalls a more down to earth reason for the change. *Conway* was close to Holyhead and the Irish ferry, and the Northern Ireland Troubles were at their height. Nearly 500 people lost their lives in that year, Bloody Sunday had seen 14 protestors shot by the army, the Provisional IRA was formed and increasing numbers of Catholics were being interred without trial. It was considered simply too dangerous for the cadets to be seen ashore in uniform.

"One Summer's evening an unspoken challenge between the Divisions took place. From the 4 floors of dormitories paper darts came sailing out of the windows. How far could we throw them, who would be first to get one to reach the strait? Someone had the ingenious idea of pinching a chart from the navigation room, taking it up to port Focsle (top floor) and casting the hugest paper dart ever into the strait! It went the whole

way! The ecstatic reception alerted Mr. Barker who caught port Foretop out of bed, saw the litter on the lawn outside, and sent them out in their pyjamas to gather up every single paper dart. They got some barracking from the rest of us..."

"I remember having expressed an interest in bugling, being given a mouthpiece by the band rate. But he refused to give me a bugle until all the calls could be played on a mouthpiece. Once achieved a very battered instrument was provided. The better you got the less dents in your bugle."

"My first bugle watch was memorable for all. As I couldn't sleep due to the fear of c***g it all up, I cat napped all night only to wake with a start, to find the time appeared to be 7.25 am. I proceeded to run down from Focsle at full pelt and bashed out Reveille perfectly. My initial pride was soon stamped on when an senior cadet captain informed me it was actually 6.25 am! Geoff Drake referred to me as the duty 'nightingale' during breakfast, and I was asked to stand up so that everyone would recognise the culprit."

1972 Winter

"After the closure announcement masters and officers kept up the academic standards very well despite their imminent redundancies, and many showed a more humane and supportive side than they had done previously. Discipline remained high and I remember coming back from Bangor on a Saturday night 30 minutes late, due to the Crossville bus breaking down outside Llanfair PG, having had three pints after an away match at Rydal - Basil Lord, wrote to our parents and put us on watch, looking over the playing fields for the last four Saturdays and Sundays of term."

1973

A cataclysmic change occurred which would have had most Old *Conways* rushing to re-enlist.

"Fifth formers were allowed to smoke off-duty in the grounds but out of sight of the main buildings and also in the designated smoking room (ex common room) on the ground floor."

Junior cadets had to resort to tradition subterfuges and one fell off the Kelvin Block parapet while sneaking a smoke behind the wall. He had to be taken to Sister with bruised ribs but survived.

"During our senior year we were sailing the 2 cutters with pleb crews. We had the plebs line the rail with buckets of water and tacked close in order to fire water broad sides. My counterpart knew I would not give way and he called 'Water' when on the windward tack, which I ignored, so when he stood on I rammed him and stove in the gunwale strake amidships on his cutter. Brookie was furious. I believe he knew what we had been doing and made us both help the Bosun replace the strake during our free time He disrated me, for the rest of the term, I was a coxswain rate."

"A new member of staff joined and there was something strange in that both his eyes were a different colour, but I don't think we cottoned on one was false. He coached the 2nd XV, and during a scrum practice I collided with him at full speed ahead. He suddenly stopped, head down and both arms outstretched as if feeling his way in the dark. Someone asked what was wrong, and he replied 'It's OK boys.' Then we spotted the empty socket where the eye used to be. I don't know whether we found it hilarious, revolting or both. Naturally, we nicknamed him Hawkeye."

The Band 1973

"The BBC came to film the school before it closed and I remember we all went sailing and rowing in a force 5-6. All capsized and I think the RAF Valley rescue helicopter was called. Not the best advertisement for a naval establishment!"

CHAPTER 37

A SEA CHANGE

Before reviewing how *Conway* faired under the Federation and Cheshire, it is important to understand what was happening in the industry she served.

An Industry Under Threat

After the second world war the words originally quoted in the 1660 Navigation Act: *"It is upon ships and sailors under the good providence of god that our wealth, safety and strength chiefly depend"* remained as true as ever, but Britain somehow allowed her reliance on a strong national merchant navy rapidly to slip away. This decline was not inevitable. From 1914 to 2003, the number of ships in the world fleet grew steadily from 24,444 to 89,960! Total tonnage went from 45.4 million gross tons to a staggering 633.32 million gross tons in the same period, but the growth was favouring other nations for a variety of reasons.

Britain's historical dominance of world shipping finally ended as the United Kingdom centric Empire became the independent Commonwealth. These countries, free to make their own decisions, formed and favoured their own merchant fleets and came to dominate regional trading. Patterns of world seaborne trade shifted to different geographical routes, in particular those to, from and within the Far East. In the process, places like Singapore, Rotterdam and Los Angeles/Long Beach would become world shipping hubs at Britain's expense.

In the late 50s, the British shipping industry was the first to feel the bite of 'outsourcing' and 'offshore working', as foreign crews were cheaper than home grown ones, though often less well trained. The increasing use of flags of convenience in the 1950s saw a wholesale transfer from UK registration. Large bulk dry goods carriers swept away fleets of small tramp ships. Ro-Ro ferries and competition from land transport encroached on coastal and short distance trade. Tankers grew to an almost unbelievable 300,000 deadweight tons, so one ship and one crew replaced what had required 25 vessels and crews in 1939. Container ships were appearing with dramatically increased carrying capacity. They were much faster and had hugely reduced turnaround times. Through the early 60s, automation and computerisation further reduced the number of seafarers needed. The volume of goods transported was increasing, but more and more cargo could be carried by fewer ships with smaller crews. By the mid 60s, air travel had all but ended passenger traffic by sea, including military trooping. Between 1956 and 1962 the tonnage of British ships laid up rose from 200,000 to 600,000 tons. Within a few years Britain provided just 9.6% of world gross shipping tonnage, third largest behind Liberia and Japan. 100 years previously it had been 63%.

British shipping companies tried to survive the storm by merging and forming consortia. In 1965, for example, Overseas Containers Ltd was formed from P&O, Alfred Holt and Co, British and Commonwealth, Clan Line, Shire Line and Furness Withy. One of these companies, Alfred Holt and Co, then merged with Elder Dempster to form Ocean Group. Over the years Glen Line, NSMO, China Mutual, China Navigation Co, Cory Bros, Paddy Henderson, Guinea Gulf,

John Swire, Swire McKinnon and McGregor Gow and Holland were all merged into the group. In 1970 the combined fleet was over 80 vessels, by 1975 there were less than 30. The deep sea fleet was moved under the Isle of Man flag and then sold off one by one. By the late 80s only a few tugs and oil offshore vessels remained, the husk of Ocean was wound up in 2001. The pattern was widespread and British shipping companies, revered worldwide, simply disappeared.

The Industry Moved On

Despite these challenges the demand for cadets was thriving. During the early 60s over 1,000 newly certified navigating officers were needed every year. In 1968 the industry recruited 1,200 navigation cadets and 800 engineer cadets. In 1972, 1,972 new cadets were employed. This burgeoning demand might have appeared a boon for *Conway* and the other pre-sea schools but the shipping companies were also changing fundamentally how they recruited and trained their officers. Throughout the 1940s and 50s *Conway* pre-sea training provided special advantages:

- It gave 12 months remission of apprenticeship time so ex-*Conway* cadets served only a 3 year period at sea not, 4 before their second mate's examination.
- 'Simply being an Old *Conway* carried a certain cachet.' Historically, without pre-sea training it was very difficult to be accepted by a first class shipping company.

"The only 'straight to sea' deck cadets I knew in my company (and there were only a few) were conspicuously related to marine superintendents, masters or chief engineers."

In short, *Conway* cadets were cheaper to train, they were more effective from the outset and achieved their mates' tickets quicker than boys going to sea straight from state schools. This suited the industry although, during the 1950s, only one in four new cadets were drawn from the pre-sea schools. All this did not mean *Conway* cadets were guaranteed places.

"The demand for cadets and junior officers seemed always to be cyclical in the post war years. Either feast or famine. In my fifth term in 1948 I can remember the Ship's company being warned by Captain Goddard that berths for cadets were becoming scarce and that everyone should work hard towards good results."

During the 60s the way shipping companies trained their deck cadets changed dramatically and phased training became the norm. A short pre-sea course (as little as 2 weeks in some cases) was followed by time at sea interspersed with periods of training ashore. A contemporary British India Steam Navigation Company's cadet prospectus put the writing firmly on the wall;

"Pre-Sea training is not essential."

Boys were increasingly employed by companies (and on full pay) from the moment they entered training, whereas *Conway* cadets made no commitment to a company until the end of their *Conway* training even though shipping companies sponsored many of their courses. Increasingly boys ceased choosing which pre-sea college they attended, they joined a company and went where employers sent them. The wise nautical colleges tailored their courses accordingly. *Conway* had early warning of this trend. In October 1959, Shell Tankers proposed to Captain Hewitt that *Conway* provide a 1 term sandwich course for 20 or so of their cadets, to provide special coaching for their

Second Mate's exam and other educational subjects. Wg. Cdr. Browne, with amazing prescience, thought the proposal

> *"should be studied carefully as it might well be the future pattern of Conway and Merchant Navy training."*

Unfortunately Shell's offer was not taken up.

Phased training became more entrenched with the introduction of the Ordinary National Diploma (OND) in Nautical Studies in 1965-6. OND studies were in 3 parts. Part 1 involved 750 hours of *post 'O' level study* ashore, and Part II, a year at sea supplemented by correspondence courses. Part III involved a further 750 hours study ashore before a final qualifying period at sea followed by the exam. Planning for the OND had been going on for years. In January 1961 a conference of sea schools agreed to adopt the course but fatally decided that they would offer only Part 1, and *not* participate in the Part II correspondence courses or Part III. *Conway's* traditional pre, sea, pre 'O' level training no longer fitted neatly into shipping companies' training plans. Captain Hewitt realised this decision posed a great threat

> *"We wanted a three piece suit but can only afford the jacket and waistcoat."*

Mr. Lord picked up responsibility for planning *Conway's* Part I offering, complicated by the need to provide a syllabus that would be acceptable in all ports and regions where the exam might eventually be taken.

By the late 60s the industry allowed boys from any school with a sufficient number of 'A' levels the same remission as for a *Conway* course. *Conway's* expensive residential courses therefore provided no advantage over a free home based secondary/comprehensive school education. Captain Hewitt estimated that pre 1968 at least 50% of cadets received assistance with fees from education authorities and/or shipping companies. Once general 'A' levels from local schools were considered the equivalent of a specialised *Conway* course for remission purposes these bodies had no reason to subsidize attendance at *Conway*. In 1961, 2 universities and 2 polytechnics started courses in nautical science, accepting entries directly from ordinary state schools. The death knell was tolling. The industry no longer needed boys with years of pre-sea training, it was happy with generalists recruited after 'O' levels. *Conway* remained wedded to 2 and 3 year pre-sea training courses. To cap it all some companies, even *Conway's* staunchest supporter Blue Funnel, were setting up their own training establishments.

Conway's drift out of the training mainstream didn't start in the mid 60s. As early as April 1958 Sir John Nicholson wrote a letter to Captain Hewitt that reflected the views of many committee members who were all deeply involved in shipping and so could judge the value of the *Conway* product first hand. He observed that shipping company entrants direct from grammar schools were often of a better calibre than *Conway* boys. He proposed that academic education should be left to ordinary schools and that boys attend *Conway* only *after* 'O' levels for a purely technical, 1 year course. In a separate meeting with marine superintendents several favoured a 1 year course. These ideas had been discussed exhaustively in 1946 and 1947 (See Chapter 18 Difficult Decisions) and kept resurfacing. Captain Hewitt and the Headmaster were strongly opposed to the idea. It meant *Conway* numbers would be almost halved to 150 and they doubted *Conway* could attract 50 boys per course, or survive on half the income. The Headmaster observed that

> *"A post GCE entry puts Conway in direct competition with 15 other schools offering (the) same course with full remission and no fees."*

Conway's staff and committee of management were well aware of the trends. They spent enormous amounts of time and effort discussing how best to respond and were in regular contact with the most senior people in the industry and government. The long struggle to build the New Block confirmed their determination to remain as the premier pre-sea training ship. Unfortunately the industry no longer needed pre-sea training of the type offered. *Conway* made many impressive changes from 1945 but not the vital ones the industry needed and so, gradually, she and all the pre-sea schools became less and less relevant in preparing for a career at sea.

The following analysis of numbers leaving over the life of the Ship demonstrates another interesting trend. More and more boys were attending *Conway* courses but fewer were going to sea. *Conway* seemed to be turning into an attractive boarding school rather than a naval recruiting ground. The 'To Sea' column includes the Royal Navies of Great Britain and other Empire and Commonwealth countries, the Royal Marines, the Merchant Navy worldwide (deck, engineer and purser departments) and pilot services:

	To Sea	Ashore	Withdrawn	Further Education	Plans Not Known
1859 to 1888	Numbers incomplete and so ommitted				
1889 to 1899	98%	1%	0%	0%	1%
1900 to 1959	91%	3%	0%	1%	4%
1960 to 1969	77%	7%	4%	11%	1%
1969 to 1971	72% to 58%	not known	not known	not known	not known
1973	34%	not known	not known	not known	not known
1974 last term	38%	11%	0%	51%	0%

Analysis of Numbers Leaving Over The Life of The Ship

By 1973 only 34% of *Conways* went to sea, but Hansard explained

> *"… by then the axe had been poised by Cheshire. Therefore, boys were leaving Conway to find education at establishments with a secure future."*

CHAPTER 38

1972–3 THE FIGHT AGAINST CLOSURE

Cheshire's Losing Battle

Two key assumptions underpinned *Conway's* viability:

- *To achieve necessary numbers cadets would have to be recruited from all over the UK and abroad.* When the Ministry granted voluntary aided status they insisted on a move towards a sixth form college with entry at 15 or 16 years of age, and away from a 3 year course with entry at age 13 or 14. Cheshire had to comply but there was no shortage of boys wishing to join. Hansard for 6th December 1973 records that

  "In 1972 … there were 800 applicants … only some 200 were interviewed, of whom 65 were accepted."

Mr. Kingsford wrote to the sub-committee that *Conway*

  "should have been full but for Cheshire putting off applicants for a 3 years course."

In 1968 the MMSA calculated *Conway* needed 310 cadets to be viable, but by 1972 there were only 180.

- ☐ *The 'home' education authority would pay to Cheshire the fees of boys attending Conway while parents paid their boarding fees of £270pa.* The Minister's approval of voluntary aided status in July 1968 was granted on the specific condition that the 'home' authorities would have the final say on whether or not to pay *Conway's* fees. Cheshire and the BSF took a huge leap of faith when they assumed that support would be forthcoming. The Labour government was replaced in 1970 and the incoming Tories were looking for cuts to meet election pledges on tax. Mrs Thatcher became Secretary of State for Education and Science in June. She immediately cut the national education budget by £200m, refocusing funding priorities on nursery and primary schools. Ted Heath's election manifesto said of secondary education:

- ☐ "We will maintain the existing rights of local education authorities to decide what is best for their area," directly re-enforcing the Labour Minister's 1968 condition. With local government and education budgets squeezed more then ever, two thirds of the education authorities in England and Wales decided not to pay Cheshire the fees of boys in their areas wishing to attend *Conway*. In 1969, 59 boys were refused places because their education authority would not pay their fees. 58 more were similarly refused in 1971. *Conway's* 1971 prospectus was clear:

  "It will be necessary for Cheshire Education Council to obtain agreement of the local education authority where the parents live before it can make arrangements for a boy to be admitted to the final examination/ interview. The reason for this is that the tuition fees, which are at present more than £400 per annum, are payable by local education authorities and cannot be paid by parents, but it is for the home authority to decide whether it will accept this responsibility."

Neither assumption was proving correct.

Under MMSA management, *Conway* had lost money since 1964 and in many years before that. Cheshire's education committee accounts show they too never came close to breaking even, despite increasing annual fees from £390 to £685 when they assumed control.

Year	Income	Expenditure	Loss
68/69	£88,047	£90,513	£2,466
69/70	£132,770	£147,827	£15,057
70/71	£134,149	£148,586	£14,437
71/72	£150,155	£169,075	£18,920
		Total Loss	£50,880

Income and Expenditure 1968-72

The largest element of cost was teachers' salaries which, under voluntary aided status, were set by the nationally agreed Burnham Scale. Projections indicated that without the financial support of the other authorities and dramatically reduced numbers Cheshire faced deficits of £37,000 in 72/73, and £54,720 in 73/74. This was unsustainable. Cheshire ratepayers could not be expected to spend their dwindling education budget subsidising boys from all over the country and abroad to attend a loss-making specialist school miles outside the county. By 1973 the situation had worsened, numbers fell to 148 of which only 20 came from the county. Cheshire could not continue with these losses and without Cheshire's involvement neither could the Federation. Cheshire's losses did not include the Federation's capital investment to bring the infrastructure up to the standards set for voluntary aided schools. They agreed *Conway* must close but not immediately, perhaps hoping for some last minute improvement. They approached the Ministry of Education and Science in November 1972 seeking a permit to cease maintaining *Conway* after August 1974. They concluded that

> *"the only possible way of granting a reprieve for the school would be for the Ministry to reverse Miss Alice Bacon's decision and to remove from us the obligation to consult with other authorities and accept boys only with their agreement."*

It would be some time before the Ministry responded so Cheshire felt obliged to announce their intentions publicly.

The announcement that *Conway* must close came like a bombshell to the cadets in the summer term of 1972.

"Basil Lord with some education bigwigs from Cheshire County Council called us all in to the Mess Hall and announced that the school was to close in the summer of 1974. The shock and disappointment was immense, and I still remember the reaction of loyal and dedicated teachers who had given so much of their lives to the old wooden mother. They showed immense dignity and strength to all the cadets, even though they had just been told they had lost their jobs and unique way of life. Many would not work again."

It must have been a double blow for Brookie and Mr. Kingsford who had seen her through the vicissitudes of the wartime blitz, the Ship's loss in 1953, recovery in the Camp, the false dawn of the New Block, new ownership and the change from ship to school. 30 years of constant struggle had come to naught.

"Although we were all bitterly disappointed and surprised at the announcement of the closure, some of us at least would be able to complete our 'O' level or 'A' level courses."

Junior cadets whose courses were expected to continue beyond the summer of 1974 would have to find other schools to continue their education.

"This is when the first links with Kelly College came about. They offered us places at their school in Tavistock, Devon so that we could complete our education. I am not sure if anyone joined Kelly College. I went for an interview but found it very uninspiring after the Conway."

A few cadets joined the following year, but were aware that they would not complete their education at *Conway*.

The *Conway* Club and parents were informed of the closure decision and both groups mobilised to try and save her.

The Conway Club's Campaign

The Club naturally did not want to see *Conway* close so, after a vote at their Annual General Meeting in October 1972, they formed a sub-committee led by Captain D Smith to consider what could be done. They focussed initially on preventing the Federation and Cheshire abandoning ship:

- Mr. P P Broadhead (19-21) a partner in Ingledew, Brown, Bennison and Garrett who specialised in shipping and marine insurance law provided, free of charge, a legal opinion on the owners' responsibilities, *Conway's* assets (leases and property) and their disposal if it closed. It gave a precise statement on the historic and extant leases, ownership responsibilities and related issues but did not identify any grounds that could be used to prevent *Conway's* closure.

- A publicity campaign was launched in the national and local press; old boys were encouraged to write to their MP seeking political support and to their local education authority asking them to pay fees for boys at *Conway*. Headlines like 'The storm that could sink HMS *Conway*' and 'Old Boys May Save *Conway*' duly appeared but did not influence those making the decisions. TEW Browne produced proposals for a TV series to demonstrate *Conway's* value to the nation.

- The Minister was asked to force education authorities to pay fees but that but was directly contrary to manifesto pledges and government policy to allow authorities *"to decide what is best for their area."*

The Ministry's reply was unambiguous

"even if Mrs Thatcher agreed the value of Conway she cannot in law force education authorities to make grants."

The iron lady did not see *Conway's* value and she was not one to support a lame duck.

- Attempts were made to persuade Cheshire to continue but the financial situation made this utterly impossible. Hansard (6th December 1973) confirms that Cheshire eventually lost £242,534 on *Conway*. A letter from the Club accepted

"there is no practical method of making Cheshire maintain Conway."

The Parents' Campaign

A Parents' Association was formed to fight closure and one of them, Mrs Pumphrey, agreed to lead the campaign. They too decided on a carefully orchestrated publicity and public relations campaign to convince Cheshire to continue. Novel ideas included a march to Parliament by a uniformed body of cadets and a personal petition by cadets to Mr. Heath, who would pipe him aboard *Morning Cloud* at Cowes to highlight the irony of closure. In the event more traditional approaches were adopted.

They met representatives of the Federation and Cheshire on 28th July 1972. While everyone agreed that

"it is desirable for ways and means to found to keep Conway open,"

in reality the parents came away believing

"the decision has to all intents and purpose been made to close the establishment and anything that follows is merely a formality."

Matters became somewhat heated when the parents suggested that Cheshire might appear to be deliberately running down numbers by advising parents of 13 and 14 year olds selected for the September 1972 course to withdraw them as they would not be able to complete their 3 year course before *Conway* closed. Cheshire vehemently denied this was their intent calling it a

"calumny on officials and councillors."

The officials explained the situation summarised at the beginning of this chapter which came as a surprise to the parents. After a brief adjournment to discuss their response the parents' stance seemed to change and they appeared to accept that Cheshire could not continue to support *Conway*. When asked if Cheshire would have any objection to another organisation taking over *Conway*,

"the question was in some measure evaded, but there was an indication that millions of pounds would be required."

Finally they sought assurances that teaching numbers would be maintained until closure. The parents' valiant aim to prevent Cheshire from withdrawing support had no more chance of success than the *Conway* Club's.

The Independent School Option

Once it was obvious that *Conway* was most likely to close, a bold step was taken. The Club and the Parents' Association joined forces to consider taking over *Conway* and following Pangbourne's example by tuning it into an independent school. From today's perspective Pangbourne made the right choice in 1964 when it become a fully independent school with a strong nautical tradition. Pangbourne's 2007 prospectus contains a clear echo of its nautical past

> *"Many aspects of the College's unique history are preserved today through ceremonial but the most important one is the continuing emphasis on leadership, self-discipline and service. These ideas may at first sound old-fashioned, but we believe that they represent the fundamental basis upon which a young person can find their place in the modern world. They contain all the elements of what is needed to become a good citizen. This is a school whose ethos and culture is very strong, and pupils here are confident and happy."*

The model clearly worked, was it feasible to emulate them in 1972?

They had huge enthusiasm for the idea. Plans were laid and studies commissioned. The school's focus would be

> *"technical expertise, self reliance, leadership, initiative and a code of right and wrong."*

Wealthy trusts would be invited to fund the school. Direct grant status would be considered. Merger with another school was a possibility. Entry at 13 and 14 years of age would continue. Old scholarships would be re-activated and new ones initiated so pupils could be sought from all walks of life, not just the better off. Pupils would be prepared for the sea and university.

The Federation were approached and indicated that they did not want to continue *Conway* themselves but they would not object if someone stepped into their place as trustees of the HMS *Conway* Cadet School Ltd. Cheshire owned the lease under which the company occupied the premises and would have to agree to assign those rights to any new undertaking. The first stumbling block came in a legal opinion

> *"It does not appear that Cheshire can be legally required by Conway (ie the company) to grant such an assignment."*

Cheshire had the whip hand. When *Conway* closed, if Cheshire had their own plans for the premises, they could prevent anyone else taking over.

Specialists were commissioned to produce a 5 year financial plan. Their very detailed report on 1st March 1974, killed all hopes stone dead. £103,335 was needed immediately for new equipment, repairs and improvements. Projected costs in year 1 (1974) of £145,000 would leap by up to £50,000 a year to £327,000 in year 5. These excluded rent that would have to be paid to Cheshire who owned the lease on the land (they informally proposed £20,000 pa) and for the transfer costs for equipment and assets owned by Cheshire. Numbers were expected to drop to just 40 in year one (*Conway* started in 1859 with 50 cadets). The Club and parents hoped to increase numbers to 312 by year 5 but their advisers thought 186 more realistic. To cover the projected costs fees would need to be average £1,800 pa over the 5 years. The advisors thought this level of fee impossible to achieve and calculated a shortfall of £500,000 over the 5-year period. The report concluded with 2 deadly observations.

> *"Additional methods of finance apart from school fees will be required"*

and

> *"The council appear to be in a position to close down the school indefinitely if they were to decide to charge excessive payment for rental of the premises or the transfer of the school equipment."*

Alternative sources of finance were vigorously pursued but in a speech to the cadets the chairman of the sub-committee reported

> *"… the Club would have needed £500,000 over 5 years to make the plan viable. The response we received, though encouraging, was not enough to underwrite this risk."*

On 29th May 1973, the sub-committee and parents admitted defeat and that alone

> *"the Club cannot make arrangements to keep Conway in being."*

The only hope now was that Mrs Thatcher could be convinced to step in with the necessary funds to save *Conway*. On 10th October 1973 the opening salvo was fired, she approved Cheshire's application to close *Conway*. It was going to be a difficult fight against a conviction politician later famous for her boast,

> *"the lady's not for turning."*

The Political Campaign

Captain Walter Elliott RN was an Old *Conway* who joined the Royal Navy after 2 attempts at the entrance exam. He represented the Royal Navy at rugby and attained the rank of Captain. When he retired, he was elected MP for Carshalton He agreed to front the political campaign that was to be cross party and not divided on party lines. 139 MPs were supportive and signed a motion calling on the government

> *"to continue the existence of this unique establishment."*

Independent expert witnesses gave advice and the press seemed sympathetic.

The campaign culminated in an adjournment debate in the House of Commons at 12.54 am, on 6th December 1973. Walter Elliott stood to face Timothy Raison, the Under Secretary of State for Education and Science, representing Margaret Thatcher. He sketched *Conway's* history and contribution not just to the sea but every walk of British life at home and abroad. He pointed out the valorous service of *Conways* over 115 years including four VCs. He stressed that *Conway* drew boys from all walks of life and that they left

"equipped to take their place in the modern world with a sense of obligation to society."

He summarised:

"Conway has fine traditions and an outstanding record of service to the nation. Demand for places at the school is high. Demand for Conway cadets by the shipping lines is strong. The standard of education is of a high order. Has this great maritime nation got its priorities so wrong that, while supporting every other type of establishment, from ballet schools to bankrupt companies, it will not support the unique training school known as HMS Conway?"

He concluded by identifying a number of ways the Ministry could intervene to save the school.

Timothy Raison responded on behalf of the government and sounded the death knell immediately

"The Secretary of State is not empowered to consider alternatives to the published (Cheshire) proposals."

He reiterated the arguments covered in the preceding paragraphs, resolutely adding nails to the coffin:

"Cheshire's economic and educational considerations;"

number applying were irrelevant as many applicants were

"not academically capable of undertaking the courses that were offered;"

Conway's remission advantage had disappeared; the Rochdale Committee questioned the value of vocational training before age 16, an increasing preference for national qualification over the *Conway* Certificate. He concluded by noting that *Conway* could become independent but no buyer had been found, and that no government financial support would be forthcoming to assist that scheme. He announced what many suspected. Cheshire intended to use the premises for their own educational purposes (*as an outdoor centre*) but would preserve the name and some of *Conway's* traditions. Cheshire owned the leases on the land and had now purchased the buildings from the Federation. The New Block cost over £400,000 to build in 1964, the Chapel another £30,000. Hansard on 6th December indicates the 1972 value was closer to £1million and that Cheshire were apparently offering £75,000 for the buildings! If they did pay that amount to the Federation the loss of £242, 534 they made on *Conway* turned a very healthy return. The debate ended at 1.24 am.

Captain Elliott made one more attempt in the House. On 11th December, with Mrs Thatcher and Timothy Raison present, he tried to re-open the debate by questioning Cheshire's motives for closing *Conway*. The parents had raised similar concerns with Cheshire and were not alone in their suspicions. In August and September 1972 two members of staff observed in private letters

"Conway is closing because Cheshire want the buildings for other purposes"

and

"Cheshire would rather use the buildings for their own pet ideas. The drama courses take over in a big way in the holidays."

That the *Conway* Centre is now one of the UK's most successful outdoor centres has given this conspiracy theory long legs, but it defies logic. If Cheshire just wanted to get their hands on the buildings and leases, close *Conway* and create an outdoor centre, the company's articles allowed them to do that from day one. Arguably, they did not even need to support the application for voluntary aided status as *Conway* could not have survived for more than a year in 1968 anyway. They did not need to work with the Federation or to try and run *Conway* for 4 years, accumulating huge debts, a massive administrative burden and probably annoying their rate payers in the process. That *Conway's* demise paralleled the significant rise in demand for council outdoor centres seems simply a fortuitous co-incidence for Cheshire. Captain Elliott's concerns were swept aside, whatever Cheshire and the Federation had agreed, Mrs Thatcher

"was not in a position to approve of them, or to be a party to them."

She apparently viewed British shipping as a sunset industry. With her final washing of hands there was now no doubt, HMS *Conway* would close after the summer term of 1974, Cheshire had their own plans for the buildings.

CHAPTER 39

1974 THE LAST HURRAH

There were just 2 more terms until closure. In 2 years numbers had collapsed from 182 to just 85 cadets. All were QBs now. Compared to the past, *Conway's* facilities had been transformed, her training was very different, her standards more demanding. But the values developed in her cadets remained the same and all Old *Conways* would have identified with the small band of men who assembled for these last sad few months. Vice Admiral Sir Arthur Power, Flag Officer Plymouth visited *Conway* during the last term and said

"how impressed he was with at the high standard being maintained in every field of endeavour."

He assessed morale as very high. Mr. Lord in his last Headmaster's report said

"I believe them to be the finest generation of Conway cadets that I have known in the last decade."

Conway now was most firmly the School not the Ship, but old traditions die hard and gulls returning to her decks and yards would have settled easily into their comforting embrace.

"I wouldn't have missed my time on the ship for anything. However, it's fair to say that few of those last cadets went to sea, and many of the parents seemed to have chosen the school for it's academic and sporting prowess as much as the nautical connection."

The cadet captains were:

Chief cadet captain	:	M C Davies
Deputy chief cadet captain	:	C R Woodward
Focsle senior cadet captain	:	N F W Faigniez
Focsle junior cadet captain	:	R G Pallett
Foretop senior cadet captain	:	N J Wand
Foretop junior cadet captain	:	T V D Woodman
Maintop senior cadet captain	:	R J Foyan
Maintop junior cadet captains	:	L Greenfield, S J Marsden
Mizzentop senior cadet captain	:	M S Grant
Mizzentop junior cadet captains	:	R L Davis, I M D Klyne

Mr. Lord was Headmaster, Mr. D Woolley his deputy. W Davidson, E Howard Davies and L Bullock were the only uniformed officers. There were 11 other teachers and the Rev. H. Chalkley was padre. The longest serving member of staff, Mr. Kingsford was housemaster of Maintop and Head of Arts.

The New Block could accommodate 230 so, half the dormitories were closed and with just 16 cadets in the sixth form most classrooms were deserted; the halls and rooms were quiet and still.

"The last year was rather poignant as half of the dorms on each floor were shut, with more than enough bed space in the remaining side (port, I think)."

The House was empty, no noisy, stumbling new chums learning the ropes, gazing on QBs with that perennial mix of admiration and dread, wondering if one day they too might appear as giants. Where once had stood a fleet of huts was now un-remarked grass. Deserted rugby fields bore no trace of the happy crew who had adapted to mud and canvas, or the generations of young men who had played rugby with fire in their bellies. Only the faint echo of cadets was to be heard at the dock. The mooring where the Ship once proudly swung was empty, though some of her giant anchors still gripped the earth with unmovable determination. Small boats lay quietly at their moorings, soon to be dispersed.

Daily routine continued, albeit as a shadow of its formal bustling self.

"When I went back to visit the school in 1974, discipline was very different from what I remembered. Naturally there were now much fewer boys and they were permitted to wear civvies around the school. The ban on smoking no longer extended to 16 year olds. I had a nice evening watching a movie on the white wall of one of the sixth form studies. A short back and sides was a thing of the past."

Cadets were still of the same breed, they obeyed most rules naturally and circumvented others with panache. Cadet captains governed daily life and punishment followed discovery.

"One dark and freezing morning the early heave-out lads were assembled on the parade ground just as first light was showing and the cadet captain of the morning stood planning exactly what form of punishment he should mete out to us unfortunates. I remember suggesting that we should all climb over the mast and organise races over the top. His reply was that if I was mad enough to sit on the truck he would find some easy task for all the party. Well being one to never let a challenge go, up I went to the 'oohs' and 'ahhs' of the others and shimmied up to the truck. I sat on it for what felt like hours but in reality was seconds scared to hell and shaking. From the cold you understand. Anyway on my return to the ground we were made to clean some internal area of the building and tea and smokes were had by all."

The hockey team was hailed as

"Probably the best hockey team we have ever had"

"probably the best hockey team we have ever had."

They played with

"rare determination and boundless energy"

winning all their matches, scoring 53 goals and conceding only nine. N J Wand captained the side with

"firm resolution and unending keenness."

Cricket, with only 14 players to chose from, faired less well and suffered heavy defeats from Rydal and Ruthin but beat Deeside and

Friars. Focsle beat Maintop 5-2 to win the Partridge Cup for interdivisional tennis. Maintop won the interdivisional Holt Badminton Cup. In the final of the very last interdivisional gig race Foretop beat Maintop by half a length. Foretop also won the final Haigh Trophy.

The faces in the last team photos gaze back out with that same mix of pleasure, confidence and physical presence all Old *Conways* remember. The same expression can be seen in every sports team photo of 10, 50 even 100 years before. These final moments saw sporting achievements the match of anything that had gone before. The 1st XV

"worked as a team and trained extremely hard all season."

And You'll Find on the Bridge a Conway Boy
Sir Clive R Woodward OBE (1969-74)

Sir Clive was forced to attend Conway by his father, largely it seems to prevent him from playing football. This coloured his whole experience and his book makes it very clear he did not enjoy his time at Conway. Despite his published statements he was a very successful cadet and was appointed the deputy chief cadet captain in his last term, a position not easily achieved by one who hates his environment. He rails against the regime yet the Headmaster remembers a different boy and a different environment to that presented. Sir Clive's books describe a Conway few others recognise and many of his compatriots lived a different experience to that he described.

Whatever his views of the life and of being forced to abandon his beloved football, Conway certainly developed his natural rugby skills and doubtless his leadership skills as well. A contemporary recalls "He was a good all-rounder and well able to get on with the senior cadets. I can quite see the Conway training in his approach to leadership."

He excelled at rugby union. "He was a centre, generally able to play anywhere in the backs - a very good kicker." Despite his apparent desire to play football, when he left Conway he continued to play rugby and only stopped when he had conquered the world. He played first for Leicester and was selected to represent England in 1980 wining 21 caps in four years. In 1985 he emigrated to Australia and played for the Sydney Premier side, Manly. By 1990 he was back in the UK and coaching Henley RFC. He had found his niche observing that "Teaching...is in my blood."

He became a successful rugby coach, moving to London Irish and then Bath. In August 1997, he was invited to become the first ever, full time coach of the England rugby union side. Conways the world over thrilled (those in Australia perhaps less so!) to see England coached to ultimate World Cup success by one of their own (no matter how reluctant).

Leaving rugby behind, he at last returned to the game taken from him in his youth, becoming Performance Director at Southampton Football Club in 2005. He left them in 2006 and took up the post of director of elite performance for the British Olympic Association.

When 'Ning Ning' Kingsford, our much loved history and rugby tutor died, a relative recalled how Sir Clive visited him one evening and quietly whisked him off a drink and a long yarn. When Mr. Kingsford's family went through his belongings they found a rugby ball signed by every member of the 2003 World Cup team. Perhaps actions speak louder than words.

And You'll Find on the Bridge a Conway Boy
Captain David Terence Smith OBE RN (1942-44)

By the time he joined Conway in 1942, David had already decided on a career in the Royal Navy. He completed his Conway course with flying colours being awarded the King's Gold Medal and the Trinity House prize in 1944. His first sea-going appointment was in Rodney, part of the 5th Battle Squadron at Scapa Flow. He moved on to the Bermuda, part of the British Pacific Fleet, taking part in the relief of Formosa, Tsingtao, Shanghai and Hong Kong. In 1946 he joined minesweepers and was involved in sweeping operations off Borneo and then Holland. From 1947 he began a specialisation in navigation and was promoted Lieutenant in 1949.

In 1950, he was loaned to the Royal New Zealand Navy and after a spell in the Mediterranean he arrived in New Zealand during their general strike in 1951. He suddenly found himself unloading merchant cargo ships in Wellington and then colliers in Westmouth and Greyport. This led to a rather unusual appointment for an RN officer, he was in charge of 6 open cast coal mines on the South Island. After the strike he served in a number of RNZN ships before returning to the UK in 1952 for a specialist navigation course. 1953 found him on the Narvik assisting in the East Coast flood relief operation. Posting followed posting from the Mediterranean to the South Atlantic and home waters. In 1959, he took up navigating duties in HM Yacht Britannia for Queen's opening of the St Lawrence Seaway. Promoted Commander in 1960 he was appointed to command the Loch Lomond in the Arabian Gulf and Persian Gulf. After a period on the Admiralty's planning staff he became second in command of the strike carrier Eagle deployed east of Suez and on the Beira Patrol. Promoted Captain in 1967, he began a series of staff appointments with the Chief of the Defence Staff. In 1973 he took up his last seagoing appointment, Commodore Amphibious Warfare to Flag Officer Carriers and Amphibious Ships. He exercised command of the UK/Netherlands Amphibious Task Group and NATO Amphibious Forces in the Mediterranean, Caribbean and on NATO's Northern Flank wearing his broad pennant in Hermes, Intrepid, Fearless and Bulwark, with amphibious ships, destroyers, frigates, naval auxiliaries and aircraft in support as necessary.

Leaving the RN in 1976, he became an Elder Brother Of Trinity House and began a second career as illustrious as his first. He worked in the Pilotage Committee, the Lights Executive, the Examiners (Navigation) Committee and attended the Admiralty and Appeal Courts at the Royal Courts of Justice. In 1987 he became the Chief Executive of the Lighthouse Service. In his spare(!) time he has undertaken considerable charitable work for the Marine Society, The Seaman's Hospital Society, The HMS Conway Trust, St Olave's Patronage Trust and the Foudroyant Trust. He is a past President of the Conway Club, a Naval member of the Royal Yacht Club, a Fellow of the Nautical Institute and a Freeman of the City of London.

In 1978, he became Chairman of the Nelson era frigate Foudroyant (ex Trincomalee), a training ship for young people in Portsmouth harbour. When training ended he masterminded her move to Hartlepool and full restoration as HMS Trincomalee, a 19th Century wooden sailing frigate at a cost of £10.5M. He was awarded an OBE for this and a special citation by the World Ship Trust for individual achievement "Through his personal and enthusiastic leadership (he) ensured that the restoration and preservation of HMS Trincomalee has been an inspiration to all who seek to preserve historic ships and the maritime heritage of the world."

Although he 'retired' in 1992, he continues much of his charitable work and his association with the Trincomalee Trust.

With so few numbers, four Colts played regularly in the 1st XV. They hosted and won the North Wales 7 a side competition, 1 cadet played in the Welsh national trials, 6 played for North Wales Schools, old rivals like Birkenhead School and Manchester Grammar were trounced. It was fitting that the last match against the Old Boys ended in a draw. The 1st XV captain, a young Clive Woodward played

"magical rugby."

In sailing, the RYA proficiency scheme was keenly pursued. Of the 85 cadets, 48 cadets achieved basic proficiency, 37 intermediate, 17 went on to advanced level and 8 achieved instructor level. The Moody Cup was won by McIlwraith, the Spittlehouse Cup by Richardson and the Harley Shield by Kenny. The interdivisional Williamson Cup was won for the last time by Maintop. The cadets won a final gig race against the Old Boys by 2 lengths.

"After being involved with sailing at Conway for over 20 years I leave with a host of memories. The MSODs, the Fifes, the old sailing cutters then more recently our modern fleet of dinghies and longboats. Between them they have enabled countless cadets to enjoy the sport of sailing … and reap the benefit of this enjoyable pastime."

The guest of honour at the final Prize Giving was Captain D. T. Smith RN (42-44) who made a fitting speech for the occasion. He was the President of the *Conway* Club and was soon afterwards deeply involved in planning a secure future for *Conway's* main artefacts. He ensured particularly that major items like the figurehead, wheel and bell found appropriate and secure homes.

The cadets paraded to choose the Queen's Gold Medallist for the 109th and last time. The qualities they sought were those

"which will make the finest sailor: cheerful submission to superiors, self respect and independence of character, kindness and protection of the weak, readiness to forgive offence, desire to conciliate the differences of others, and above all, fearless devotion to duty and unflinching truthfulness."

M C Davies - Last Chief Cadet Captain and QGM Winner

They choose the chief cadet captain, M C Davies and it was presented to him by the Queen in a private audience at Buckingham Palace on 17th July 1974. A complete list of winners is in *Appendix E*. Some years later the Queen later graciously agreed to rename the medal as the 'Queen's *Conway* Gold Medal' and to transfer its award to the Canadian Coastguard College.

On the last Tuesday of term, all 85 cadets, 4 old boys and 8 masters assembled at the dock for a final cruise to Aber Menai. They manned all 25 sailing dinghies, gigs, motorboats and rescue boats and departed at 4.00 pm

"Off Port Dinorwic the ebb against a force 5 wind was creating a nasty sea. The sailing was hard and the cadets proved to themselves that a 7 mile beat to windward requires stamina, skill and the right gear."

By 7.00 pm, all were ashore at Aber Menai for a barbeque, sing song and tug of war against the staff, which the staff won. At 10.00 pm, everyone embarked for the return journey. A mast had been rigged in one of the gigs and under a square sail she was back in the dock in 1 hour and 10 minutes. It was dark but, with a following wind and the tide under them, they made good progress and arrived back safely.

"Conway started under sail and it was appropriate that her entire company should take part in her final major evolution - under sail."

But before paying off there was to be one last sad day.

CHAPTER 40

THURSDAY 11ᵀᴴ JULY 1974: PAYING OFF DAY

As the sun set on Wednesday 10th July 1974 outside the New Block, *Conway's* ensign was lowered for the last time to the sound of the buglers from the band. The next morning, cadets and staff prepared for her last day, a service at Liverpool Cathedral followed by a *Conway* Club lunch

In the words of Mr. Lord

"It has seemed most appropriate that Conway, which began her life on the Mersey, should as it were return there from exile to take her leave of that great seaport and country which feels she had served her purpose."

The empty river, derelict docks and silent wharves reflected one reason why *Conway* had run her course.

Liverpool cathedral was full of Old *Conways*, staff, parents, friends and shipping representatives. The ceremony remembered the foundation of *Conway*, gave thanks for the spirit of loyalty and adventure shown by former cadets on the high seas, under the sea, on land and in the air, in peace and war. It acknowledged the service and guidance of governors and staff. The intercessions were:

LIVERPOOL CATHEDRAL

THANKSGIVING SERVICE
AND
LAYING UP OF THE COLOURS
OF
H.M.S. CONWAY
MERCHANT NAVY CADET SCHOOL

THURSDAY, 11th JULY, 1974
at 11 a.m.

Cover of Thanksgiving Service

- For the foresight and inspiration of the members of the Mercantile Marine Services Association, which led the school's foundation in 1859.

- For the shipowners of Liverpool, whose generosity in early and subsequent days, enabled this inspiration to become a reality.

- For their Lords Commissioners of the Admiralty, through whose practical support the first three ships were provided.

- For the support given by successive Sovereigns, who through the annual award of the gold medal have encouraged high ideals and standards and the formation of qualities that make the finest sailor.

- For all staff, both professional and academic, and those who have voluntarily served on the governing body and their devoted service to the ideals of HMS *Conway*.

- For all Old *Conways* who have been called to higher service, especially those who died on active service during the two world wars.

- For all other Old *Conways* who have tried to live up to and pass on to others the ideals learnt during their training onboard.

A final prayer was offered up:

> *"Almighty and Eternal God, whose way is on the deep, we commend to Thy Fatherly care all that go down to the sea in ships and occupy their business in great waters: the officers and men of the Royal Navy and Merchant Navy; all lighthouse keepers, coastguards and pilots; the men of the fishing fleets and the crews of lifeboats; and all the workers in docks and harbours. Help them, in whatever lies before them, to quit themselves like men: if there be any duty may they do it with cheerfulness; if any danger may they face it with courage, knowing Thy hand is in all things and all things are in Thy hands."*

> *"The most poignant moment was when the colour party, in a hushed cathedral slow marched down the aisle to hand over the colours for laying up in the cathedral."*

The sermon was preached by the Archbishop of Wales who took Philippians 4, 9 (NEB) as his theme

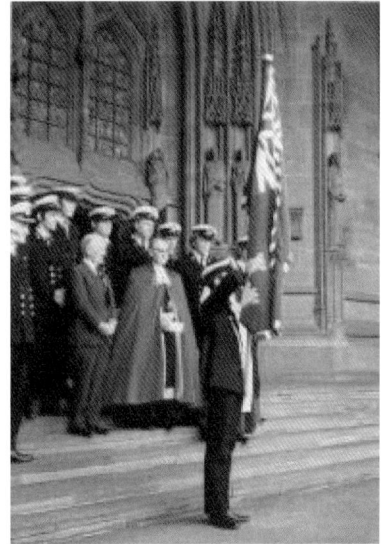

Ensign Outside The Cathedral

> *"The lessons I taught you, the tradition I have passed on, all that you heard me say or saw me do, put into practice."*

He summed up what it means to be a *Conway* Boy

> *"… the formation of character … experience of what it means to be members of a single community in which each person depends on all the others and is responsible for them. The motivation that puts the interests of others above their own. Their extraordinary affection for their old school is the best proof that experience of life has made them endorse for themselves the value taught to them in their early days."*

> *"At the end of the service the cadets lined the aisles as the packed congregation went out – a most emotional moment."*

The *Conway* Club hosted lunch in *Royal Iris*. She was wearing the *Conway* ensign. All hands mustered on deck for Colours and, as a cadet bugler sounded Sunset, the ensign was lowered for the last time. The ships in port, many dressed overall for the occasion, blew their sirens and cheered her on her way. As seagulls circled overhead, those assembled sang the *Conway* song and gave a rousing Hullabaloo to send her over the bar to meet her waiting sons.

> *Where the tide runs in from the open sea,*
> *The good ship Conway rides,*
> *No more she fights the enemy,*
> *No more she takes the tides,*
> *But dear as of old to our hearts is she,*
> *For she caught us and taught us to sail o'er the waters,*
> *So we love her, none other, our old Wooden Mother,*
> *O the Conway's the one ship for you and for me!*
> *When I came to her I was four foot three,*

My heart was beating fast.
I saw her first quite tearfully,
But kept them down at last,
But soon I was settled and sang with glee,
To bewail her, no sailor, would dare so to fail her,
We find later we rate her a splendid old Mater,
O the Conway's the one ship for you and for me!

When I left her at last and I went to sea,
A lump was in my throat,
I watched her fade all mistily,
God bless the dear old boat,
And dear to the hearts of her sons is she,
For she made us, displayed us, on fighters and traders,
Ev'ry rover, all over, from Chili to Dover,
Sings, the Conway's the one ship for you and for me!

Chorus
Carry on, carry on, till the last day's gone,
And the old ship knows you no more.
O East and West and North and South,
From Rio Bay to Mersey mouth,
From every distant sea and shore,
You'll here the cry,

"Ship ahoy, Ship ahoy!"
And you'll find on the bridge a Conway boy,
So for love of the ship that sends us forth,
From East and West and South and North,
Till the last tide turns and the last day's gone
Carry on, Carry on, Carry on.

CHAPTER 41

1982 OLD CONWAYS AND THE FALKLANDS CAMPAIGN

In 1982, when the Argentinean invaders of the Falkland Islands surrendered, the BBC assembled a collection of service chiefs and politicians to comment.

> *"They paid tribute to the fighting services, the dockyard maties, those getting the stores together, indeed everyone concerned save one – the Merchant Navy."*

The Merchant Navy actually played a critical role, indeed the British task force could never have made it to the Falklands or sustained the invasion without the merchant fleet and her sailors. The task force comprised 114 ships of which 37 were from the Royal Navy, 77 were from the Merchant Navy; 25 Royal Fleet Auxiliaries and 52 chartered commercial vessels, all manned by civilian crews. Many Old *Conways* were involved, including the Masters of 10 of the task force's vessels. As the Falklands Campaign is described well elsewhere, I have simply listed Old *Conways'* involvement by role or vessel as appropriate.

Discovery of the Invasion and Initial Response, Steve Martin (1970-73) and Brian Lockwood (1972-74)

The first report of the invasion was made by Steve Martin (1970-73), the British Antarctic Survey's base commander in the Falklands. On 19th March four of his scientists, including Brian Lockwood (1972-74), visited South Georgia, an uninhabited British island 800 miles from the Falklands, and were surprised to find an Argentinean ship at anchor and around 50 men ashore. Steve was advised of their presence and he informed the Governor. At the Governor's request Steve travelled to South Georgia to investigate but the Argentineans refused to co-operate with him. On 24th March, 24 Royal Marine commandoes landed to back him up. On 25th March, significant numbers of Argentinean troops were landed on South Georgia and an unofficial incursion escalated into a military invasion. By 3rd April the invasion of the Falkland Islands proper was complete and the British troops on South Georgia, along with Steve Martin and Brian Lockwood, were arrested, questioned and transferred to Tierra del Fuego where they were imprisoned. Well treated, they were eventually flown back to the UK via Montevideo.

Assistant Chief of Defence Staff (Operations), Mod HQ London, Vice Admiral Sir David Brown KCB RN (1941- 45)

The British Government decided that the islands would be recaptured by force and a war cabinet was formed. At the Ministry of Defence, Admiral Sir John Fieldhouse was given overall command and began planning the campaign on behalf of the Chief of the Defence Staff (CDS), Admiral Sir Terrance Lewin. The Assistant Chief of Defence Staff (Operations), Old *Conway* Vice Admiral Sir David Brown KCB RN (1941- 45) was appointed to liaise between the CDS and Admiral Fieldhouse. He digested Admiral Fieldhouse's plans and information into a form that could be presented by the CDS to the war cabinet, and then translated war cabinet decisions into operational directives that he relayed back to Admiral Fieldhouse.

"The job was really one of politico/military interface, presentation of the military view, speed/time/distance constraints, information flow, operational directives for special forces, trouble shooting, and perhaps most complex of all was the Rules of Engagement. The latter was an interpretation of whether HM Government was escalating, retaining the status quo, or de-escalating, and in case specific rules had to be signalled to Commanding Officers of HM ships and aircraft, giving clear and positive guidance as to what could or could not be done."

Admiral Brown's job lasted throughout the campaign.

Deputy Chief of Fleet Support, Rear Admiral Edwards MVO RN (1941-44)

Everything needed to get the troops and their equipment to the Falklands, to land them and then support them ashore until the islands were liberated, had to be carried in the 114 vessels of the task force. Each ship had its own complex mix of stores, spares, victuals, fuel and armaments, much of which had to be purchased on the open market, delivered to stores depots across the UK and then moved to the dockyard where each ship was being fitted out. Rear Admiral Edwards MVO RN (1941-44) as Deputy Chief of Fleet Support played a key role in this vital and huge logistical task.

Preparing The Royal Fleet Auxiliary, Captain C G Butterworth (1941-43)

The Royal Fleet Auxiliary (RFA) would provide the core of the task force's support ships so the RFA's Marine Superintendent, Captain C G Butterworth (1941-43), suddenly found himself working long hours to get them back to the UK, provisioned and fitted out in time. He assembled and despatched 25 ships against seemingly impossible deadlines.

In Hermes as Chief of Staff to the Joint Service Commander of the task force, Vice Admiral Sir Peter Woodhead RN (54-57)

Sir Peter was recalled from leave and appointed to support the force commander, Rear Admiral Woodhouse. The force had already departed so he had to fly to Ascension and rendezvous with Hermes there. Such was the enormous amount of work of planning the landing and all that goes with it, that Sir Peter and another officer stood watch and watch as Group Warfare Officer concentrating on running the task force, which at any one time numbered up to 80 vessels, and overseeing almost constant use of the flight deck.

Queen Elizabeth 2 (QEII), Chief Officer, R W Warwick (1956-57)

The majority of the task force were requisitioned civilian ships, including the *QEII*. Her Chief Officer, R W Warwick (1956-57) kept a diary of events. In just 18 days she was stripped of everything relating to her civilian cruising role, converted into a troopship and fitted with helicopter landing pads. She was loaded with ammunition, military equipment and vehicles covered every spare deck space, and finally, on 12th May, she embarked 3,000 soldiers and airmen, the most passengers she had ever carried. Off Portsmouth, 2 Sea King helicopters landed onboard and were secured for the journey south. Her transition to troopship was complete,

"live firing exercises … every part of the ship is in use for some form of training … every unit onboard has a time slot for jogging (in army boots) – the noise is incredible, it is playing havoc with the decks – the caulking is lifting out all over the place."

And You'll Find on the Bridge a Conway Boy
Vice Admiral Sir David Brown KCB RN (1941- 45)

On Conway, Brown was at or near the top of his intake in several subjects, won prizes and was a cadet captain. Poor eyesight meant that it took him 5 attempts to get into the Royal Navy. His determination won him a place in the last week of the second world war, at the age of 17. He became a specialist in anti-submarine warfare and commanded eight vessels, from a gunboat to frigates, a frigate squadron, and finally took charge of one of the latest guided missile destroyers. He saw active service as an operations officer in the confrontation with Indonesia in the 1960s, and held several staff posts, including with NATO.

Deep defence cuts in the late 1960s, had effectively confined the Royal Navy to the north Atlantic and the Mediterranean. In the early 1970s, Brown, as Director of Naval Operations and Trade, successfully argued the case for annual naval forays to such areas as the Far East and the South Atlantic. This revival of the old custom of "showing the flag" would remind the world of Britain's abiding foreign interests and once again attract recruits to "Join the navy and see the world." A series of deployments east and south of Suez ensued.

Margaret Thatcher's first administration removed the last vestige of a naval presence in the South Atlantic and the Argentinean junta thought that the Falklands were theirs for the taking. When the Argentinean army invaded the Falklands Thatcher was furious but frustrated. There was much wringing of hands until Admiral Sir Henry Leach, the chief of naval staff, marched into parliament in full uniform and persuaded Thatcher that the navy should dispatch a task force to take back the Falklands. Rear Admiral Brown was in the key post of Assistant Chief of Defence Staff (Operations) and it fell to him to brief the daily meetings of the war cabinet in London on events in the South Atlantic. His briefings impressed Thatcher and all who heard them.

He ran a tight ship and drove his juniors hard. His inability to suffer fools gladly extended to the top of the service and probably explained why such a gifted officer never made full Admiral. He was once called aboard Vanguard, flagship of Admiral Sir Philip Vian, the C-in-C, Home Fleet. Vian was furious because Brown's ship had failed to dip its colours in salute to him as it entered harbour. After being bawled out at considerable volume, Brown coolly replied that, as a ship's Captain, he was entitled to be piped aboard the flagship and had therefore not been properly saluted either.

His last position was as Flag Officer, Plymouth, before he retired in 1985 with a KCB.

A Conway's commitment to deckwork never fails!

As they moved south towards Ascension Island, all vessels were completely blacked out. On the QEII all windows and portholes were covered, even navigating lights were extinguished so she could advance undetected. After Ascension, radio silence was imposed. The loss of the Atlantic Conveyor suddenly brought home

"the reality of the situation that we find ourselves in."

The *QEII* was despatched to South Georgia and anchored in Cumberland Bay East from where she would disembark troops, equipment and stores into other vessels for landing on the Falklands, before transitioning into a hospital ship. On 22nd May Major General J Moore CB OBE MC Commander Land Forces and his staff boarded the *QEII* and set up their headquarters. Under threat from air attack, and still carrying 60 tons of ammunition she was ordered back to sea and steamed off towards Ascension Island. From there it was decided she should return to Southampton, undertaking replenishment at sea under extremely difficult sea conditions to load fuel and offload ammunition. On 12th June, she arrived in the Solent and was welcomed by the Queen Mother in the Royal Yacht and 6,000 spectators along the shore. Military personnel and the injured were disembarked, the ship was released from military service and the crew quietly went about their business to prepare for a refit.

Norland, Chief Officer R B Lough (1961-63)

The rest of the task force made for the Falklands to land the relief force. *Norland* was a large North Sea ferry fitted out as a troopship at Hull and Portsmouth but basically unsuited to the seas around the Falklands. She travelled independently to Ascension where she joined the rest of the Task Force. She was carrying 2 Para and so, inevitably, was going to be in the thick of the action. On 21st May, Norland, with Chief Officer R B Lough (1961-63) as pilot, led the warships *Plymouth*, *Intrepid* and *Fearless*, and the *Canberra*, *Stromness*, *Europic Ferry* and *Fort Austen* into San Carlos Bay for the first forced landing on the Falklands.

> *"Norland led in case the channels were mined, as she was considered to be the most expendable of the ships."*

The Paras disembarked into landing craft and went ashore to begin the land campaign to expel the Argentineans. After disembarkation *Norland* led the whole fleet into San Carlos Water where they anchored. *Norland* and others then began a shuttle service carrying new waves of troops from the *QEII* at South Georgia to San Carlos Water and repatriating prisoners to Montevideo. She entered San Carlos water 5 separate times, always under threat of air attack. The next 4 days saw frequent bombing attacks by Argentinean planes. *Ardent* and *Antelope* were sunk close to *Norland* and she had

> *"one near miss on 24th when two 500 pound bombs landed close alongside."*

With all British forces ashore, she evacuated thousands of prisoners from Port Stanley to the mainland at one time disembarking 2,000 of them at Puerto Madryn in Argentina! Eventually, on 24th June, survivors of 2 and 3 Para were embarked and taken to Ascension from where they flown home. She returned to Port Stanley with relief troops and remained there as a South Atlantic ferry. In August RB Lough was appointed master of *Norland*.

> *"Norland was very lucky to have survived as the Argentinean Air Force was very good and gave us quite a hard time … I must say looking back it was 95% hard work, 5% sheer terror, but I wouldn't have missed it for the world."*

In October Admiral Fieldhouse awarded him a citation

> *"…for his willingness, initiative and fortitude in ensuring the successful achievement of Norland's task."*

Geesport, Master Capt G de Ferry Foster (1954-56)

Geestport was chartered as a 'Forward Support Ship' and she too immediately underwent a number of modifications, including fitting of a helicopter flight deck to facilitate transfer of stores and replenishment at sea. After loading she set off for the South Atlantic by a devious route. When they entered the British Total Exclusion Zone there was a heavy concentration of icebergs

"never less than 57 within a 12 mile radius of the ship … at times it was hard to find a way through them."

Icebergs, atrocious weather and the threat of Argentinean attack meant little sleep for the Old Man. They remained in the Zone for almost 3 months, visiting most scenes of action and completing 58 stores transfers to HM ships and others. At one stage she was alongside *Avalonia Star* whose master was Old *Conway* Captain AW Kinghorn. The return home was flat out at an average speed of 20.02 knots. They were the 43rd ship to return to Portsmouth but still received a tremendous welcome home from the Royal Navy,

"The decks of all HM Ships and shore establishments were manned and gave us 3 cheers as we passed, the sight of Hermes flight deck manned for us is something I will never forget."

Europic Ferry, Master Captain W Clarke OBE (1959-62), Chief Officer Norman Bamford (1961-63), Second Officer Alan Burns (1948-50). One of the soldiers onboard was Staff Sergeant RL Peacock (1969-71)

Europic Ferry must have seemed like a mini *Conway* reunion, with no less than 4 old boys onboard. She embarked equipment and personnel from 2 Para, the RAMC and 656 Squadron AAC, including several vehicles and 3 helicopters, plus a large reserve of ammunition. On the journey south her Master exercised the crew regularly to determine the best conditions for helicopter deck landings and to

"gave serious thought on how to prepare the ship for war."

They travelled south with the ill fated *Atlantic Conveyor*, but they separated at Ascension and *Europic Ferry* left on 7th as part of a much larger group.

"When Defence Watches were instituted, the ship's company were divided into 2 watches so that half the crew were up and alert at any time. Personnel remained in their clothing at all times. Glass fittings were taped up to prevent shattering and furniture was securely lashed down. Extra lookouts were posted and the engine room manning increased."

On 18th May, they joined the main task force in the total exclusion zone and experienced their first 'Action Stations', warnings of submarine attacks. They were part of the main amphibious landing force including *Norland*, *Canberra* and the assault ships *Fearless* and *Intrepid*. They entered San Carlos Bay and immediately offloaded a battery of artillery. Suddenly the air was full of Argentinean Mirages, Skyhawks and Pucaras first attacking the beachhead, *Norland* and *Canberra* but soon turning their attention to *Europic Ferry*. There were a number of near misses and *Europic Ferry* fired back with her small compliment of machine guns. The rest of the day was spent offloading equipment and acting as a helicopter operating deck.

"As we waited for the setting sun to bring an end to the air attacks, all onboard had now realised the meaning of the 'longest day.'"

Over the following days they embarked more materiel from other vessels for San Carlos Bay and then transferred it ashore. At one point they suffered 36 hours of continuous force 10 and 11 storms. Finally, they landed stores and troops to re-establish communications at Port Stanley before returning to the UK.

Baltic Ferry, Master Captain E Harrison (1954-56), Second Officer Bill Langton (1967-69)

When Captain Harrison was asked to take *Baltic Ferry* to the South Atlantic he readily agreed

"surmising that we would probably get no nearer than South Georgia."

They departed UK on 9th May, carrying elements of the 5th Infantry Brigade and considerable quantities of hazardous materials like kerosene, petrol, ammunition and phosphorous and other missiles and helicopters. They completed over 1,000 helicopter deck landings over the next 4 months. *Baltic's* job was to land the second wave of troops and supplies. They entered San Carlos bay in darkness and offloaded without incident. 2 further visits were made, delivering more ammunition and fuel the second with heavy air attacks during which *Plymouth* was damaged and moored nearby. When the engineers reported noises outside the hull, sabotage was feared but it turned out to be a false alarm. Once hostilities were over the crew were relieved and flown home.

RFA Fort Grange, Master Captain DGM Averill CBE (1941-43)

After loading maximum cargo in record time, Captain Averill sailed from the UK for the South Atlantic accompanied by C flight of 824 Squadron and their Sea Kings. On arrival, as the first Royal Fleet Auxiliary (RFA) in the total exclusion zone, 8 very hectic days were spent replenishing 25 vessels in the task force. Subsequently she moved into Bomb Alley to supply the beach head and other vessels. As a specialist re-supply ship, the next few weeks saw non-stop activity supplying the troops and re-supplying themselves from later waves of vessels arriving from the UK. She spent 105 days in the total exclusion zone completing 389 transfers including 700,000 pounds of potatoes, half a million eggs, 10,500 gallons of draught beer and 504,000 cans of beer. Helicopters made 933 day deck landings and 165 night landings.

RFA Sir Tristram, Master Captain G Green (1949-51)

"I was Master of Sir Tristram at Fitzroy Creek (or as the press has it - Bluff Cove) where she was bombed and set on fire, along with her sister ship Sir Galahad. It was a whole new experience, and have the need to replace my Conway tie plus of course everything else."

He says no more. They were attacked by Sky Hawks, 51 people were killed and 46 injured. Captain Green was decorated for his service. His citation reads:

"She was the first ship to make the run to Fitzroy. The task had to be unescorted and meant lying at anchor by day off Fitzroy in an exposed position without benefit of adequate air defence or warning. It was while there that the ship, still well loaded with ammunition, came under fierce surprise air attack and suffered the damage that caused her to be damaged on fire. It is greatly to Captain Green's credit that he was successful

in getting all his people off the ship with the exception of 2 seamen killed. Captain Green, by his personal example and courage throughout the period, inspired his crew to do all that was asked of them, far beyond the normal call of duty."

A number of other Old *Conways* were present but details of their service are not known.

Lycaon, Master Captain H Lawton (1951-52)
Arrow, Lt Commander M Manning RN (1962-64)
Avalonia Star, Master Captain A Kinghorn (1949-51)
British Dart, Master Captain JAM Taylor (1947-49)
RFA Tidespring, Master Captain S Redmond OBE (1953-55)
RFA Engadine, Master Captain Christopher Smith (1951-53)
British Pilot, Master Captain J Taylor (1947-49)
At St Helena P Hughes (1968-70)

And You'll Find on the Bridge a Conway Boy
Captain Christopher Smith QGM (1953-55)

Christopher was one of the small group of cadets in the Ship when she grounded and he was one of the first ashore in the doomed attempts to refloat her. After Conway he served with a Dutch shipping line and then British companies before joining the Royal Fleet Auxiliary (RFA) in 1961. He obtained his Master's ticket in 1965.

As chief officer of the helicopter support ship Engadine, he was awarded the Queen's Gallantry Medal for the decisive role he played in the salvage of a stricken merchantman in the Channel during a gale in December 1981. The 4,000-tonne motor vessel Melpol was ablaze and drifting in gale-force winds and heavy seas 35 miles southeast of the Isle of Wight. With the fire raging unchecked, Smith and PO Olley were winched onboard from a helicopter to assess whether she could be saved. Deciding she could, Smith led a team of volunteers back onboard. They had been able to bring only limited fire-fighting equipment with them. Below decks Melpol had been reduced to a tangle of twisted metal, with ladders and bulkheads melted in the intense heat. All electrical wiring had been burnt through, so the team had to rely on its own portable light sources. It took them almost 8 hours to bring the blaze under control, during which time they extinguished fires in the engine room and accommodation areas. They then connected tows to 2 salvage tugs enabling the ship to be taken in tow and brought to safety. The official citation read "Chief Officer Smith displayed courage, leadership and professional skills of the highest order during this most difficult operation and by his resourcefulness enabled the ship to be saved."

Only four months later Engadine joined the Falklands task force as a support ship for helicopters during the campaign to liberate the islands from their Argentine occupiers. Engadine provided helicopter maintenance and accommodation for ground crew in San Carlos Water throughout the period of the intense Argentinean air attacks. In a 36 year career with the RFA Smith also saw service in many other theatres of international conflict, including the Gulf, Malaysia and Lebanon. He retired in 1997, eventually living in a 70 foot canal narrow boat with his wife and a very raucous parrot. He died in 2007.

CHAPTER 42

A PROUD TRADITION CONTINUES

90% of world trade is still borne by sea and Britain's dependence on maritime trade remains undiminished. Sea transport is Britain's third largest service sector earner, adding some £2.6 billion net to our balance of payments every year, yet the size of the fleet continues to dwindle. The 1998 Government white paper 'British Shipping: Charting A New Course' showed that the size of the UK owned fleet of trading vessels of over 500 gross tonnes fell from a peak of around 50.8 million tonnes deadweight (dwt) in 1975 to 10.8 million dwt in 1997.

> *"The proportion of the UK owned trading fleet registered in the UK is now only 20%; up to the late 1970s it was almost unknown for UK-owned ships to be registered outside of the UK."*

Between 1980 and 1997, the number of British officers fell by 78% and

> *"will continue to decline from about 17,000 in 1998 to about 9,000 by 2012."*

This despite the fact that

> *"the increasing international shortage of qualified seafarers …. creates great opportunities for well-trained and experienced British seafarers at sea and ashore, both at home and abroad."*

The white paper anticipated a need for only 500 cadets per annum from 1998, a quarter of that in 1972, observing

> *"a large number of British shipping companies, particularly the smaller ones, continue to seek (or passively enjoy) short-term competitive cost advantage by opting not to train seafarers."*

By 2006, Britain was tenth in the world fleet league table and the largest British registered fleet was the Royal Fleet Auxiliary.

Country	Ships In Fleet
Japan	3,962
Greece	3,032
Germany	2,321
China	1,999
USA	1,963
Russia	1,872
Norway	1,458
Singapore	1,122
Netherlands	1,016
UK	957

World's Top 10 Merchant Shipping Fleets In 2006

The need for well trained young people desiring a career at sea remained so the British Shipping Federation (BSF) still had to ensure a steady supply of suitable candidates. Although *Conway* (the establishment) had paid off and could no longer help meet that demand, 1974 was not actually her end. The governing entity (the *Conway* Cadet School Ltd) remained 'in being' but went into limbo. The BSF's John Weight and Cadet Committee (whose members included Old *Conways* Captain Don Houghton (53-55) and John Hughes (54-56)) were all determined that *Conway's* fine traditions should not be lost. The committee resolved that any residue from *Conway's* accounts, basically the funds paid by Cheshire County Council for the purchase of the New Block, should be used to perpetuate her name and ideals. In April 1980, after a 6 year gestation period, they finally achieved their goals when the *Conway* Cadet School was formerly renamed The *Conway* Merchant Navy Trust. *Conway* was thus re-awakened with the aims of

The Trust's Crest

> *"supporting the training of young people for a career at sea ... to maintain the same aspirations, values and vision perceived in Liverpool all those years ago."*

The Trust is a registered charity run now with the co-operation of the UK Chamber of Shipping. It offers full sponsorship to a limited number of young men and women each year who become *Conway* Cadets to train as deck or engineer officers. There are 2 sets of interviews each year. Training can be up to degree level, lasts from 3 to 4 years, and consists of alternating periods at sea and study at one of the UK's maritime colleges/universities. Shore based training includes

Conway's Original

> *"theoretical studies and use of the latest computer controlled engine room, radar and navigation simulators; and practical training in the important areas of safety, survival and fire fighting. All schemes followed by Conway Cadets are approved by the Merchant Navy Training Board and the Marine and Coastguard Agency."*

Seagoing time obviously focuses on practical training and cadets can experience a number of different British shipping companies and ship types.

> *"Cadets need a commitment to hard work and personal qualities which accept the challenge of developing technology. They must be physically fit, get on easily with fellow trainees, have good teamwork skills and a high degree of personal responsibility,"*

which all sounds rather familiar.

The training, environment and expectations of these modern *Conway* Cadets is totally different to that experienced in the New Block, just as New Block training was not the same as that in the Ship. *Conway* training was always evolving and adapting. Life on the Menai Strait was totally different to life on the Mersey. Training for sail was a world away from that for early steam ships. The growth in technical equipment and electronic aids on the bridge has transformed navigation. Vessels just keep getting bigger and bigger. The capacity of some large modern 'box boats' exceeds that of whole shipping companies in the past. While every *Conway* cadet knew how to use a sextant and had mastered the art of dead reckoning, today's mariners would be hard pushed to find a sextant

and global positioning satellites place vessels to within a few feet anywhere, anytime. Life at sea has changed completely and so has training for that life. The pattern of training now resembles very closely what Mr Lord was trying to achieve, and what HMS *Conway* would have been forced to adopt if she had survived. The thread that joined 'our' generations of *Conway* cadets is drawn very thin but the *Conway* Merchant Navy Trust *is* our direct successor committed to perpetuating *Conway's* ideals and standards. Today the *Conway* Merchant Navy Trust is an independent charity, of which 12 of the 17 trustees are Old *Conways*, and the chair is always an Old *Conway*, further maintaining the link with the past.

Old *Conways* often reflect on the eventual demise of the last *Conway* cadet but they should rest easy. The 'HMS' has been lost, but a steady trickle of *Conway* cadets is again training for a career at sea. May it always be so.

APPENDIX A

GLOSSARY

This Glossary serves two purposes. It provides a very short explanation of standard naval terminology/abbreviations used in the text, and it decodes the *Conway* specific slang words/terminology in everyday use in the Ship. The meaning of some slang terms changed over the years.

Abaft	Behind.
Aft	1. The back or stern end of a ship.
	2. Towards the back of anything.
Andes	One of the list of ships' names adopted for one of the dormitories at the House.
Band Shag	Member of the band and/or 'free thinker.'
Bertha	One of the seats in a rowing gig or cutter.
Big Stink	The large motorboat.
Bilge Cod	Fish.
Bishop	A derisory term meaning out of date or old fashioned.
Bitts	Short, heavy oaken 'crucifixes' around which the various cordage controlling the movement of the mainsail would be secured.
Blu Flu	Alfred Holt's Blue Funnel Line.
Boris	An unclean cadet.
Boris Box	In the New Block, each cadet had a chest of drawers for their belongings so the old sea chests were superfluous. Rather than throw them away, they were cut down in size, placed at the foot of each bunk and used to store dirty laundry until wash day. The term Boris meant an unclean cadet so the boxes were soon nicknamed Boris Boxes.
Bow	The very front of a vessel.
Bright Work	Any polished metal
Bright Work Juice	Brasso.
BSF	British Shipping Federation.
Bug Juice	Hair oil.
Bulkhead	Wall.
Cab	The second gig.
Cadet Captain	Conway's naval equivalent of a school prefect.
Carry On	A two note bugle call in the Ship to indicate that the previous 'Still' and order were complete, and that normal activity could be resumed: Tuh, tuuuuuuu
CCC	Chief Cadet Captain, interchangeable with CPO.
Cdr	Commander.
Cheese Crap	Cheese and potatoes.

Chum	A friend. Hence a new chum was a newly joined cadet.
Climb Zion	To rush up to the Focsle chased by senior cadets.
Clout(S)	Pieces of threadbare bedcovers or cloth, which cadets would slide around on to improve the shine of their section of deck and to avoid damage to it.
Colours	1. The act of raising the ensign in the morning. 2. Badge awarded for notable prowess in a sport.
Condenny/Conny	Condensed milk.
Cossack	One of the list of ships' names used from 1943 to 1949 to group cadets for sporting competitions.
Covered Wagon	Fruit tart.
Cow Juice	Milk.
CPO	Chief Cadet Captain. Interchangeable with CCC.
Cuts	Being struck over the backside with the Teaser.
Cutter	A 10 or 12 oared pulling boat that could also be rigged for sailing.
DCCC	Deputy Chief Cadet Captain, interchangeable with DCPO.
DCPO	Deputy Chief Cadet Captain, interchangeable with DCCC.
Dead Man's Leg	Jam roly poly.
Dead Man's Tool	Long suet pudding with sultanas.
Deadeyes For Square?	Shall I pass at Divisions?
"Deck!"	A request to pass over a part of the ship 'owned' by a Top other than the requester's own.
Deck	Floor.
Deckhead	Ceiling.
Ditching The Gash	Throwing out the rubbish.
Division	A grouping of cadets, originally by size but later for sporting and other competitive purposes. Interchangeable with Top.
Divisions	Parade and inspection of all cadets.
DMT	Abbreviation for Dead Man's Tool
Fife	One of two Fife designed sailing boats.
First Spare!	Request for any uneaten food.
Focsle	Pronounced 'folk-sul' 1. Abbreviation of forecastle, the area in the bows of a ship. 2. One of the Divisions.
Forrad	Forward or towards the front.
Foretop	One of the Divisions.
Fresh Juice	Water.
Frig About	To fool around.
G	The special bugle note sounded five minutes before Division in the Ship. It was also used in series with other calls, eg with the 'Cutters Away' call to indicate which cutter was required.

Gaff	A small fore and aft yard angled upwards from the mizzen mast.
Galley	Kitchen.
Galley Trogs	Welsh kitchen staff.
Gangway	1. A passageway.
	2. Mind your backs! Gangway please when addressing seniors.
Gash	Rubbish.
Gig	A six oared pulling boat.
Glyn Garth	The Anglesey landing stage near the Ship's Bangor moorings.
Grease	Butter.
Grit	Sugar.
Groyse, To	To spit.
Hawse Pipes	Two openings in the bows of a ship through which the anchor cable passes.
Heads	Toilets.
Heave Round	1. Proceed vigorously.
	2. Cleaning ship
HMS	His/Her Majesty's Ship.
Holy Joe	One who is good at Scripture.
The House	The north end of the Marquis of Anglesey's home (Plas Newydd) used by cadets. Officially called the Nelson Block.
Howe	One of the list of ships' names used from 1943 to 1949 to group cadets for sporting competitions.
JCC(s)	Junior Cadet Captain(s)
Jervis Bay	One of the list of ships' names adopted for one of the dormitories at the House.
Juice Barge	Special boat used every day to collect water for the Ship.
Kelvin Block	The converted stable block at Plas Newydd.
King Of The Woods	The most powerful QB, later the QB most other cadets thought should have been a cadet captain.
Knacker/Knackering	To borrow something with little intention of returning it. Quiet different to stealing, which was an unforgivable thing.
Ladder	Stairs
Lambie	Mizzentopman.
Light Oh!	Request for more light called to anyone who blocks the light.
Lt. Lieutenant.	
Lt. Cdr.	Lieutenant Commander.
Lt Col.	Lieutenant Colonel
Mauritania	One of the list of ships' names adopted for one of the dormitories at the House.
Meat Crap	Meat and potatoes.
Mess Clout	The weekly duster supplied to each mess.

Mess Deck	Restaurant; ok, in deference to Old Conways now clutching their sides with laughter, the place where meals were served.
MN	Merchant Navy.
MMSA	Mercantile Marine Services Association.
MMSS	Mercantile Marine School Ship
Mooch	Walking around (the deck) in company but with no real purpose.
MSOD	Menai Strait One Design sailing dinghy.
Murphy	Half a baked potato.
Muster	To line up/queue for any purpose.
Nelson Block	See the House.
Nervey	Impertinent.
Nestor	One of the list of ships' names adopted for one of the dormitories at the House.
New Block	The new purpose built shore establishment opened in 1964.
New Chum	New cadet just joined the ship.
Niffle	To smoke.
Nix A Buff	Look out - someone has broken wind!
Nix Oh!	1. A warning that someone in authority is approaching! 2. Mind your back!
No 1/Number 1	One of the three motorboats.
No 2/Number 2	One of the three motorboats.
Nursery	Area of the Ship reserved for new chums.
Old Conway	Old *Conway*.
Ohio	One of the list of ships' names used from 1943 to group cadets for sporting competitions. In 1949 the system was abandoned and this name was adopted for one of the dormitories at the House.
Orontes	One of the list of ships' names adopted for one of the dormitories at the House.
PD	Port Dinorwic
Pinnace	The largest of the three motorboats.
Pipe Down	Keep quiet.
Piss-Quicks	Cadets who sadly wet their hammocks and so were required to sling in a row near the night heads in the Ship.
Pleb(S)	New Chums and other junior cadets in their first couple of terms.
PO	Petty Officer
Poop (Deck)	The upper most deck at the stern of a vessel.
Port	1. The left side of a vessel, building etc., looking forward. 2. An opening in the side of the Ship.
Pretty Spare Chum	Bullshit.

QB	Quarter Boy or cadet in his last term whose Conway course has gained him one year's remission of his four year apprenticeship at sea.
Rangitiki	One of the list of ships' names adopted for one of the dormitories at the House.
Rate	A cadet captain of any rank.
Rawlpindi	One of the list of ships' names used from 1943 to group cadets for sporting competitions. In 1949 the system was abandoned and this name was adopted for one of the dormitories at the House.
RCN	Royal Canadian Navy.
RD	Reserve Decoration, awarded for service in the RNR.
REAN	Royal East African Navy.
Reefers	Best RNR uniforms.
Returning Gash!	The Yak tub was emptied over the side. If anything was blown back towards the ship the cry "Returning Gash!" was used to warn others.
Rig	Appropriate/required clothing for an activity.
Rigging	The complex system of ropes and blocks, which kept masts and yards in place and, which allowed masts and sails to be to be manoeuvred for sailing.
RIN	Royal Indian Navy.
RN	Royal Navy.
RNR	Royal Naval Reserve.
Ronuk	1. Floor polish. 2. Floor polishing machine.
SCC(s)	Senior Cadet Captain(s).
Scouse	Irish stew (obvious really).
Sea Lion	One of the list of ships' names used from 1943 to 1949 to group cadets for sporting competitions.
Senior Hand	Senior cadet.
Shag	1. The shape a cadet bent his cap into, the more independently minded the individual - the greater the shag in his cap. 2. A cadet one would expect to have a massive shag in his cap!
Shit On A Raft	Kidneys or liver on toast.
Sick Bay	That portion of the Ship, right aft on the lower deck, where Sister ministered to sick cadets. Later this was moved ashore into the Nelson Block.
Skilley	Tea (any hot drink in earlier years).
Slack Party	A group of cadets performing a punishment activity.
Slash Creek	Secluded inlet on the Anglesey side of the strait between Plas Newydd and Port Dinorwic.

Sling	To rig a hammock ready for the night.
Slippery Hitch	So hitching a hammock that the owner falls to the deck when he gets into his hammock.
Small Stink	The small motorboat.
Soduk/Soddack/Sawduk	Bread.
Soduk For A Spread	Usually heard right after the bread load came aboard the old ship.
Spell	Period of time usually of work.
Spello	A rest from work.
Spooky	Lt. Cdr. (previously Lt) John Brooke Smith aka Brookie.
Spread	Jam
Squeaker	A small, noisy cadet.
Squit	A small cadet.
Starboard	The right side of a vessel, building etc., looking forward.
Stars Out	1. To go red in the face. 2. To express incredulity.
Stay	A large tarred rope angled down from a mast to the deck, which helped keep the mast in place.
Stern	The very back of a vessel.
Still	The special bugle call in the Ship instructing everyone to be quiet and listen to the following order. It was four notes, a G plus three ascending notes: Tum, tu-tu-tuuuu.
Stow /Stowed	1. To Put something into storage. 2. To stop doing something.
Suction	Suction was the equivalent of modern brown-nosing. When anybody obtained an unusual favour it was always put down to suction, often accompanied by horrible sucking noises, rather like a pump running dry.
Sweep	An area of the ship that a cadet was responsible for cleaning and maintaining, every cadet had one.
(To) Sweep	To clean.
Tarted Out	A poor specimen.
Teaser	A ropes end used to inflict corporal punishment.
Tesco	Whitewash.
The Huts	The temporary wooden huts built on the site of the Marquis of Anglesey's old dairy farm to accommodate cadets while the New Block was built, they lasted from 1953 to 1963.
The Ship	The wooden wall sailing ship of the line ex HMS Nile used as the floating home for Conway until she was lost in 1953
The Tents	The temporary camp site erected for the summer term of 1953 after the loss of the Ship.
Toe Nail Pie	A stodgy pudding with bits in.

"Top Please!"	A request to pass through a part of the ship owned by a Top other than the requester's own.
Top	1. The platform where two sections of mast joined and from where marines could fire down on sailors in enemy ships.
	2. A part of the Ship.
	3. A grouping of cadets, originally by size but later for organisational, sporting and other competitive purposes. Interchangeable with Division.
Train Crash	Tinned tomatoes on toast.
Truck	The small wooden plate in the very top of each mast.
Vulch, To	See Vulture.
Vulture	A Cadet eying your plate in the hope you might have left something worth eating.
Water Lilly	Cadet who wets the hammock.
Whales	Sardines.
Yack/Yak	Rubbish or dirt.
Yack Tub	Old barrel ends fitted with rope handles on either side, and used as rubbish containers.
Yard	A wooden beam attached to a mast from which sails were originally hung.
Yuck	Pilchards in tomato sauce.
Zion's Hill	The old Focsle head (pre1938).

APPENDIX B

SHIP'S LOG – HMS CONWAY

Royal Navy Vessels Called Conway.

To date the Royal Navy has named 5 vessels HMS *Conway*.

The original was a frigate laid down in 1813 at Frindesbury opposite Rochester on the Medway. She was launched in 1814. She is variously classified as a ship sloop, or a brig sloop. Length 108.4 feet, 444 tons BOM. She had a crew of 150. Her armament was 26 eight pounders on the upper deck, 18 thirty two pounders on the quarter deck, 6 twelve pounders and 2 twelve pounders on the Focsle. She saw service in the North and South Atlantic and the Pacific and was sold in 1825.

The second HMS *Conway* was a 26 gun frigate launched in 1832 and loaned to the MMSA as the first training ship called *Conway* Her service before and after being loaned to the MMSA is summarised below.

The third and fourth *Conway*s were replacement vessels lent by the Royal Navy to the MMSA and renamed *Conway* (previously *Winchester* and *Nile*). They are described in Appendices C and D.

In 1915, during the first world war a trawler was requisitioned from merchant service by the Admiralty and given the name HMS *Conway*. The duration of her commission is not known but for a while at least there were 2 Royal Navy vessels with the same name!

2 other Royal Navy vessels were given the name HMS *Conway Castle* and are often confused with HMS *Conway*. From 1804 to 1809 an HMS *Conway Castle* (54 tons) was hired as an Irish Gun Vessel. Details are very sparse but it seems she was hired for use against the French. In 1939 during the second world war trawler FY 509 was requisitioned and renamed HMS *Conway Castle*. She was returned to her owner in October 1945. She was probably used in mine laying/clearing duties and as an inshore convoy escort.

Other Conways

Further confusion arises over a US Navy destroyer called USS *Conway* (DD-70). She was one of the fifth group of ships provided under the Lend Lease agreement between the UK and the USA. She was turned over to the Royal Navy at Halifax, Nova Scotia, renamed HMS *Lewes* and commissioned into the Royal Navy 23rd October 1940. She was scuttled on 25th May 1946 off Australia.

Finally there were a number of commercial trading vessels called *Conway* including:

- 1846 to 1870, the Royal Mail Steamship Company had a 895 ton wooden passenger paddle steamer, the RMS *Conway* built by William Pitcher of Northfleet. On 20 Oct 1867, she was grounded during the great St. Thomas hurricane and her masts and funnel blown off the ship. She was depicted on a Belize Stamp in 1985.

- 1851 to 1875, a clipper ship named *Conway* was built by Owens and Duncan at Portland, St John, New Brunswick, Canada. She was mainly an Australian emigrant ship and many Australian records mistakenly document her frequent arrivals and departures as HMS *Conway*.

- Between 1904 and 1930, the Royal Mail Steamship Company has another RMS *Conway* in which many *Conway* cadets served. She was 2,650 tons and built of steel by Armstrong, Whitworth, Newcastle.

'Our' HMS Conway 26 (1836-61).

1828

Conway was laid down at Chatham Royal Naval Dockyard on London's River Thames as a sixth rate man of war of 652 tons and twenty-six guns. She was designed by Sir Robert Seppings and like all vessels of her size she was nicknamed a Jackass or Donkey Frigate. This was a derogatory term because the difference between her type and a 'real' frigate was like the difference between a donkey and a race-horse. She was a 3 masted ship with 1 covered main gun deck. Her full complement was 175 men and boys.

1832 February

Conway was launched and her first captain was Capt. Henry Eden RN. He took her to Plymouth, Port Royal, Jamaica and back. By the end of the year she had joined a Franco-British fleet blockading the ports of Holland to induce the Dutch to drop their defiance of the great powers over the future of Belgium.

1835

Conway spent many years in the Pacific. In June she was at Lima, Peru and Charles Darwin dispatched two boxes of his samples and many letters back to the UK in *Conway* immediately before leaving for the Galapagos in *Beagle*.

Late 1830s

Under her new master, Captain C R Drinkwater Bethune RN, *Conway* had a surveying role on the Australian, New Zealand and Chinese stations. He charted Port Underwood, a South Island whaling port before sailing to the Rewa River (near Suva), Fiji. Whilst there she charted the Conway Reef (21 44 S 174 38 E) - today more often known by its Fijian name Ceva-I-Ra.

1840 July

In the 1830s, Britain was probably the largest drugs trafficker in the world. Although laws were passed in England to prevent internal drugs trade huge amount of opium were exported from India to China by the British East India Company. The effects on Chinese society were devastating in terms of pure human misery and tragedy. In an effort to stem the trade, the Chinese government made opium illegal in 1836 and began aggressively to close down the opium dens, destroying stockpiles and storage facilities and pursuing the British traders. Outraged at the loss of property and unwilling to submit British citizens to Chinese justice Britain declared war on China beginning the Opium War of 1840. *Conway* was in the fleet sent to attack Canton. They captured the northern harbour of Chusan. Fighting continued until May 1841 when the Chinese were soundly beaten. Canton paid a £6m indemnity for the loss of British property. The money was paid over to Captain Bethune who returned with it in *Conway* to the UK.

Conway's remaining service covered Queenstown, Southern Africa, Madagascar and China. In 1858 she was a coastguard vessel at Devonport.

1859-61

Loaned to the Liverpool MMSA for use as the training ship *Conway*.

1861 November

The MMSA replaced her by a larger Royal Navy vessel and the two ships exchanged names. Now HMS Winchester, she was returned to the Admiralty who despatched her to Aberdeen as the RNR drill ship. By 1876 she had been replaced by HMS *Clyde*. It is assumed that at some point she was scrapped, presumably at Aberdeen.

APPENDIX C

SHIP'S LOG – HMS WINCHESTER

The first HMS *Conway* quickly proved to be too small so the Admiralty was asked to provide a larger ship. They agreed to loan HMS *Winchester*.

HMS Winchester

1816

Winchester was laid down at Woolwich on the River Thames, London as a Java Class fourth rate sixty gun frigate. She was equipped with 16 forty-two pound guns, 8 carronades and 36 twenty four pound guns. She was described as a perfect gem in hull and rigging, not at all like most short, wide and shallow British warships of the fourth rate. Her lines were sharp, approaching those of a clipper, yet she could carry tons of foodstuffs, fresh water and enough materiel to keep her at sea for months. She was well sparred and crossed 3 skysail yards. She weighed 487 tons, was 173 feet long overall, with a beam of 44 feet and 6 inches. Her full compliment was 450 men and boys. She was launched on 21 June 1822.

1831

Lord William Paget was appointed captain and took her to the West Indies. He was the brother of the Marquis of Anglesey and he erected the statue of Admiral Lord Nelson that stands on the banks of the strait below the Britannia Bridge.

1833

Out of commission at Chatham.

1834-38

Winchester was on the East Indies station. For some reason, the seven logbooks for these years are in the US Library of Congress. In 1837 she became the flagship of Rear Admiral Sir Frederick Maitland and on the 19th through the 21st October 1837, she was off Entry Island (now known as Kapiti Island), New Zealand. She returned to the UK in 1838.

1840

Under Captain John Parker she was the flagship of Vice Ad. Sir Thomas Harvey, on the North America and West Indies station. Early in 1842 she had a new captain, Thomas W. Carter and returned to the UK via the Cape of Good Hope. She was refitted in March and by August was back on the North America and West Indies station.

1852

Engaged in the Burmese War. On 9th October, she was part of a mixed naval/military force that captured Prome. During 1853-4 she sailed all over the Far East visiting Rangoon, Madras, Singapore, Borneo and Hong Kong. During one encounter with Burmese insurgents on the Irrawaddy River *Winchester*'s Captain Granville Gower Loch RN was killed. His replacement was Edward Sholto Douglas (a nephew of the Marchioness of Queensberry) but he was invalided off the ship on 20th February in Rangoon. He was sent home in *Hastings* but she was lost off the Ascension Island. His body was recovered and he was buried on the island.

1854

Sir James Stirling took command of *Winchester* in 1854 and spent several months pursuing pirate junks, which were preying on other shipping around Hong Kong. On 16th February, her boats captured 7 pirate junks off Lema Island, Hong Kong, and on 2nd November she destroyed 9 pirate junks in Tynmoun Bay near Hong Kong. The pursuit of pirates took her along the south coast of China and up the Pearl River towards Canton. *Winchester*'s gunnery officer was Louis Charles Henry Tonge RN whose family lived near Calne in Wiltshire. His memoirs, stored in Wiltshire and Swindon History Centre, Chippenham describe these events in graphic and exciting detail.

1855

On 25th March, *Winchester*'s boats destroyed nine pirate junks in Port Shelter. On 29th October she participated with British and US warships in the capture of Canton landing a naval brigade and members of the Royal Artillery.

1856.

On promotion to Admiral, Stirling made *Winchester* his flagship. On 6th November 6 of her boats assisted in freeing the French ship *Folly* on the Canton River and destroyed 21 war junks. Later that year having moved further north, her crew were the first British sailors to set eyes on the dramatic natural harbour of Vladivostok when *Winchester* sailed in during the Crimean War. According to contemporary chronicler, Nikolai Matveyev, the English visitors named the bay Port May.

1857-61

She was on harbour service at Chatham. It was from here that the Admiralty loaned her to the Liverpool MMSA where she was renamed and served as the second HMS *Conway*.

1861-76

Conway was going from strength to strength and in 1876 she was judged too small for *future* needs. The Admiralty agreed to replace her with a larger ship, HMS *Nile*. On 12 July 1876 the two ships exchanged names. The second HMS *Conway*, originally HMS *Winchester* became HMS *Nile* and was towed from the Mersey to Devonport by the paddle frigate *Valorious*, arriving on the 24th.

1876 September 1st

The Admiralty renamed her HMS *Mount Edgcumbe*.

1877 June 28th.

She was loaned as the '*Mount Edgcumbe* Industrial Training Ship' for Homeless and Destitute Boys. There is an old naval tradition that when a ship's name is changed, the reason for the change should be explained to the ship. This poor vessel must have been a very patient lady as she had in turn been HMS *Winchester*, HMS *Conway*, HMS *Nile*, HMS *Mount Edgcumbe* and now became plain *Mount Edgcumbe*, generally abbreviated to *Edgcumbe*. She was moored below the famous Royal Albert Railway Bridge on the river Tamar.

1920 December 4th

Mount Edgcumbe closed and for a short period the ship became a depot ship for Devonport dockyard.

1921 April 8th

She was sold, towed across Plymouth Sound to Queen Anne's Battery and broken up.

APPENDIX D

SHIP'S LOG HMS NILE

Several Royal Navy vessels have been named *Nile*, reflecting the iconic status of one of Nelson's most famous victories. At one point in 1800, two quite distinct hired vessels called *Nile* seem to have been in commission at the same time, both stationed on the South Coast.

HMS Nile, 16 Guns (lugger)

This first *Nile* was a hired vessel described as a lugger carrying 16 guns. On 13th January 1800, her captain, Lt. Whitehead, was ashore sick so the master, Stephen Butcher, was in command when he captured the French lugger *Modere* from Boulogne, one of a small fleet of French vessels preying on English shipping in the Channel. On 7th July, *Nile* supported a night attack by fire ships on French frigates in the Dunkirk Roads under Captain Inman in *Andromeda*. Using smugglers as pilots, Inman brought the whole squadron through the Roads without loss. *Nile* was stationed as a leading mark at Gravelines Hook to assist with the navigation. On 8th July, she was involved in the capture of *Desiree*, a 38 gun frigate, in Dunkirk Roads. Three other frigates escaped.

On 2nd November 1800, with Lt. Whitehead still sick ashore, Mr. Butcher fell in with the French privateer cutter *Renard* off Folkestone at nine o'clock in the evening. He captured her as she was about to board a laden British merchantman.

HMS Nile, 12 guns (cutter)

Just to confuse matters, this apparent second *Nile* was also in service in the Channel during November 1800. She was described as a hired cutter carrying 12 guns and her commander was Lt. George Argles. As the last reference found to the 16 gun *Nile* (lugger) was for 2nd November 1800, and the first reference to the 12 gun *Nile* (cutter) was for 7th November 1800 it is possible that the lugger was paid off and replaced by the cutter in the few days between the 2nd and 7th. Alternatively, the 2 vessels might have been one and the same; the sick Whitehead being replaced by Argles and her armament reduced.

Her role for the next 4 years was to intercept French supplies in the Channel, much of that time in company with the smaller *Lurcher*. She was in almost constant contact with the French operating close inshore around Morbihan and Port Navale. She was in many fierce engagements capturing or destroying several French warships, often very close inshore under the fire of shore batteries. On one occasion *Nile* and *Lurcher* attacked a convoy of 15 or 16 sail capturing 9 trading vessels taking brandy and wine from Bordeaux to Brest.

1805 was another battling year for the little *Nile*. On 22nd July she was with Sir Robert Calder's squadron at the action with the combined fleets off Ushant. Later, in a major action with the French and Spanish 150 miles WNW of Ferol, *Nile* captured 2 Spanish ships.

The record is not entirely clear, but it appears that in 1806 *Nile* was purchased by the Admiralty. By 1807, she was at Spithead before finally being sold in 1810.

HMS *Nile 1826 – 1876.*

'Our' *Nile* was designed by Sir Robert Seppings in response to a perceived threat from a new breed of American frigates. They had the manoeuvrability and speed of traditional frigates with the firepower and size of a larger ship of the line. They were akin to a modern tank with the agility of a mini. She was one of three 'Rodney' class, two deck, second rate sailing line of battle ships. The other two vessels in the class were *Rodney* and *London*. She was laid down in October 1826 at HM Dockyard, Plymouth. To help imagine her size, she was slightly larger than *Victory* now preserved at Portsmouth. Their sizes and capabilities are compared in the following table.

	HMS *Nile*	HMS *Victory*
Extreme Length (Figurehead to Taffrail)	240 feet 6.5 inches	226 feet 6 inches
Length of Bowsprit	102 feet	110 feet
Overall Length (Bowsprit to Taffrail)	346 feet 6.5 inches	336 feet 6 inches
Beam	53 feet 6 inches	51 feet 10 inches
Depth in Hold	23 feet	21 feet 6 inches
Draught	22 feet	21 feet 6 inches
Burthen Weight	2,622 tons	2,162 22/94 tons
Height of Foremast (waterline to truck)	182 feet	182 feet
Height of Mainmast (waterline to truck)	195 feet	205 feet
Height of Mizzenmast (waterline to truck)	168 feet (she carried an unusually large Spanker sail)	152 feet
Length of Main Yard	105 feet	102 feet
Number of Sails	37	37
Maximum Recorded Speed	13.5 knots, just over 15.5 miles per hour	10 - 11 knots, approx., 12 miles per hour
Armament	2nd Rate Ship of 92 guns, ten 8 inch and eighty-two 30 pounders	1st Rate Ship of 100 guns, but 110 at Trafalgar - two 68 pound carronades, thirty 32 pounders, twenty eight 24 pounders, six 18 pounders and forty four 12 pounders
Weight of Broadside	1,652 pounds	1148 lbs at Trafalgar
Crew	850 men and boys	850 men and boys
Construction Costs	£86,197, including £41,665 to arm, rig and equip her	£63,176
Launched	1839	1765

Comparison of HMS Nile and HMS Victory

Nile's full complement of 850 men and boys comprised:

Officers	40
Chief Petty Officers (POs)	9
First class POs	41
Second class POs	78
Leading seamen	40
Wrights and artificers	32
Servants and stewards	51
Marines	150
Boys first class	46
Boys second class	24
Engine room	27
Seamen	312

It was originally planned that *Nile* would be launched in July 1834 at the same time as *Pique*. Although she was ready, the launch was cancelled, the launching gear was removed and she remained on the slip for another five years. Seppings replacement took some time to be convinced that her novel rounded stern was a sensible design. *Nile* was eventually launched at 6.09 pm on Saturday 28th June 1839 on the anniversary of Queen Victoria's coronation. A very large crowd, estimated at around 50,000, gathered to watch. She was launched by Miss Warren the Dockyard Admiral's daughter. The press observed she

"looked very fine on the water,"

but she went straight into reserve at Devonport where she languished unused for the next 13 years.

In 1845, the French launched *Pomone* a sailing frigate with supplementary steam power and a screw. She proved successful and the French started converting a number of sailing warships to steam power. The Admiralty had been trialling steam in a number of smaller vessels but now decided they had to respond to the threat of French screw frigates. *Nile* was chosen for a trial. On 14th December 1852, she was docked in Devonport to be converted into a screw ship with an engine, boiler, propeller and funnel. Conversion took over a year and cost £63,837. When *Nile* emerged from dry-dock on 30th January 1854, she had been fitted with a Seaward and Capel 928ihp engine. The engine and boiler were accommodated in the hold where space was also turned over to coal storage. Her coal boxes held 262 tons of coal. A single demountable funnel was placed between the fore and main masts. The propeller shaft ran in a specially created tunnel from the engine out through the stern of the ship. The propeller was detachable and held in a metal cage called a banjo that slid vertically in rails inserted between the rudder and the stern post. When not in use the propeller was raised vertically out of the water in its banjo. In use, a special flange on the propeller shaft ensured a sound engagement with the propeller. The shaft was in 2 parts, 1 fixed to the engine and 1 that could be forced out into the propeller from inside the ship. Thus engaged the 2 sections of shaft were joined by a special collar. This, seeming Heath Robinson, approach was designed by Francis Pettit Smith and actually widely adopted. An identical mechanism, chosen by Brunel for the SS *Great Britain*, can be viewed in that ship's museum at Bristol in the UK.

With all her new machinery, her displacement increased to 4,375 tons. When she was finally commissioned for sea in February 1854 it was as an auxiliary powered sailing vessel, not a pure sailing vessel, so many lists of Royal Navy sailing vessels exclude her. Between 16th and 18th April 1854, she underwent steam trials in Stokes Bay, achieving a speed of almost seven knots. On commission her engine was only used close to port or inshore and she rarely achieved more than 2 - 5 knots under power. By comparison, she regularly achieved 9 - 12 knots under sail alone.

Nile represented a revolution in naval tradition. Ships would no longer rely on the vagaries of the wind and the sailing skills of their crews. Waters once closed or too dangerous for sailing vessels now became accessible. But most important of all, the Royal Navy's fighting strategy and tactics honed over hundreds of years became obsolete with the first turn of *Nile's* screw. A whole new operating vocabulary had to be developed along with new skills. It would take a while for the navy to adjust but with *Nile*, 'line of battle' ships, and all that name implied, simply became battleships. The new machine would soon be tested in war.

1854

On 27th March, war was declared on Russia beginning what we now call the Crimean War. On 3rd May Nile sailed for the Gulf of Finland to join the Baltic Squadron. She left the Baltic on 19th October 1854 before the winter freeze (nature's blockade being far more effective and much cheaper than the Royal Navy!) and returned to Devonport via Kiel which she left on 7th December after a brief stop over. Shortly after arriving at Devonport she was involved in a minor collision so on 23rd December she went into dry dock for repairs.

Nile off Seskar

1855

By 13th April, she was back in Kiel en-route for the Baltic. In May *Nile* led the inshore squadron into the Gulf to an anchorage in Biorko Sound. She engaged the Russians on several occasions capturing or destroying large numbers of vessels and supplies. On 17th June she was off Seskar on the Baltic near Cronstadt, guarding the approaches to St Petersburg. Her Captain was John Wilson Carmichael. On 26th Oct, with the winter freeze again imminent, she left via Kiel for Devonport. The war ended shortly afterwards.

1856-57

On 23rd April, *Nile* participated in Queen Victoria's Grand Fleet Review at Spithead to mark the end of the Crimean War.

The rest of this period was spent patrolling the North American and East Indies stations from her base in Halifax, Nova Scotia.

1858

She was based in Queenstown as flagship for Admiral Chads.

1859

Nile toured various ports including Greenock, and Liverpool as a recruiting ship open to visitors. By an interesting co-incidence on 3rd July she arrived on the Mersey and moored very near the first HMS *Conway* then awaiting her first new chums and official opening. On 1st August, Nile's band played at the opening of HMS *Conway*. *Conway* cadets visited *Nile* for gun-drill, cutlass-drill, rifle drill and more mundane

"instructions in knotting, splicing, the lead-line, compass and the wheel."

Nile in Hurricane

On 4-5th November, she was in the Atlantic and caught in a hurricane in North Atlantic. She suffered considerable damage and lost all her sails and much equipment. At one point she rolled onto her side and was in danger of foundering but fortunately her engine mountings held and she somehow managed to right herself. Mast, sails and rudder damage were so great it took until 26th November to make port in Cork. It took many months to repair the damage.

1860-63

She was again flagship on the North American station based in Halifax.

1863

Nile was involved indirectly in the American Civil War. The battle of Gettysburg in July marked the highpoint of the Confederacy who appeared to be winning the war. Britain had supplied them with the *Alabama* armed raider and there were strong rumours that Britain would support the Confederacy. On 15th September the Union's Foreign Secretary Seward issued a notice to all consulates decrying Britain and France's belief that the Union could not win and that secession was

Nile as Flagship at Halifax

likely. *Nile* was flagship of the North American Squadron, Rear Admiral Milne was CinC. Public Records Office records show there was steady communication between Milne, the Admiralty and the Duke Of Somerset - the First Lord Of The Admiralty from 1861 discussing the capacity, readiness and potential response of the North American Squadron to any interference with British merchant shipping. The New York Times archives record that on 29th September Milne in *Nile* visited New York along with what is described as *"the Russian Fleet."*

They remained for over 4 weeks during which they were very well received by the people of New York and were entertained to balls and other events – the local businessmen (Roosevelts, Astors and Browns) forming a special committee for the purpose. *Nile* was open for visits by New Yorkers. Significantly, on 12th-15th October Milne and Secretary Seward visited a number of fortifications together. There are suggestions that this visit was a cover for high level negotiations with the Union which would decide finally whether or not Britain remained neutral in the American Civil War. I can find no direct evidence to support this claim but would be interested to hear from anyone who can shed light on the matter. Whatever the purpose of the *Nile's* visit, Britain remained neutral and, by sheer weight of numbers and armament production capabilities, the Union eventually ground the South down.

1864 April 18th

Nile returned to Spithead and on 23rd she was placed in reserve at Devonport. Her logs for the period 1860 to 1864 are held by the National Archives of Canada.

1876

The Admiralty agreed to exchange *Nile* for the *Conway* (ex *Winchester*). *Conway's* Captain Franklin inspected *Nile* and recommended a number of changes and improvements. Between 20th March and 13th May, her engines, boilers, underwater fittings and funnel were removed so she might be loaned to the MMSA as a replacement for the second HMS *Conway*. The Admiralty carried out many other renovations to the ship including replacement masts and jib (the foremast being the old main mast of HMS *Satellite*) and the remainder from HMS *Jason*. She was towed out of Devonport on 20th June by *Valorous*, a paddle frigate, arriving on the Mersey on 23rd June. Many spars were transferred from the second Conway. *Nile* was renamed *Conway*.

Nile Prior to Conversion for Conway

1953 April 14th

She ran aground whilst being towed through the dangerous Swellies in the Menai Strait, Anglesey, North Wales. She settled as the tide fell, broke her back and was declared a constructive total loss. She lay on the shore below the Menai Suspension Bridge, gradually deteriorating, whilst legal battles raged around her about responsibility for her removal.

1956 October 30th

Conway (Nile) now almost 150 years old was burnt to the waterline whilst being dismantled. The remains of her hull lie on the bottom of the Swellies close to the Menai Suspension Bridge to this day.

One More HMS Nile.

On 27th March 1885, at Pembroke Dockyard a new HMS *Nile* launched. She was a steel armoured battleship of the Hamilton Programme and predicted to be the last battleship ever built. *Nile* and her sister ship, *Trafalgar*, were the immediate predecessors of the Royal Sovereign Class of battleship and carried their heavy guns in armoured turrets. In 1893 this vessel was part of the fleet off Tripoli when *Victoria* was rammed and sunk by *Camperdown* on 22nd June. She was eventually sold for breaking in 1912.

The name *Nile* has not been used since.

APPENDIX E

GOLD MEDAL WINNERS

* Medal presented by the monarch in person (Prince of Wales in 1931)
+ Medal winner later became Captain Superintendent.

Queen's Medallists
1865	Oswald Hilmark
1866	Wm Pettyman
1867	W A Cowley
1868	E Le M Robinson
1869	Frederick Fawcett
1870	W G Glennie
1871	Henry Wood
1872	G D Freeth
1873	J M Harvey
1874	Thomas Fairfield
1875	Martin Frampton
1876	George R Cox
1877	C H Herbert
1878	S C Dawson
1879	T G Proctor
1880	J G King
1881	W F Searle
1882	Alfred Howard
1883	G C Macpherson
1884	A S Gibb
1885	T S Earl
1886	J C Humfrey
1887	John Craven
1888	Albert Smith
1889	G A Tribe
1890	W B Wilkinson
1891	R S M Curran
1892	R V Peel
1893	Joseph Hudson
1894	A W Michie
1895	H Glynn Williams
1896	E D Drury
1897	A J May
1898	W F Reeve
1899	F W W Jackson
1900	A G Robertson

King's Medallists
1901	Arthur Watson
1902	F A Richardson+
1903	E C Holmes
1904	W A Galbraith*
1905	A G Foote
1906	J W Trees
1907	T M Goddard+
1908	A C P B Cope
1909	A H Hicks
1910	J C K Dowding
1911	T Q Studd
1912	G D Moore
1913	R Reffell*
1914	W R Pittis
1915	R J H Williams
1916	C S Hamer
1917	N H Bowyer
1918	B F Skinner
1919	L Scott Evans
1920	R Ellis
1921	C W W Hill
1922	T E Fernie
1923	A J Wilkie
1924	J H Houghton*
1925	F J Allen
1926	J E Woolfenden
1927	C C Ellison*
1928	R N Hoppins
1929	D G Clutterbuck
1930	W R Harley
1931	G W R Graves*
1932	W F Ross
1933	J H L Allen
1934	H C Kirby
1935	J L Rigge
1936	R E Hutson
1937	K H Martin
1938	C H Hayes

1939	C Ogilvy
1940	J B Harboard
1941	J F Leseur
1942	G W Bateman
1943	R G Bayer
1944	D T Smith
1945	L G Carnham
1946	R P Royan
1947	D W Stewart
1948	B J C Taylor
1949	J C Naylor
1950	A J F Manton
1951	J St H Webber

Queen's Medallists
1952	N Boland
1953	P C T Potter
1954	R G Methven
1955	J W Perry
1956	R P Blythe
1957	M De B Bennett
1958	S F Hasan
1959	R K Cringle
1960	D R Martin
1961	M P Warner
1962	D C Jones
1963	A H Carson
1964	M E Davies
1965	A G L Chippendale
1966	G S Symes
1967	C G Massie Taylor
1968	R J Lansdell
1969	I D Lawson
1970	D Sandy
1971	A Abbott
1972	C H Plummer
1973	M C Davies*

APPENDIX F

NUMBERS OF CADETS

Year	Date	No. of Cadets
1859	1st August	17
	20th December	20
1860	February	102
	30th June	79
	1st August	114
1861	December	62
1862	-	102
1862	30th June	107
1863	-	117
1864	-	126
1865	-	117
1866	-	108
1867	June	94
1867	Later in the year	89
1868	June	95
1868	Later in the year	123
1869	-	122
1870	-	125
1870	later	115
1871	Average for year	113
1871	Maximum number	123
1873	Average for year	127
1873	On 1st February the 1000th cadet joined	na
1874	Average for year	114
1876	Average for year	123
1876	later	163
1878	January	175
1879	Average for year	178
1880	Average for period	157
1881	Maximum	162
1882-83	Average for period	172

Year	Date	No. of Cadets
1884	Average for period	176
1885	On 1st February the 2000th cadet joined	na
1888	Average for year	153
1889	Average for year	207
1891	Average for year	199
1893	17th April	160
1896	In April the 3000th cadet joined	na
1911	June	200
1916	In April the 5000th cadet joined	na
1917	Average for year	220
1928	The 6000th cadet joined	na
1933	The smallest intake ever, just 7 new chums	-
1934	July	130
1934	Summer	106
1939		180
1940	-	250
1941	-	221
1942	-	242
1945	-	250
1947	-	260
1948	-	250
1949	Easter and summer terms	275
1950	-	270
1950	End of year	"Near 300"
1964	average	307
1972		182
1974	10th July (paying off day)	85

APPENDIX G

TOPS AND TERMS

Cadets were always organised into the broad equivalent of boarding school houses. There were two main grouping criteria and the balance between them changed significantly several times over the life of the Ship:

- The concept of a 'term'; the intake of new chums who joined at the same time. For some the 'term,' or class, was the dominant unit and its composition hardly changed for the duration of their courses. At other periods, the composition of the 'term' changed significantly over time as new boys joined, left, specialised in different subjects etc.

- The other grouping was that of a 'top' or 'division' whereby every cadet was allocated to one of four 'tops: Focsle, Foretop, Maintop and Mizzentop. For many years there was a fifth 'top,' the Hold Party, although this later became just a general overflow dormitory at the Nelson Block. For two short periods in the 1940s when numbers were very high, there was a sixth top called Quarterdeck. 'Tops' existed first to group boys of similar physical ability for sail drill but later were to facilitate sporting, deckwork, recreational, boating and other competitive events.

The changing priorities of these criteria over the years caused considerable confusion when cadets from one period discussed arrangements in other years. One thing remained constant; new chums in their first term were always accommodated separately from the rest of the cadets.

From 1859 until the 1890s, sail drill was regularly practiced and each top was responsible for handling a particular mast's sails. New cadets were therefore allocated to a top based on their size and apparent ability to handle that top's sails. The 'term' grouping was of little relevance especially in the very early years when sojourns varied from a term or two, to years.

Sail drill ended in the 1890s and from then on, the 'term' grouping dominated. Each intake of new chums remained largely together, bunked together and left together as QBs. The 'top' concept became just a device for indicting seniority, as each calendar term the 'terms' actually progressed from one top to another. Arrangements were slightly different for 'small and skinny' cadets, those promoted as cadet captains and the RN Class, but basically your term was a very distinct grouping, largely unchanged from when you joined as a new chum, to when you left as a QB.

Arrangements changed again in 1949 with the opening of the shore establishment, and reverted more to the arrangements from 1859 to the 1890s, in that cadets were allocated to, and stayed in one top ie intakes no longer all bunked together for the duration. However the 'intake term' still remained a largely unchanged grouping from start to finish.

By the New Block years things were very muddled.

"I joined in summer 64 with a load of other new chums that I can clearly identify as my 'intake term' but then it gets a bit difficult. We were a big intake and so split randomly into two academic classes. We were also allocated randomly to one of the four divisions, Focsle, Foretop, Maintop and Mizzentop. Some were on a two year course, some a 3 year course and a few added a year for 'A' levels. By the end of our second term (Christmas 1964) we had many people in our term (or class) who were from later 'intake terms.' After two years some of my 'intake term' left, and after 3 years the majority left. For some reason, I was counted (and photographed) as one of the Easter 67 QBs, and as one of the July 67 QBs even though I had absolutely no intention of leaving in those terms. Both these sets of QBs were a complete mis-mash of 'intake terms' and perversely some of my 'intake term' are not in either of those QB groups. I stayed on after my 3 year course for another year to complete 'A' Levels and left finally as a real QB in July 68. My final "term" or class and QB grouping had people who joined with me and people who joined up to two years after me!"

The rest of this appendix describes the specific arrangements discovered to date and, where possible, the reasons for adopting that grouping.

Founding

In the very earliest days after the founding, cadets were organised simply into port and starboard watches. During the morning one watch would be below at school, the other on deck or aloft for nautical training. In the afternoon they swapped places.

Until the 1890s

Cadets would regularly practice sail drill on the fore, main and mizzen masts. They were allocated to work on either the port or starboard sides. Therefore a number of regular units called tops were established:

> port and starboard Foretop.
> port and starboard Maintop.
> port and starboard Mizzentop.

The size of the gear on each mast varied so it was necessary to organise cadets so they were physically capable of handling the sails to which they were allocated. For the first fifty years or so, the new chums spent their first term together in port or starboard Focsle. After that their term would be split up and each cadet would proceed to a top in accordance with his size. If he grew he would proceed into other tops. The largest boys became port or starboard Maintopmen; the main mast having the heaviest gear. Tops therefore consisted of cadets from a number of different terms.

From the 1890s

At some point, with the demise of sail drill in the 1890s, the practice changed so that terms stayed together for the full two years of their course. On joining new chums were still assigned to port or starboard Focsle but thereafter they remained together as a term and progressed through the tops in a set order. This method would ring the changes as to working on different decks/parts of Ship. The only exceptions were those who had gone to make up numbers in the Hold Party (a supernumerary mixture of different terms), or who had become cadet captains over other tops, or the various supernumerary cadet captains. Each top had a senior and a junior cadet captain.

Until 1915

At an indeterminate date after the 1890s and until 1915, the system was revised again so that new chums were all placed in Focsle. After one term together they were separated by size. The biggest boys moved to Maintop, the smallest to Mizzentop and the rest to Foretop.

From 1915

New chums at the end of their first term went either to port or starboard Mizzen (if small or skinny) until their final term, whilst the rest stayed together in their term but moved in succession through the other tops. This change to the top system was to reflect the fact that cadets remained together as a term for academic classes.

By 1937

The progression changed to be from Focsle to port Main to port Fore, then starboard Fore and finally starboard Main as QBs unless they became cadet captains or joined the band when they moved to Hold.

By 1939

New chums joined either port or starboard Focsle for their 1st term. After that they progressed as follows:

2nd term either starboard Foretop, Mizzentop, Quarterdeck (band) or Hold.
3rd term: port Maintop.
4th term: port Foretop.
5th and 6th terms: starboard Maintop.

1943

The situation of having tops composed of all one seniority did not lend itself to internal competitive sport, so the cadet captains designed and introduced a system of 'ships' or 'divisions' to encourage sporting competition:

Cossack wore black.
Howe wore grey.
Nestor wore blue.
Ohio wore yellow.
Rawlpindi wore red.
Sea Lion wore green.

Several of these merchant ships' names were re-incarnated as dormitory names when shore based accommodation opened in 1953.

1945/46

1st term: New Chums joined either port or starboard Focsle. For larger intakes Quarterdeck might be reintroduced.

2nd term: starboard Foretop.
3rd term: port Maintop.
4th term: port Foretop.
5th term: starboard Maintop.
6th term: starboard Maintop.

Mizzentop was reserved for the smallest cadets where they remained until they grew! There was also a Hold Party and Foreguard although their purpose has not been determined.

After 1946

1st term: New Chums joined either port or starboard Focsle.
2nd term: starboard Maintop.
3rd term: starboard Foretop.
4th term: port Maintop.
5th term: port Foretop.
6th term: Hold.

Mizzentop was reserved for the smallest cadets where they remained until they grew!

By 1948

New chums joined either port or starboard Focsle for their 1st term. In their 2nd term smaller cadets went into port or starboard Mizzentop and a few went into the Hold division. The rest went en bloc into what had been the senior top of the previous term.

"Thus in the summer term of 1949 we (who had been port and starboard Focsles) went en bloc into starboard Foretop. Our part of ship was the starboard upper deck. We stayed together for the rest of our time in the ship, being depleted by promotions to cadet captains."

1949 Easter Term

There was a large intake so the Quarterdeck division was formed containing the surplus new chums.

1949 September

With the opening of the Nelson Block, new chums spent at least their first term ashore and were placed into one of five divisions i.e. Focsle, Foretop, Maintop, Mizzentop and Hold, and in either the port or starboard watch. They remained in their allocated division and watch throughout their course. Those already onboard stayed in their current divisions for the remainder of their time onboard.

By the early 1960s

New chums were placed directly into one of four tops/divisions, Focsle, Foretop, Maintop and Mizzentop and to the port or starboard watch where they remained for the duration of their course. Each top was identified by a coloured band on the neck and arms of cadets' tee shirts. Focsle was gold, Foretop red, Maintop blue and Mizzentop green. They remained somewhat cocooned from older cadets by being accommodated in the House, although shortage of space meant that a few were allocated immediately to senior dormitories. Hold was just a temporary grouping at the House; one large dorm for the excess numbers that could not be accommodated in each tops' dorms. The system of allocation to a top seems to have been in blocks of 3 - 5 cadets by their cadet number. The Christmas 64 Watch Bill for example shows cadets 41 to 43 in Focsle (Andes dorm), 55 to 59 in Focsle (Nestor dorm), 110 to 112 in Foretop (Rawlpindi dorm) and 66 to 70 in Mizzen (Jervis Bay dorm). For some reason there are gaps in the numbering sequence eg there was no 73, 101 or 113.

"My number was 72 and I was in a Focsle dorm in the house with most of my term, but 73 to 76 were also Focsle and my term but slept in the New Block."

1972.

Cadets were still organised in 4 Divisions but the traditional port and starboard watches were now called platoons. This arrangement continued until closure.

APPENDIX H

A CAREER AT SEA

Shipping Companies

Conway cadets served in the following shipping lines, navies and maritime organisations around the world. The list is necessarily incomplete! OK Worcesters, beat this:

1.	A Nicholls & Co	35.	Bank Line
2.	A W Rainford	36.	Baron Line
3.	Abram Lyle & Sons	37.	Batavian Petroleum Maatschippi
4.	Abu Dhabi National Tanker Co	38.	Beaver Line (Canada)
5.	Adelaide Steamship Co	39.	Ben Line
6.	Alcan Inc Bulk Shipping	40.	Berthing Master (Port Rashid, Dubai)
7.	Alfred Holt & Co	41.	BHP Ltd
8.	Alcan Shipping (Montreal)	42.	Bibby Line
9.	All Red Line (San Francisco)	43.	Black Star (Ghana)
10.	Ambra Management	44.	Blue Funnel Line
11.	American President Lines	45.	Blue Star Line
12.	Anchor Line	46.	Blystad Shipping (USA)
13.	Andrew Weir Shipping	47.	Bohannen Line (Panama)
14.	Angfartygs A/B Tirfing (Sweden)	48.	Bolton Steamship Co
15.	Anglo American Oil Co	49.	Booker Line
16.	Anglo Saxon Petroleum Co	50.	Booth Line
17.	ANL Alltrans	51.	Bowater Steamship Company
18.	Aran Ferries	52.	BP Tanker Co
19.	Argyle Shipping Co (Bermuda)	53.	Branch Line
20.	Arklow Shipping	54.	Bridge Line
21.	Arya National Shipping Company (Iran)	55.	Bristol City Line
22.	Asiatic Steam Navigation Co (Singapore)	56.	Bristol Steam Navigation Co
23.	ASP Ship Management Group	57.	Britain Steamship Co Ltd
24.	Associated Container Transportation	58.	British Antarctic Survey
25.	Associated Steamships (Australia)	59.	British & Argentine Steam Nav Co
26.	Astoria Shipping Co	60.	British & Burma Steam Nav Co
27.	Athell Line	61.	British & Commonwealth Line
28.	Atlantic Container Line (ACL)	62.	British & Eastern
29.	Atlantic Steam Navigation Co	63.	British Channel Island Ferries
30.	Austasia Line (Singapore)	64.	British Columbia Ferries
31.	Australia National Line	65.	British India Steam Nav Co
32.	Australian Territory Liner Services	66.	British Rail Hovercraft Ltd (Seaspeed)
33.	Balfour & Williamson	67.	British Rail Marine Dept
34.	Baltic Shipping Co	68.	British Rail South West

69. British Shipowners Company
70. British Steamship Co
71. British Tanker Co Ltd
72. British Underwater Engineering
73. Britship (IOM) Ltd
74. Brocklebank Line
75. Broken Hill Line (NSW)
76. Brook line
77. Brookes Bell & Co
78. BT Marine
79. BUE Marine
80. Bullard King
81. Buries Marks
82. Burmah Oil Co.(Tankers) Ltd
83. Burns Philp (Australia) Pty Ltd
84. Butterfield & Swires China Steam Nav Co
85. C Y Tung Line
86. Cable & Wireless
87. Cairn Line
88. Caladonian MacBraynes
89. Canada Steamship Lines (Montreal)
90. Canadian British Aluminum Co
91. Canadian Coast Guard Service
92. Canadian Government Merchant Marine
93. Canadian Hydrographic Service
94. Canadian Pacific Steamship Co
95. Canadian Steamship Co
96. Caltex Tankers
97. Caribean Molasses Co.
98. Caribbean Shipping (Texas)
99. Carisbrooke Shipping
100. Carmichaels & Stewart
101. Cayzar Irvine
102. Ceina Mutual SS Co
103. Ceol Mor Shipping
104. Ceres Hellenic Shipping (Piraeus)
105. Cermar Shipping, Dublin
106. Ceylon Shipping Corporation
107. Chagargeur-Delmar (France)
108. Chambers & Co
109. Chandris Tankers
110. Charles Hills
111. Charles Wille (Cardiff)
112. Chevron Tankship (UK)
113. China Maritime Customs
114. China Navigation Company
115. Chinese Maritime Customs
116. City Line
117. City of Cork Steamship Co
118. City of Dublin Steam Nav Co
119. Clan Line Steamers
120. Coast Line
121. Coldwell Line (Hong Kong)
122. Colonial Sugar Refining Co (Sydney)
123. Columbus Line
124. Comben, Longstaff & Co
125. Commercial Cable Co
126. Commodore Shipping (Guernsey)
127. Common Brothers
128. Commonwealth Lighthouse Service
129. Comprehensive Shipping
130. Constantine Line
131. Continental Line
132. Conway Line (NI) (founder of)
133. Cook Strait Ferries (NZ)
134. Corfields
135. Cork-Swansea Ferries
136. Cowasjee Line (Karachi)
137. Crawford and Rowat Line (Canada)
138. Crawley Tugs (Los Angeles)
139. Crusader Shipping Co
140. Cunard Cargo Shipping
141. Cunard Steam Ship Co
142. Currie Line
143. Dalraida Steam Packet Company (founder of)
144. De Wolf Shipping
145. Delta Shipping (Gothenburg)
146. Dene Shipping Company
147. Denholm (Bermuda)
148. Dept of Energy Mines & Resources (Canada)
149. Devitt & Moore
150. Donaldson Line
151. C G Dunn & Co (Liverpool)

152. Dundalk Port Authority
153. Eagle Container Line
154. Eagle Oil Shipping Co
155. Eagle Tugs, Mombasa
156. East & West Steamship Co
157. Eastbound Line
158. Eastern Telegraph Co
159. Elder Dempster Lines
160. Elders & Fyffes Line
161. Egyptian Navy
162. Ellerman & Bucknell Shipping
163. Ellerman Lines
164. Ellerman Hall Line
165. Ellermans Wilson Line
166. Engen Oil
167. Esso Petroleum Co. Ltd
168. Eureka Shipping (Piraeus)
169. European Marine Contractors
170. Everett Steamship Co (Calcutta)
171. Evergreen Line
172. F C Strick & Co Ltd
173. F Laeisz (Hamburg)
174. Far East Hydrofoil Co. Ltd (Hong Kong)
175. Fast Cat Ferries Ltd (NZ)
176. Federal Offshore Services (Nova Scotia)
177. Federal Steam Navigation Company
178. Finanglia Ferries
179. Fishers
180. Fleet Air Arm
181. Foss Shipping
182. Freight Express Seacon
183. FT Everard
184. Furness Withy & Co Ltd
185. Fyffes Group
186. G M Steve & Co
187. G S Milne & Co
188. GPO Cable Ships
189. Gardline Shipping
190. Gas Pac Shipping Co (Tonga)
191. Geest Line
192. General Maritime S.A. (Casablanca)
193. General Steam Navigation Co
194. George Horsley & Co (West Hartlepool)

195. General Steam Navigation Co
196. Gillison & Chadwick (Liverpool)
197. Glen & Shire Line
198. Global Chemical Tankers (Torshavn, Faroe Islands)
199. Global Marine Inc (Los Angeles)
200. Gold Star Line (Hong Kong)
201. Golden Bay Cement Company (NZ)
202. Golden Line (Singapore)
203. Gracie, Beazley & Co
204. Gray McKenzie (Bahrein and Dubai)
205. Great White Fleet
206. Green R Line (South Africa)
207. Griffin Shipping (Hong Kong)
208. Gulf Line
209. Gulf Oil
210. Gulf Steamships
211. Guinea Gulf Line
212. Gustaf Erikson Line
213. HM Cableship Service
214. HM Coastguard
215. HMTelegraph Ships
216. Hadden & Co (Singapore)
217. Hadley Shipping Co
218. Hain Steamship Company
219. Hall Line
220. Harley Mullion (Hong Kong)
221. Harrison Crossfield Medal (Sumatra)
222. Harrison Line
223. Hayes Shipping
224. Head-Donaldson Line (Belfast)
225. Hedlams
226. Hella Carribean Steamship Company
227. Henderson Line
228. Henry F Watt
229. Hogarth & Son
230. Holland Africa Line
231. Holm Shipping (New Zealand)
232. Holyhead And Kingstown Royal Mail Service
233. Hong Kong & Borneo Shipping Co
234. Hong Kong Macau Hydrofoil Co
235. Hong Kong Marine Police

236. Houlder Brothers
237. HoverKaz inc
238. Hovertravel Ltd
239. Howard Smith (Sydney Australia)
240. Hudson Steam Navigation Company
241. Hugh Roberts and Sons (Newcastle)
242. Hugli River Survey Steamers
243. Hull Gates Shipping Co
244. IFR Services
245. Indo-China Steam Navigation Co
246. Inland Waterway Transport Co
247. Inspector of Irish Lights
248. Interisland Line (NZ)
249. International Chartering plc
250. International Marine Services (Dubai)
251. International Maritime Transport
252. Iranian Navy
253. Iredale & Porter
254. Irish Shipping Co
255. Irrawaddy Flotilla Co (Rangoon)
256. Isbrandtson Line
257. Isle of Man Steam Packet Co
258. Isle of Wight Ferries
259. Ivanavire
260. J Edgar & Co
261. J Hardie & Co
262. J Heron & Co
263. J Nourse & Co
264. J S Fry & Co
265. Jamaican Coast Guard
266. James Chambers & Co
267. James Fisher & Son
268. James Nourse Ltd
269. Jardine Matheson
270. Jebsons International
271. Jessmar Shipping (Great Yarmouth)
272. John Steward
273. Johnson Line
274. Jones Brothers & Co (Cardiff)
275. Jordain Shipping
276. K Steamship Co
277. Kapal
278. Kenny & Mahon
279. Kent Line
280. Kenya & Uganda Railway Marine
281. Kerr Steamship Company (Canada)
282. King Line
283. Kingston Steam Trawling
284. KKK Line
285. Kristian Jebson (Bergen)
286. Kuwait Oil Tanker Co
287. Kuwait Shipping
288. Landing & Shipping Co (Mombasa)
289. Lagos Shipping Co Ltd
290. Lamport & Holt Line
291. Lang & Fuller
292. Larrinaga Steamship Co
293. Leyland Line
294. Libyan Navy
295. Lion Shipping (Singapore)
296. Liverpool & North Wales Steamship Co
297. Liverpool Towing Co
298. Loch Line
299. Lockett & Wilson
300. London & Overseas Freighters
301. Lord Line (Belfast)
302. Low Line
303. Lund & Co
304. Lykes Line
305. Lyle Shipping Co
306. MacAndrews & Co
307. McCay Shipping (Canada)
308. McCowen & Cross
309. McGregor Gow & Co
310. Maersk Co
311. Mainland Market Deliveries
312. Mairsh Supply Service (Copenhagen)
313. Malasian Navy
314. Malaysian International Shipping Corp
315. Manchester Liners
316. Manchester Ship Canal Co
317. Manx Line
318. Marconi Co
319. Marico Marine (New Zealand)
320. Marine Exploration Ltd
321. Marine Survey Dept (Cayman Islands)

322. Marine Survey of India
323. Maritime Fruit Carriers
324. Maritime Services Board (NSW)
325. Mavroleon & Co
326. Medomsley Lin
327. Meridian Marine Management
328. Merlion Shipping Agency (Singapore)
329. Meteorological Office (UK)
330. Michalinos
331. Mitchells of Woolwich
332. Milton Marine Management
333. Ministry of Defence (UK)
334. Mitsui OK Line
335. Mobil Shipping
336. Mogul Line
337. Mollers
338. Montgomery
339. Montreal Shipping Co
340. Moore-McCormick Lines
341. Moss Line
342. Moss Hutchison Line
343. Muhne Drilling
344. Mullisons (Hong Kong)
345. Nash Dredging/Van Hattum en
     Blankevoort b.v.
346. Natal Line
347. National Bulk Carriers
348. Natural Environment Research
     Council Fleet
349. National Sea Rescue Institute
     (South Africa)
350. Nautilus Steam Navigation Co
351. Nederlandsche Stoomvaart Maatschappij
     Oceaan
352. Neptune Orient
353. Neptune Ship Mgt
354. Nerdrum Shipping
355. New Guinea Australia Line
356. New Zealand Shipping Co
357. Newcastle Shipping Federation
358. Newgate Shipping
359. Nigerian Marine
360. Nigerian National Line
361. Nigerian Port Authority
362. Noble Denton
363. Nomis Shipping Company
364. Norships Ocean Carriers
365. North Shipping Co
366. North Thames Gas Board
367. Northern Marine
368. Northern Shipping NZ
369. Northumberland Ferries (Canada)
370. NYK Line
371. Nyasaland Railway Lake Service
372. New Zealand Rail Ferries
373. OIL Ltd
374. Ocean Cruise Lines
375. Ocean Fleets
376. Ocean Inchcape
377. Ocean Tramping Co Ltd (Hong Kong)
378. Ocean Transport & Trading
379. Ocean Weather Service
380. Offshore Marine
381. Orient Line
382. Orient Overseas Line
383. Orkney Island Shipping Co
384. OT Africa Line
385. Overseas Container Line
386. Overseas Tankship (UK) Ltd
387. Oxidental & Orient Line
388. P Henderson Line
389. P & O Ferries
390. P & O New Zealand Ltd
391. P & O Steam Navigation Co
392. PNSL
393. Pacific Express Line
394. Pacific Forum Line
395. Pacific Steam Navigation Company
396. Pakistan Merchant Navy
397. Pakistan Navy
398. Pakistan River Steamers
399. Palestine Police Marine Division
400. Palm Line
401. Palmer Marin
402. Palmer Surveys (Gt. Yarmouth)
403. Pan Ocean

404. Pan Ocean Chemical Tanker Line
405. Papayanni Line
406. Pandoro
407. Papuan Liner Services
408. Pedder & Mylchreest
409. Persian Gulf Lightering Service
410. Pilot - Bengal
411. Pilot - Boston, Lincs
412. Pilot - Brisbane, Australia
413. Pilot - Canadian Atlantic
414. Pilot - Cinque Ports
415. Pilot - Clyde
416. Pilot - Dartmouth
417. Pilot - Dee (Chester)
418. Pilot - Dover (Superintendent)
419. Pilot - English Channel
420. Pilot - Falmouth
421. Pilot - Freemantle
422. Pilot - Great Barrier Reef
423. Pilot - Hoogly River, Calcutta
424. Pilot - Humber
425. Pilot - Isle of Wight (Superintendent)
426. Pilot - Jebel Dhanna, U.A.E
427. Pilot - Kharg Island
428. Pilot - Lagos/Port Harcourt
429. Pilot - Liverpool
430. Pilot - London
431. Pilot - Manchester Ship Canal
432. Pilot - Moulmein, Burma
433. Pilot - Nigeria Port Authority
434. Pilot - North Sea
435. Pilot - Panama Canal
436. Pilot - Penang, Malaysia
437. Pilot - Port Jackson/Sydney
438. Pilot - Port of Spain
439. Pilot - Port Pirie (S Aus)
440. Pilot - Queensland Coast/Torres Strait
441. Pilot - Rockhampton & Port Alma, Australia
442. Pilot - San Francisco bar
443. Pilot - St Lawrence Seaway
444. Pilot - Sidon, Lebanon
445. Pilot - Singapore
446. Pilot - Southampton
447. Pilot - Suez Canal
448. Pilot - Swansea & Port Talbot
449. Pilot - Tees
450. Pilot - Townsville, Australia
451. Pilot - Trent
452. Pilot - Trinidad
453. Pilot - Tyne
454. Pilot - Yangtze River
455. Pilot - Yarmouth & Southwold
456. Port Line
457. Potter Bros (Liverpool)
458. Prince Line
459. Queensland Shipping Co
460. R Ropner & Co Ltd
461. R A Lapthorne & Co
462. Rathbone Bros
463. Rea Tugs Ltd
464. Reardon Smith and Sons Ltd
465. Red Funnel Steamers
466. Rederi Nord (Hamburg)
467. Regent Petroleum Tankship Co
468. Rennies Coasters (South Africa)
469. Ropner Line
470. Royal Army Service Corps Fleet
471. Royal Australian Air Force (Marine Section)
472. Royal Australian Navy
473. Royal Australian Naval Reserve
474. Royal Canadian Mounted Police Maritime Div
475. Royal Canadian Navy
476. Royal Ceylonese Navy
477. Royal Corps of Transport Maritime Sqn
478. Royal Fleet Auxiliary
479. Royal Indian Navy
480. Royal Indian Navy Volunteer Reserve
481. Royal Mail Steam Packet Co
482. Royal Malaysian Navy
483. Royal Marines
484. Royal Maritime Auxiliary Service
485. Royal National Lifeboat Institution
486. Royal Naval Engineering Service

487. Royal Naval Patrol Service
488. Royal Navy
489. Royal Navy of Oman
490. Royal Naval Reserve (RNR)
491. Royal Naval Volunteer Reserve
492. Royal Naval Volunteer Supplementary Reserve
493. Royal New Zealand Navy
494. Royal Yacht Squadron, Sultanate of Oman
495. Royden Line
496. SBM (Monaco)
497. SCNZ
498. Safmarine (Cape Town)
499. Saga Line
500. Saguenay Shipping
501. Saguenay Terminals SS Co
502. Saint Line (South America)
503. Salen/Whitco
504. Salmon Troller (West Coast of Canada)
505. Salveson of Leith
506. Scindia Steam Navigation Co
507. Scottish Fisheries Protection
508. Scottish Ship Management
509. Sea-Land Service Inc (USA)
510. Seaglen Shipping NZ
511. Seahorse Ship Management
512. Sealion Shipping
513. Seaspeed (BRH Ltd)
514. Seatrain Lines (New York)
515. Seaworkx of Den Helder
516. Shaw Savill & Albion Co Ltd
517. Shell Company (New Zealand)
518. Shell Tankers
519. Shipping Corporation of NZ
520. Shire (Welsh) line (Glasgow)
521. Silver Line
522. Singapore Straits Line
523. Smit International
524. Smit-Pentow (Durban, South Africa)
525. Smith Line
526. South African Marine Corporation
527. South African Navy
528. South African Naval Reserve
529. South America Line
530. Southern Nigerian Marine
531. Southern Shipping Lines (Australia)
532. Soviet Navy
533. St Helena Shipping
534. St Lucia Coastguard/Police Marine Unit/ Drug Enforcement/Fisheries Protection Force (founder of)
535. Stag Line
536. Star Offshore Services, Aberdeen
537. Star Shipping (Canada)
538. Starline Cruises
539. Stateships of Western Australia
540. Stena Sealink
541. Stephenson Clark Line
542. Stolt-Neilson (Denmark)
543. Straits Steamship Co (Singapore)
544. Strick Line
545. Stuart & Douglas
546. Stuntbrand Mail Steamship Co
547. Sub Sea Seven
548. Sugar Line
549. Sun Shipping Co
550. Superclubs
551. Svenska Orient Linien (Sweden)
552. Svitzer
553. T & J Harrison
554. T & W Smith (Newcastle)
555. Tarakohe Shipping (NZ)
556. Tasman Express Line
557. Tay Ferries
558. Tedfords (Belfast)
559. Teekay Tankers
560. Texaco Overseas Tankships
561. Terrazzo Ship Co (Niagara USA)
562. Thomas Watson
563. Thompson & Co
564. Thompson Anderson & Co
565. Thor Dahl (Norway)
566. Tidewater International (Australia)
567. TNT
568. Tolka Shipping, Dublin

569. Tonga Copra Board
570. Townsend Ferries
571. Trader Navigation
572. Trans Oceanic Steamship Co
573. Transport Ferry Co
574. Tranz Rail
575. Trawlerman
576. Trident Tankers
577. Trinder Anderson & Co
578. Trinity House
579. Tristan Da Cuhna Dev Corp
580. Tung Group
581. Turnbull Scotts
582. Turner Morrison & Co (Calcutta)
583. Tyser Line
584. Ulster Steamship Company
585. Uiterwyk Corp. (Tampa)
586. Unicorn Lines
587. Unicorn Tankers
588. United Arab Shipping
589. Union Castle Mail Steamship Co
590. Union Company of NZ
591. Union Steam
592. Union Steamship Company
       (New Zealand)
593. Union Transpot
594. United Africa Line
595. United Arab Shipping
596. United Baltic Corporation
597. United States Line
598. United States Coastguard Auxiliary
599. United States Navy

600. United Towing, Hull
601. Upper Lakes Shipping, Toronto
602. Vela International (Dubai)
603. Vergocean
604. Victoria Shipping Co (Borneo)
605. Vitoil (Geneva)
606. W Holyman & Co
607. W Price & Co
608. W Watkins (Tugs) Ltd
609. W R Thomas & Co
610. Wallems SMS (Isle of Man)
611. Watts & Watts & Co
612. Waverley Line
613. West Australian Stateship
614. West Australian Steamships Co
615. Western Canada Steamships
616. West India & Pacific
617. Western Telegraph Co
618. Westminster Dredging
619. Whartons of Gunness
620. Whitco/Salen UK
621. White Star Line
622. Wightlink
623. Wholesale Society (Tarawa)
624. William Thomas Line
625. Williamson, Milligan and Co
626. Wilson Line
627. Wimpy Marine
628. Witherby Semanship International
629. World Wide Shipping Co
630. Yangste River Steamers
631. Yeoward Line
632. Zapata Marine Services (Italy)

Maritime Training Establishments

Old *Conways* have put their skills to good use training others:

Adventure Youth Sea Training Trust
   (Chairman)
Arethusa (Captain)
Arkabar Sea School (on River Murray, South
   Aus) set up by OCs in 1963.
Asia Pacific Maritime Centre

Auckland (NZ) Navigation School
Australian Maritime College
BISN Cadet Ship (master)
Cadet Training Blue Funnel Line
Canadian Coast Guard College
Chindwara Cadet Ship

Dept of Maritime Studies, Brunel College, Bristol

Dept of Maritime Studies, Glasgow College of Nautical Studies

Dept of Navigation, Riversdell College, Liverpool

Dufferin (India's equivalent of Conway) Captain Superintendent

Endeavor (Replica of Captain Cook's barque) Stockton on Tees

Faculty of Maritime Transport & Engineering, Australian Maritime College

Falmouth Sailing & Seamanship School

Fleetwood Nautical College

General Botha, South Africa (captain superintendent, Chief Offcier, Padre and several others)

Glasgow College of Nautical Studies

Georgian College, Canada

Great Lakes International Marine Training Centre

HMS Worcester (now we know why OWs are also such 'stout fellows')

Hong Kong Navigation School

Hull Nautical College

Hull Trinity House Navigation School

Indefatigable School

Institute of Marine Studies, University of Plymouth

International Association of Navigation Schools

James Watt Sea Training School Greenock (captain superintendent)

King George VII Nautical College (Essex)

Leith Nautical College

Libyan Navy Instructor

Liverpool Nautical School (Founder)

Liverpool Polytechnic (Navigation Dept)

Marine Society Education & Training Committee

Maritime Command Pacific Training Division (Canada)

Maritime Studies Dept. of UWIST, Cardiff

Merchant Navy Training Board

National Nautical School, Portishead (Captain Superintendent)

National Sea Training College

Nautical Studies, Georgian College, Ontario

Navigation and Seamanship courses, Department of Further Education, South Australia

Northern Ireland Polytechnic (School of Navigation)

New Zealand Shipping Co Cadet Training Ship (Master)

Nova Scotia Nautical Institute

Ocean Fleets Training Establishments

Outward Bound Sea School, Aberdovey

Pangbourne School (Governor)

Papua New Guinea Maritime College

Plymouth School of Maritime Studies

Port Jackson Cadet Ship (Master)

RAN Naval Apprentice Training Establishment

Royal Canadian Naval College

Royal Canadian Navy Naval Operations School

Royal Canadian Navy Sea Training Staff

Royal Corps of Transport Maritime Training Squadron

Royal Indian Navy Training Center, Karachi

RNC Dartmouth (4 serving together at one time)

Royal Yacht Association Instructor

Russell Coates Nautical School, Branscombe, Dorest (Captain Superintendnet)

Sail Training Association

School of Maritime Studies, Plymouth

School of Navigation, Sydney Technical College

Schools Afloat

Seamans Training Centre, Hong Kong

Sir John Cass Nautical School, London

Sir Winston Churchill (Bosun)

Southampton School of Navigation (Governor)

Southampton University, UK advanced
    maritime management course

Smith Junior Nautical School, Cardiff

Spirit of Adventure Sail Training (Founder)

Survival Systems Training Ltd

Technikon, Durban

Trinity House Cadet Training

Unicorn Training School, Durban

Vancouver Navigation School (Chief
    Instructor)

Warsash Nautical College *Uniformed Services and Units*

Old *Conways* have served in the following (RN Ships are not named individually as they are too numerous to list).

1. 1st Dragoon Guards
2. 3rd Group Royal Engineers Water Tpt
3. 4 Flying School RAF (CO)
4. 15/19 Kings Royal Hussars
5. 19 Tank Transporter Sqn RCT
6. 27 Regt RCT
7. 27 Squadron RAF (NW Frontier, India)
8. 30th Lancers
9. 42nd Company Imperial Yeomanry (Herts)
10. 205 Flying Boat Sqn RAF (Australia)
11. Austrian Army
12. Australian Army
13. Birmigham Police (Chief Constable)
14. Border Regt
15. British South African Police in Rhodesia
16. The Buffs Burma Army
17. Canadian Mounted Rifles
18. Cape Town Highlanders
19. Ceylon Planters Regt
20. China Maritime Customs
21. Coldstream Guards
22. Coventry City Police Force Devon & Cornwall Light Infantry
23. Devonshire Regt
24. Dublin Fusiliers
25. East Yorkshire Regt
26. Egyptian Navy
27. Fire Service (UK)
28. Fleet Air Arm
29. French Maquis Gibraltar Contraband Service
30. Gilbert & Ellice Islands Police Force
31. Gloucestershire Regt
32. Greater Manchester Ambulance Service
33. Hampshire Constabulary
34. Hampshire Rifles
35. HM Cableship Service
36. HM Coastguard
37. HQ BAOR
38. HQ British Commonwealth Force
39. Hong Kong Marine Police
40. Hong Kong Police Force (from 1997)
41. Inland Waterway Transport Co
42. Inns of Court Rifles
43. Jamaican Coast Guard
44. Green Howards (Lt Col)
45. Indian Army
46. Indian Cavalry
47. Iranian Navy
48. Kent Regt
49. Kenya Police
50. King Edward's Horse
51. King George's Own Central Indian Horse
52. Kings Liverpool Rifles
53. Kitcheners Horse Lancashire Fusiliers
54. Lancashire Militia
55. Leicestershire Regt
56. Leinster Regt
57. Libyan Navy
58. Liverpool Police
59. Liverpool Scottish
60. London Regt
61. Long Range Desert Group
62. Malaysian Navy
63. Manchester Regt

64. Metropolitan Police
65. MOD HQ
66. MOD Police
67. NATO HQ
68. NATO (NAMMA)
69. New Zealand Army
70. New Zealand Fire Service
71. Northern Rhodesia Police Force
72. Northumberland Police Force
73. North West Mounted Police (Canada)
74. Nottinghamshire Constabulary
75. Pakistan Navy Parachute Regiment
76. Palestine Police Force 1922
77. Palestine Police Marine Division
78. Polish Air Force
79. Princess Patricia's Canadian Light Infantry
80. Prison Service (UK) Punjab Regt
81. The Queen's Own Gurkha Logistic Regiment
82. RDA Rifles (Bermuda?)
83. Rhodesian Police
84. Royal Air Force
85. RAFR
86. RAFVR
87. Royal Army Medical Corps
88. Royal Army of Oman
89. Royal Army Pay Corps Royal Army Service Corps
90. Royal Artillery
91. Royal Australian Air Force
92. Royal Australian Air Force (Marine Section)
93. Royal Australian Navy
94. Royal Australian Naval Reserve
95. Royal Canadian Air Force
96. Royal Canadian Mounted Police
97. Royal Canadian Mounted Police Maritime Division
98. Royal Canadian Navy
99. Royal Canadian Navy Reserve
100. Royal Canadian Navy Volunteer Reserve
101. Royal Ceylonese Navy
102. Royal Corps of Signals
103. Royal Corps of Transport Maritime Squadron
104. Royal Electrical & Mechanical Engineers

105. Royal Engineers
106. Royal Fleet Auxiliary
107. Royal Flying Corps
108. Royal Hong Kong Police (1968-1997)
109. Royal Indian Navy
110. Royal Indian Navy Volunteer Reserve
111. Royal Irish Constabulary
112. Royal Jersey Light Infantry
113. Royal Malaysian Navy
114. Royal Maritime Auxiliary Service
115. Royal Military Academy Sandhurst
116. Royal Marines
117. Royal National Lifeboat Institution
118. Royal Naval Engineering Service
119. Royal Navy (RN)
120. Royal Navy of Oman
121. Royal Naval Mediterranean Fleet Clearance Diving Team
122. Royal Naval Reserve
123. Royal Naval Patrol Service
124. Royal Naval Supply & Transport Service
125. Royal Naval Volunteer Reserve
126. Royal Naval Volunteer Supplementary Reserve
127. Royal New Zealand Air Force
128. Royal New Zealand Armoured Regiment (New Zealand Scottish)
129. Royal New Zealand Navy
130. Royal New Zealand Naval Reserve
131. Royal Norfolk Regiment
132. Royal Scots Dragoon Guards
133. Royal Tank Corps
134. Royal Warwickshire Regt
135. Royal Welsh Fusiliers (RWF)
136. Royal Yacht Squadron
137. Sultanate of Oman
138. SAS
139. Seaforth Highlanders
140. Seinde Cavalry Regiment
141. Shropshire Light Infantry
142. SOE
143. South African Light Horse
144. South African Navy
145. South African Naval Reserve
146. South Lancashire Regt

147. South Staffordshire Regt
148. Soviet Navy?
149. St Lucia Coastguard/Police Marine Unit/ Drug Enforcement/Fisheries Protection Force (founder of)
150. Suffolk Regiment
151. Thornycrofts Horse (SA)
152. Trinity House
153. Trucial Oman Scouts
154. US Army Reserve Officer Training Corps
155. US Coastguard Auxiliary
156. US Navy
157. US Naval Reserve Yorkshire & Lancashire Regt
158. Yorkshire Regt
159. Zambian Police Force

Other Fields of Endeavour

Some Old *Conways* never went to sea, others eventually came ashore. They've turned their hands to almost every job imaginable:

1. Accountant Actor
2. Advertising Manager
3. Agricultural Research Council
2. Airline Pilot
3. Air Surveyor
4. Air Traffic Controller
5. Antique Dealer
6. Architect
7. Art Silk Spinner
8. Author (See Bibliography for list and details)
9. Bagpipe Teacher (Scots College, Sydney)
10. Bank Manager
11. Banker
12. Barrister
13. Blast Furnace Foreman
14. Bolton Metropolitan College
15. Bookseller
16. Brewery Manager (and Founder)
17. Brewery Sales Manager
18. British Aerospace
19. Building Society
20. Bulldozer Driver
21. Cargo Surveyor
22. Cattle Rancher (South America)
23. Chandlery Manager
24. Chartered Company Secretary
25. Clinical Hypnotist
26. Chartered Acountant
27. Commonwealth Secretariat
28. Computer Consultant
29. Condominium Manager, Florida, USA
30. Consultant Histopathologist
31. Cowman
32. Diplomat
33. District Manager for C&A stores
34. Diver
35. Eastern Caribbean Regional Security System
36. Editor Staffordshire Life
37. Electrician
38. Estate Agent
39. Estate Worker
40. Film Director Hammer Horror Films
41. Fireman
42. Fish & Chip Shop Proprietor
43. Florist
44. Freight Forwarding
45. Game Conservancy
46. Ghillie
47. Gold Miner (NSW)
48. GP
49. Health Shop
50. High Court Judge
51. Hod Carrier
52. Honey Farmer
53. Hotelier
54. House Father
55. Hydrographer
56. Hypnotherapist
57. Insurance Consultant

58. International Harvester
69. Journalist
60. Jumbo Jet Pilot
61. Justice of the Peace
62. Landscape Gardener
63. Launderette Operator
64. Lawyer
65. Legal Advisor,
66. Saudi Ports Authority
67. Liferaft Surveyor
68. Lloyds Insurance Broker
69. Lord Lieutenant of Anglesey
70. Management Consultant
71. Managing Director
72. Marine Hydrographer
73. Marine Surveyor
74. Market Gardener
75. Marketing Manager
76. Master Baker
77. Mauritius Ministry of Housing and Land
78. Mechanical Engineer
79. Member House of Commons
80. Member House of Lords
81. Meterological Officer
82. Mining Engineering
83. Ministry of Overseas Development
84. Mosquito Pilot
85. Music Publisher
86. New Zealand Kiwifruit Marketing Board
87. Operations Officer/Manager
88. Organisation of Eastern Caribbean States
89. Patent Agent
90. Personnel Manager
91. Poet Laureate

92. Port Inspector
93. Poultry Farmer
94. Prison Officer
95. Professional Father Christmas
96. Publican (A few of these!)
97. Radio Broadcaster and Documentary Writer (South Africa)
98. Recruitment Consultant
99. Residential Care Home
100. Restauranteur
101. Rock Musician
102. Rothmans International Tobacco Ltd
103. Salesman
104. Silver Fox Farmer
105. Statistician
106. Stevedoring Superintendent/Manager
107. Systems Analyst
108. Taxi Driver
109. Tea Planter, Assam
110. Teacher
111. Textiles Company
112. Timber Importer
113. Trade Union Secretary
114. Translator
115. Tree Surgeon
116. Trinidad and Tobago Hydrographic Unit
117. TV Comedy writer
118. TV Presenter
119. United Nations Development Programme
120. United Nations World Food Program (Rome, Italy)
121. Vicar
122. Vintner/Wine Merchant
123. Wool Merchant

APPENDIX I

LOSS OF THE SHIP – SUPPORTING PAPERS

Chapters 23 and 24 describe the loss of the Ship in 1953. They include references to a number of source documents, which can be found online at hmsconway.org. Attachments I-1 and I-2 are sufficiently important to be reproduced here. Attachments I-3 and I-4 provide very useful background information.

Attachment I-1:	Report of The Sub-Committee Appointed To Ascertain The Facts of The Stranding of The *Conway*.
Attachment I-2:	Report to Rea Towing By Capt Durrant of Rea Towing.
Attachments I-3 to I-6	Menai Strait at A Glance.
	Mean Spring Tidal Conditions In The Menai Strait.
	Synoptic Weather Chart.
	Kerr's Chart of the Swelly Channel.

ATTACHMENT I-1:
REPORT OF THE SUB-COMMITTEE APPOINTED TO ASCERTAIN THE FACTS OF THE STRANDING OF THE CONWAY.

The original document is not of good enough quality to scan so the following pages provide a verbatim transcript of the original. The original's punctuation and most formatting have been maintained but the transcript occupies less space than the original because of the font size and spacing used.

Present:-   Mr Brian Heathcote (in the chair)
            Captain G Ayre
            Mr L. O'Brien Harding
            Mr A. Rigby Hughes
            Captain A.G. Peterkin
            Mr Alfred Wilson

Lord Norbury was prevented by illness from attending.

Captain James Nelson was with the Committee for part of the sittings as Adviser.

The Committee heard from the following gentlemen, who all took part in the operation:-

Captain E. Hewitt   (HMS "Conway")
Mr R.J. Jones   (Trinity House Pilot)
Captain Durrant   (Rea Towing Company)
Skipper Brown   (Ahead tug "Dongarth")
Skipper Cooper   (astern tug "Minegarth")
Mr. Miller   (Liverpool Pilot)

Preparation

Captain Hewitt began to ascertain available data to assist in planning the move from the moorings off Plas Newyyd to those prepared off Bangor as early as April, 1952. He consulted many times the Harbourmaster of Caernarvon, Captain Rees Thomas, on both the navigation of the channel and the tidal data. He obtained tidal data also from Dr. Doodson, of Bidston Observatory. The information he obtained was that slack water at the Tubular Bridge was about 10 to 15 minutes before high water at Caernarvon Bar. He planned to make the passage between the two bridges during this period of slack water, so as to be clear of the Suspension Bridge before the Southgoing stream commenced to run. Captain Thomas's recommendation was to be at the Tubular Bridge at 9.25 am, and he anticipated slack water for the next 10 to 15 minutes. Captain Hewitt planned to be at the Tubular Bridge at 9.20 to have something in hand. On several occasions he went to the Tubular Bridge and checked for himself that the water slacked there 10 minutes before the time given. He had also made a number of passages through the Swellies himself, both at high, slack and low water. He knew from the old log books of the previous passage of *"Conway"* through the Swellies that she made the passage between the bridges going South in 13 minutes, and decided to allow 15 for the

passage North between the same points. He then checked his times in the *"Conway"* motor boat at
41/2 knots, starting at the time he had planned for the operation, though not at the highest H.W.
and with a light Easterly wind both outside and inside the Straits. He went through without difficulty,
turning under the Suspension Bridge. Captain Durrant, Mr. Brooke Smith and Mr Miller were with
him on this occasion. A further passage by boat was made about one hour before low water on
Monday, April 13th, by Captain Hewitt and the tug masters, and it was followed by a final briefing
meeting onboard *"Conway,"* at which were present Captain Hewitt, Pilot Miller, Captains Durrant,
Duff (the Senior Master of Rea Towing Co.), Brown and Cooper. The exact timings were finally
fixed, and stress was laid on the critical point of the timetable which was the time under the Tubular
Bridge at 9.20 am It was agreed that the nine cables between the bridges would be covered in 156
minutes, towing at 4 knots, by which time the S.W. running stream would have achieved a rate of 4
knots. This was based on observations by Captain Hewitt and Mr Miller. Captain Durrant stated that
it had previously been confirmed by the local pilot, though no occasion was mentioned in which a
full conference of all concerned included the local pilot. The only occasion mentioned in which the
local pilot took part was when Captain Durrant, Mr Miller, Captains Duff and the local pilots (father
and son) went down to the water's edge and watched the turn of the tide.

It is pertinent here to quote the extract from the tidal notes on the Admiralty Chart of the
Swellies, No. 1464 –

> *"Between the bridges the stream runs to the S.W. for 6¾ hours from 1 hour before H.W. at Menai, to 1½
> hours before L.W.; and to the N.E. for 5¾ hours from 1¾ hours before L.W. to 1 hour before H.W. 7 to
> 8 knots at Springs, 5 knots at Neaps. Slack water ¼ hour at Springs, ½ hour at Neaps."*

On the day in question H.W. at Menai Bridge was 10.53 am If the tidal data is accurate, slack water,
which occurs at the termination of the Northgoing stream, should have been from 9.38 to 9.53 am,
when the Southgoing stream would commence at 9.53 at Menai Suspension Bridge. It would seem,
therefore, that the *timing* of the passage as planned was correct.

There was some discussion at the final briefing conference as to the disposition of the tugs. It was
decided that "Minegarth" should remain astern to give steering power or to bring up as necessary.
The tugmasters confirmed, in answer to questions, that "Dongarth" was fully able to tow *"Conway"*
with "Minegarth" trailing astern against the anticipated 4 knot stream. Pilot Jones stated that he asked
for three tugs, but was assured that two were ample for the job. He admitted that his experience of
towed ships was negligible. It was also decided, after discussion, that the astern tug should make fast
stern to stern, and not tug bow to *"Conway"* stern. Discussion also took place on whether the astern
tug should be slipped at any point and transferred to assists the ahead tug after clearing the Swellies.
It transpired that all parties concerned were satisfied as to the ability of "Dongarth" to tow to the
scheduled times under the circumstances detailed above, but Captain Durrant and the tugmasters
stated at the enquiry that they doubted whether any of their tugs could singly have towed *"Conway"*
through the current they actually encountered.

In addition to the existing marks Captain Hewitt himself laid three extra buoys to assist the navigation
of the channel. These proved effective and helpful.

All orders from *"Conway"* were relayed to both tugs by Marconi "walkie-talkie," manned in *"Conway"* by Mr Miller, who transmitted the orders given by Captain Hewitt and Mr Jones. At all times interchange of communication was satisfactory between *"Conway"* and the ahead tug, but messages could only be sent from *"Conway"* to the astern tug, and not vice versa, the tug acknowledging reception and understanding of messages by whistle signal. A simple semaphore system was agreed in case of failure of the communication system. The need for it did not arise.

Operation

April 14th, 1953, was the second of three successive days of highest Springs during which the operation was possible at that time of year. At Plas Newydd on that morning it was clear and sunny, with a flat calm and a light breeze. Cables were hove in at about 6.30 am, the ship put on slips and the tugs made fast. At 8.23 *"Conway"* was slipped.

Onboard *"Conway"* were Captain Hewitt in command with Pilot Jones. Mr Miller was on the fo'c'sle head to pass orders to the tugs. The pilot's son, also a local pilot, was in the ahead tug, with Captain Duff in the astern tug. Pilot Jones in his statement gave the wind as N.W. force 2/3, and the draughts of the *"Conway"* as 21 feet forward and 21 feet 6 inches aft. Captain Hewitt gave the draught as 19 feet 6 inches forward and 20 feet aft. Her displacement was 4,300 tons.

The ship was turned easily and there was still a good following tide. The pilot checked with Captain Hewitt that the time of arrival at the Tubular Bridge was 9.20. The passage to the Tubular Bridge was uneventful, the tugs towing easily to arrive at the Bridge at the agreed time. *"Conway"* had her bows under the Tubular Bridge at 9.23 am Pilot Jones agreed in his statement that, if anything, *"Conway"* was early rather than late at the bridge. The ship was headed up for the narrow channel between Price's Point and Swelly Rock, and Captain Hewitt stated that this is the place where the tide runs most strongly. He remarked that she was not going very fast, but appeared to be making good headway. Pilot Jones gives the time when *"Conway"* was abeam Price's Point Beacon, about half way between the bridges, as 12 minutes after passing the Tubular Bridge. Abeam of Swelly Rock, Pilot Jones states that the wind had veered to the N.E., but this is doubtful, other observers agree that the wind remained N.W. but was increasing in force. He asked for more power, and then suggested to Captain Hewitt that *"Conway"* be taken back stern first through the Swellies. The Captain decided against this, and witnesses at our enquiry agreed on the impossibility of this under the prevailing conditions. Clear of the Swelly Rock prudent navigation demands that the ship should haul to the Northward in order to get an offing for the centre of the Suspension Bridge. Observers noted what they remarked a to be a sheer to port at this time, but this was undoubtedly a deliberate attempt to get the ship into position. *"Conway"* was now stationary, and the order was given, with Pilot Jones' concurrence, to let go the stern tug and make fast forrad. This manoeuvre was clearly foreseen in the preliminary conference. Captain Duff replied that the tug could not get under the port bow of *"Conway"* under the conditions, so decided to go ahead of the forward tug and tow in line ahead. The manoeuvre was brilliantly executed, but with both tugs towing forward the ship made little headway. The "Dongarth" was now held head and stern by tow ropes, and had little power of manoeuvre in face of the wind and tide. At some time between 10.20 and 10.30 am, with both tugs towing ahead but making little impression, when abreast of the Platters Rocks the *"Conway"* took a sudden and violent sheer to starboard, took charge, and went ashore over the Platters in a matter of seconds. Continuous straining on the tow lines at full speed for a further 10 minutes had no result. It was realised that the *"Conway"* was hard and fast, and, on orders for the ship, the towing hawsers were slipped from the tugs.

Observations.

1. **Tow Ropes.** Captain Hewitt stated that the tow rope from *"Minegarth"* to *"Dongarth"* broke, and a second rope was then passed. It would seem from the statements of the tugmasters that two ropes were out between the tugs, an 8" and a 6" rope. The 6" rope broke, but at no time after the "Minegarth" had made fast to the *"Dongarth"* were the two ships unconnected by tow rope. The break occurred at the last sheer of *"Conway,"* and was in no way contributory to the disaster.

2. **Wind.** Photographs taken at the time of stranding show the direction of the smoke from the tugs almost parallel to the fore and aft line of the *"Conway." "Conway"* was heading 118° when aground. The wind would seem to be about 300°, i.e. a point W. of N.W. We do not agree that the wind was N.E. at any time during the passage.

   An extract from the Liverpool Pilot Log Book on Tuesday, 14th April, is –
   8 am   N.W wind Force 6
   10 am   N.W. wind Force 6
   Noon   N.W. wind Force 7

3. **Tide.** The Master of the astern tug stated that his tug, when light, had a speed of 10 knots. He said, referring to the time when he let go "Conway's" stern, approximately at 10.10 am, "I put the telegraph to full speed and she finished up about 400 feet astern of the "Conway." She was going every once she could go, but was still going astern. The tide was most severe."

   In Captain Durrant's written statement to his Owners (attached) *(Attachment I-2)* he states that, at about 9.40 am, observing the operation form the Suspension Bridge, he made careful observation of the rate of passage of floating kelp borne on the tide, and estimated the stream to be 8 to 10 knots in a Southerly direction. He describes it as having the character of a race. Pilot Jones, in answer to questions, said that as the ship came along the conditions became abnormal. Mr Miller speaks of the tide as not being a true tide, but a confused mass of water running at a fast speed. Shore observers speak of something in the nature of a bore coming Southwards as the *"Conway"* took her last sheer.

   It is somewhat surprising to us that the party had no knowledge of the stormy conditions prevailing at sea at the time *"Conway"* was to make the passage. Local knowledge may well have been that, under such circumstances, abnormal conditions might be encountered. It seems clear, from the time *"Conway"* took to do 6 cables (9.23 to 10.10), that something very unusual was taking place, possibly a strong undercurrent, which is known to occur in the channel, or that there was little or no stand of tide.

   A third tug, sent from Liverpool a t about 2 pm to assist towing off, was unable to make the passage owing to weather and was forced to return.

4. **Tugs.** Had those concerned felt the least alarm about the ability of the tugs supplied to carry out the operation successfully under normal conditions, there was both opportunity and time to

rectify matters. All concerned were agreed that the tugs were sufficient for the job, as nothing but a 4 knot tide was mentioned at the conferences. The Admiralty Chart Tidal Notices indicate the expectation of 7/8 knot S.W. running stream, whereas in the Southbound voyage of *"Conway"* she would not have encountered more than a 5 knot N. running stream. It was not feasible to have one ahead tug on each bow, with on stern tug, owing to the narrowness of the channel. At no material time were the tugs short of coal or without a full head of steam.

5. **Ranger.** The ranger was standing by off Bangor with the moorings to which *"Conway"* was proceeding. Had she been required to come to the assistance of *"Conway"* those moorings would have had to be let go, and *"Conway"* would have been unable top moor at all. In any case, in those waters and under the conditions encountered it would have been impossible for *"Ranger"* to give any assistance whatsoever.

Report ends.

ATTACHMENT I-2:
REPORT TO REA TOWING BY CAPTAIN
DURRANT OF REA TOWING.

This report was produced for Rea Towing who subsequently made it available to the investigating sub committee. The original document is not of good enough quality to scan so the following pages provide a verbatim transcript of the original. The original's punctuation and most formatting have been maintained but the transcript occupies less space than the original because of the font size and spacing used.

16th May 1953

HMS "CONWAY"

Preliminary

We were first advised by letter from Messrs. Alfred Holt and Co., dated 13th February 1953, signed by Mr. Dickie, of the projected movement, in two stages, of HMS *"Conway"* from Menai Straits to Birkenhead.

The first stage (from Plas Newydd northward to Bangor) was planned to coincide with the period of Spring tides, April 13th – 14th – 15th and we were requested to have 2 tugs available for the various moves, also one of the Tug Masters who was present when the *"Conway"* made her previous move.

On March 24th the Writer, in company with Mr Miller (Pilot instructed by Messrs Alfred Holt and Co., to act as liaison between *"Conway,"* Menai Pilots, Tugs, etc.) and Captain Duff (Rea Towing Company Supervisory Tug Master) met Mr. Dickie to discuss plans. It was then arranged that the above named – except Mr. Dickie – would proceed to Menai on March 30th to complete arrangements, on the spot, withy Captain Hewitt, HMS *"Conway,"* the Caernarvon Harbour Master and Menai Pilots.

All aspects of the operation were discussed at this meeting. Tuesday, April 14th was decided upon as the date for the move, subject to suitable weather conditions, and a timetable was agreed upon. It was further agreed that the tugs *"Dongarth"* (Capt. F.A. Brown) and "Minegarth" (Capt. F. Cooper) – being the same tugs and Masters engaged on the previous move, should be employed for the current impending move.

A final briefing meeting, to include the Tug Masters, was arranged for onboard HMS *"Conway"* for Monday, April 13th, the day prior to the move (See memo addressed to Mr Madders dated march 31st 1953 – copy attached) *(Editor's note: No copy of this memo has been found)*

The tugs duly arrived in the Menai Straits early Monday, April 13th, their Captains in the early afternoon and about one hour before low water accompanying Captain Hewitt on a further tour of inspection through the Swellies Channel by motor launch.

On its return down channel from this inspection, the launch called at the Plas Newydd landing to pick up Messrs. Duff, Miller, Pope (Marconi Representative) and self, all proceeding onboard *"Conway"* for the meeting as arranged.

(Present at meeting: Captain Hewitt, Pilot Miller, Captains Brown, Cooper, Duff and Durrant.

At this meeting the exact timing of each point of the move was finally fixed and agreed upon. It was stressed that the critical point of the timetable was the time of passing under the Britannia (Railway) Tubular Bridge which was to be 9.20 am This was the estimated time of High Water at that point, to be followed by a slack water period of ten (10) minutes between the north east running FLOOD tide and its change to the south west running EBB tide.

The 10 minutes slack water period was calculated to be sufficient to tow the *"Conway"* through the most dangerous part of the Swellies Channel with a maximum clearance of 4 feet of water over the SWELLIES ROCK. *(Editor's Note: The last two words are hand written corrections to the original text made by Captain Durrant completely overwriting his original words.)*

It was estimated that the nine cables between the Tubular Bridge and the Menai Suspension Bridge, through the Swellies Channel, would be covered in approximately 15 minutes – i.e. towing at approximately 4 knots – by which time the south west running EBB tide would have attained a rate of 4 knots. This rate was based upon observations by Captain Hewitt and Pilot Miller – previously confirmed by the local Pilots, Jones, Senior and Junior. The Admiralty Chart - No.1464 – for the Menai Strait gives a tidal rate of 7 – 8 knots for the Swellies Channel at Spring Tides).

It was arranged that the *"Dongarth,"* Capt. Brown, would make fast at the head of the *"Conway,"* and the *"Minegarth,"* Capt. Copper, would make fast at the stern end. The question of the *"Minegarth"* remaining at the stern throughout the tow, or slipping and transferring to assist the *"Dongarth"* at the forward end, after clearing the Swellies, was discussed. It was decided that the *"Minegarth"* would remain astern, to provide steering power, or for bringing up, as necessary.

Questioned as to the *"Dongarth's"* ability to tow both the *"Conway"* plus the "Minegarth" trailing astern, against the anticipated 4-knot tide, Captain Brown confirmed the opinion of Captains Duff and Cooper that the *"Dongarth"* was capable of doing so. Times of making fast the tugs to the *"Conway"* and slipping the *"Conway's"* moorings were confirmed.

(N.B. In the actual operation the agreed timetable was strictly maintained up to the time of passing under the Tubular Bridge).

The Radio Telephone set supplied by Messrs Marconi limited and transported to Menai by one of the tugs, was fitted onboard *"Conway"* during the afternoon, satisfactory tests being carried out with the tugs anchored down channel.

Tuesday, 14ᵗʰ April 1953 – Moving and Stranding of The "Conway"

The early morning weather was fine and bright with a light North Westerly wind blowing across the Straits. Conditions appeared almost ideal for the operation and no suggestion was made – so far as the Writer is aware – or seemed necessary – of postponing the operation.

The two tugs left their anchorage off Port Dinorwic at 6.30 am and were alongside the *"Conway"* at 7 am They were made fast as arranged between 7 and 8 am and the *"Conway"* slipped her moorings at 8.15 am The *"Conway"* was then heading South stemming the flood tide, the tugs proceeded to swing her, in order to bring her head North, between 8.15 am and 8.35 am

She moved easily when under way, with comparatively little effort from the tugs.

The tow proceeded slowly northward on the last of the flood tide being held in check off Pwllfanogl in the northerly bend of the Straits south of the Tubular Bridge, from approximately 8.45 to 9.15 am ready for passing under the Tubular Bridge at the appointed time of 9.20 am Headway was resumed at 9.15 am and the passage under the Bridge was duly made at 9.20 am

By this time the North Westerly wind had freshened considerably and it was noted by a local pilot stationed under the Tubular Bridge that the anticipated 10 minute slack did not materialise. The south going EBB set in immediately after High Water at 9.20 am

The Swellies channel was safely negotiated but at a slower speed than estimated, and diminishing as the EBB tide gathered momentum.

It has been calculated that the tow would pass under the north easterly bridge, i.e. the Suspension Bridge, not later than 9.35 to 9.45 am, but at the latter time it was still a matter of 300-400 yards short, or westward, of the bridge.

(N.B. For the purpose of recording the Writer's point of vantage it should be stated that, from the time of making the tugs fast until passing under the Tubular Bridge, the operation was followed and viewed from a *"Conway"* motor launch. The remainder of the operation, until its final phase, was viewed from a point on the Suspension Bridge immediately over the centre of the channel, and under which the tow was due to pass.)

As stated above, it could be seen at 9.40 am, looking from the Suspension Bridge, that the tow was practically stationary, with the forward tug, "Dongarth," towing at full speed against the tide but making no progress. In this situation, apart from minor tacks form port or starboard, the *"Conway"* continued to be held, head on to the tide, but edging gradually towards the Carnarvonshire side, under the pressure of the strong north westerly wind against her port side.

Carful observation of the rate of passage of floating kelp borne by the tide, which appeared to have the character of a race, indicated a tidal strength of at least 8 to 10 knots.

At approximately 10.15 am the stern tug was slipped, and with great difficulty was manoeuvred to a position ahead of the forward tug, i.e. the "Dongarth," a new 6" rope being passed from the stern of the "Minegarth" to the forward end of the "Dongarth" in order to hold the two tugs in position, end on to one another, while a heavier (also new) 8" rope was passed ahead from the "Dongarth."

Under the strong tidal conditions prevailing it would have been impossible to place the "Minegarth" under the bluff bow of the *"Conway"* in a position to pass or receive a towing line direct from the ship, and likewise impossible for the crew of the ship, owing to her design, to make a speedy connection through the small hawse holes half way down her bows.

The "Minegarth" then took up the strain ahead of the "Dongarth," the combined efforts of the two tugs, towing in line ahead of the *"Conway,"* produced a slight but noticeable headway towards the Bridge.

The "Dongarth," held head and stern by tow ropes, was severely hampered in her manoeuvring power, and at one point was listed to her gunwale in her efforts to hold the *"Conway"* up to wind and tide.

At 10.30 am, without warning, when *"Conway"* was abreast of the Platters Rocks, and there appeared to be good hope of the tow making the Bridge and passing through, she took a violent sheer to starboard, apparently forced by an eddy of overwhelming strength. Her forward end passed over the Platters, the ship's forefoot digging into the bank adjacent to and shoreward of the Rocks. This disastrous sheer occurred, and was concluded in a matter of seconds.

As the tow lines eased momentarily the ensuing and suddenly increased strain caused the *"Minegarth's"* 6" line to part, but her 8" line, plus *"Dongarth's"* two hawsers connected direct to the *"Conway,"* continued to hold. The tugs were eased over to a position in which the hawsers were leading aft across the *"Conway's"* bows, and from where they continued their efforts to haul her stem off the bank. These efforts were restricted by the necessity, and difficulty, of ke3eping the tugs head on to the racing tide, plus the very small radius of action available in the rocky channel.

After a further 10 minutes or so of continuous straining on the tow lines, at full speed, it was realised that the *"Conway"* was ashore hard and fast, and that any further effort on the part of the tugs must be unavailing. On orders from the ship the towing hawses were slipped from the tugs and they proceeded to Menai Pier to await developments.

Conclusion:

Tentative arrangements were made for an attempt to refloat the ship on the pm High Tide at 9.45 pm, the tugs being ordered to be prepared to stand by again at 8.30 pm

A third tug was ordered from Liverpool to provide additional assistance, but after leaving the Mersey at 2.30 pm the tug, the *"Grassgarth,"* was forced to return to port owing to bad weather. Arrangements were made to despatch another tug, if possible, from Liverpool at midnight, this order being cancelled at 8.30 pm, deteriorating conditions onboard the *"Conway"* having forced the conclusion that further attempts to tow her off the bank would be useless.

She was stranded with approximately three-quarters of her forward length grounded on a sloping bank of rock and gravel, the remaining stern part being unsupported and suspended over 31 feet of water at low tide.

When the p.m. flood tide made, it was seen that the ship failed to lift and was making water, which, before High Water, was pouring in through the lowest of the stern ports.

The Writer earlier in the day had made contact at Menai with Capt. Nelson, Nautical Advisor to Mr. Lawrence Holt, and with him boarded the *"Conway"* during the afternoon just before Low Water. The outlook then appeared very bad, with the after end of the ship sagging downwards from the main mast aft and a continuous sound of twisting, cracking and rending timber, and rushing water below.

Mr. Lawrence Holt, Messrs. Wilson (MMSA), Mr Heathcote and Mr Wilson (Alfred Holt Construction Dept.) arrived at about 5.30 pm, viewed the ship from the beach, where her fore part was then high and dry, and then adjourned to await a further inspection an hour before High Water at 8.45 pm

At this late stage (8.45 pm Tuesday, April 14th) conditions onboard were very much worse than previously and the ship was later abandoned for the night.

At low tide, 5 am on the following morning (Wednesday, 15th April) a further inspection of the ship's interior was made by Mr. L.D. Holt and party, plus representatives of the Liverpool and Glasgow Salvage Association following which a decision was made to call off, for the present, any further attempt at refloating.

The tugs *"Dongarth"* and "MN sailed from Menai Bridge on their return voyage to Liverpool, at 9 pm Wednesday, 15th April, arriving Gladstone Dock 3.30 pm

On Thursday evening April 16th 1953 Mr. Alfred Wilson (M.M.S.A.) secretary of the *"Conway"* Committee, in a Press statement declared HMS *"Conway"* a total loss.

Note:

Tugs' Equipment lost or damaged:

	(1 4" Towing Wire	(25 faths)	
	(1 12" Towing Spring	(45 faths)	) new
Ex	(1 8" Rope (Sisal)	(60 faths)	)
"Dongarth"	(1 6" " "	(30 faths)	

damaged and jammed under "Conway's stem"

	(1 4" Towing Wire	(25 faths)
"Minegarth"	(1 12" " Spring	(45 faths)
	(1 8" Rope (Sisal)	(60 faths)

retained on stern mooring deck of *"Conway"* when tug slipped.

Total values – approx. £320.

The report is signed by Captain Durrant.

ATTACHMENT I-3:
MENAI STRAIT AT A GLANCE.

ATTACHMENT I-4:
MEAN SPRING TIDAL CONDITIONS IN THE MENAI STRAIT.

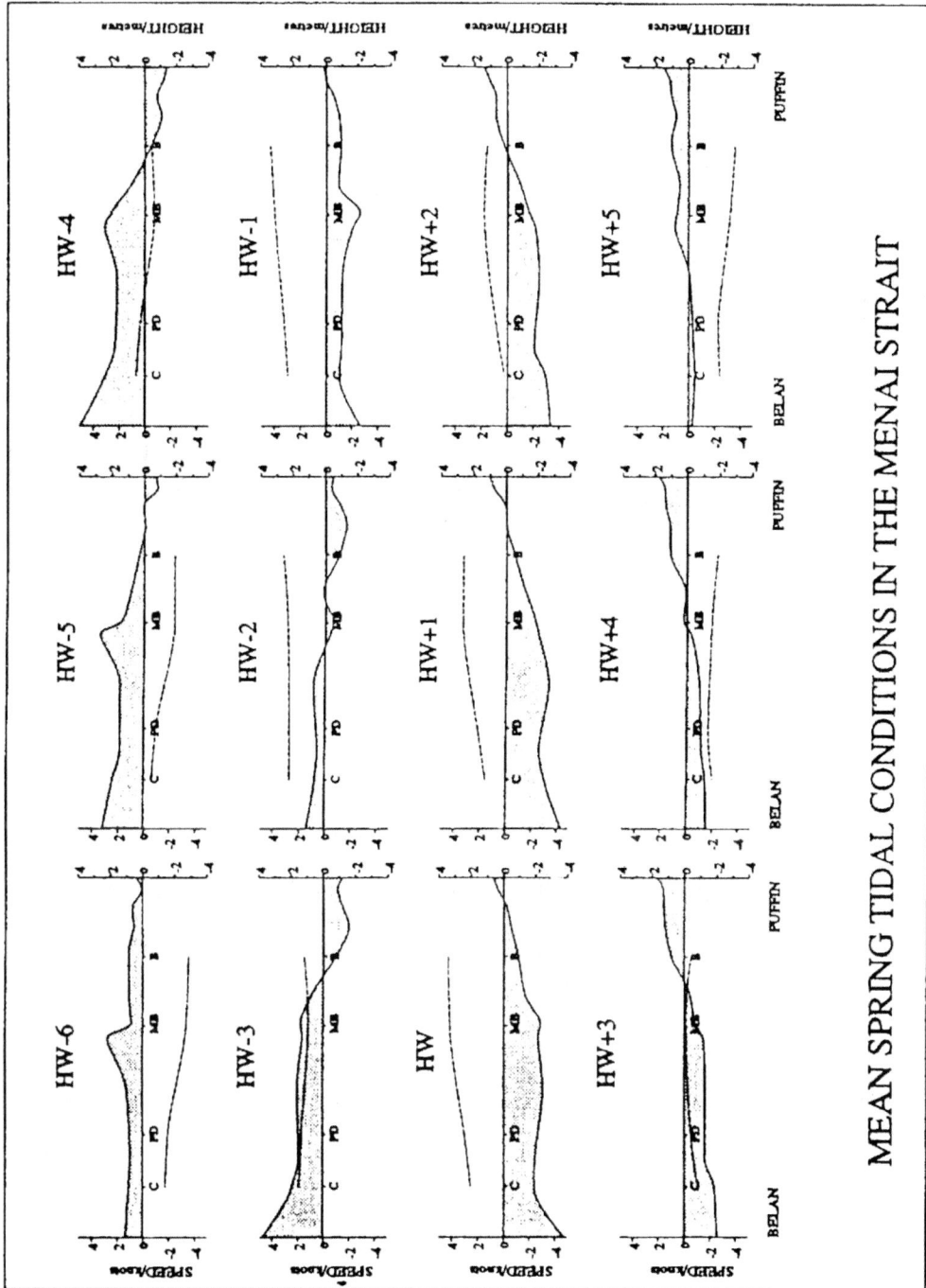

MEAN SPRING TIDAL CONDITIONS IN THE MENAI STRAIT

ATTACHMENT I-5:
SYNOPTIC WEATHER CHART.

GENERAL SYNOPTIC DEVELOPMENT:-
The depression between Iceland and Norway and the anticyclone to Southwest of the British Isles have remained almost stationary. A small depression developed over Scotland yesterday and moved southeastwards into the North Sea. The cold north to north west air stream has persisted over the whole country.

Issued at Mid-day. today Tuesday 14th April, 1953

FORECAST FOR BRITISH ISLES until noon tomorrow :- there will be bright intervals and showers in all districts but in eastern districts of England and Scotland more continuous rain or sleet will occur in some places with snow on the high ground. The showers will be heavy with hail in places and scattered thunderstorms may occur in southwest England and the Midlands, while the showers is of snow on high ground in the north.

ATTACHMENT I-6:
KERR'S CHART OF THE SWELLY CHANNEL.

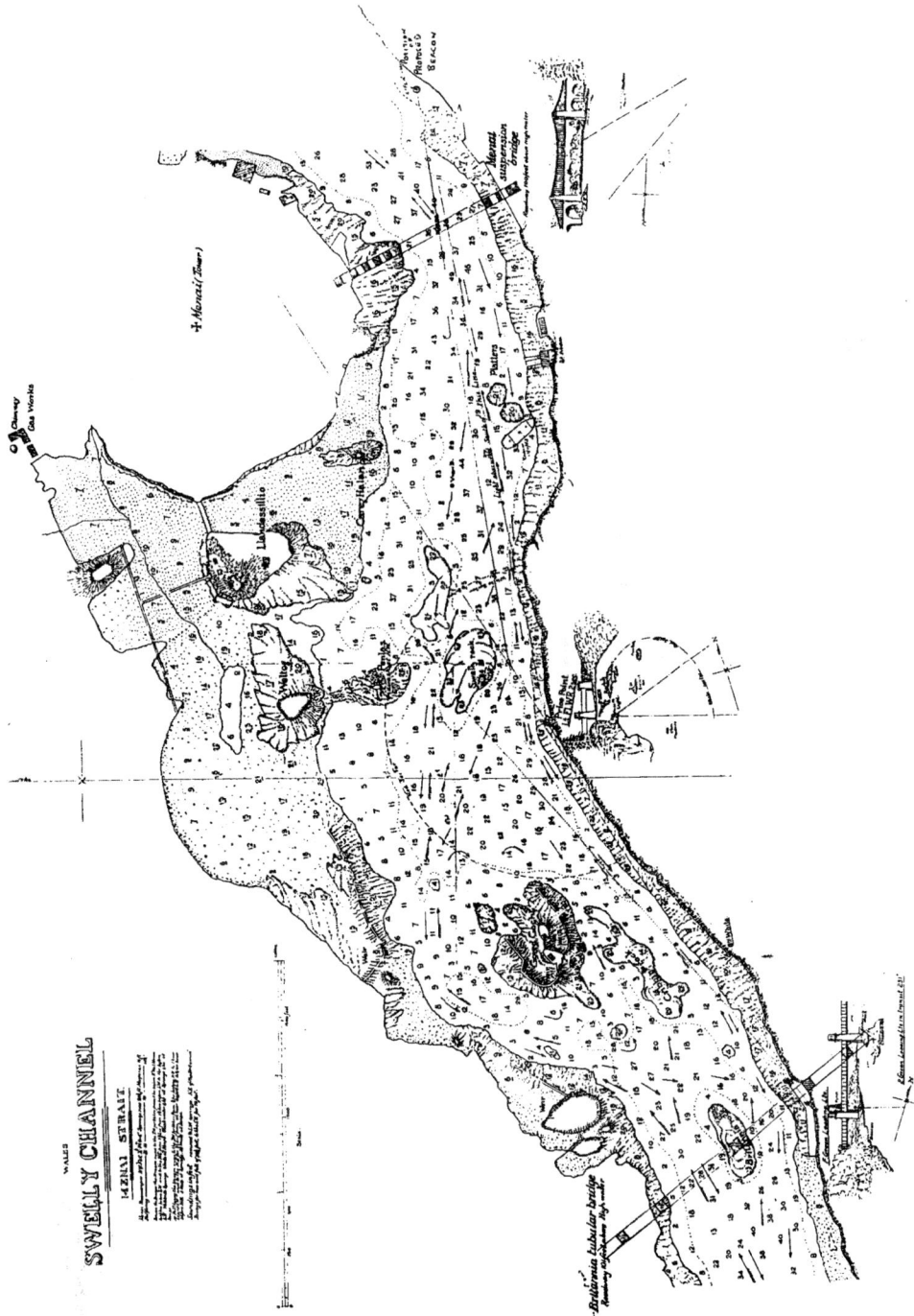

APPENDIX J

CAPTAIN SUPERINTENDENTS AND HEADMASTERS

Captain Superintendents

There were ten Captain Superintendents from 1859 to 1968 when the Headmaster took charge of the Ship.

1. May 1859 - Apr 1860 — Captain Charles Powell He resigned after a number of tragic losses in his family.
2. Apr 1860 - Feb 1862 — Captain Alfred Royer RN.
3. Feb 1862 - 1871 — Captain Richard Mowll RN (Old Mobby) who had previously been Chief Officer.
4. 1871 - 30 Sep 1881 — Captain Edward Franklin RN. Promoted Rear Admiral on retirement
5. 1 Oct 1881 - 1903 — Lt. Archibald Miller RN (Lippy). Died in his cabin.
6. 1903 - 1927 — Captain H Broadbent RNR (1880-81). First ex-Conway to return as Captain.
7. 1927 - 14 June 1934 — Commander F A Richardson DSC RN (00-02).
8. 14 June - September 1934 — Montague Douglas RD RNR (Monty) - the Conway's Chief Officer was Acting Captain.
9. September 1934 - 1949 — Captain T M Goddard RD RN (05-07). Captain of South Africa Training Ship General Botha in 1921.
10. 1949 - July 1968 — Capt Eric Hewitt RD RNR (19-21)

Headmasters

There were Headmasters in the ship throughout her life.

1. 2nd Aug 1859 - 30th Jun 1863 — Mr. Thomas Dobson BA. Taught navigation, maths and the use of nautical instruments. In 1863 he moved to be Head of Hexham High School.
2. 1st Jul 1863 - 31 Aug 1892 — Mr. Charles Barton (Bummy)
3. 1 Sep 1892 - 31 Jul 1898 — Mr. Joseph H. Light (Charlie)
4. 1 Sept 1898 - 1 Mar 1911 — Mr. James Stuart
5. 1 Apr 1911 - 31 July 1923 — Mr. James Morgan
6. 1 Aug 1923 - 3 Sep 1943 — Mr. Thomas P. Marchant BA
7. 4 Sep 1943 - 31 Aug 1939 — Mr. Tom E.W. Browne B.Sc. (TEWB)
8. 1 Sep 1939 - 30 Nov 1945 — Mr. Robert H. Carter BA.(Bog Brush) Acting Headmaster
9. 1 Dec 1945 - 31 Jul 1964 — Mr. Tom E.W. Browne B.Sc. (TEWB)
10. 1 Aug 1964 - 17 Jul 1974 — Mr. Basil Lord MA

Headmaster 'In Command'

July 1968 – 17 Jul 1974

The post of Captain Superintendent ended in 1968 and the Headmaster assumed his duties and command of the establishment. It is appropriate therefore to acknowledge Mr Lord's special position as more than just Headmaster in these years.